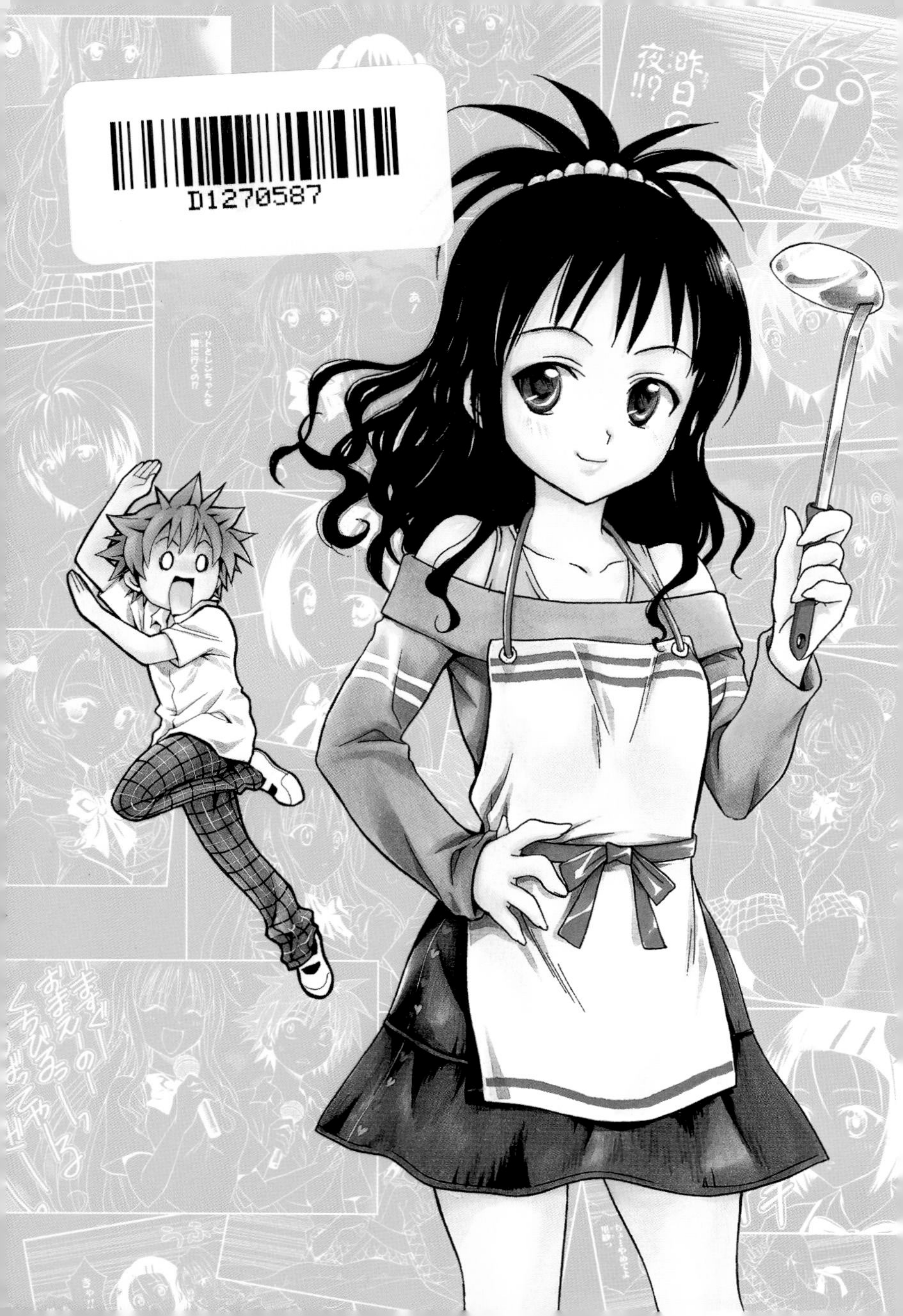

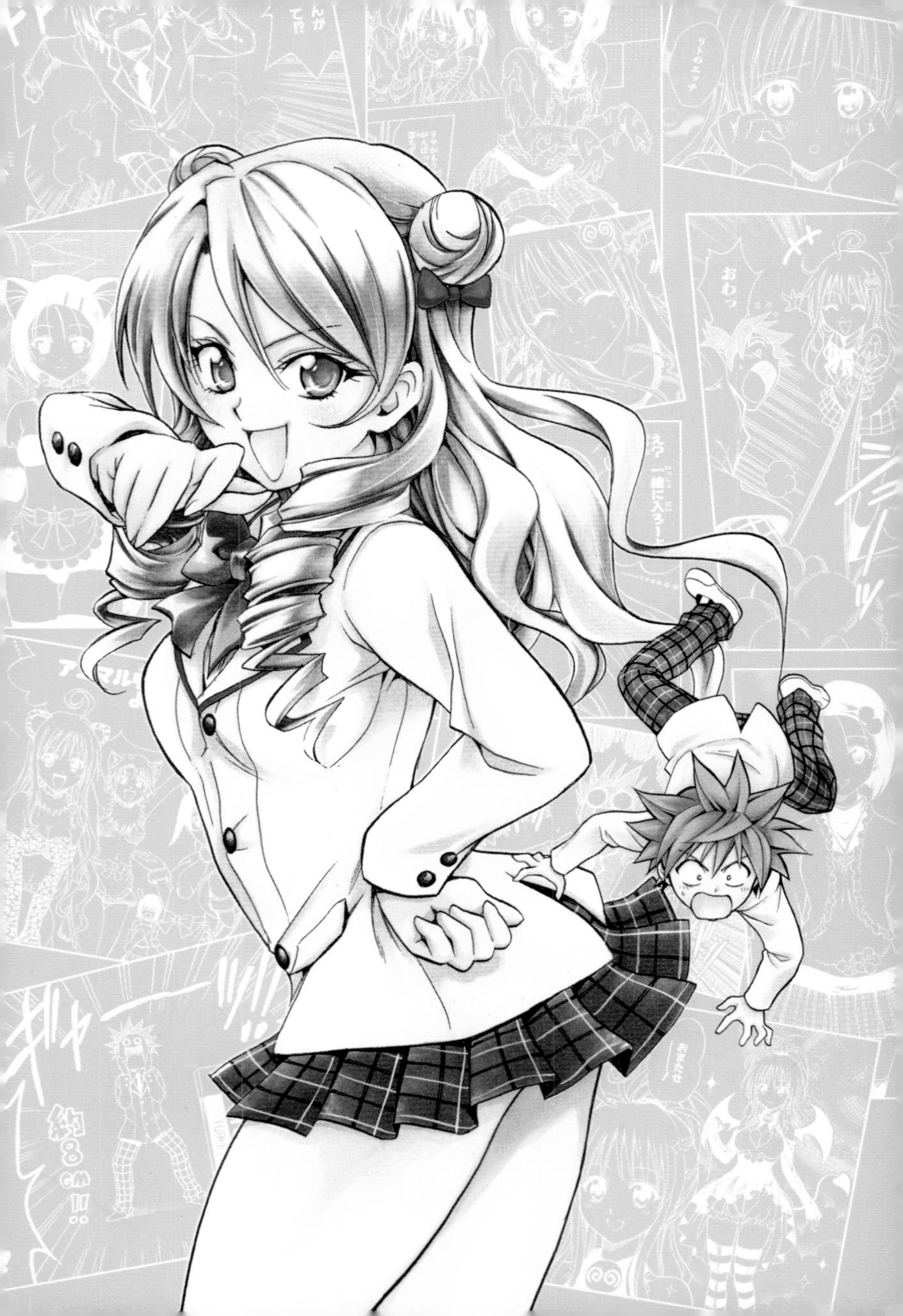
おわっ
約8cm!!

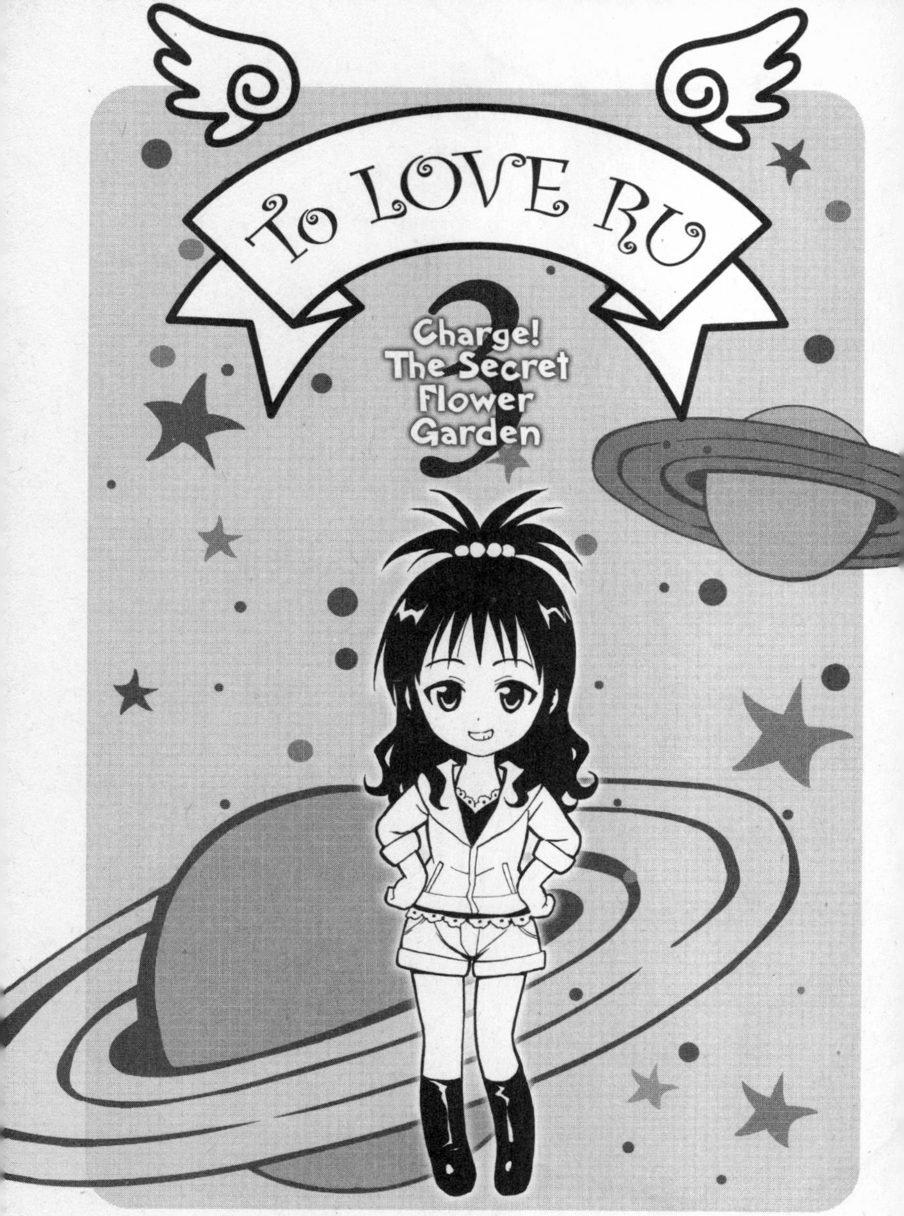
To LOVE RU
3
Charge! The Secret Flower Garden

Story: Saki Hasemi Art: Kentaro Yabuki

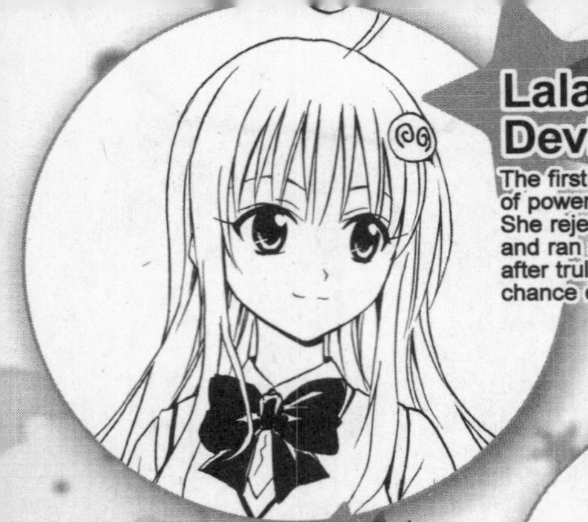

Lala Satalin Deviluke

The first princess of Planet Deviluke, seat of power for the entire Milky Way Galaxy. She rejected the suitors her father selected and ran away from home to Earth. However, after truly falling for Rito, whom she met in a chance encounter, they started living together!

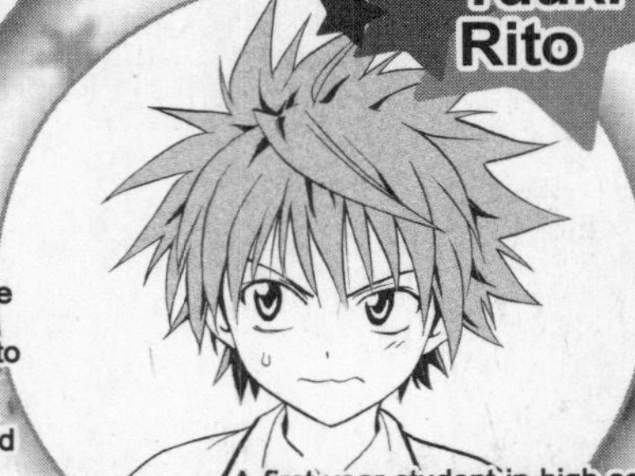

Yuuki Rito

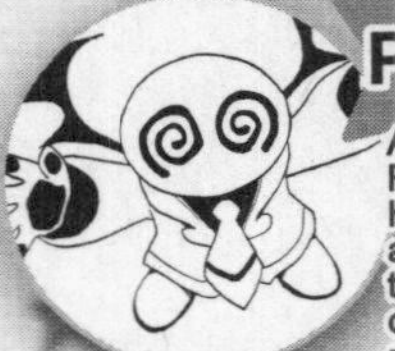

Peke

A Universal Costume Robot, built by Lala. He can transform into a variety of shapes, taking the form of a dress, a uniform, and more.

A first year student in high school. As it turns out, a sudden bath-time encounter with Lala after she warped away from her ship has led to them living together! A late-bloomer in matters of love, he was in the middle of trying to confess his feelings for Haruna, the girl he'd been crushing on since middle school. But in the heat of the moment, he accidentally confessed to Lala, who had appeared between them, and ended up becoming her fiancé.

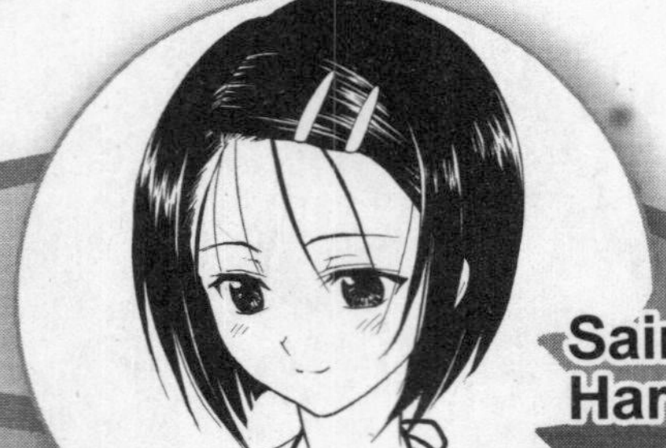

Sairenji Haruna

A girl who has been in the same class as Rito since middle school and secretly likes him?! She is a quiet, mild-mannered, prim-and-proper beauty. However, she does hide a certain quirk...!

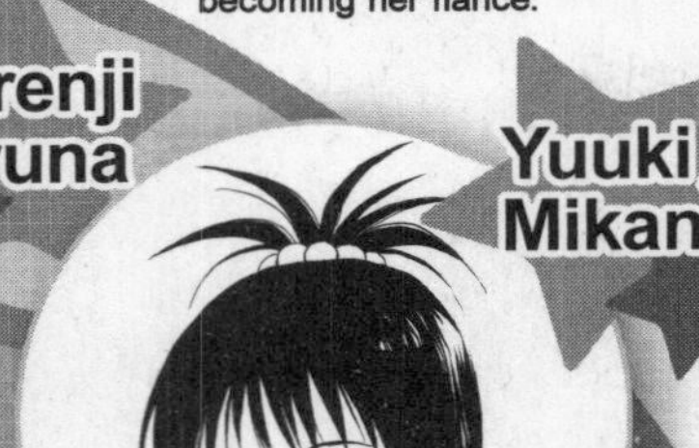

Yuuki Mikan

Rito's little sister. Rather than taking issue with the whole "Lala is an alien" thing, she welcomes her into their home with open arms. Mikan had to grow up fast, and is quite a stable, level-headed person.

Characters & Story

To LOVE-Ru

Super-sweet, super-innocent Rito, along with Planet Deviluke's Princess Lala--the girl whose beauty is the pride of the cosmos--and Rito's classmate Haruna, are woven together throughout this cute, teensy-bit naughty, slapstick romantic comedy!!

Zastin

Commander of the Deviluke Royal Guard. A man who is said to be Planet Deviluke's most powerful warrior, but in reality...

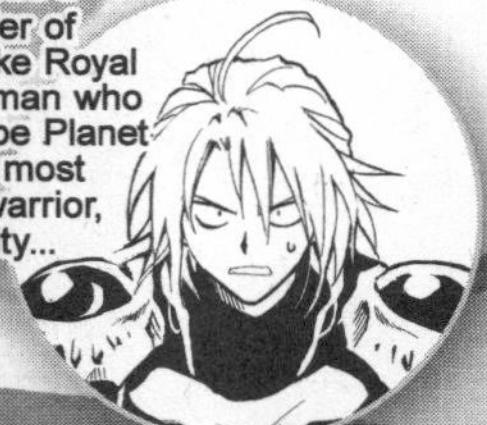

King of Deviluke

The king of Planet Devliuke. Has no qualms about utterly annihilating the worlds of those who disappoint him. So far, only his voice has appeared. This ever-growing, ever-more-horrifying visage is merely the product of Rito's imagination.

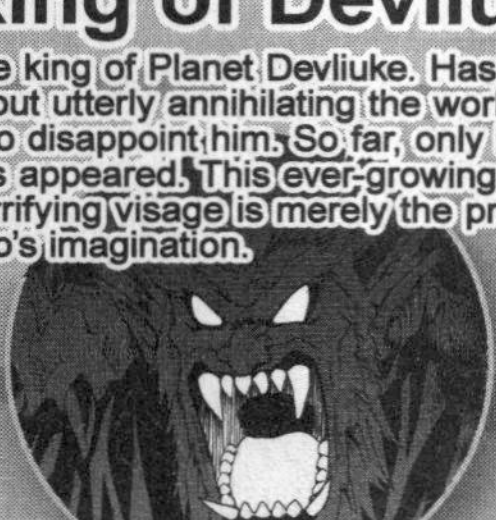

To LOVE Ru

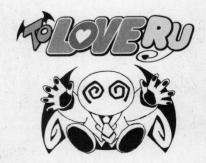

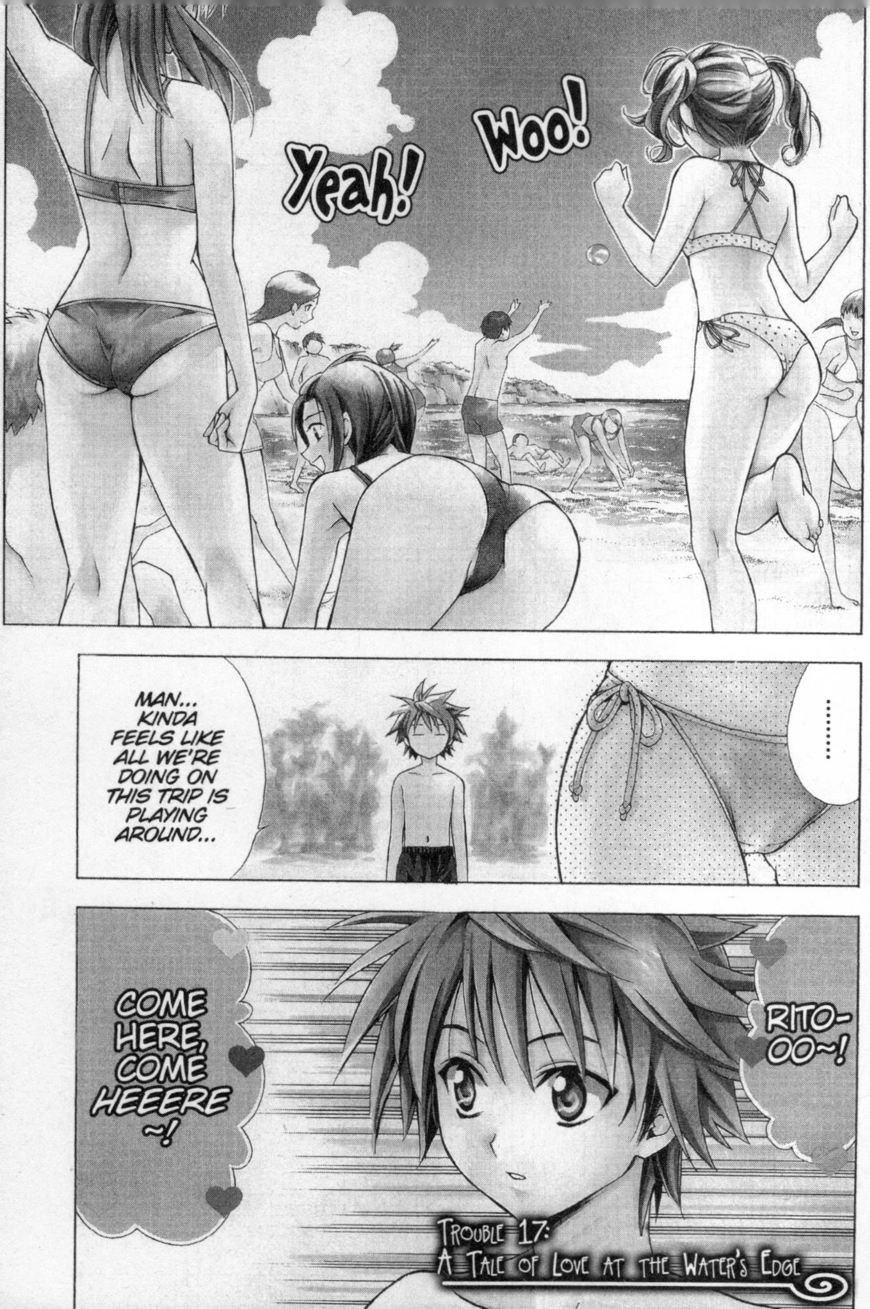
Woo!
Yeah!
......
MAN... KINDA FEELS LIKE ALL WE'RE DOING ON THIS TRIP IS PLAYING AROUND...
RITO-OO~!
COME HERE, COME HEEERE ~!
Trouble 17: A Tale of Love at the Water's Edge

Trouble 17: A Tale of Love at the Water's Edge

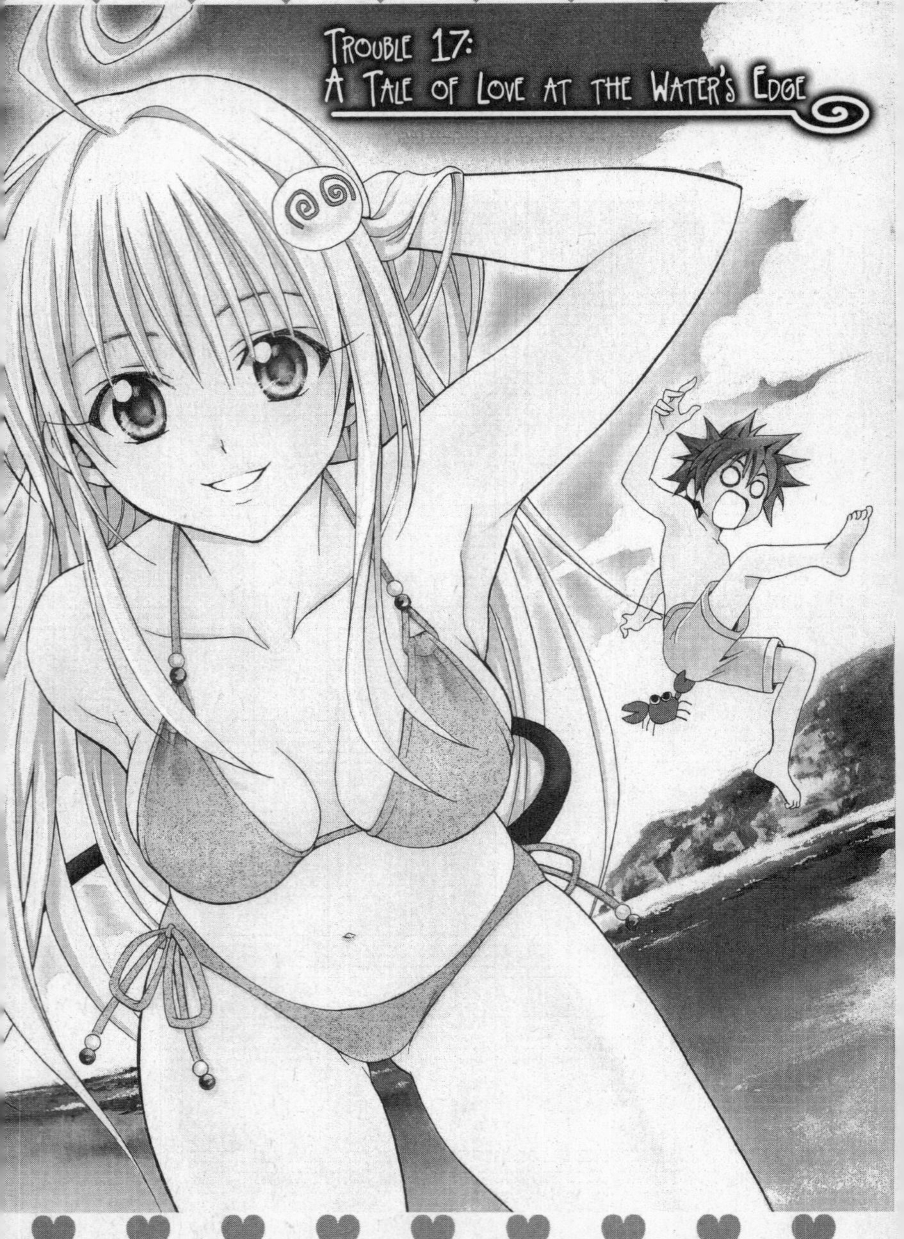

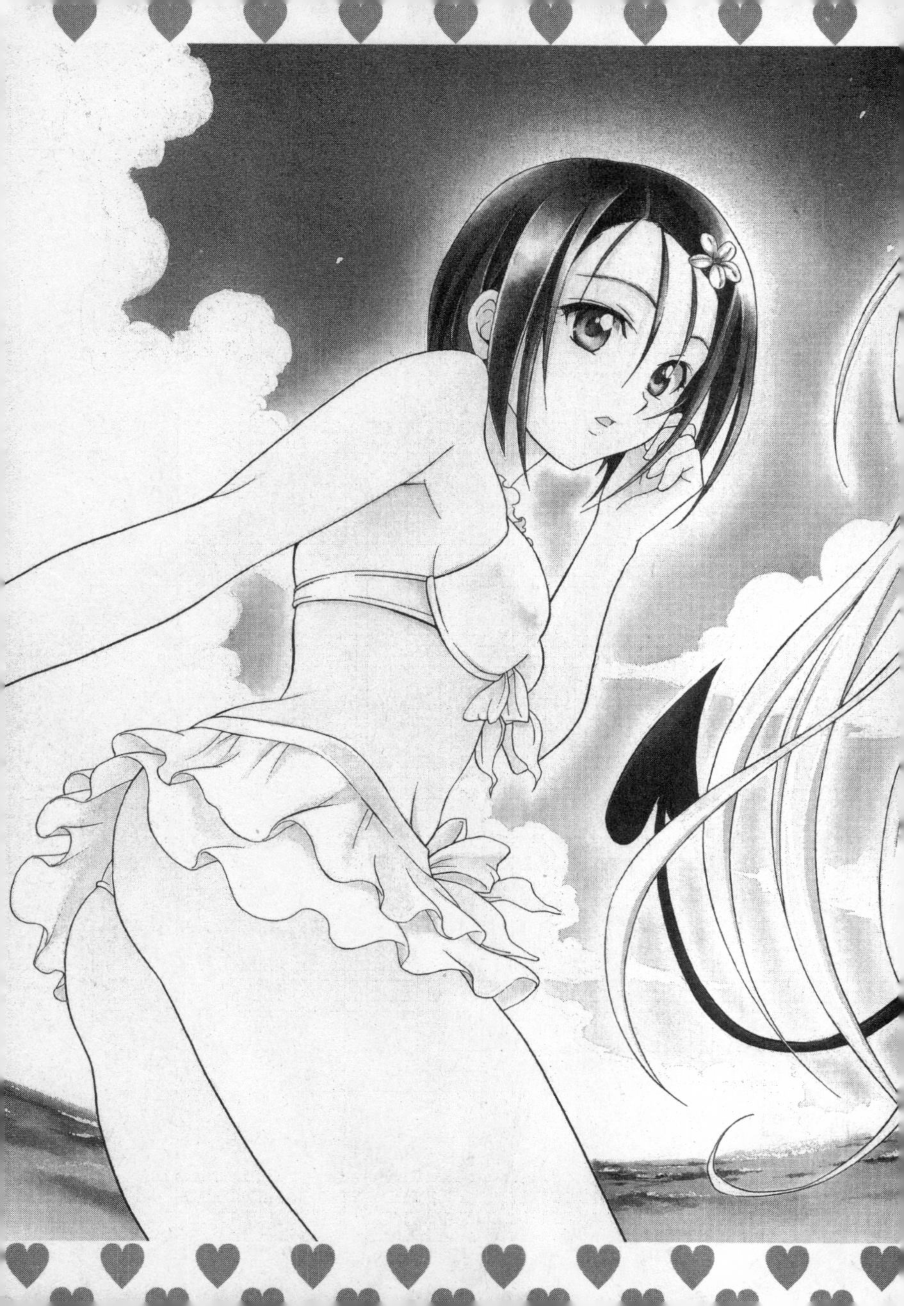

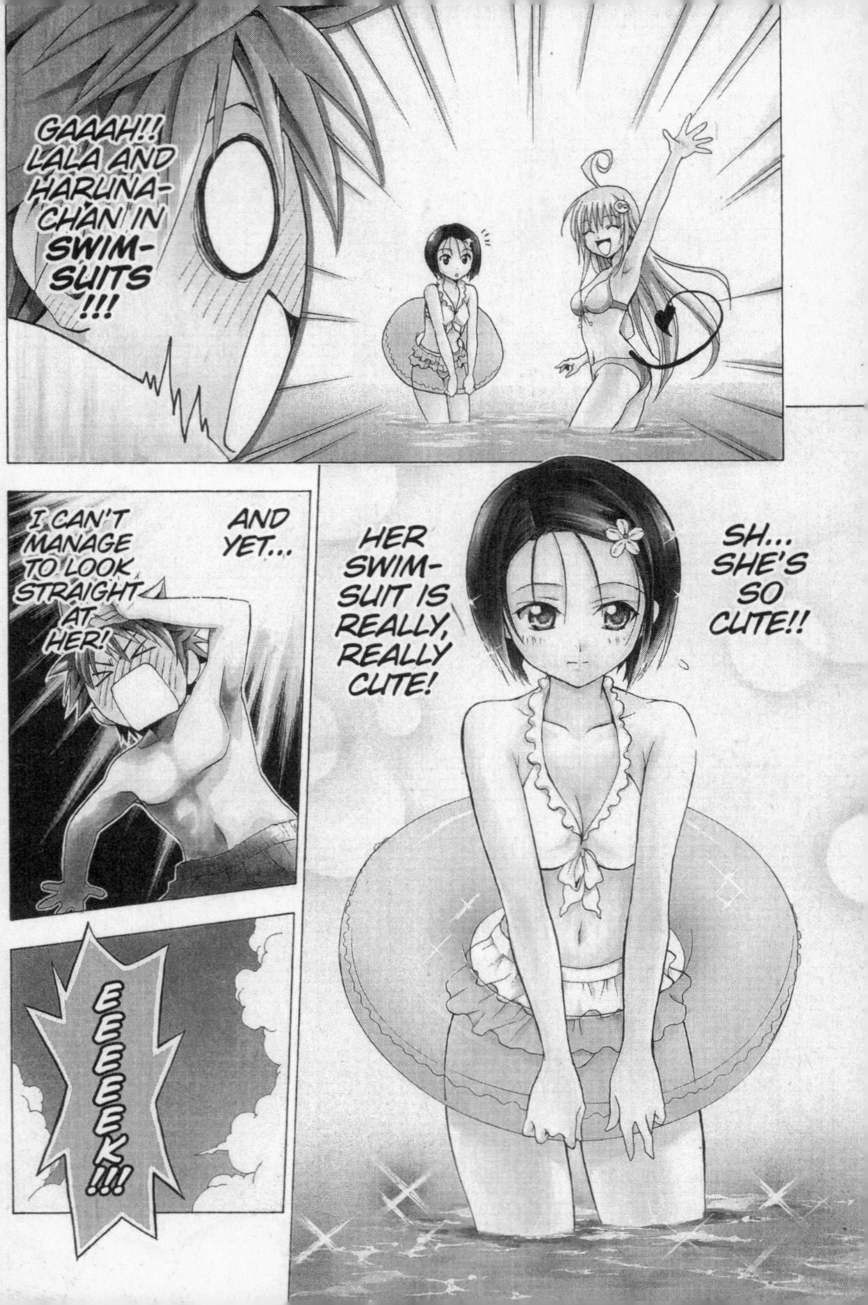
GAAAH!! LALA AND HARUNA-CHAN IN SWIM-SUITS!!!
SH... SHE'S SO CUTE!!
HER SWIM-SUIT IS REALLY, REALLY CUTE!
AND YET...
I CAN'T MANAGE TO LOOK STRAIGHT AT HER!
EEEEEEK!!!

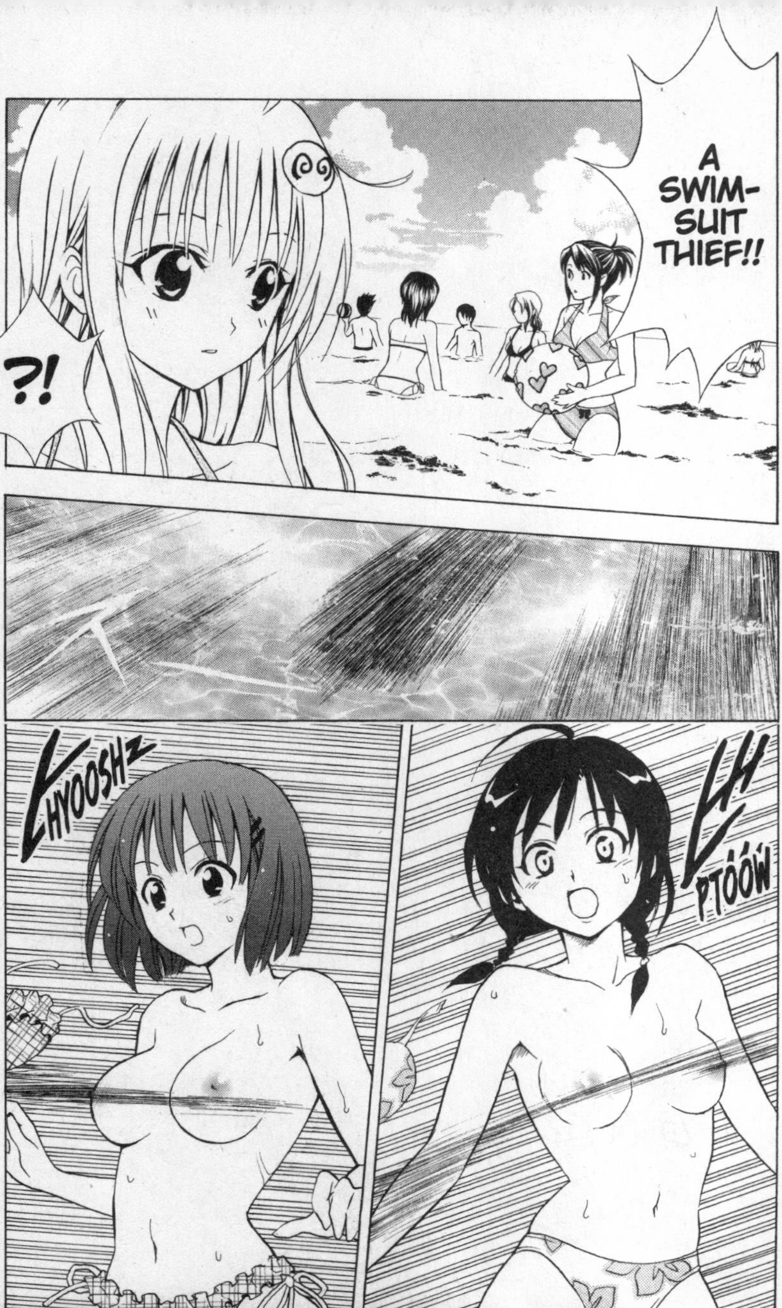
A SWIM-SUIT THIEF!!
?!
PTOOW
HYOOSH

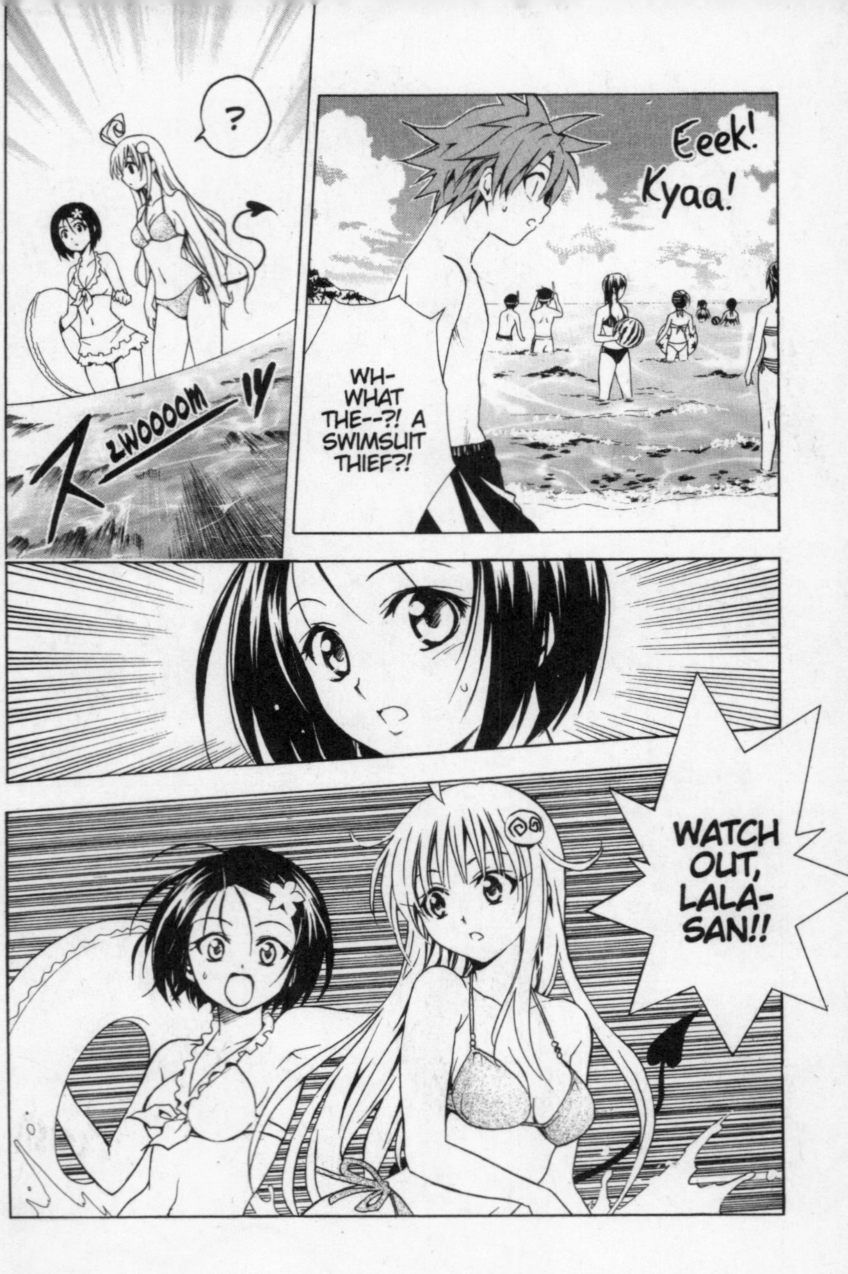
Eeek! Kyaa!
WH-WHAT THE--?! A SWIMSUIT THIEF?!
?
ZWOOOOM
WATCH OUT, LALA-SAN!!

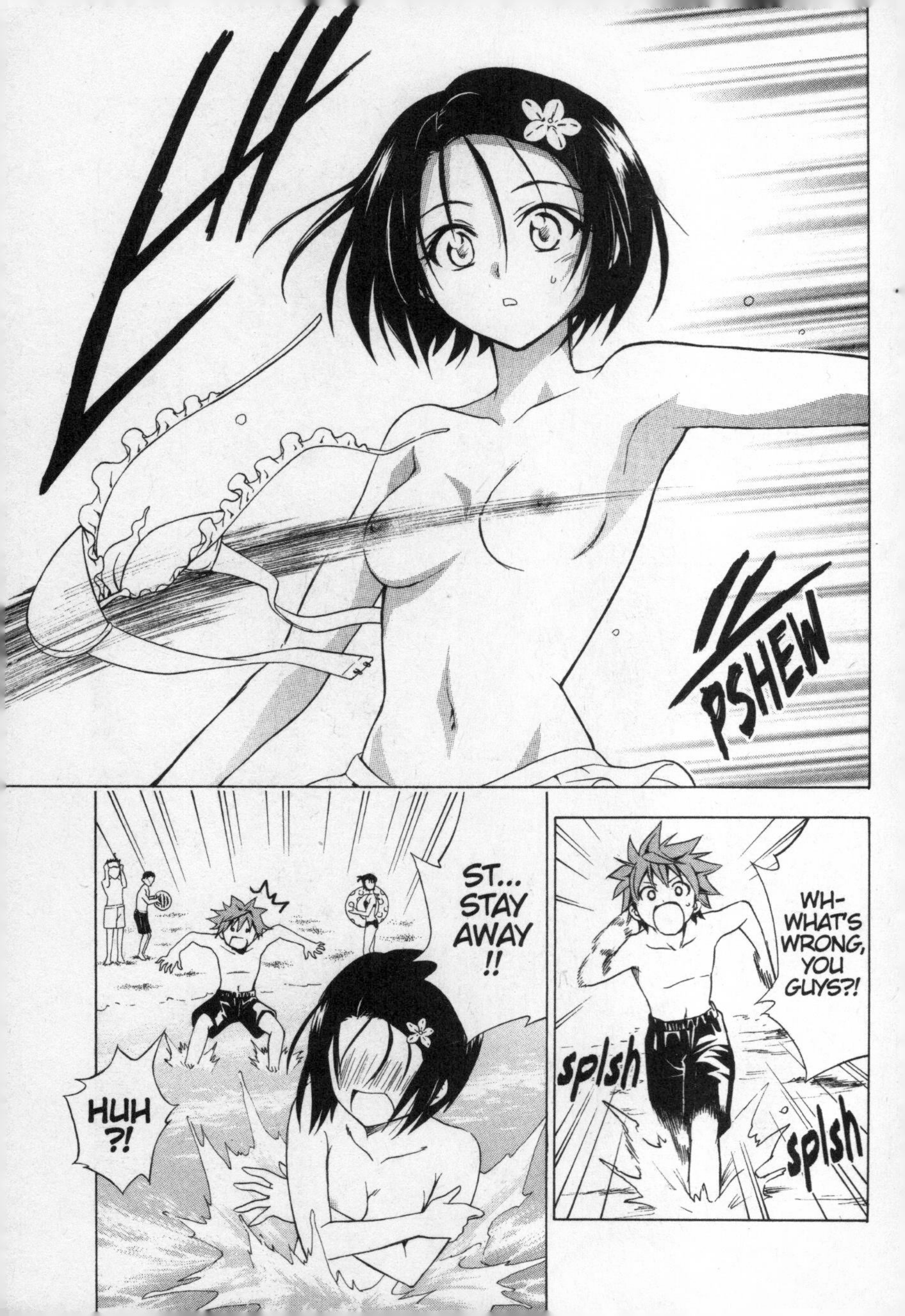
PSHEW
WH- WHAT'S WRONG, YOU GUYS?!
splsh
splsh
ST... STAY AWAY !!
HUH ?!

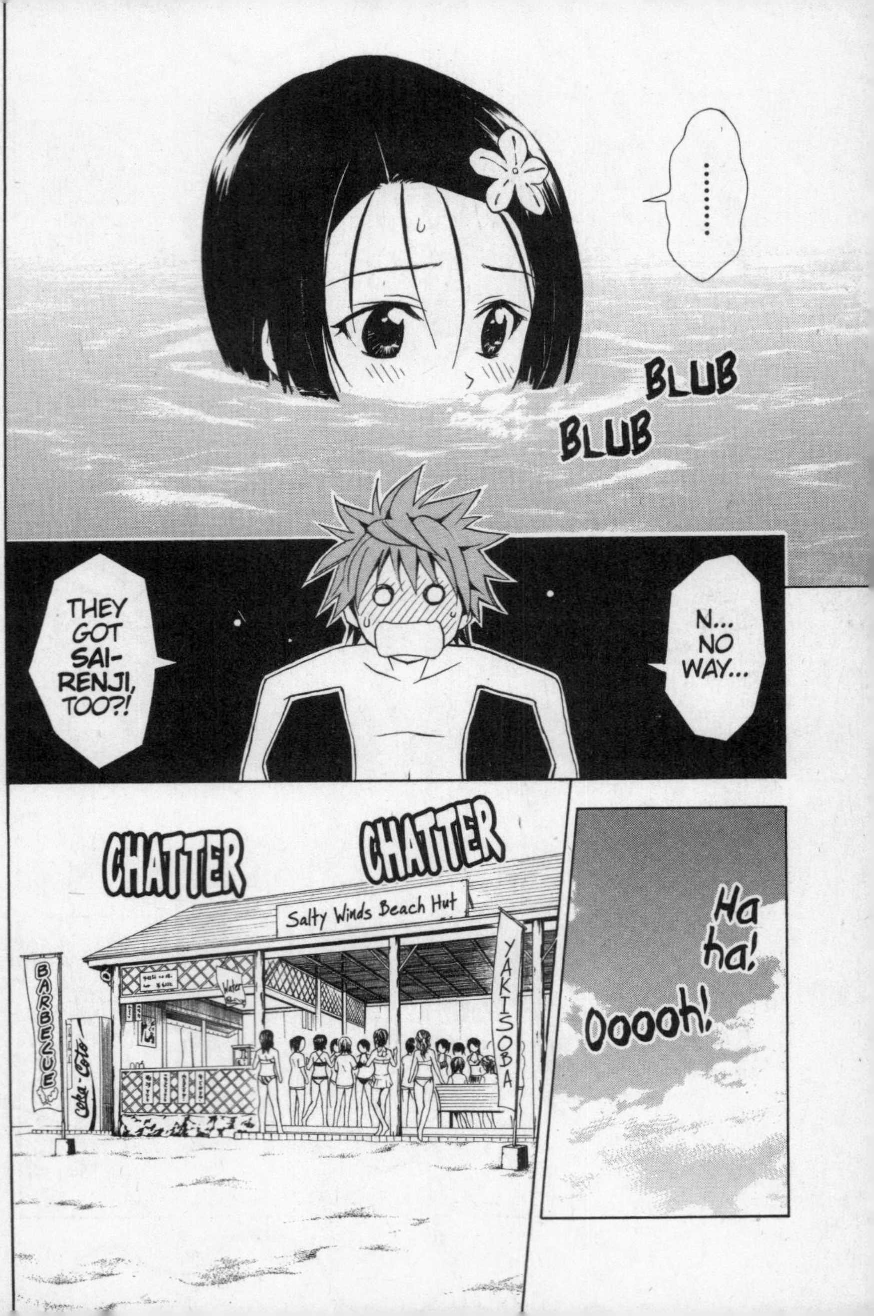
......
BLUB
BLUB
N... NO WAY...
THEY GOT SAI-RENJI, TOO?!
Ha ha!
Ooooh!
CHATTER
CHATTER
Salty Winds Beach Hut
YAKISOBA
Water
BARBECUE
Coka-Cota

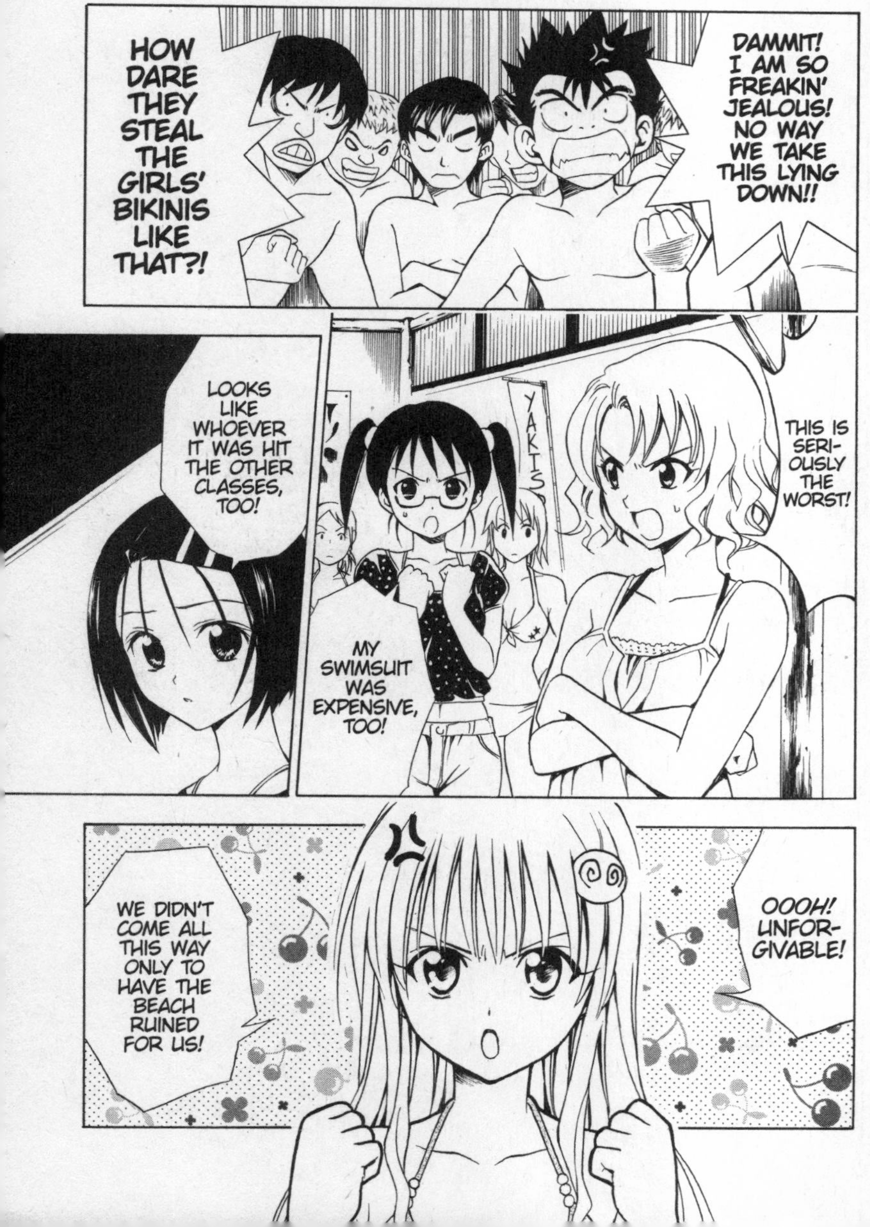
DAMMIT! I AM SO FREAKIN' JEALOUS! NO WAY WE TAKE THIS LYING DOWN!!
HOW DARE THEY STEAL THE GIRLS' BIKINIS LIKE THAT?!
THIS IS SERIOUSLY THE WORST!
MY SWIMSUIT WAS EXPENSIVE, TOO!
LOOKS LIKE WHOEVER IT WAS HIT THE OTHER CLASSES, TOO!
OOOH! UNFORGIVABLE!
WE DIDN'T COME ALL THIS WAY ONLY TO HAVE THE BEACH RUINED FOR US!

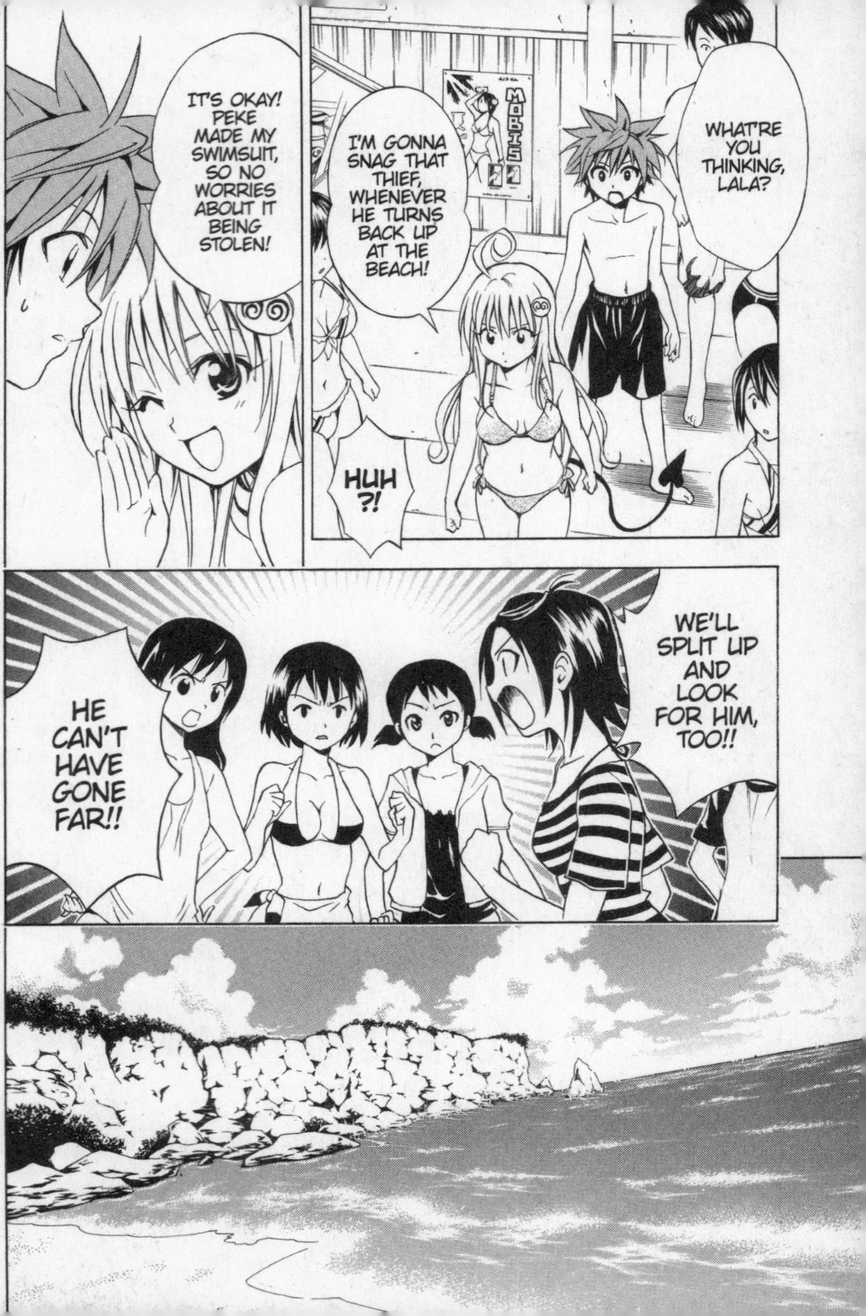
WHAT'RE YOU THINKING, LALA?
I'M GONNA SNAG THAT THIEF, WHENEVER HE TURNS BACK UP AT THE BEACH!
HUH ?!
IT'S OKAY! PEKE MADE MY SWIMSUIT, SO NO WORRIES ABOUT IT BEING STOLEN!
WE'LL SPLIT UP AND LOOK FOR HIM, TOO!!
HE CAN'T HAVE GONE FAR!!

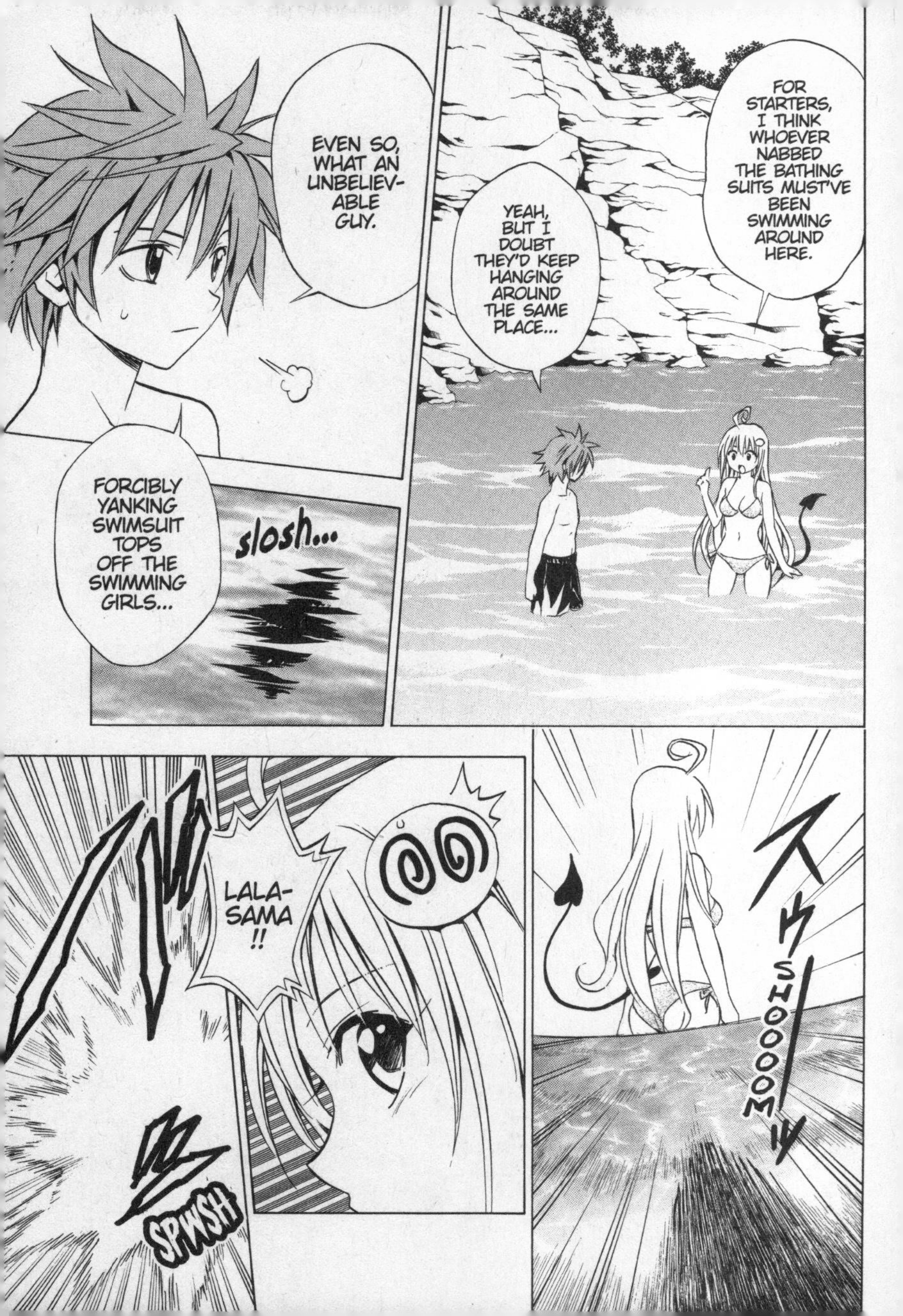
FOR STARTERS, I THINK WHOEVER NABBED THE BATHING SUITS MUST'VE BEEN SWIMMING AROUND HERE.
YEAH, BUT I DOUBT THEY'D KEEP HANGING AROUND THE SAME PLACE...
EVEN SO, WHAT AN UNBELIEV-ABLE GUY.
FORCIBLY YANKING SWIMSUIT TOPS OFF THE SWIMMING GIRLS...
slosh...
SHOOOOOM
LALA-SAMA!!
SPWSH

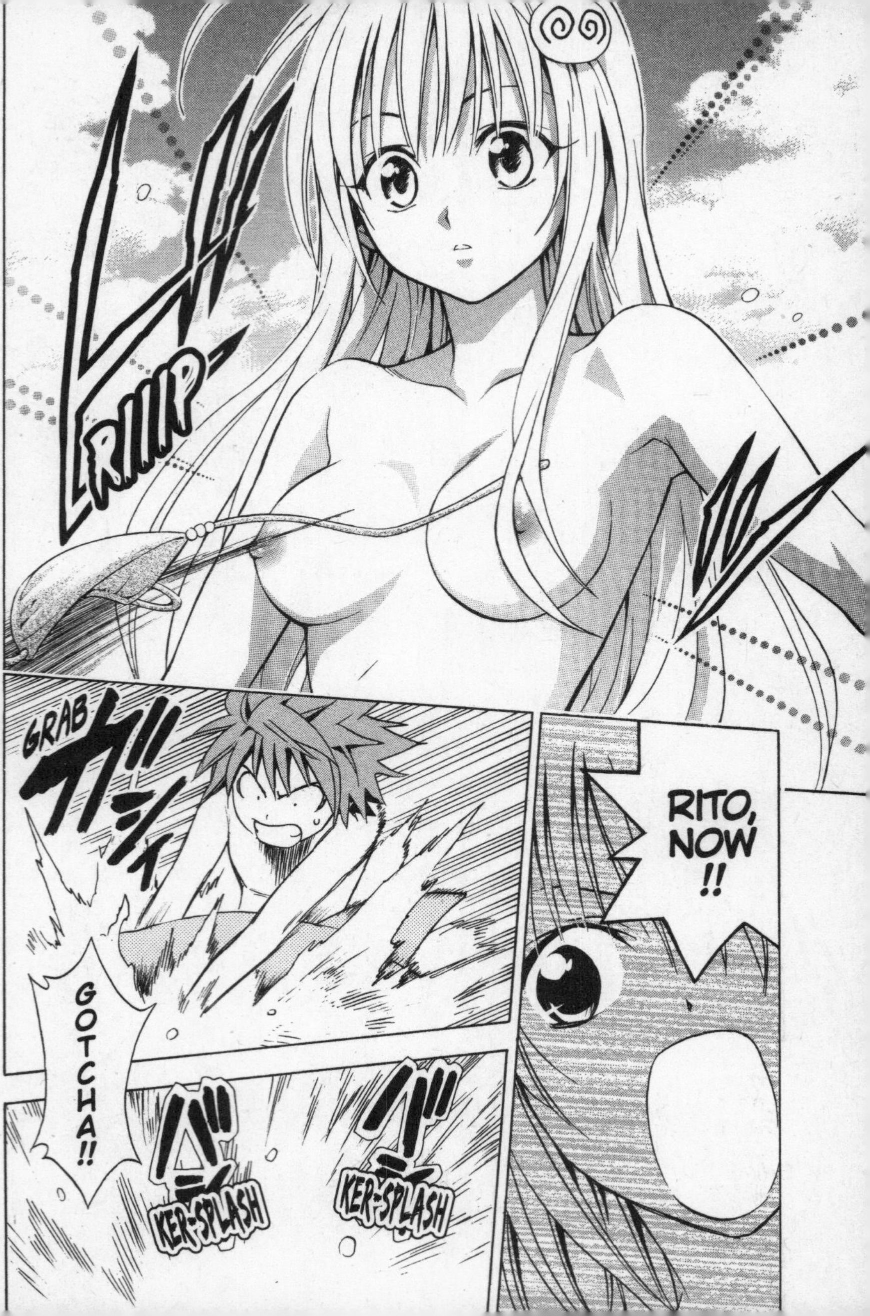
RIIIP
RITO, NOW!!
GRAB
GOTCHA!!
KER-SPLASH
KER-SPLASH

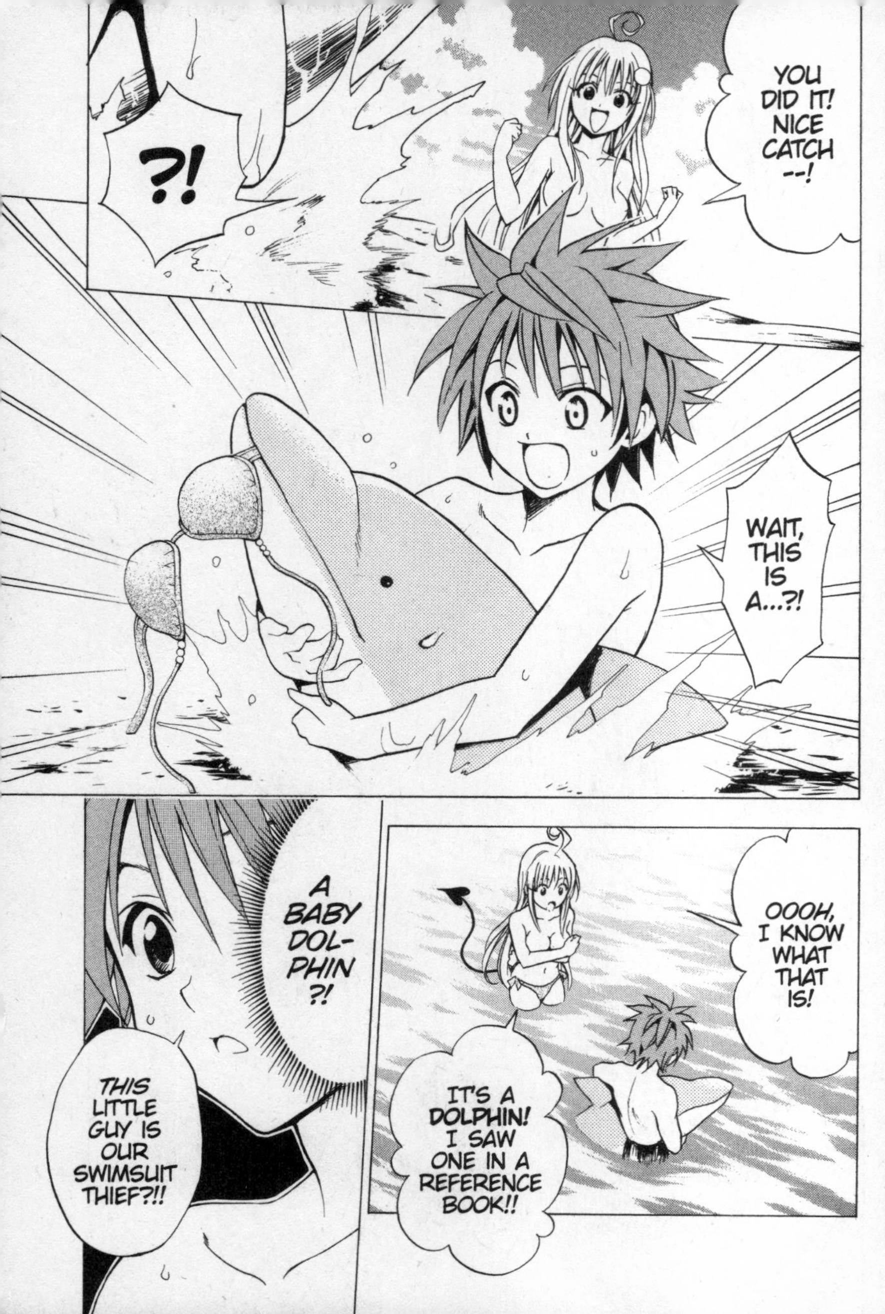

YOU DID IT! NICE CATCH--!
?!
WAIT, THIS IS A...?!
OOOH, I KNOW WHAT THAT IS!
IT'S A DOLPHIN! I SAW ONE IN A REFERENCE BOOK!!
A BABY DOL-PHIN?!
THIS LITTLE GUY IS OUR SWIMSUIT THIEF?!!

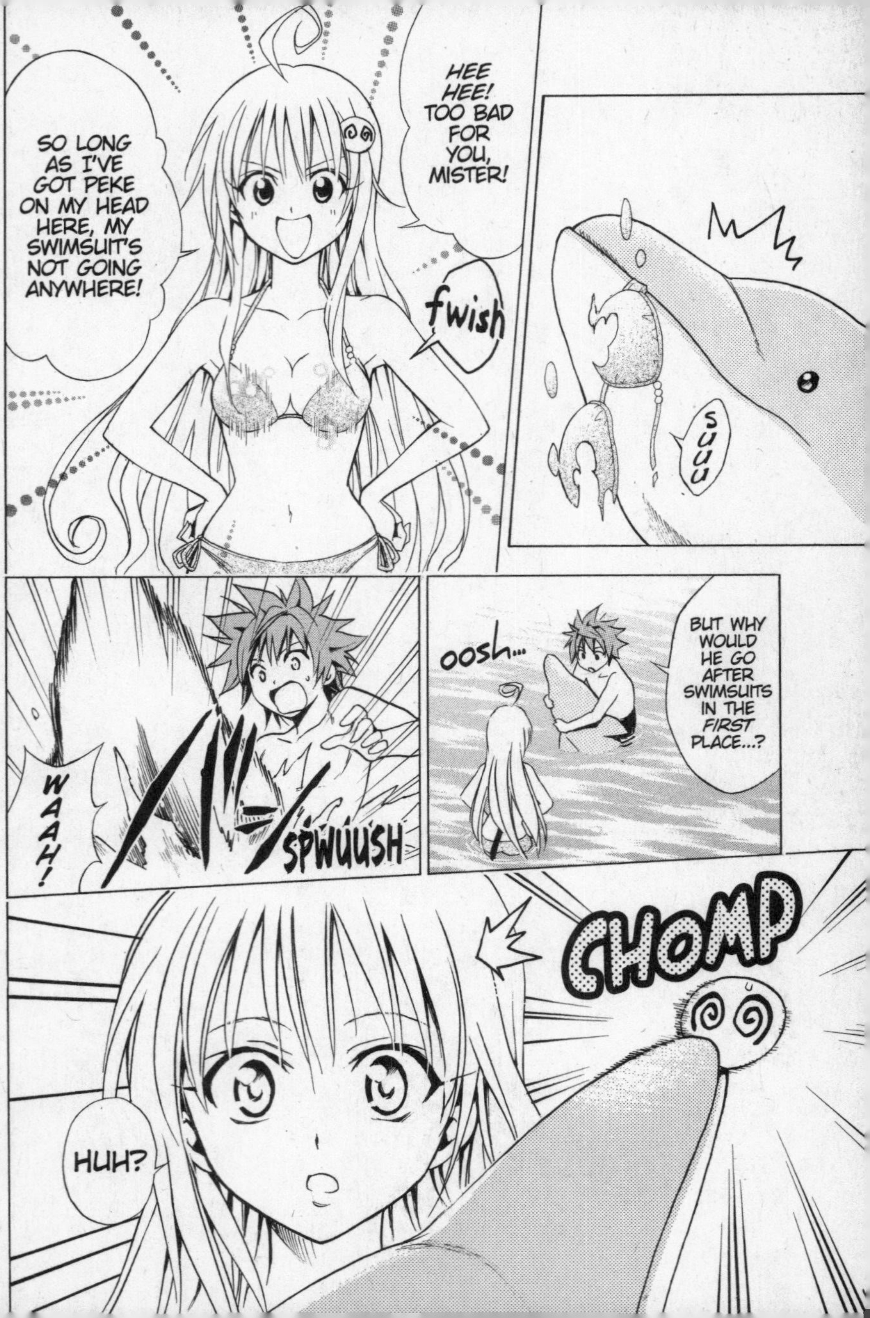
HEE HEE! TOO BAD FOR YOU, MISTER!
SO LONG AS I'VE GOT PEKE ON MY HEAD HERE, MY SWIMSUIT'S NOT GOING ANYWHERE!
fwish
SUUU
BUT WHY WOULD HE GO AFTER SWIMSUITS IN THE *FIRST* PLACE...?
oosh...
SPWUUSH
WAAAH!
CHOMP
HUH?

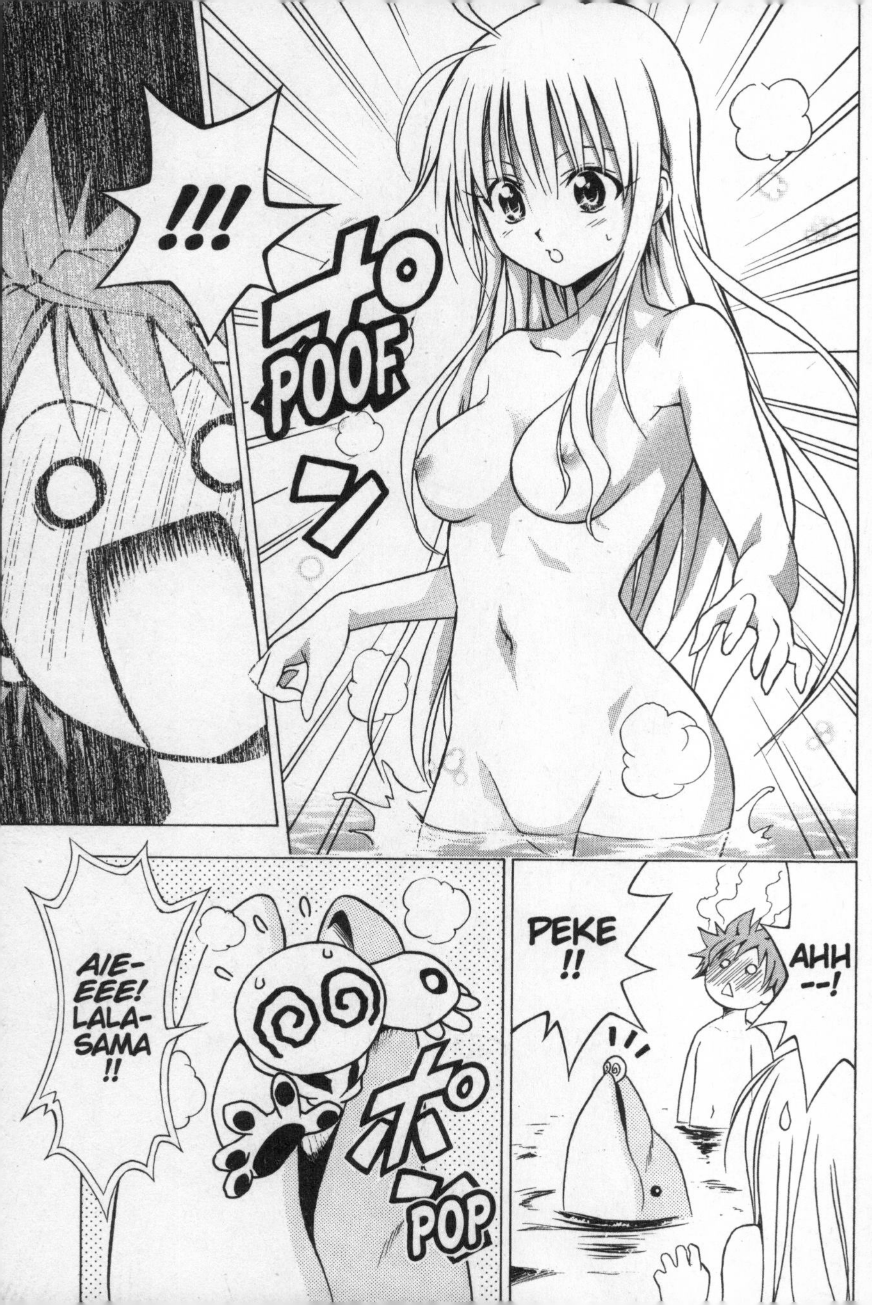
!!!
POOF
AHH --!
PEKE !!
AIE-EEE! LALA-SAMA !!
POP

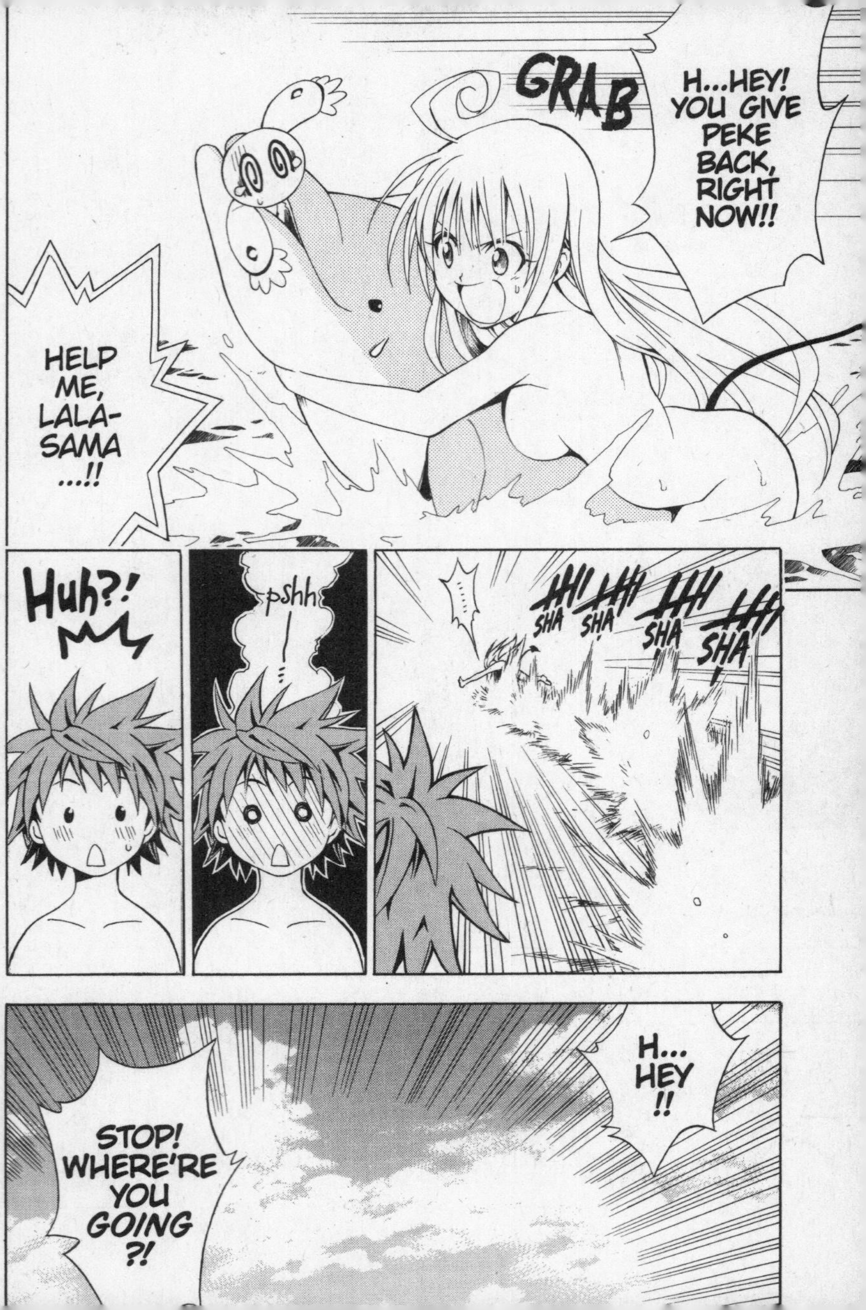
H...HEY! YOU GIVE PEKE BACK, RIGHT NOW!!
GRAB
HELP ME, LALA-SAMA...!!
SHA SHA SHA SHA
pshh
Huh?!
H... HEY!!
STOP! WHERE'RE YOU GOING?!

I LOST THEM...

WHERE DID THOSE TWO GET OFF TO...?

slosh...

splsh splssh

OVER HERE! QUICK!!

RITOOOO!

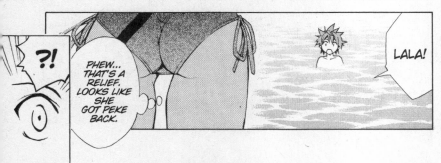

?!

PHEW... THAT'S A RELIEF. LOOKS LIKE SHE GOT PEKE BACK.

LALA!

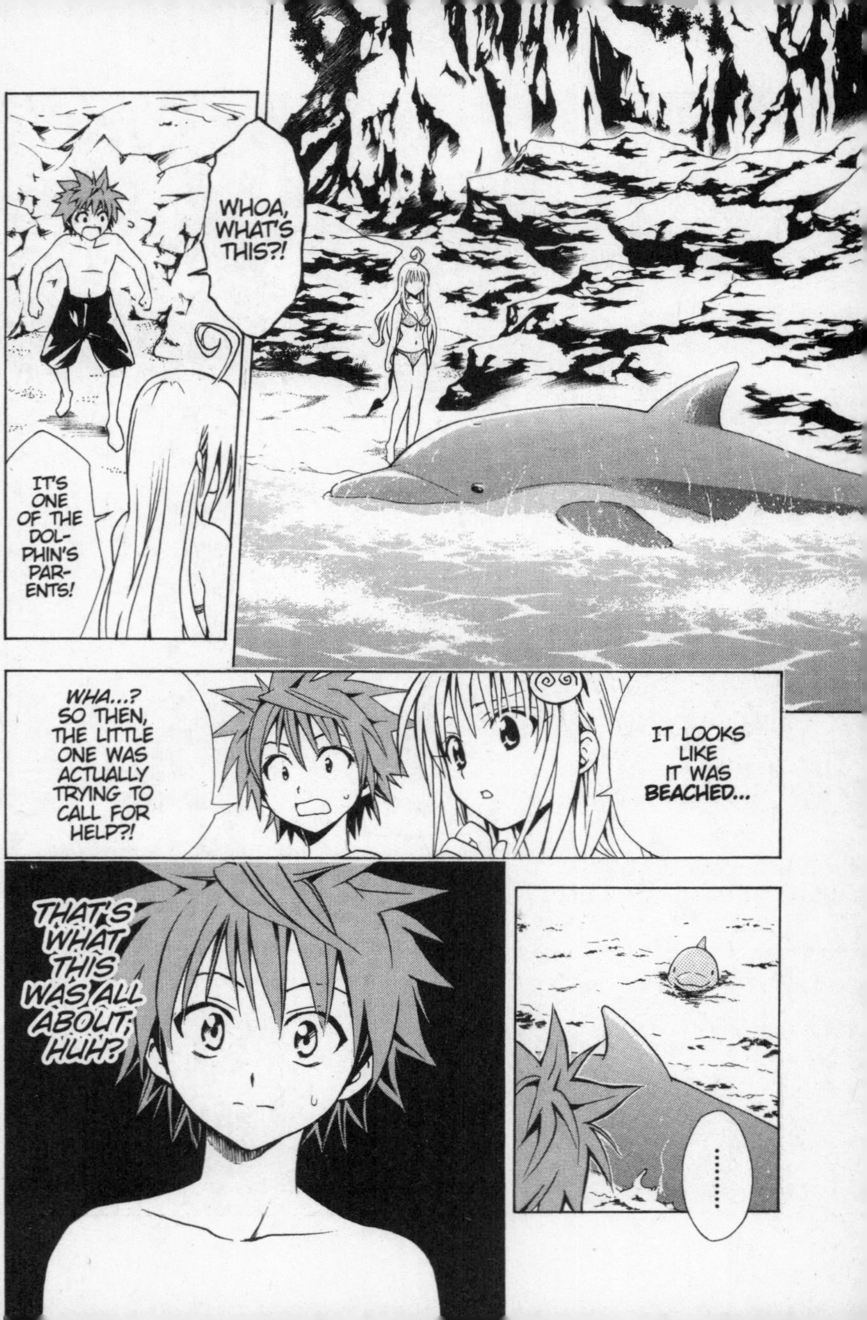
WHOA, WHAT'S THIS?!
IT'S ONE OF THE DOL-PHIN'S PAR-ENTS!
IT LOOKS LIKE IT WAS BEACHED...
WHA...? SO THEN, THE LITTLE ONE WAS ACTUALLY TRYING TO CALL FOR HELP?!
......
THAT'S WHAT THIS WAS ALL ABOUT, HUH?

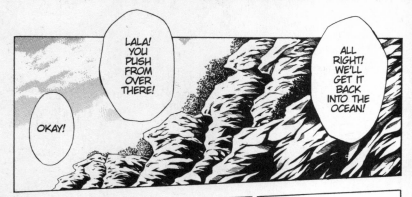

ALL RIGHT! WE'LL GET IT BACK INTO THE OCEAN!
LALA! YOU PUSH FROM OVER THERE!
OKAY!
eee-ee!
I CAN'T SEE ANY BIG INJURIES--LOOKS LIKE IT'LL BE JUST FINE!
SEEMS LIKE BOTH PARENT AND CHILD ARE TRYING TO THANK US.
......

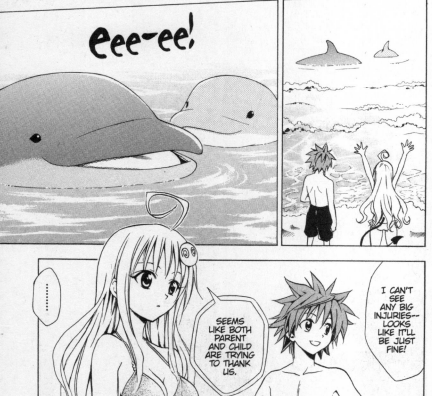

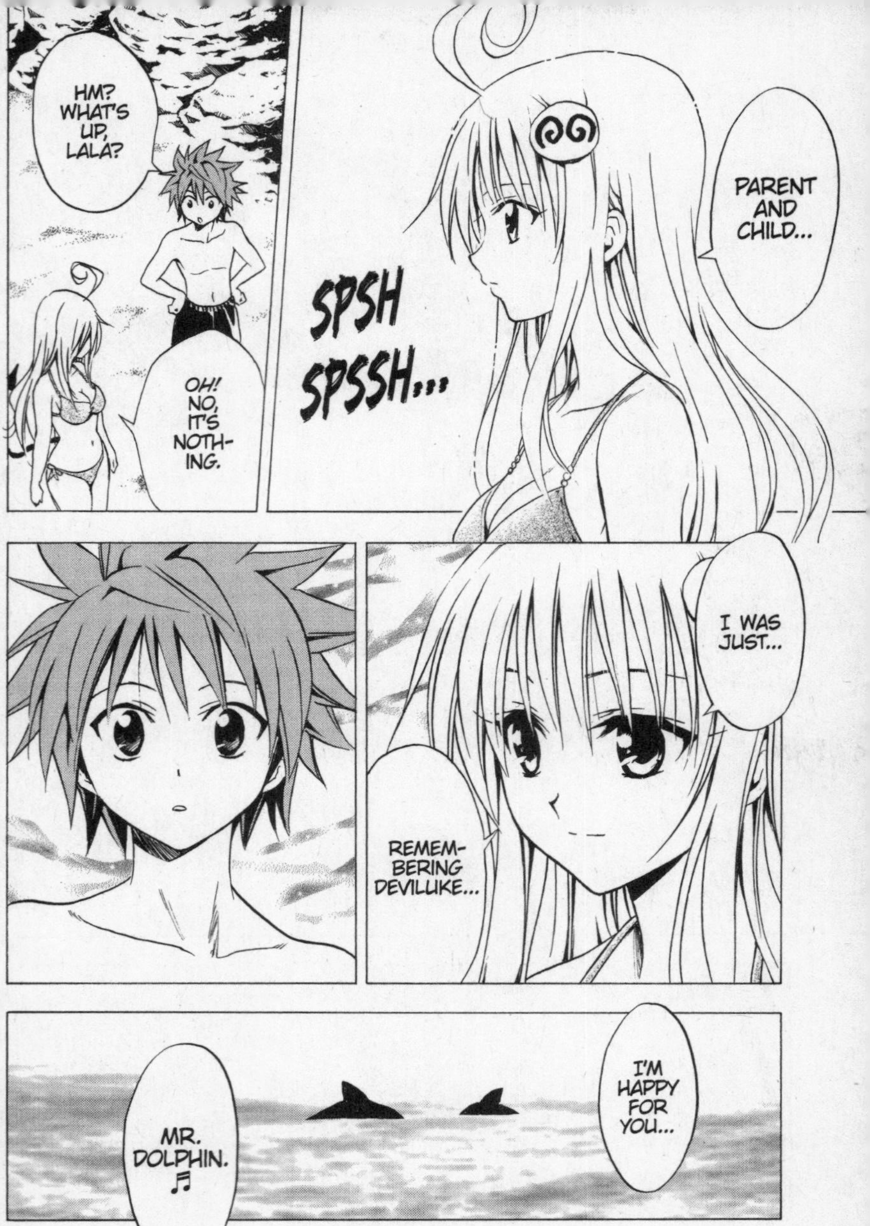
PARENT AND CHILD...
SPSH SPSSH...
HM? WHAT'S UP, LALA?
OH! NO, IT'S NOTH-ING.
I WAS JUST...
REMEM-BERING DEVILUKE...
I'M HAPPY FOR YOU...
MR. DOLPHIN. ♬

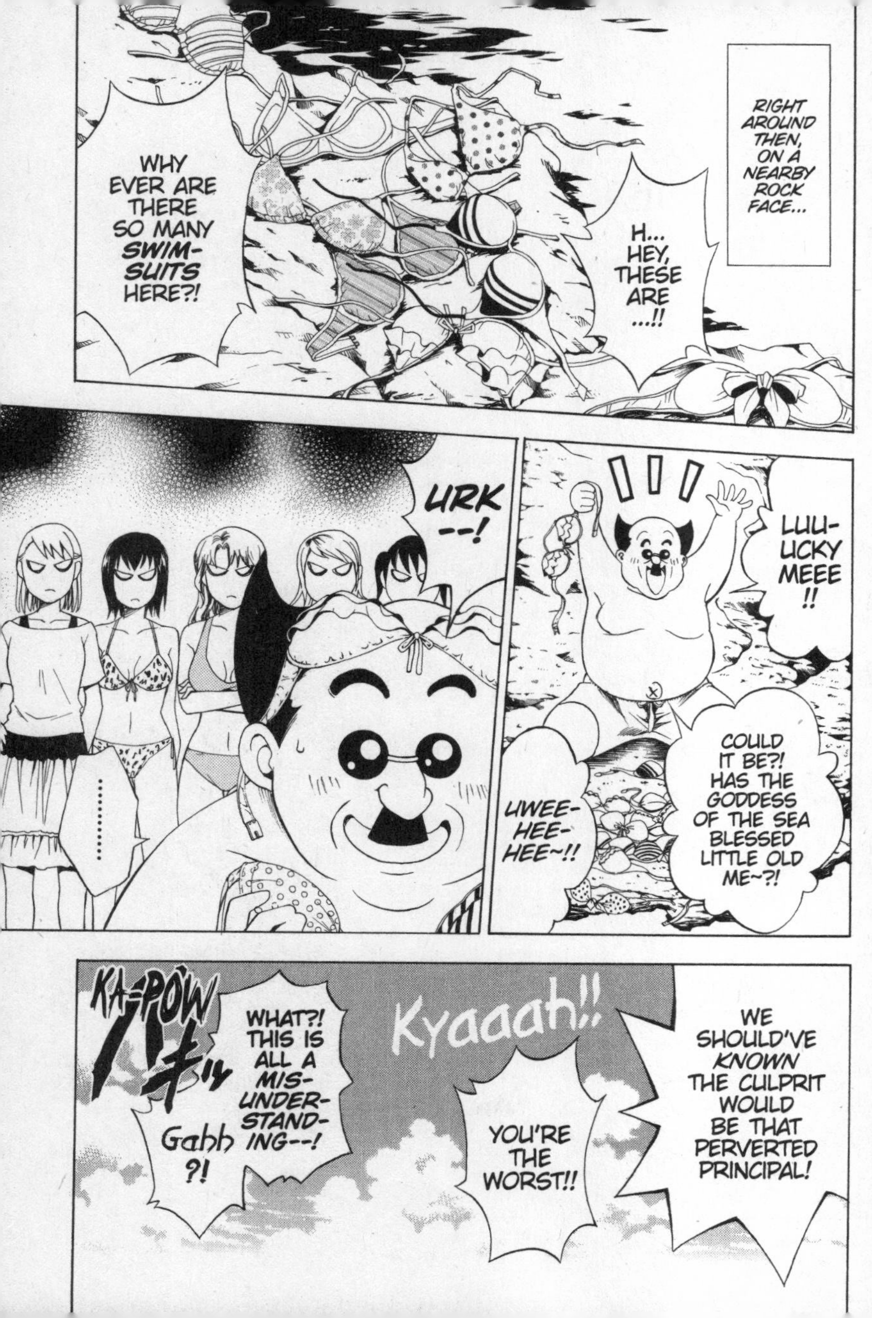
RIGHT AROUND THEN, ON A NEARBY ROCK FACE...
H... HEY, THESE ARE ...!!
WHY EVER ARE THERE SO MANY *SWIM-SUITS* HERE?!
LUU-UCKY MEEE !!
COULD IT BE?! HAS THE GODDESS OF THE SEA BLESSED LITTLE OLD ME~?!
UWEE-HEE-HEE~!!
URK --!
......
WE SHOULD'VE *KNOWN* THE CULPRIT WOULD BE THAT PERVERTED PRINCIPAL!
YOU'RE THE WORST!!
Kyaaah!!
WHAT?! THIS IS ALL A MIS-UNDER-STANDING--!
KA-POW
Gahh ?!

Character File

1
Yuuki Mikan

Let's see... Starting with this volume, we're going to write some introductions for the side characters. Or maybe you could call them "backstories." These will appear in every volume, like this one.

The decision to do so came about kind of like this:

Yabuki: Could you *pleeeease* write a chapter about Mikan? She's on the cover of Volume 3!
Hasemi: Say what?! SHE IS?!

● ● ● ● ● ● ● ● ● ● ● ● ● ● ●

So, let's start the first of these off with Rito's little sister, Mikan.

She was among the earliest characters we conceived of. We thought, "Well, we don't have a little sister character!" and so, she was born. Because of that, thinking her up and creating her wasn't the difficult part. Instead it was crafting the character's personality that caused a lot of suffering... Or rather, what caused the most confusion was the question of how she would refer to Rito. "Oniichan" kept popping into my head, right up until the end. Ultimately, we landed on just having her call him "Rito," though... *(ha ha)*.

Beyond that, what we were most mindful of was to give her an impish but irresistible charm--and to make her cute! We are always conscious of that as we write her.

Even though she's quite steadfast, at her core, she's still an elementary school student. She wants to enjoy herself and mess with Rito... That's kind of her vibe. And even as the story proceeds, and she slowly starts to get an inkling of who Rito's dream girl is, she still doesn't have any qualms about teasing him over it. That's first and foremost how we depict her.

● ● ● ● ● ● ● ● ● ● ● ● ● ● ● ●

☆ Mikan's Main Story

I've actually invented and abandoned a number of stories for Mikan. I've learned a few things from my attempts to write about her. If I advance the story from her perspective, no matter what I do, Lala and Haruna end up getting left behind. And there ends up being not much interaction with other characters, so the scope of the story becomes narrower than usual. So, I don't really know when I'll write a story using her, but when the *AHA!* moment comes, I'll be sure to do it justice, so please take a long-term view on this one! (Man, I'd really like to create some friends for Mikan, too...)

● ● ● ● ● ● ● ● ● ● ● ● ● ● ● ●

So, we'll write comments like this for the girl on the cover of the next volume, too. Guess it would've been nice if we'd done that from the start, huh...? (regretful laugh)

Hasemi

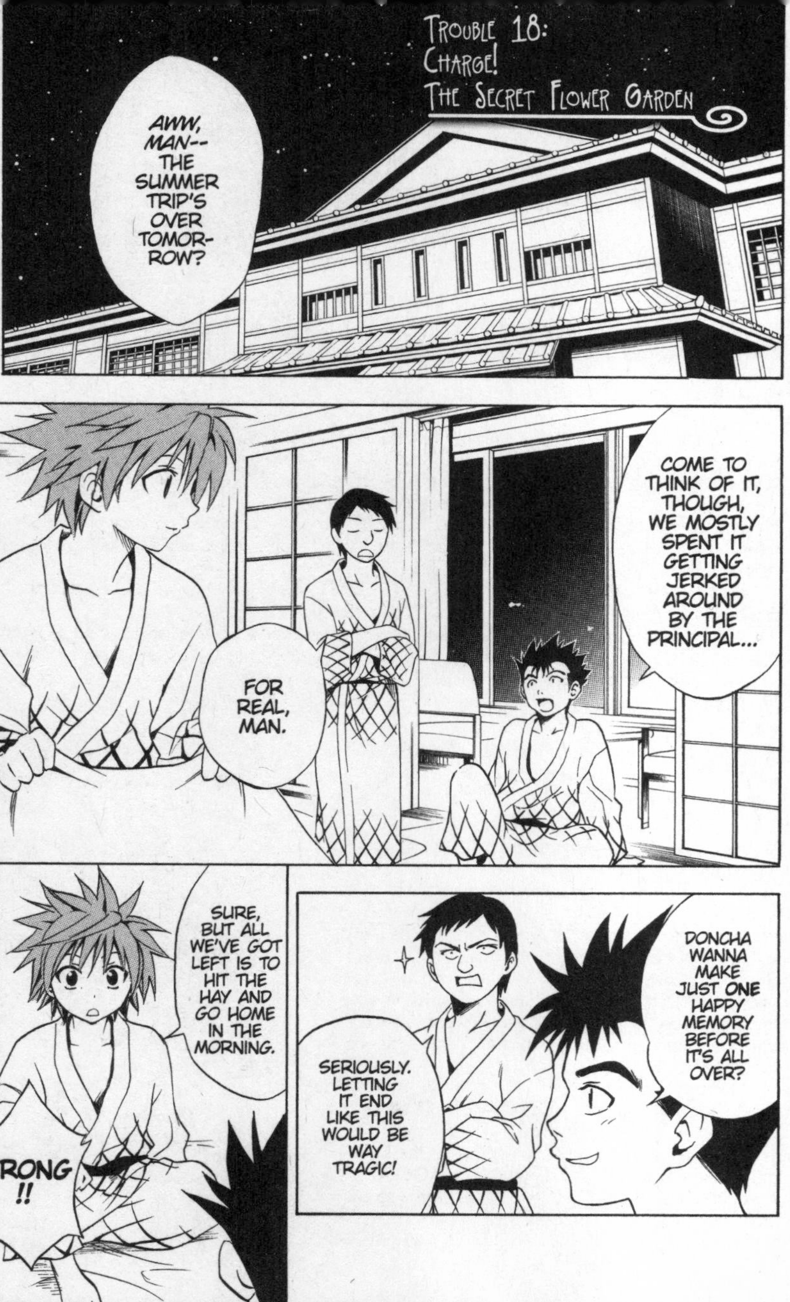
TROUBLE 18: CHARGE! THE SECRET FLOWER GARDEN
AWW, MAN-- THE SUMMER TRIP'S OVER TOMOR-ROW?
COME TO THINK OF IT, THOUGH, WE MOSTLY SPENT IT GETTING JERKED AROUND BY THE PRINCIPAL...
FOR REAL, MAN.
DONCHA WANNA MAKE JUST ONE HAPPY MEMORY BEFORE IT'S ALL OVER?
SERIOUSLY. LETTING IT END LIKE THIS WOULD BE WAY TRAGIC!
SURE, BUT ALL WE'VE GOT LEFT IS TO HIT THE HAY AND GO HOME IN THE MORNING.
WRONG!!

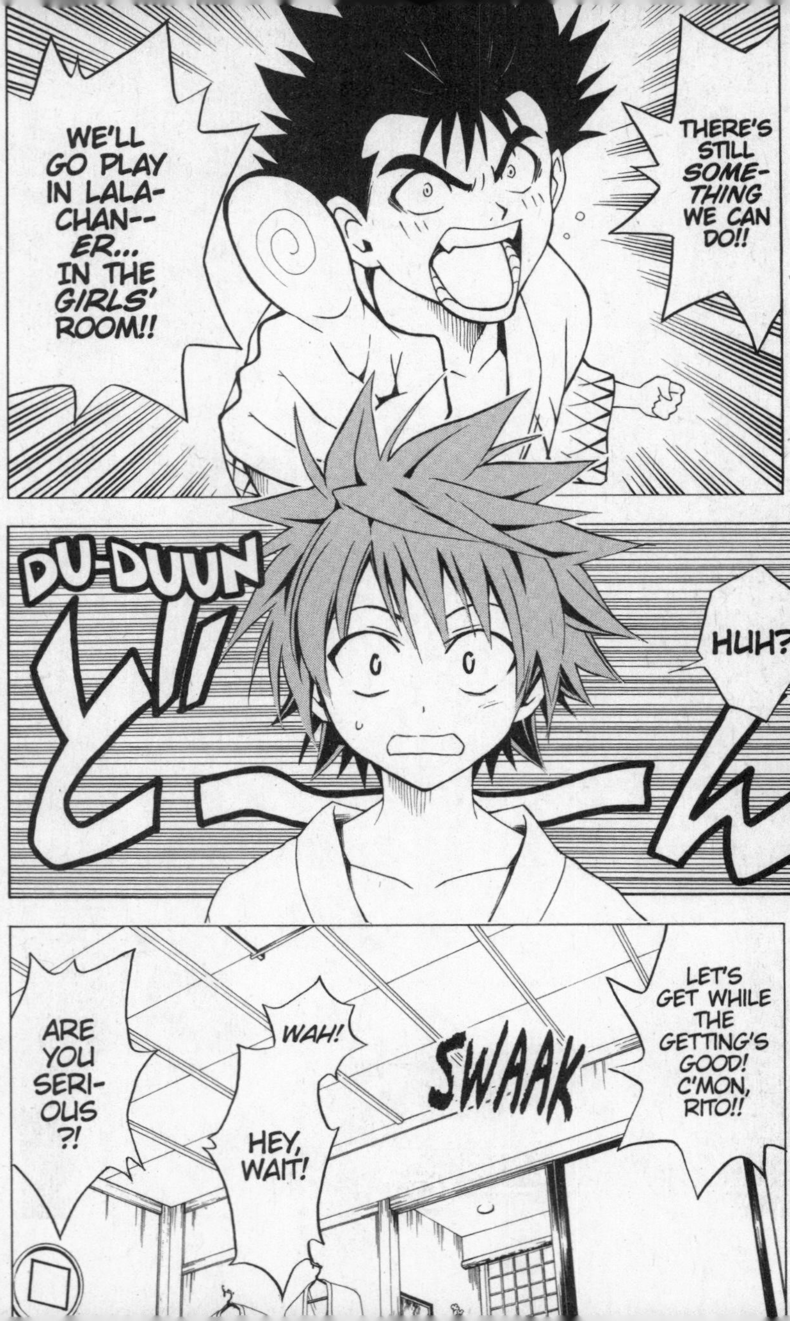
THERE'S STILL SOMETHING WE CAN DO!!
WE'LL GO PLAY IN LALA-CHAN-- ER... IN THE GIRLS' ROOM!!
HUH?
DU-DUUN
LET'S GET WHILE THE GETTING'S GOOD! C'MON, RITO!!
SWAAK
WAH!
HEY, WAIT!
ARE YOU SERIOUS?!

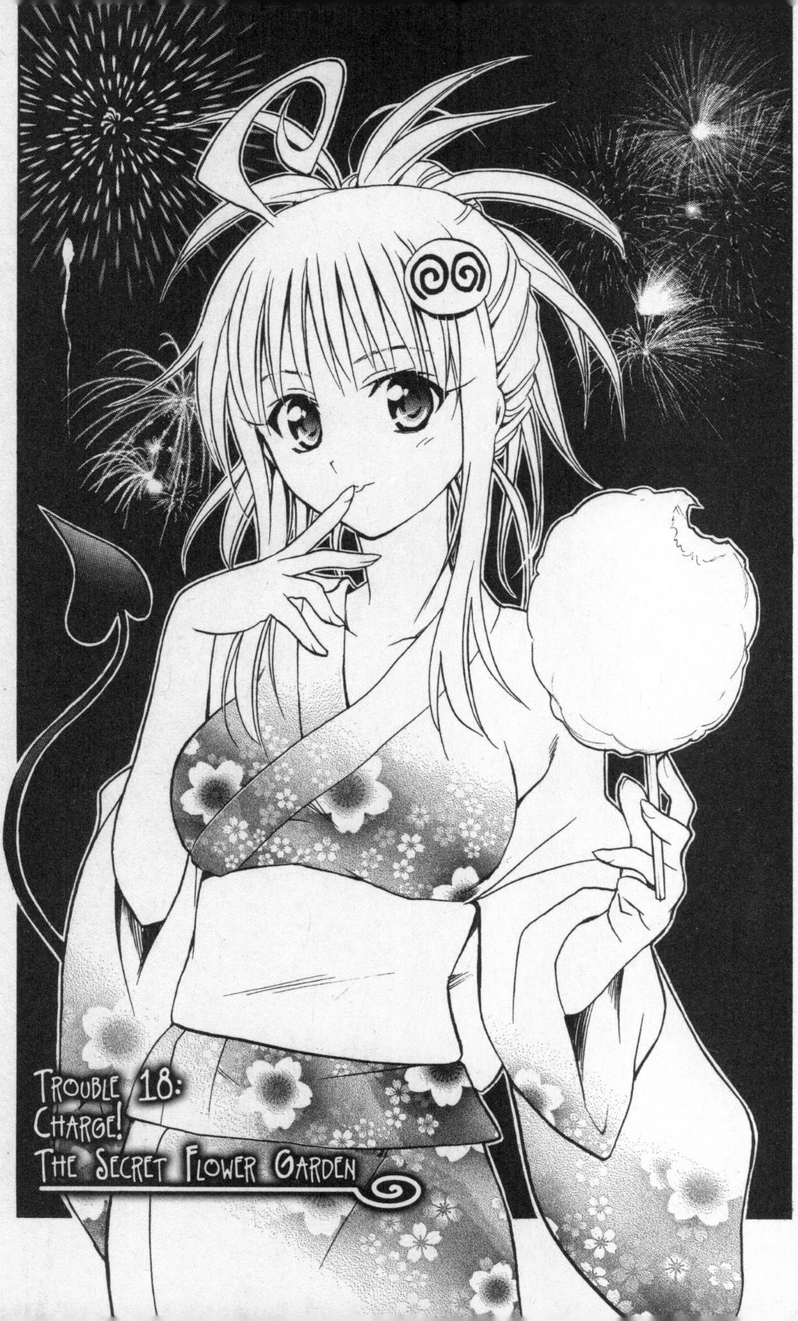

TROUBLE 18:
CHARGE!
THE SECRET FLOWER GARDEN

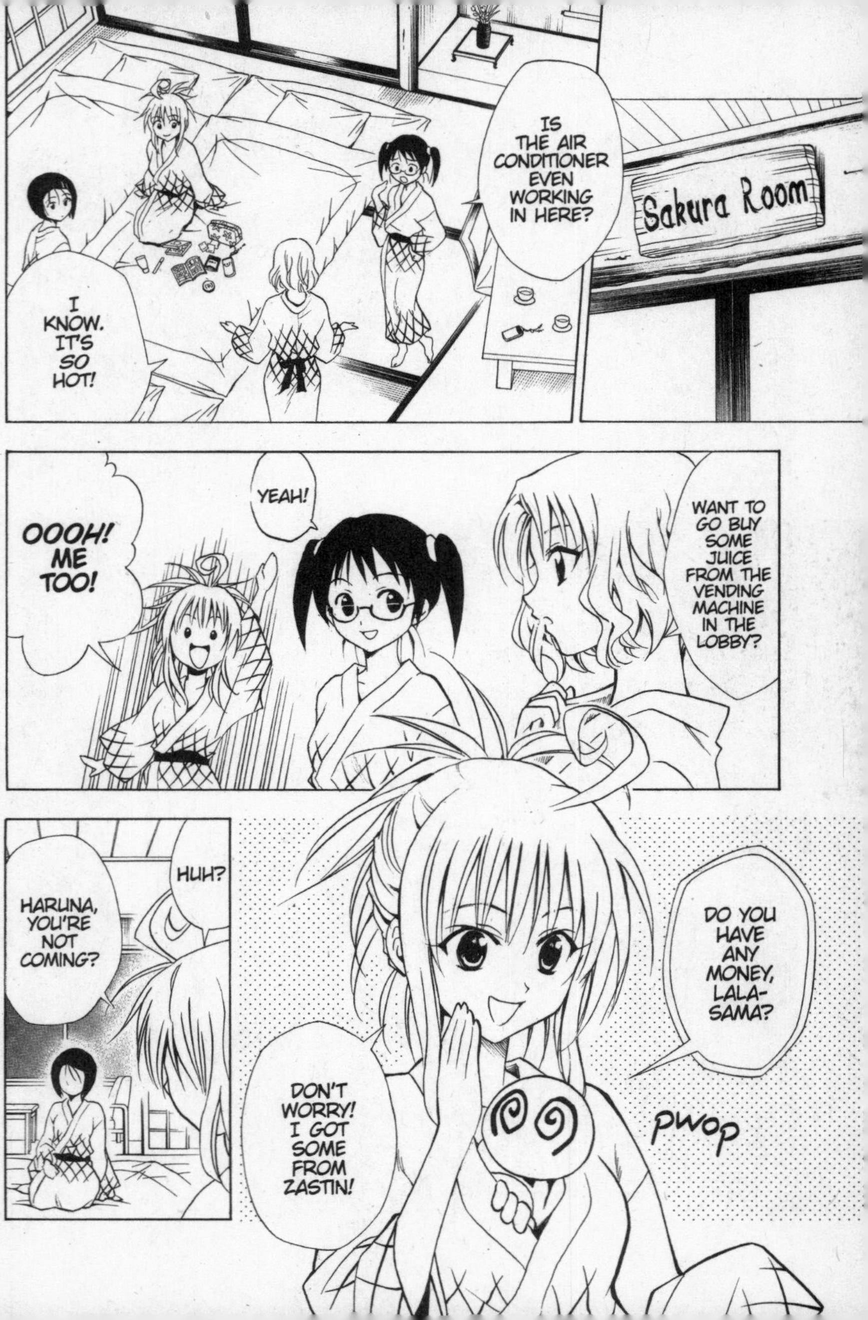
Sakura Room
IS THE AIR CONDITIONER EVEN WORKING IN HERE?
I KNOW. IT'S SO HOT!
WANT TO GO BUY SOME JUICE FROM THE VENDING MACHINE IN THE LOBBY?
YEAH!
OOOH! ME TOO!
DO YOU HAVE ANY MONEY, LALA-SAMA?
pwop
DON'T WORRY! I GOT SOME FROM ZASTIN!
HUH?
HARUNA, YOU'RE NOT COMING?

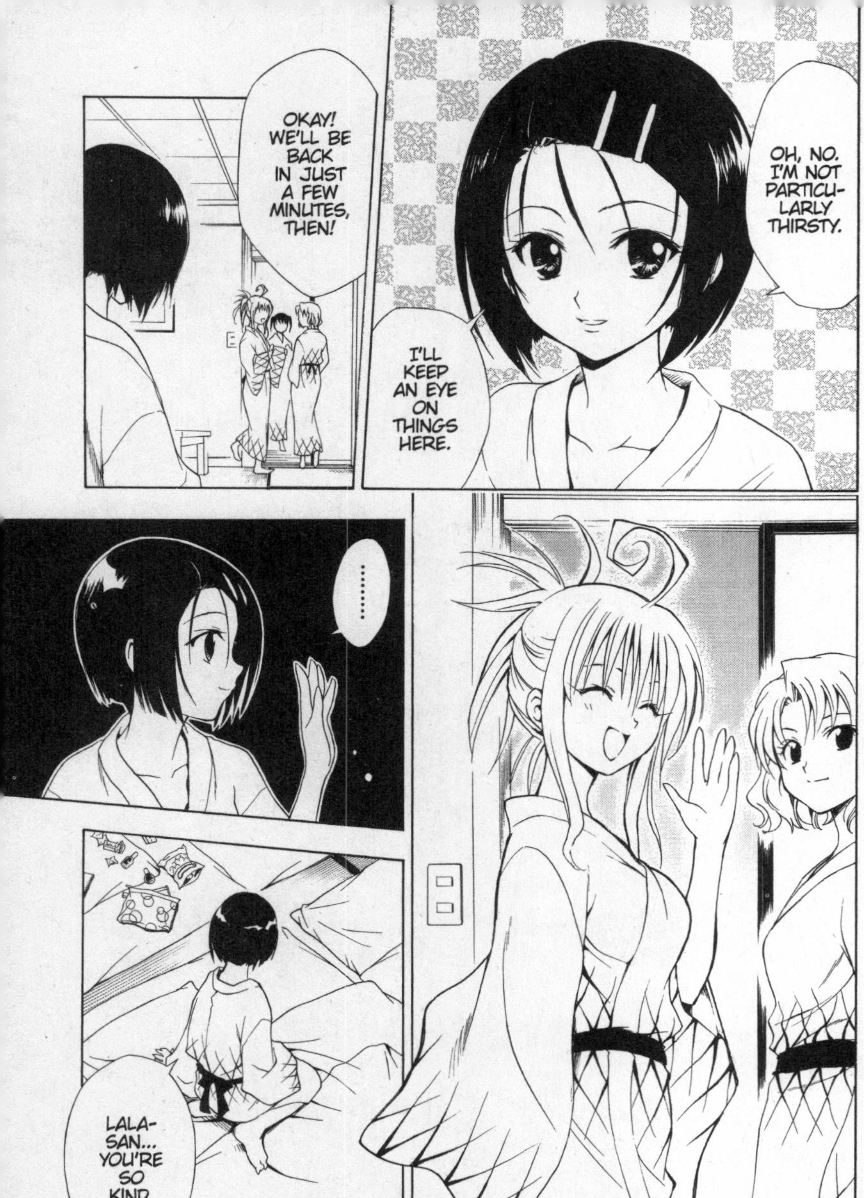
OH, NO. I'M NOT PARTICU-LARLY THIRSTY.
I'LL KEEP AN EYE ON THINGS HERE.
OKAY! WE'LL BE BACK IN JUST A FEW MINUTES, THEN!
......
LALA-SAN... YOU'RE SO KIND.

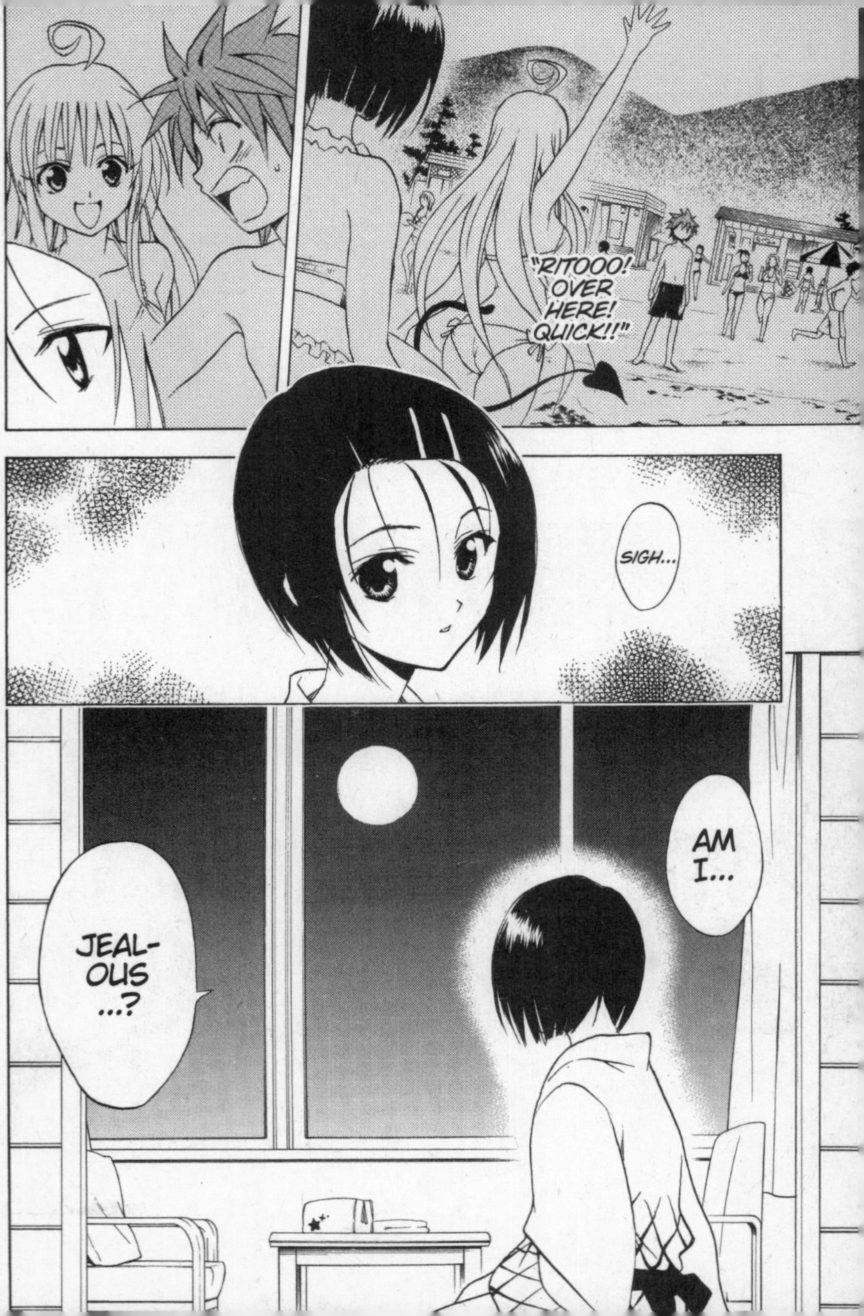
"RITOOO! OVER HERE! QUICK!!"
SIGH...
AM I...
JEAL-OUS ...?

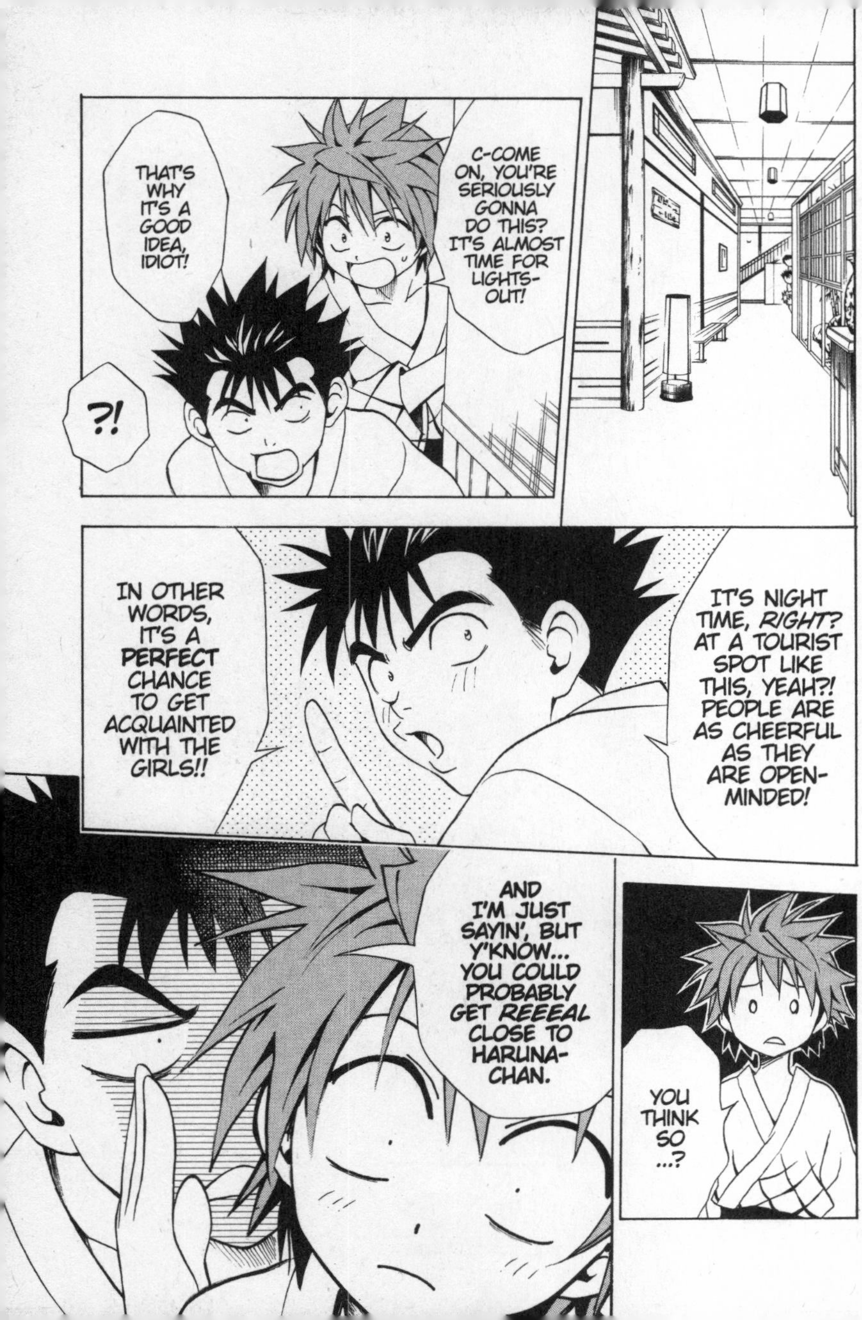
C-COME ON, YOU'RE SERIOUSLY GONNA DO THIS? IT'S ALMOST TIME FOR LIGHTS-OUT!
THAT'S WHY IT'S A GOOD IDEA, IDIOT!
?!
IT'S NIGHT TIME, *RIGHT?* AT A TOURIST SPOT LIKE THIS, YEAH?! PEOPLE ARE AS CHEERFUL AS THEY ARE OPEN-MINDED!
IN OTHER WORDS, IT'S A **PERFECT CHANCE** TO GET ACQUAINTED WITH THE GIRLS!!
AND I'M JUST SAYIN', BUT Y'KNOW... YOU COULD PROBABLY GET *REEEAL* CLOSE TO HARUNA-CHAN.
YOU THINK SO ...?

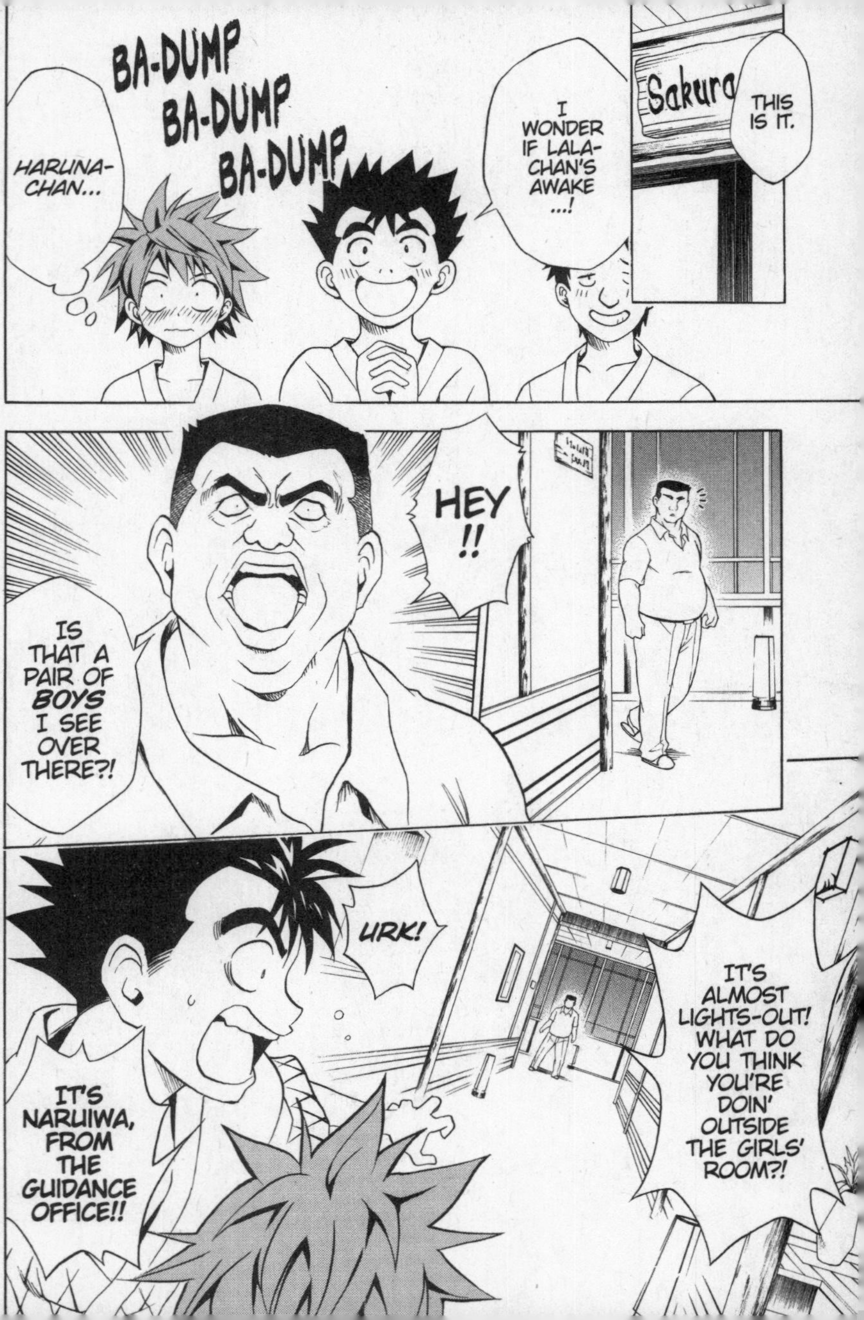
Sakura
THIS IS IT.
I WONDER IF LALA-CHAN'S AWAKE ...!
BA-DUMP BA-DUMP BA-DUMP
HARUNA-CHAN...
HEY !!
IS THAT A PAIR OF BOYS I SEE OVER THERE?!
IT'S ALMOST LIGHTS-OUT! WHAT DO YOU THINK YOU'RE DOIN' OUTSIDE THE GIRLS' ROOM?!
URK!
IT'S NARUIWA, FROM THE GUIDANCE OFFICE!!

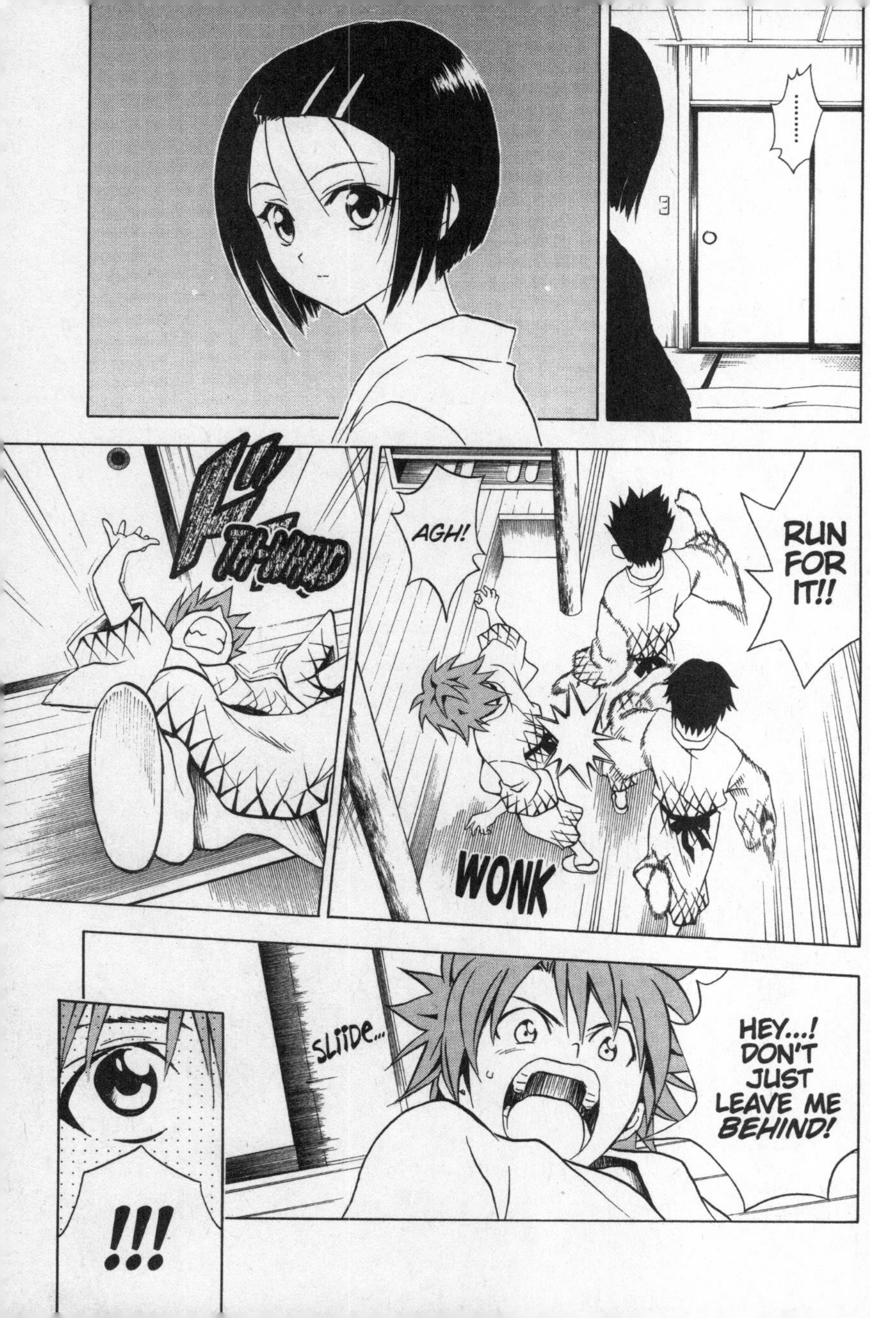
......
RUN FOR IT!!
AGH!
WONK
HEY...! DON'T JUST LEAVE ME BEHIND!
SLIIDE...
!!!

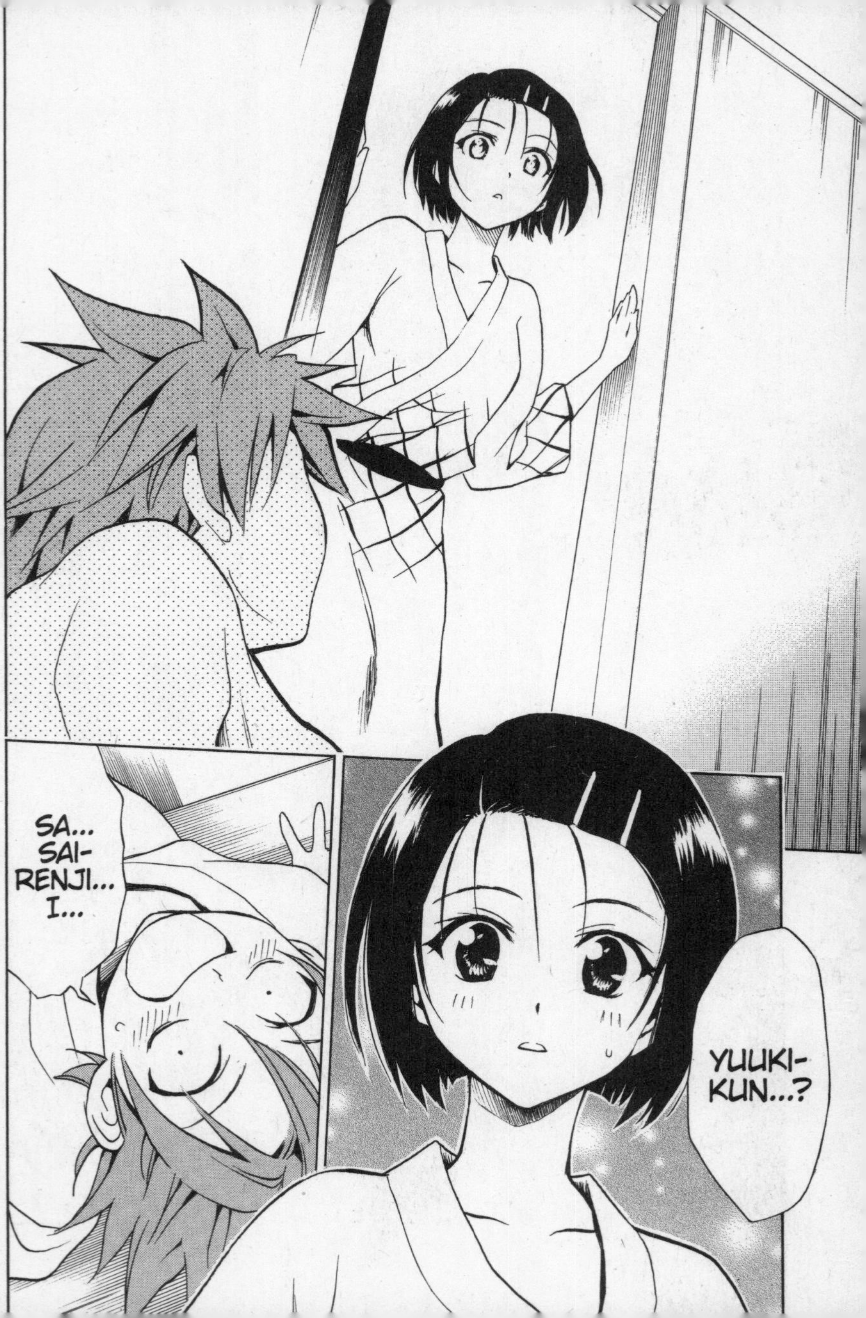
YUUKI-KUN...?
SA... SAI-RENJI... I...

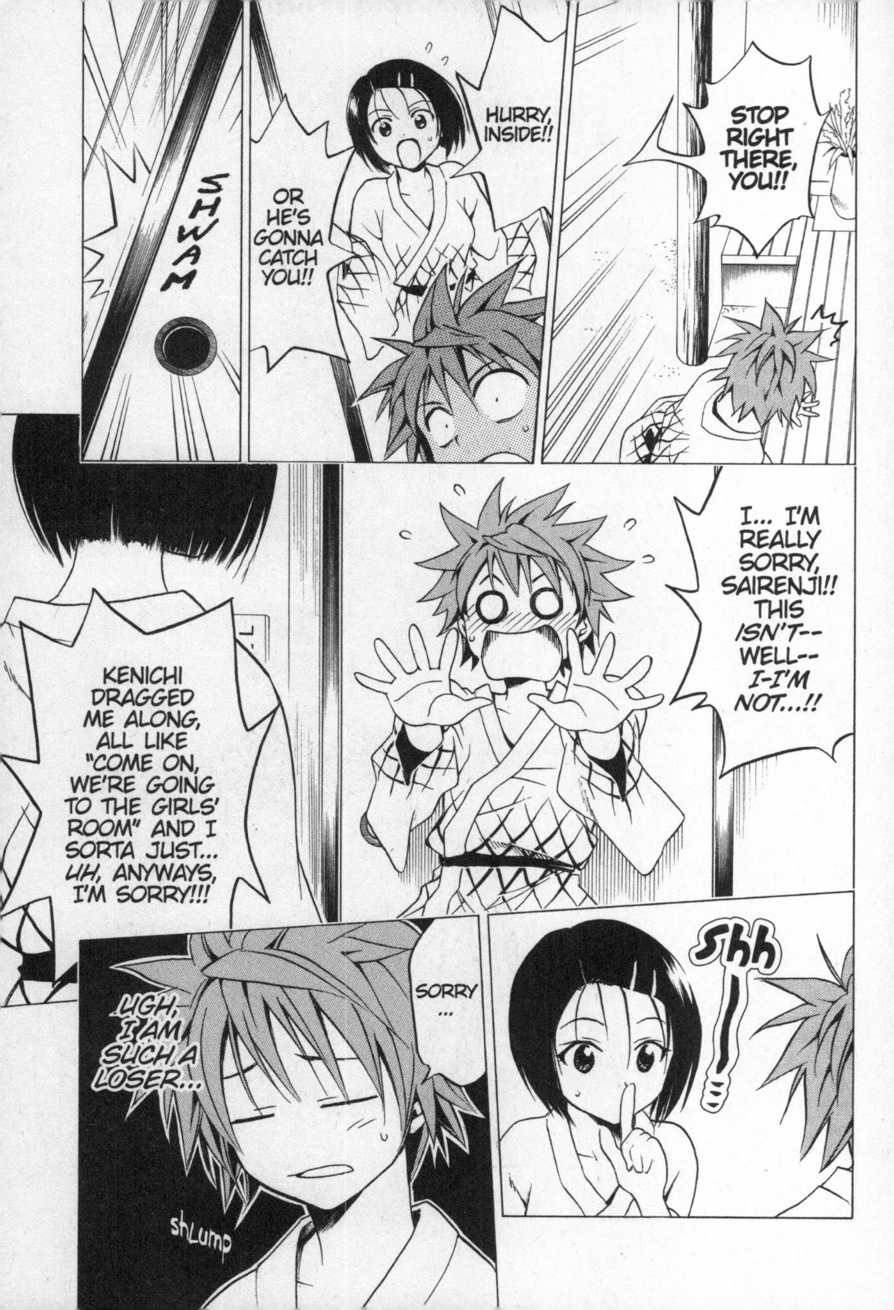
STOP RIGHT THERE, YOU!!
HURRY, INSIDE!!
OR HE'S GONNA CATCH YOU!!
SHWAM
I... I'M REALLY SORRY, SAIRENJI!! THIS *ISN'T*-- WELL-- *I-I'M NOT*...!!
KENICHI DRAGGED ME ALONG, ALL LIKE "COME ON, WE'RE GOING TO THE GIRLS' ROOM" AND I SORTA JUST... UH, ANYWAYS, I'M SORRY!!!
Shh
SORRY ...
UGH, I AM SUCH A LOSER...
shLump

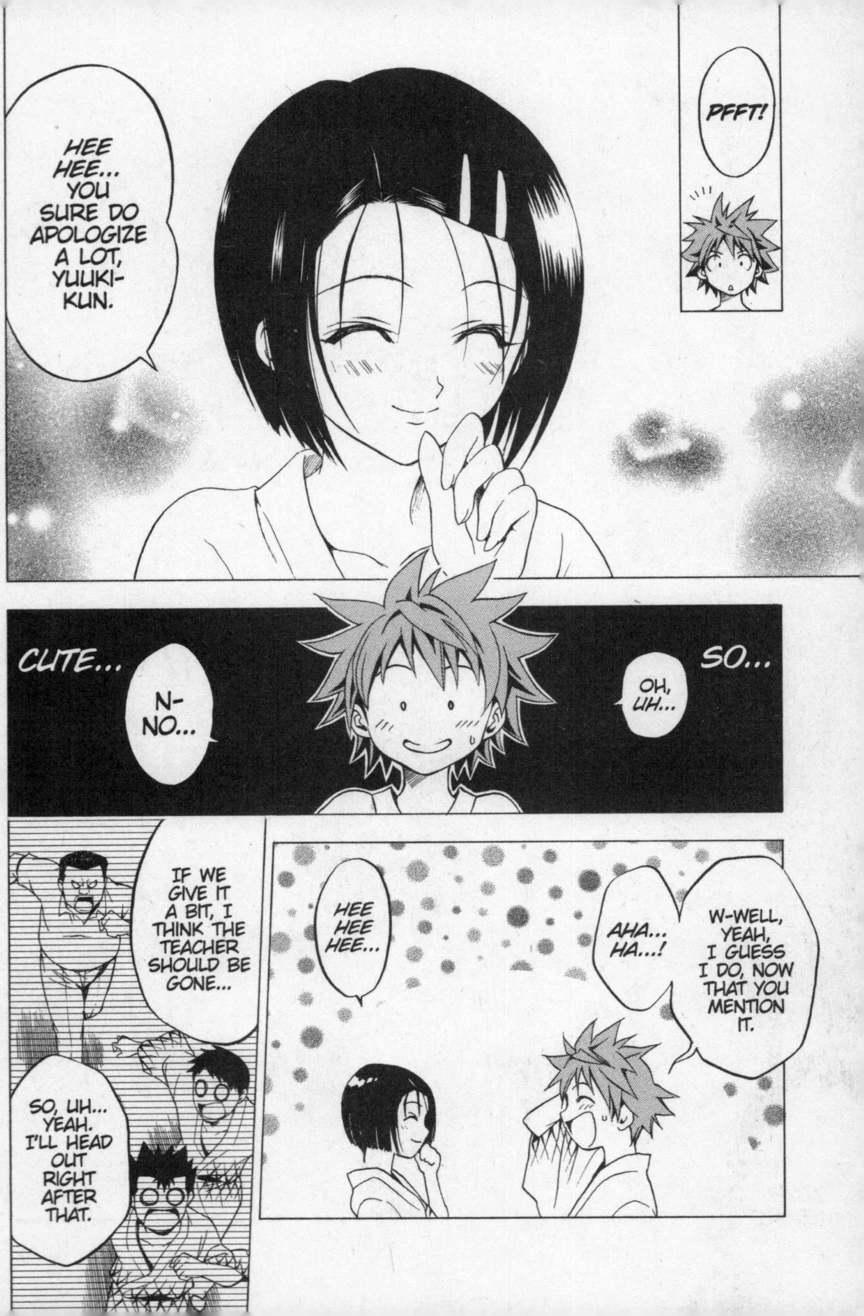
PFFT!
HEE HEE... YOU SURE DO APOLOGIZE A LOT, YUUKI-KUN.
SO...
OH, UH...
CUTE...
N-NO...
W-WELL, YEAH, I GUESS I DO, NOW THAT YOU MENTION IT.
AHA... HA...!
HEE HEE HEE...
IF WE GIVE IT A BIT, I THINK THE TEACHER SHOULD BE GONE...
SO, UH... YEAH. I'LL HEAD OUT RIGHT AFTER THAT.

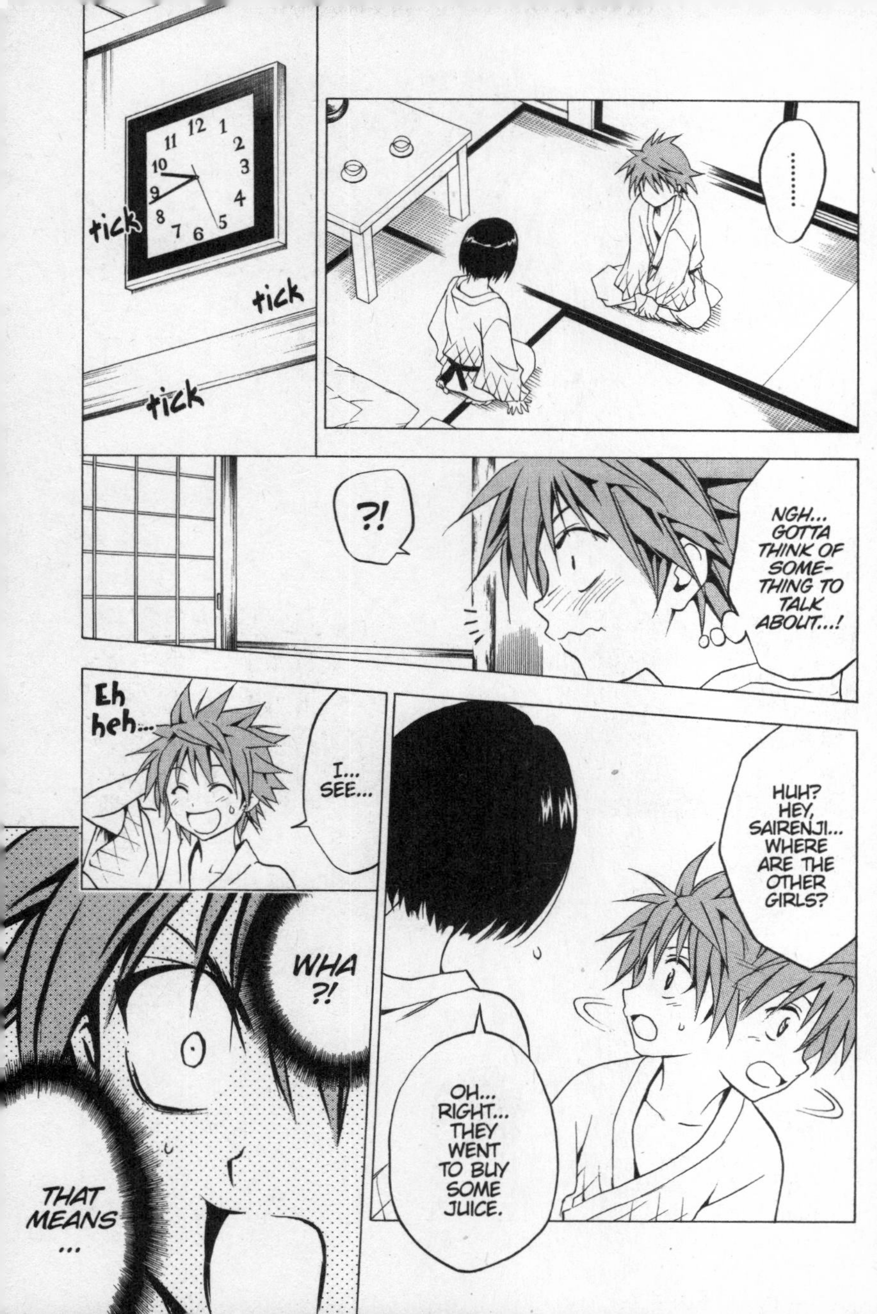
......
tick
tick
tick
NGH... GOTTA THINK OF SOME-THING TO TALK ABOUT...!
?!
HUH? HEY, SAIRENJI... WHERE ARE THE OTHER GIRLS?
OH... RIGHT... THEY WENT TO BUY SOME JUICE.
I... SEE...
Eh heh...
WHA ?!
THAT MEANS ...

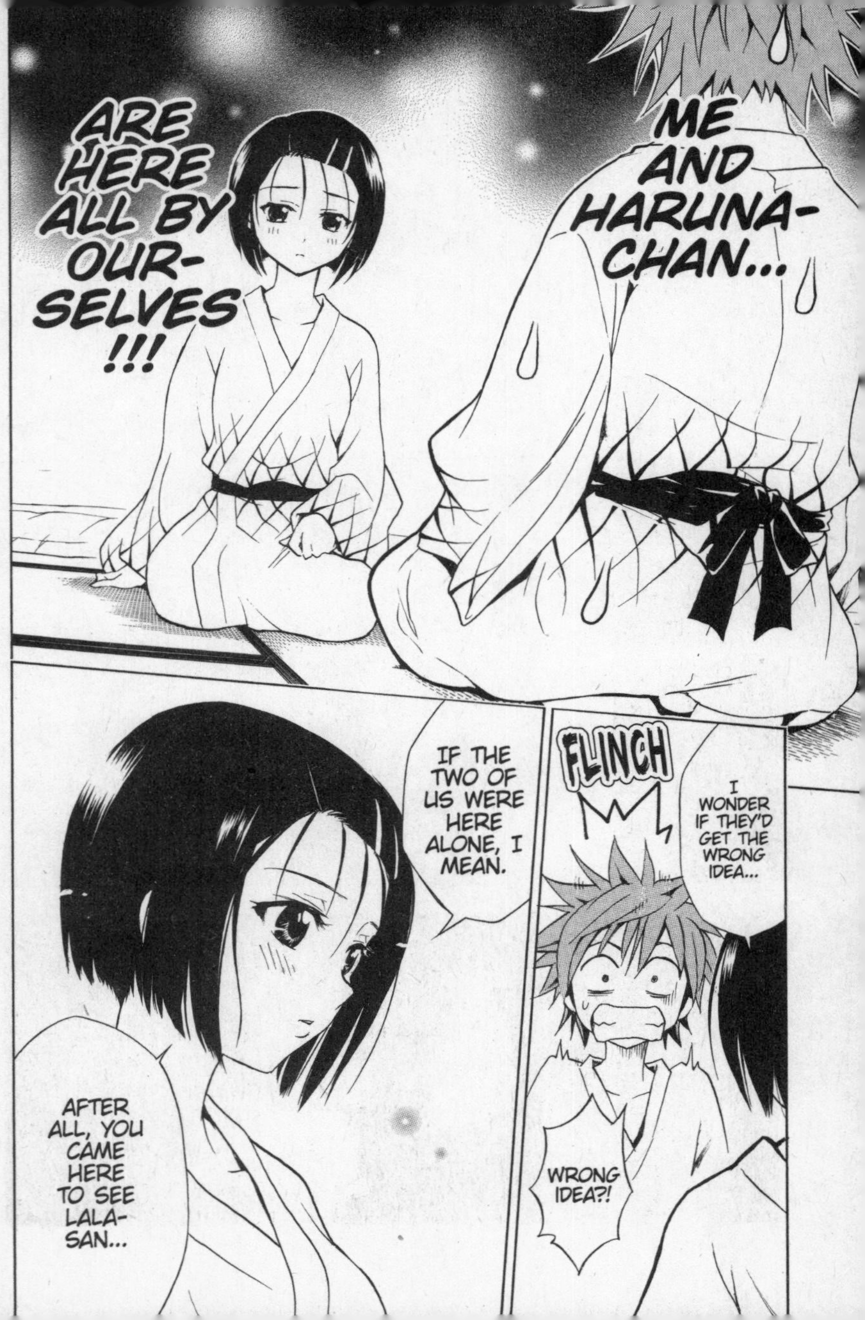
ME AND HARUNA-CHAN...
ARE HERE ALL BY OURSELVES!!!
I WONDER IF THEY'D GET THE WRONG IDEA...
FLINCH
WRONG IDEA?!
IF THE TWO OF US WERE HERE ALONE, I MEAN.
AFTER ALL, YOU CAME HERE TO SEE LALA-SAN...

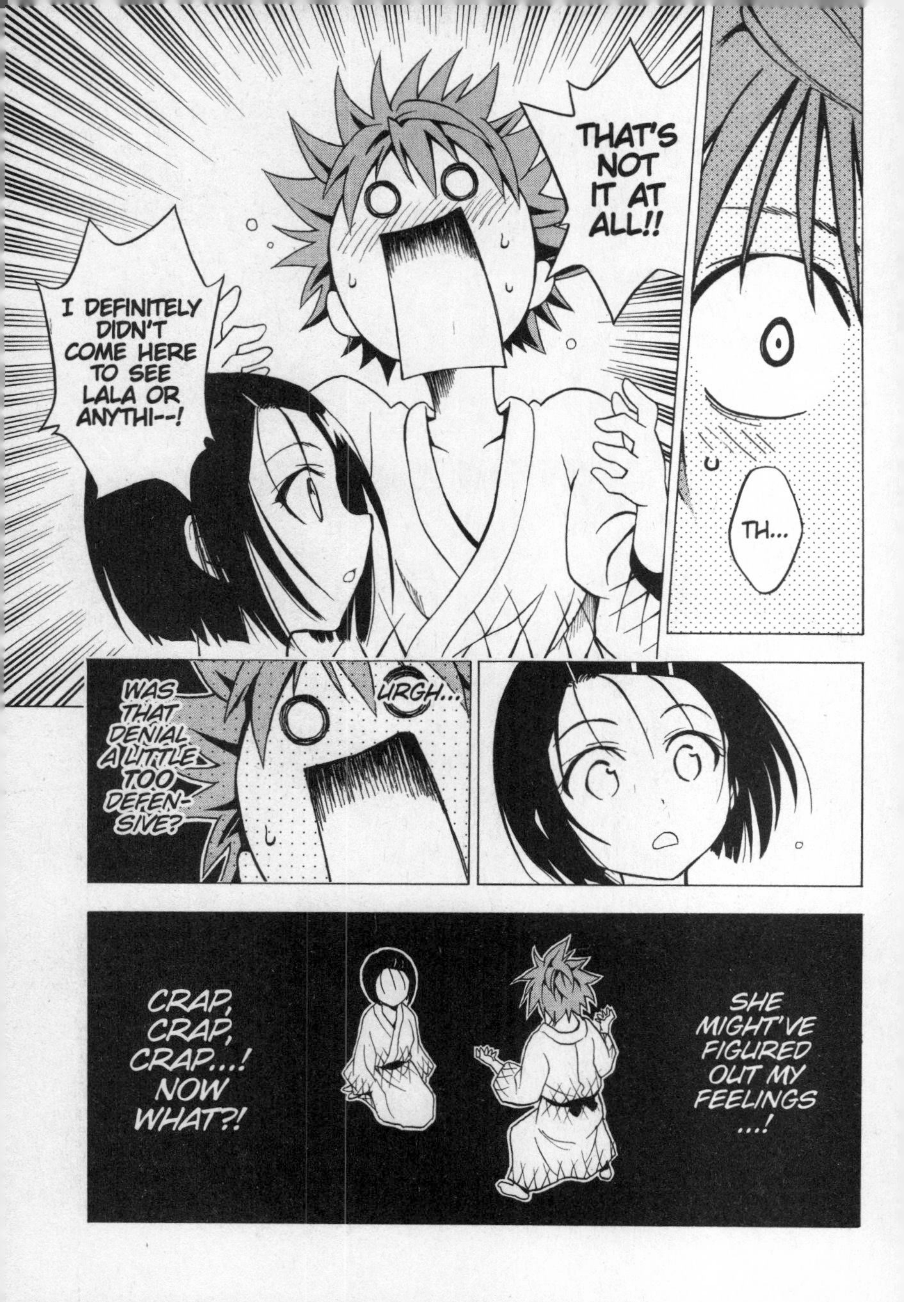
TH...
THAT'S NOT IT AT ALL!!
I DEFINITELY DIDN'T COME HERE TO SEE LALA OR ANYTHI--!
URGH...
WAS THAT DENIAL A LITTLE TOO DEFEN-SIVE?
SHE MIGHT'VE FIGURED OUT MY FEELINGS ...!
CRAP, CRAP, CRAP...! NOW WHAT?!

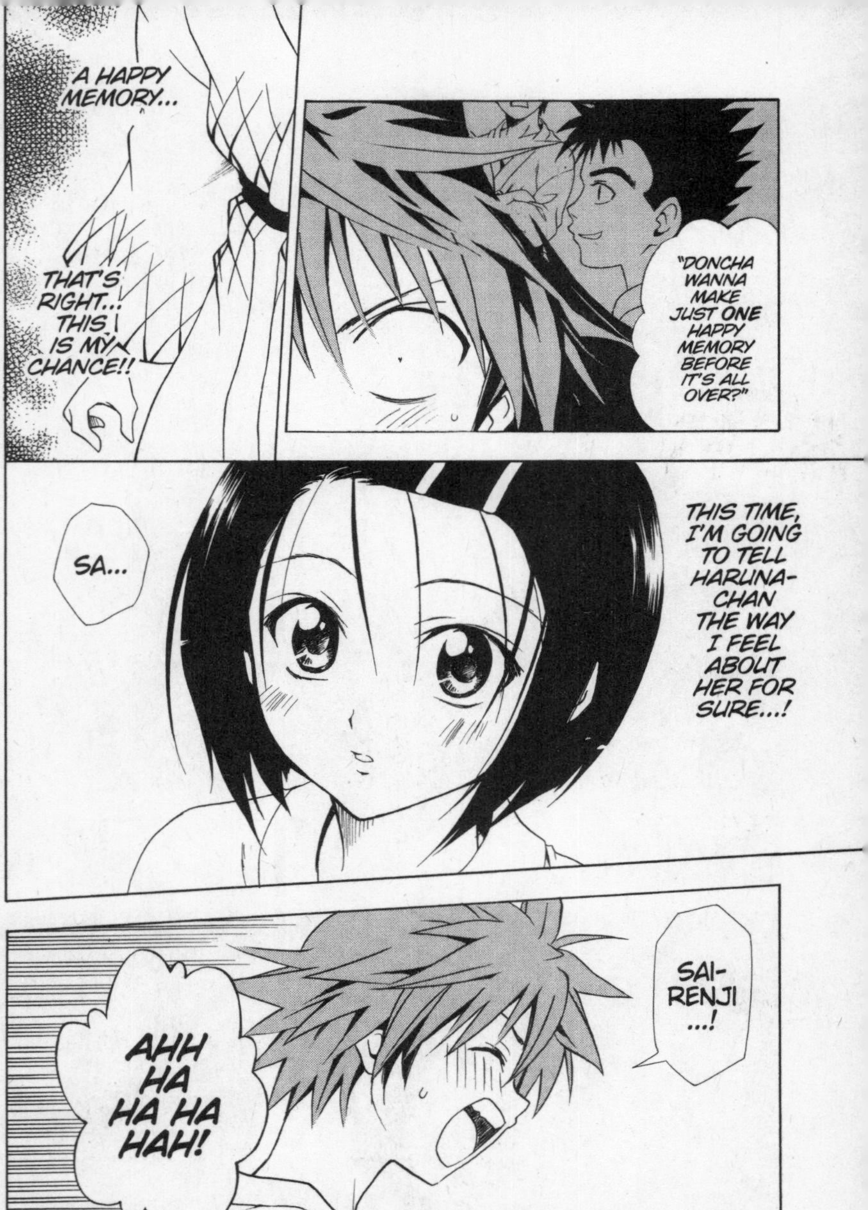
"DONCHA WANNA MAKE JUST ONE HAPPY MEMORY BEFORE IT'S ALL OVER?"
A HAPPY MEMORY...
THAT'S RIGHT... THIS IS MY CHANCE!!
THIS TIME, I'M GOING TO TELL HARUNA-CHAN THE WAY I FEEL ABOUT HER FOR SURE...!
SA...
SAI-RENJI ...!
AHH HA HA HA HAH!

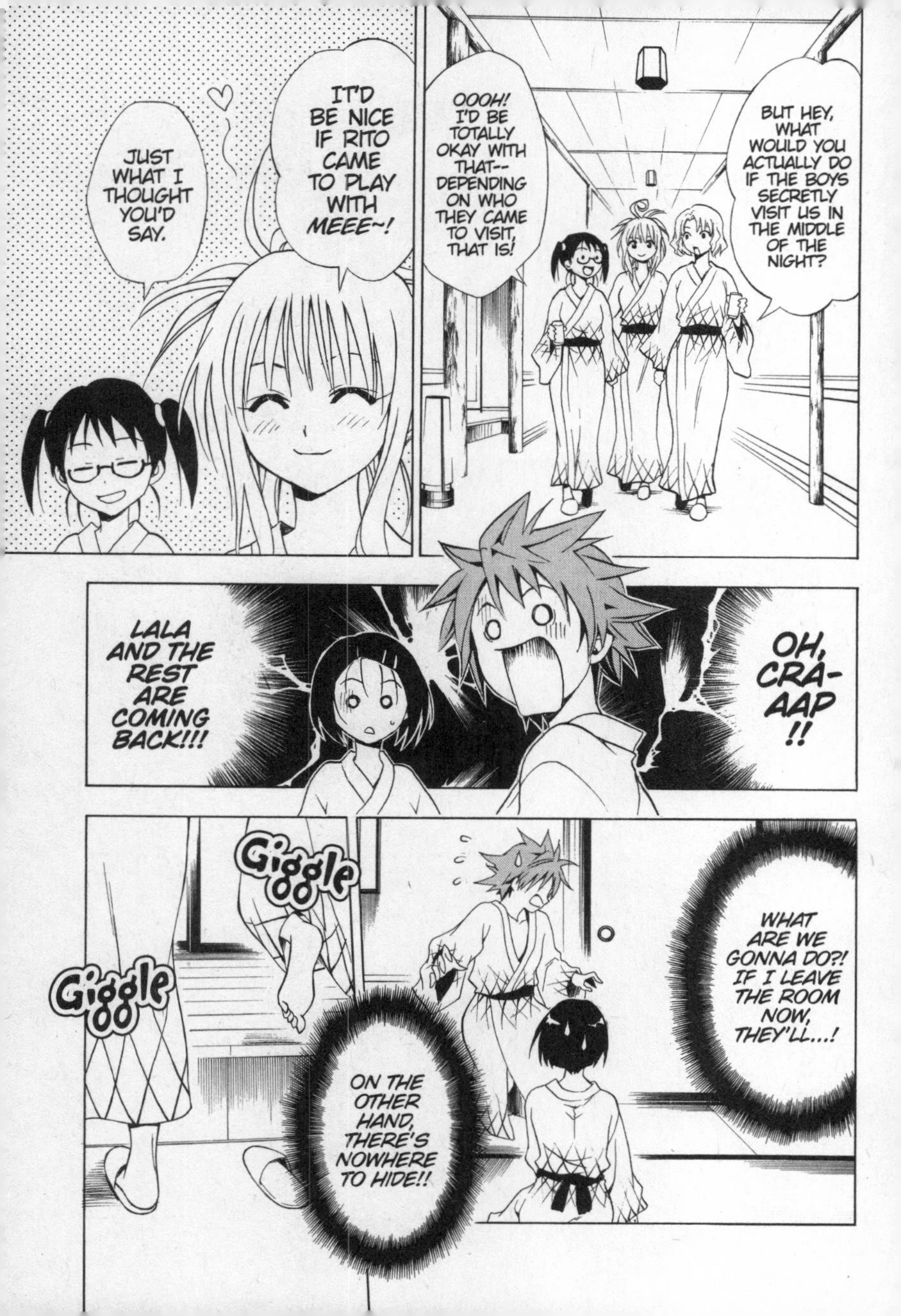
BUT HEY, WHAT WOULD YOU ACTUALLY DO IF THE BOYS SECRETLY VISIT US IN THE MIDDLE OF THE NIGHT?
OOOH! I'D BE TOTALLY OKAY WITH THAT--DEPENDING ON WHO THEY CAME TO VISIT, THAT IS!
IT'D BE NICE IF RITO CAME TO PLAY WITH MEEE~!
JUST WHAT I THOUGHT YOU'D SAY.
OH, CRA-AAP!!
LALA AND THE REST ARE COMING BACK!!!
WHAT ARE WE GONNA DO?! IF I LEAVE THE ROOM NOW, THEY'LL...!
Giggle
ON THE OTHER HAND, THERE'S NOWHERE TO HIDE!!
Giggle

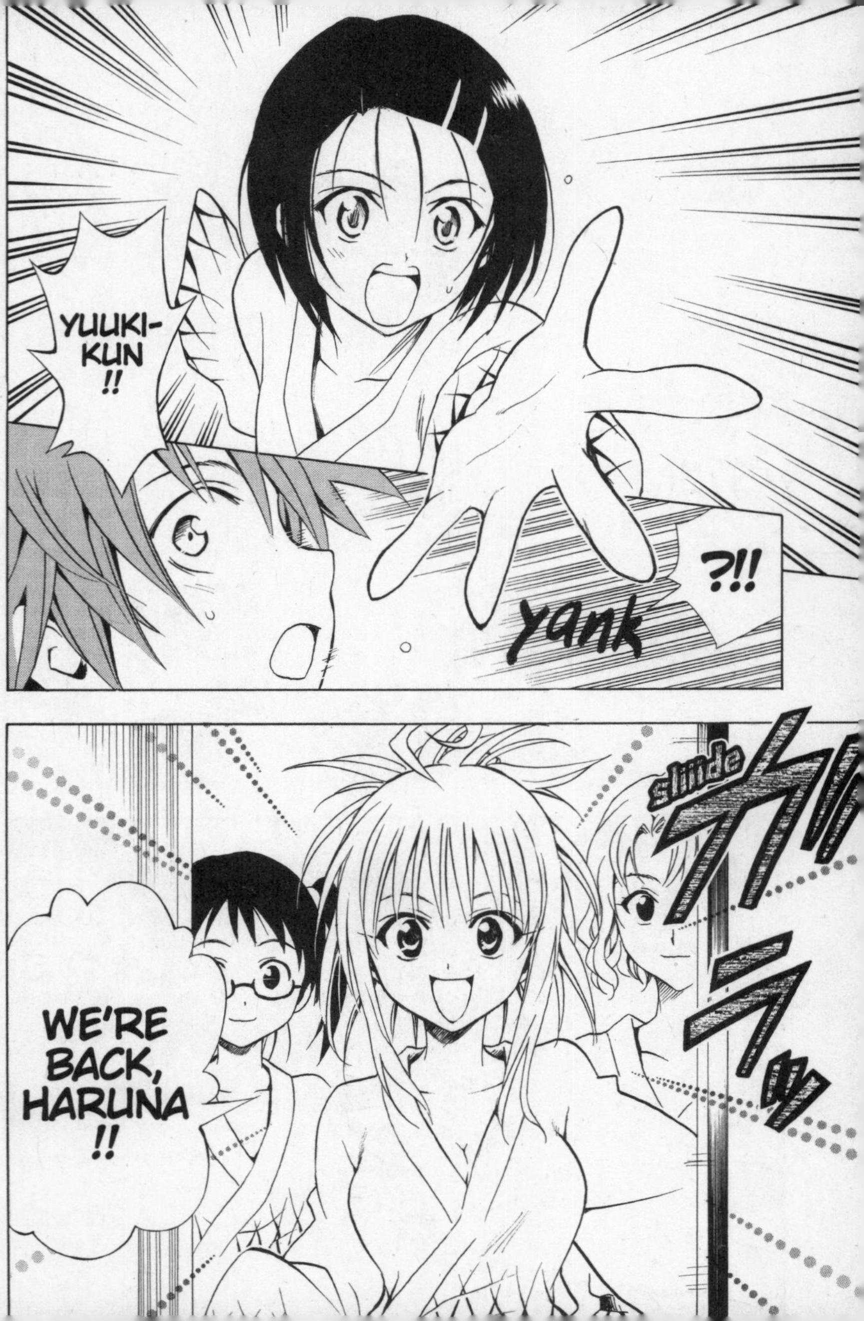
YUUKI-KUN!!
?!!
yank
slide
WE'RE BACK, HARUNA!!

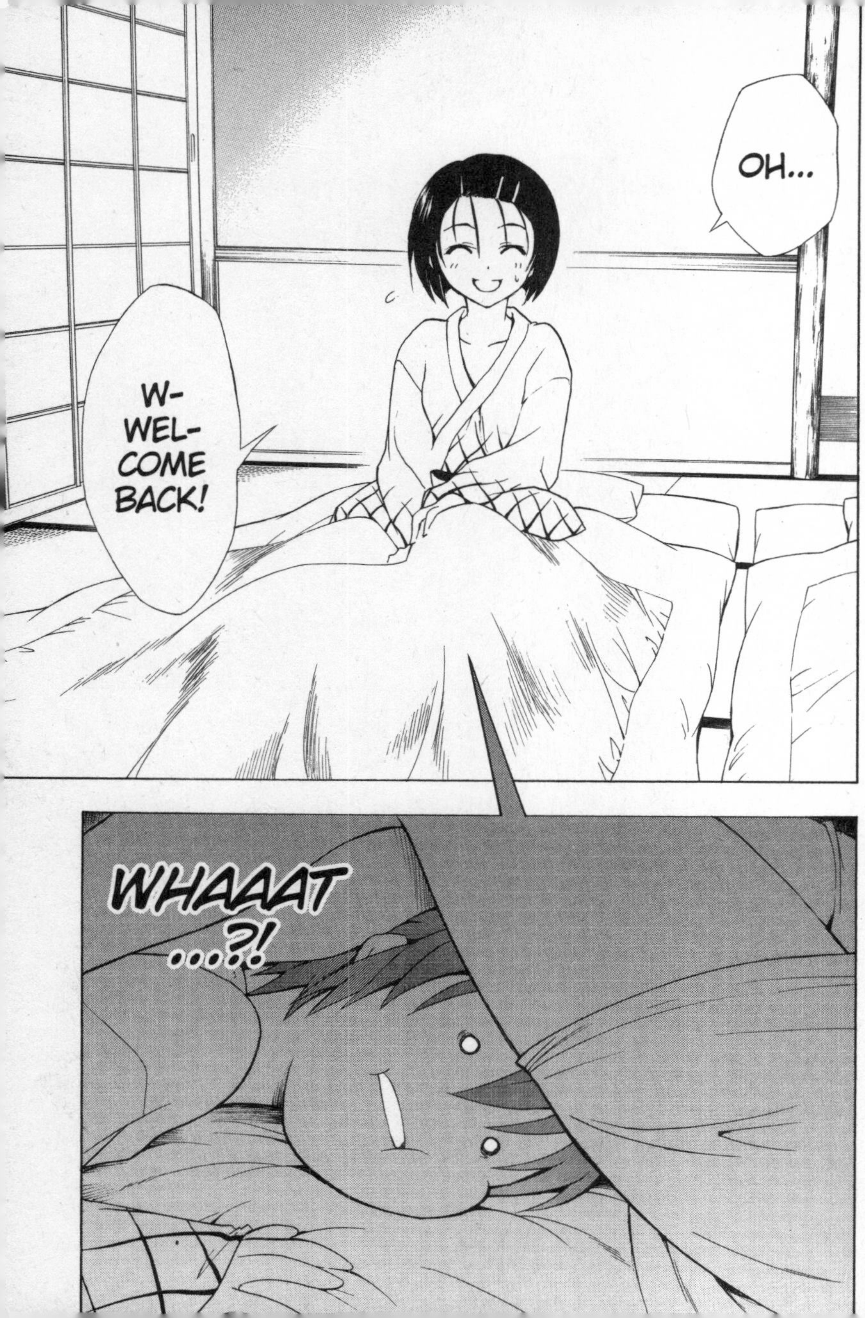
OH...
W-WEL-COME BACK!
WHAAAT ...?!

To LOVE Ru

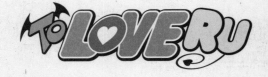

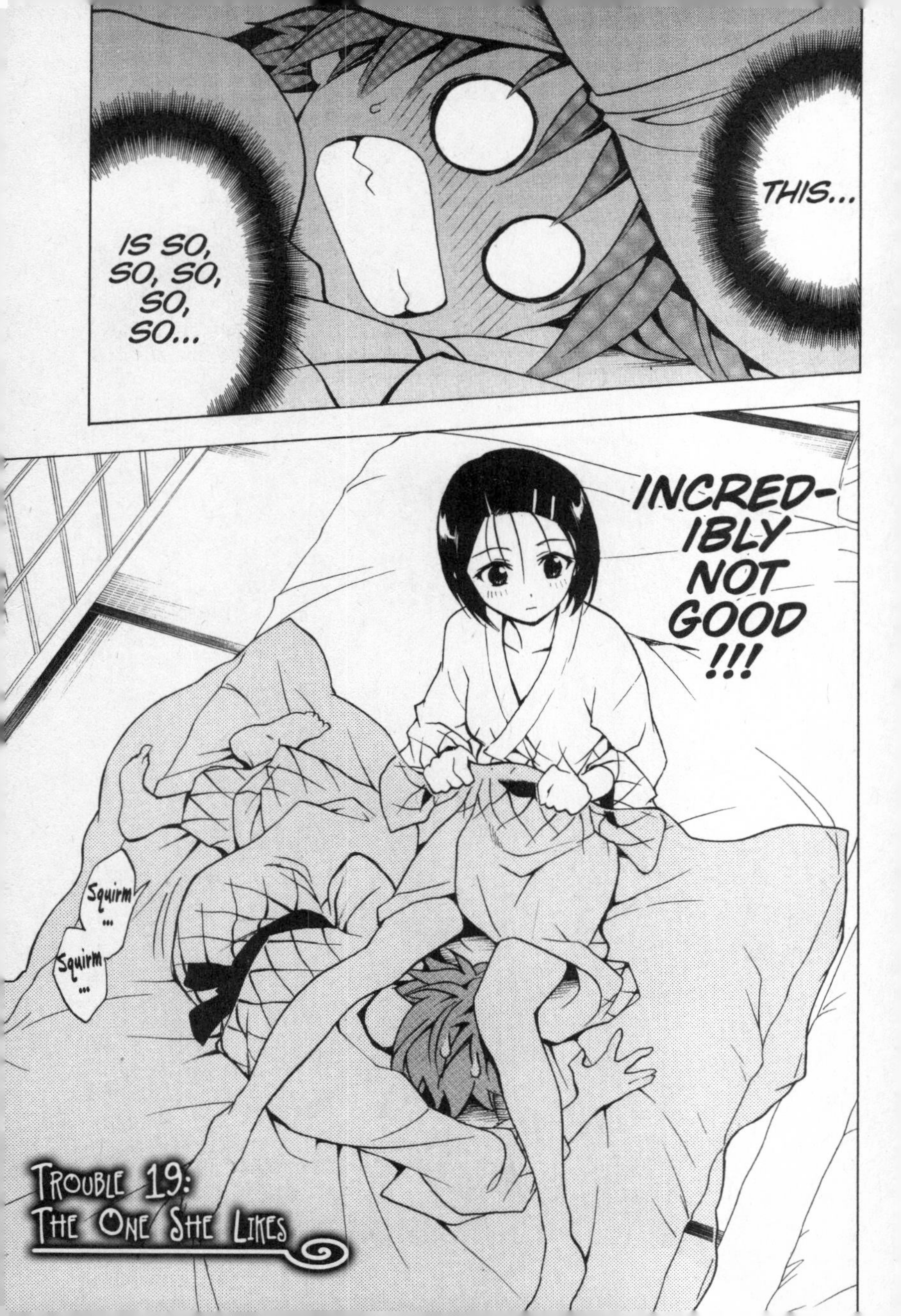
THIS...
IS SO, SO, SO, SO, SO...
INCREDIBLY NOT GOOD!!!
Squirm... Squirm...
TROUBLE 19: THE ONE SHE LIKES

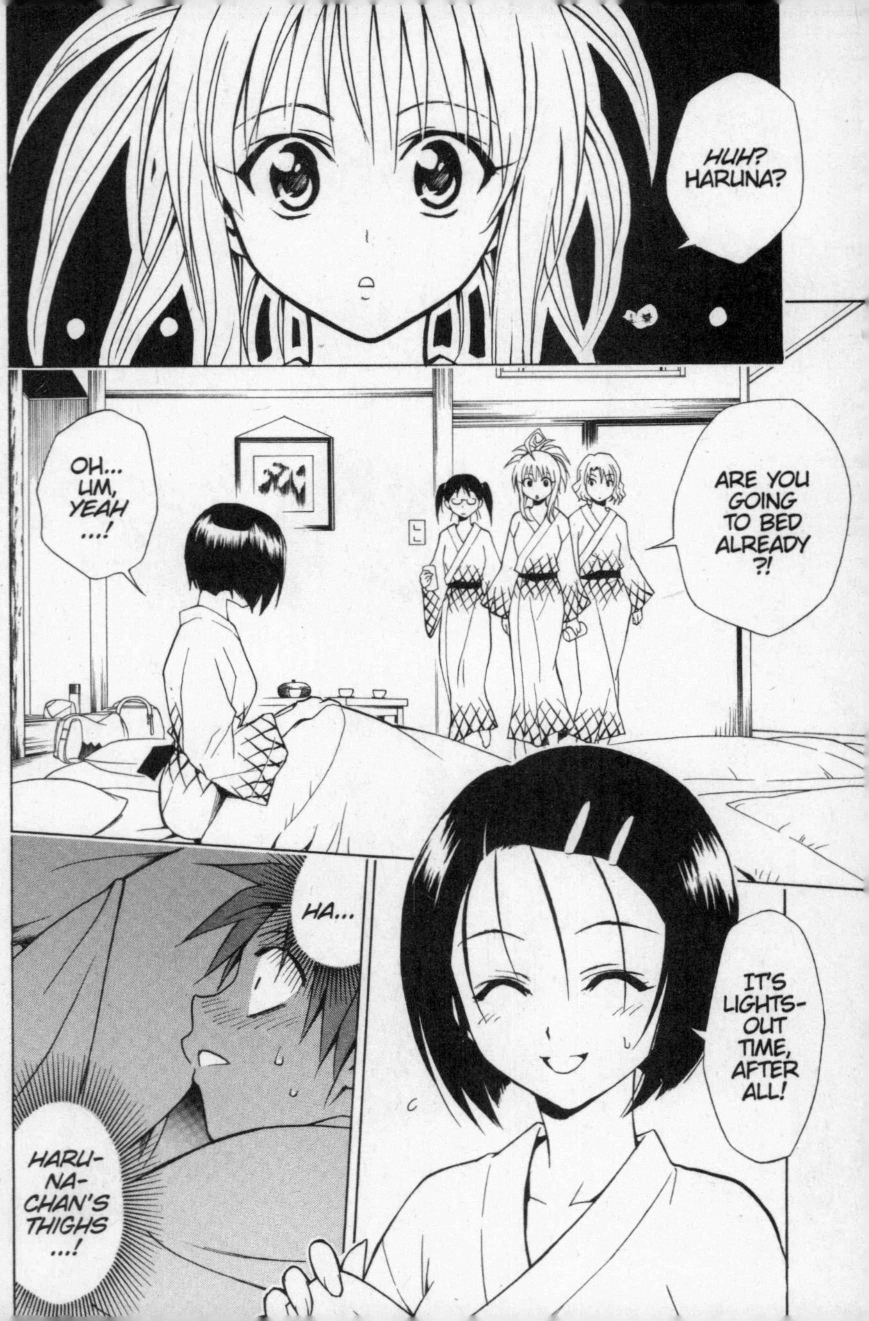
HUH? HARUNA?
ARE YOU GOING TO BED ALREADY?!
OH... UM, YEAH...!
IT'S LIGHTS-OUT TIME, AFTER ALL!
HA...
HARUNA-CHAN'S THIGHS...!

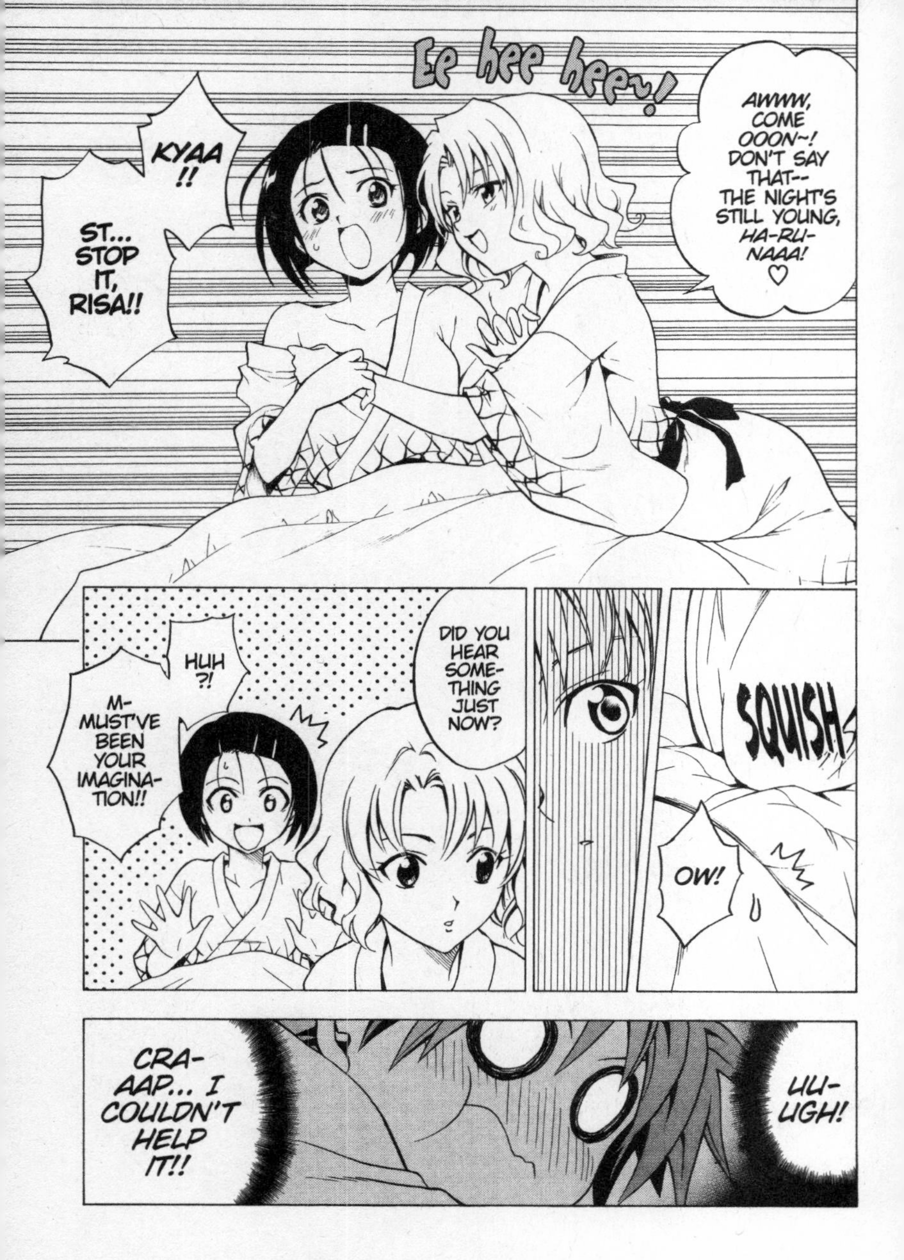
Ee hee hee~!
AWWW, COME OOON~! DON'T SAY THAT-- THE NIGHT'S STILL YOUNG, HA-RU-NAAA! ♡
KYAA!!
ST... STOP IT, RISA!!
SQUISH
OW!
DID YOU HEAR SOMETHING JUST NOW?
HUH ?!
M-MUST'VE BEEN YOUR IMAGINATION!!
UU-UGH!
CRA-AAP... I COULDN'T HELP IT!!

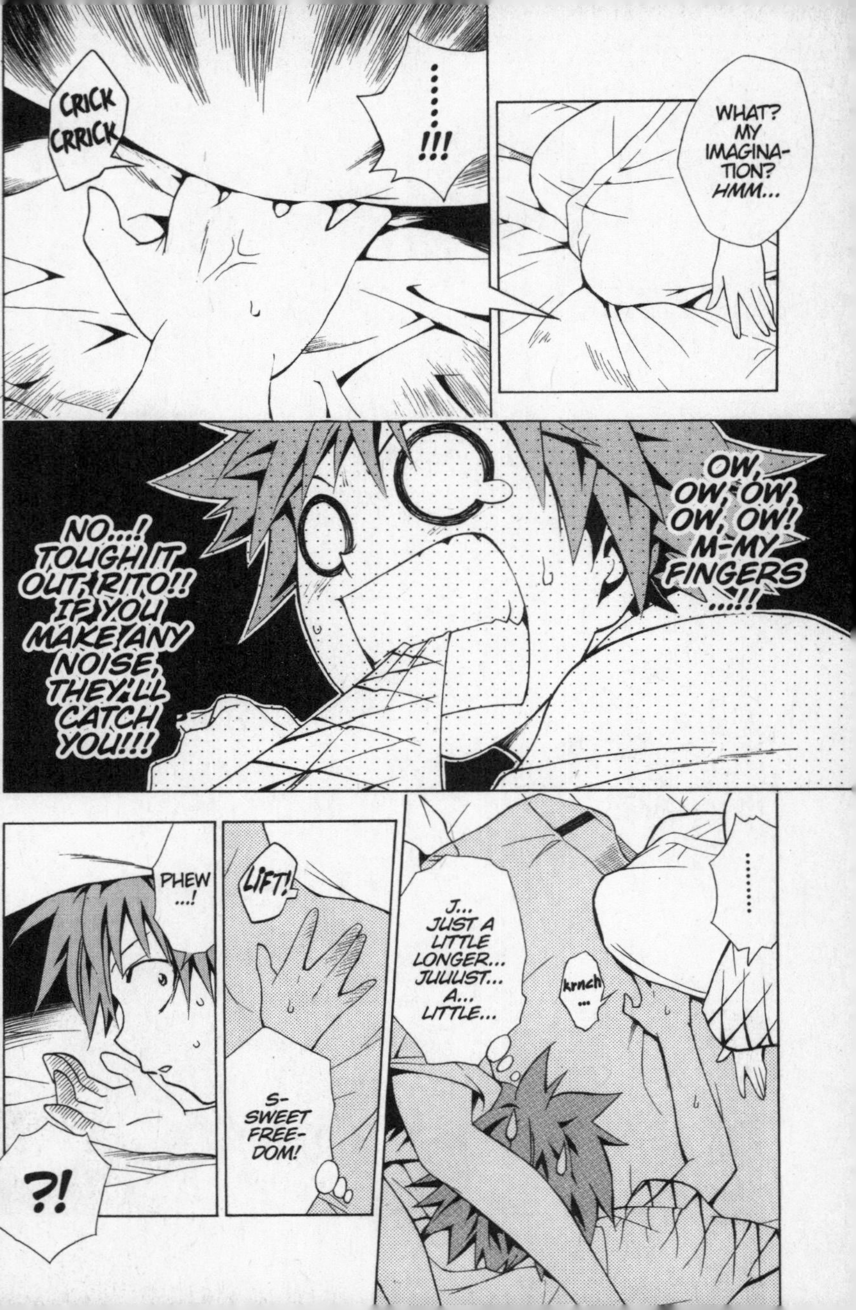
WHAT? MY IMAGINATION? HMM...
......!!!
CRICK CRRICK
OW, OW, OW, OW, OW! M-MY FINGERS ...!!
NO...! TOUGH IT OUT, RITO!! IF YOU MAKE ANY NOISE, THEY'LL CATCH YOU!!!
......
J... JUST A LITTLE LONGER... JUUUST... A... LITTLE...
krnch ...
LIFT!
S-SWEET FREE-DOM!
PHEW ...!
?!

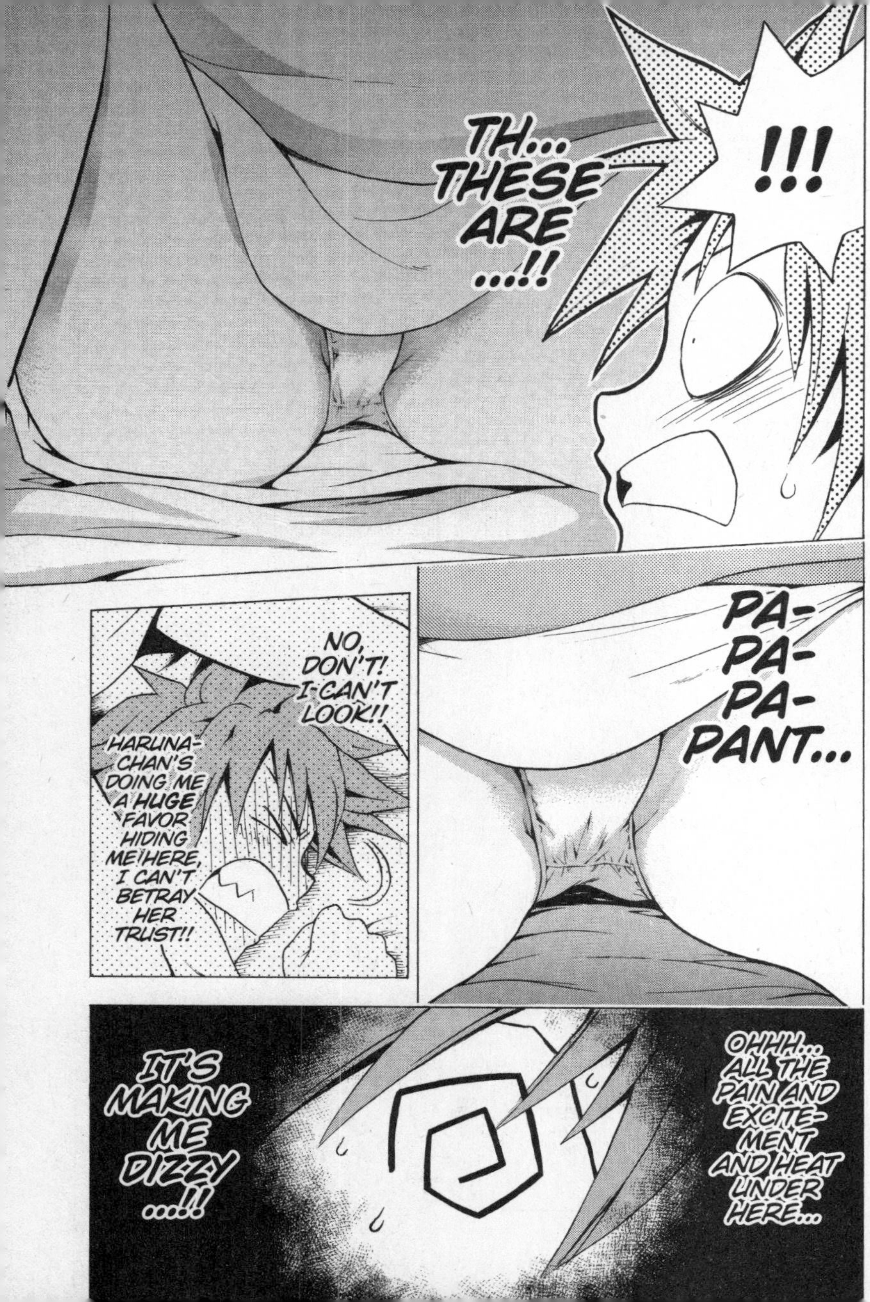
!!!
TH... THESE ARE ...!!
PA-PA-PA-PANT...
NO, DON'T! I CAN'T LOOK!!
HARUNA-CHAN'S DOING ME A HUGE FAVOR HIDING ME HERE, I CAN'T BETRAY HER TRUST!!
OHHH... ALL THE PAIN AND EXCITE-MENT AND HEAT UNDER HERE...
IT'S MAKING ME DIZZY ...!!

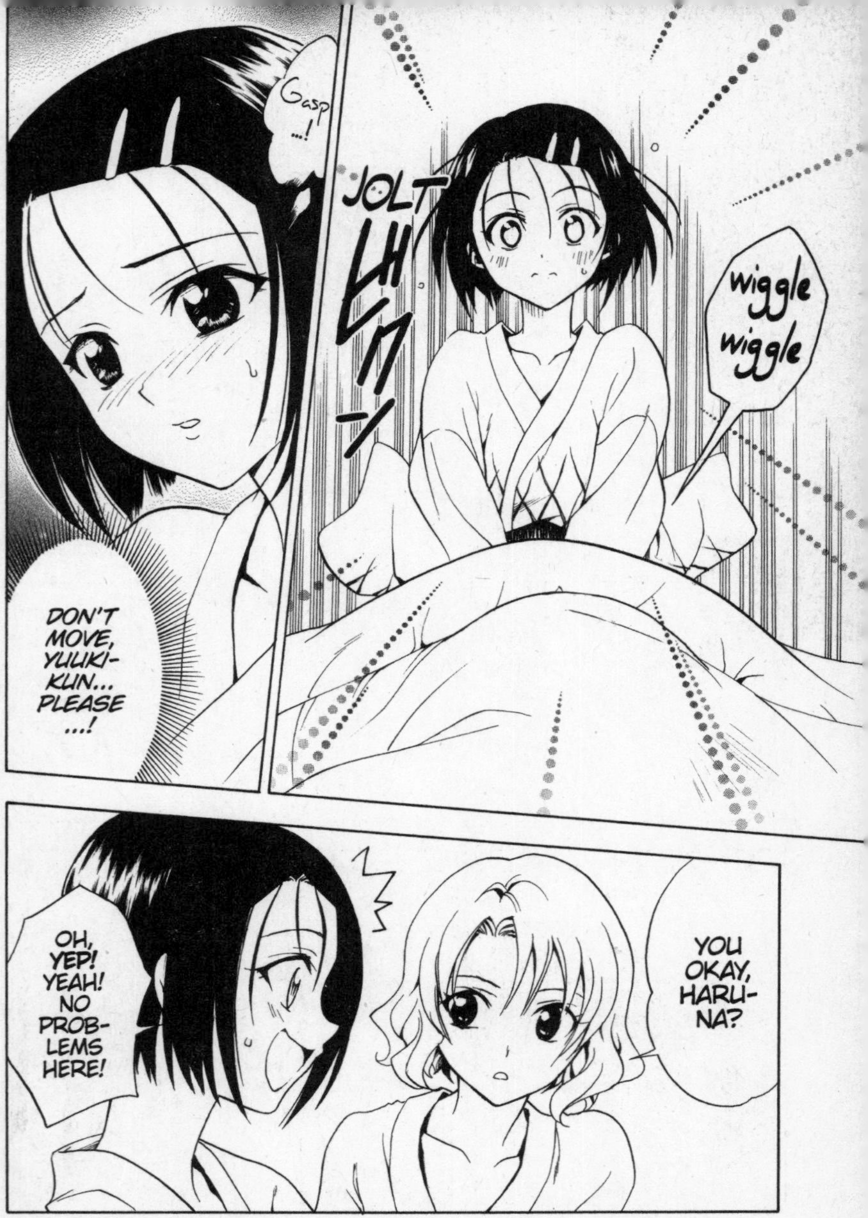
wiggle wiggle
JOLT
Gasp ...!
DON'T MOVE, YUUKI-KUN... PLEASE ...!
YOU OKAY, HARUNA?
OH, YEP! YEAH! NO PROBLEMS HERE!

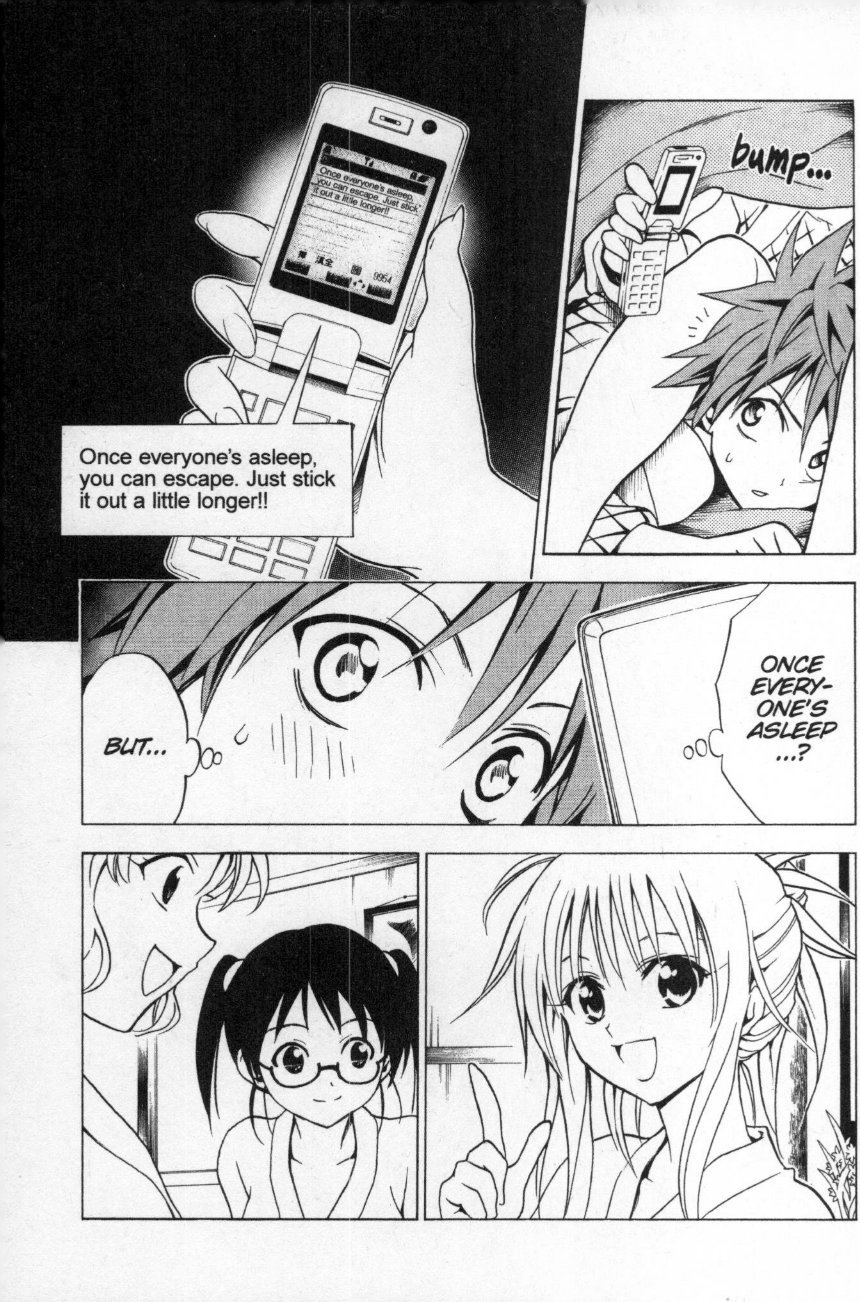
bump...
Once everyone's asleep, you can escape. Just stick it out a little longer!!
Once everyone's asleep, you can escape. Just stick it out a little longer!!
ONCE EVERY-ONE'S ASLEEP ...?
BUT...

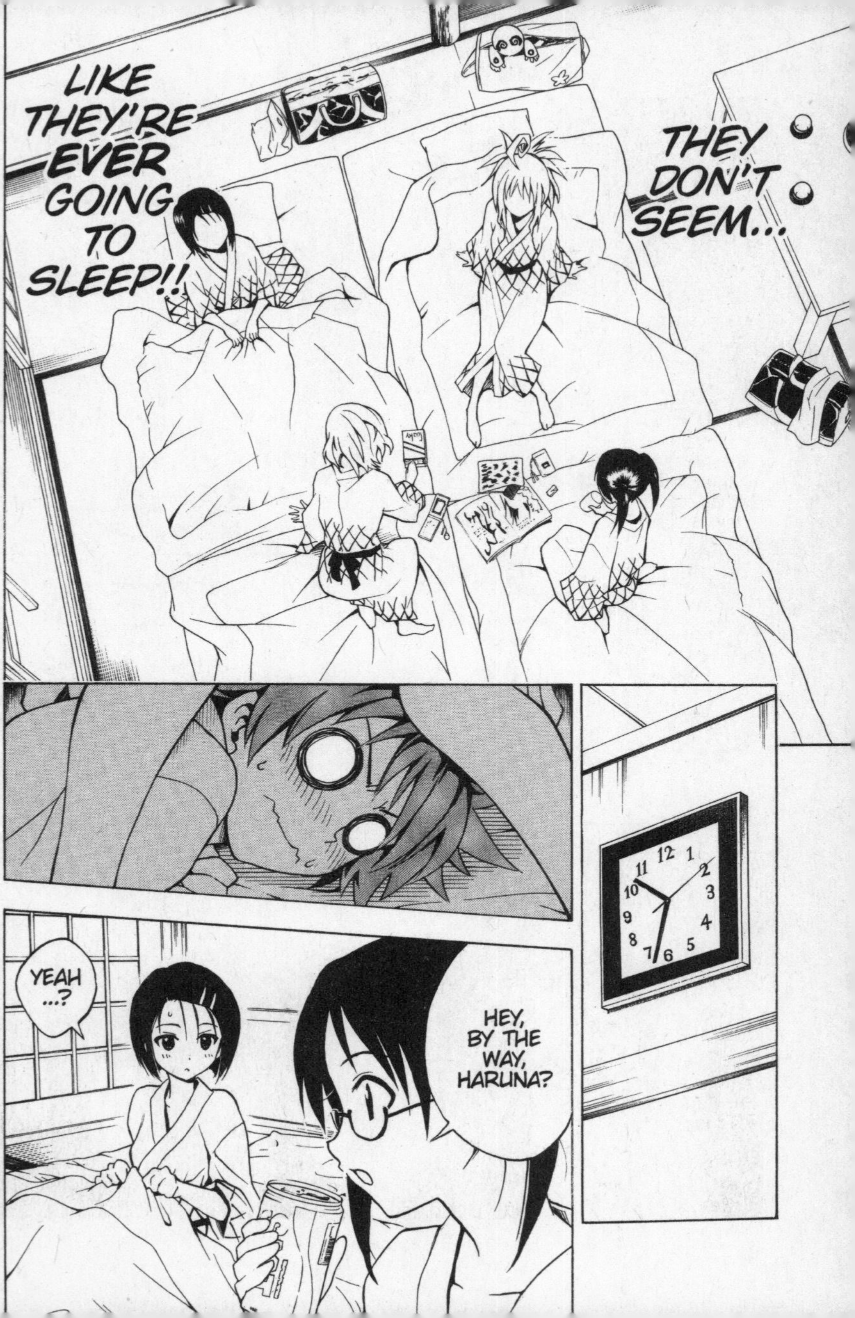
THEY DON'T SEEM...
LIKE THEY'RE EVER GOING TO SLEEP!!
HEY, BY THE WAY, HARUNA?
YEAH ...?

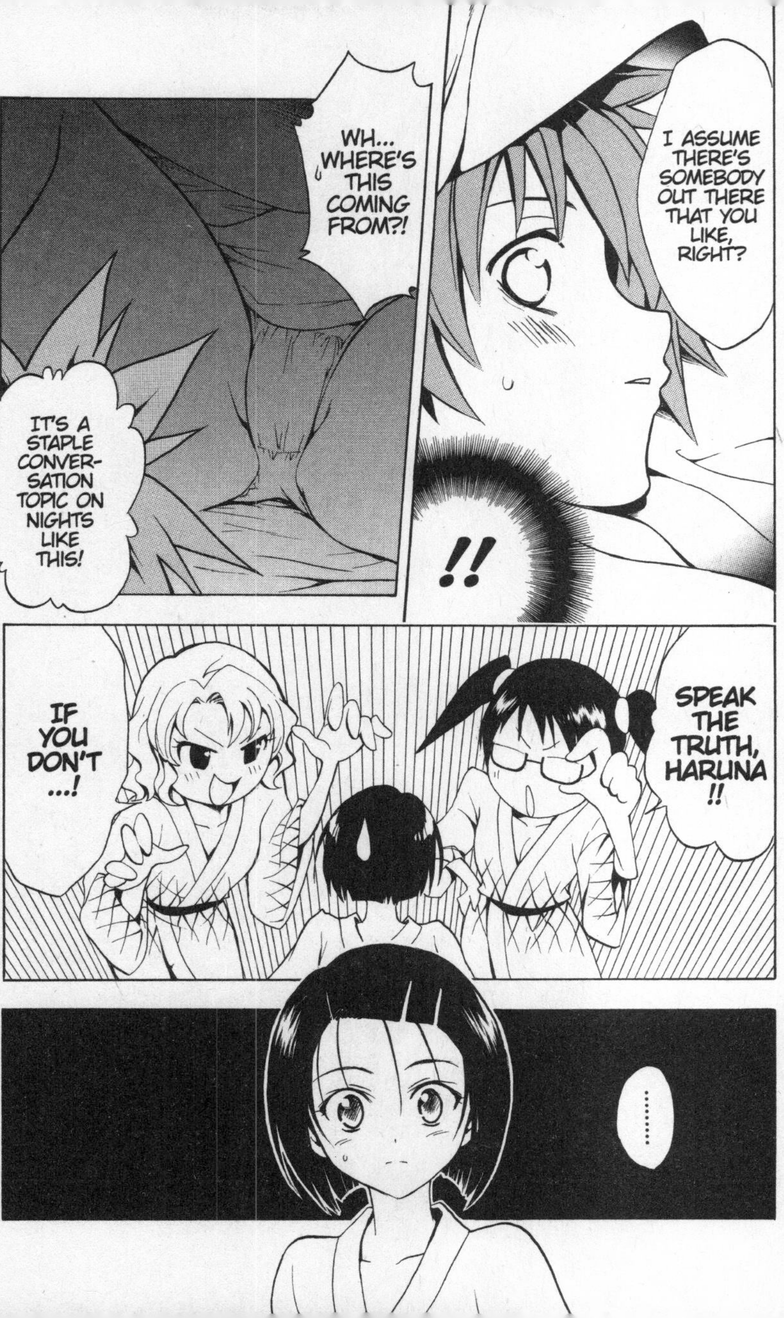
I ASSUME THERE'S SOMEBODY OUT THERE THAT YOU LIKE, RIGHT?
!!
WH... WHERE'S THIS COMING FROM?!
IT'S A STAPLE CONVERSATION TOPIC ON NIGHTS LIKE THIS!
SPEAK THE TRUTH, HARUNA!!
IF YOU DON'T...!
....

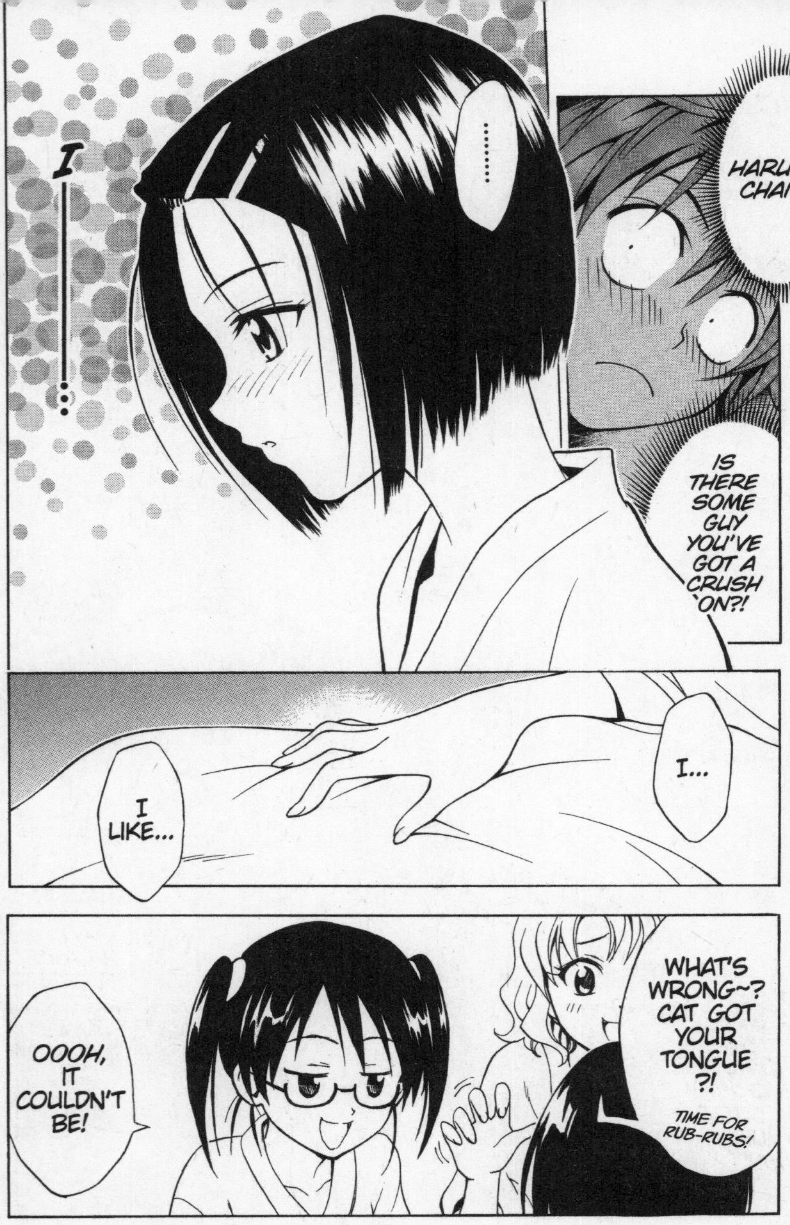
HARUNA-CHAN...
IS THERE SOME GUY YOU'VE GOT A CRUSH ON?!
......
I—...
I...
I LIKE...
WHAT'S WRONG~? CAT GOT YOUR TONGUE?!
TIME FOR RUB-RUBS!
OOOH, IT COULDN'T BE!

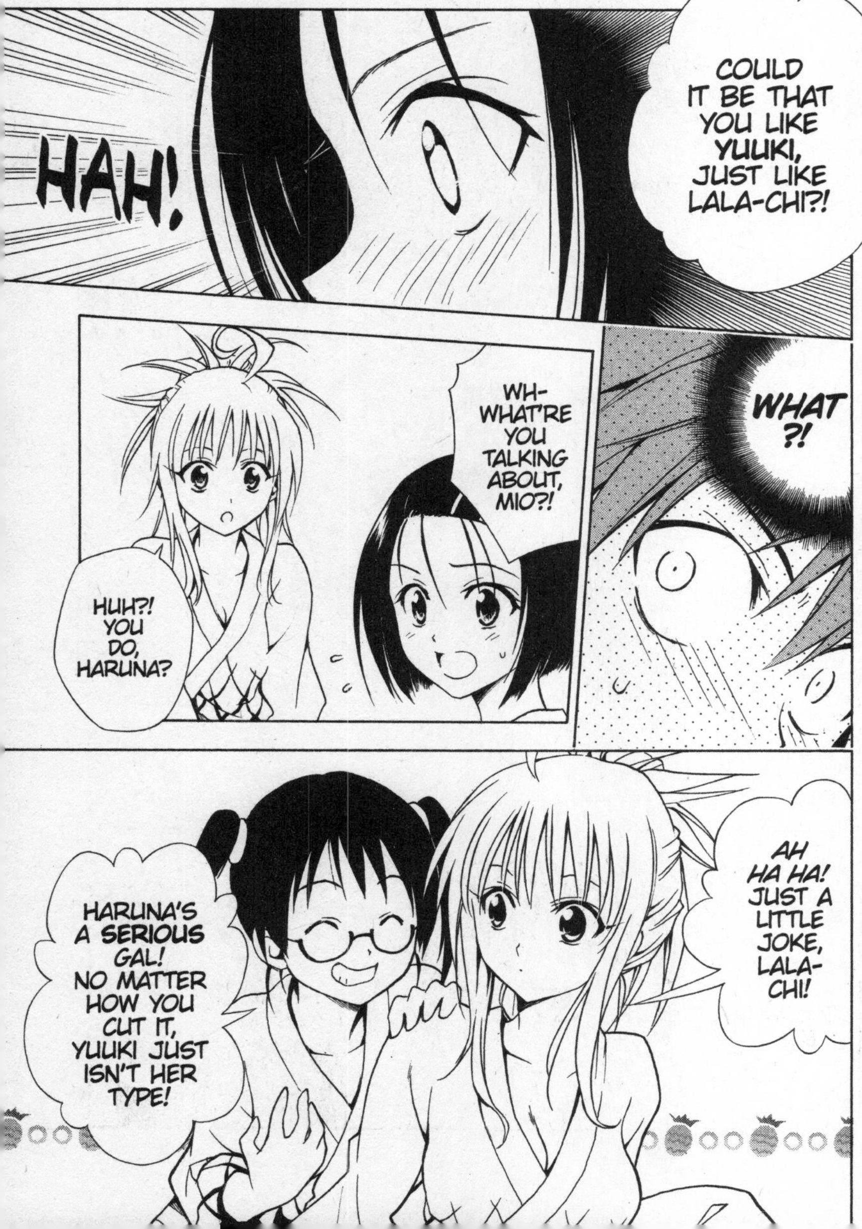
COULD IT BE THAT YOU LIKE YUUKI, JUST LIKE LALA-CHI?!
HAH!
WHAT ?!
WH- WHAT'RE YOU TALKING ABOUT, MIO?!
HUH?! YOU DO, HARUNA?
AH HA HA! JUST A LITTLE JOKE, LALA-CHI!
HARUNA'S A SERIOUS GAL! NO MATTER HOW YOU CUT IT, YUUKI JUST ISN'T HER TYPE!

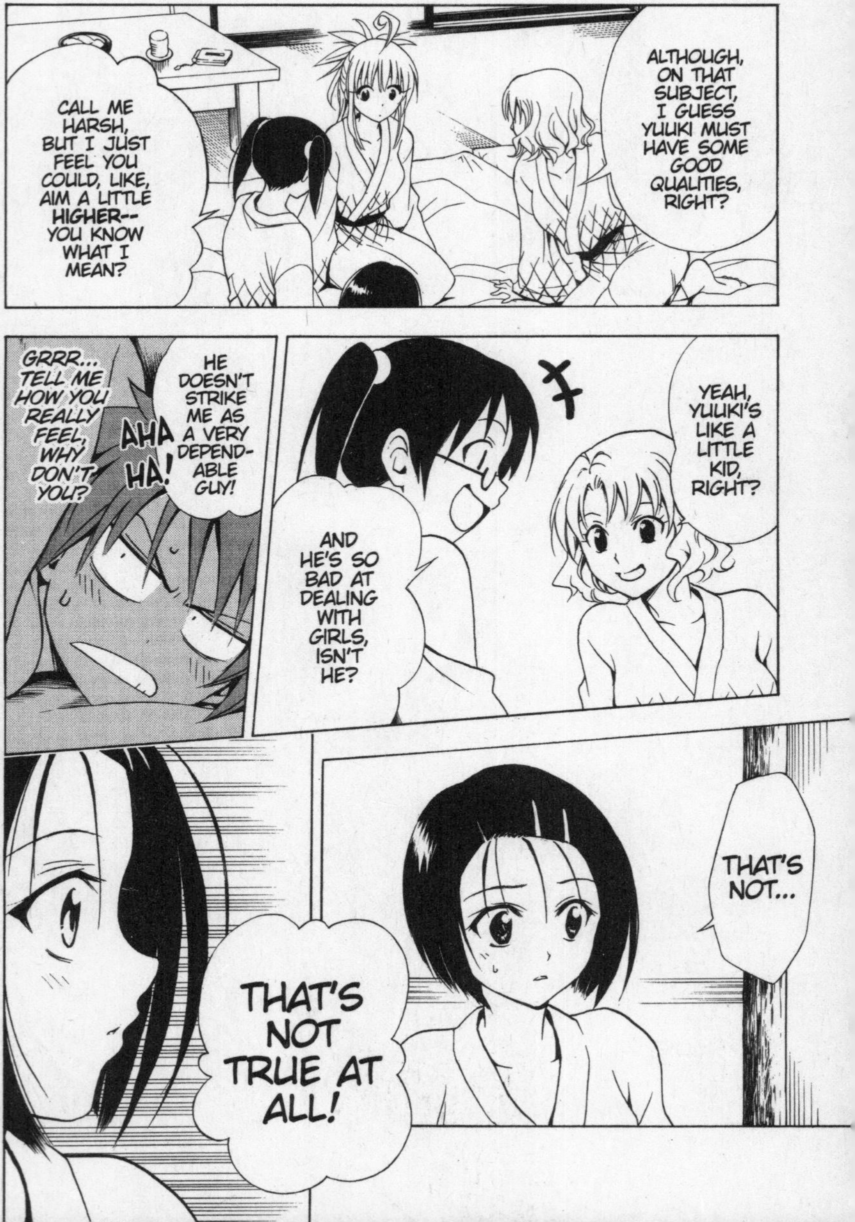
ALTHOUGH, ON THAT SUBJECT, I GUESS YUUKI MUST HAVE SOME GOOD QUALITIES, RIGHT?
CALL ME HARSH, BUT I JUST FEEL YOU COULD, LIKE, AIM A LITTLE HIGHER-- YOU KNOW WHAT I MEAN?
YEAH, YUUKI'S LIKE A LITTLE KID, RIGHT?
AND HE'S SO BAD AT DEALING WITH GIRLS, ISN'T HE?
HE DOESN'T STRIKE ME AS A VERY DEPEND-ABLE GUY!
AHA HA!
GRRR... TELL ME HOW YOU REALLY FEEL, WHY DON'T YOU?
THAT'S NOT...
THAT'S NOT TRUE AT ALL!

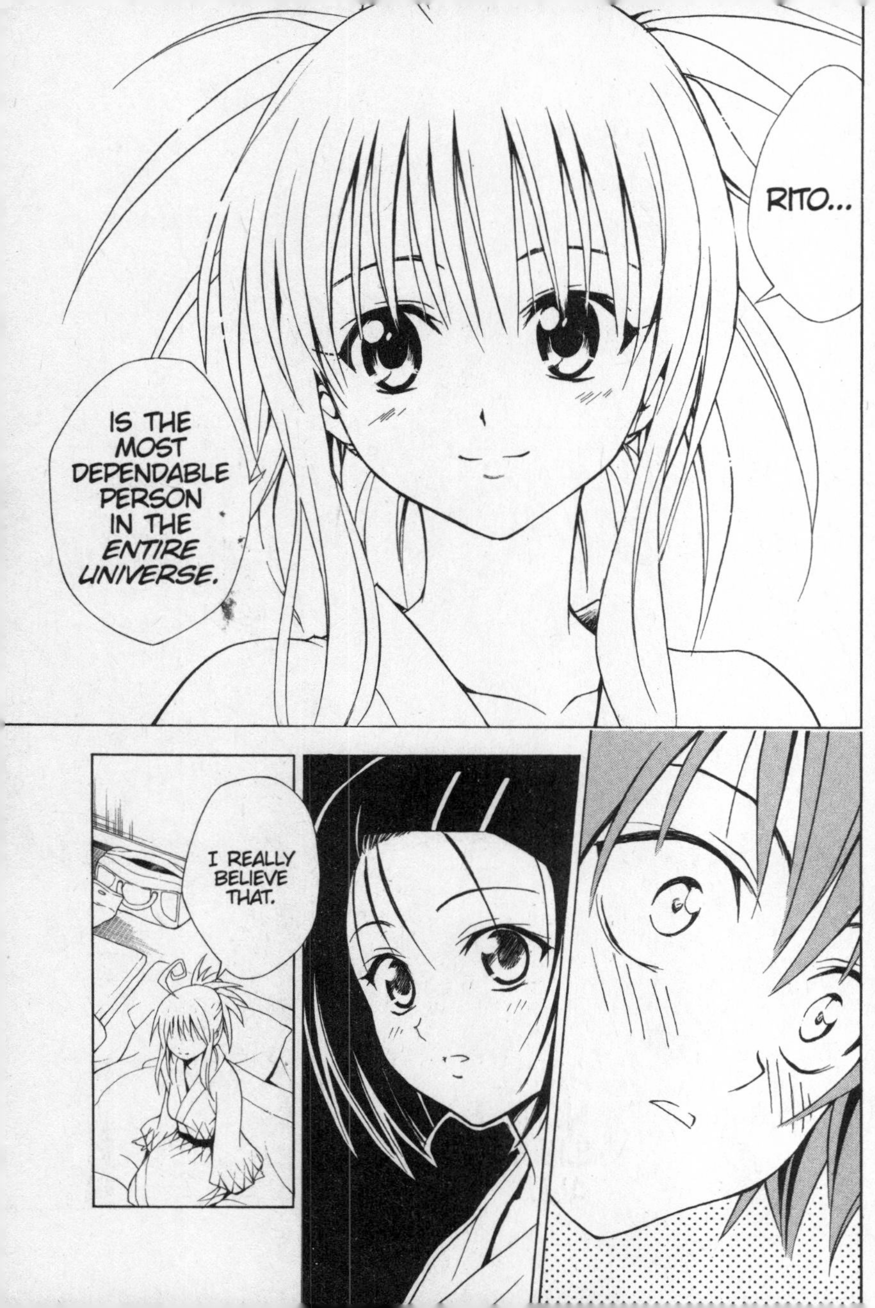
RITO...
IS THE MOST DEPENDABLE PERSON IN THE *ENTIRE* UNIVERSE.
I REALLY BELIEVE THAT.

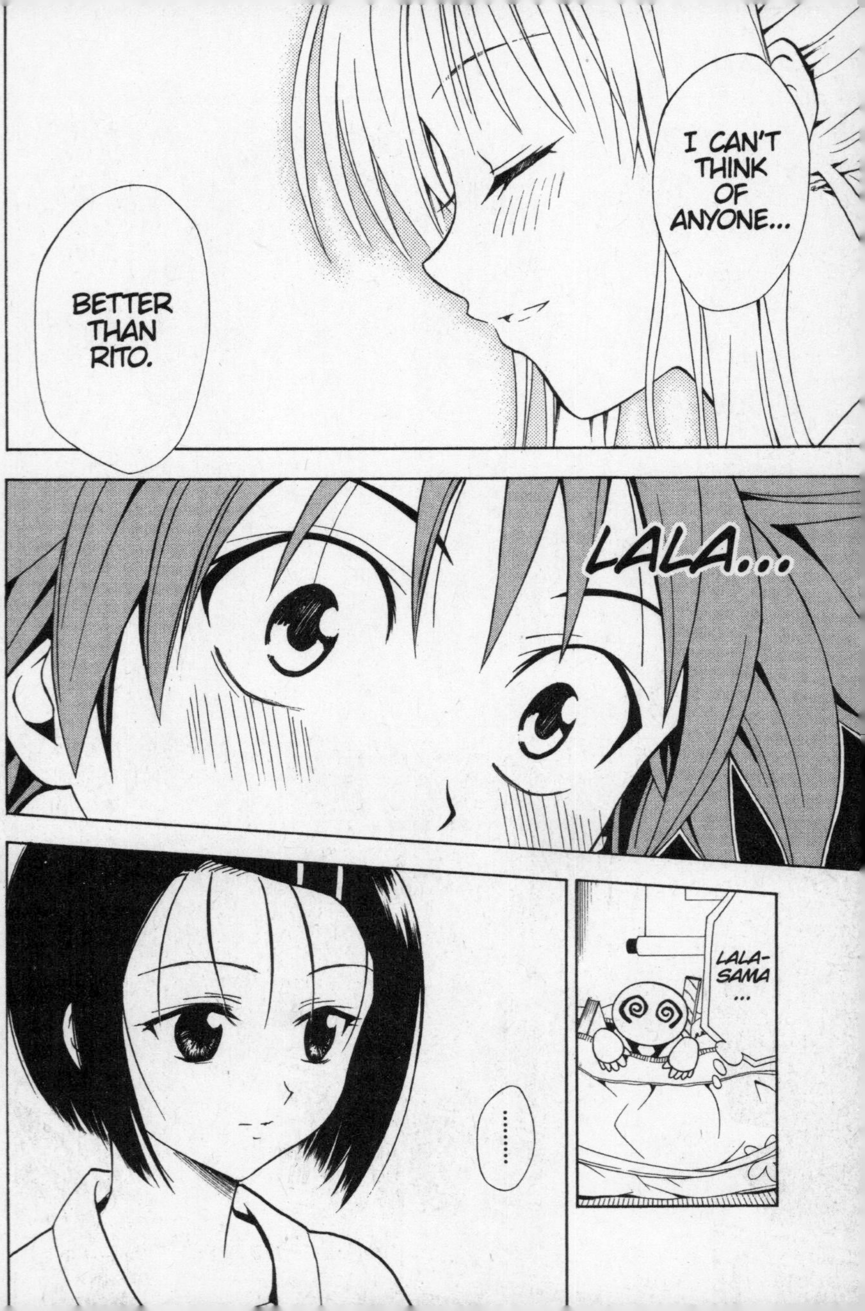
I CAN'T THINK OF ANYONE...
BETTER THAN RITO.
LALA...
LALA-SAMA ...
....

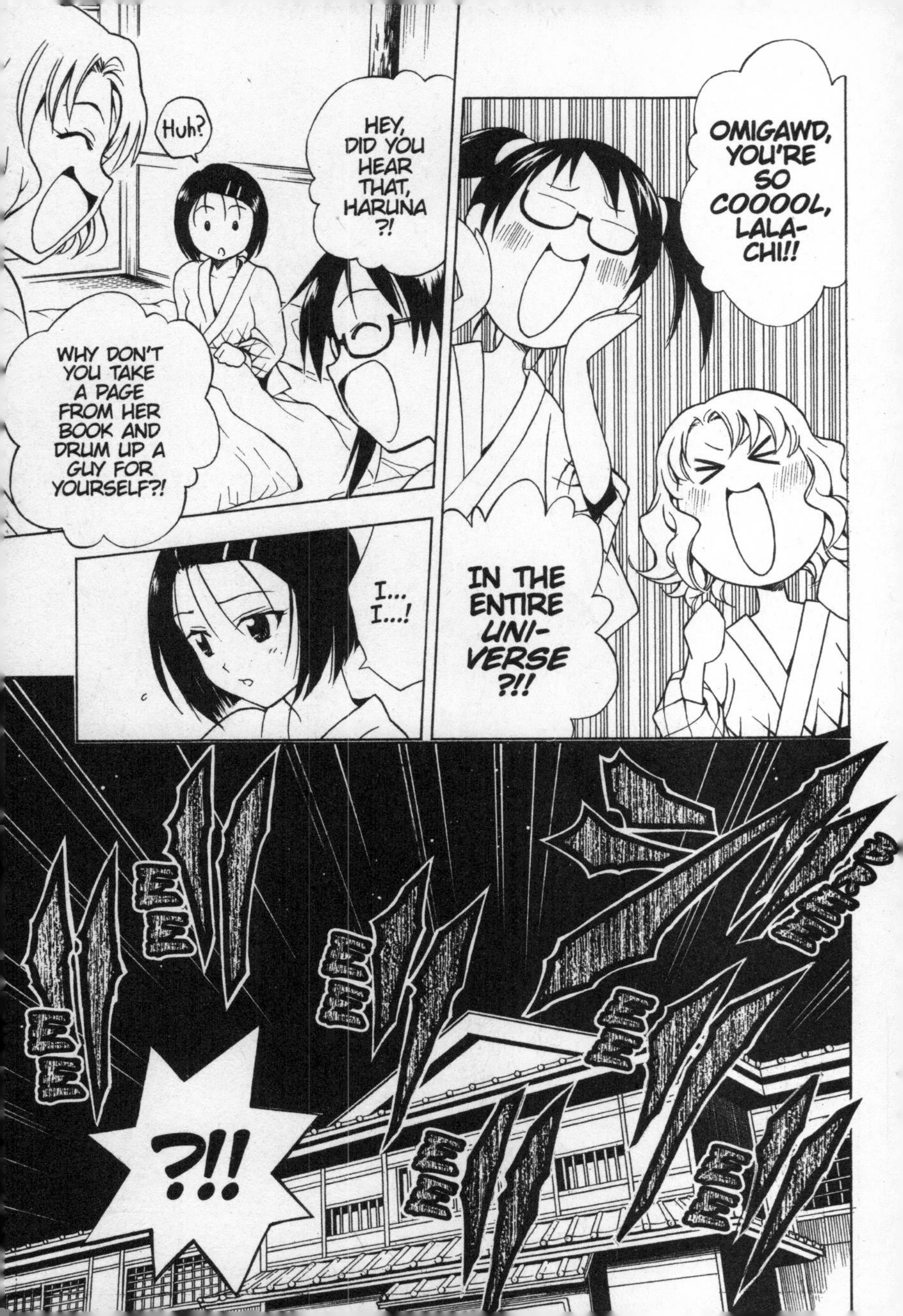
OMIGAWD, YOU'RE SO COOOOL, LALA-CHI!!
IN THE ENTIRE UNI-VERSE ?!!
HEY, DID YOU HEAR THAT, HARUNA ?!
Huh?
WHY DON'T YOU TAKE A PAGE FROM HER BOOK AND DRUM UP A GUY FOR YOURSELF?!
I..., I...!
?!!

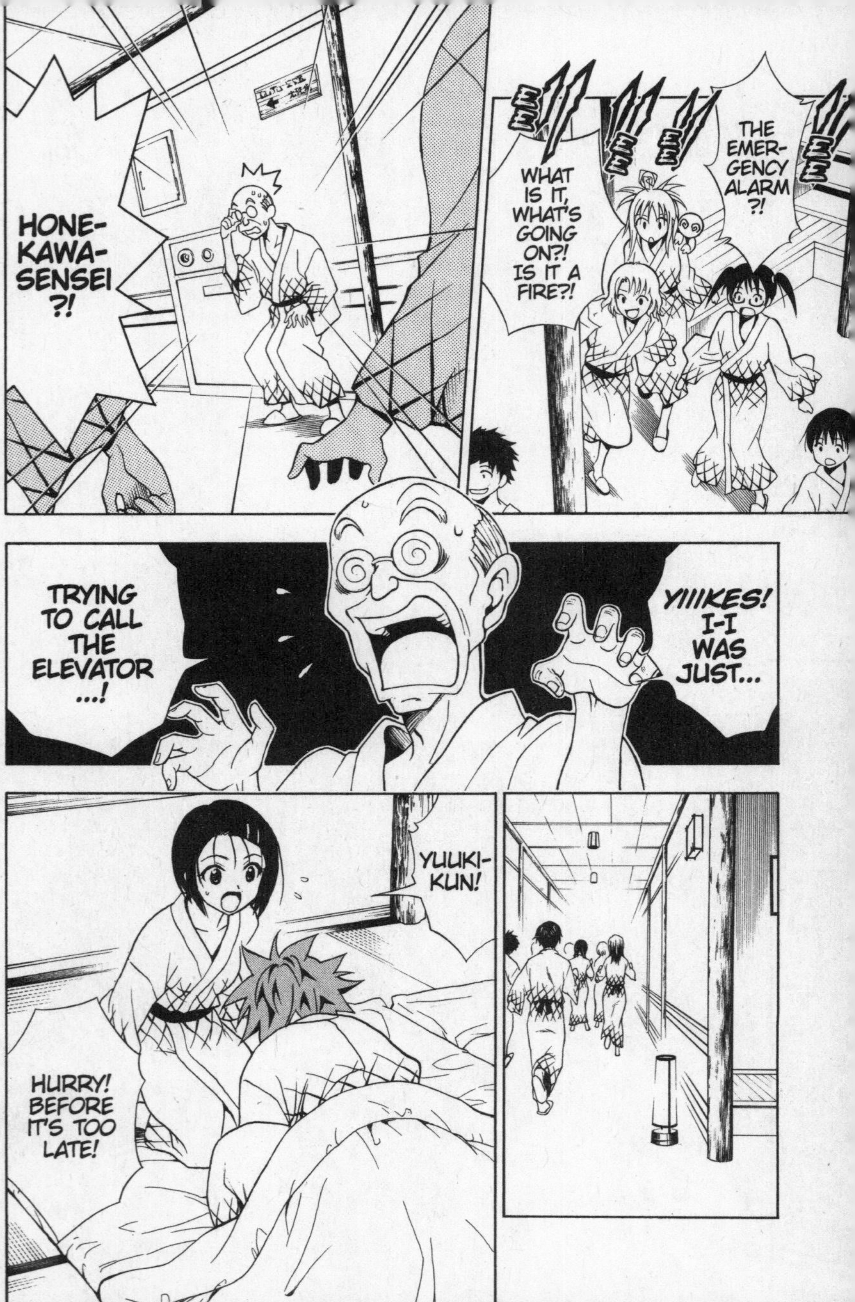
THE EMERGENCY ALARM?!
WHAT IS IT, WHAT'S GOING ON?! IS IT A FIRE?!
HONEKAWA-SENSEI?!
YIIIKES! I-I WAS JUST...
TRYING TO CALL THE ELEVATOR...!
YUUKI-KUN!
HURRY! BEFORE IT'S TOO LATE!

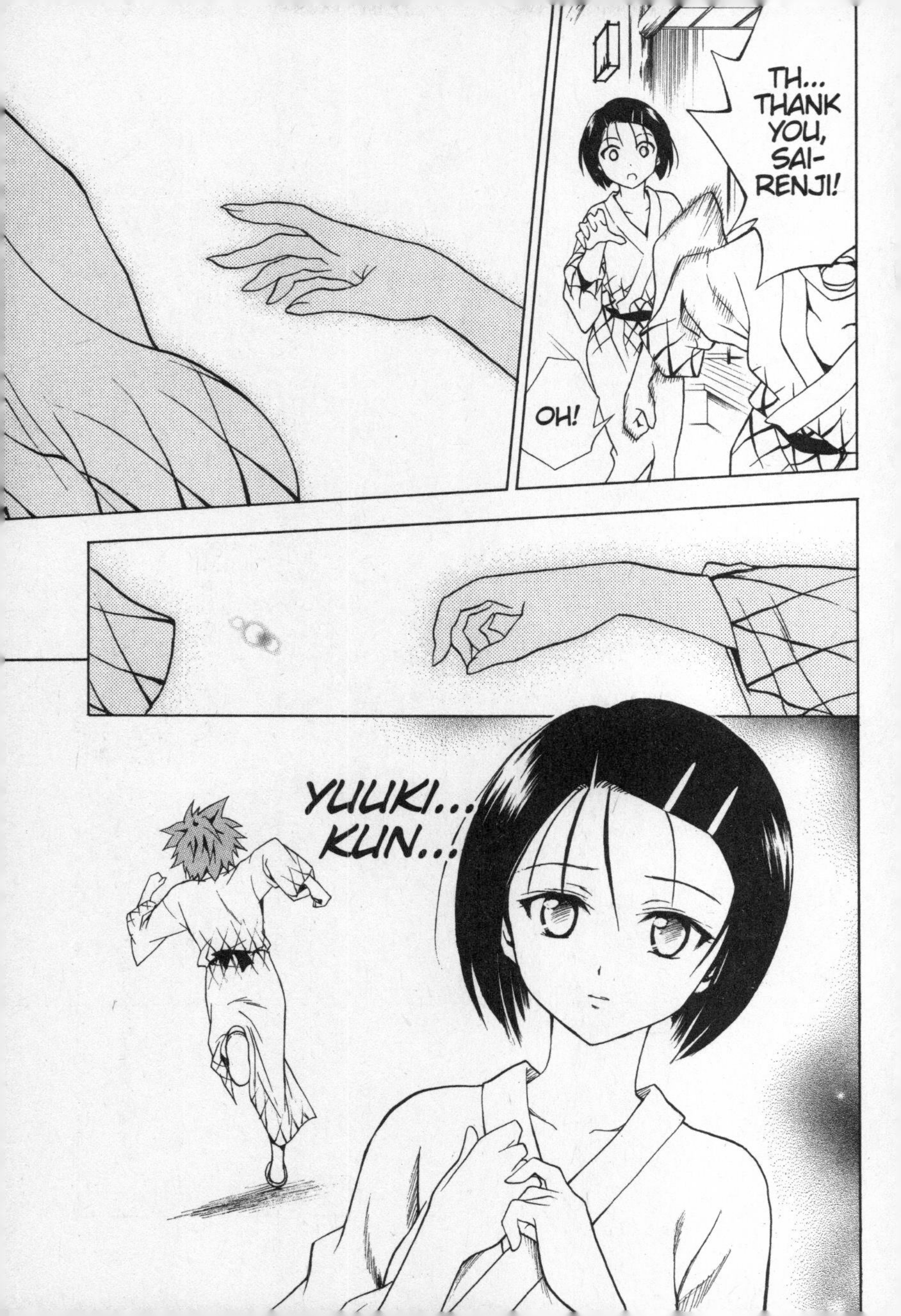
TH... THANK YOU, SAI-RENJI!
OH!
YUUKI... KUN...!

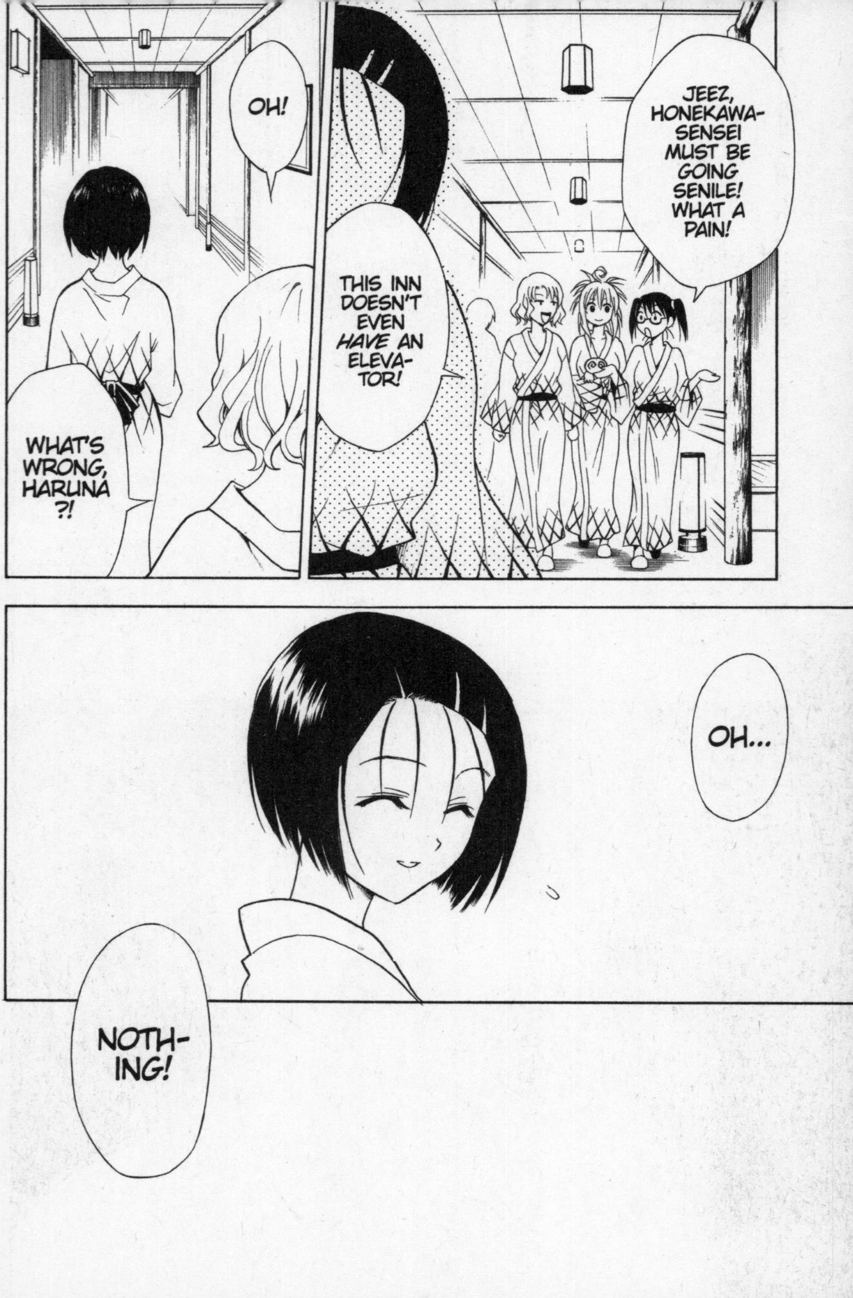
JEEZ, HONEKAWA-SENSEI MUST BE GOING SENILE! WHAT A PAIN!
THIS INN DOESN'T EVEN *HAVE* AN ELEVATOR!
OH!
WHAT'S WRONG, HARUNA?!
OH...
NOTH-ING!

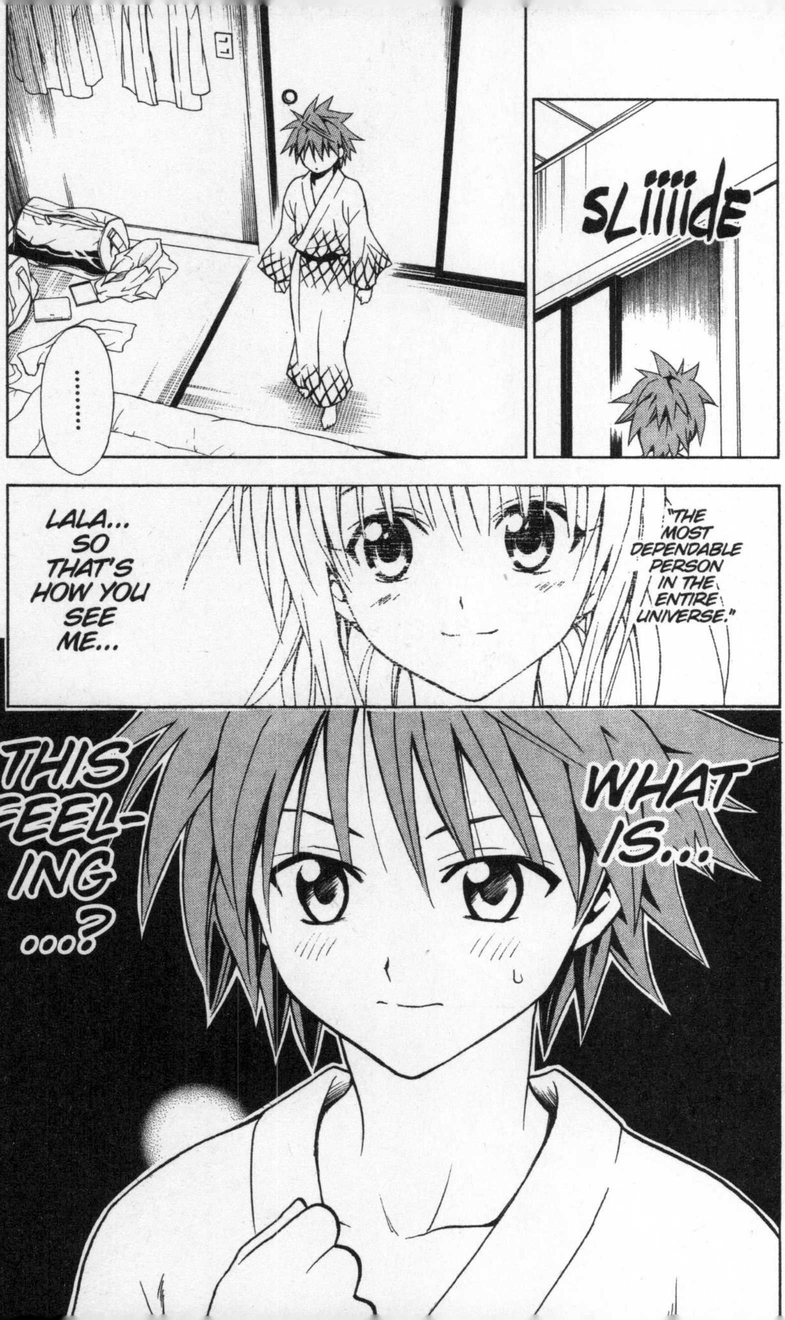
SLIIIIDE
......
"THE MOST DEPENDABLE PERSON IN THE ENTIRE UNIVERSE."
LALA... SO THAT'S HOW YOU SEE ME...
WHAT IS...
THIS FEEL-ING ...?

To LOVE Ru

Trouble 20: The Transfer Student Who Calls The Storm

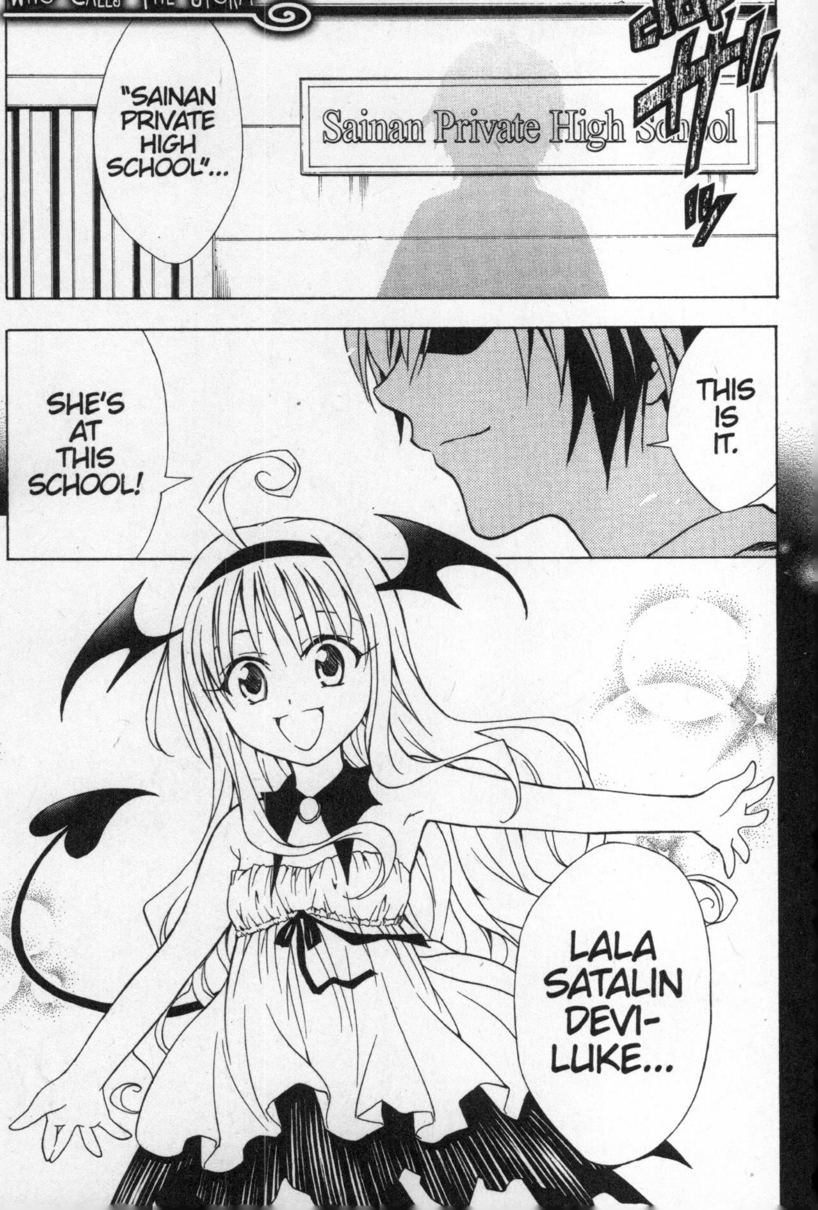
clap
Sainan Private High School
"SAINAN PRIVATE HIGH SCHOOL"...
THIS IS IT.
SHE'S AT THIS SCHOOL!
LALA SATALIN DEVI-LUKE...

TROUBLE 20:
THE TRANSFER STUDENT WHO CALLS THE STORM

Lala, Age 6 - Royal Palace of Deviluke

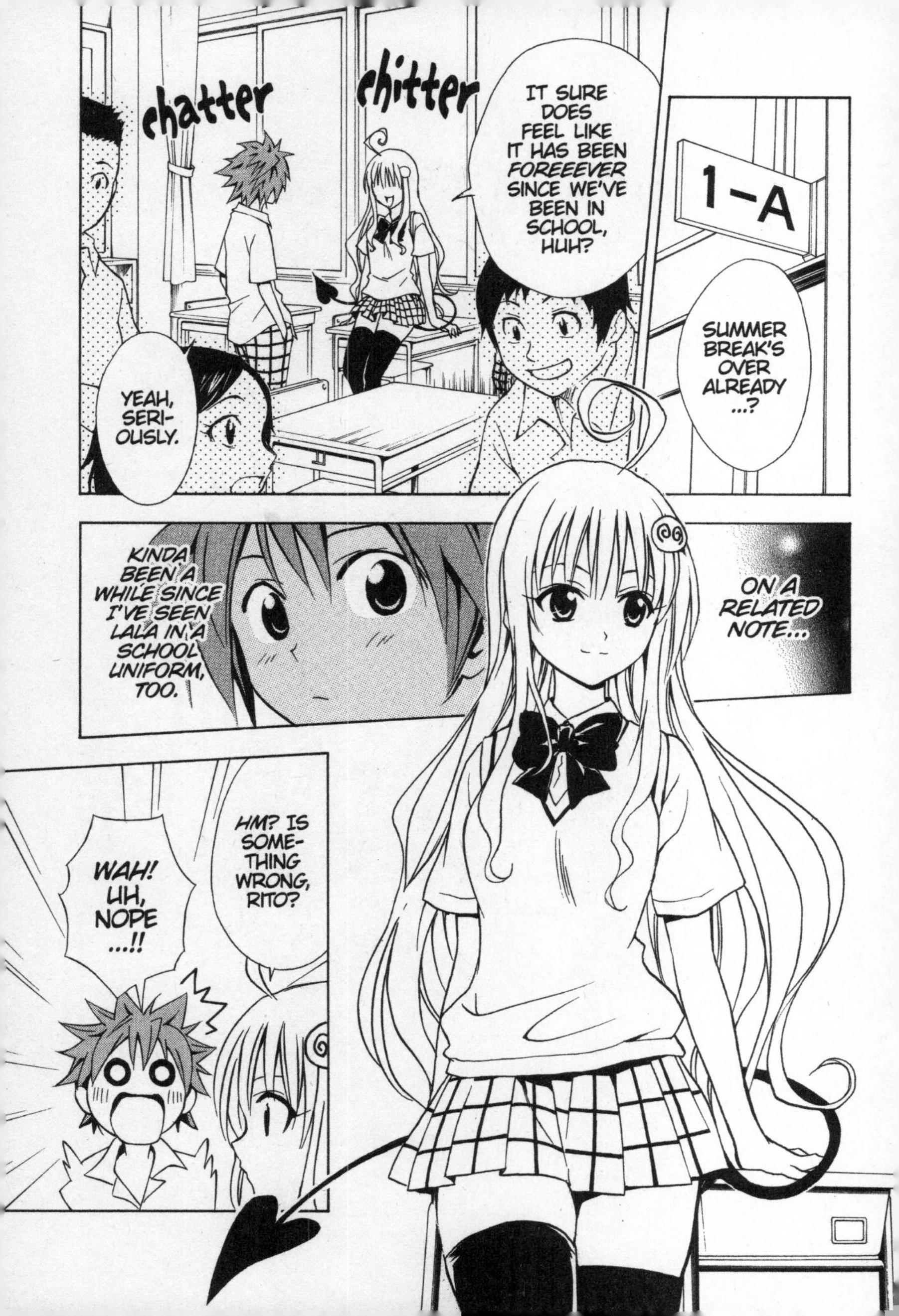
1-A
SUMMER BREAK'S OVER ALREADY ...?
IT SURE DOES FEEL LIKE IT HAS BEEN FOREEEVER SINCE WE'VE BEEN IN SCHOOL, HUH?
chitter
chatter
YEAH, SERI-OUSLY.
ON A RELATED NOTE...
KINDA BEEN A WHILE SINCE I'VE SEEN LALA IN A SCHOOL UNIFORM, TOO.
HM? IS SOME-THING WRONG, RITO?
WAH! UH, NOPE ...!!

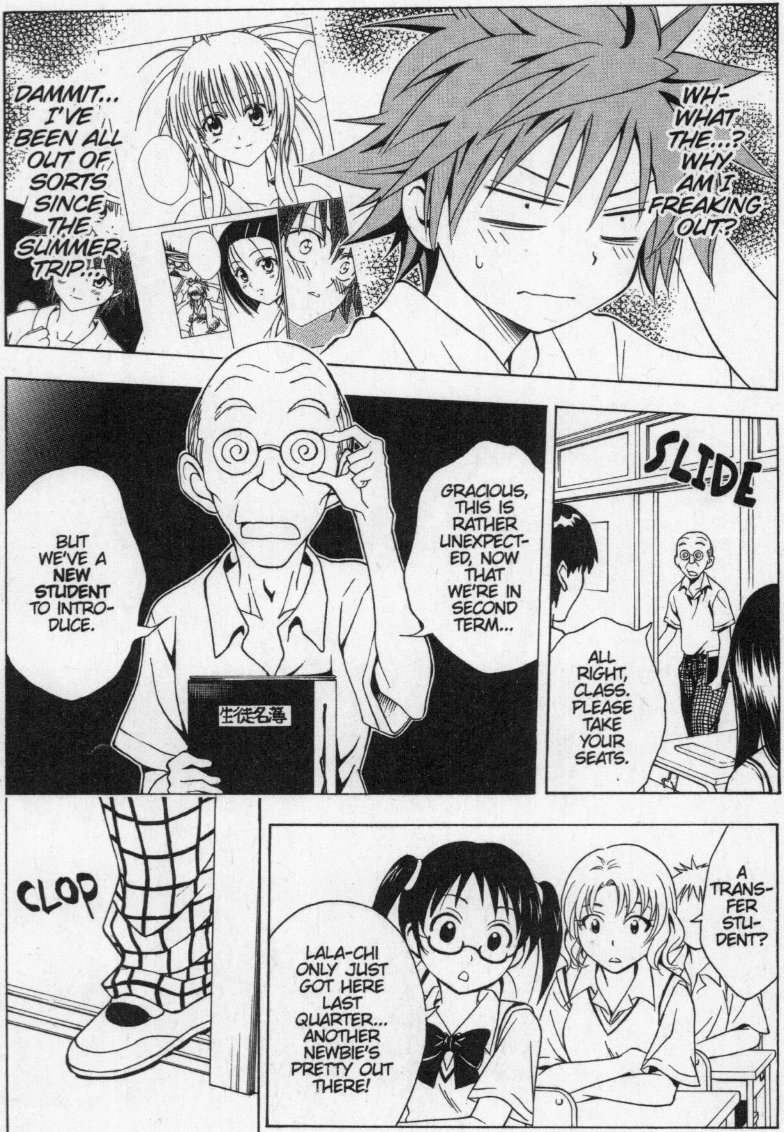
WH-WHAT THE...? WHY AM I FREAKING OUT?
DAMMIT... I'VE BEEN ALL OUT OF SORTS SINCE THE SUMMER TRIP...
SLIDE
ALL RIGHT, CLASS. PLEASE TAKE YOUR SEATS.
GRACIOUS, THIS IS RATHER UNEXPECTED, NOW THAT WE'RE IN SECOND TERM...
BUT WE'VE A NEW STUDENT TO INTRODUCE.
生徒名簿
A TRANSFER STUDENT?
LALA-CHI ONLY JUST GOT HERE LAST QUARTER... ANOTHER NEWBIE'S PRETTY OUT THERE!
CLOP

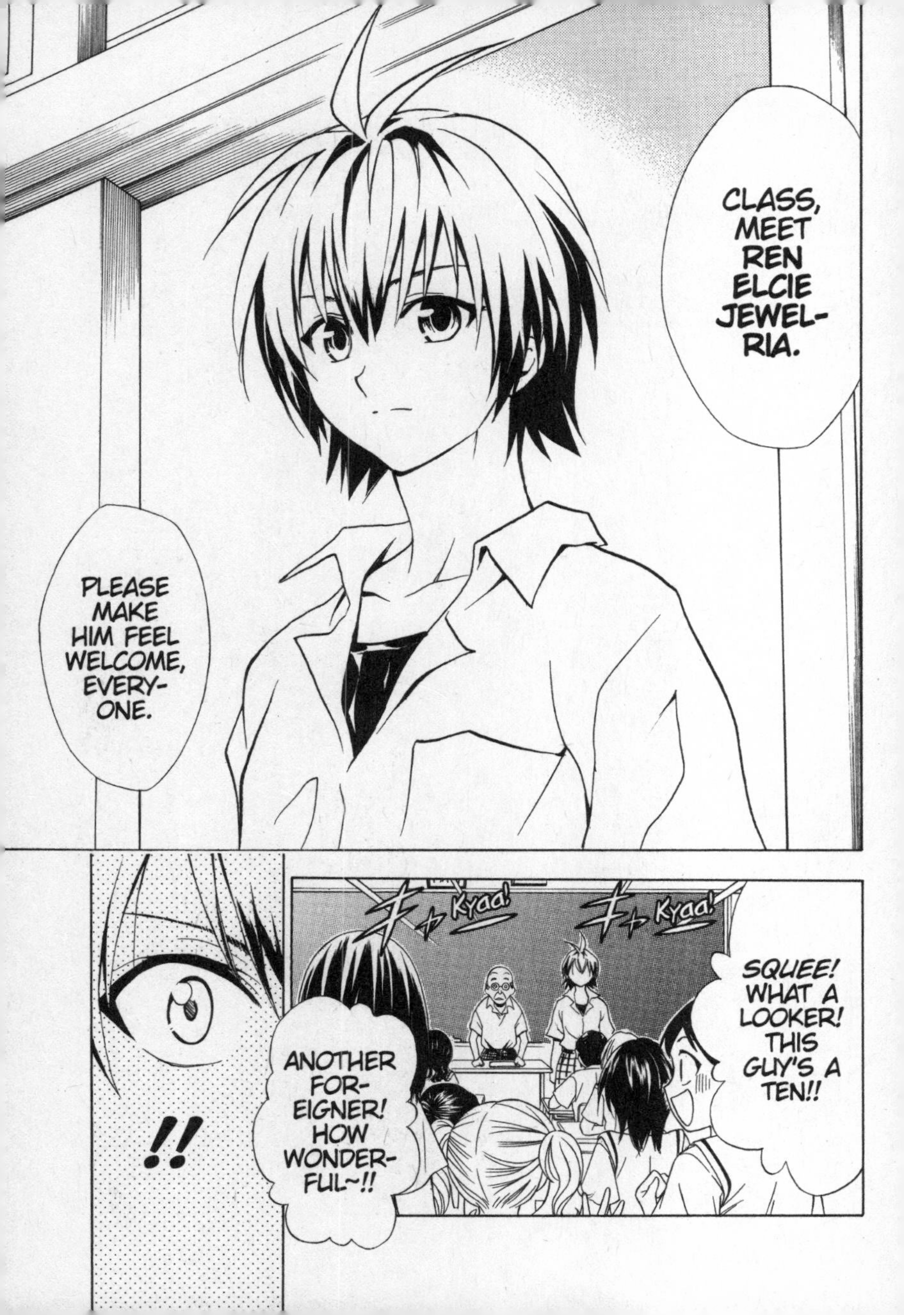
CLASS, MEET REN ELCIE JEWEL-RIA.
PLEASE MAKE HIM FEEL WELCOME, EVERY-ONE.
Kyaa!
Kyaa!
SQUEE! WHAT A LOOKER! THIS GUY'S A TEN!!
ANOTHER FOR-EIGNER! HOW WONDER-FUL~!!
!!

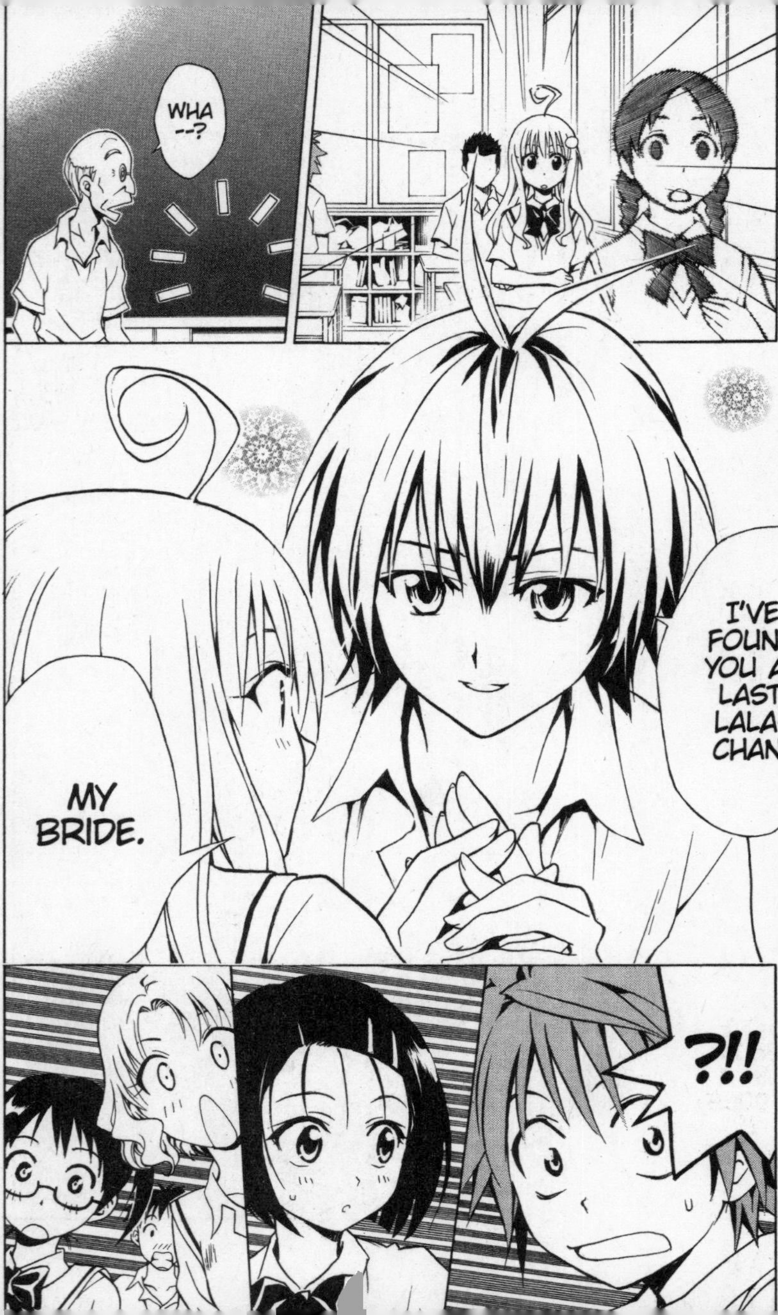
WHA --?
I'VE FOUND YOU AT LAST, LALA-CHAN.
MY BRIDE.
?!!

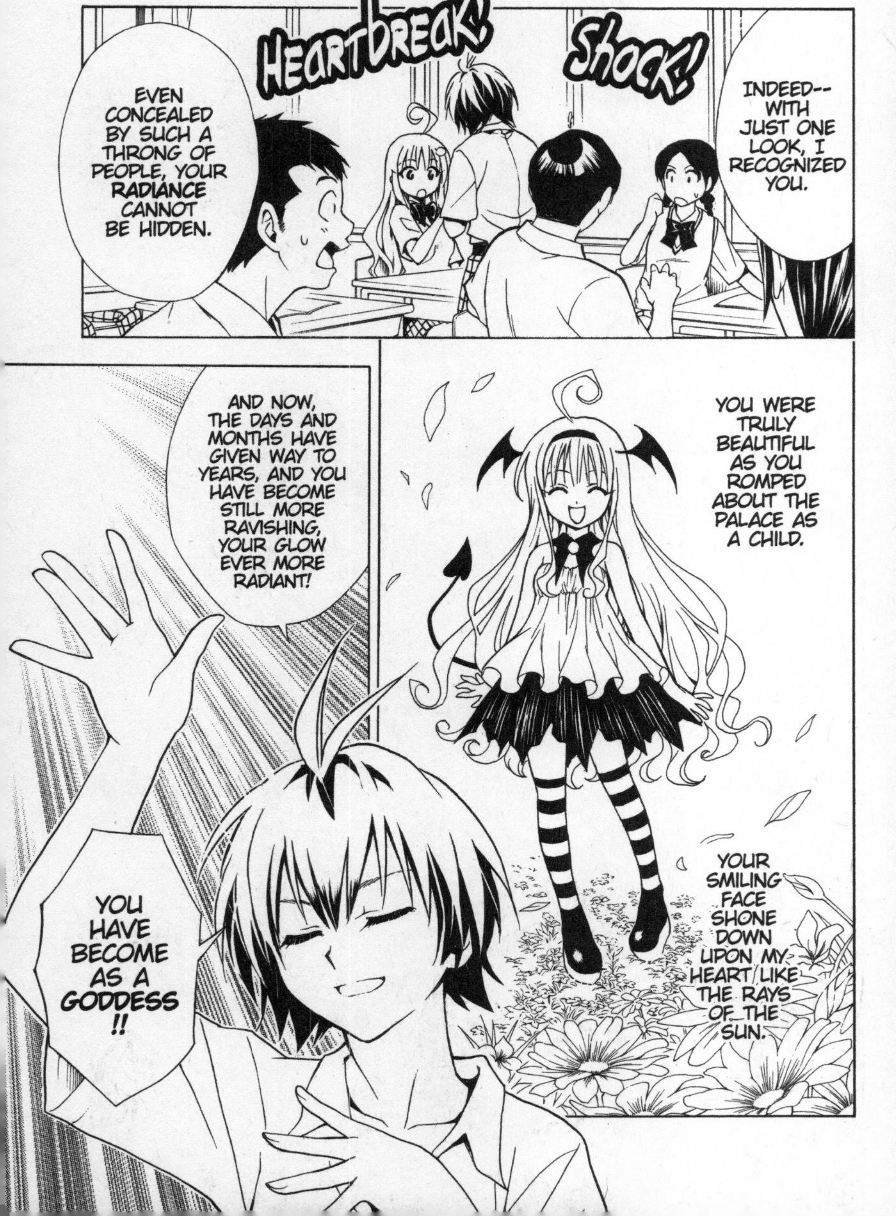
INDEED-- WITH JUST ONE LOOK, I RECOGNIZED YOU.
Shock!
HEARTBREAK!
EVEN CONCEALED BY SUCH A THRONG OF PEOPLE, YOUR RADIANCE CANNOT BE HIDDEN.
YOU WERE TRULY BEAUTIFUL AS YOU ROMPED ABOUT THE PALACE AS A CHILD.
YOUR SMILING FACE SHONE DOWN UPON MY HEART LIKE THE RAYS OF THE SUN.
AND NOW, THE DAYS AND MONTHS HAVE GIVEN WAY TO YEARS, AND YOU HAVE BECOME STILL MORE RAVISHING, YOUR GLOW EVER MORE RADIANT!
YOU HAVE BECOME AS A GODDESS !!

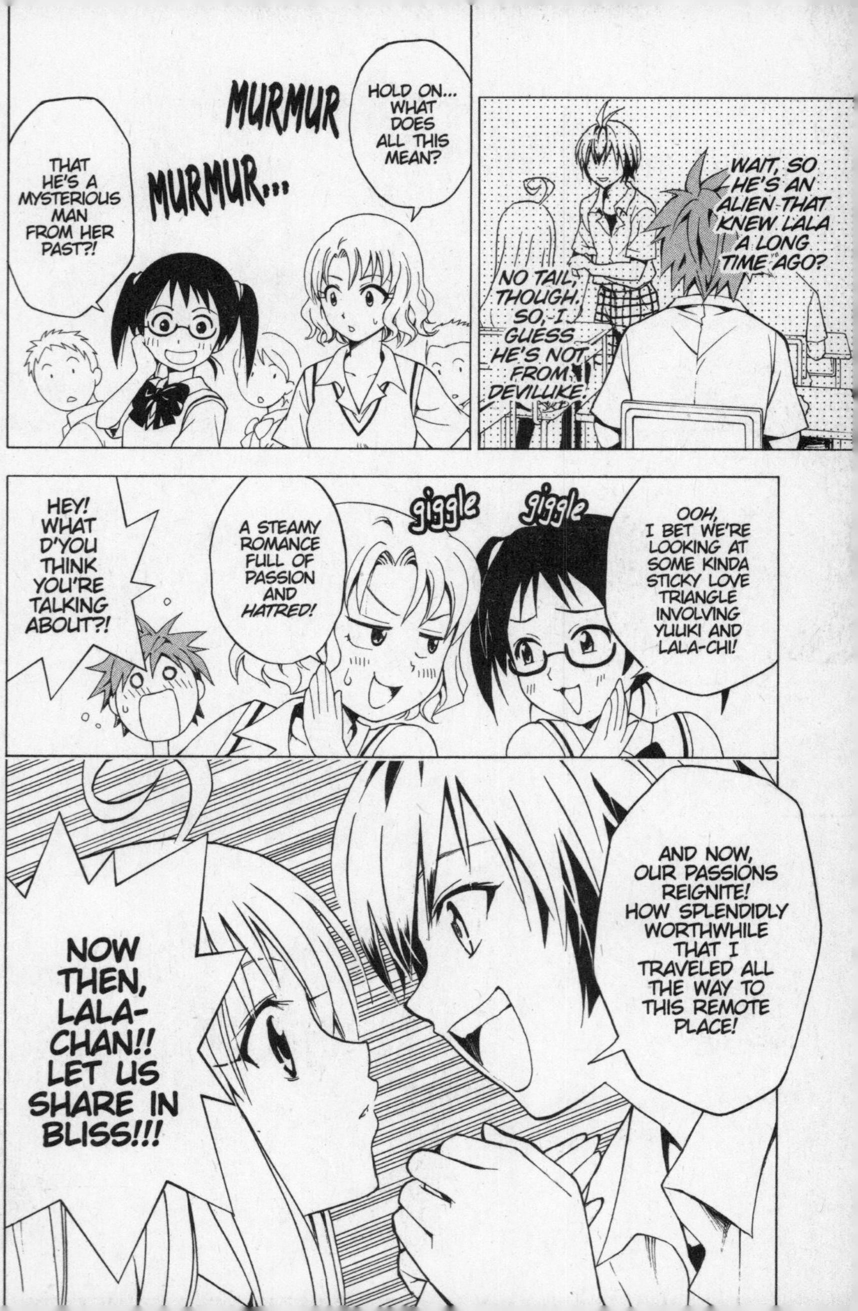
WAIT, SO HE'S AN ALIEN THAT KNEW LALA A LONG TIME AGO?
NO TAIL, THOUGH. SO, I GUESS HE'S NOT FROM DEVILUKE.
HOLD ON... WHAT DOES ALL THIS MEAN?
MURMUR
MURMUR...
THAT HE'S A MYSTERIOUS MAN FROM HER PAST?!
OOH, I BET WE'RE LOOKING AT SOME KINDA STICKY LOVE TRIANGLE INVOLVING YUUKI AND LALA-CHI!
giggle
giggle
A STEAMY ROMANCE FULL OF PASSION AND HATRED!
HEY! WHAT D'YOU THINK YOU'RE TALKING ABOUT?!
AND NOW, OUR PASSIONS REIGNITE! HOW SPLENDIDLY WORTHWHILE THAT I TRAVELED ALL THE WAY TO THIS REMOTE PLACE!
NOW THEN, LALA-CHAN!! LET US SHARE IN BLISS!!!

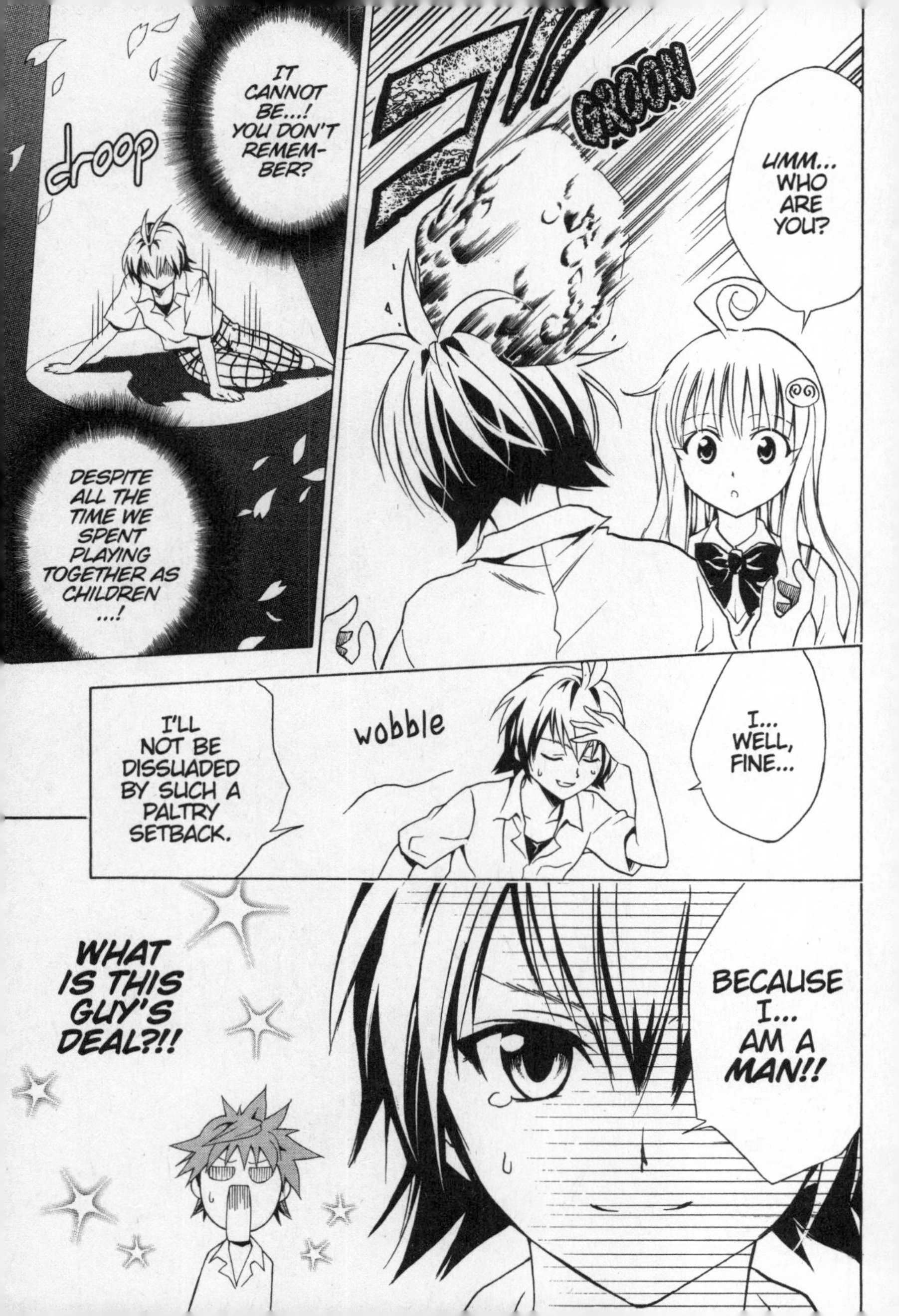
UMM... WHO ARE YOU?
GROON
IT CANNOT BE...! YOU DON'T REMEMBER?
droop
DESPITE ALL THE TIME WE SPENT PLAYING TOGETHER AS CHILDREN ...!
I... WELL, FINE...
wobble
I'LL NOT BE DISSUADED BY SUCH A PALTRY SETBACK.
BECAUSE I... AM A MAN!!
WHAT IS THIS GUY'S DEAL?!!

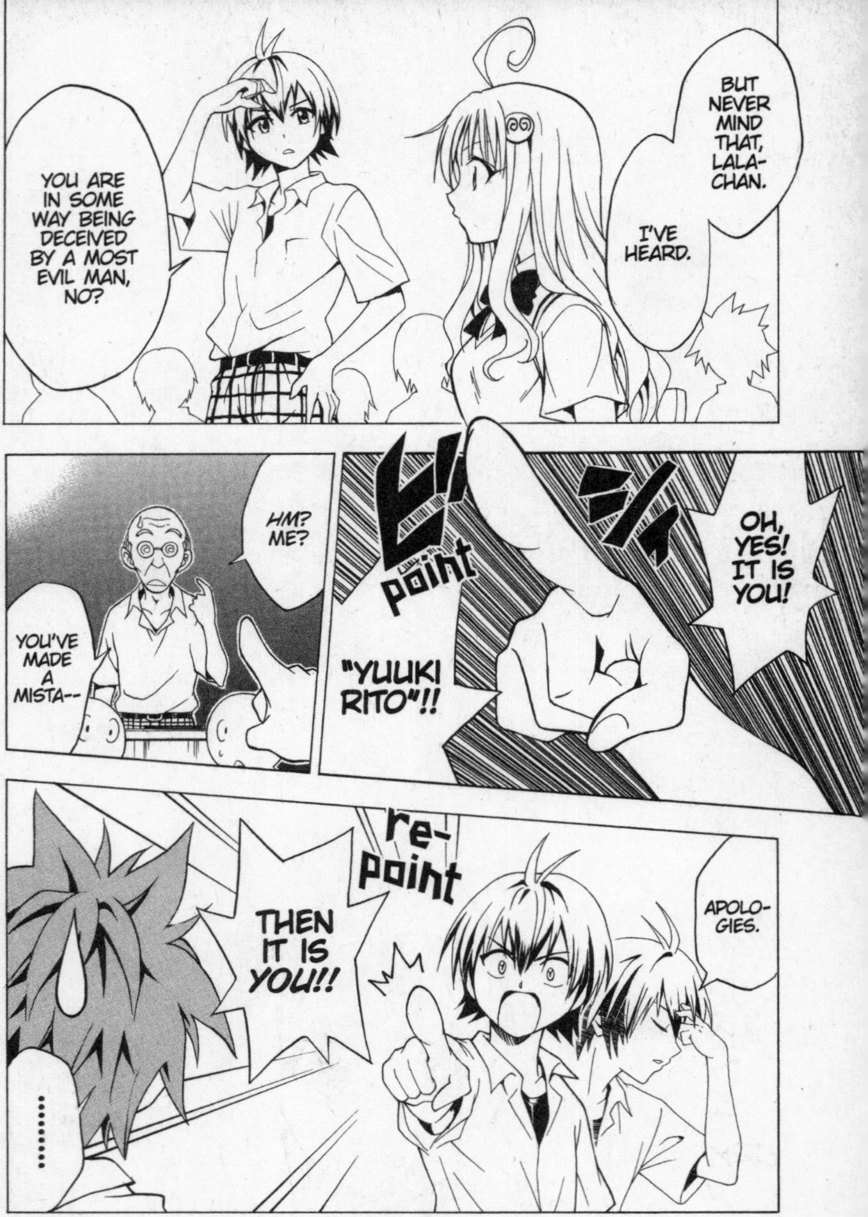
BUT NEVER MIND THAT, LALA-CHAN.
I'VE HEARD.
YOU ARE IN SOME WAY BEING DECEIVED BY A MOST EVIL MAN, NO?
ビシィ
point
OH, YES! IT IS YOU!
"YUUKI RITO"!!
HM? ME?
YOU'VE MADE A MISTA--
APOLOGIES.
re-point
THEN IT IS YOU!!
....

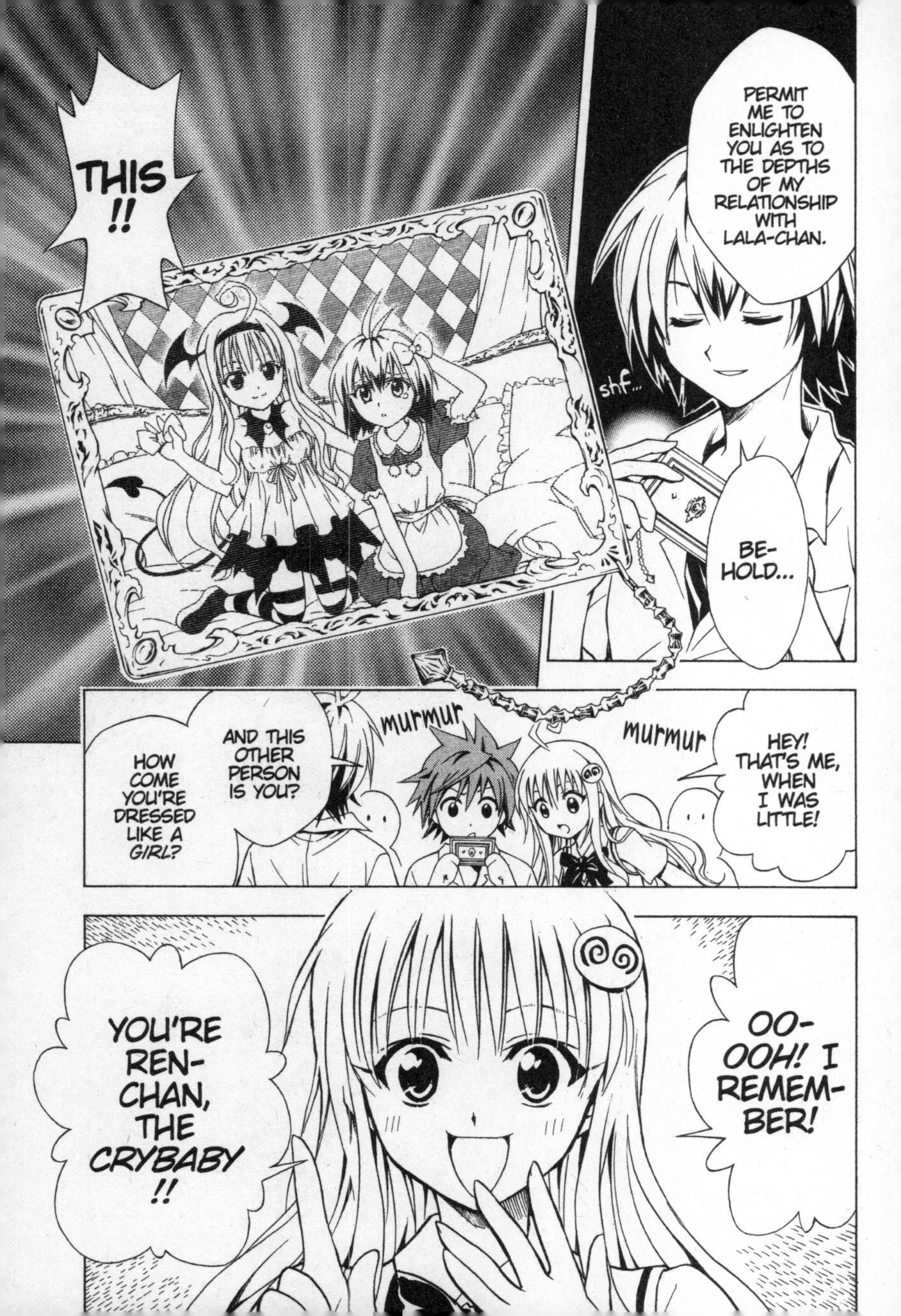
PERMIT ME TO ENLIGHTEN YOU AS TO THE DEPTHS OF MY RELATIONSHIP WITH LALA-CHAN.
shf...
BE-HOLD...
THIS !!
HEY! THAT'S ME, WHEN I WAS LITTLE!
murmur
murmur
AND THIS OTHER PERSON IS YOU?
HOW COME YOU'RE DRESSED LIKE A GIRL?
OO-OOH! I REMEM-BER!
YOU'RE REN-CHAN, THE CRYBABY !!

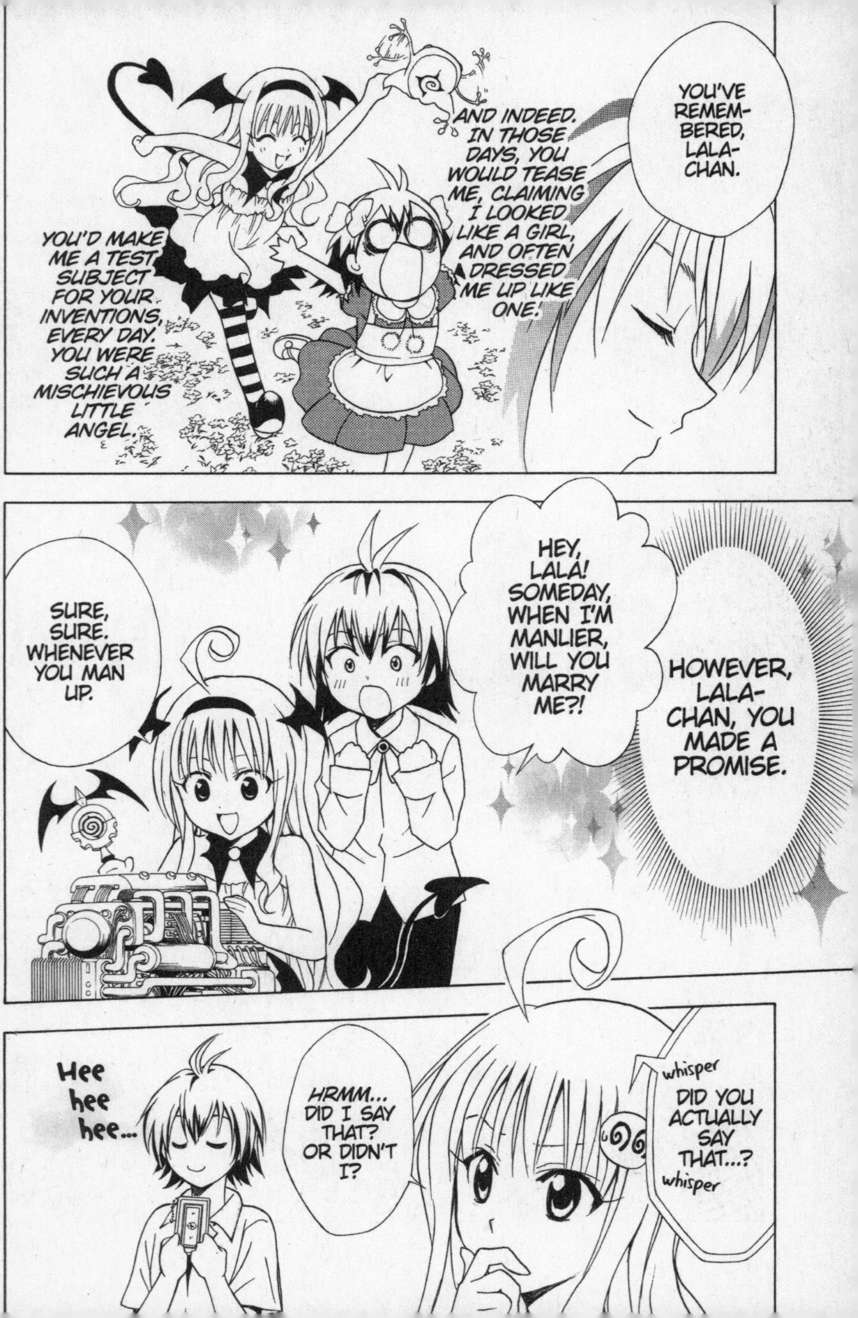

YOU'VE REMEMBERED, LALA-CHAN.
AND INDEED. IN THOSE DAYS, YOU WOULD TEASE ME, CLAIMING I LOOKED LIKE A GIRL, AND OFTEN DRESSED ME UP LIKE ONE!
YOU'D MAKE ME A TEST SUBJECT FOR YOUR INVENTIONS, EVERY DAY. YOU WERE SUCH A MISCHIEVOUS LITTLE ANGEL.
HOWEVER, LALA-CHAN, YOU MADE A PROMISE.
HEY, LALA! SOMEDAY, WHEN I'M MANLIER, WILL YOU MARRY ME?!
SURE, SURE. WHENEVER YOU MAN UP.
whisper
DID YOU ACTUALLY SAY THAT...?
whisper
HRMM... DID I SAY THAT? OR DIDN'T I?
Hee hee hee...

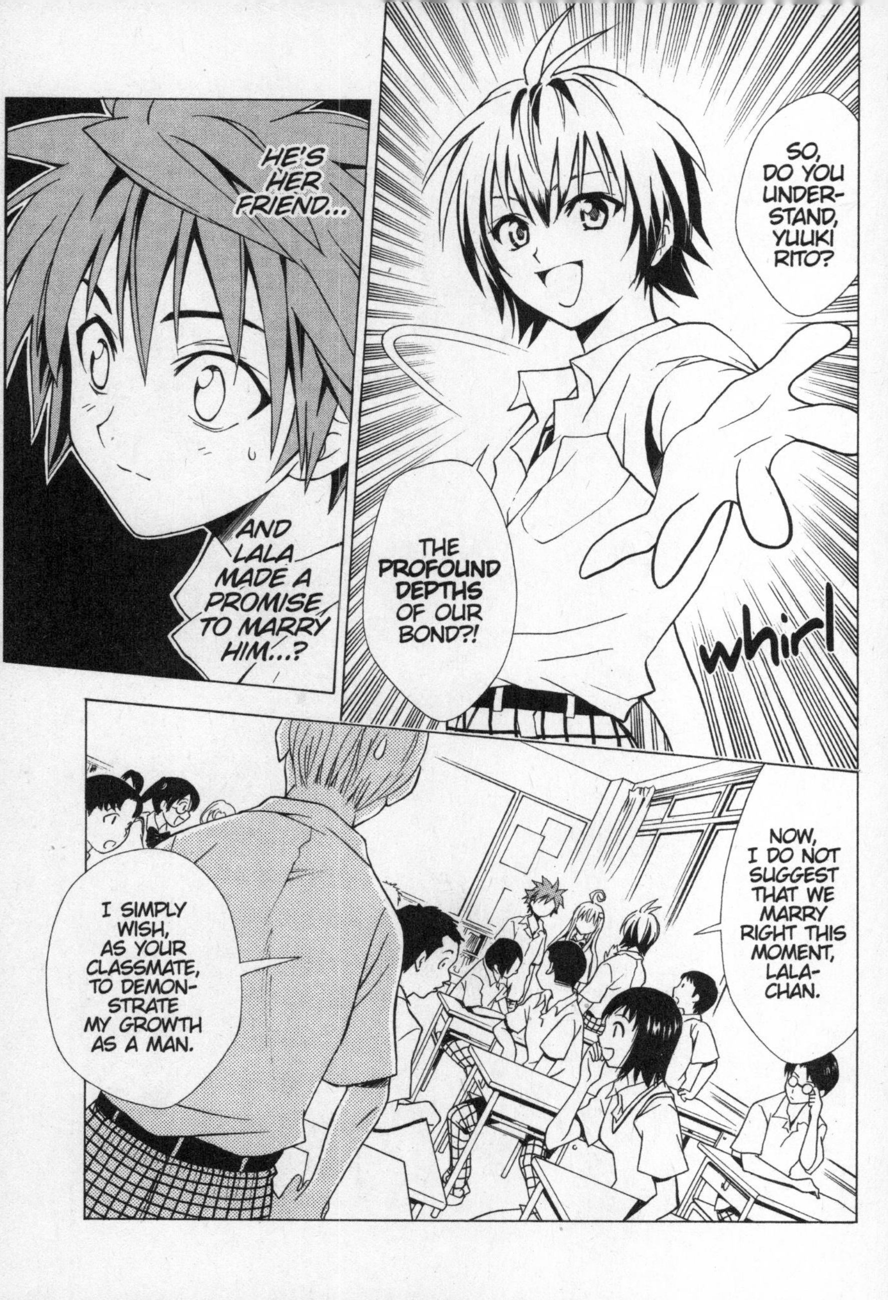
SO, DO YOU UNDER-STAND, YUUKI RITO?
THE PROFOUND DEPTHS OF OUR BOND?!
whirl
HE'S HER FRIEND...
AND LALA MADE A PROMISE TO MARRY HIM...?
NOW, I DO NOT SUGGEST THAT WE MARRY RIGHT THIS MOMENT, LALA-CHAN.
I SIMPLY WISH, AS YOUR CLASSMATE, TO DEMON-STRATE MY GROWTH AS A MAN.

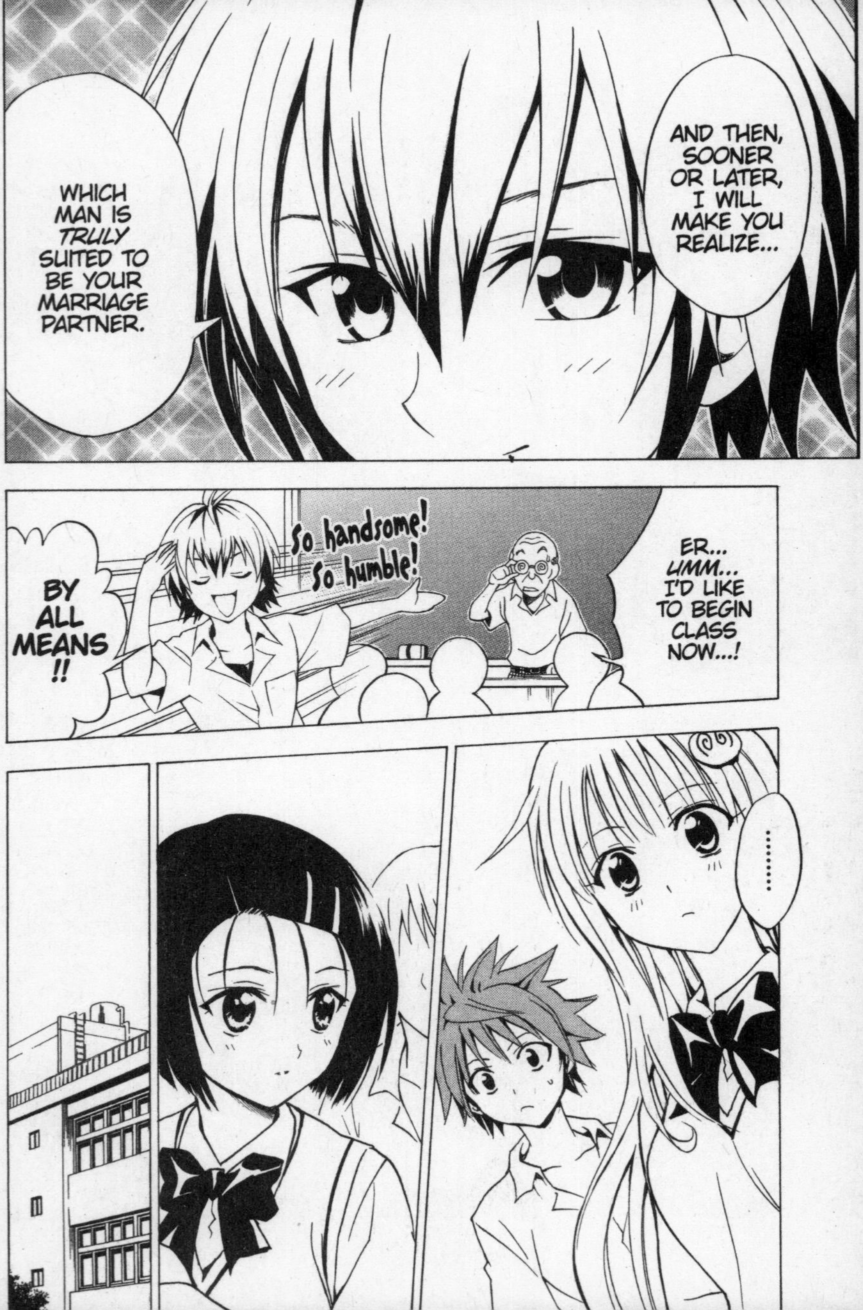
AND THEN, SOONER OR LATER, I WILL MAKE YOU REALIZE...
WHICH MAN IS *TRULY* SUITED TO BE YOUR MARRIAGE PARTNER.
ER... *UMM...* I'D LIKE TO BEGIN CLASS NOW...!
So handsome! So humble!
BY ALL MEANS !!
......

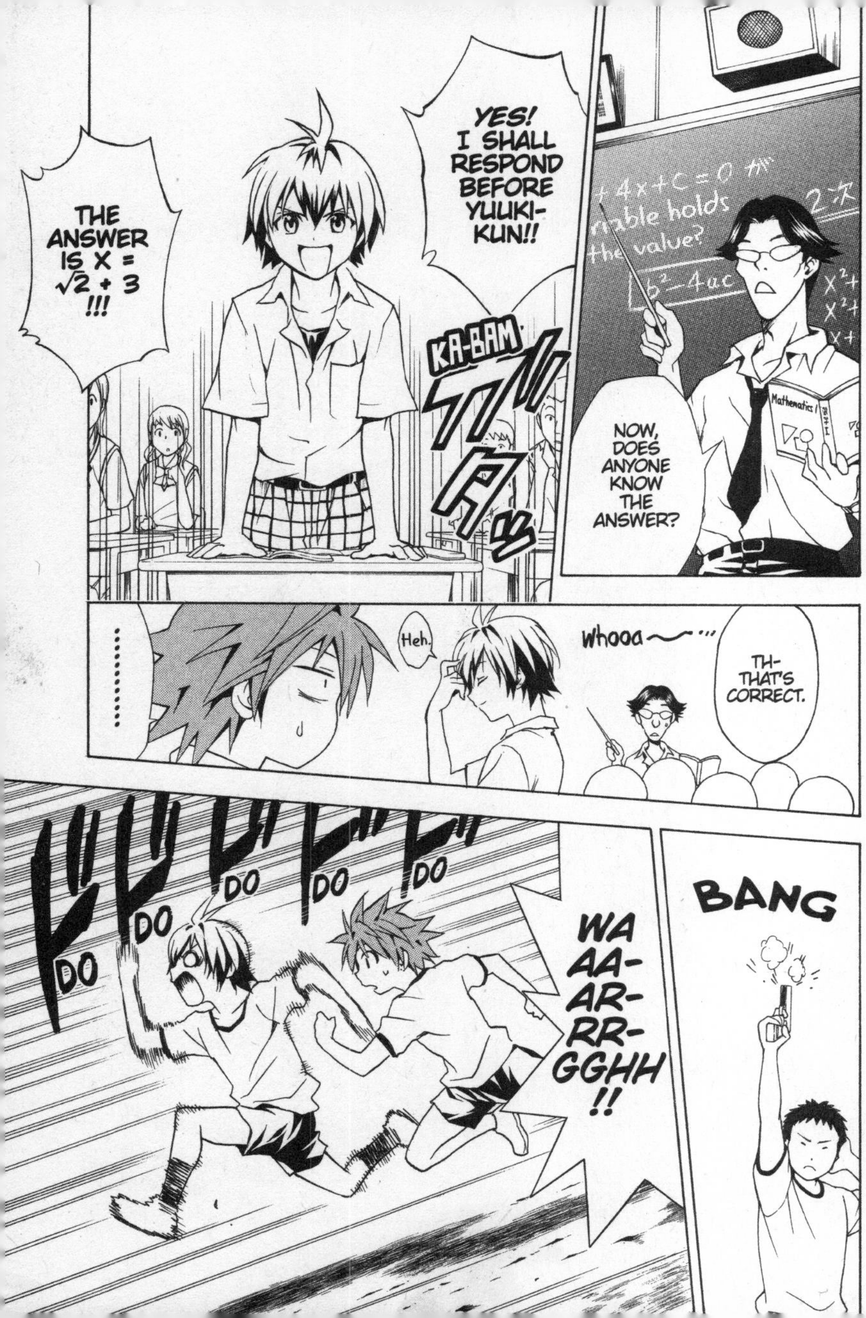
NOW, DOES ANYONE KNOW THE ANSWER?
KA-BAM
YES! I SHALL RESPOND BEFORE YUUKI-KUN!!
THE ANSWER IS X = √2 + 3 !!!
TH- THAT'S CORRECT.
Whooa~...
Heh.
....
BANG
WA AA- AR- RR- GGHH !!
DO
DO
DO
DO
DO

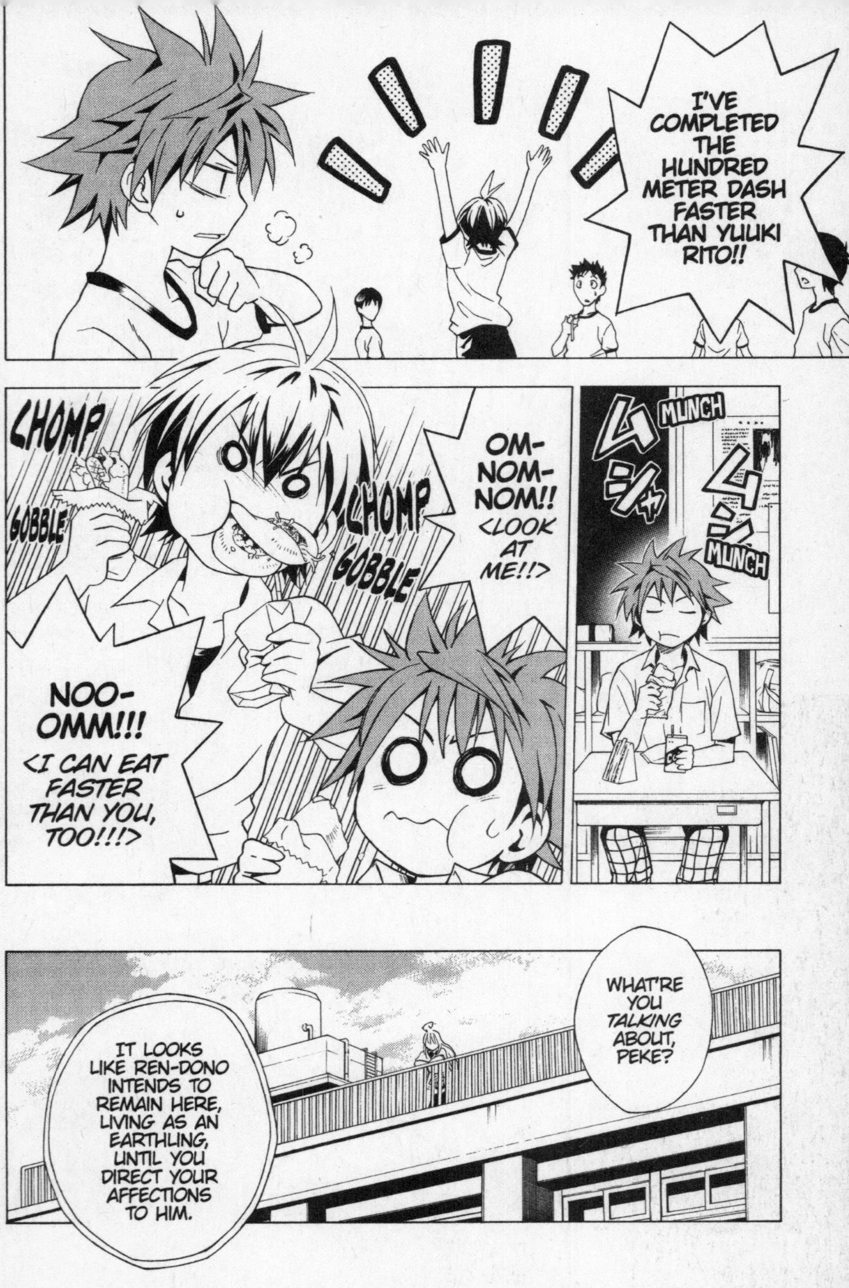
I'VE COMPLETED THE HUNDRED METER DASH FASTER THAN YUUKI RITO!!
MUNCH
MUNCH
OM-NOM-NOM!! <LOOK AT ME!!>
CHOMP
CHOMP
GOBBLE
GOBBLE
NOO-OMM!!! <I CAN EAT FASTER THAN YOU, TOO!!!>
WHAT'RE YOU TALKING ABOUT, PEKE?
IT LOOKS LIKE REN-DONO INTENDS TO REMAIN HERE, LIVING AS AN EARTHLING, UNTIL YOU DIRECT YOUR AFFECTIONS TO HIM.

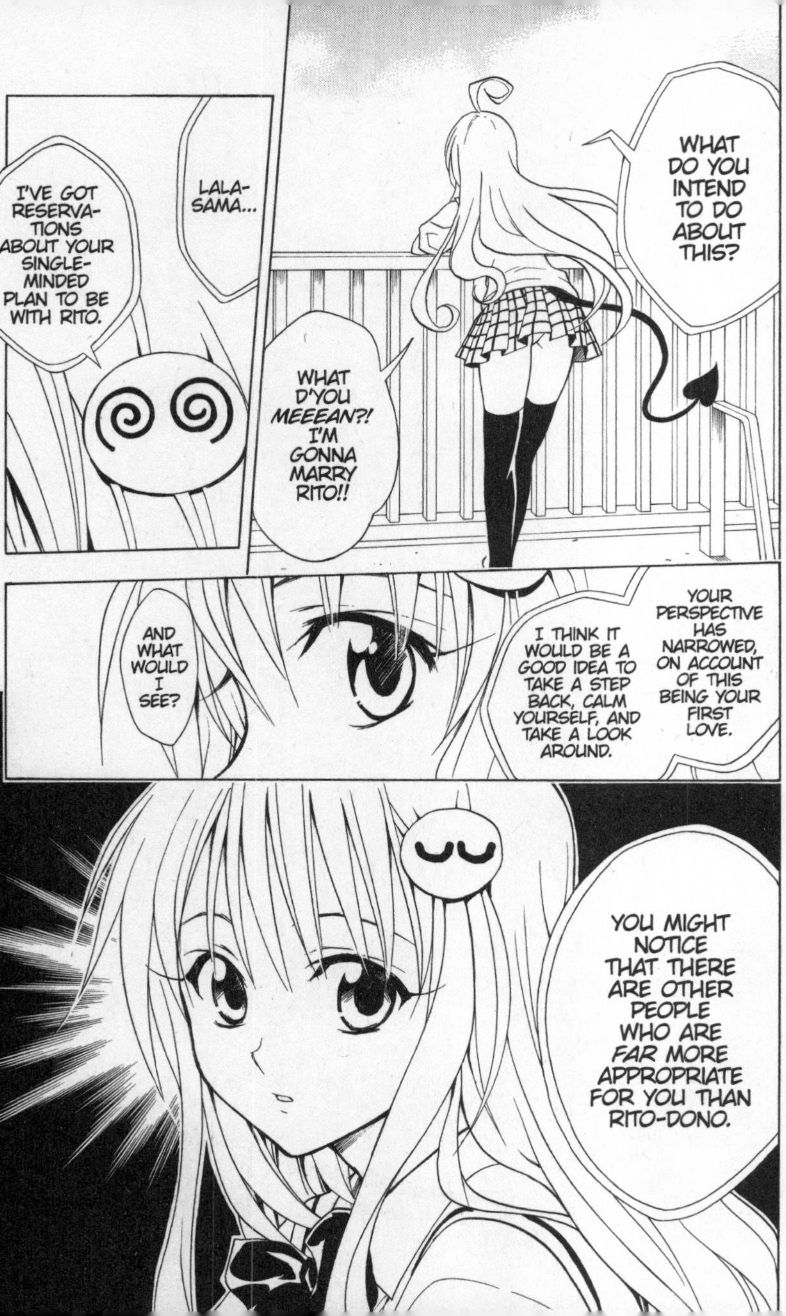
WHAT DO YOU INTEND TO DO ABOUT THIS?
WHAT D'YOU *MEEEAN*?! I'M GONNA MARRY RITO!!
LALA-SAMA...
I'VE GOT RESERVA-TIONS ABOUT YOUR SINGLE-MINDED PLAN TO BE WITH RITO.
YOUR PERSPECTIVE HAS NARROWED, ON ACCOUNT OF THIS BEING YOUR FIRST LOVE.
I THINK IT WOULD BE A GOOD IDEA TO TAKE A STEP BACK, CALM YOURSELF, AND TAKE A LOOK AROUND.
AND WHAT WOULD I SEE?
YOU MIGHT NOTICE THAT THERE ARE OTHER PEOPLE WHO ARE *FAR* MORE APPROPRIATE FOR YOU THAN RITO-DONO.

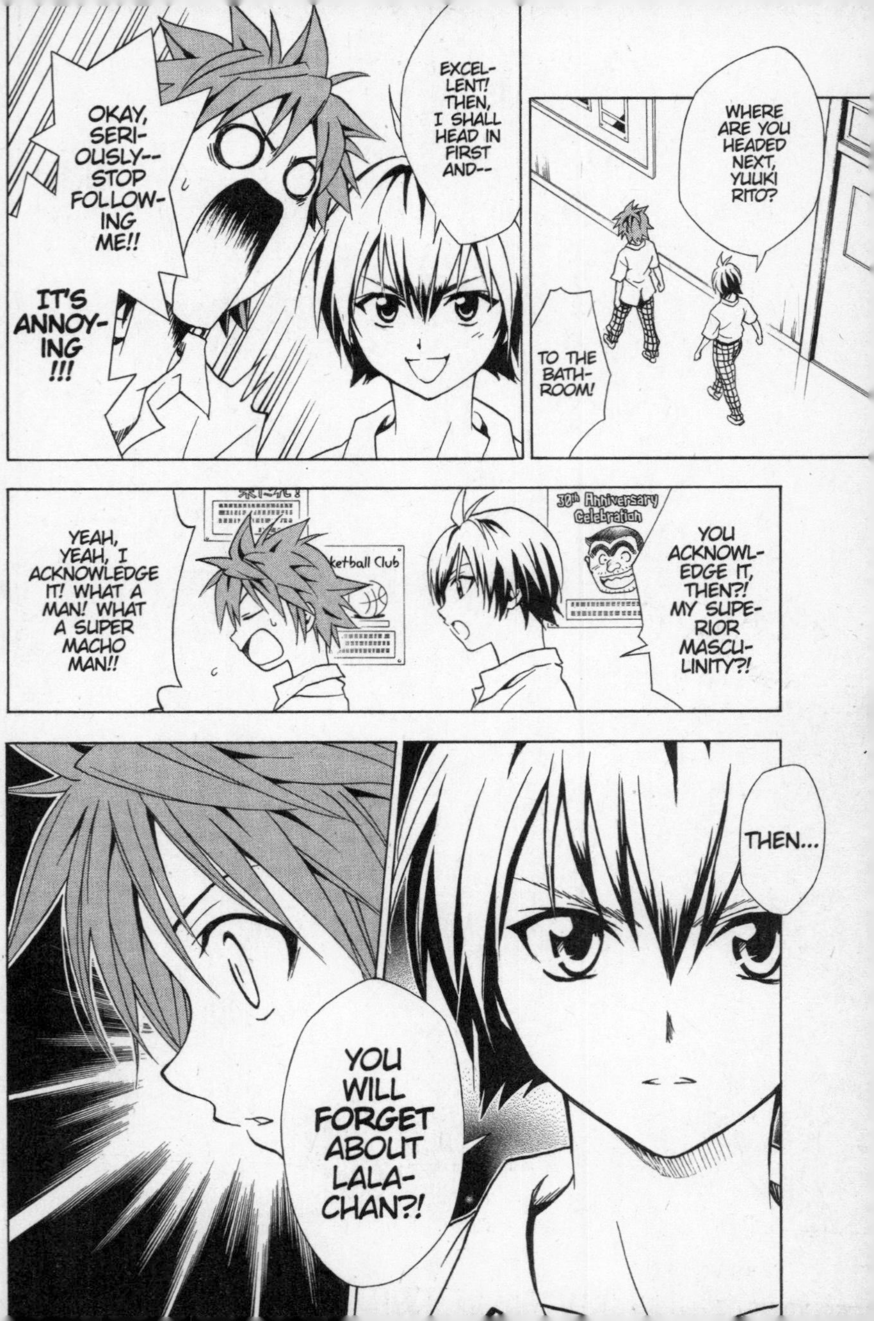
WHERE ARE YOU HEADED NEXT, YUUKI RITO?
TO THE BATH-ROOM!
EXCEL-LENT! THEN, I SHALL HEAD IN FIRST AND--
OKAY, SERI-OUSLY--STOP FOLLOW-ING ME!!
IT'S ANNOY-ING!!!
30th Anniversary Celebration
YOU ACKNOWL-EDGE IT, THEN?! MY SUPE-RIOR MASCU-LINITY?!
ketball Club
YEAH, YEAH, I ACKNOWLEDGE IT! WHAT A MAN! WHAT A SUPER MACHO MAN!!
THEN...
YOU WILL FORGET ABOUT LALA-CHAN?!

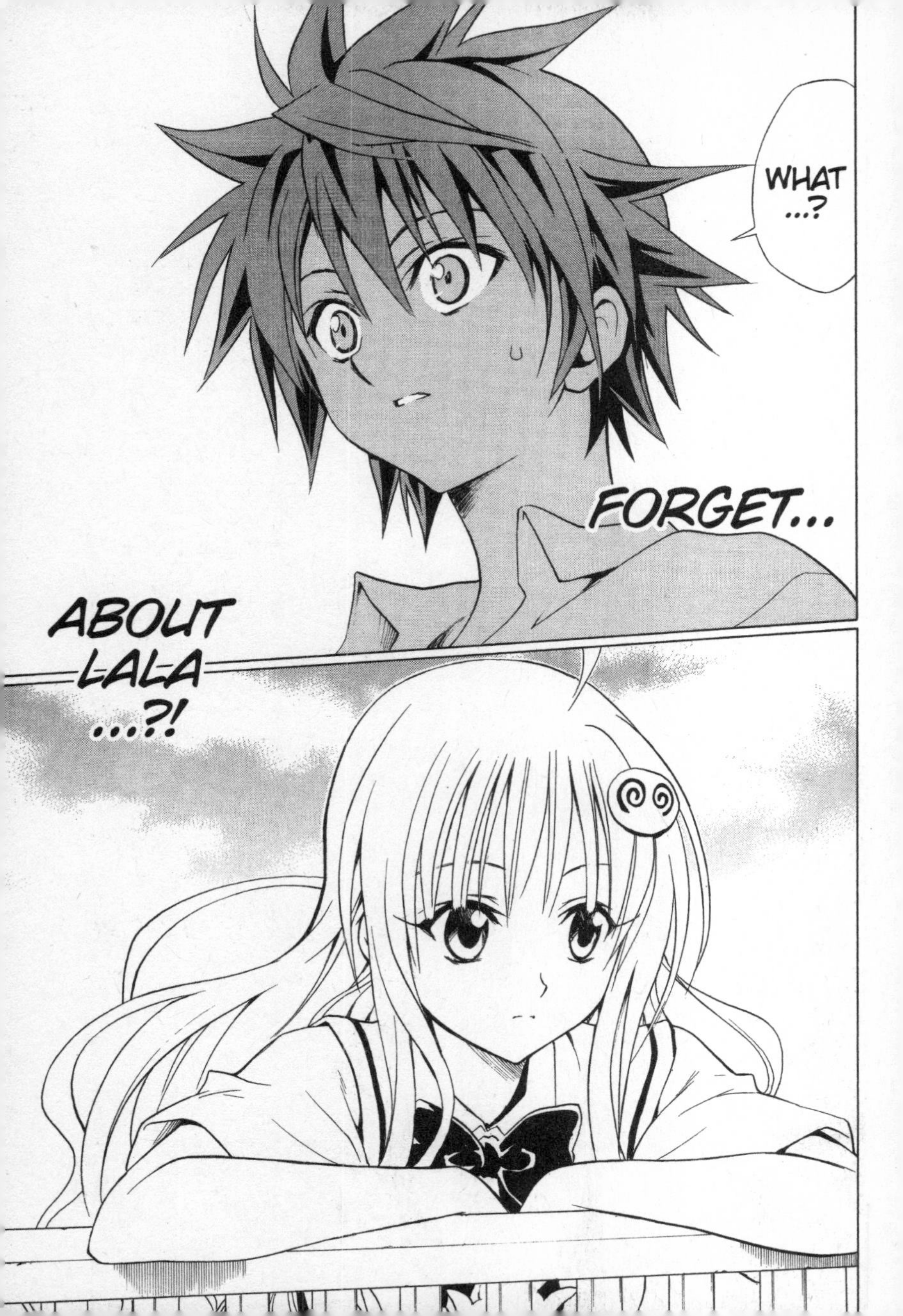
WHAT ...?
FORGET...
ABOUT LALA ...?!

To LOVE Ru

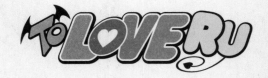

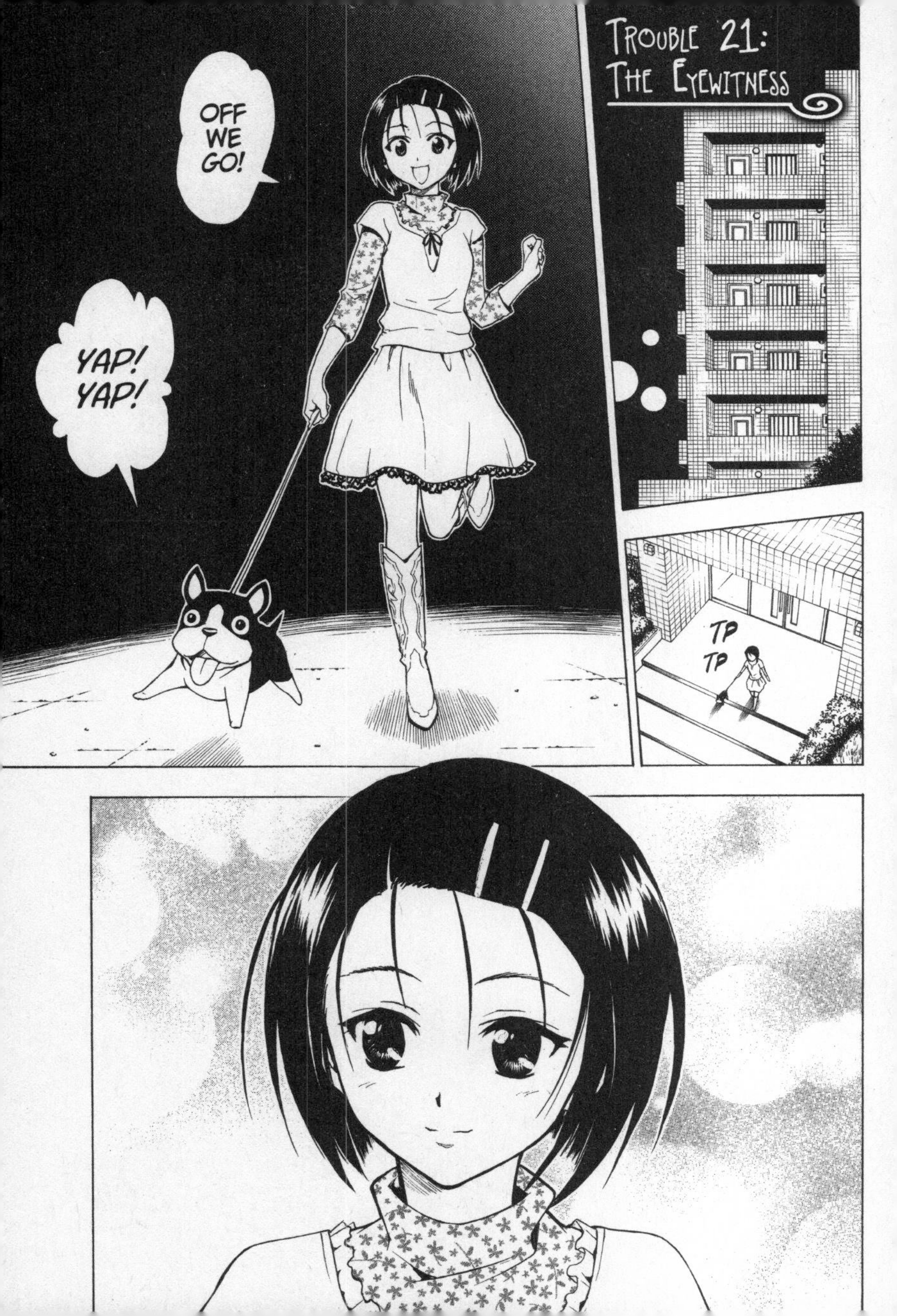
TROUBLE 21:
THE EYEWITNESS
TP
TP
OFF WE GO!
YAP! YAP!

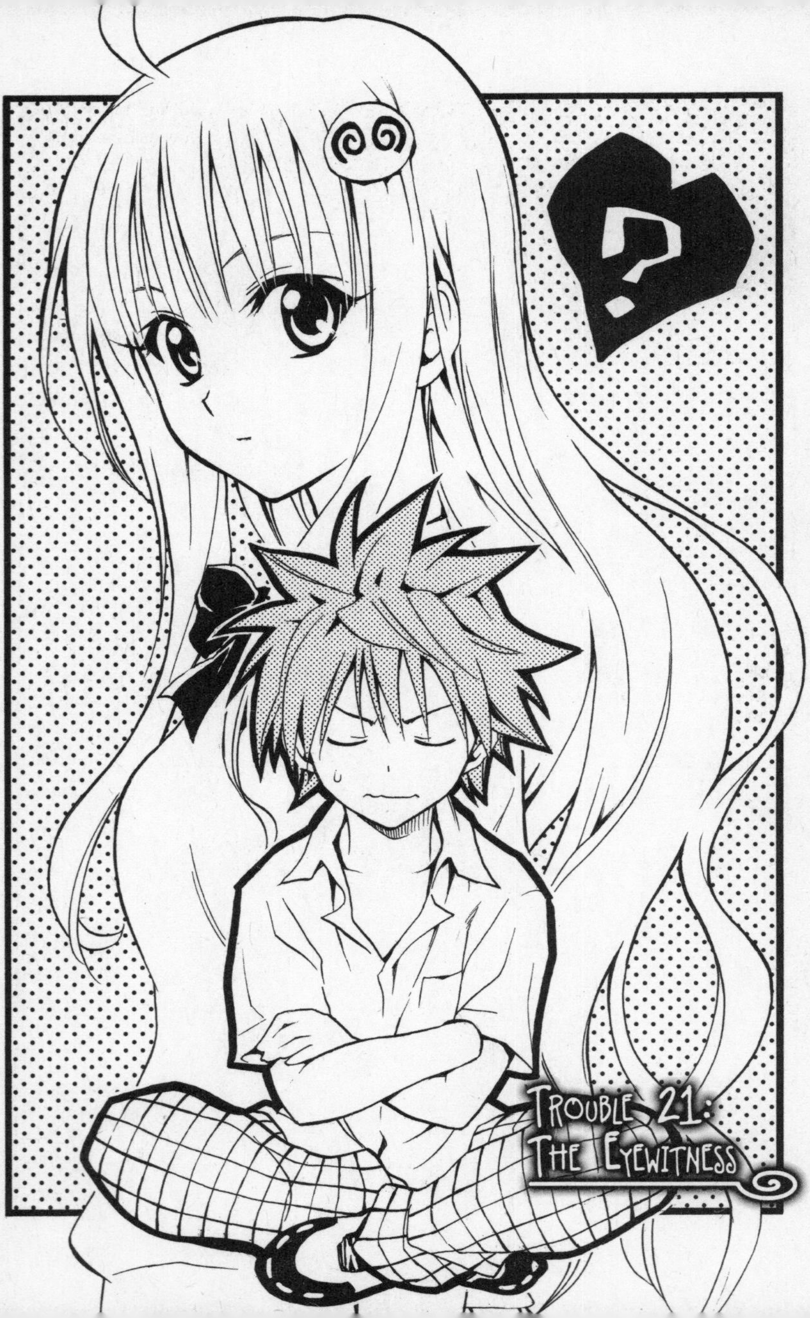
?
Trouble 21:
The Eyewitness

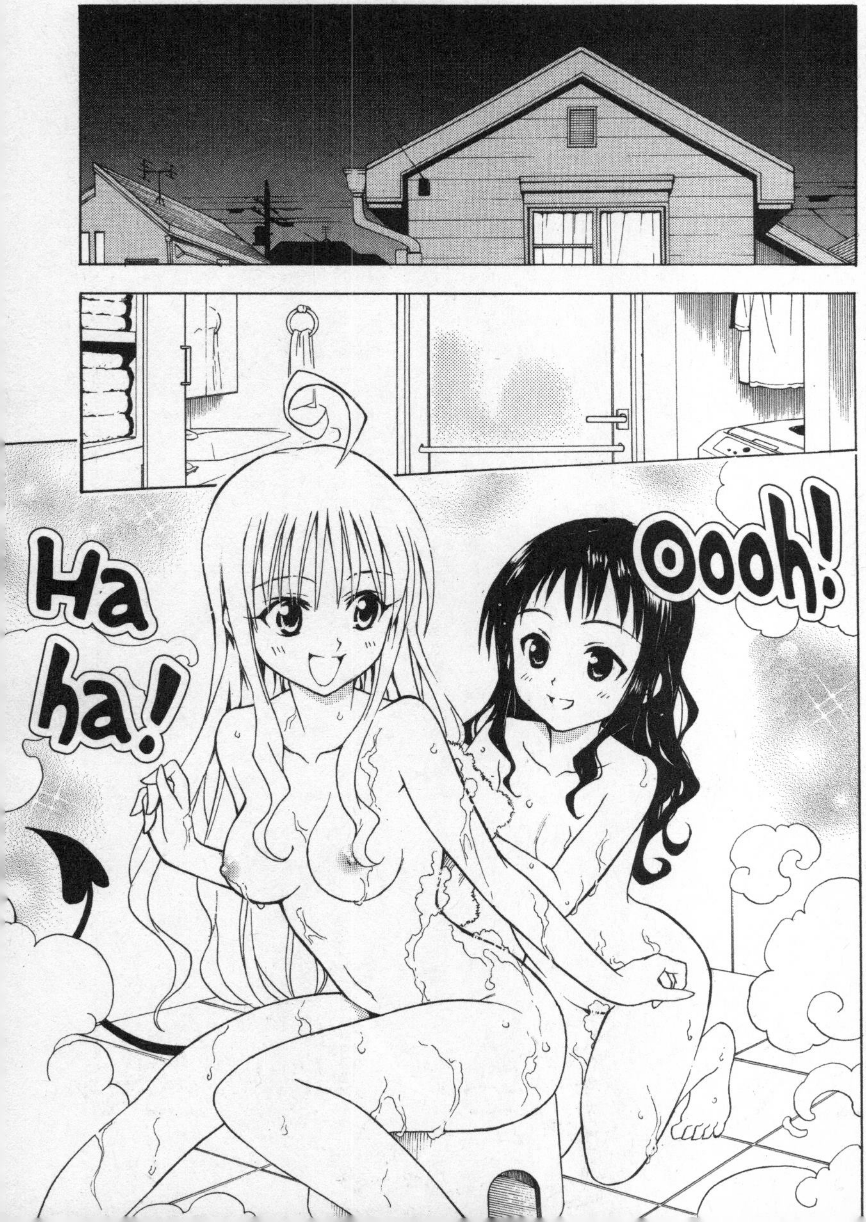
Oooh!
Ha ha!

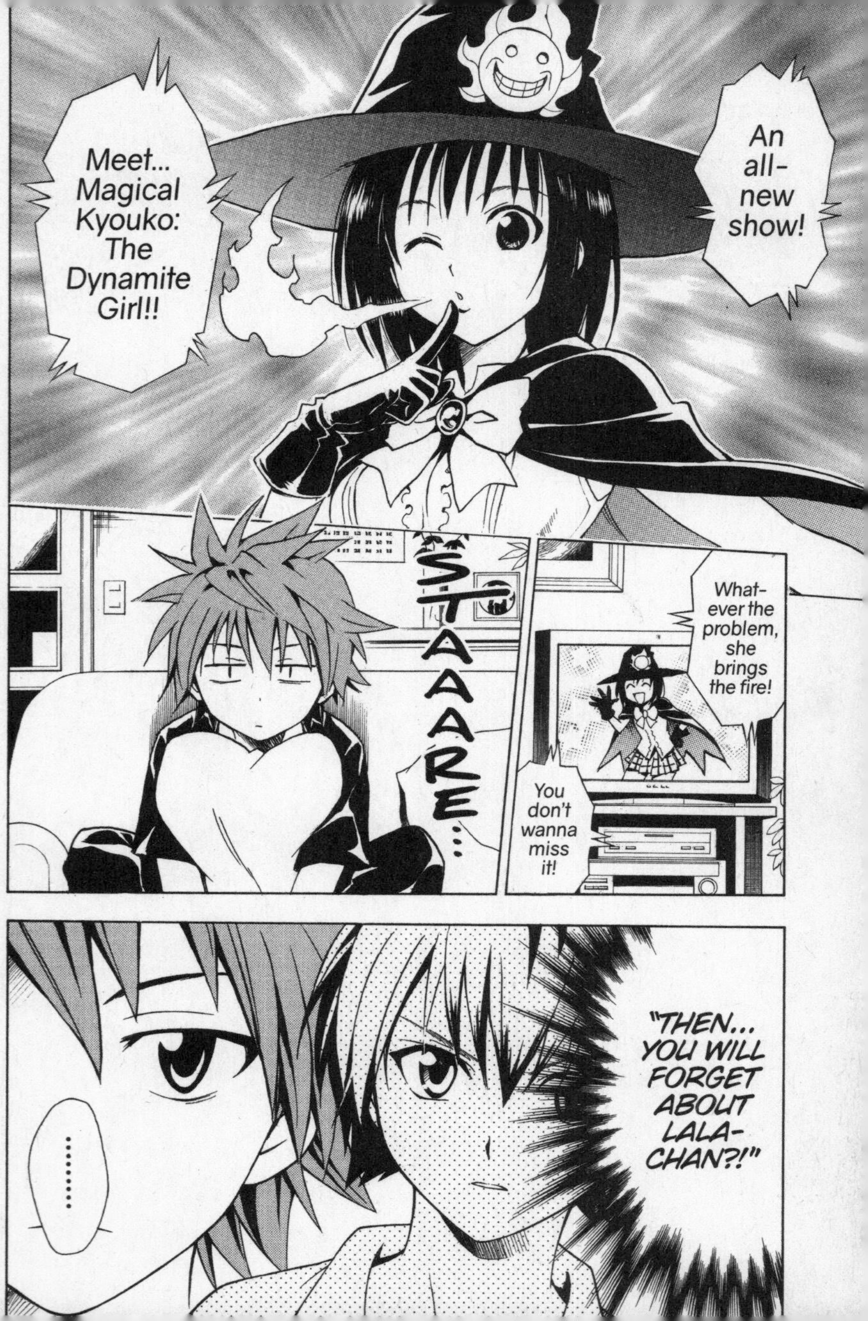
An all-new show!
Meet... Magical Kyouko: The Dynamite Girl!!
Whatever the problem, she brings the fire!
You don't wanna miss it!
STAARE...
"THEN... YOU WILL FORGET ABOUT LALA-CHAN?!"
....

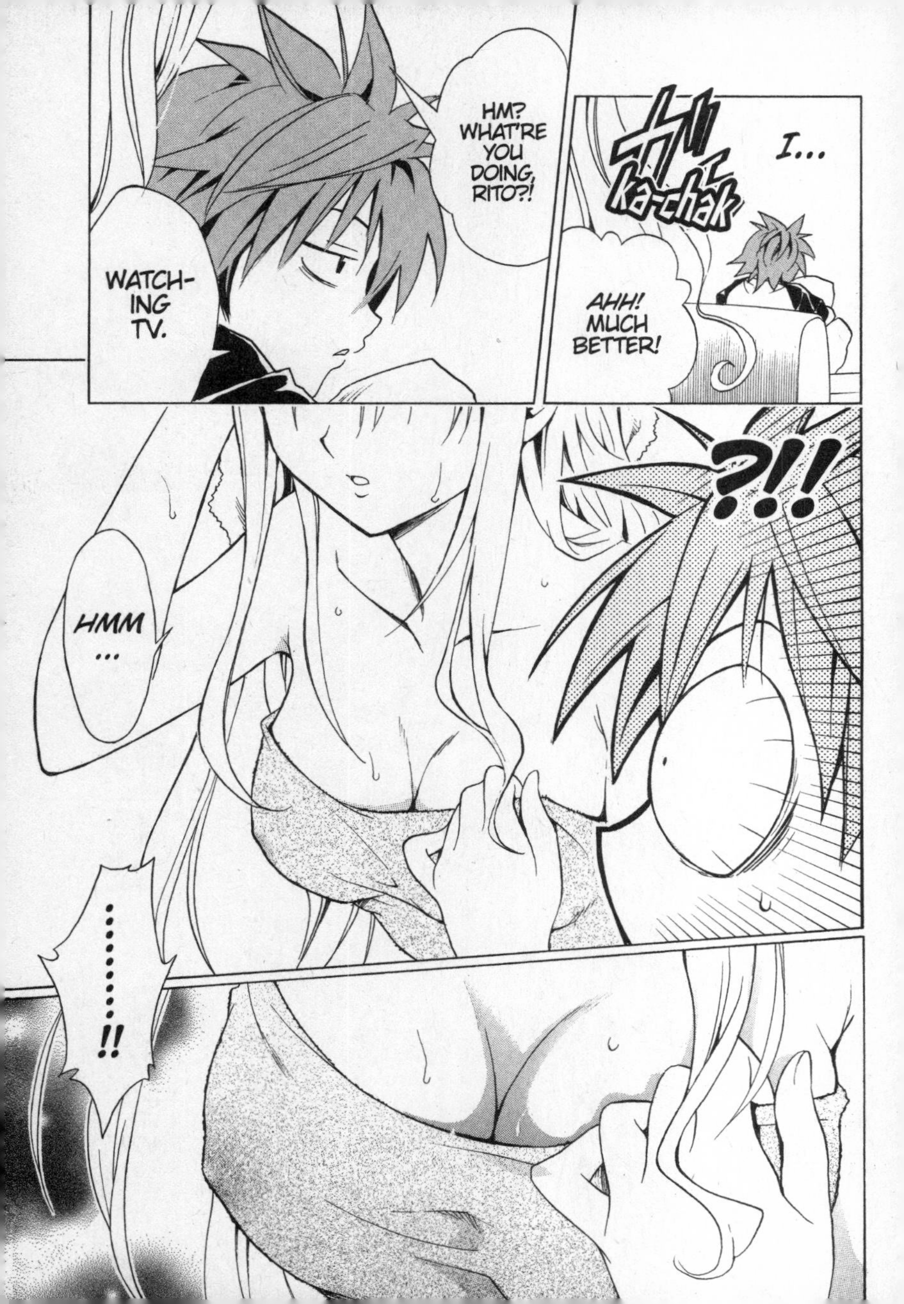
I...
Ka-chak
AHH! MUCH BETTER!
HM? WHAT'RE YOU DOING, RITO?!
WATCH-ING TV.
?!!
HMM...
......!!

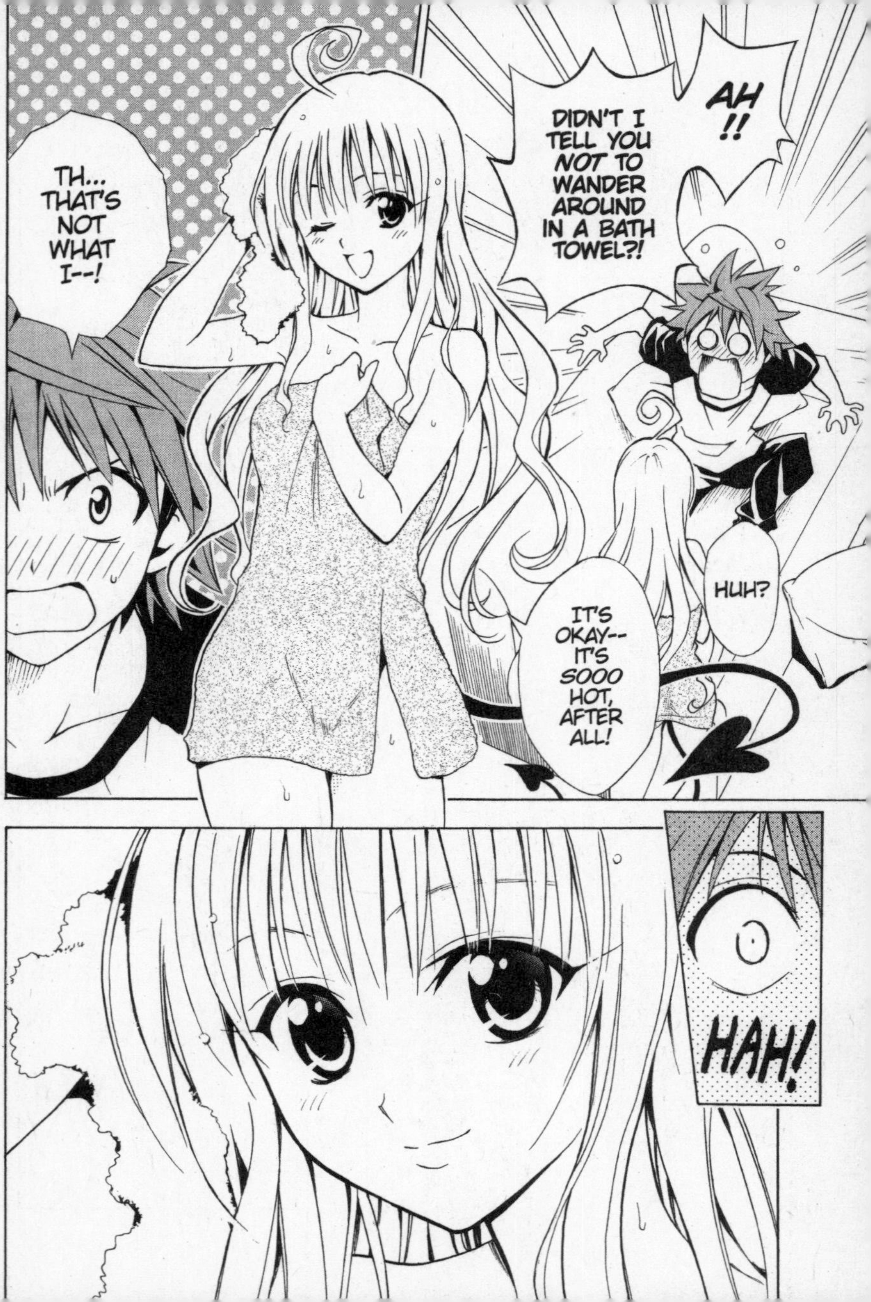
AH!!
DIDN'T I TELL YOU *NOT* TO WANDER AROUND IN A BATH TOWEL?!
HUH?
IT'S OKAY-- IT'S *SOOO* HOT, AFTER ALL!
TH... THAT'S NOT WHAT I--!
HAH!

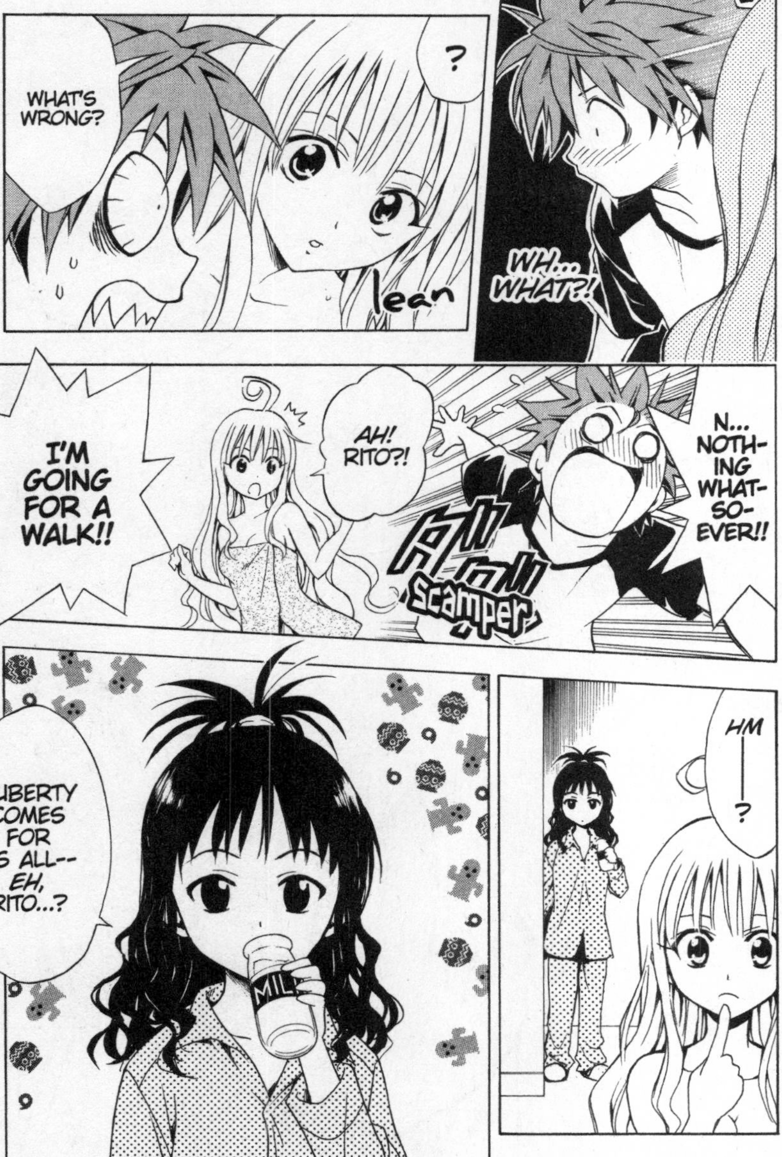
WH... WHAT?!
?
WHAT'S WRONG?
lean
N... NOTHING WHATSOEVER!!
scamper
AH! RITO?!
I'M GOING FOR A WALK!!
HM—?
PUBERTY COMES FOR US ALL-- EH, RITO...?

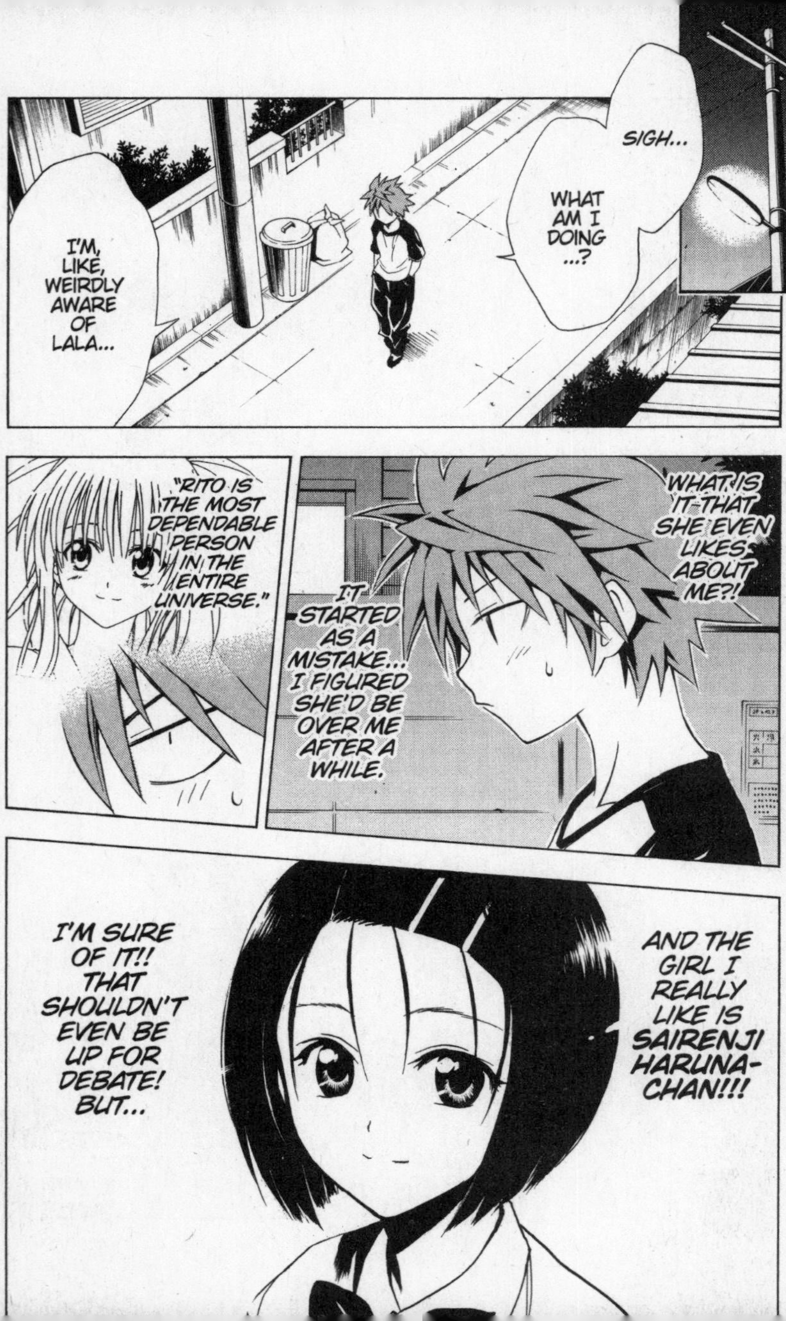
SIGH...
WHAT AM I DOING ...?
I'M, LIKE, WEIRDLY AWARE OF LALA...
WHAT IS IT THAT SHE EVEN LIKES ABOUT ME?!
IT STARTED AS A MISTAKE... I FIGURED SHE'D BE OVER ME AFTER A WHILE.
"RITO IS THE MOST DEPENDABLE PERSON IN THE ENTIRE UNIVERSE."
AND THE GIRL I REALLY LIKE IS SAIRENJI HARUNA-CHAN!!!
I'M SURE OF IT!! THAT SHOULDN'T EVEN BE UP FOR DEBATE! BUT...

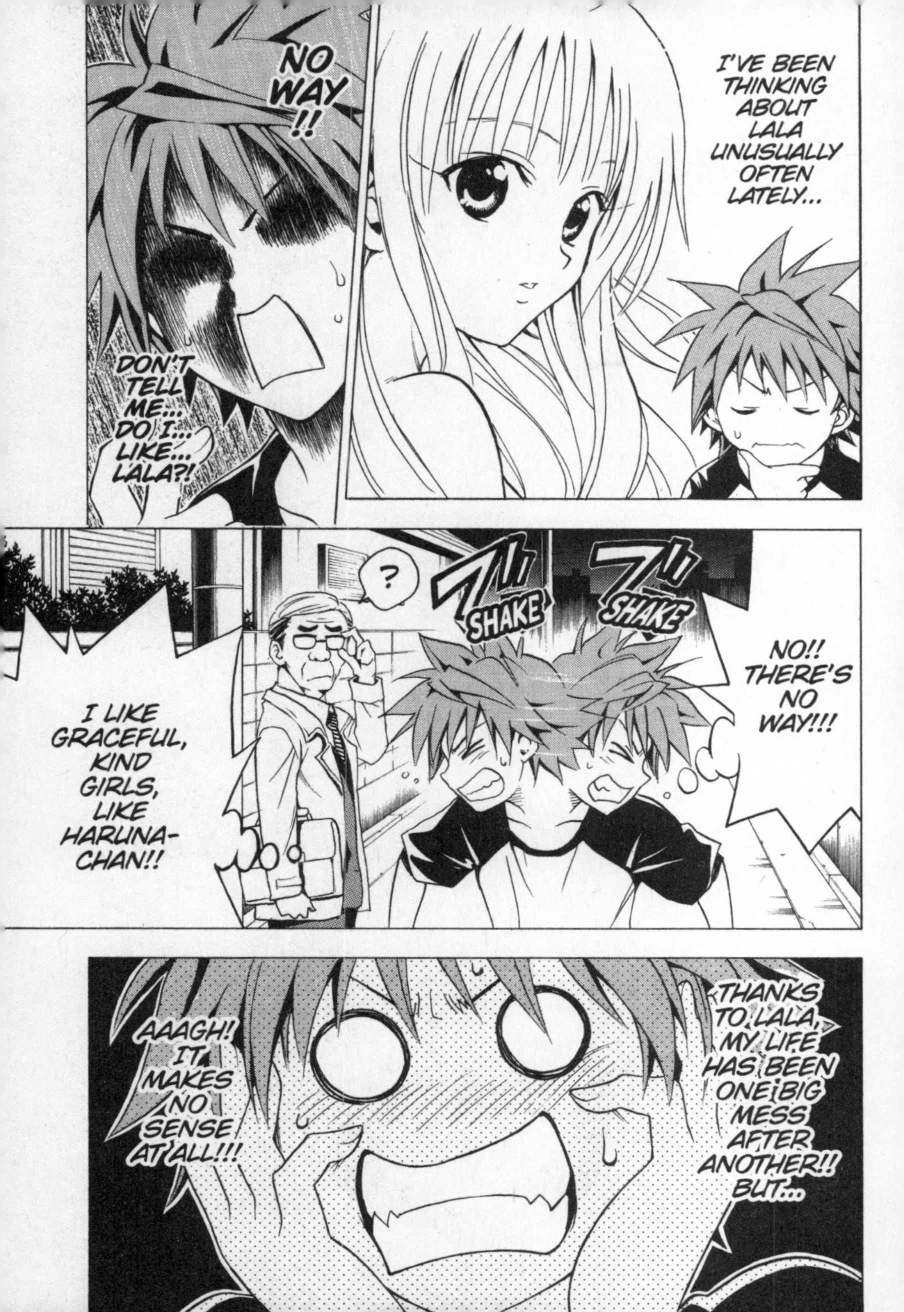
I'VE BEEN THINKING ABOUT LALA UNUSUALLY OFTEN LATELY...
NO WAY!!
DON'T TELL ME... DO I... LIKE... LALA?!
NO!! THERE'S NO WAY!!!
SHAKE
SHAKE
?
I LIKE GRACEFUL, KIND GIRLS, LIKE HARUNA-CHAN!!
THANKS TO LALA, MY LIFE HAS BEEN ONE BIG MESS AFTER ANOTHER!! BUT...
AAAGH! IT MAKES NO SENSE AT ALL!!!

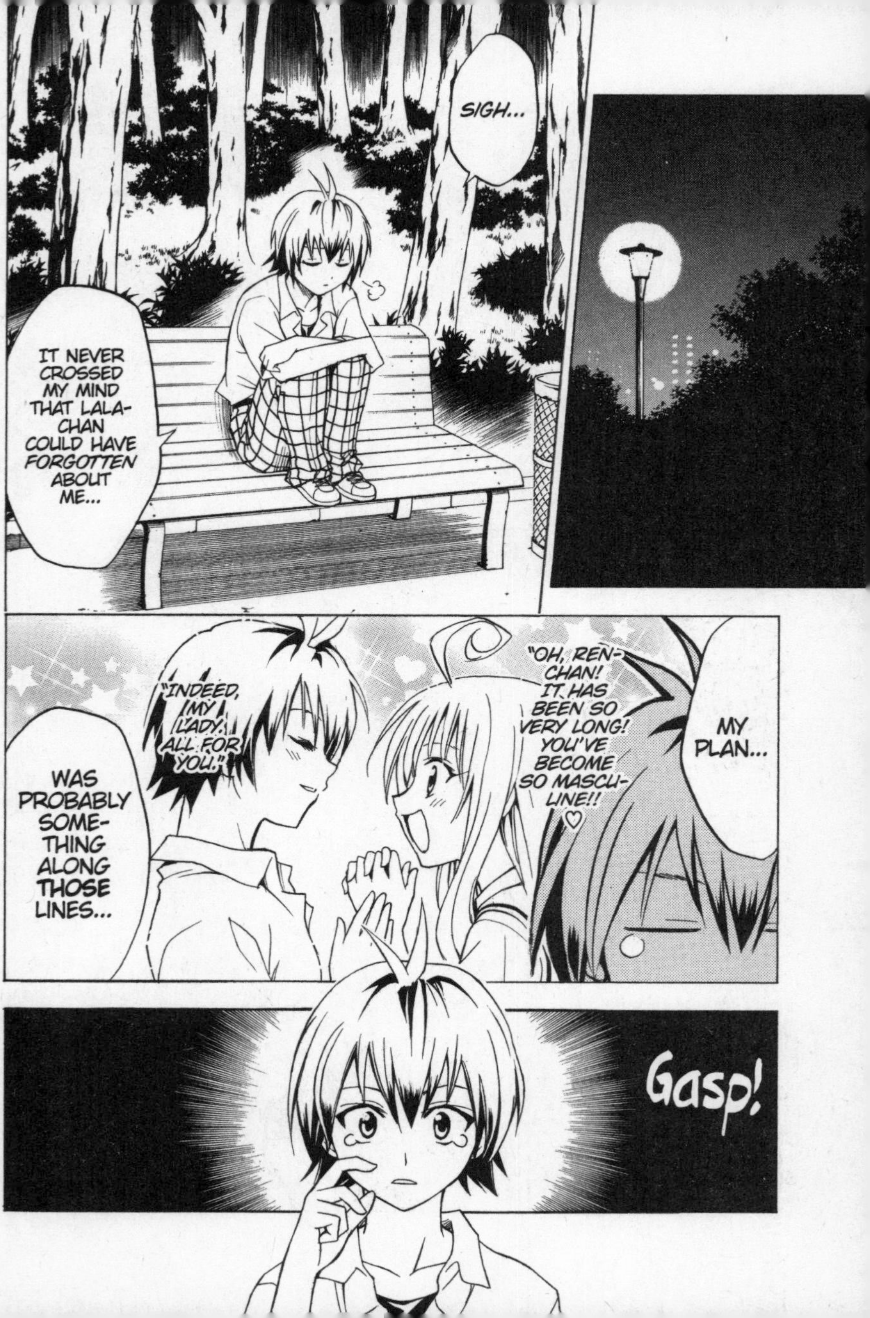
SIGH...
IT NEVER CROSSED MY MIND THAT LALA-CHAN COULD HAVE FORGOTTEN ABOUT ME...
MY PLAN...
"OH, REN-CHAN! IT HAS BEEN SO VERY LONG! YOU'VE BECOME SO MASCU-LINE!! ♡
"INDEED, MY LADY. ALL FOR YOU."
WAS PROBABLY SOME-THING ALONG THOSE LINES...
Gasp!

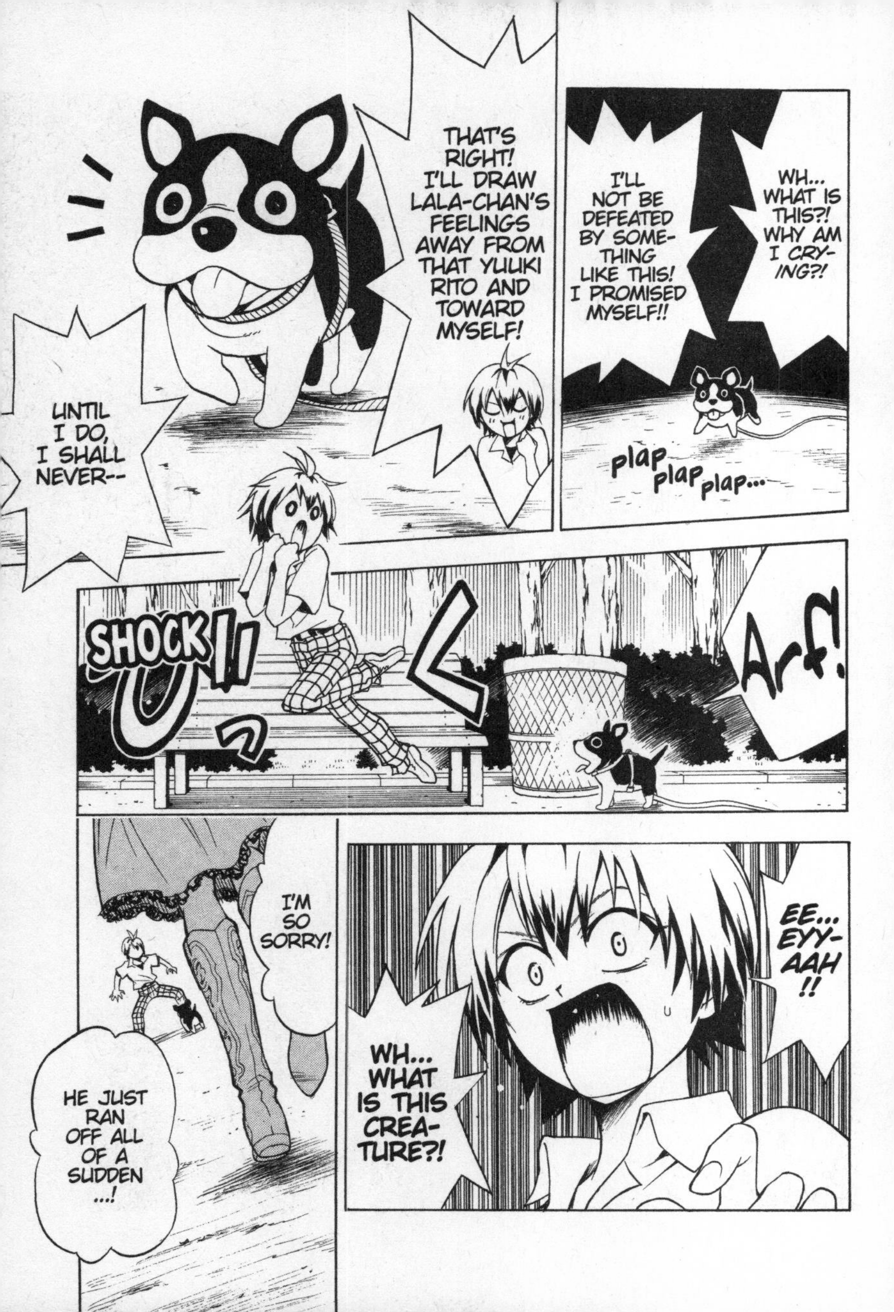
WH... WHAT IS THIS?! WHY AM I CRY-ING?!
I'LL NOT BE DEFEATED BY SOME-THING LIKE THIS! I PROMISED MYSELF!!
plap plap plap...
THAT'S RIGHT! I'LL DRAW LALA-CHAN'S FEELINGS AWAY FROM THAT YUUKI RITO AND TOWARD MYSELF!
UNTIL I DO, I SHALL NEVER--
Arf!
SHOCK
EE... EYY-AAH!!
WH... WHAT IS THIS CREA-TURE?!
I'M SO SORRY!
HE JUST RAN OFF ALL OF A SUDDEN ...!

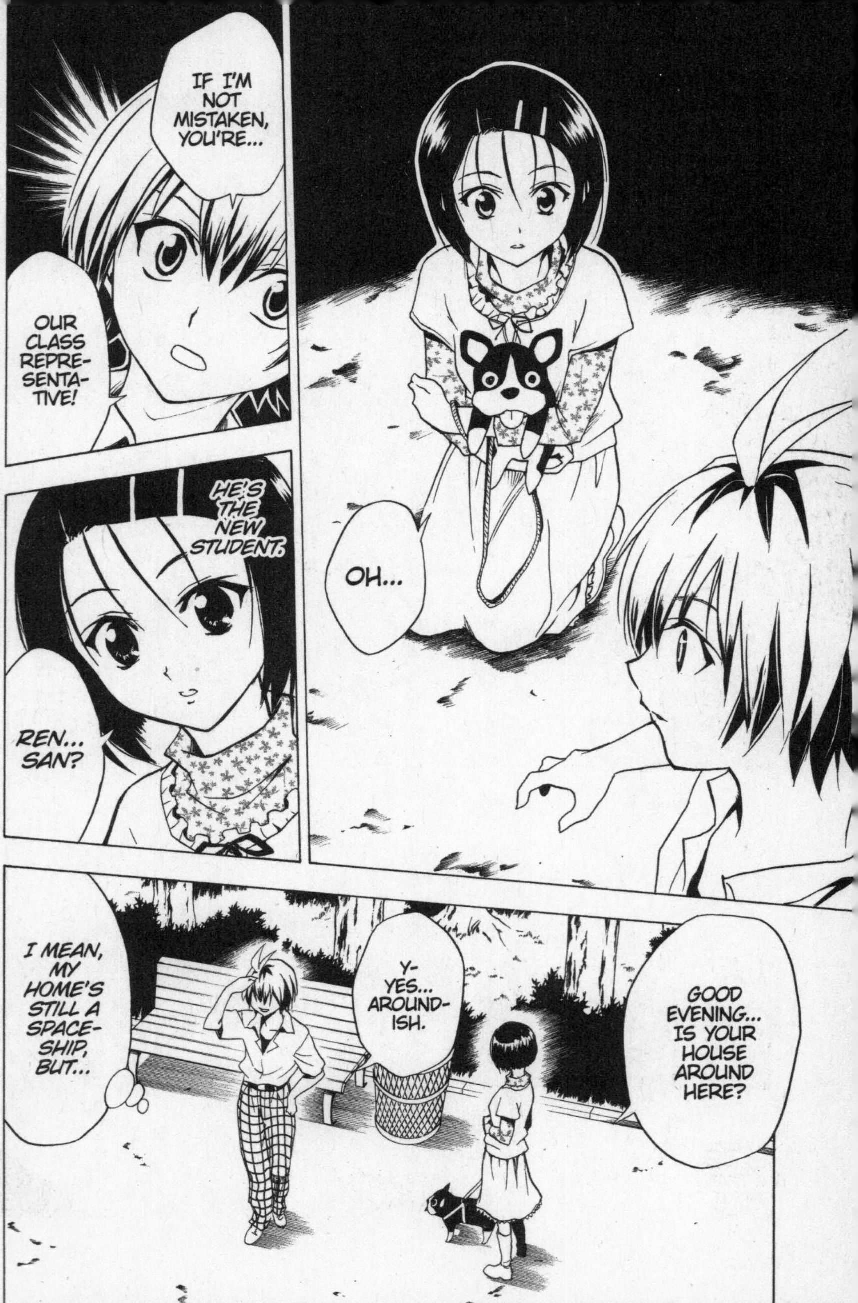
OH...
IF I'M NOT MISTAKEN, YOU'RE...
OUR CLASS REPRE-SENTA-TIVE!
HE'S THE NEW STUDENT.
REN... SAN?
GOOD EVENING... IS YOUR HOUSE AROUND HERE?
Y-YES... AROUND-ISH.
I MEAN, MY HOME'S STILL A SPACE-SHIP, BUT...

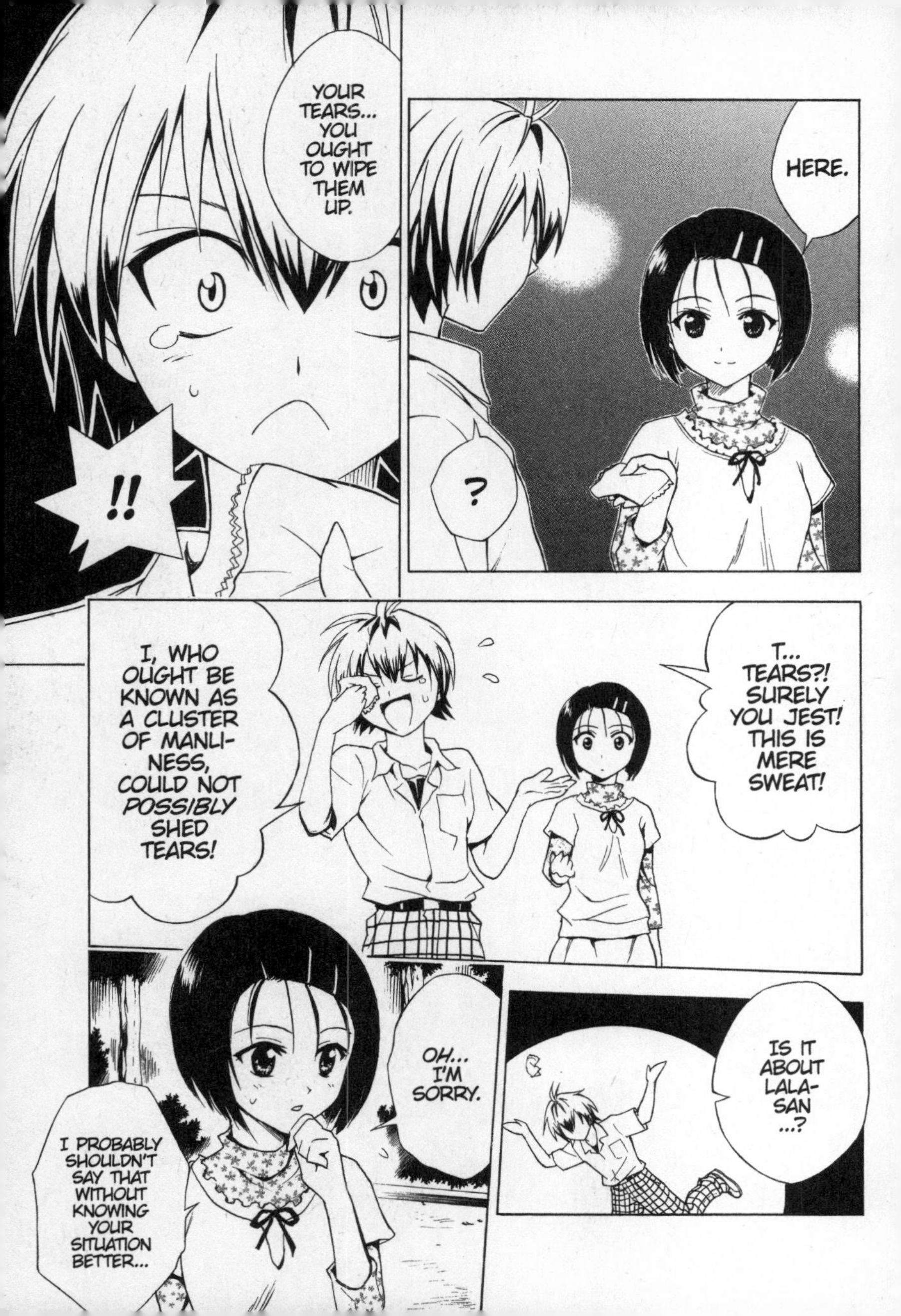
HERE.
?
YOUR TEARS... YOU OUGHT TO WIPE THEM UP.
!!
T... TEARS?! SURELY YOU JEST! THIS IS MERE SWEAT!
I, WHO OUGHT BE KNOWN AS A CLUSTER OF MANLI-NESS, COULD NOT *POSSIBLY* SHED TEARS!
IS IT ABOUT LALA-SAN ...?
OH... I'M SORRY.
I PROBABLY SHOULDN'T SAY THAT WITHOUT KNOWING YOUR SITUATION BETTER...

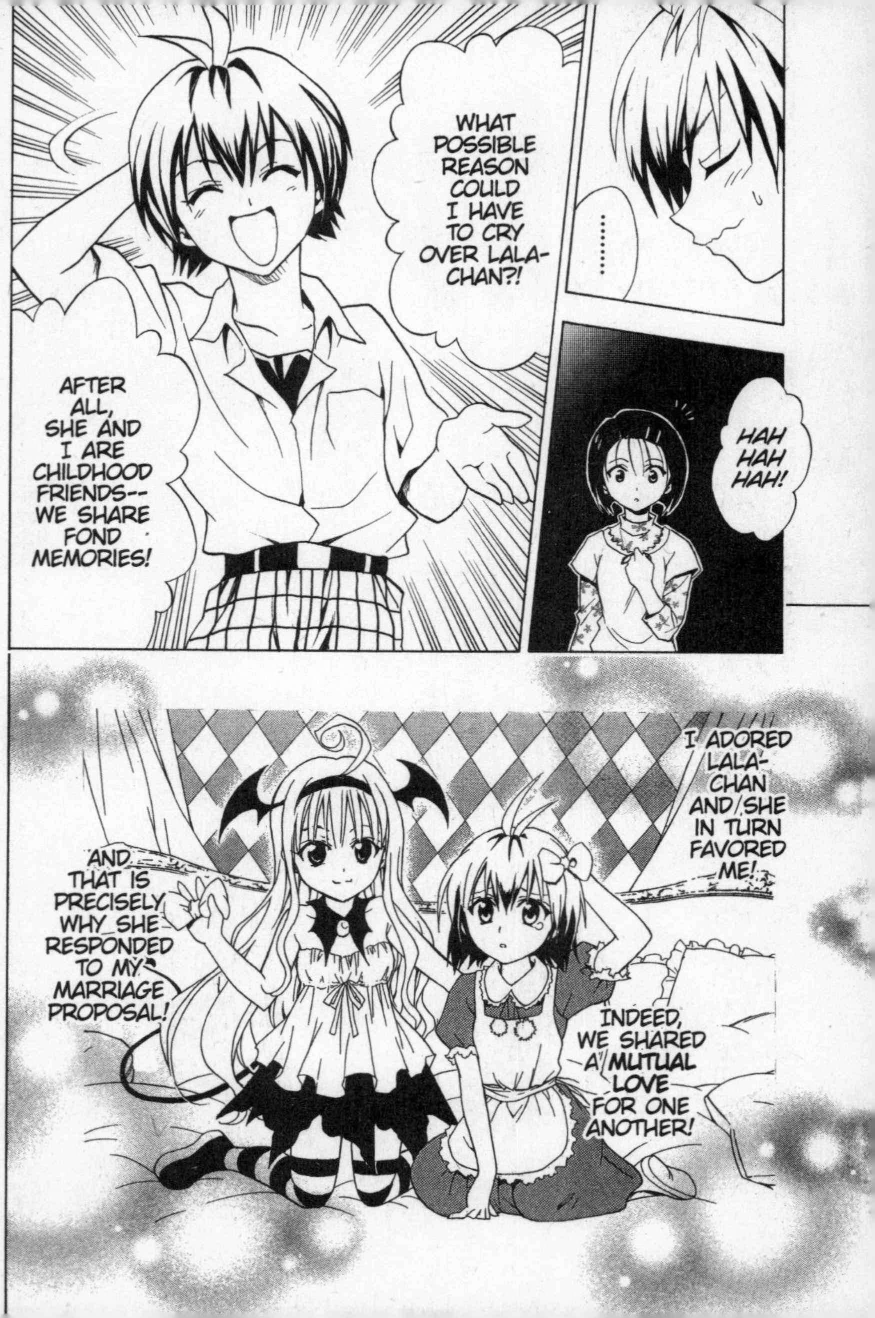
......
HAH HAH HAH!
WHAT POSSIBLE REASON COULD I HAVE TO CRY OVER LALA-CHAN?!
AFTER ALL, SHE AND I ARE CHILDHOOD FRIENDS-- WE SHARE FOND MEMORIES!
I ADORED LALA-CHAN AND SHE IN TURN FAVORED ME!
INDEED, WE SHARED A MUTUAL LOVE FOR ONE ANOTHER!
AND THAT IS PRECISELY WHY SHE RESPONDED TO MY MARRIAGE PROPOSAL!

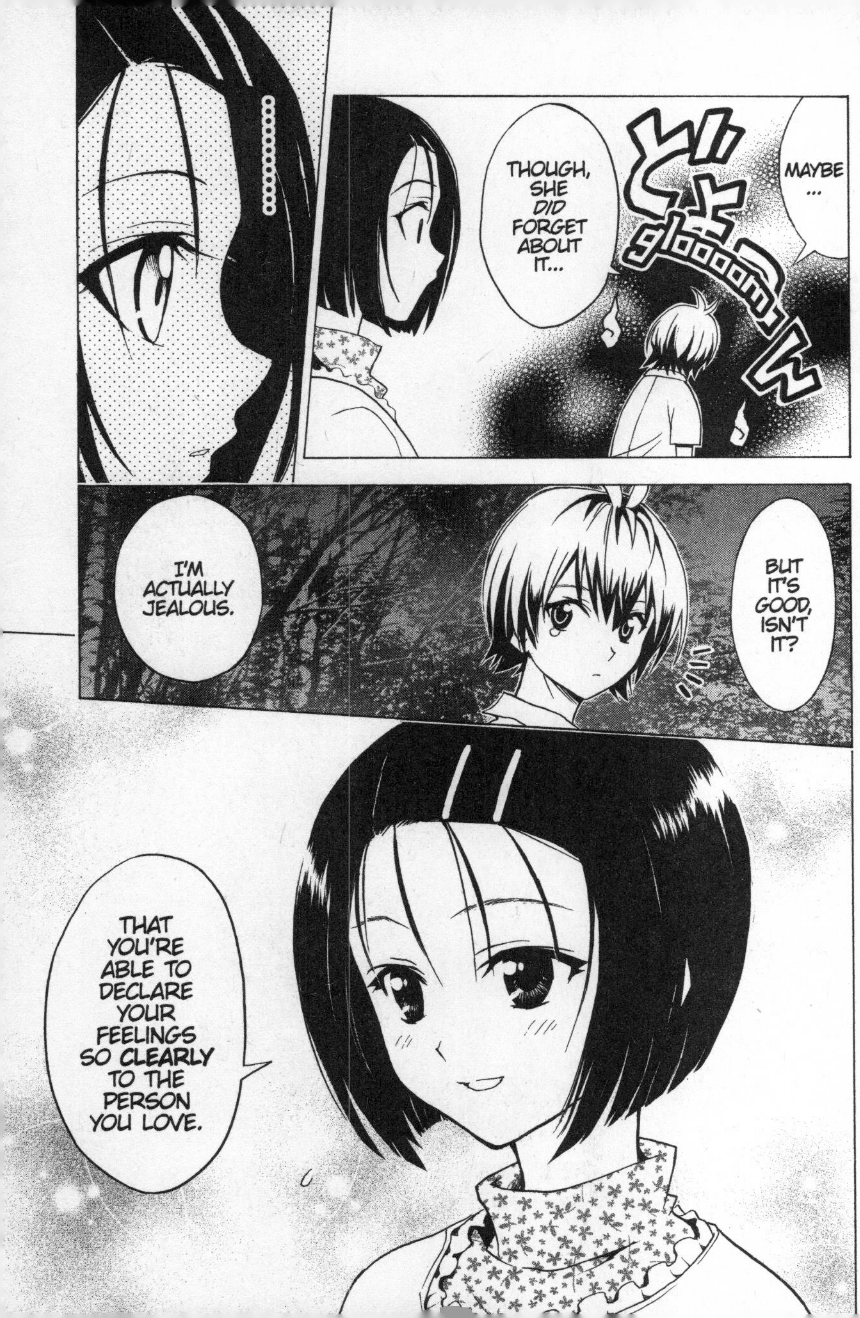
MAYBE ...
どよ
glooom
THOUGH, SHE *DID* FORGET ABOUT IT...
BUT IT'S GOOD, ISN'T IT?
I'M ACTUALLY JEALOUS.
THAT YOU'RE ABLE TO DECLARE YOUR FEELINGS SO CLEARLY TO THE PERSON YOU LOVE.

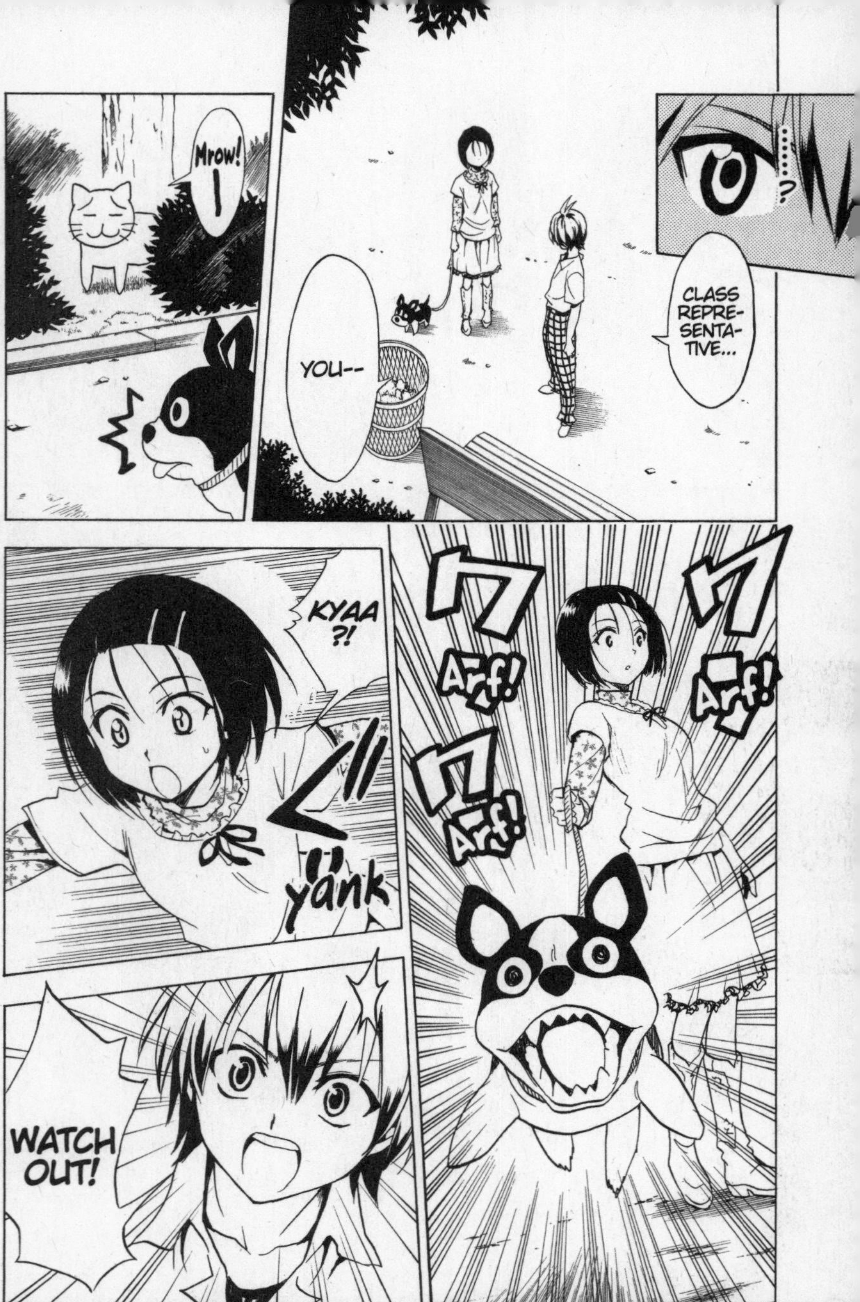
......?
CLASS REPRESENTATIVE...
YOU--
Mrow!
Arf!
Arf!
Arf!
KYAA?!
yank
WATCH OUT!

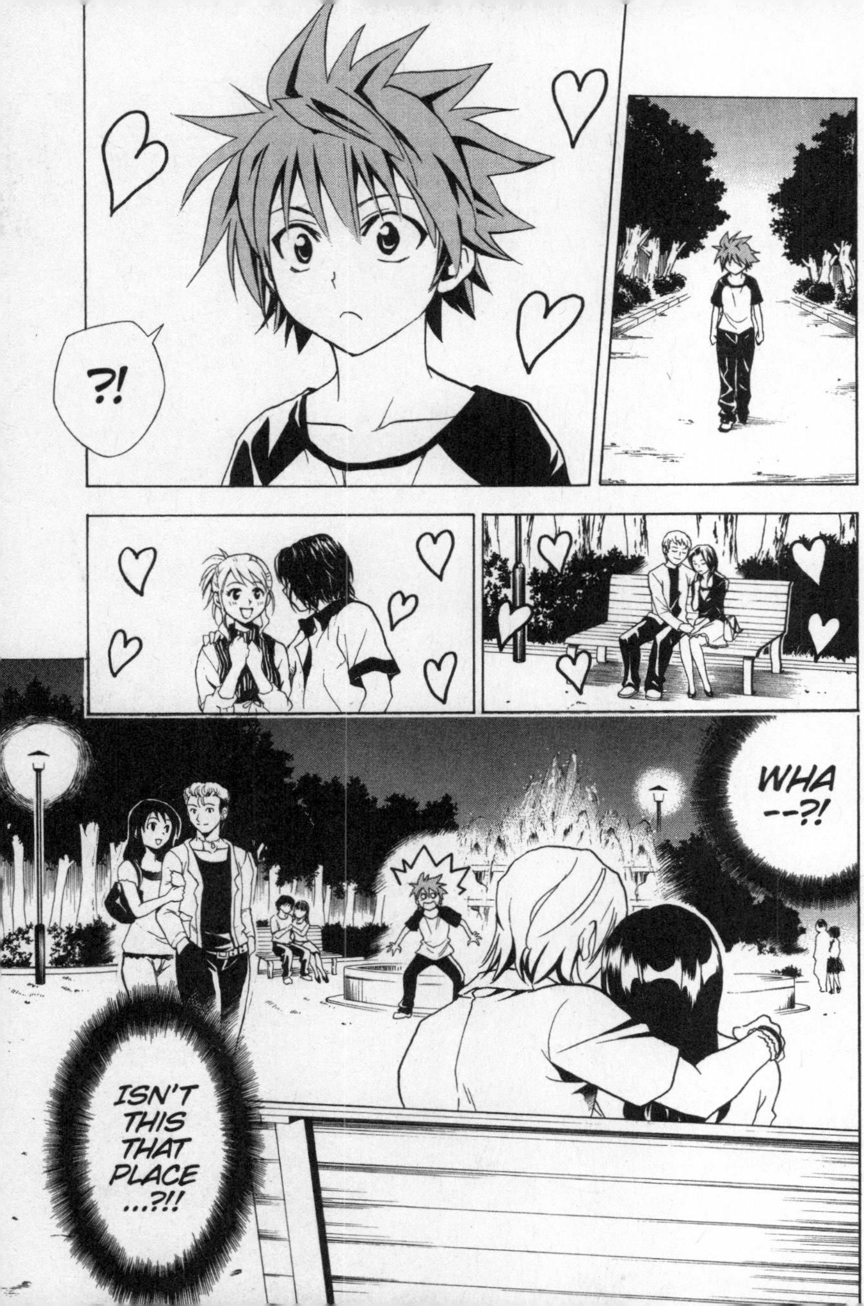
?!
WHA --?!
ISN'T THIS THAT PLACE ...?!!

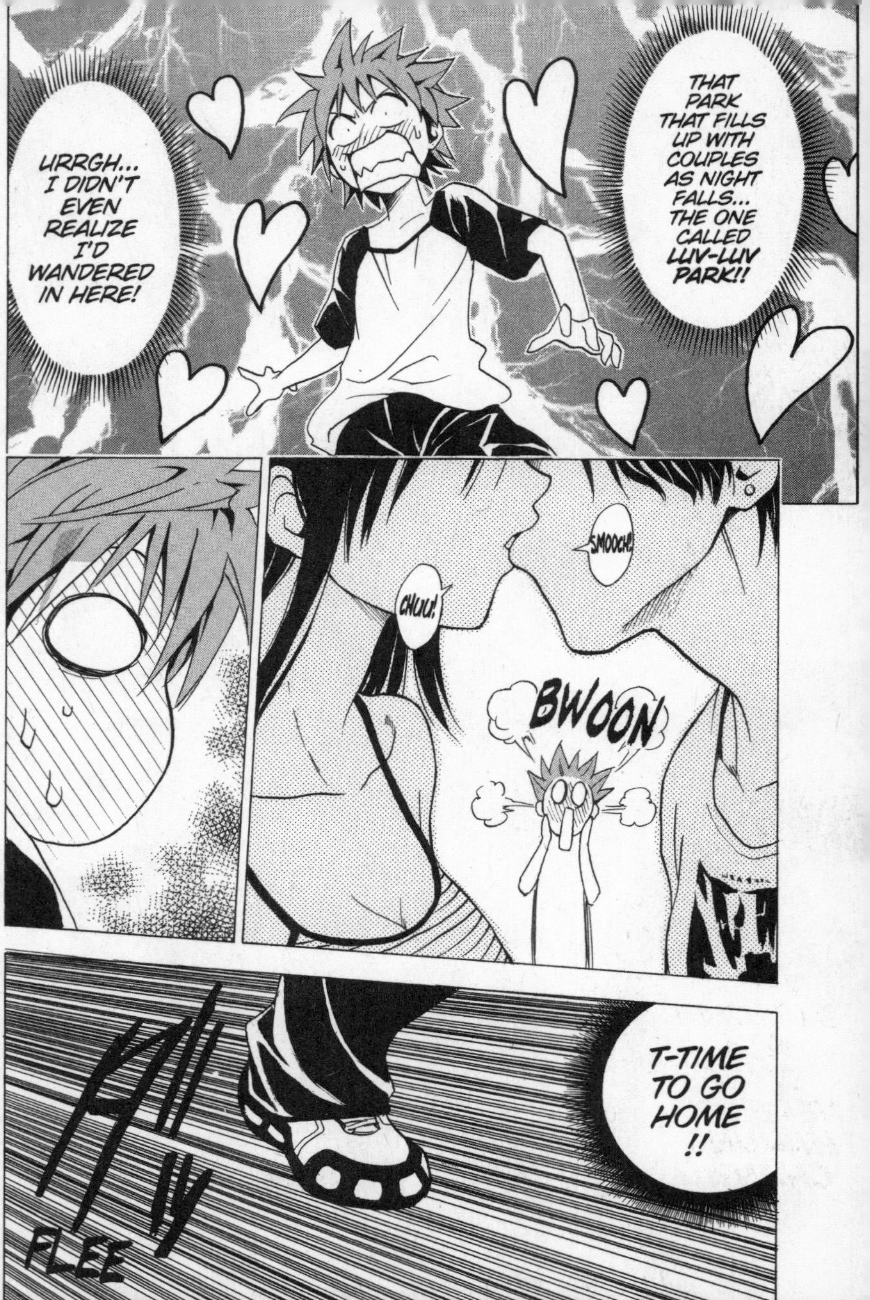
THAT PARK THAT FILLS UP WITH COUPLES AS NIGHT FALLS... THE ONE CALLED LUV-LUV PARK!!
URRGH... I DIDN'T EVEN REALIZE I'D WANDERED IN HERE!
SMOOCH!
CHUU!
BWOON
T-TIME TO GO HOME!!
FLEE

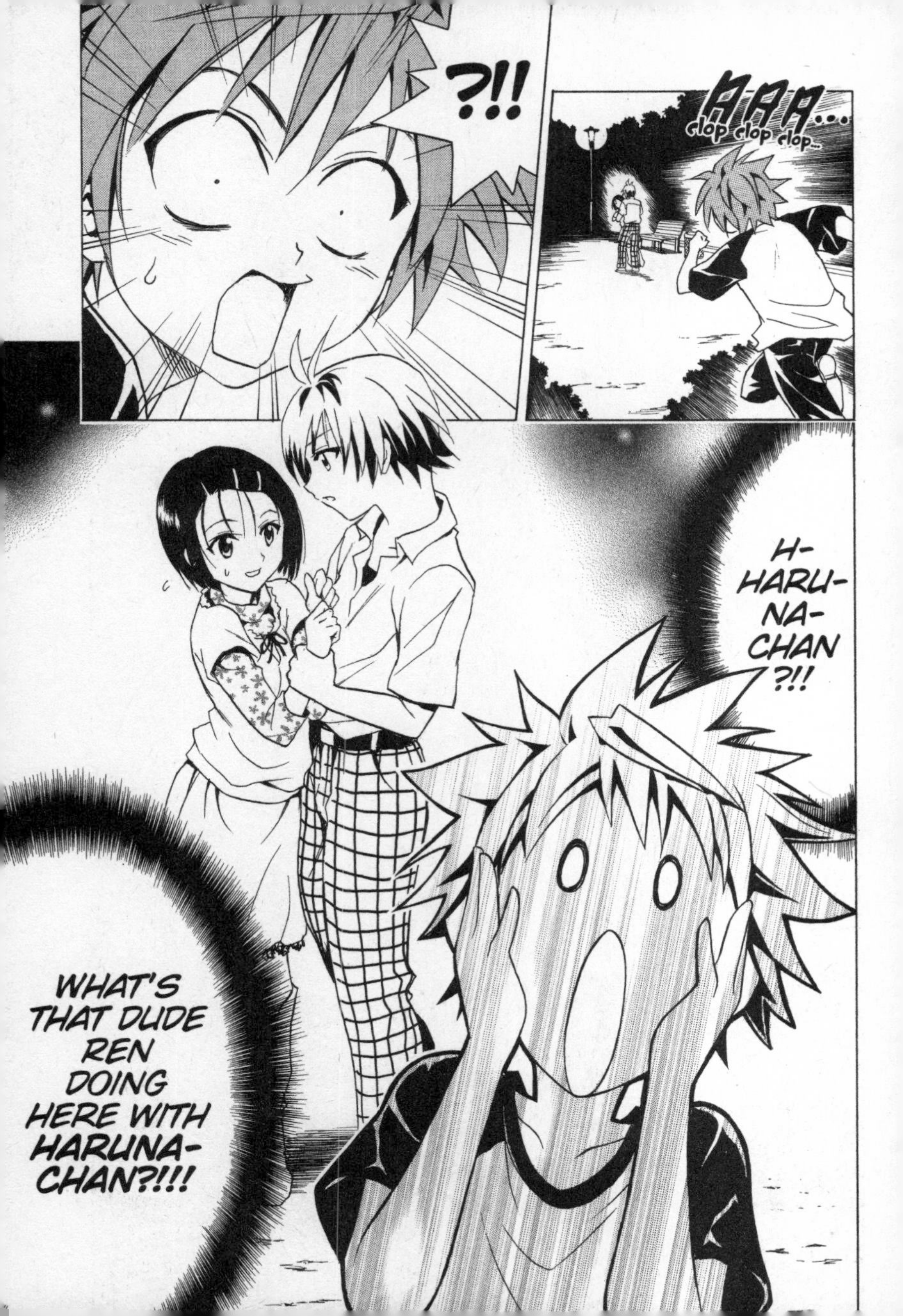
AAA...
clop clop clop...
?!!
H-HARU-NA-CHAN?!!
WHAT'S THAT DUDE REN DOING HERE WITH HARUNA-CHAN?!!!

To LOVE Ru

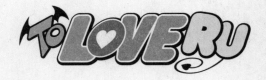

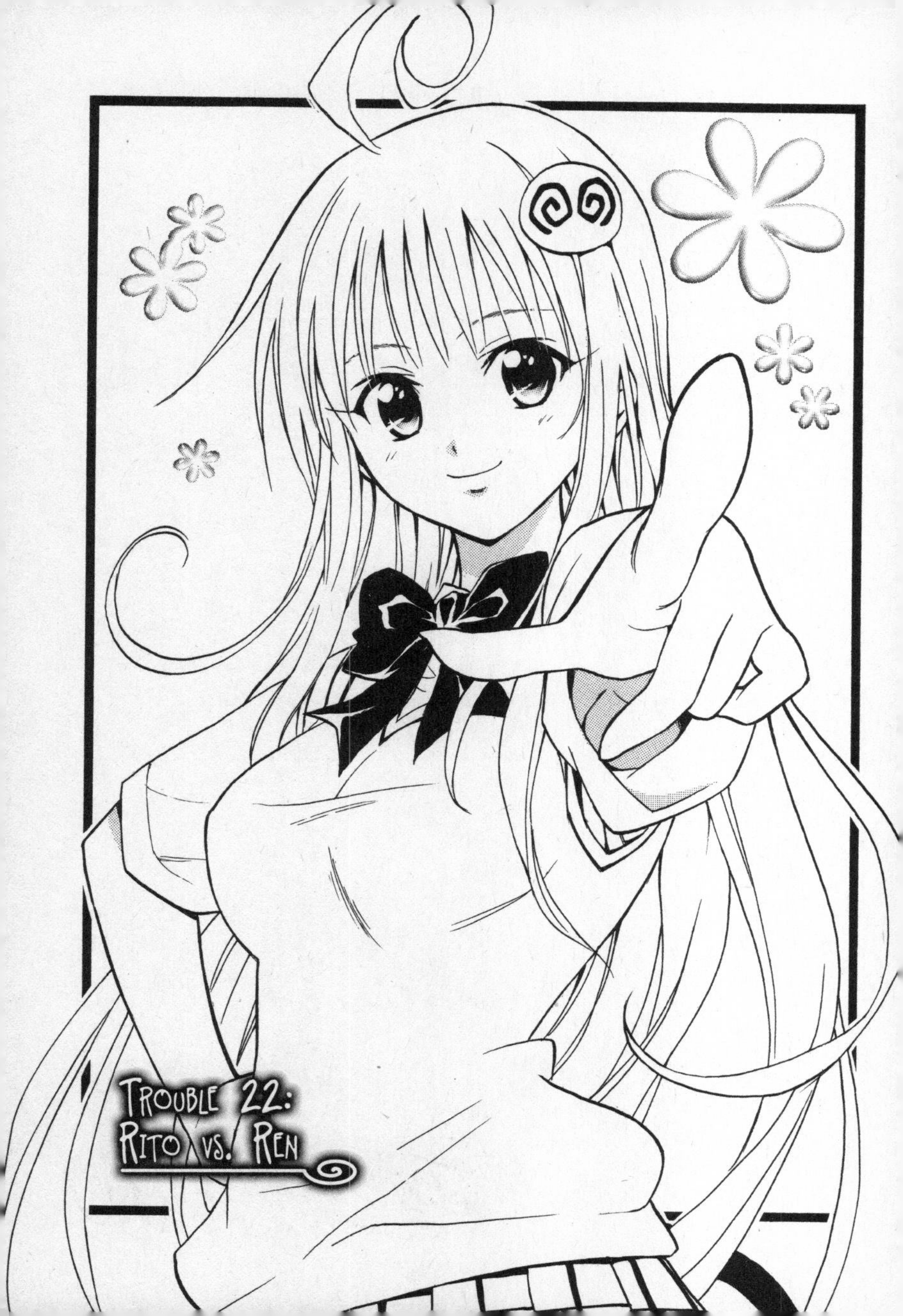
TROUBLE 22:
RITO VS. REN

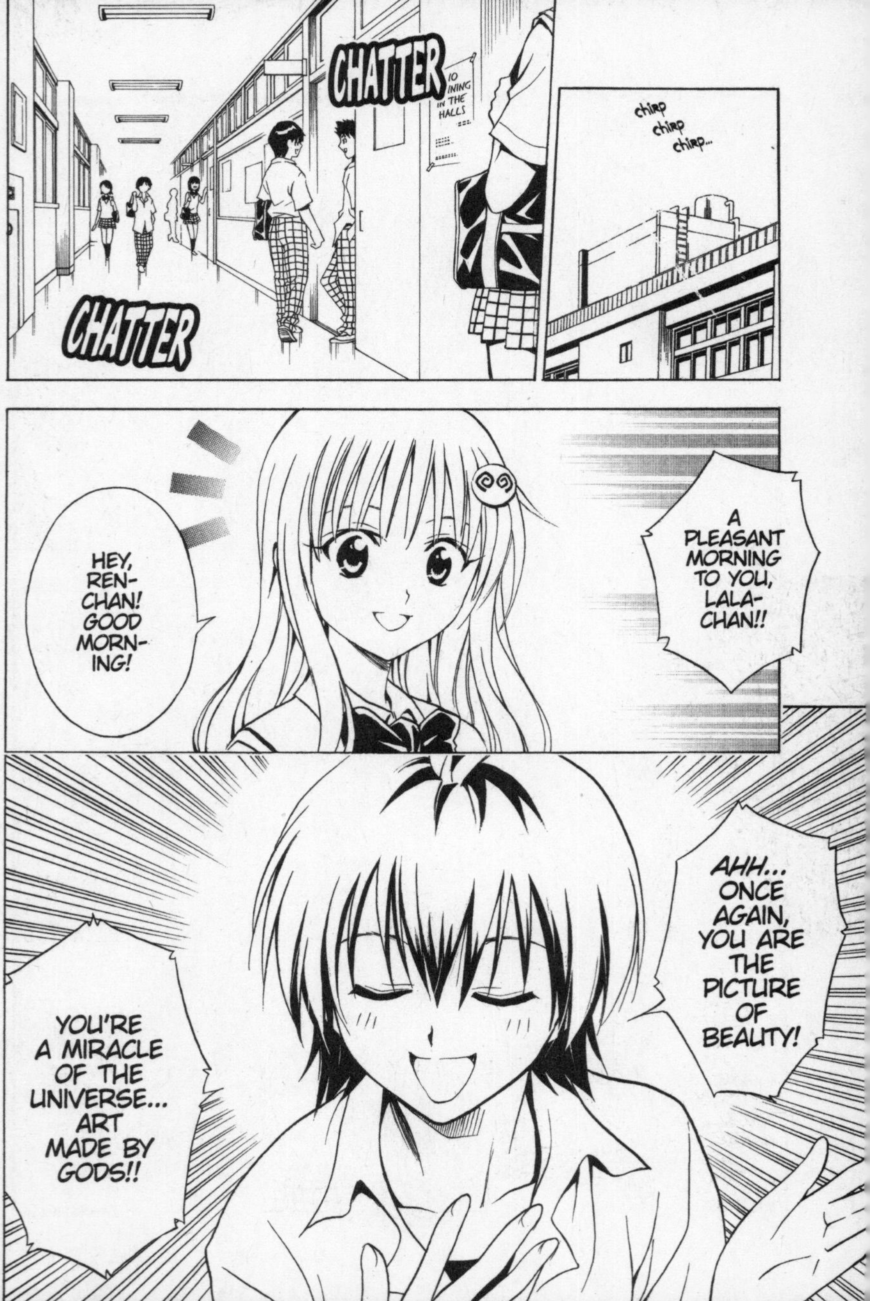
chirp chirp chirp...
CHATTER
CHATTER
A PLEASANT MORNING TO YOU, LALA-CHAN!!
HEY, REN-CHAN! GOOD MORNING!
AHH... ONCE AGAIN, YOU ARE THE PICTURE OF BEAUTY!
YOU'RE A MIRACLE OF THE UNIVERSE... ART MADE BY GODS!!

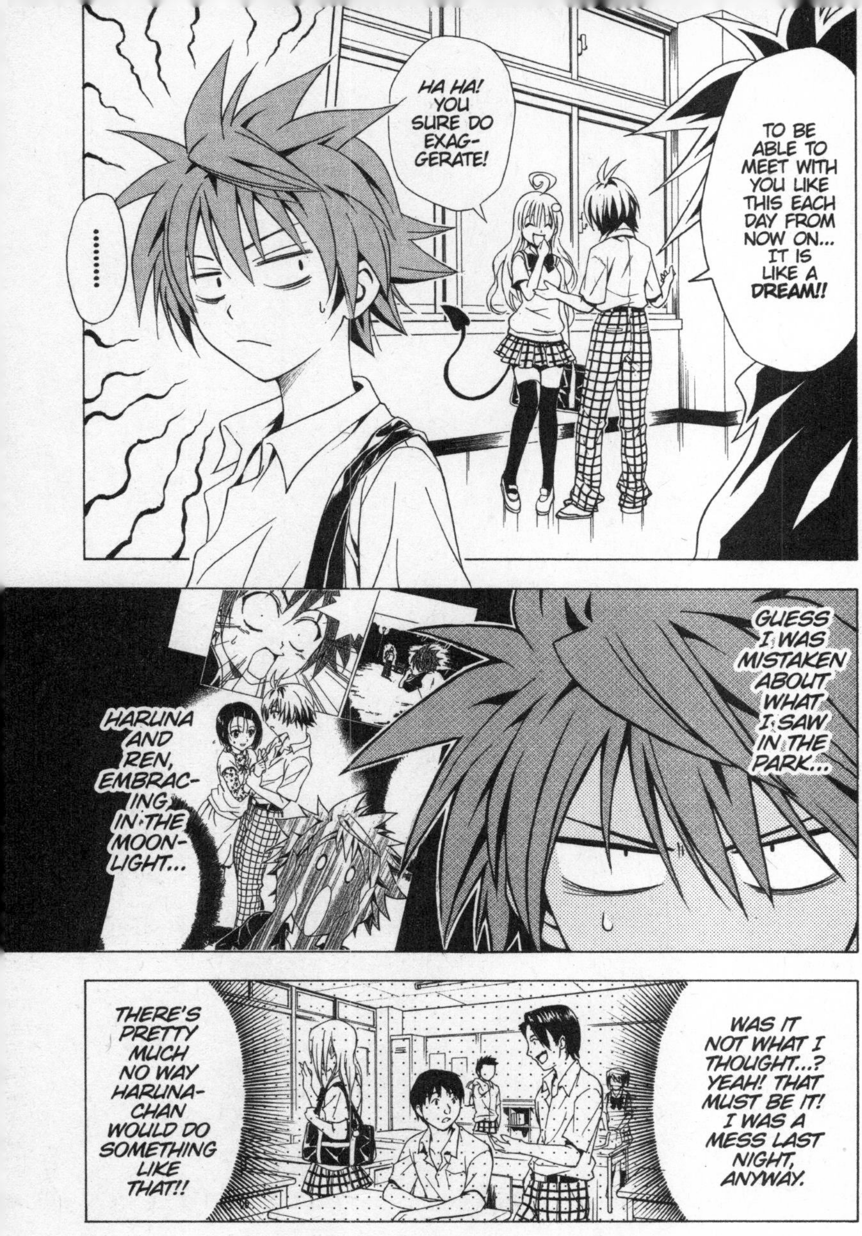
TO BE ABLE TO MEET WITH YOU LIKE THIS EACH DAY FROM NOW ON... IT IS LIKE A DREAM!!
HA HA! YOU SURE DO EXAG-GERATE!
....
GUESS I WAS MISTAKEN ABOUT WHAT I SAW IN THE PARK...
HARUNA AND REN, EMBRACING IN THE MOONLIGHT...
WAS IT NOT WHAT I THOUGHT...? YEAH! THAT MUST BE IT! I WAS A MESS LAST NIGHT, ANYWAY.
THERE'S PRETTY MUCH NO WAY HARUNA-CHAN WOULD DO SOMETHING LIKE THAT!!

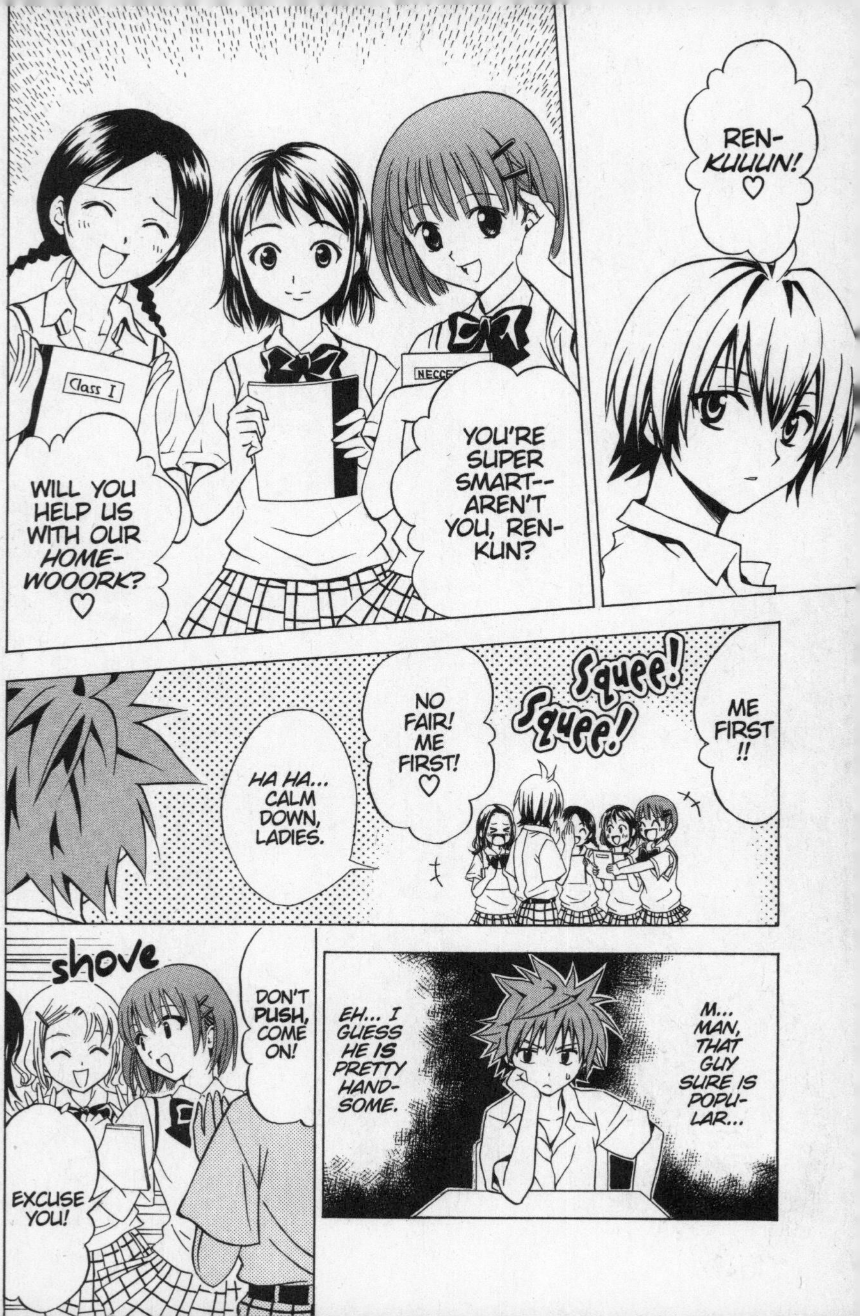
REN-KUUUN! ♡
YOU'RE SUPER SMART--AREN'T YOU, REN-KUN?
Class I
WILL YOU HELP US WITH OUR HOME-WOOORK? ♡
ME FIRST !!
Squee! Squee!
NO FAIR! ME FIRST! ♡
HA HA... CALM DOWN, LADIES.
M... MAN, THAT GUY SURE IS POPU-LAR...
EH... I GUESS HE IS PRETTY HAND-SOME.
DON'T PUSH, COME ON!
shove
EXCUSE YOU!

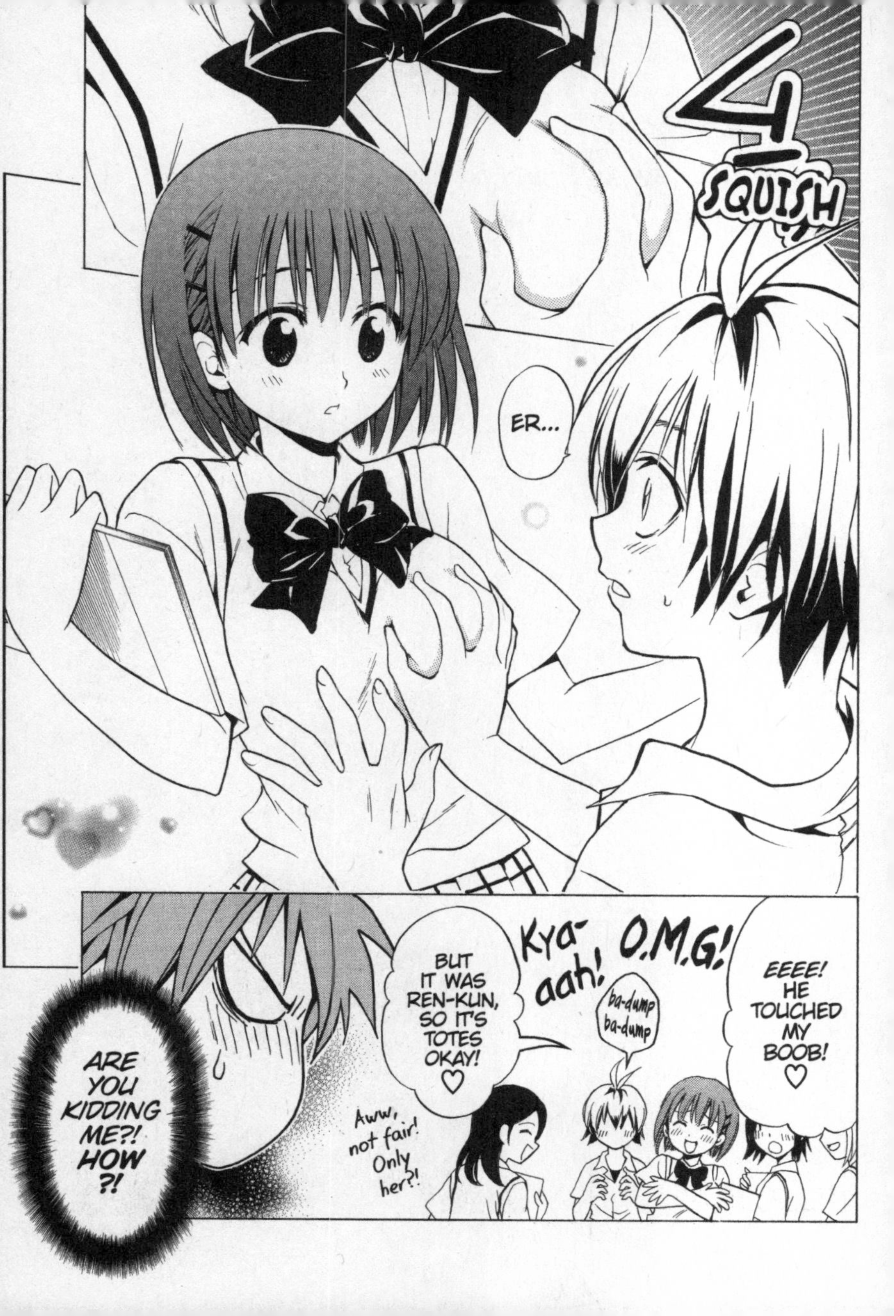
SQUISH
ER...
EEEE! HE TOUCHED MY BOOB! ♡
O.M.G!
ba-dump ba-dump
Kya-aah!
BUT IT WAS REN-KUN, SO IT'S TOTES OKAY! ♡
Aww, not fair! Only her?!
ARE YOU KIDDING ME?! HOW?!

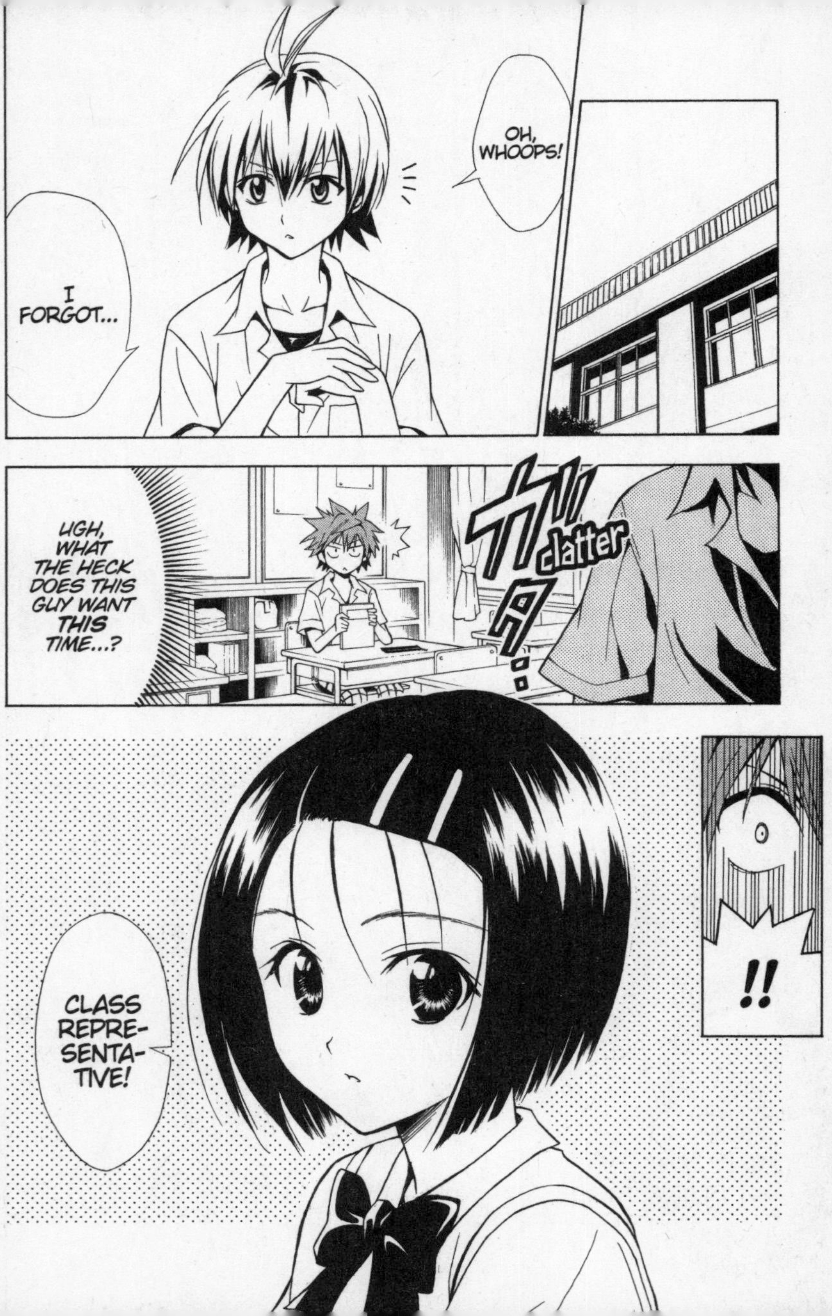
OH, WHOOPS!
I FORGOT...
clatter
UGH, WHAT THE HECK DOES THIS GUY WANT THIS TIME...?
!!
CLASS REPRESENTATIVE!

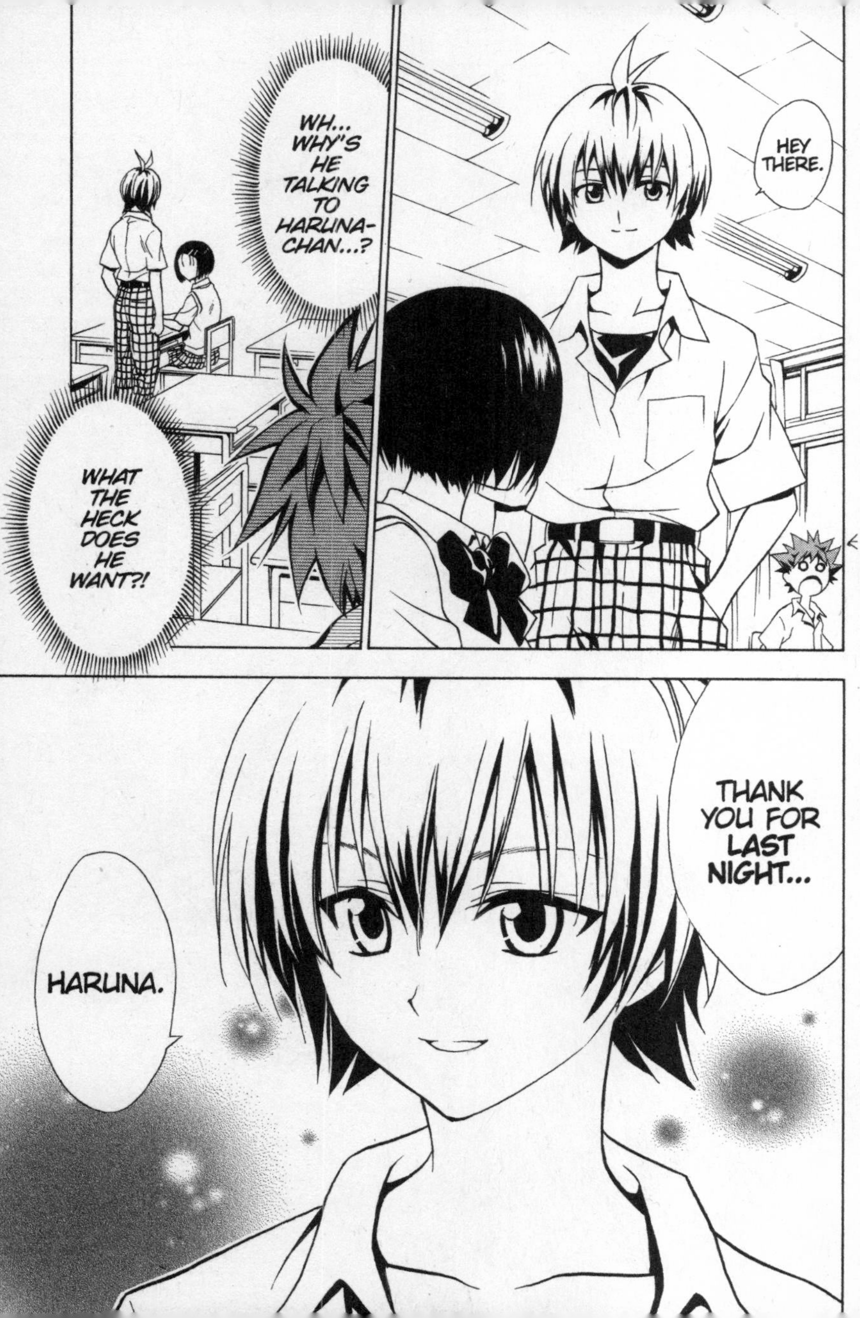
HEY THERE.
WH... WHY'S HE TALKING TO HARUNA-CHAN...?
WHAT THE HECK DOES HE WANT?!
THANK YOU FOR LAST NIGHT...
HARUNA.

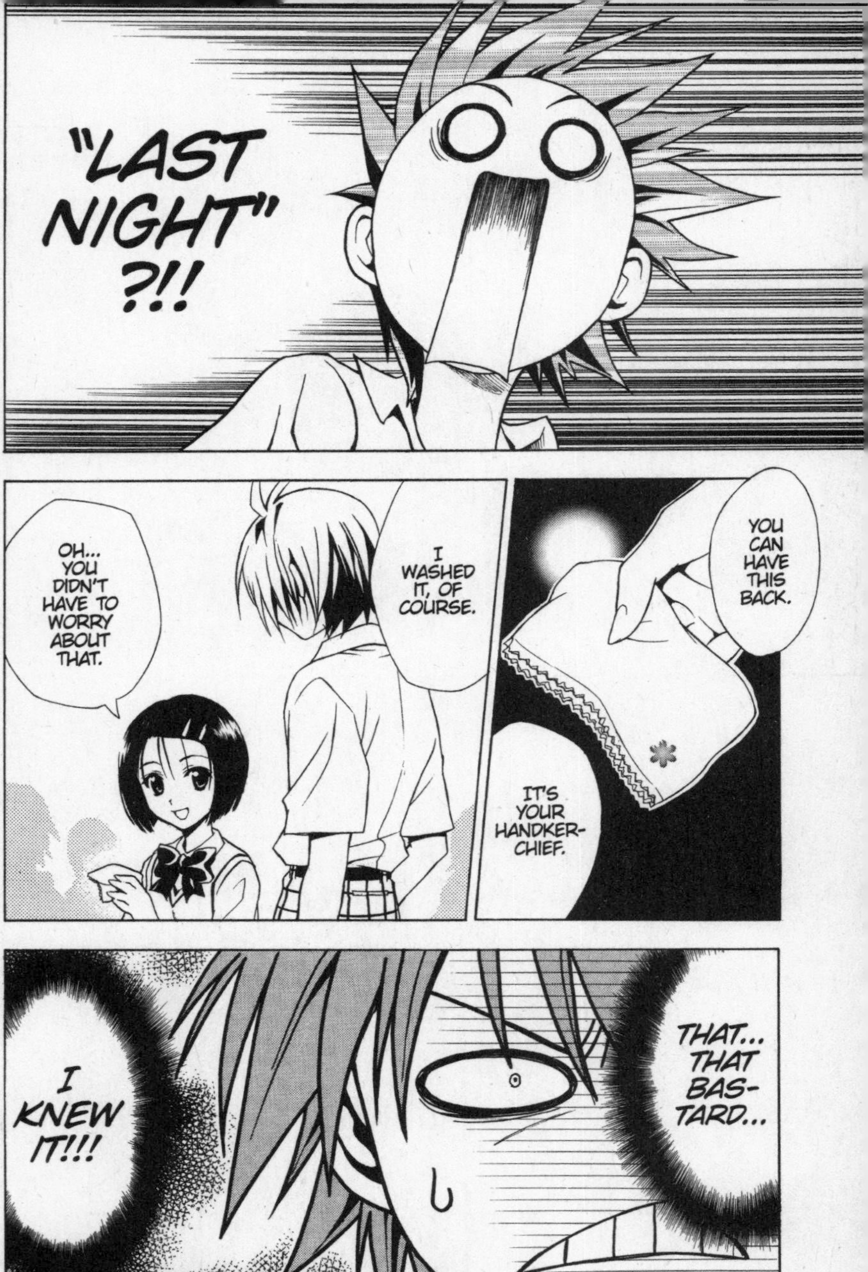
"LAST NIGHT" ?!!
YOU CAN HAVE THIS BACK.
IT'S YOUR HANDKER-CHIEF.
I WASHED IT, OF COURSE.
OH... YOU DIDN'T HAVE TO WORRY ABOUT THAT.
THAT... THAT BAS-TARD...
I KNEW IT!!!

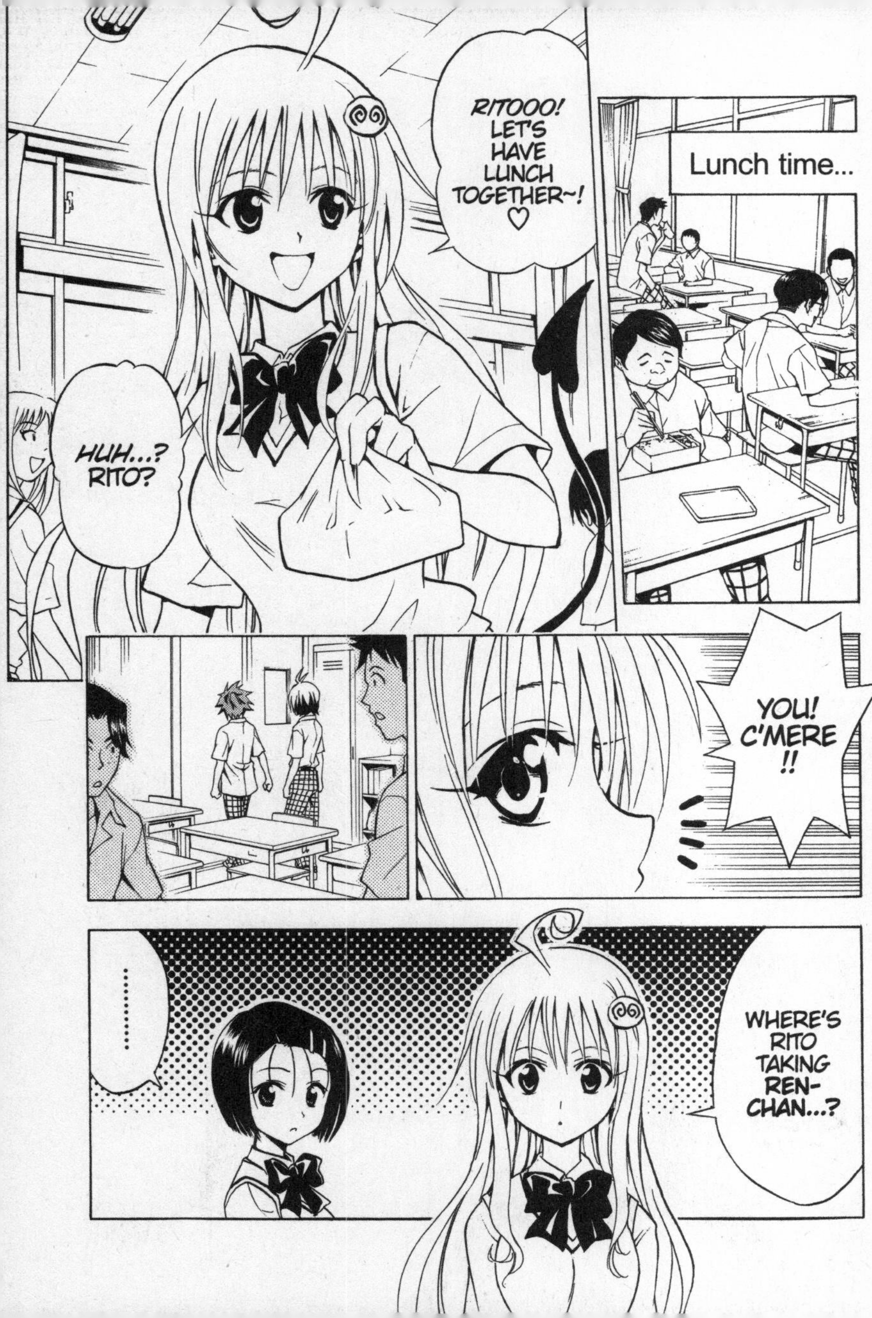
Lunch time...
RITOOO! LET'S HAVE LUNCH TOGETHER~! ♡
HUH...? RITO?
YOU! C'MERE !!
WHERE'S RITO TAKING REN-CHAN...?
......

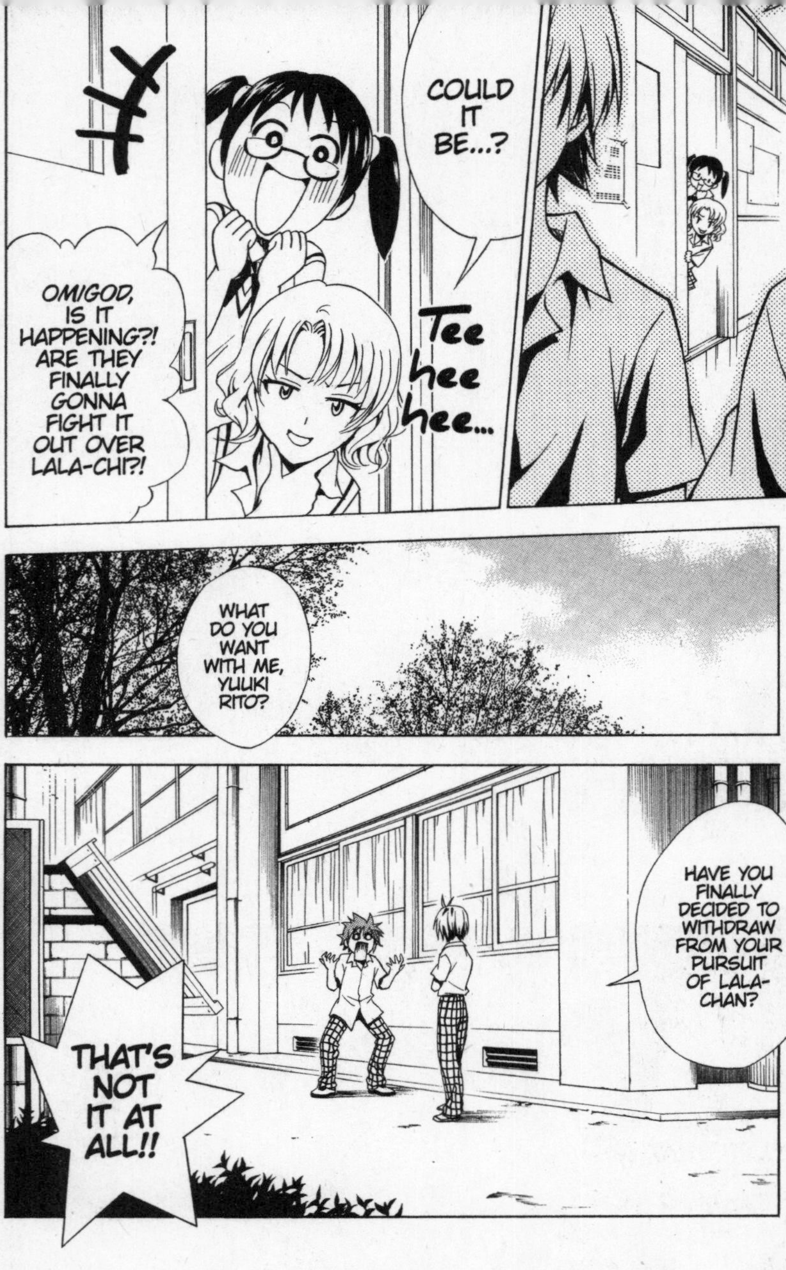
COULD IT BE...?
Tee hee hee...
OMIGOD, IS IT HAPPENING?! ARE THEY FINALLY GONNA FIGHT IT OUT OVER LALA-CHI?!
WHAT DO YOU WANT WITH ME, YUUKI RITO?
HAVE YOU FINALLY DECIDED TO WITHDRAW FROM YOUR PURSUIT OF LALA-CHAN?
THAT'S NOT IT AT ALL!!

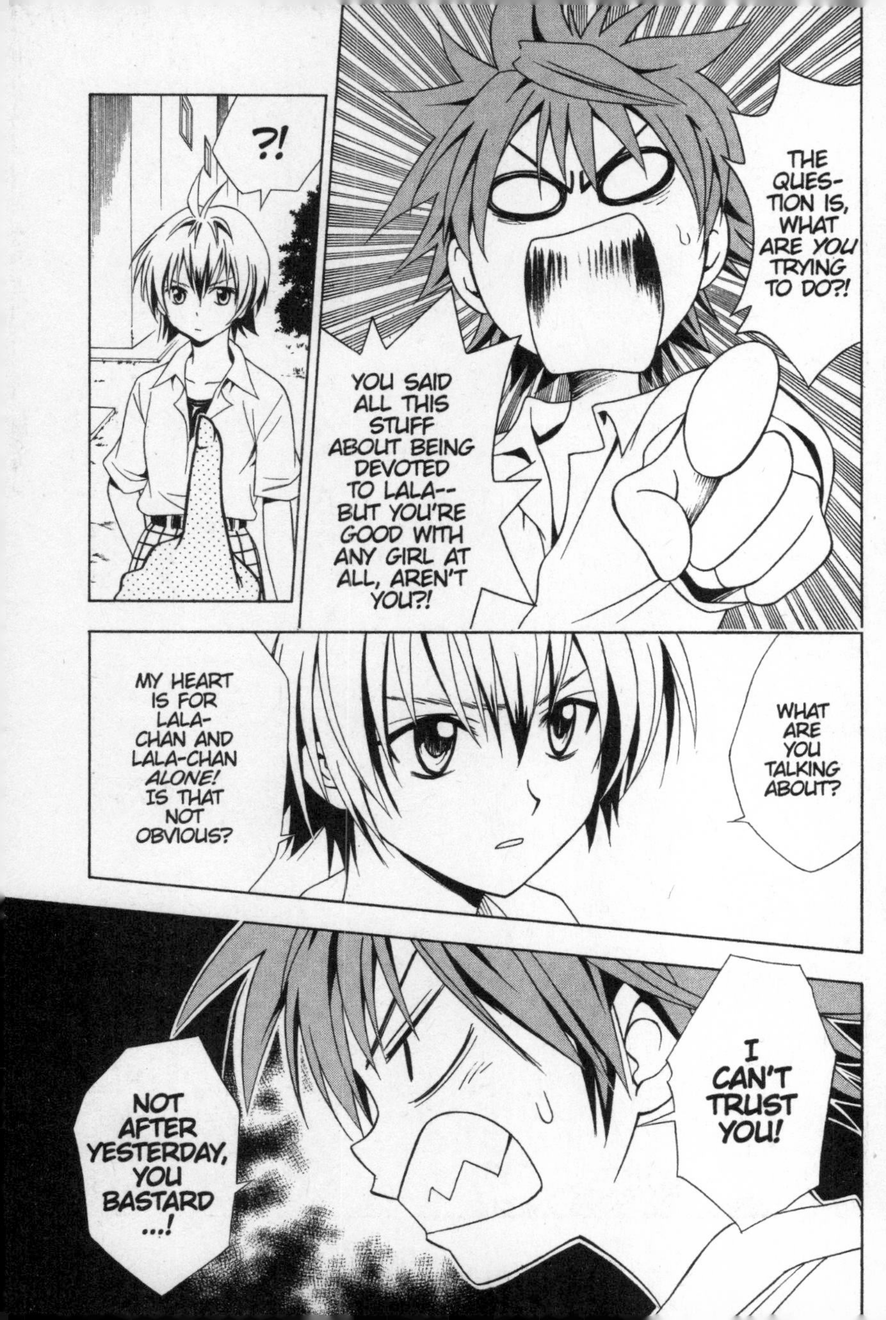
THE QUES-TION IS, WHAT ARE *YOU* TRYING TO DO?!
YOU SAID ALL THIS STUFF ABOUT BEING DEVOTED TO LALA-- BUT YOU'RE GOOD WITH ANY GIRL AT ALL, AREN'T YOU?!
?!
WHAT ARE YOU TALKING ABOUT?
MY HEART IS FOR LALA-CHAN AND LALA-CHAN *ALONE!* IS THAT NOT OBVIOUS?
I CAN'T TRUST YOU!
NOT AFTER YESTERDAY, YOU BASTARD ...!

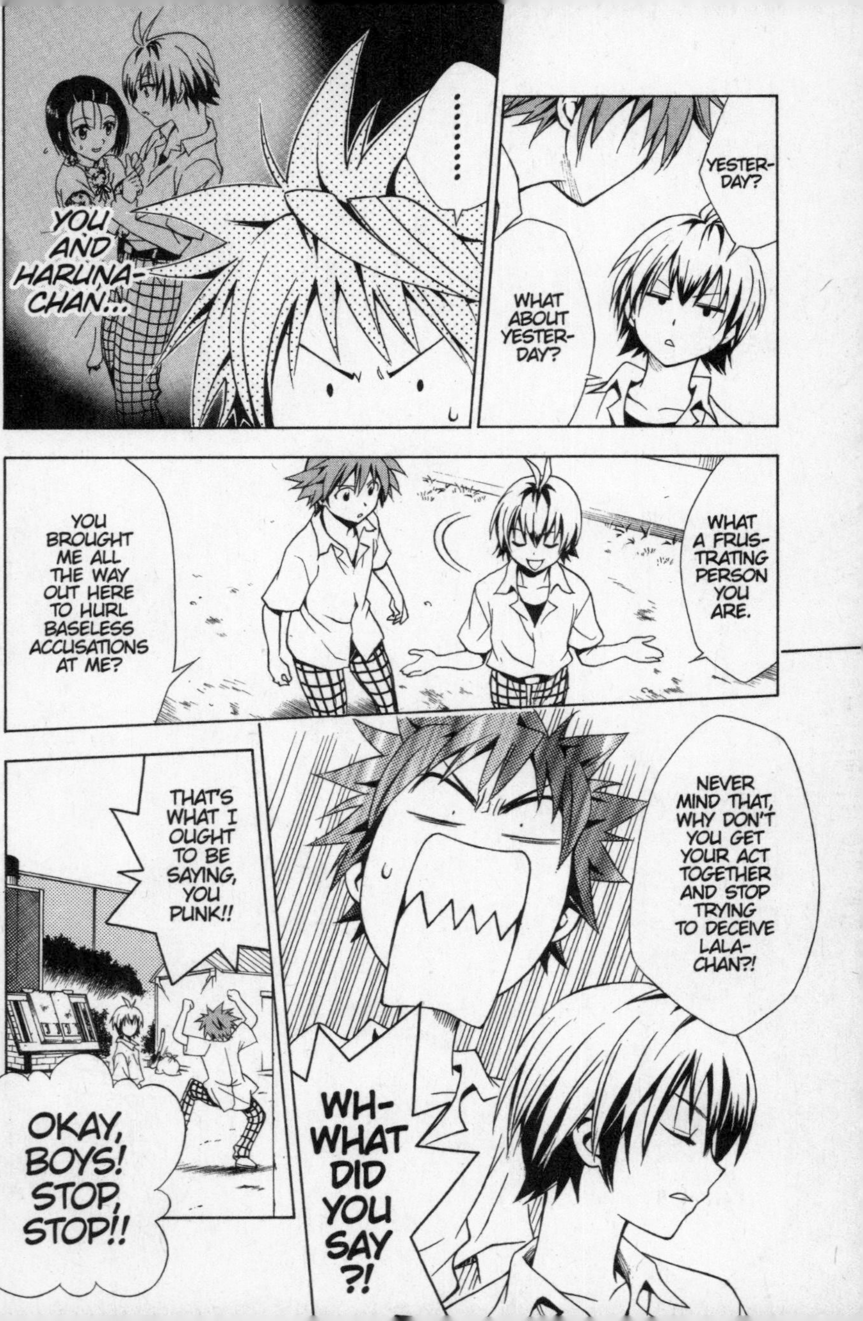
YESTER-DAY?
WHAT ABOUT YESTER-DAY?
......
YOU AND HARUNA-CHAN...
WHAT A FRUS-TRATING PERSON YOU ARE.
YOU BROUGHT ME ALL THE WAY OUT HERE TO HURL BASELESS ACCUSATIONS AT ME?
NEVER MIND THAT, WHY DON'T YOU GET YOUR ACT TOGETHER AND STOP TRYING TO DECEIVE LALA-CHAN?!
WH-WHAT DID YOU SAY?!
THAT'S WHAT I OUGHT TO BE SAYING, YOU PUNK!!
OKAY, BOYS! STOP, STOP!!

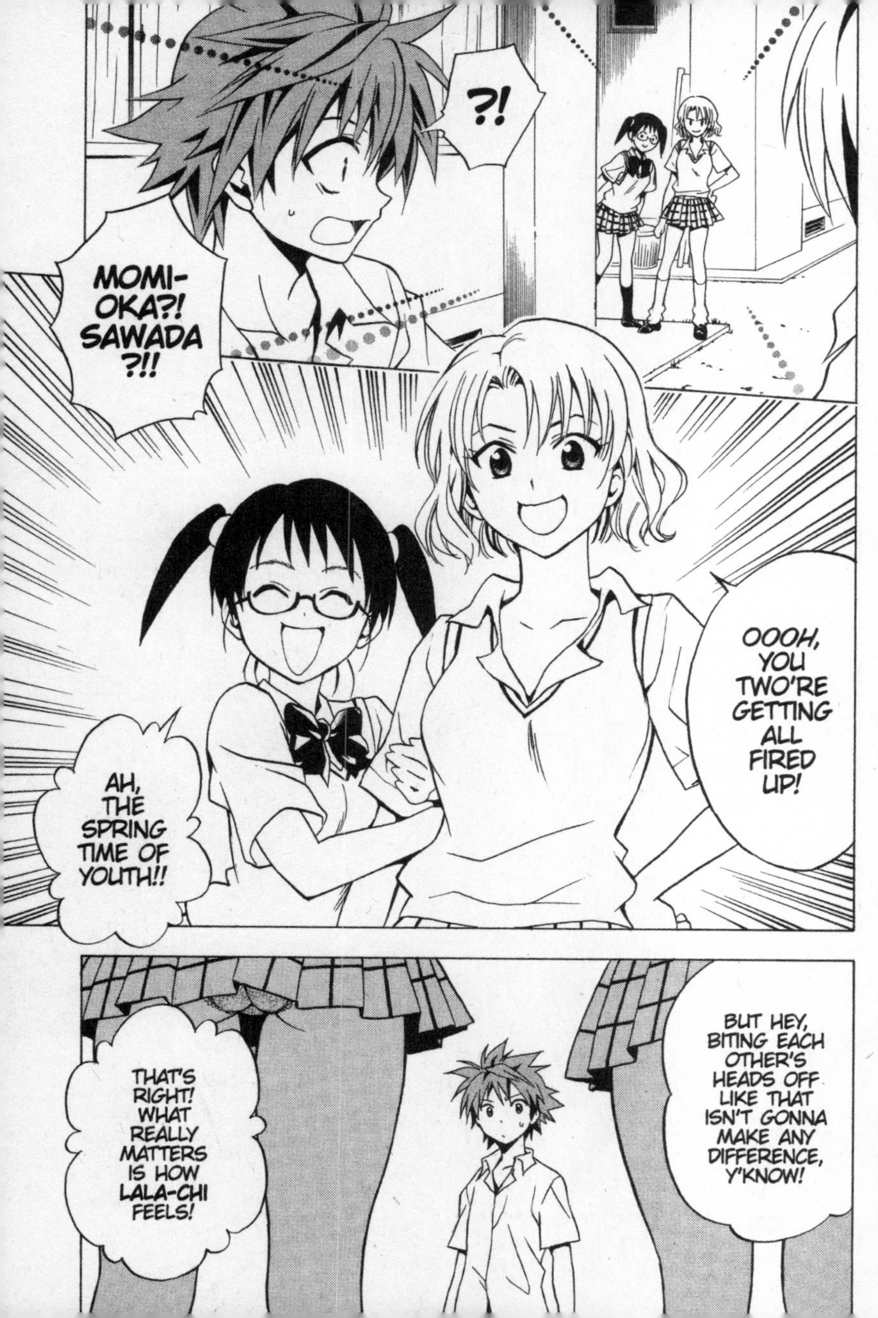
?!
MOMI-OKA?! SAWADA?!!
OOOH, YOU TWO'RE GETTING ALL FIRED UP!
AH, THE SPRING TIME OF YOUTH!!
BUT HEY, BITING EACH OTHER'S HEADS OFF LIKE THAT ISN'T GONNA MAKE ANY DIFFERENCE, Y'KNOW!
THAT'S RIGHT! WHAT REALLY MATTERS IS HOW LALA-CHI FEELS!

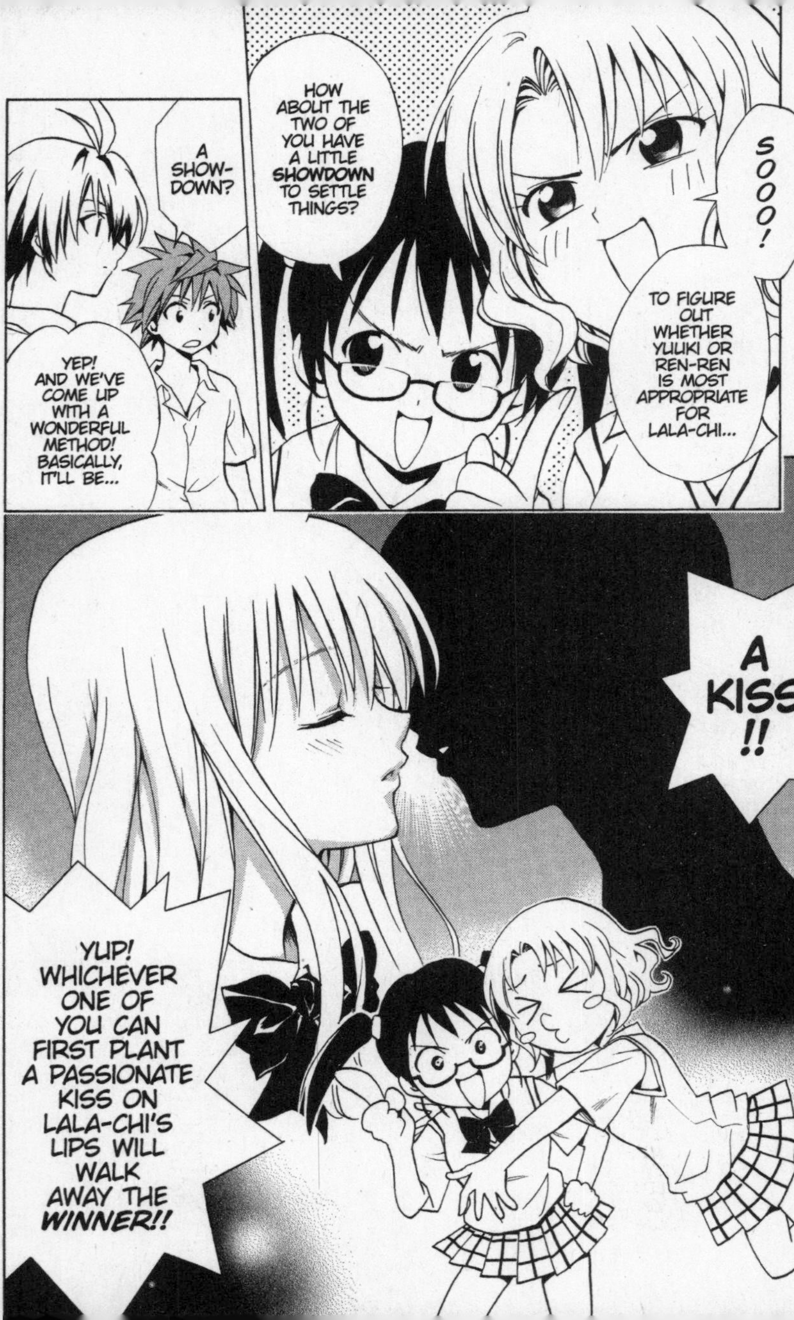
SOOOO!
TO FIGURE OUT WHETHER YUUKI OR REN-REN IS MOST APPROPRIATE FOR LALA-CHI...
HOW ABOUT THE TWO OF YOU HAVE A LITTLE SHOWDOWN TO SETTLE THINGS?
A SHOW-DOWN?
YEP! AND WE'VE COME UP WITH A WONDERFUL METHOD! BASICALLY, IT'LL BE...
A KISS!!
YUP! WHICHEVER ONE OF YOU CAN FIRST PLANT A PASSIONATE KISS ON LALA-CHI'S LIPS WILL WALK AWAY THE WINNER!!

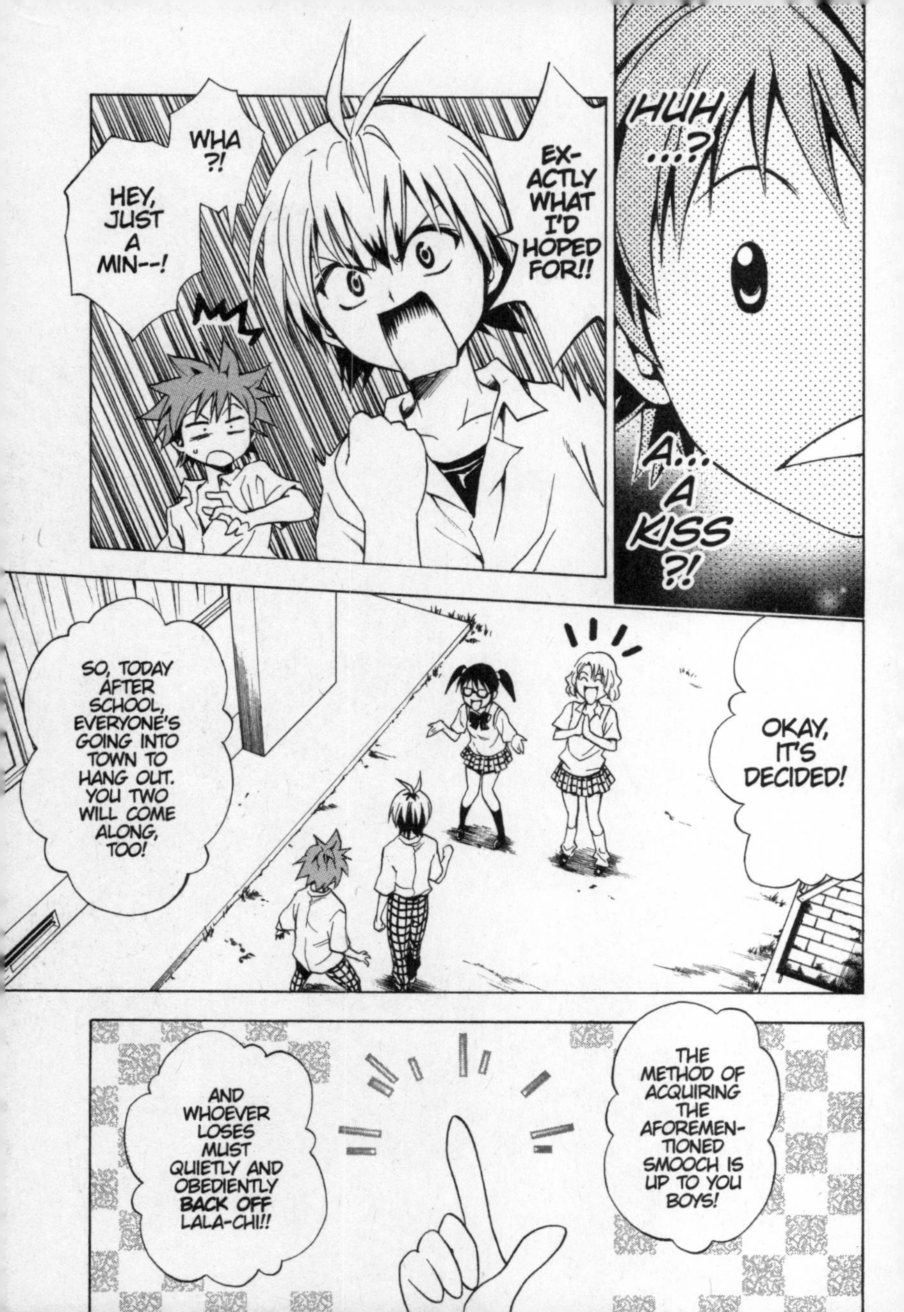
HUH ...?
A... A KISS ?!
EX-ACTLY WHAT I'D HOPED FOR!!
WHA ?!
HEY, JUST A MIN--!
OKAY, IT'S DECIDED!
SO, TODAY AFTER SCHOOL, EVERYONE'S GOING INTO TOWN TO HANG OUT. YOU TWO WILL COME ALONG, TOO!
THE METHOD OF ACQUIRING THE AFOREMEN-TIONED SMOOCH IS UP TO YOU BOYS!
AND WHOEVER LOSES MUST QUIETLY AND OBEDIENTLY BACK OFF LALA-CHI!!

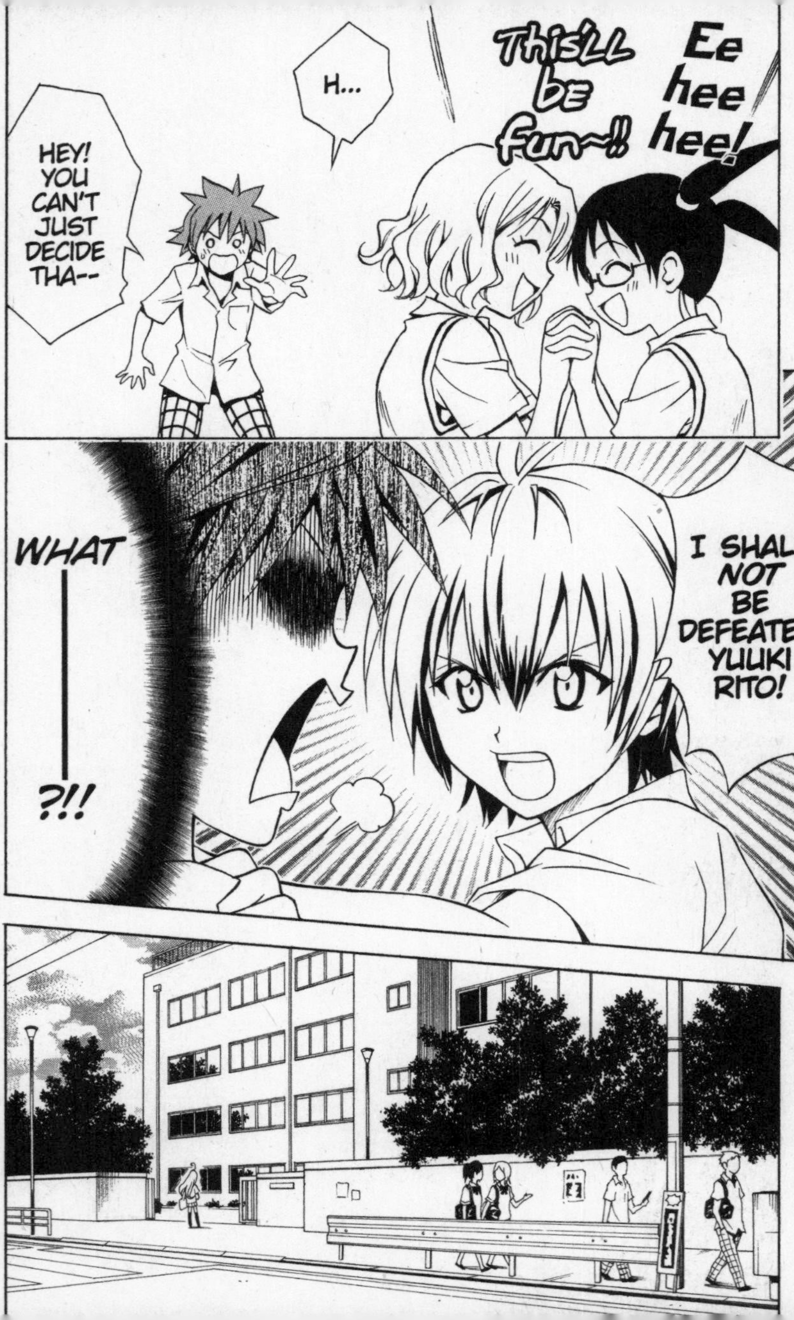
Ee hee hee!
This'll be fun~!!
H...
HEY! YOU CAN'T JUST DECIDE THA--
I SHALL NOT BE DEFEATED, YUUKI RITO!
WHAT ?!!

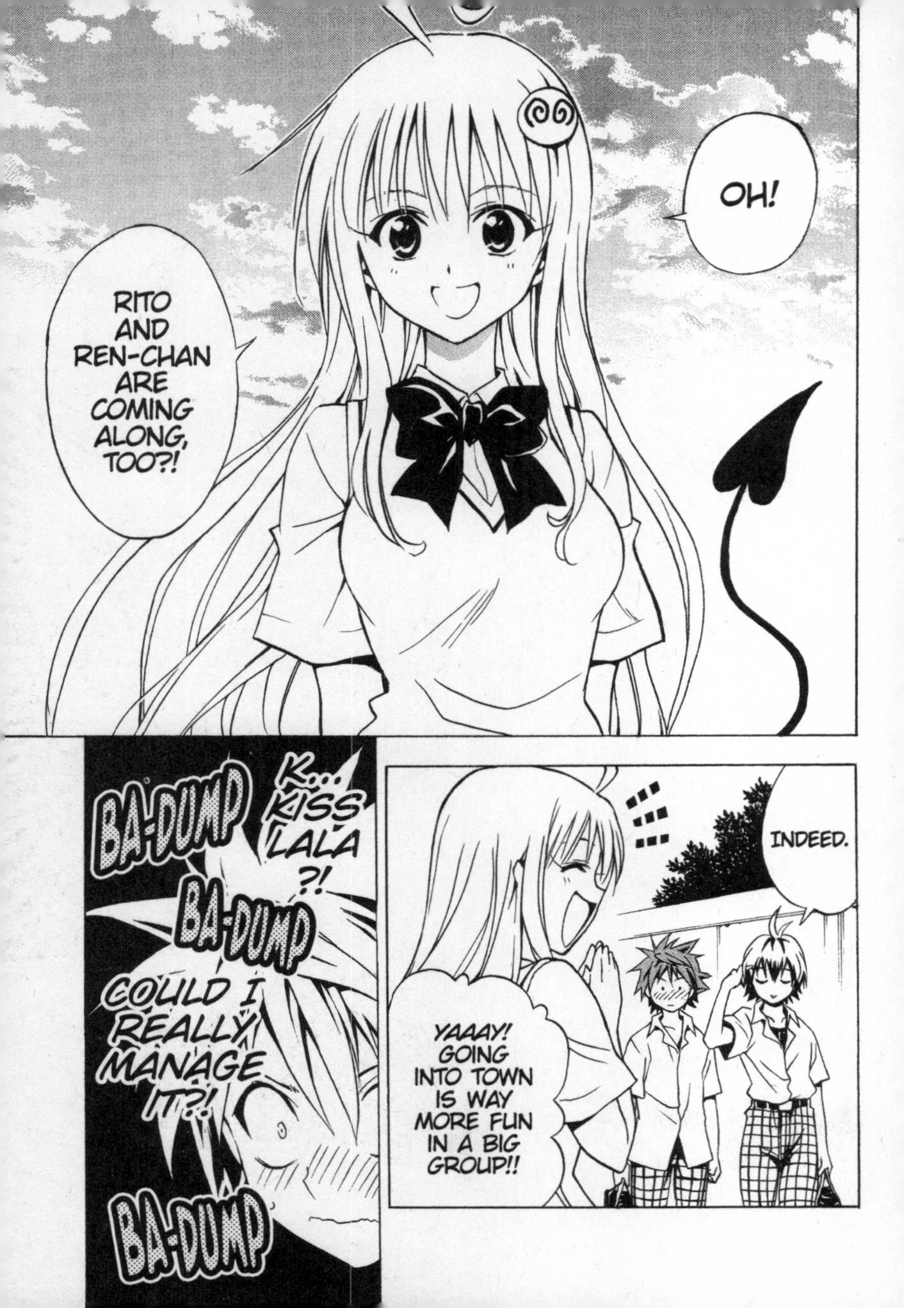
OH!
RITO AND REN-CHAN ARE COMING ALONG, TOO?!
INDEED.
YAAAY! GOING INTO TOWN IS WAY MORE FUN IN A BIG GROUP!!
K... KISS LALA ?!
BA-DUMP
BA-DUMP
COULD I REALLY MANAGE IT?!
BA-DUMP

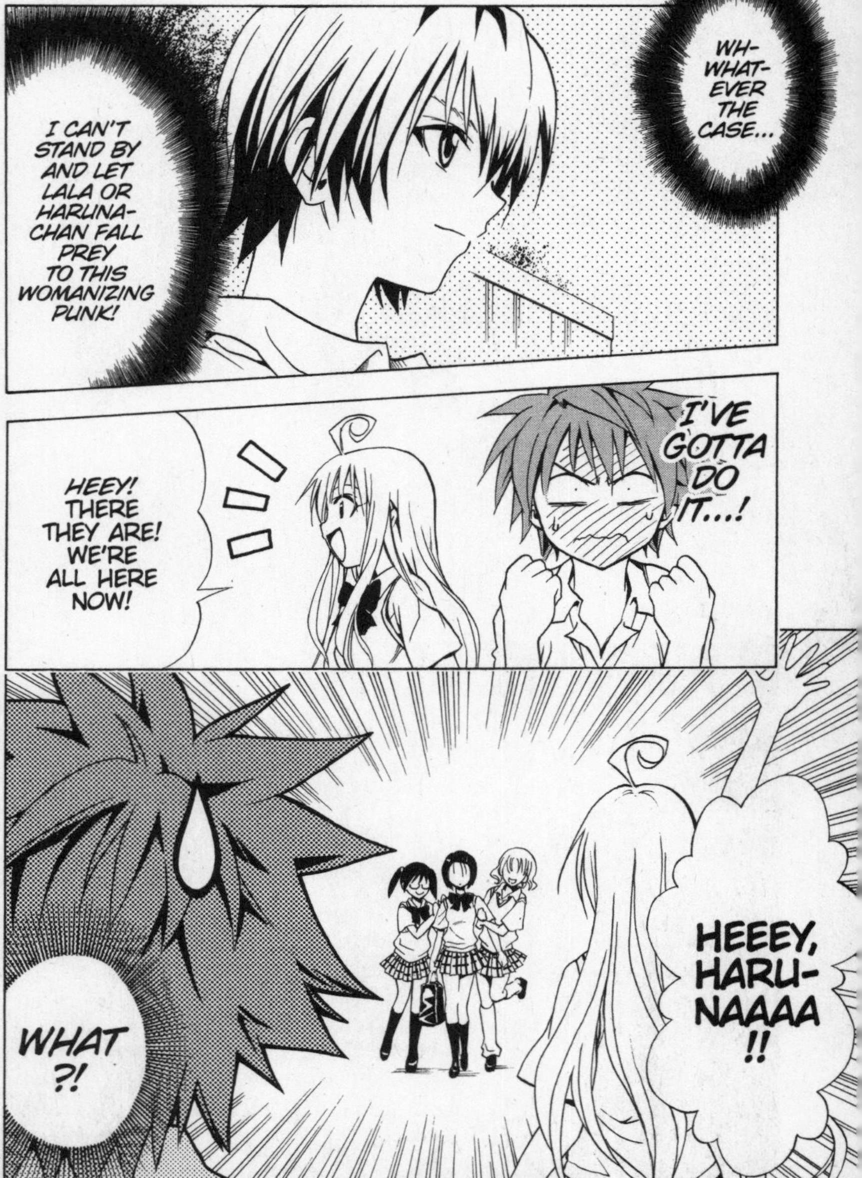
WH- WHAT-EVER THE CASE...
I CAN'T STAND BY AND LET LALA OR HARUNA-CHAN FALL PREY TO THIS WOMANIZING PUNK!
I'VE GOTTA DO IT...!
HEEY! THERE THEY ARE! WE'RE ALL HERE NOW!
HEEEY, HARU-NAAAA!!
WHAT?!

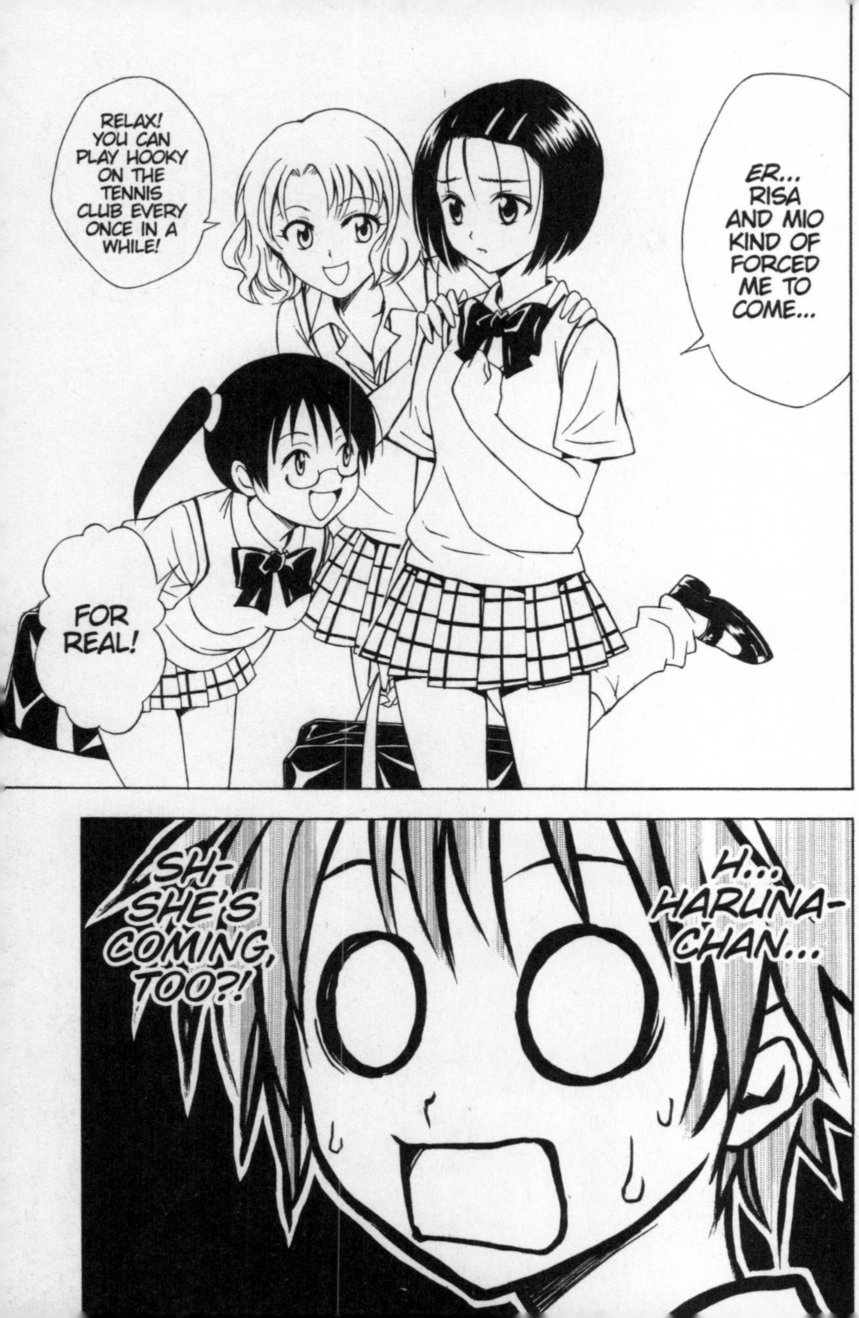
ER... RISA AND MIO KIND OF FORCED ME TO COME...
RELAX! YOU CAN PLAY HOOKY ON THE TENNIS CLUB EVERY ONCE IN A WHILE!
FOR REAL!
H... HARUNA-CHAN...
SH-SHE'S COMING, TOO?!

To LOVE Ru

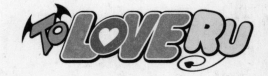

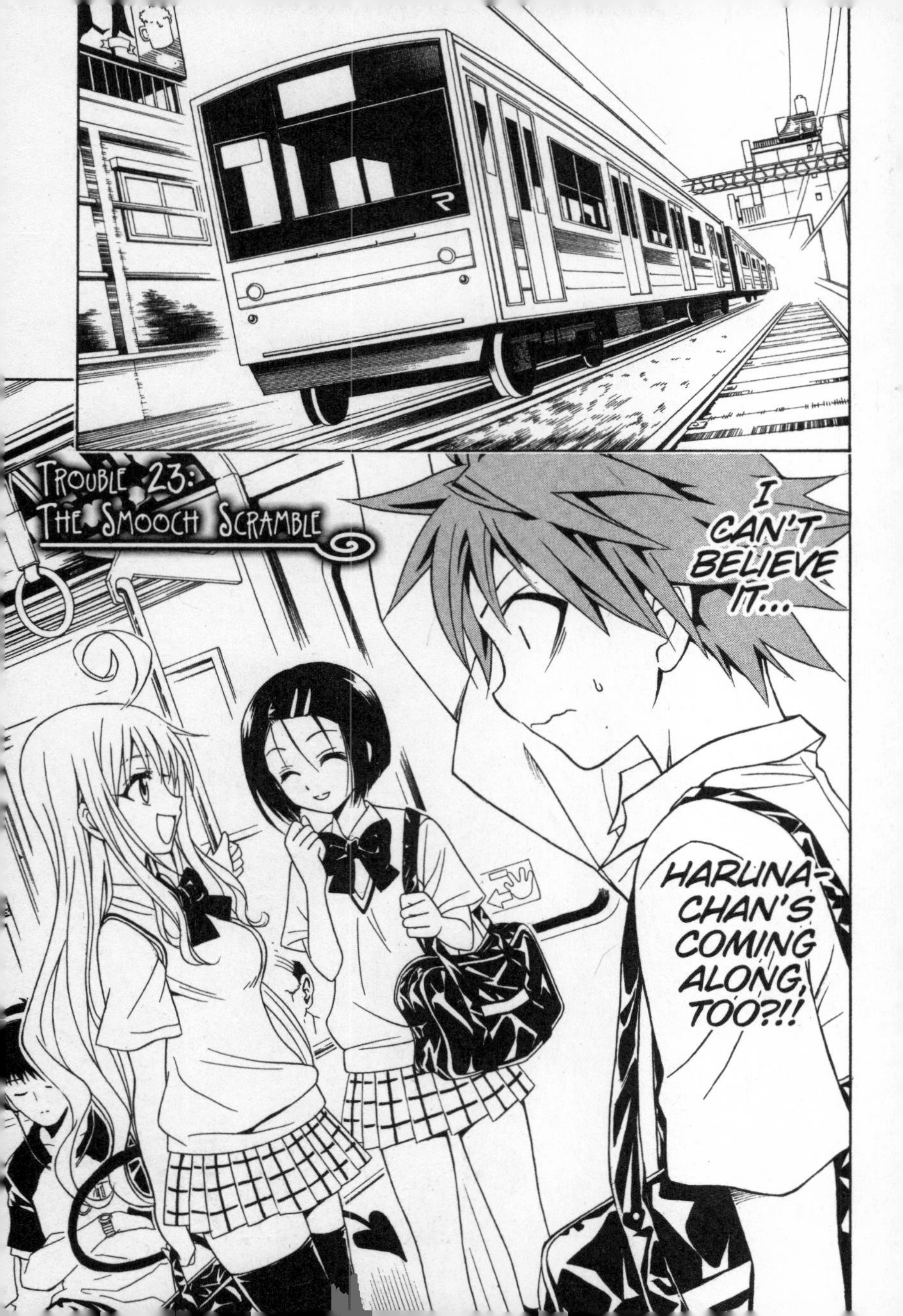
Trouble 23: The Smooch Scramble
I can't believe it...
Haruna-chan's coming along, too?!!

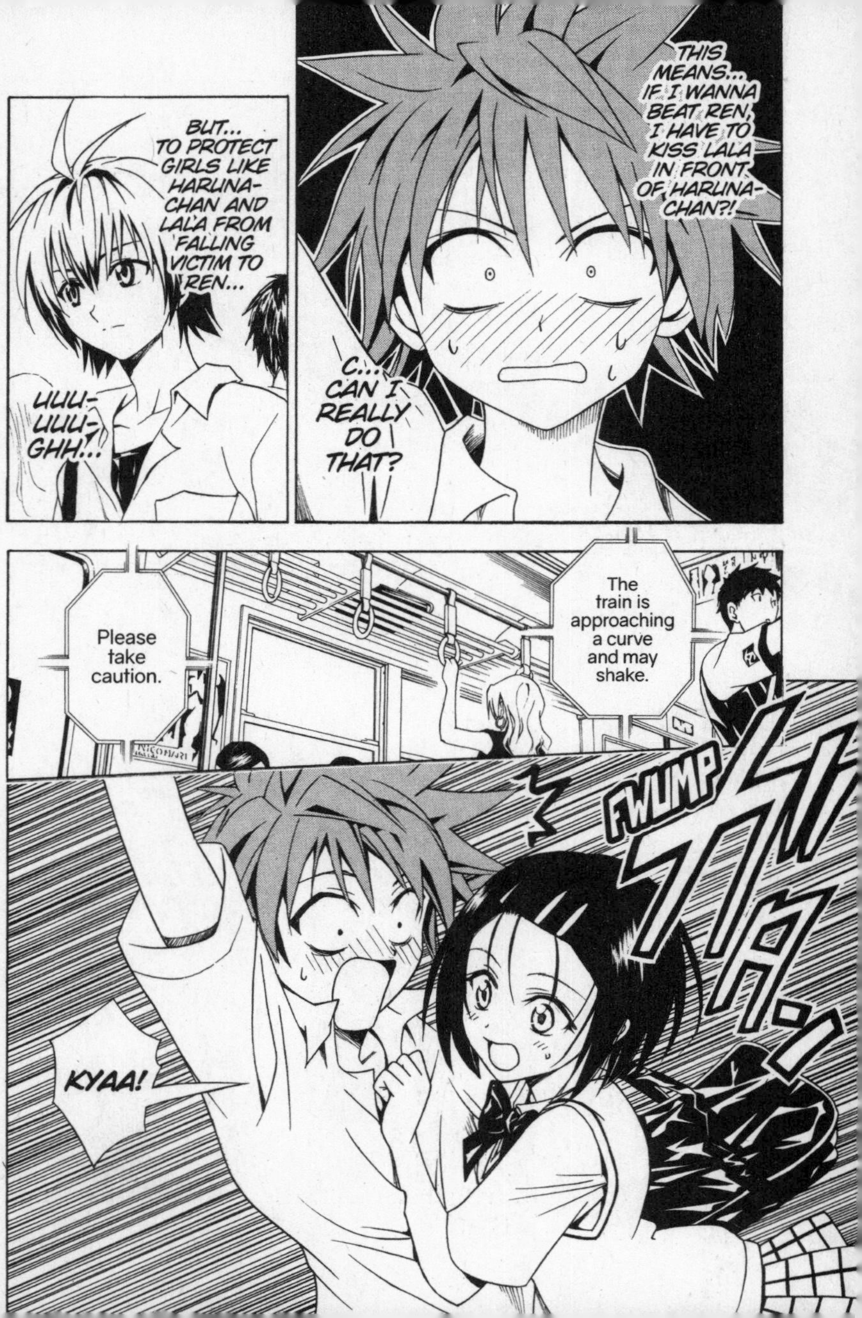
THIS MEANS... IF I WANNA BEAT REN, I HAVE TO KISS LALA IN FRONT OF HARUNA-CHAN?!
C... CAN I REALLY DO THAT?
BUT... TO PROTECT GIRLS LIKE HARUNA-CHAN AND LALA FROM FALLING VICTIM TO REN...
UUU-UUU-GHH...
The train is approaching a curve and may shake.
Please take caution.
FWUMP
KYAA!

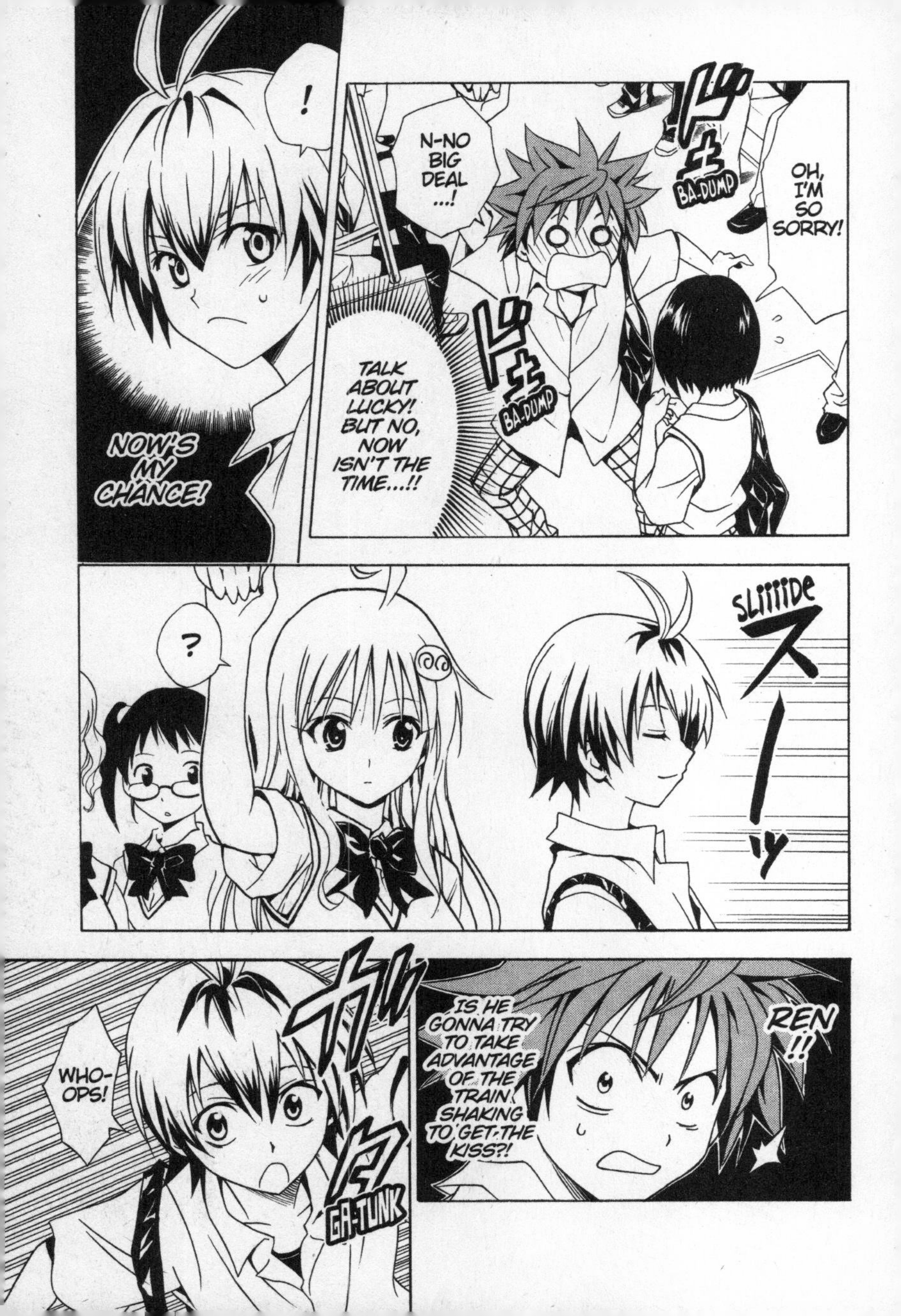
OH, I'M SO SORRY!
BA-DUMP
N-NO BIG DEAL ...!
BA-DUMP
TALK ABOUT LUCKY! BUT NO, NOW ISN'T THE TIME...!!
!
NOW'S MY CHANCE!
SLIIIIDE
?
REN!!
IS HE GONNA TRY TO TAKE ADVANTAGE OF THE TRAIN SHAKING TO GET THE KISS?!
WHO-OPS!
GA-TUNK

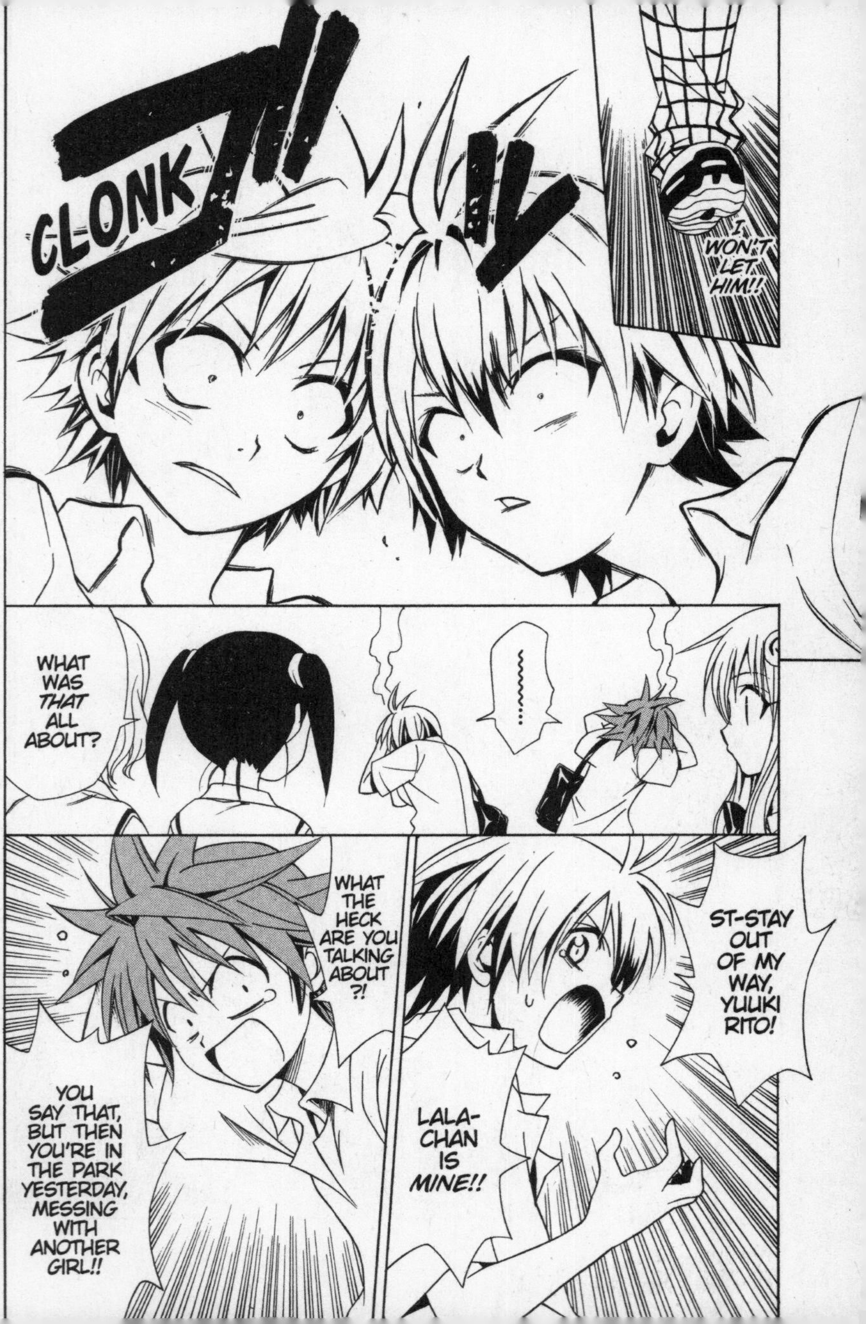
I WON'T LET HIM!!
CLONK
......
WHAT WAS *THAT* ALL ABOUT?
ST-STAY OUT OF MY WAY, YUUKI RITO!
LALA-CHAN IS *MINE!!*
WHAT THE HECK ARE YOU TALKING ABOUT ?!
YOU SAY THAT, BUT THEN YOU'RE IN THE PARK YESTERDAY, MESSING WITH ANOTHER GIRL!!

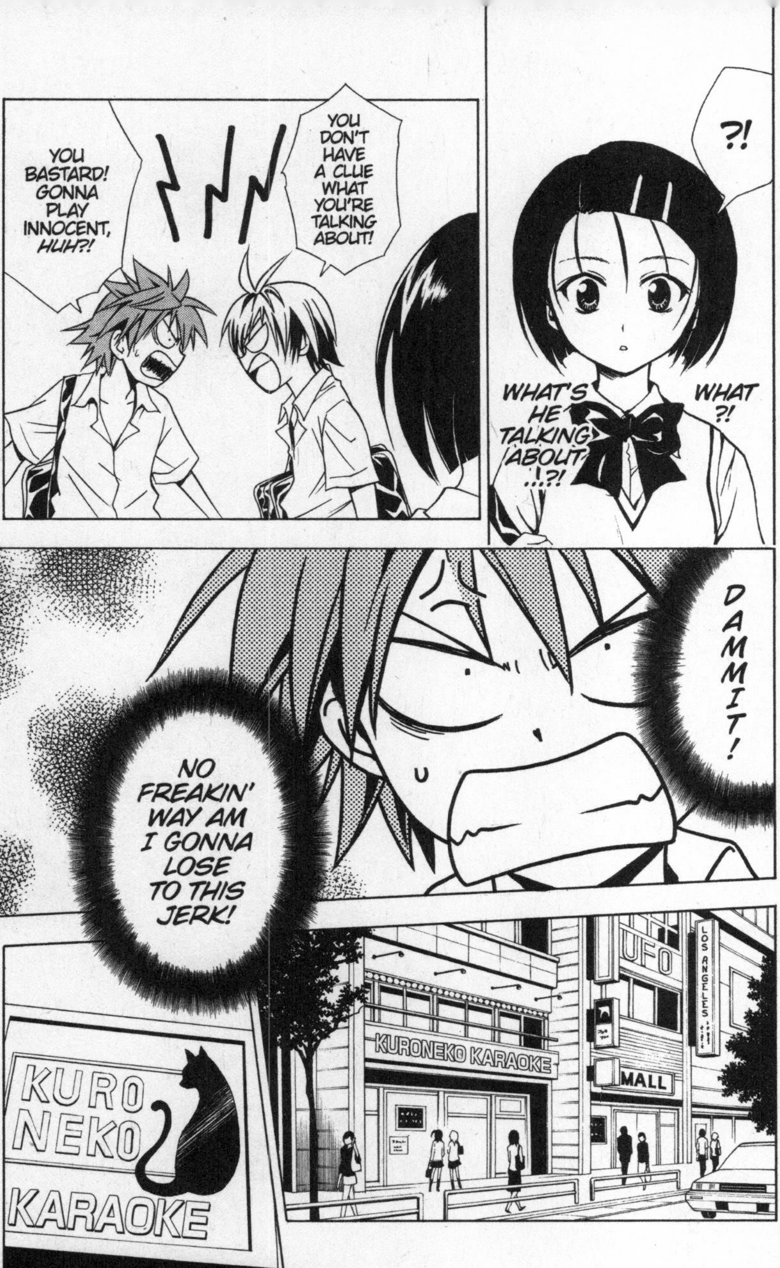
?!
WHAT ?!
WHAT'S HE TALKING ABOUT ...!?!
YOU DON'T HAVE A CLUE WHAT YOU'RE TALKING ABOUT!
YOU BASTARD! GONNA PLAY INNOCENT, HUH?!
DAMMIT!
NO FREAKIN' WAY AM I GONNA LOSE TO THIS JERK!
LOS ANGELES
UFO
KURONEKO KARAOKE
MALL
KURO NEKO KARAOKE

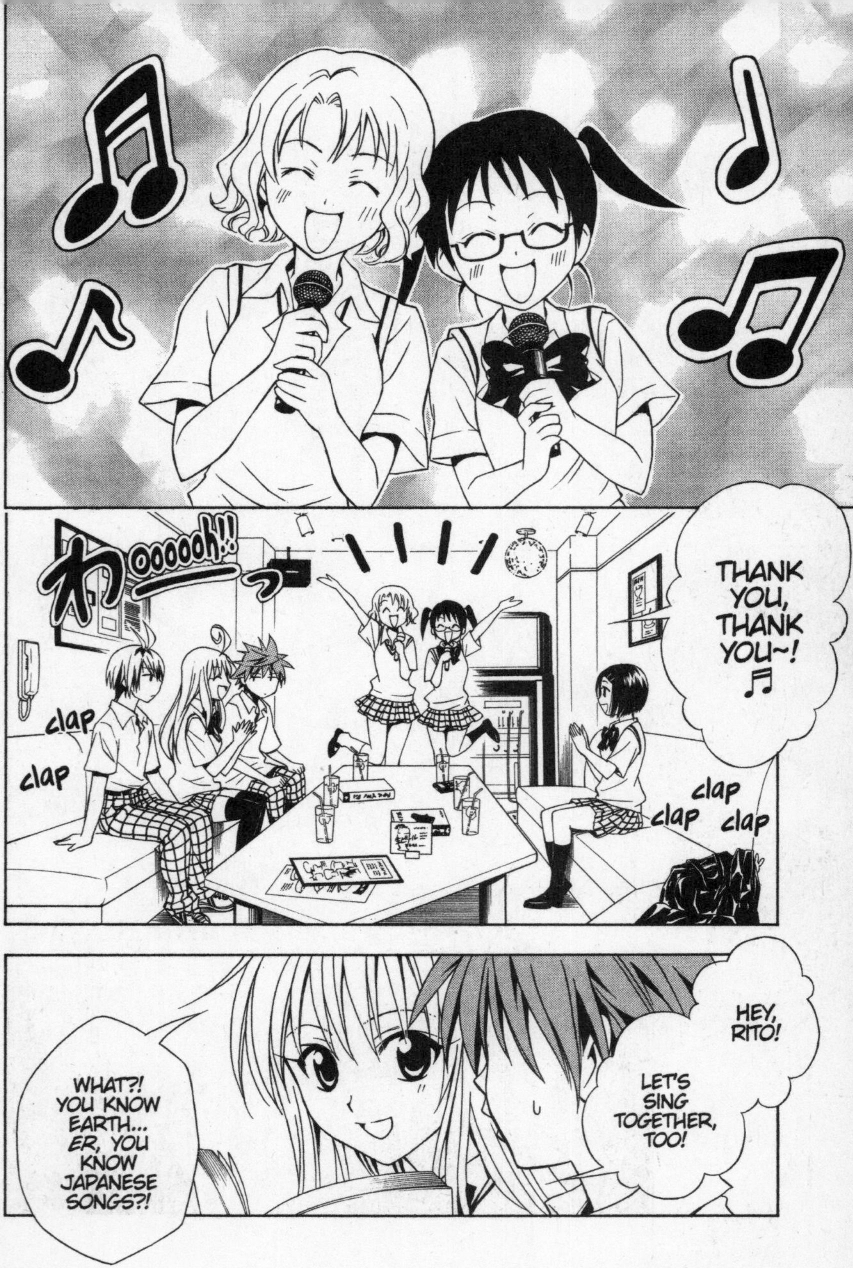
THANK YOU, THANK YOU~! ♬
わーーっ oooooh!!
clap
clap
clap
clap
clap
HEY, RITO!
LET'S SING TOGETHER, TOO!
WHAT?! YOU KNOW EARTH... ER, YOU KNOW JAPANESE SONGS?!

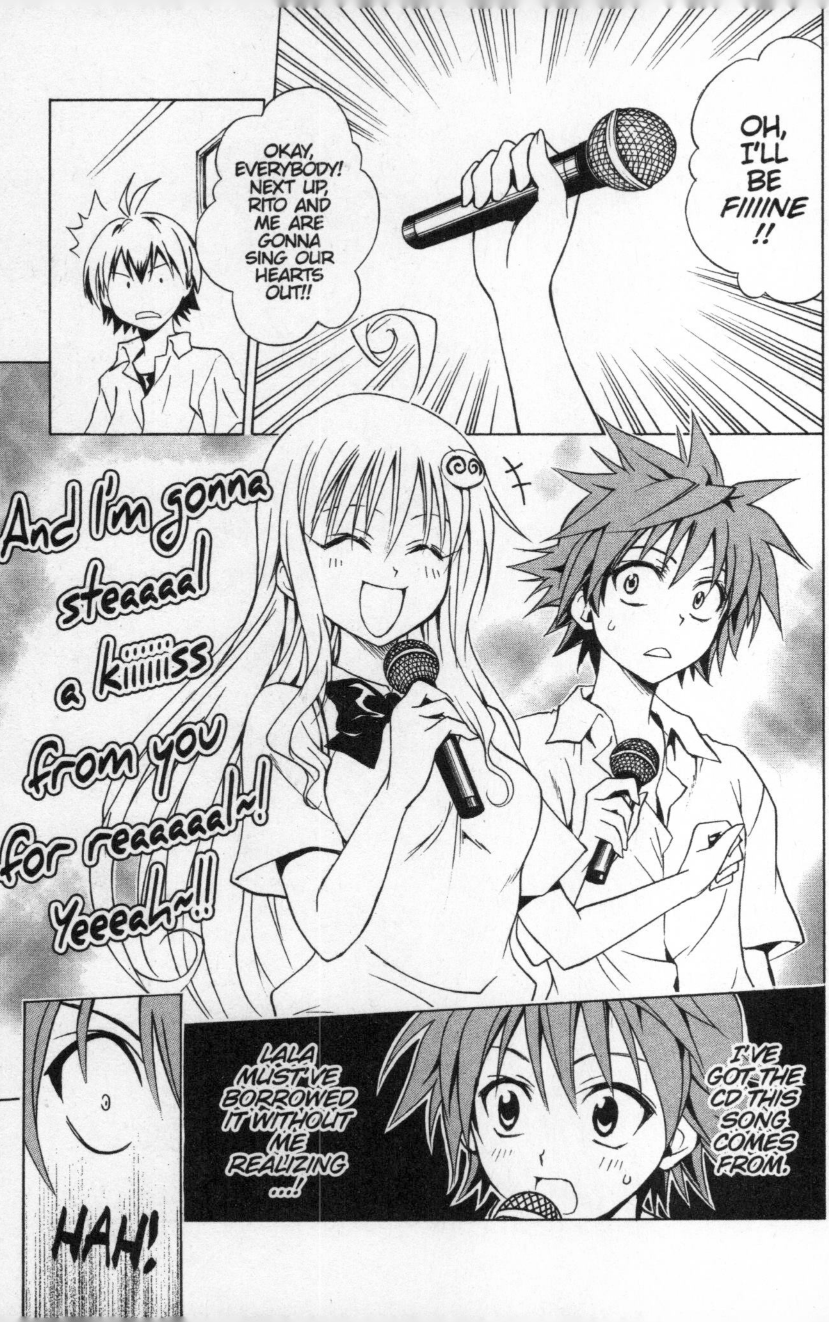
OH, I'LL BE FIIIINE!!
OKAY, EVERYBODY! NEXT UP, RITO AND ME ARE GONNA SING OUR HEARTS OUT!!
And I'm gonna steaaaal a kiiiiiiss from you for reaaaaal~! Yeeeah~!!
I'VE GOT THE CD THIS SONG COMES FROM.
LALA MUST'VE BORROWED IT WITHOUT ME REALIZING ...!
HAH!

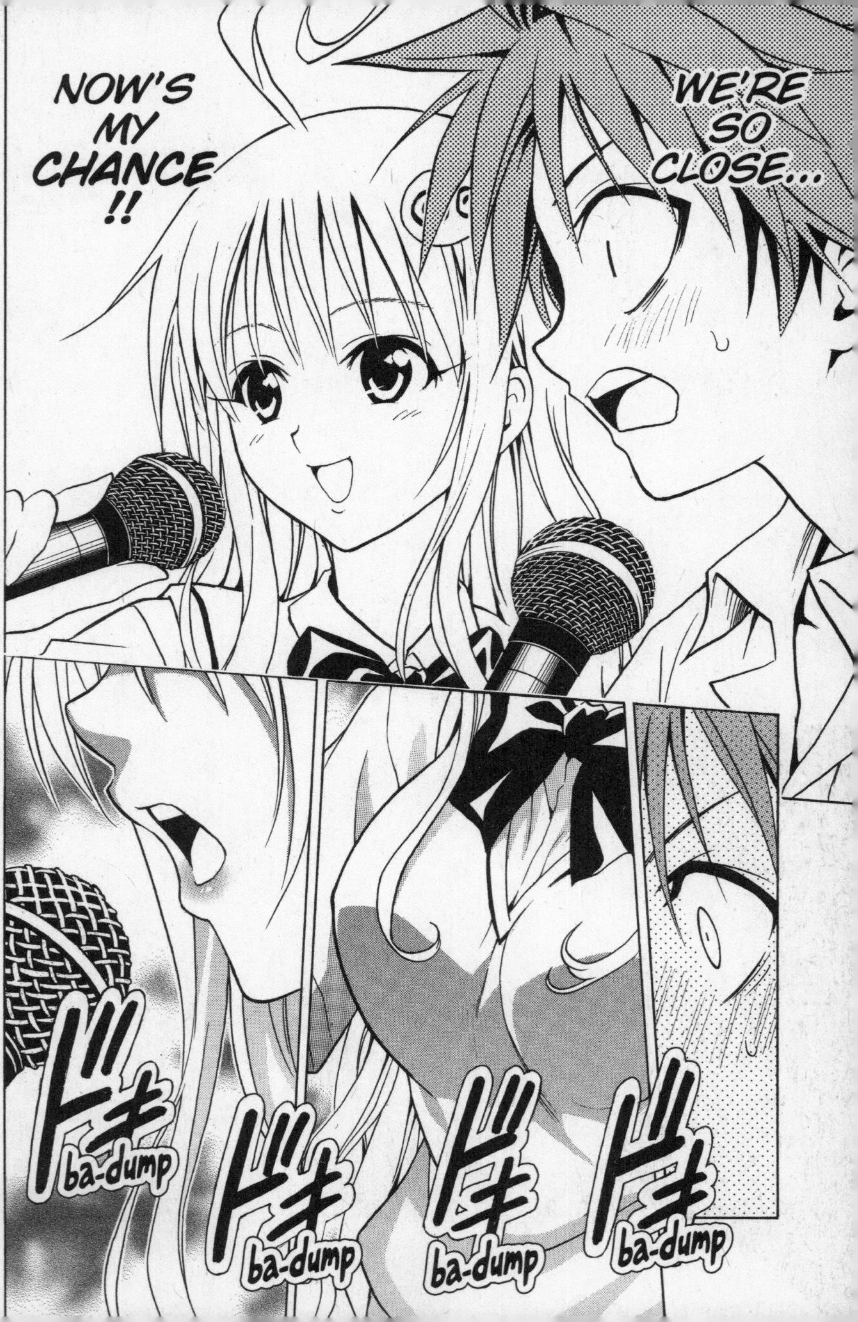
WE'RE SO CLOSE...
NOW'S MY CHANCE !!
ドキ ba-dump
ドキ ba-dump
ドキ ba-dump
ドキ ba-dump

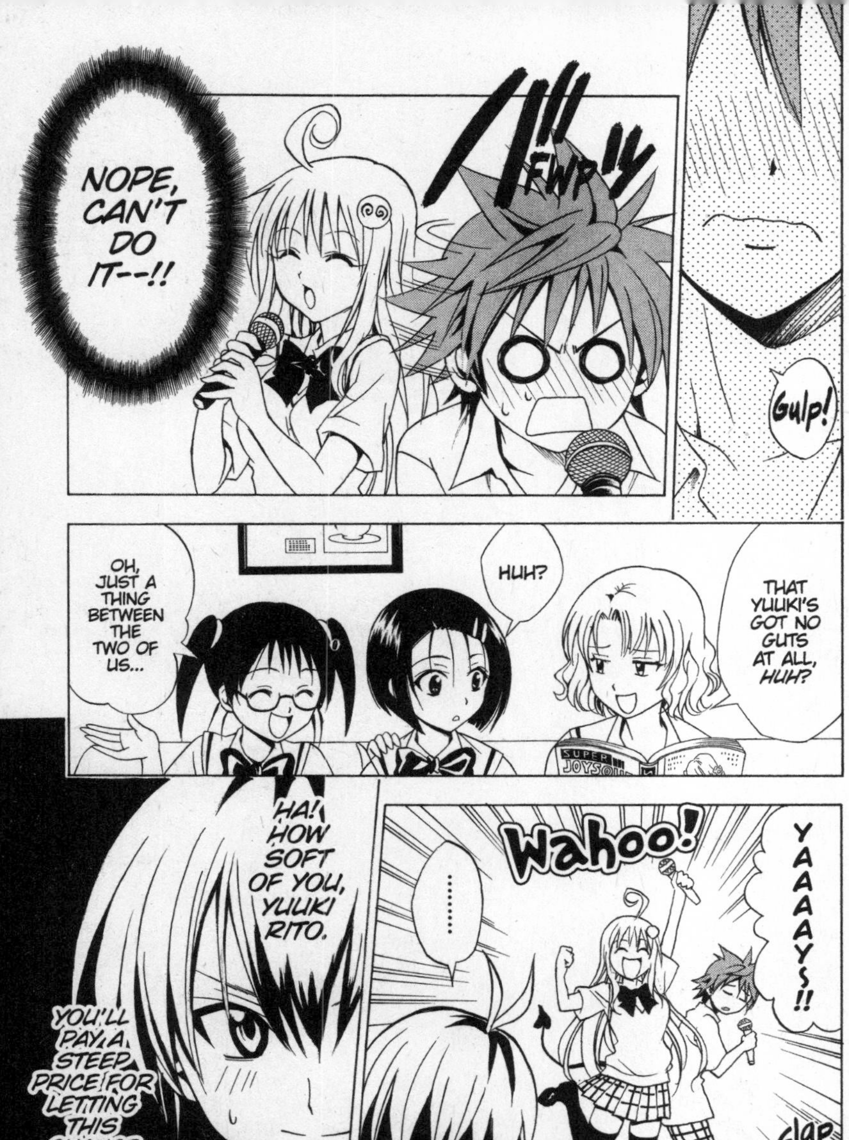
Gulp!
FWP
NOPE, CAN'T DO IT--!!
THAT YUUKI'S GOT NO GUTS AT ALL, HUH?
HUH?
OH, JUST A THING BETWEEN THE TWO OF US...
YAAAAAYS!!
Wahoo!
....
clap
clap
HA! HOW SOFT OF YOU, YUUKI RITO.
YOU'LL PAY A STEEP PRICE FOR LETTING THIS CHANCE SLIP BY...

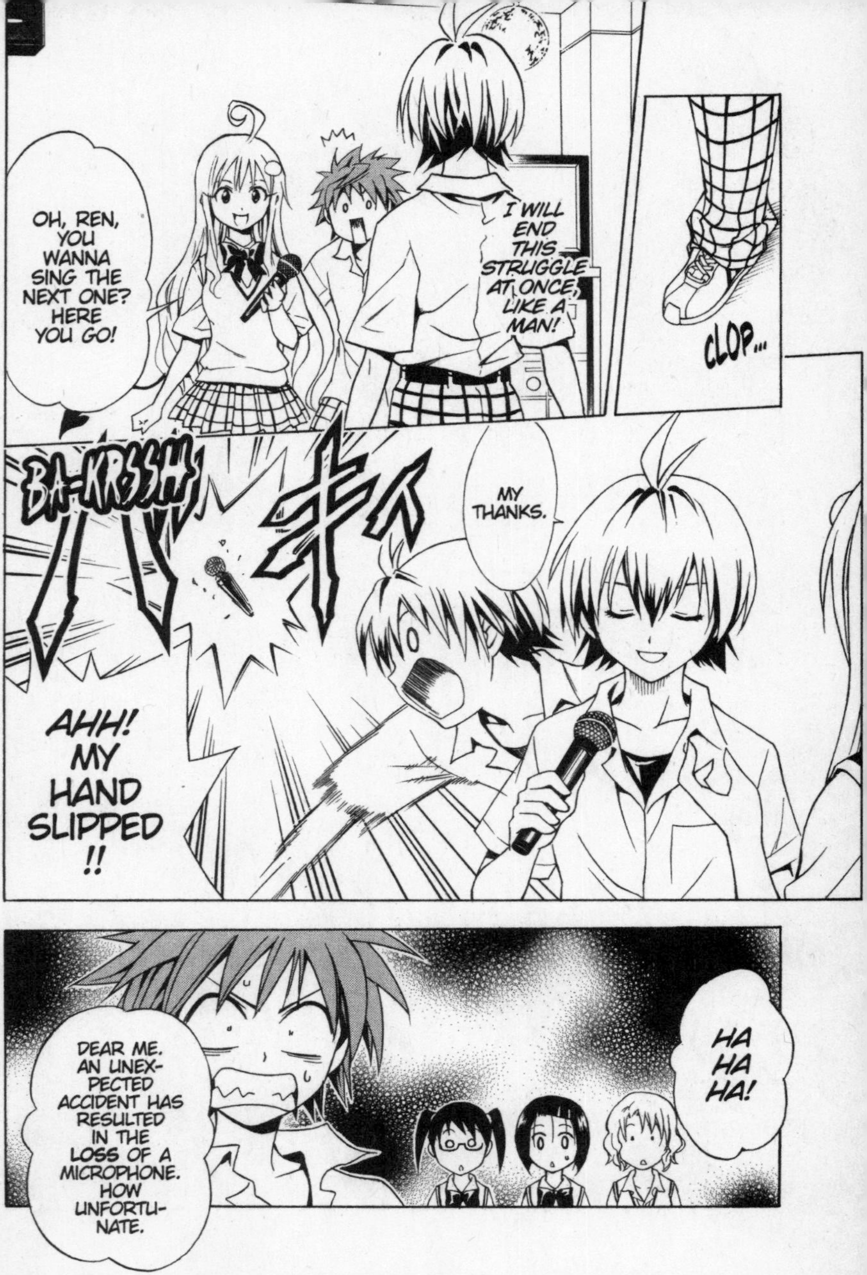
CLOP...
I WILL END THIS STRUGGLE AT ONCE, LIKE A MAN!
OH, REN, YOU WANNA SING THE NEXT ONE? HERE YOU GO!
MY THANKS.
BA-KRSSH
AHH! MY HAND SLIPPED !!
HA HA HA!
DEAR ME. AN UNEX-PECTED ACCIDENT HAS RESULTED IN THE LOSS OF A MICROPHONE. HOW UNFORTU-NATE.

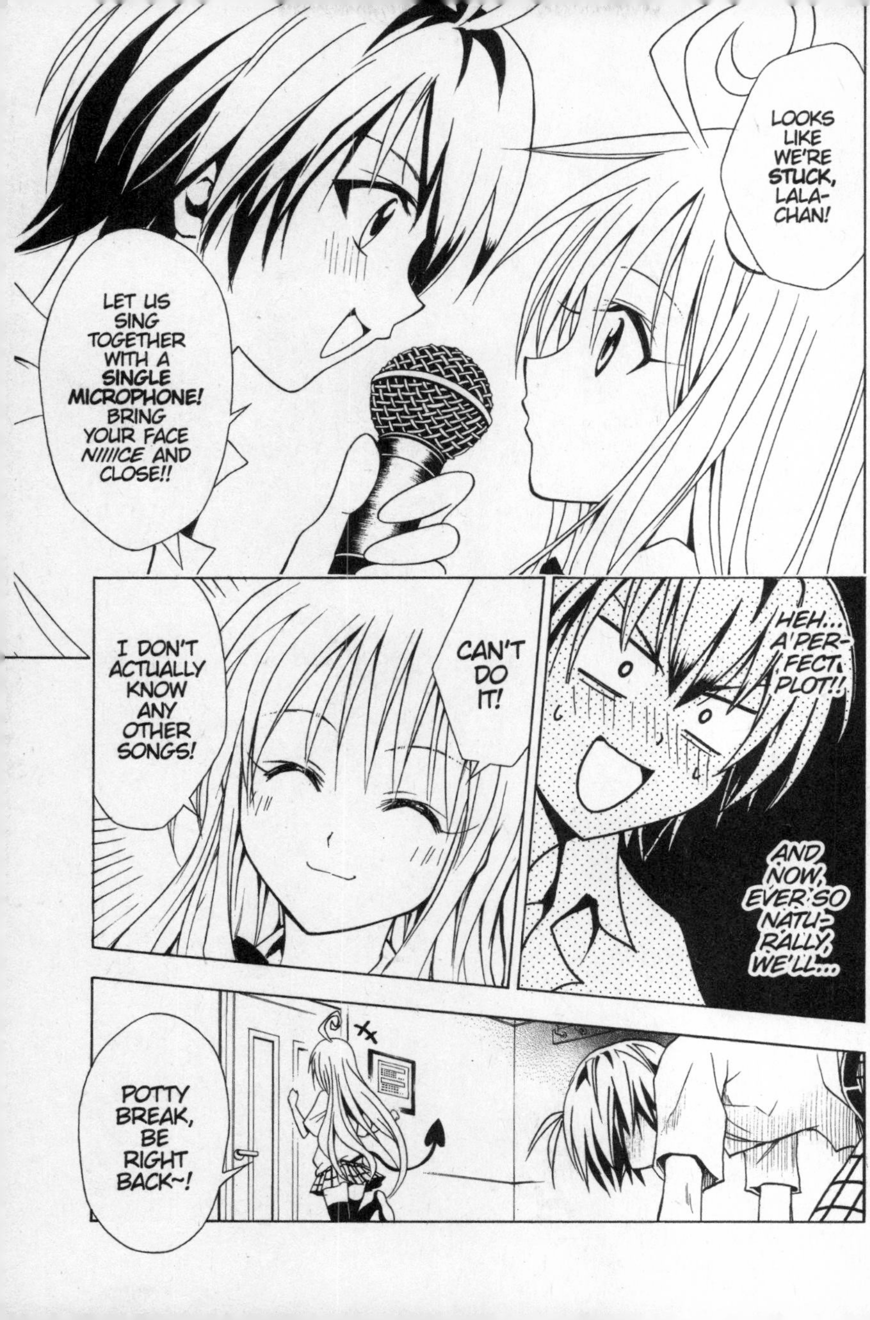
LOOKS LIKE WE'RE STUCK, LALA-CHAN!
LET US SING TOGETHER WITH A SINGLE MICROPHONE! BRING YOUR FACE NIIIICE AND CLOSE!!
HEH... A PERFECT PLOT!!
AND NOW, EVER SO NATURALLY, WE'LL...
CAN'T DO IT!
I DON'T ACTUALLY KNOW ANY OTHER SONGS!
POTTY BREAK, BE RIGHT BACK~!

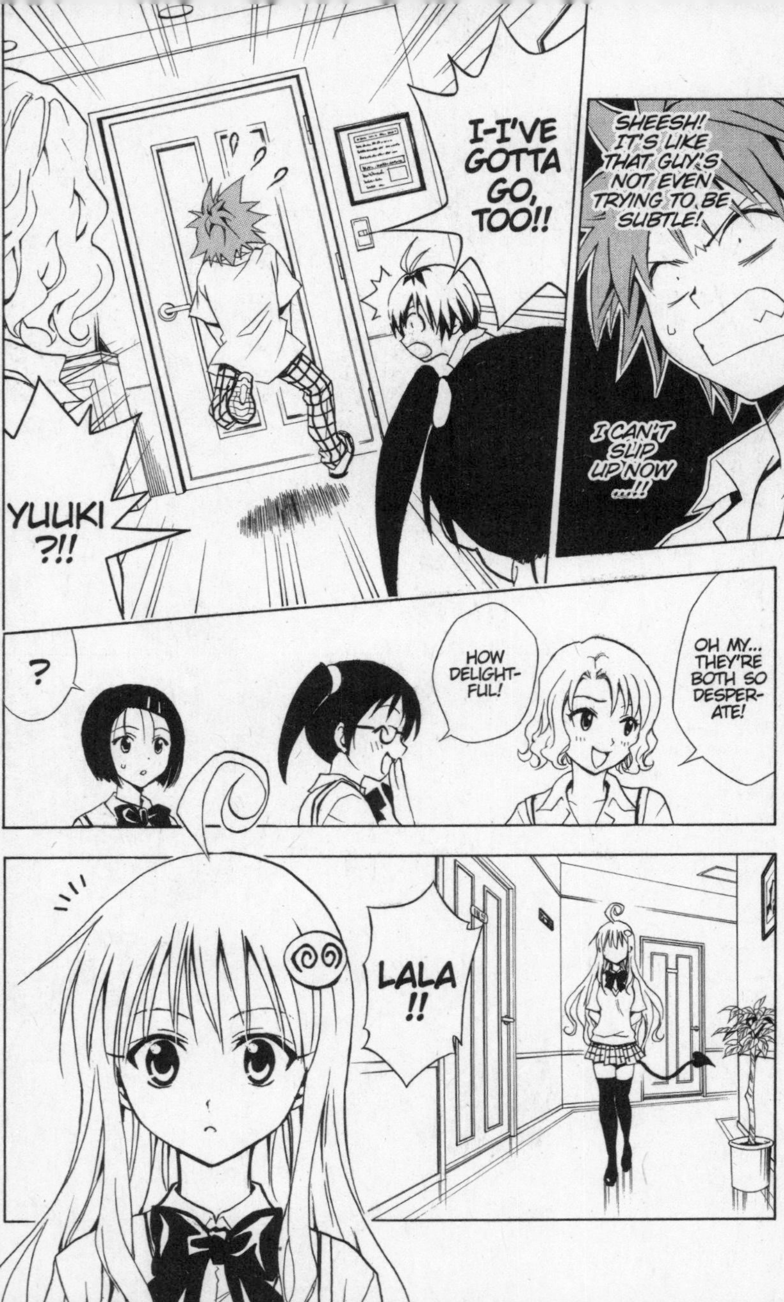
SHEESH! IT'S LIKE THAT GUY'S NOT EVEN TRYING TO BE SUBTLE!
I CAN'T SLIP UP NOW ...!!
I-I'VE GOTTA GO, TOO!!
YUUKI ?!!
OH MY... THEY'RE BOTH SO DESPERATE!
HOW DELIGHTFUL!
?
LALA !!

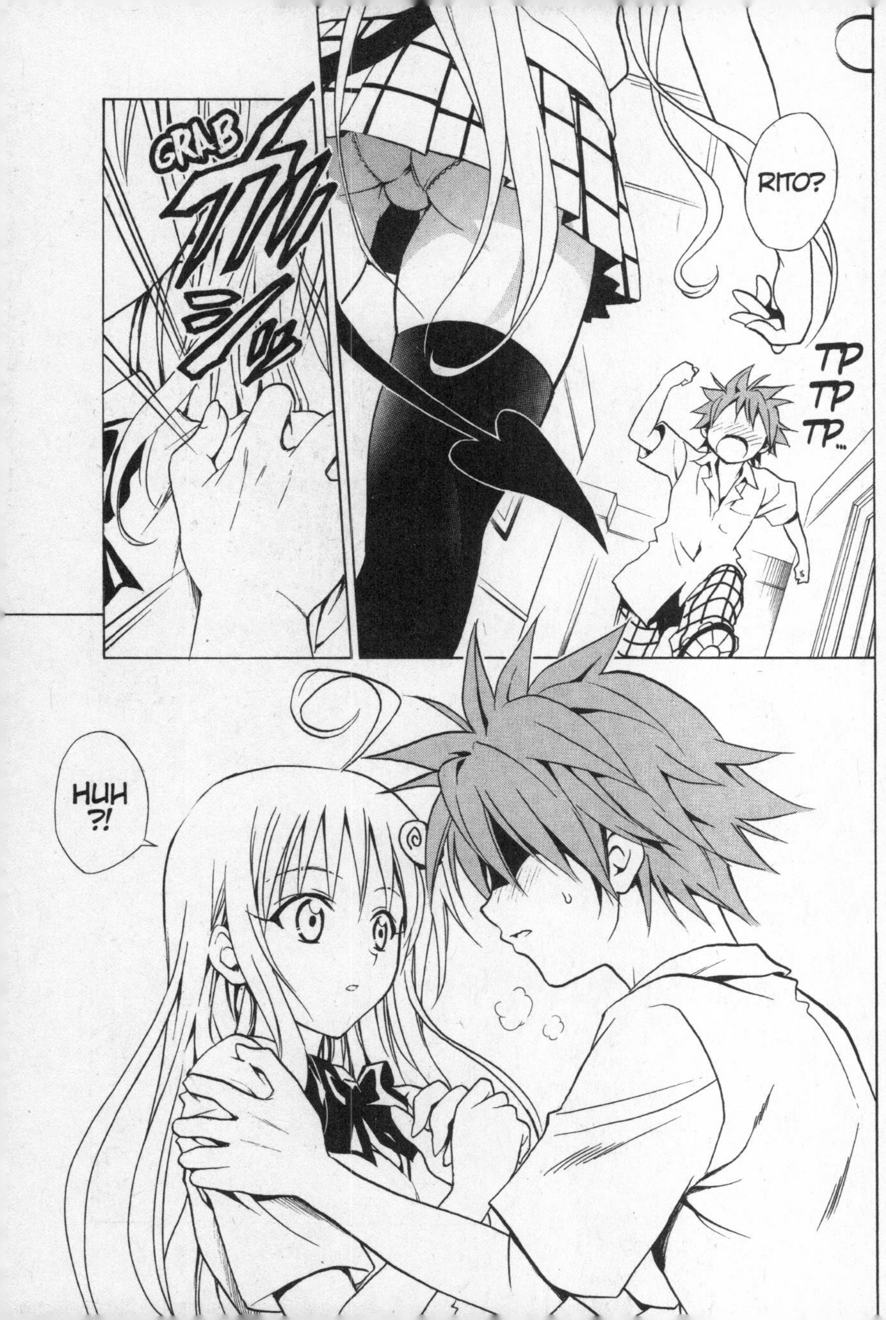
RITO?
TP TP TP...
GRAB
HUH ?!

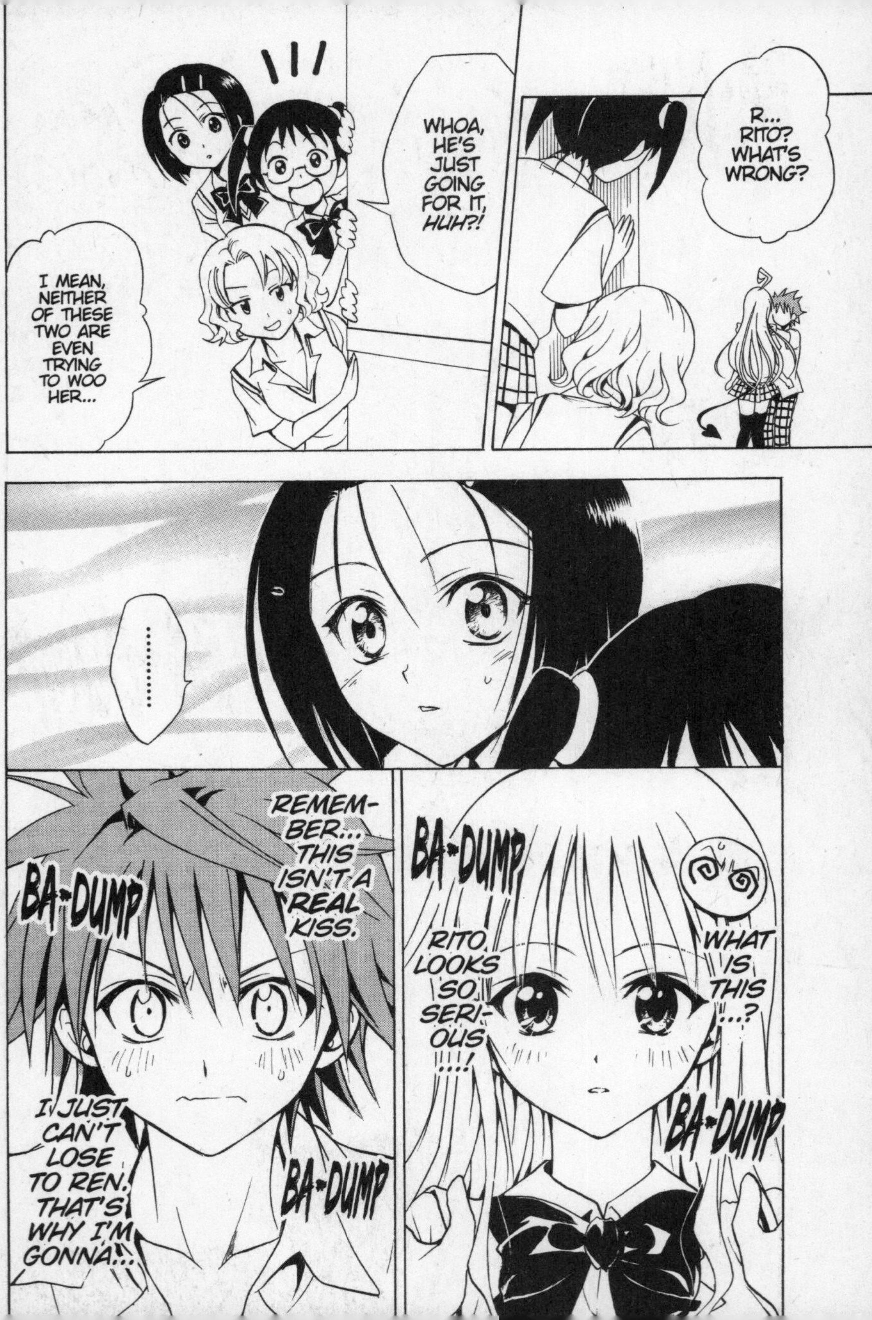
R... RITO? WHAT'S WRONG?
WHOA, HE'S JUST GOING FOR IT, HUH?!
I MEAN, NEITHER OF THESE TWO ARE EVEN TRYING TO WOO HER...
......
BA-DUMP
WHAT IS THIS...?
RITO LOOKS SO SERIOUS...!!
BA-DUMP
REMEMBER... THIS ISN'T A REAL KISS.
BA-DUMP
I JUST CAN'T LOSE TO REN. THAT'S WHY I'M GONNA...!
BA-DUMP

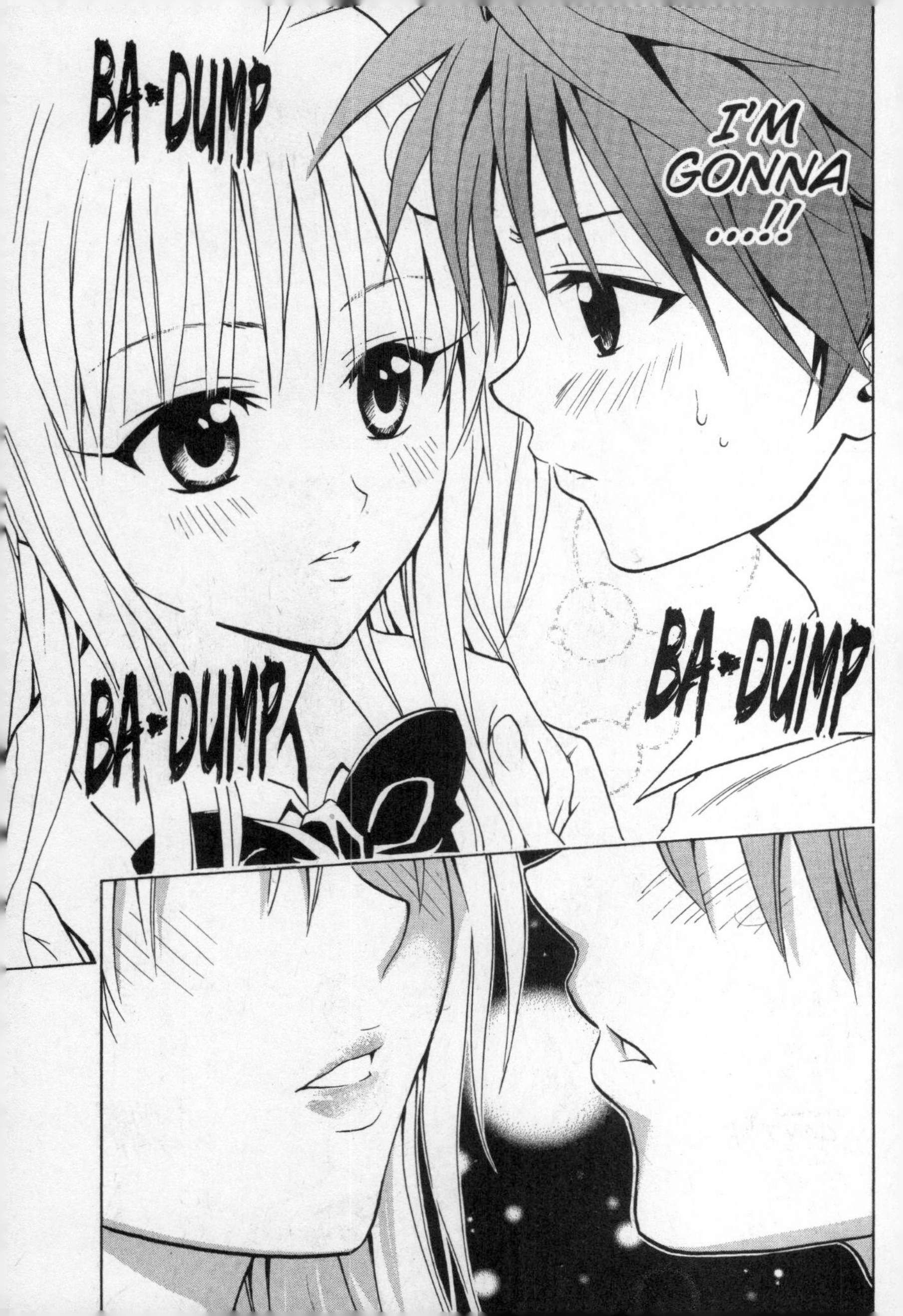
I'M GONNA ...!!
BA-DUMP
BA-DUMP
BA-DUMP

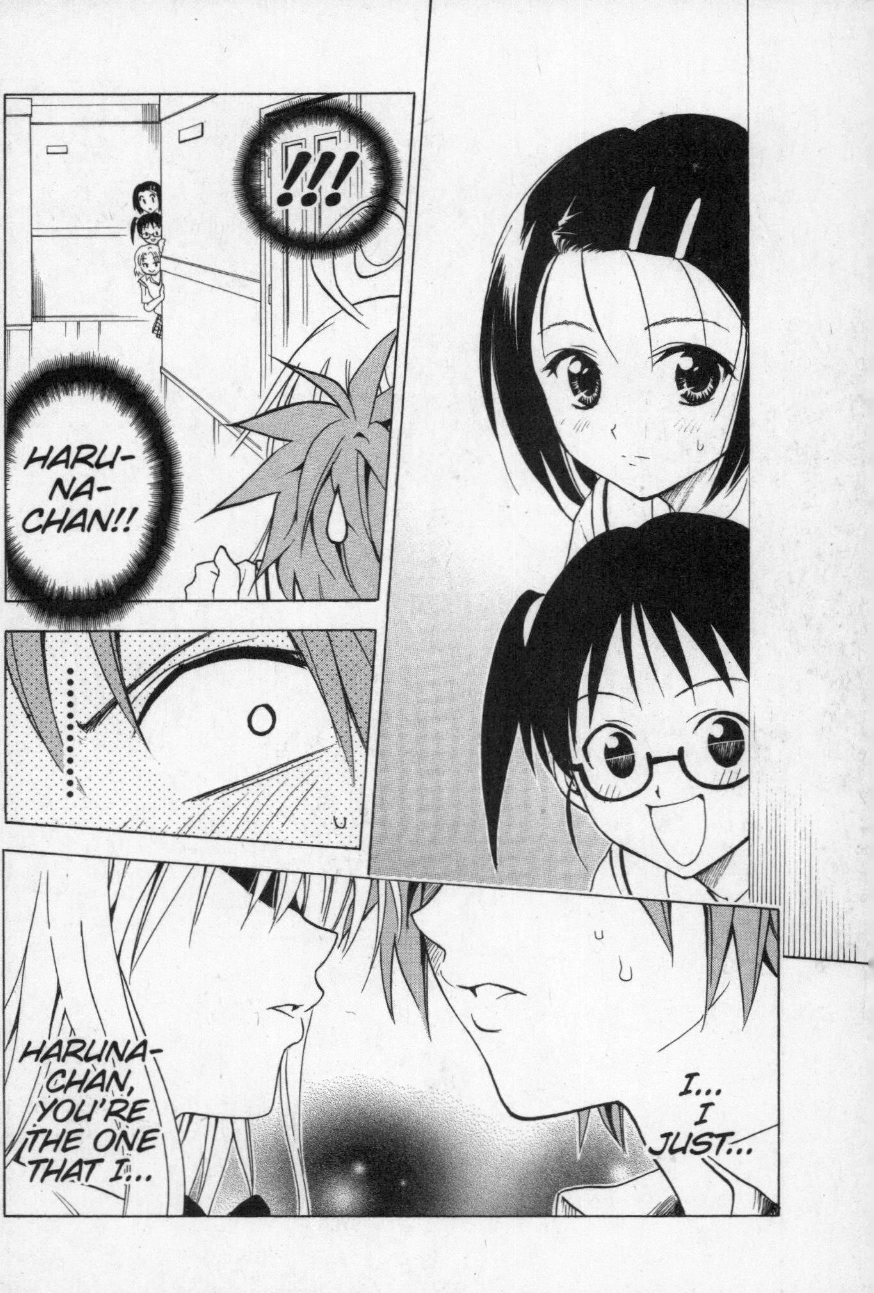
!!!
HARU-NA-CHAN!!
......
I... I JUST...
HARUNA-CHAN, YOU'RE THE ONE THAT I...

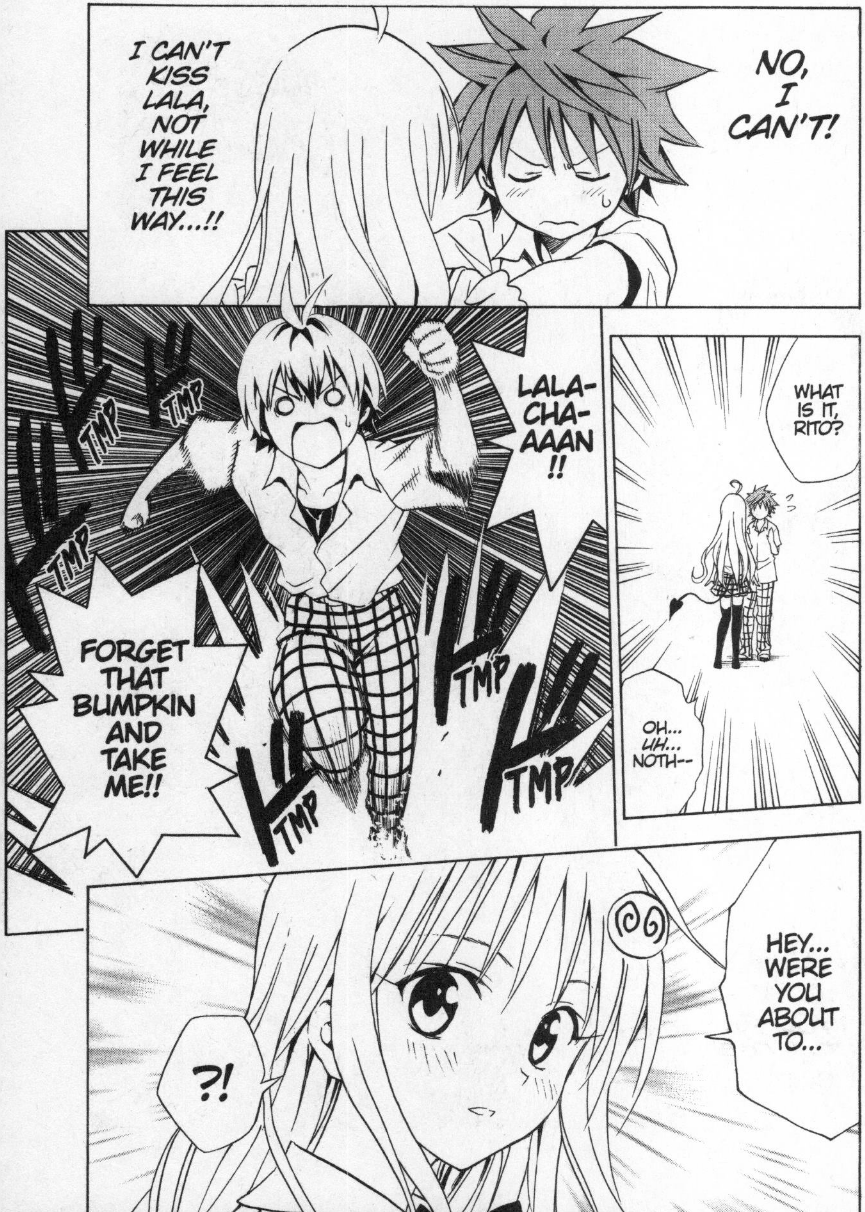
NO, I CAN'T!
I CAN'T KISS LALA, NOT WHILE I FEEL THIS WAY...!!
WHAT IS IT, RITO?
OH... UH... NOTH--
LALA-CHA-AAAN!!
TMP
TMP
TMP
TMP
FORGET THAT BUMPKIN AND TAKE ME!!
TMP
TMP
TMP
HEY... WERE YOU ABOUT TO...
?!

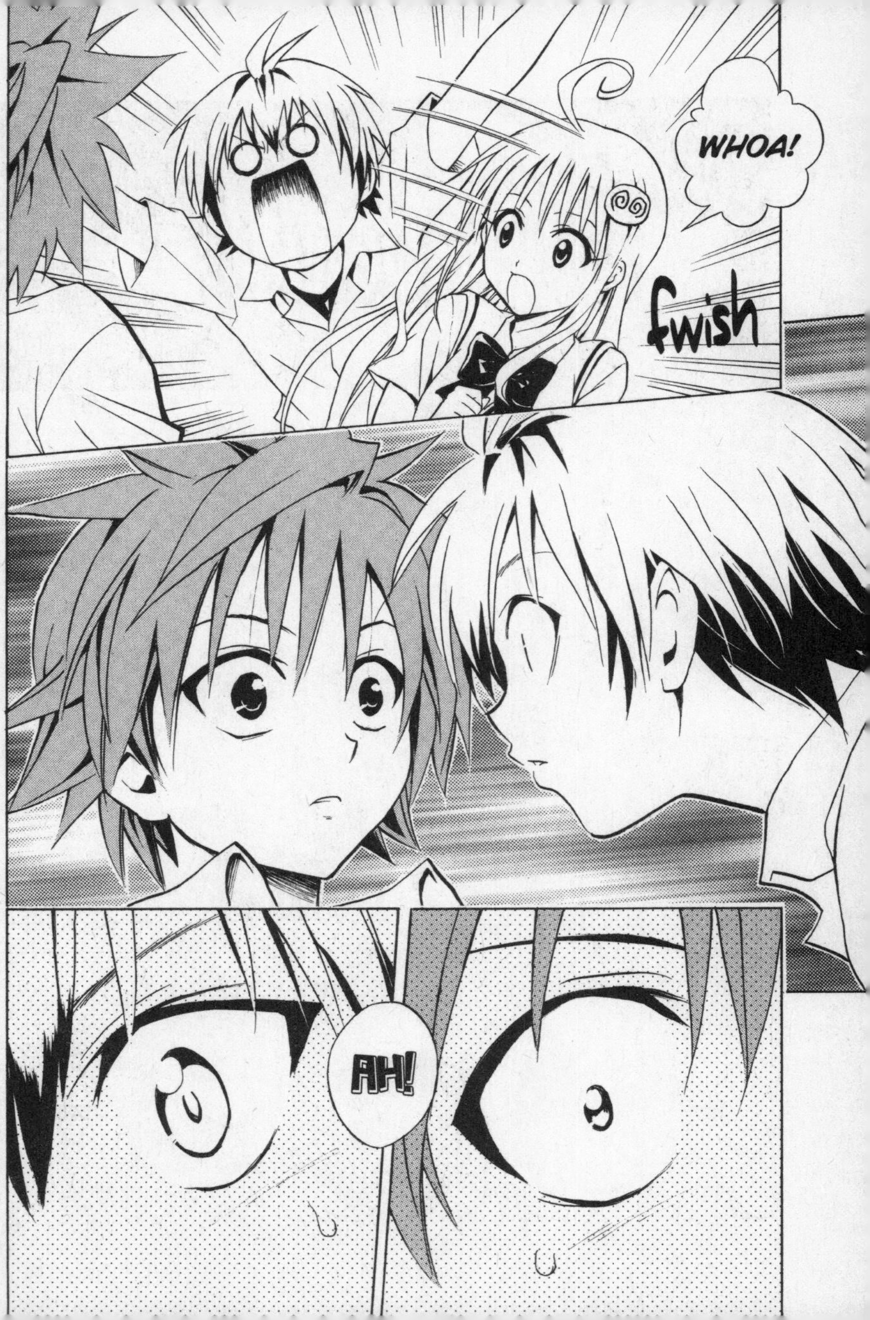
WHOA!
fwish
AH!

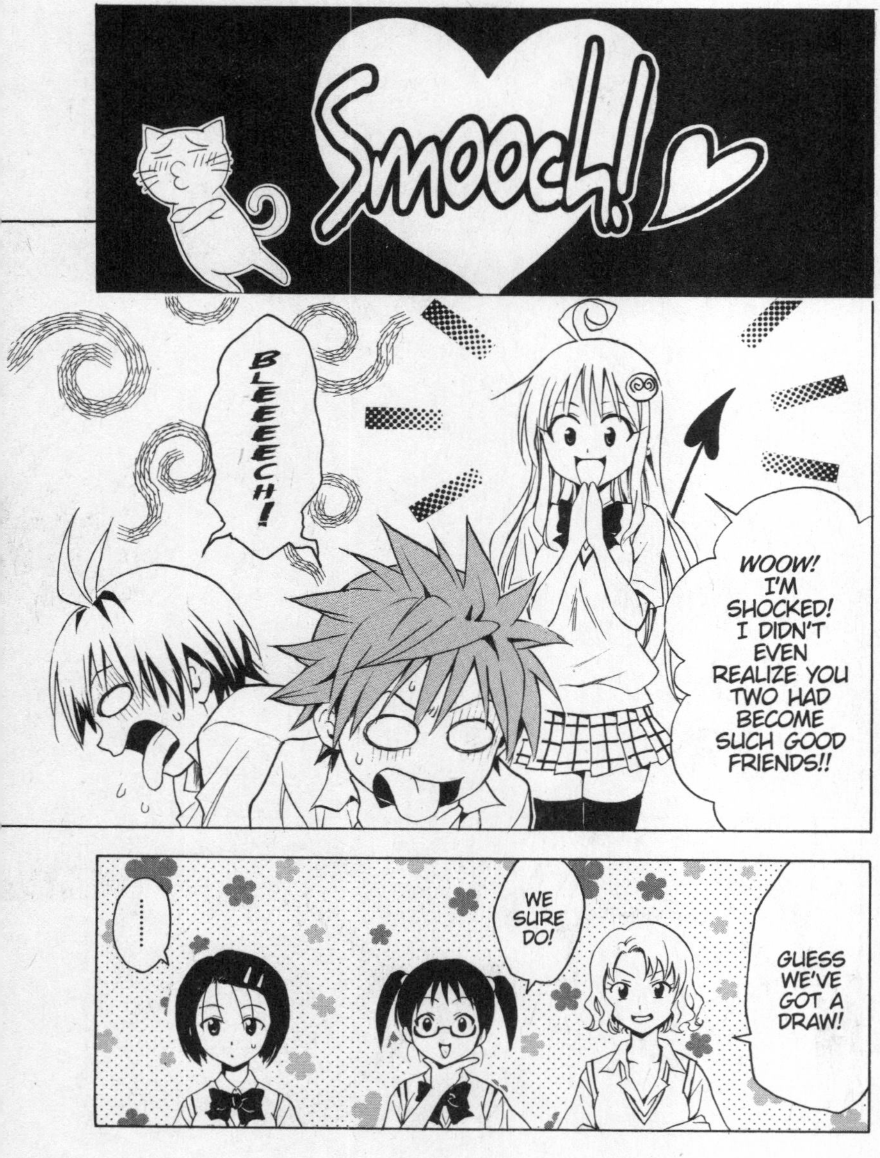
SMOOCH!
WOOW! I'M SHOCKED! I DIDN'T EVEN REALIZE YOU TWO HAD BECOME SUCH GOOD FRIENDS!!
BLEEEEECH!
GUESS WE'VE GOT A DRAW!
WE SURE DO!
....

To LOVE Ru

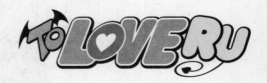

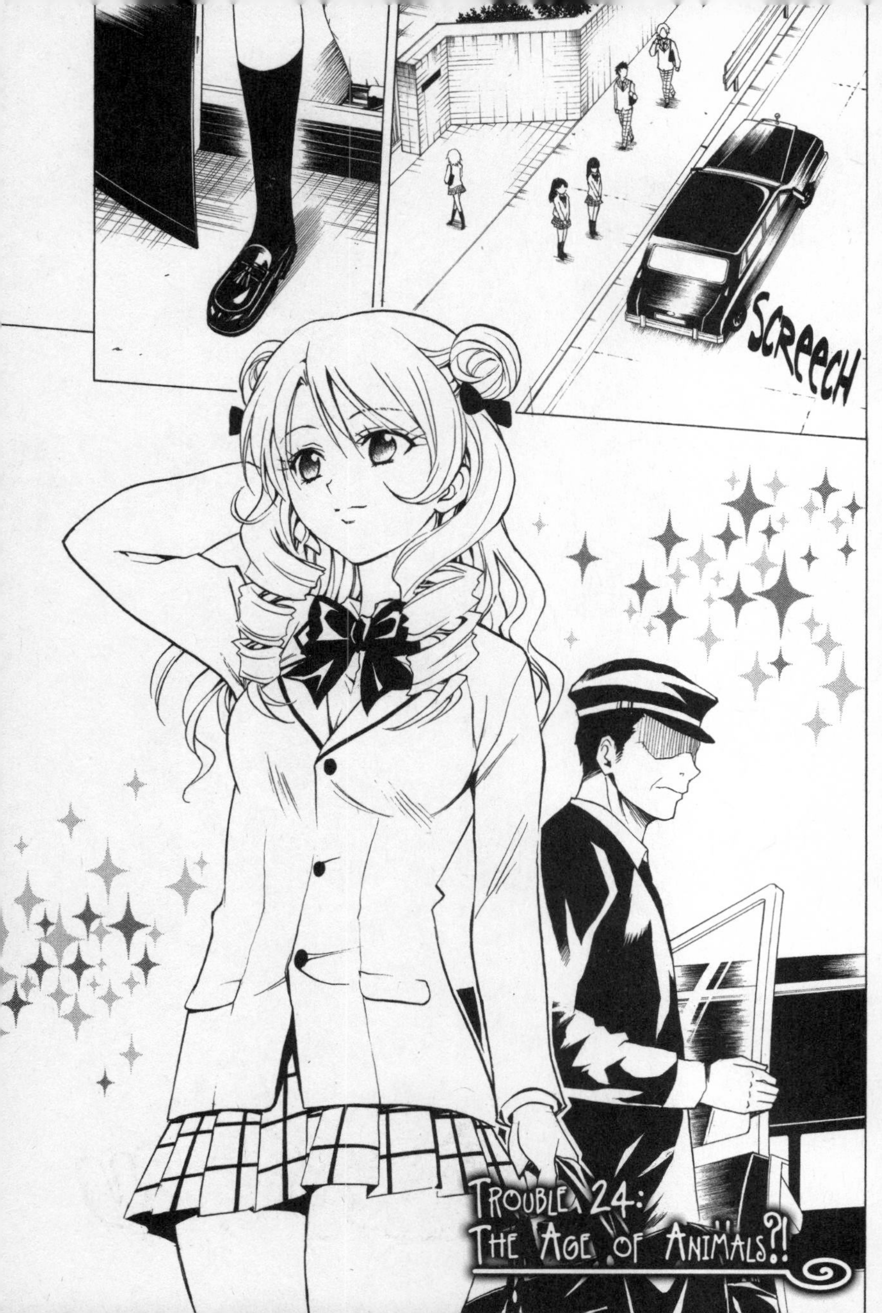
SCREECH
TROUBLE 24:
THE AGE OF ANIMALS?!

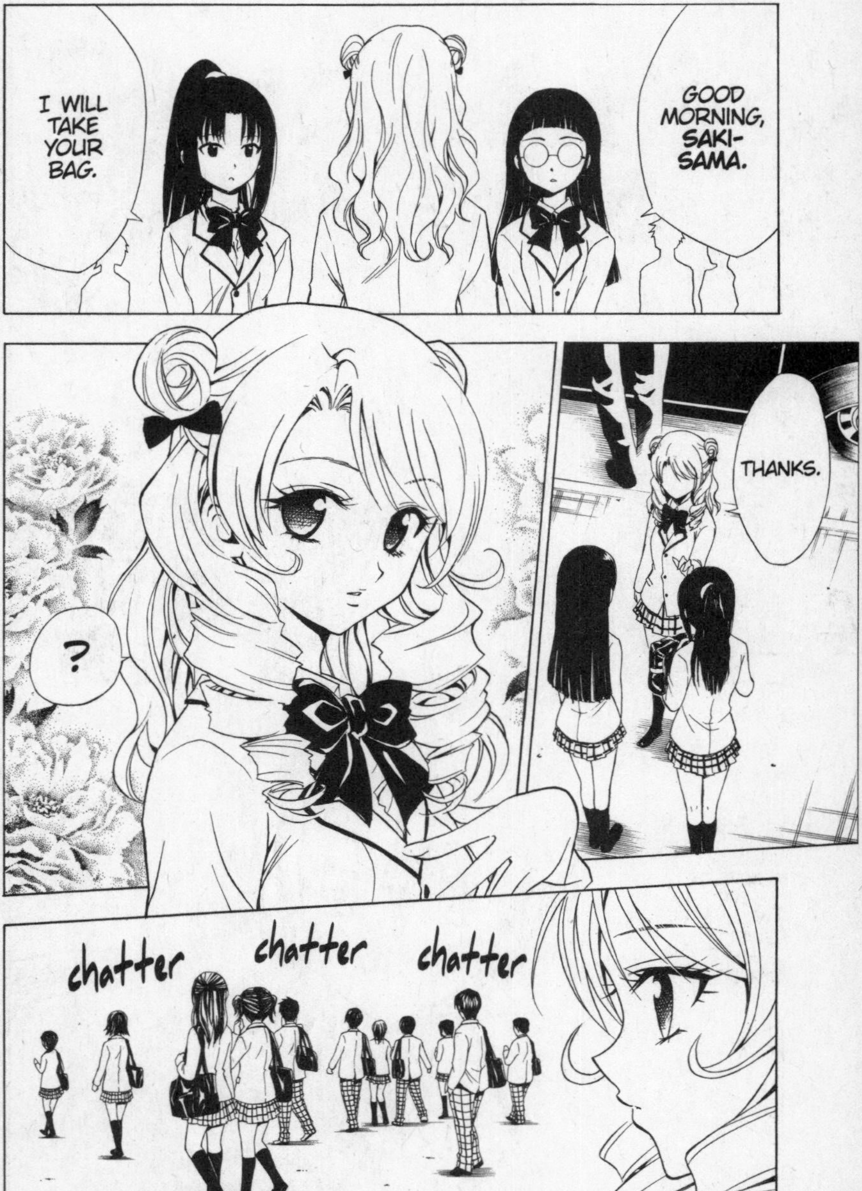
GOOD MORNING, SAKI-SAMA.
I WILL TAKE YOUR BAG.
THANKS.
?
chatter chatter chatter

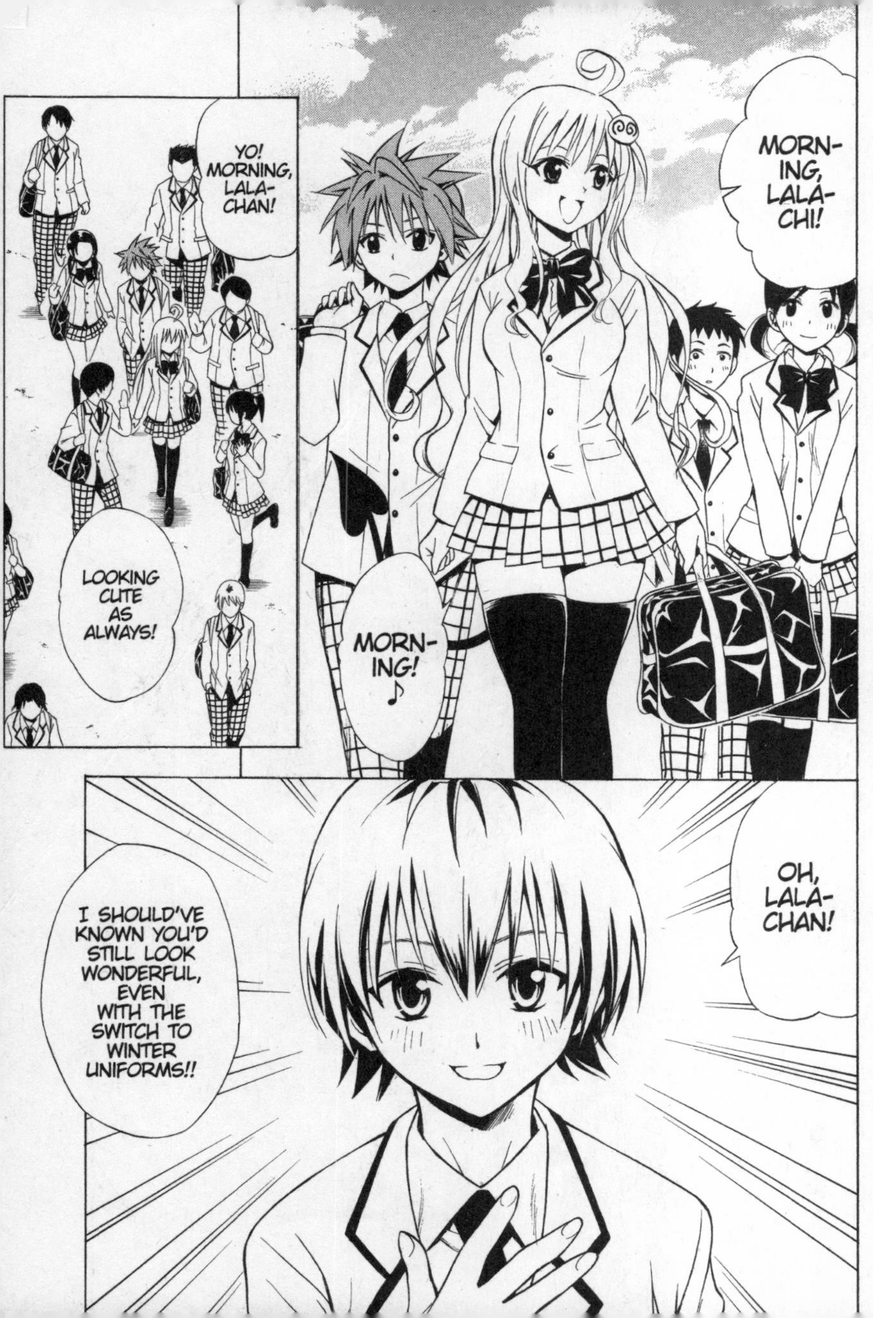
MORNING, LALA-CHI!
MORNING! ♪
YO! MORNING, LALA-CHAN!
LOOKING CUTE AS ALWAYS!
OH, LALA-CHAN!
I SHOULD'VE KNOWN YOU'D STILL LOOK WONDERFUL, EVEN WITH THE SWITCH TO WINTER UNIFORMS!!

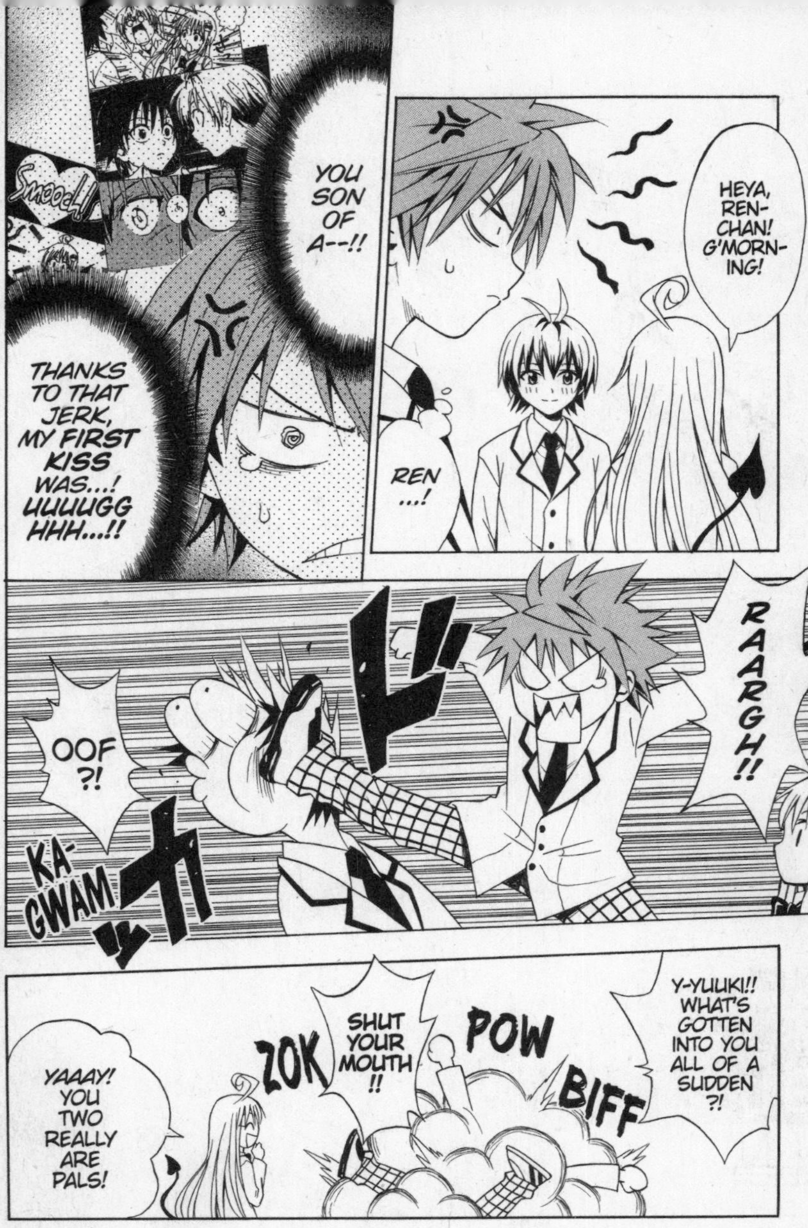
HEYA, REN-CHAN! G'MORNING!
REN...!
YOU SON OF A--!!
THANKS TO THAT JERK, MY FIRST KISS WAS...! UUUUGGHHH...!!
Smooch!
RAARGH!!
OOF?!
KA-GWAM!!
Y-YUUKI!! WHAT'S GOTTEN INTO YOU ALL OF A SUDDEN?!
BIFF
POW
SHUT YOUR MOUTH!!
ZOK
YAAAY! YOU TWO REALLY ARE PALS!

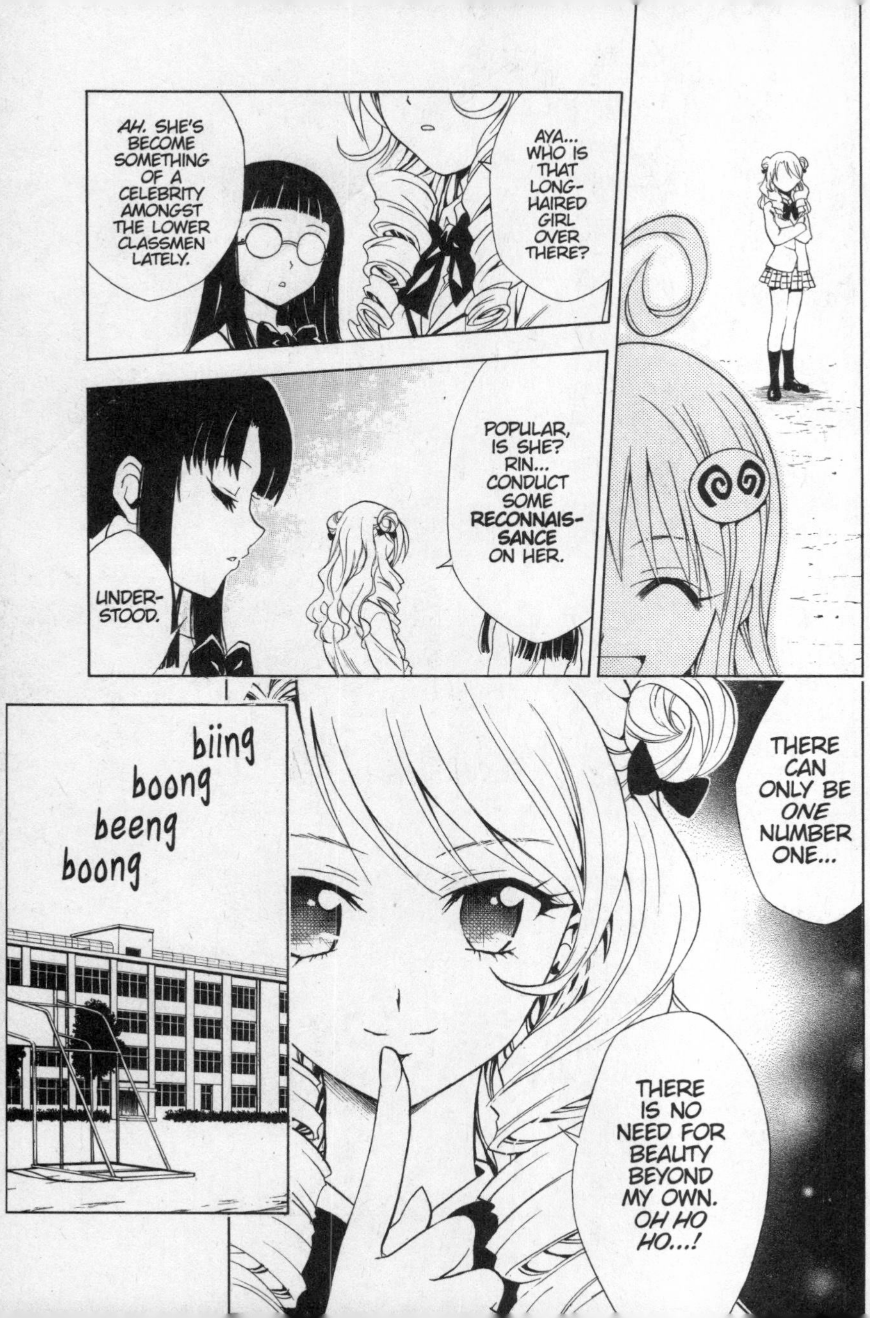
AYA... WHO IS THAT LONG-HAIRED GIRL OVER THERE?
AH. SHE'S BECOME SOMETHING OF A CELEBRITY AMONGST THE LOWER CLASSMEN LATELY.
POPULAR, IS SHE? RIN... CONDUCT SOME RECONNAISSANCE ON HER.
UNDERSTOOD.
THERE CAN ONLY BE *ONE* NUMBER ONE...
THERE IS NO NEED FOR BEAUTY BEYOND MY OWN. *OH HO HO...!*
biing boong beeng boong

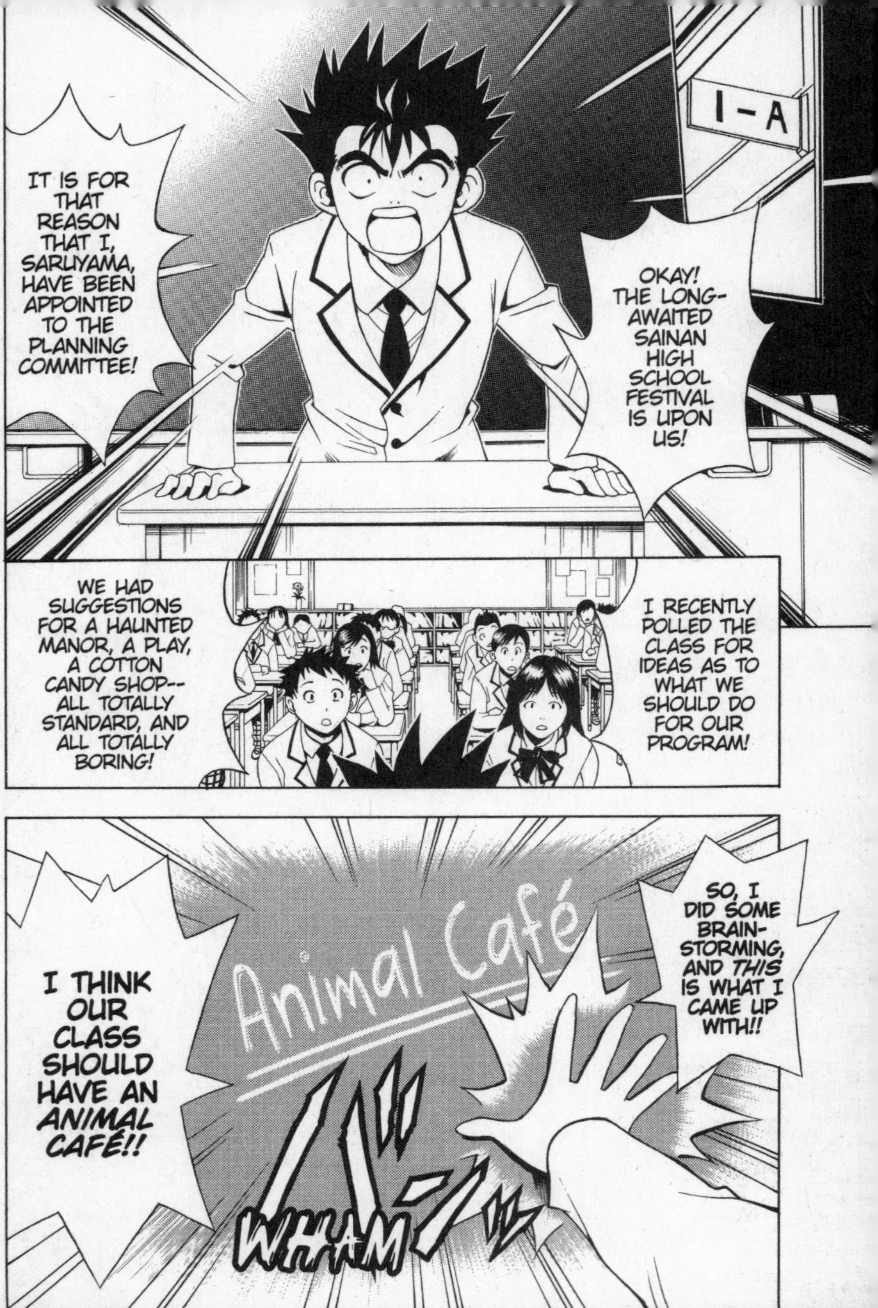
1-A
OKAY! THE LONG-AWAITED SAINAN HIGH SCHOOL FESTIVAL IS UPON US!
IT IS FOR THAT REASON THAT I, SARUYAMA, HAVE BEEN APPOINTED TO THE PLANNING COMMITTEE!
I RECENTLY POLLED THE CLASS FOR IDEAS AS TO WHAT WE SHOULD DO FOR OUR PROGRAM!
WE HAD SUGGESTIONS FOR A HAUNTED MANOR, A PLAY, A COTTON CANDY SHOP--ALL TOTALLY STANDARD, AND ALL TOTALLY BORING!
SO, I DID SOME BRAIN-STORMING, AND *THIS* IS WHAT I CAME UP WITH!!
Animal Café
I THINK OUR CLASS SHOULD HAVE AN *ANIMAL CAFÉ!!*
WHAM

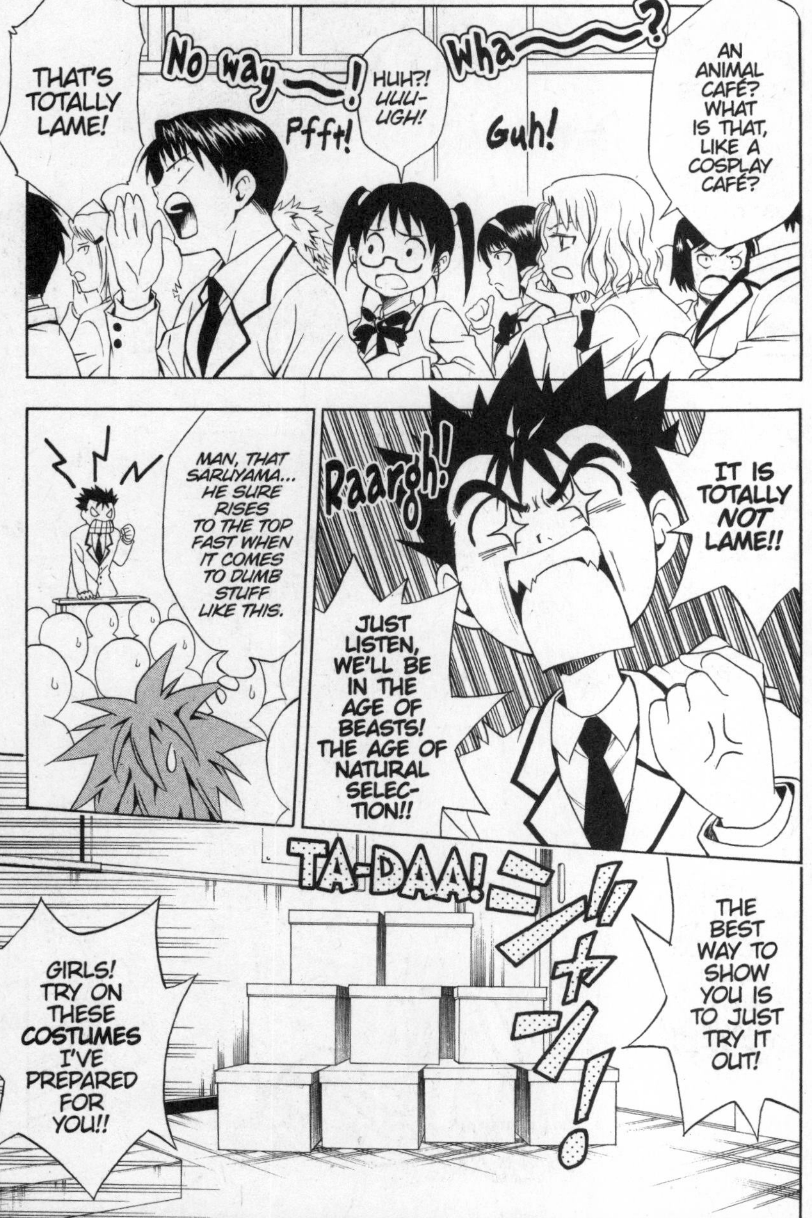

AN ANIMAL CAFÉ? WHAT IS THAT, LIKE A COSPLAY CAFÉ?
Wha——?
Guh!
HUH?! UUU-UGH!
Pfft!
No way——!
THAT'S TOTALLY LAME!
IT IS TOTALLY NOT LAME!!
Raargh!
JUST LISTEN, WE'LL BE IN THE AGE OF BEASTS! THE AGE OF NATURAL SELEC-TION!!
MAN, THAT SARUYAMA... HE SURE RISES TO THE TOP FAST WHEN IT COMES TO DUMB STUFF LIKE THIS.
TA-DAA!
THE BEST WAY TO SHOW YOU IS TO JUST TRY IT OUT!
GIRLS! TRY ON THESE COSTUMES I'VE PREPARED FOR YOU!!

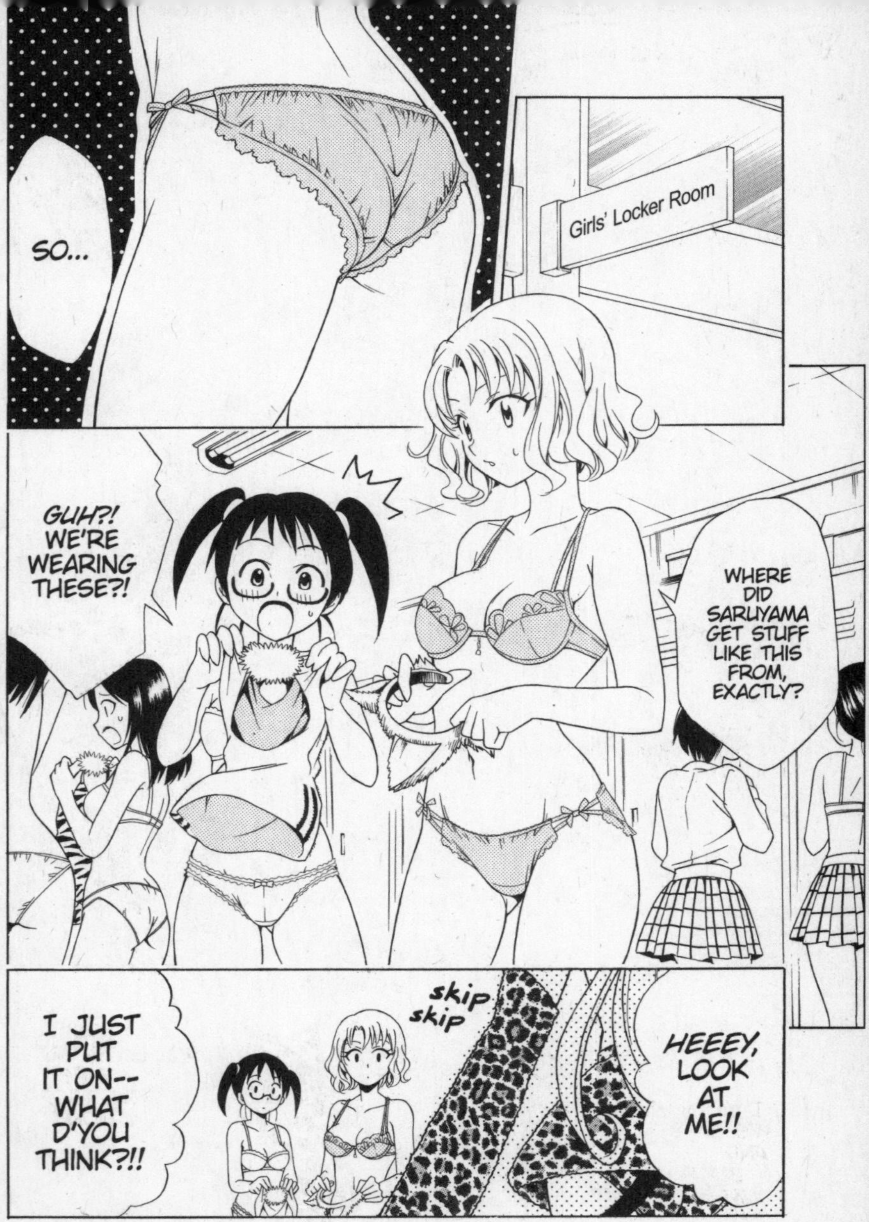
Girls' Locker Room
SO...
WHERE DID SARUYAMA GET STUFF LIKE THIS FROM, EXACTLY?
GUH?! WE'RE WEARING THESE?!
HEEEY, LOOK AT ME!!
skip skip
I JUST PUT IT ON-- WHAT D'YOU THINK?!!

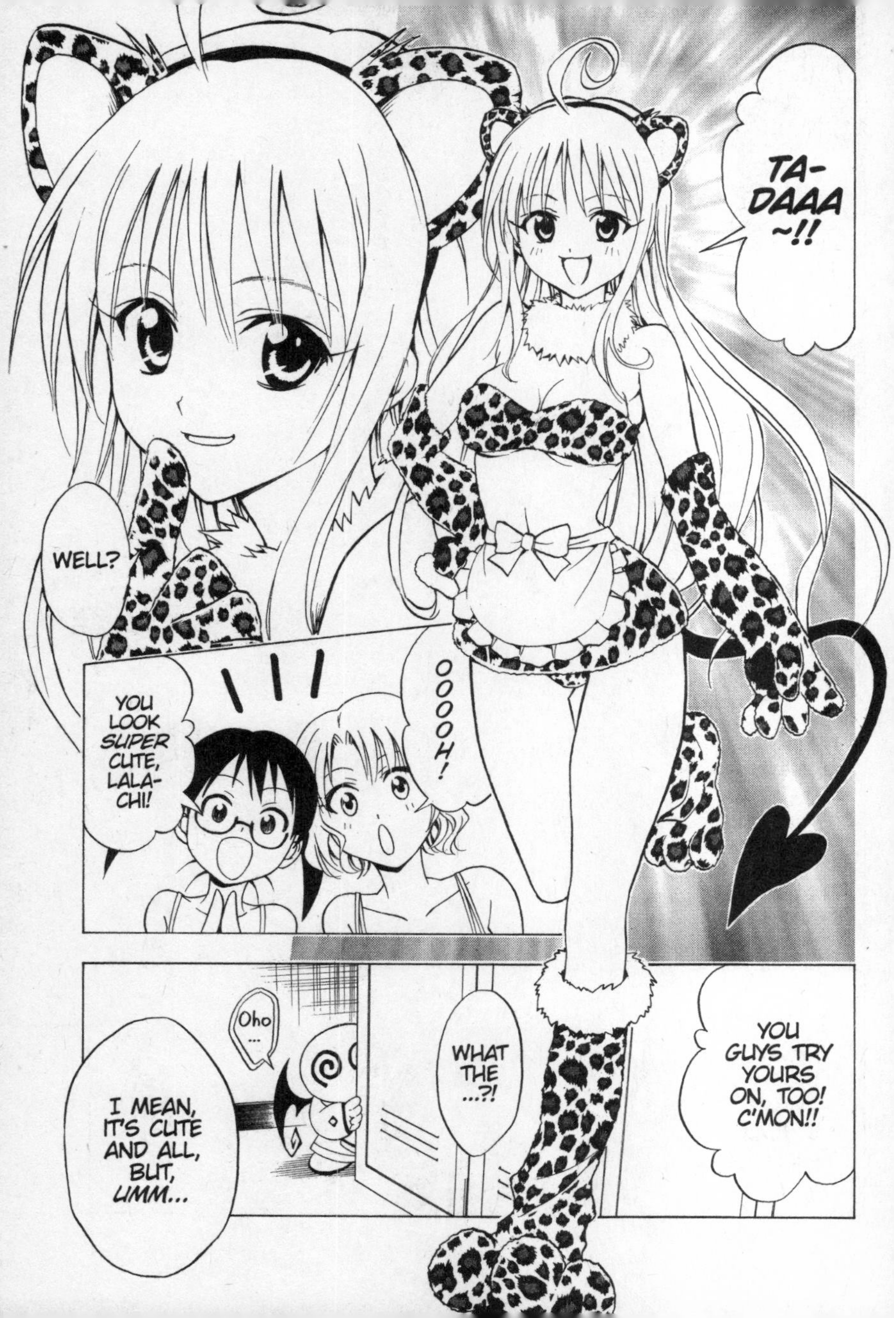
TA-DAAA~!!
WELL?
OOOOOH!
YOU LOOK SUPER CUTE, LALA-CHI!
YOU GUYS TRY YOURS ON, TOO! C'MON!!
WHAT THE ...?!
Oho ...
I MEAN, IT'S CUTE AND ALL, BUT, UMM...

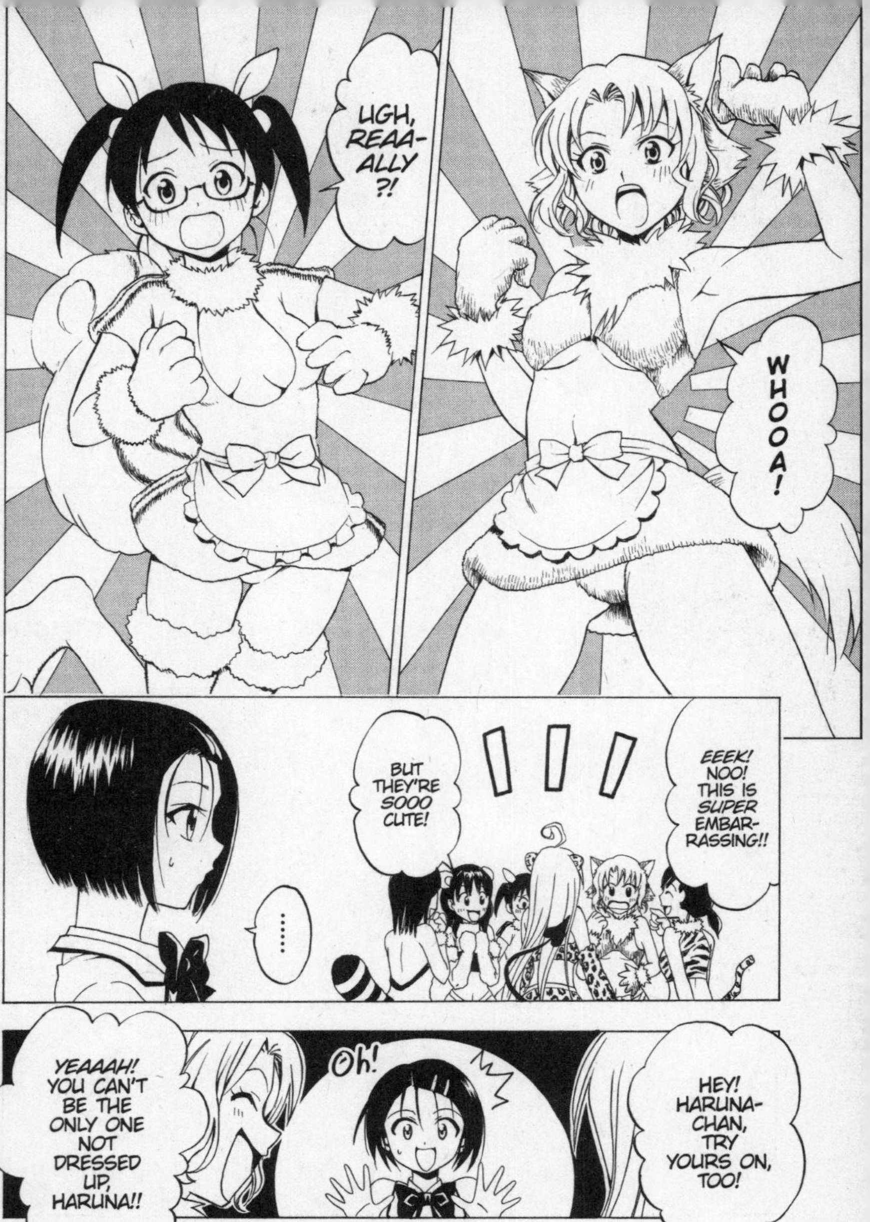
WHOOA!
UGH, REAA-ALLY?!
EEEK! NOO! THIS IS SUPER EMBARRASSING!!
BUT THEY'RE SOOO CUTE!
......
HEY! HARUNA-CHAN, TRY YOURS ON, TOO!
Oh!
YEAAAH! YOU CAN'T BE THE ONLY ONE NOT DRESSED UP, HARUNA!!

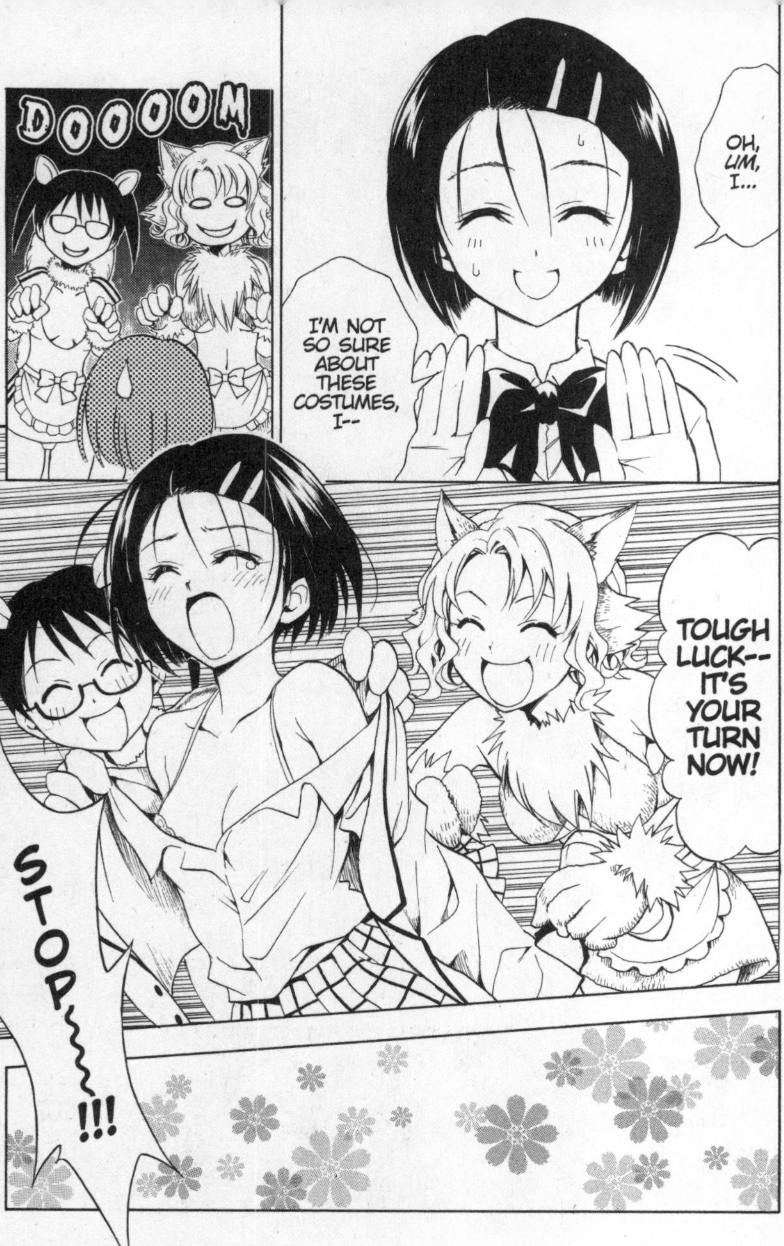
OH, UM, I...
I'M NOT SO SURE ABOUT THESE COSTUMES, I--
DOOOOM
TOUGH LUCK-- IT'S YOUR TURN NOW!
STOP~~~!!!

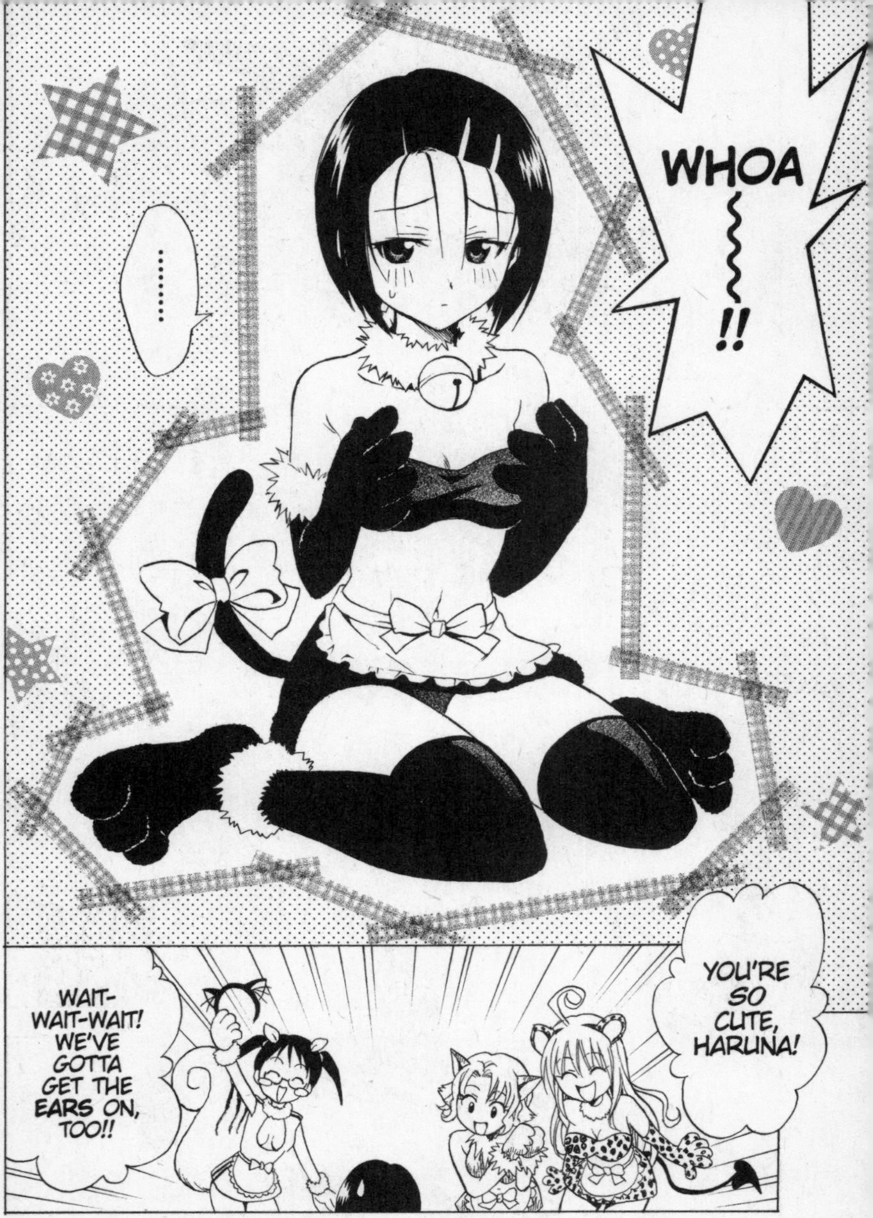
WHOA ~~~!!
......
YOU'RE SO CUTE, HARUNA!
WAIT-WAIT-WAIT! WE'VE GOTTA GET THE EARS ON, TOO!!

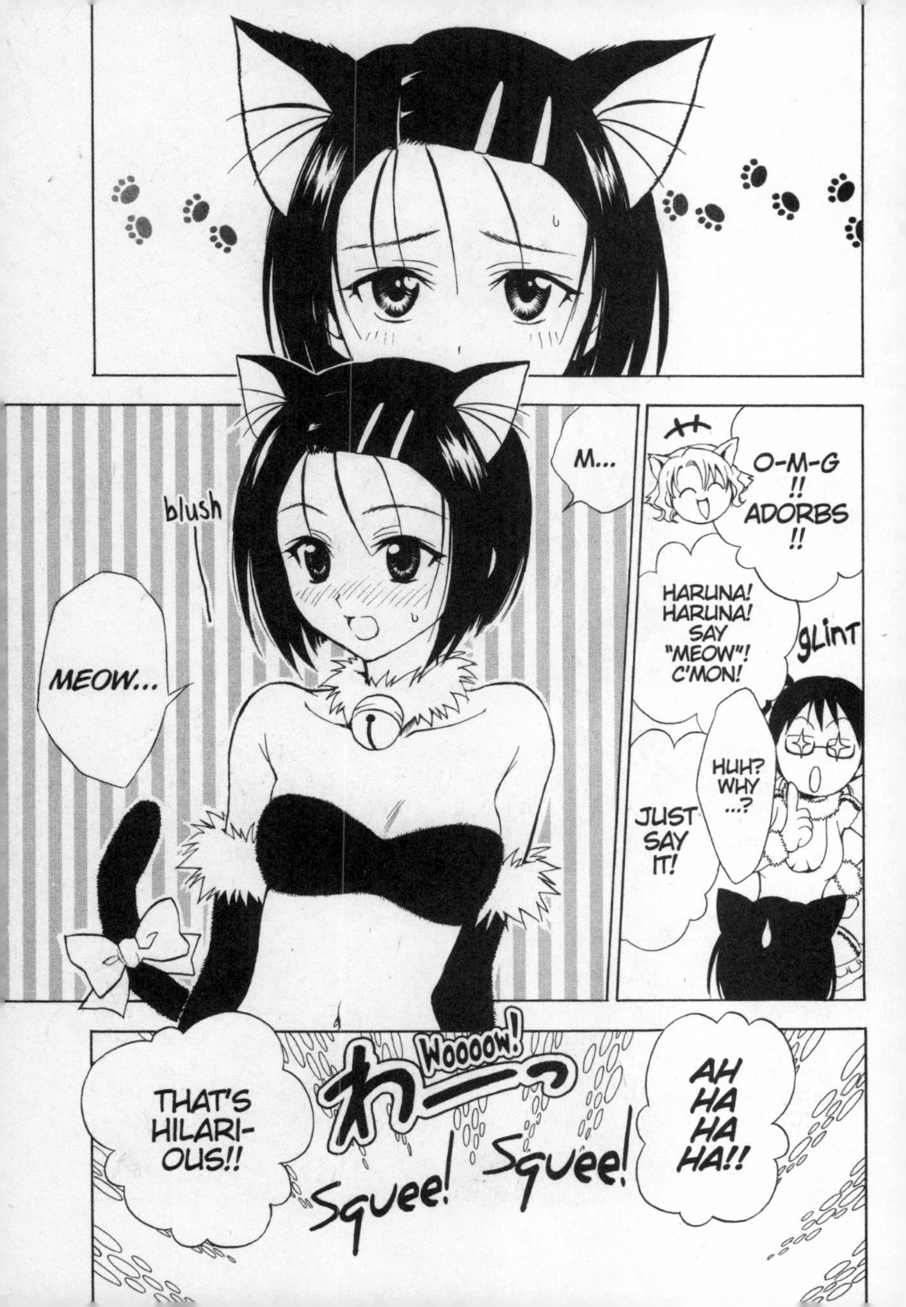
O-M-G!! ADORBS!!
HARUNA! HARUNA! SAY "MEOW"! C'MON!
gLint
HUH? WHY ...?
JUST SAY IT!
M...
blush
MEOW...
AH HA HA HA!!
Squee!
Squee!
わーっ
Woooow!
THAT'S HILARI-OUS!!

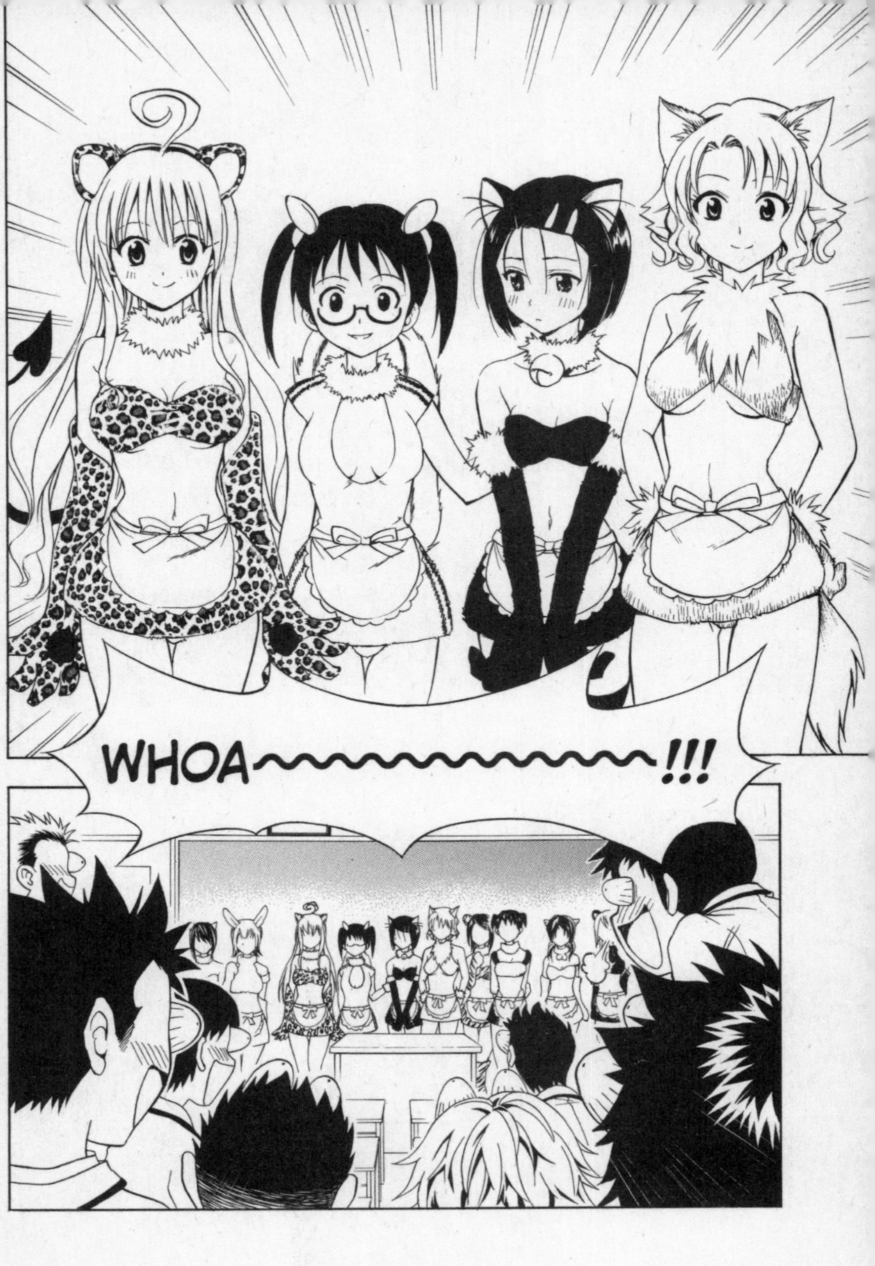
WHOA~~~~~~~~~~~~~~~!!!

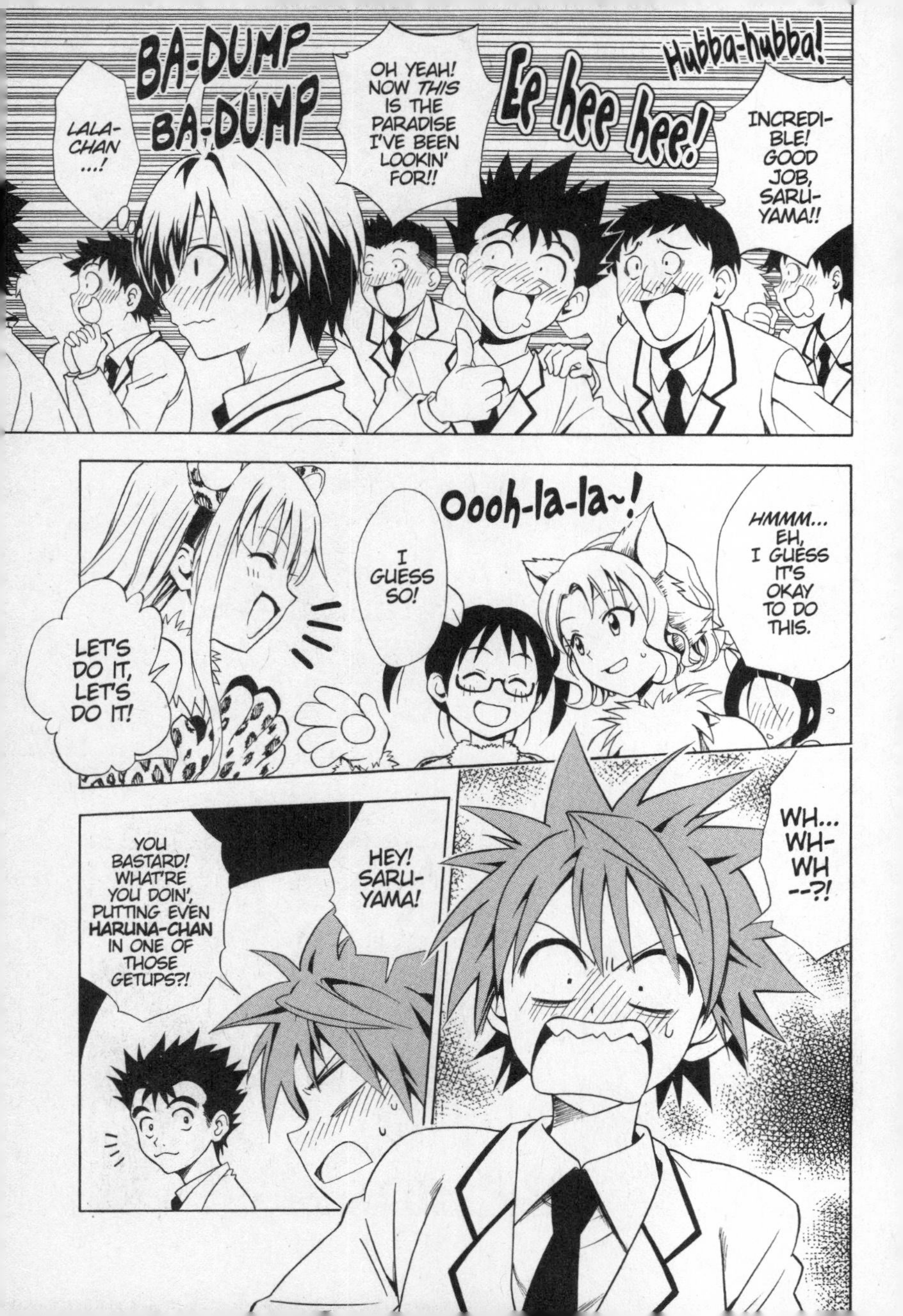
Hubba-hubba!
INCREDIBLE! GOOD JOB, SARUYAMA!!
Ee hee hee!
OH YEAH! NOW THIS IS THE PARADISE I'VE BEEN LOOKIN' FOR!!
BA-DUMP BA-DUMP
LALA-CHAN ...!
HMMM... EH, I GUESS IT'S OKAY TO DO THIS.
Oooh-la-la~!
I GUESS SO!
LET'S DO IT, LET'S DO IT!
WH... WH-WH --?!
HEY! SARUYAMA!
YOU BASTARD! WHAT'RE YOU DOIN', PUTTING EVEN HARUNA-CHAN IN ONE OF THOSE GETUPS?!

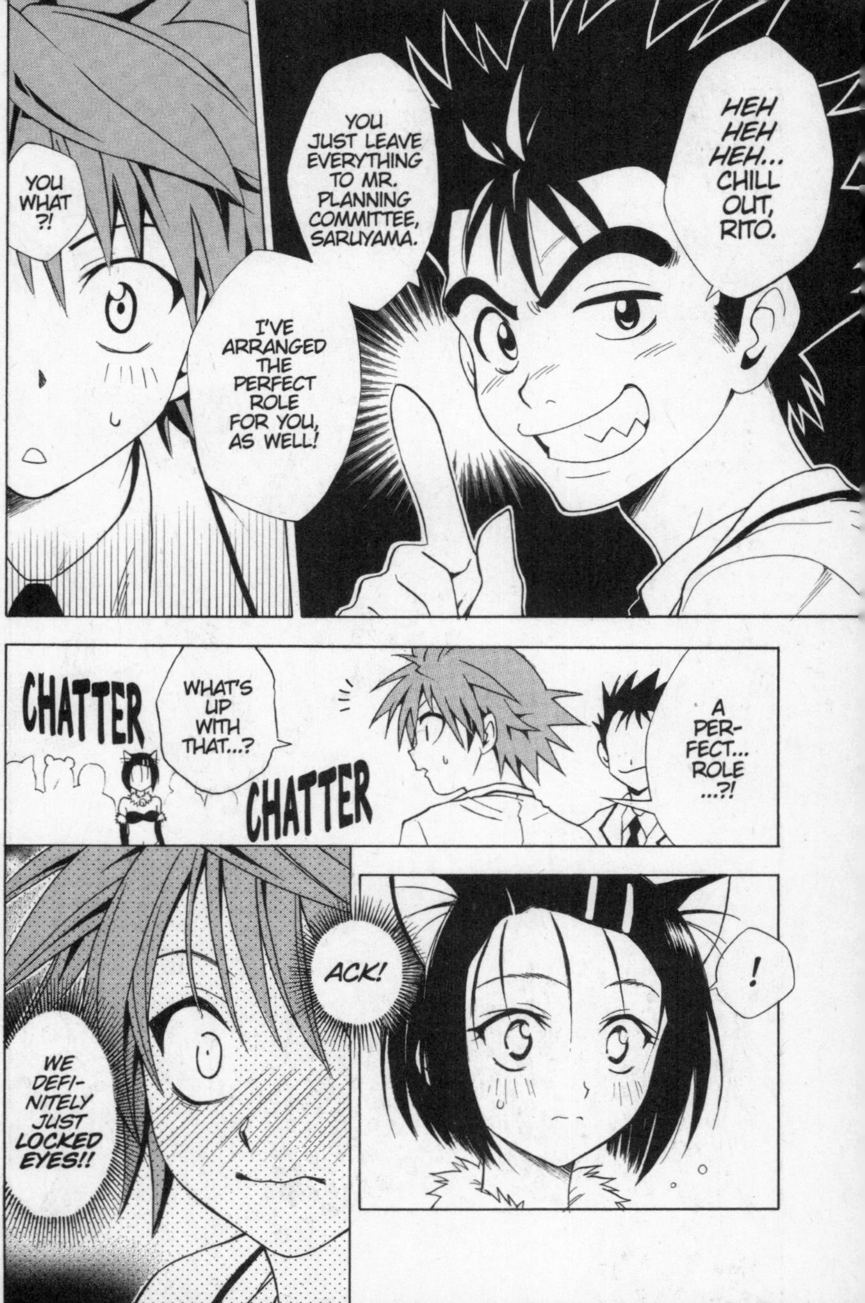
HEH HEH HEH... CHILL OUT, RITO.
YOU JUST LEAVE EVERYTHING TO MR. PLANNING COMMITTEE, SARUYAMA.
I'VE ARRANGED THE PERFECT ROLE FOR YOU, AS WELL!
YOU WHAT ?!
A PER-FECT... ROLE ...?!
CHATTER
WHAT'S UP WITH THAT...?
CHATTER
!
ACK!
WE DEFI-NITELY JUST LOCKED EYES!!

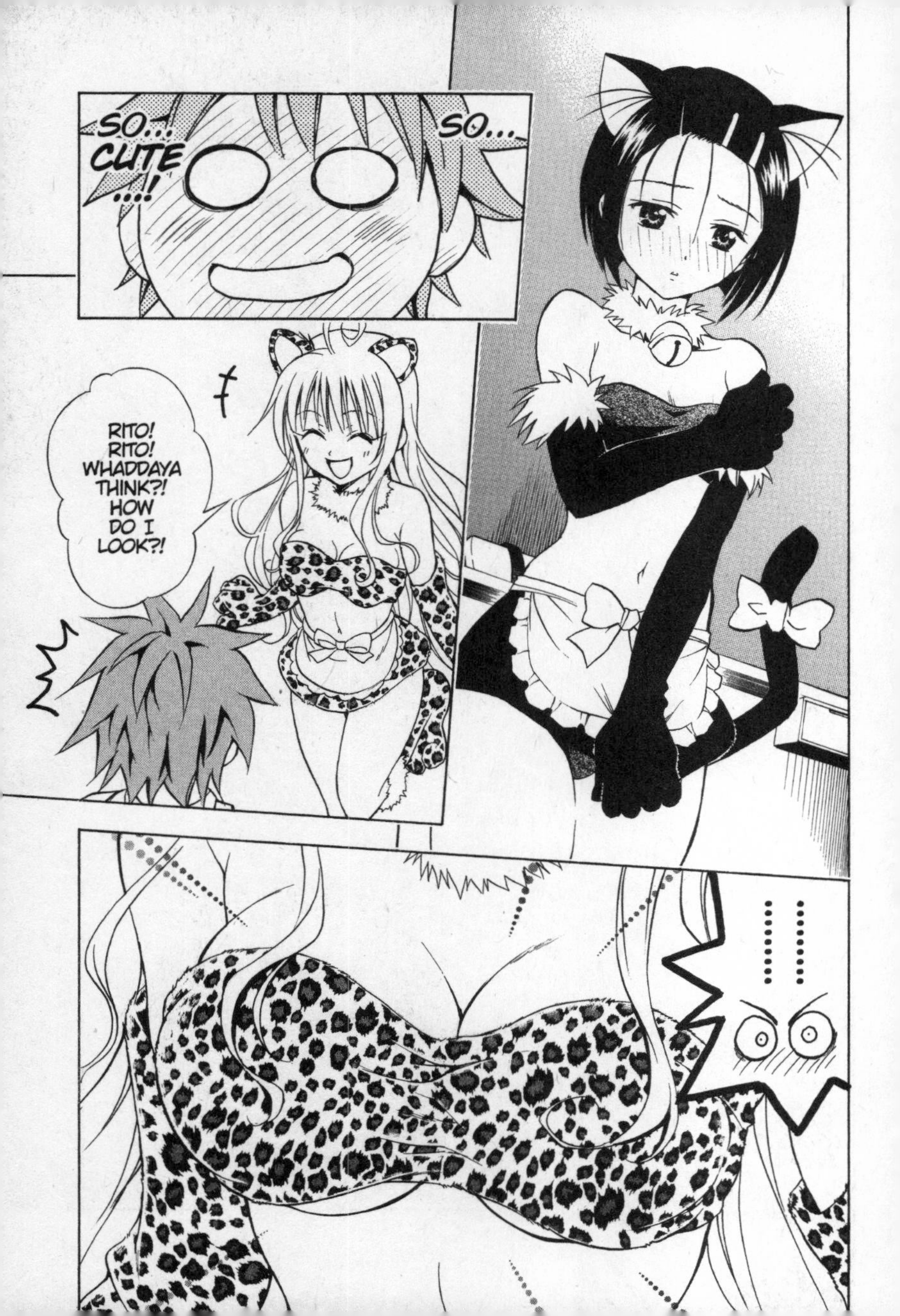
SO...
SO... CUTE...!!
RITO! RITO! WHADDAYA THINK?! HOW DO I LOOK?!

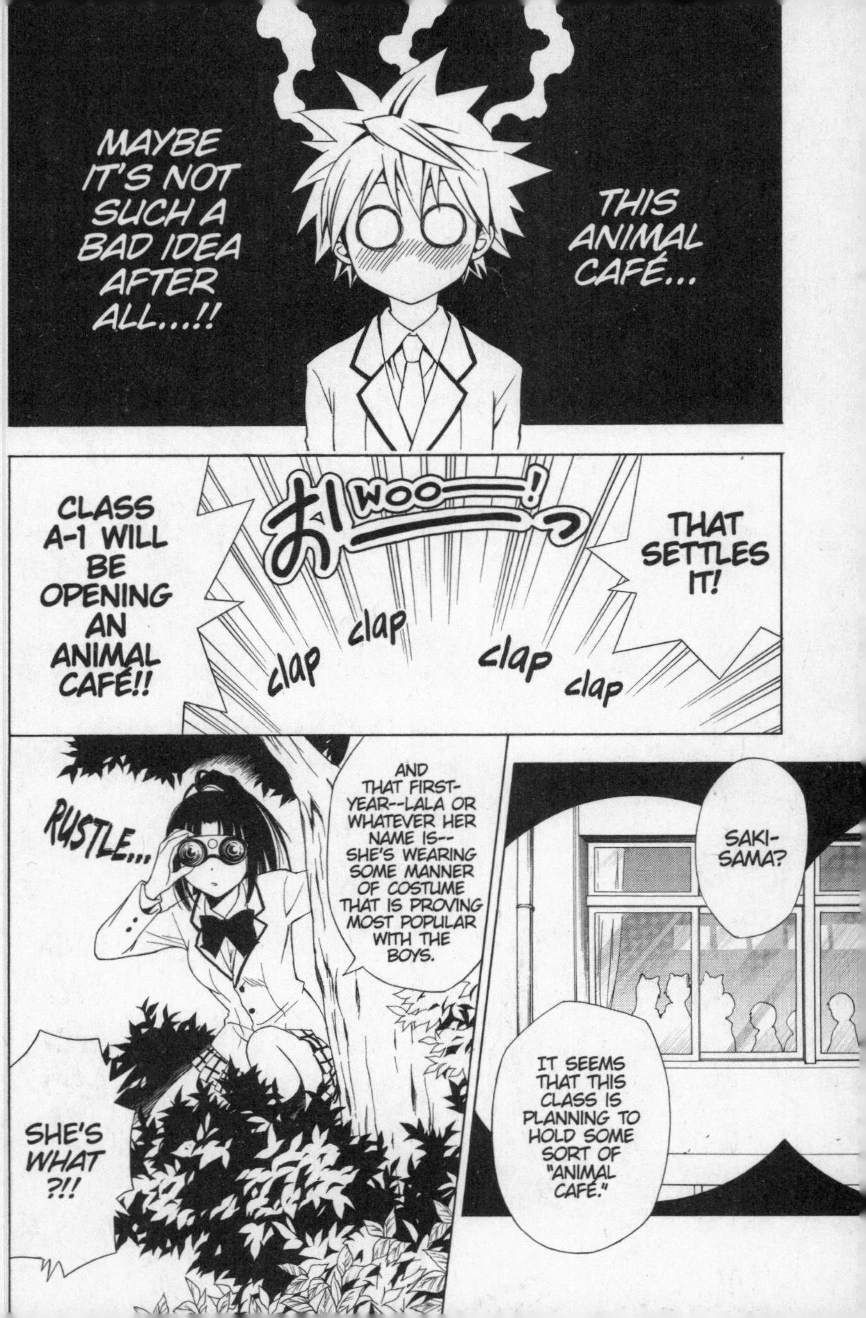

THIS ANIMAL CAFÉ...
MAYBE IT'S NOT SUCH A BAD IDEA AFTER ALL...!!
THAT SETTLES IT!
お WOO——! っ
CLASS A-1 WILL BE OPENING AN ANIMAL CAFÉ!!
clap
clap
clap
clap
SAKI-SAMA?
IT SEEMS THAT THIS CLASS IS PLANNING TO HOLD SOME SORT OF "ANIMAL CAFÉ."
AND THAT FIRST-YEAR--LALA OR WHATEVER HER NAME IS--SHE'S WEARING SOME MANNER OF COSTUME THAT IS PROVING MOST POPULAR WITH THE BOYS.
RUSTLE...
SHE'S WHAT?!!

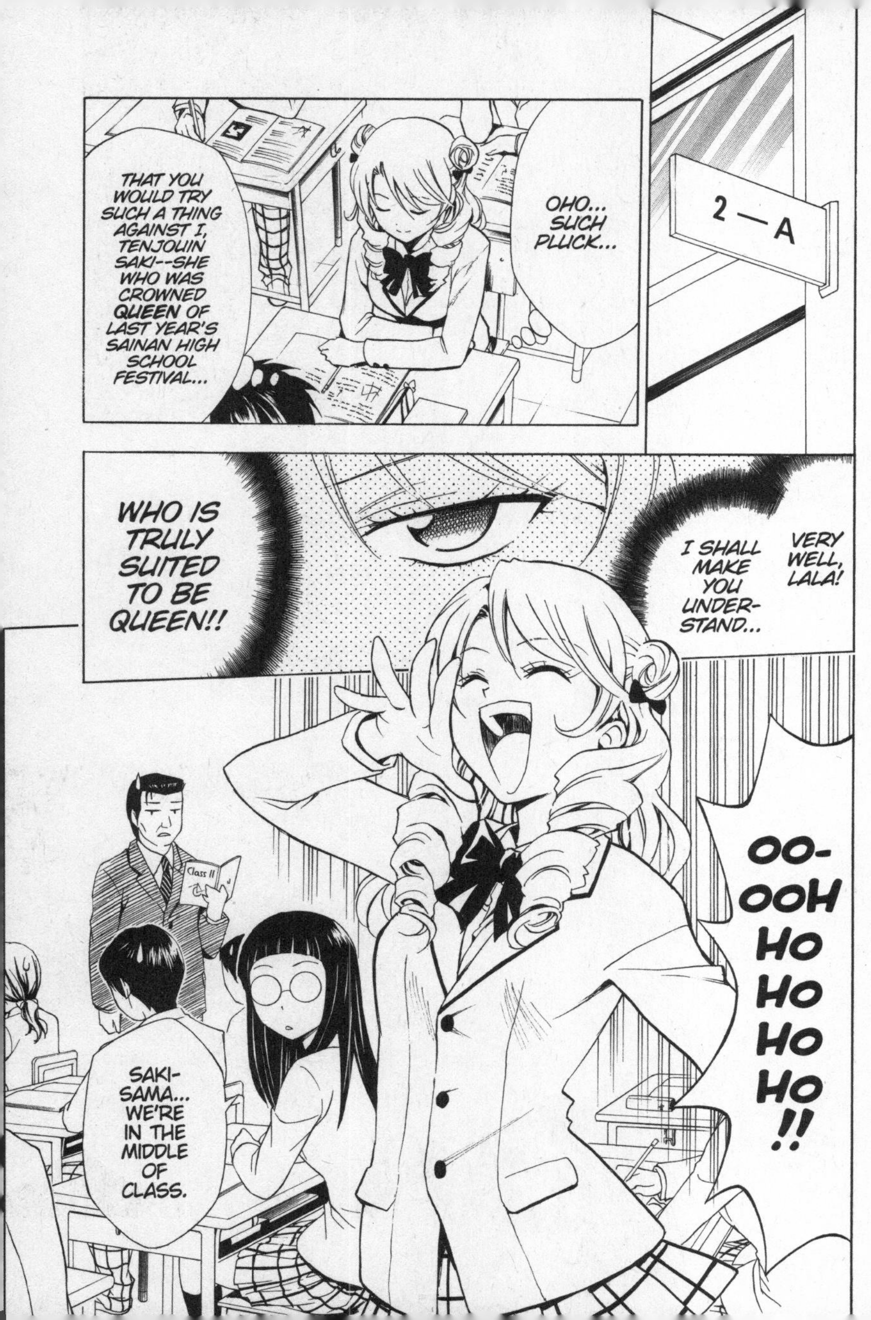

2—A
OHO... SUCH PLUCK...
THAT YOU WOULD TRY SUCH A THING AGAINST I, TENJOUIN SAKI--SHE WHO WAS CROWNED QUEEN OF LAST YEAR'S SAINAN HIGH SCHOOL FESTIVAL...
VERY WELL, LALA!
I SHALL MAKE YOU UNDER-STAND...
WHO IS TRULY SUITED TO BE QUEEN!!
OO-OOH HO HO HO HO!!
Class II
SAKI-SAMA... WE'RE IN THE MIDDLE OF CLASS.

To Love Ru Gaiden: Galaxy Legend ☆ Zastin –Chapter 3–

PRESENTED BY SAKI HASEMI

Zastin and his three subordinates were in the living room of Studio Saibai, enjoying a break just after sending their most recent work to the presses. Buwatts was speaking to Maul, who had a cup of green tea in his hand.

"Sure, Saibai-sensei has so much energy... But I just can't take any more..."

"Don't complain like that. It's thanks to Saibai-sensei that we've gotten so much better at drawing!"

"I've...got a bunch of calluses on my hands, now..."

Hearing those words, Zastin closely examined his own hands.

"Commander Zastin!"

"Hm? What is it, Buwatts?"

"What is this thing...?"

Adorning the living room bookshelf was a doll, which he picked up.

"Hmm... Some kind of little girl's toy, it seems."

"Oh!"

With a terrible expression, Maul cried out, clearly trying to snatch the doll away.

"Whooa!"

The suddenness of the movement set Zastin's heart racing.

As he pinned his right hand to his chest, he asked.

"Wh-what is it, Maul?"

"THIS IS A LIMITED-EDITION MAGAZINE-ONLY FIGURE FROM THE POPULAR TOKUSATSU SHOW MAGICAL KYOUKO! WHY WOULD IT BE IN A PLACE LIKE THIS?!"

"Limited...edition?"

"Yes, the production company was the popular 'TAO,' and it's a limited-run Gouda Kunio. Maaan, it's incredible!"

"I see. I don't really get it, but you're certainly quite knowledgeable on this subject..."

Buwatts begins to whisper in the now-impressed Zastin's ear. "Commander... Recently, it appears that Maul has become obsessed with Earth culture. He consumes huge amounts of anime and manga, and it seems he's eager to propagate it when we return to Deviluke..."

"What?! That's wonderful, though! Cultural exchange with other worlds... (Yup!) Maul has certainly grown..."

"Wheee! SO CUUUTE!"

However, looking at Maul, delighted and off in his own little world, made Buwatts worry.

"Um... It seems that it's a very limited slice of Earth's culture that he's looking to spread, though..."

Meanwhile, on a spaceship headed to Earth, chasing Zastin...

"Wait! What is this place?"

"Who knows... Where, indeed?"

"Commander Zastin... We'll be there to see you soon..."

(They were totally lost.)

To be continued...

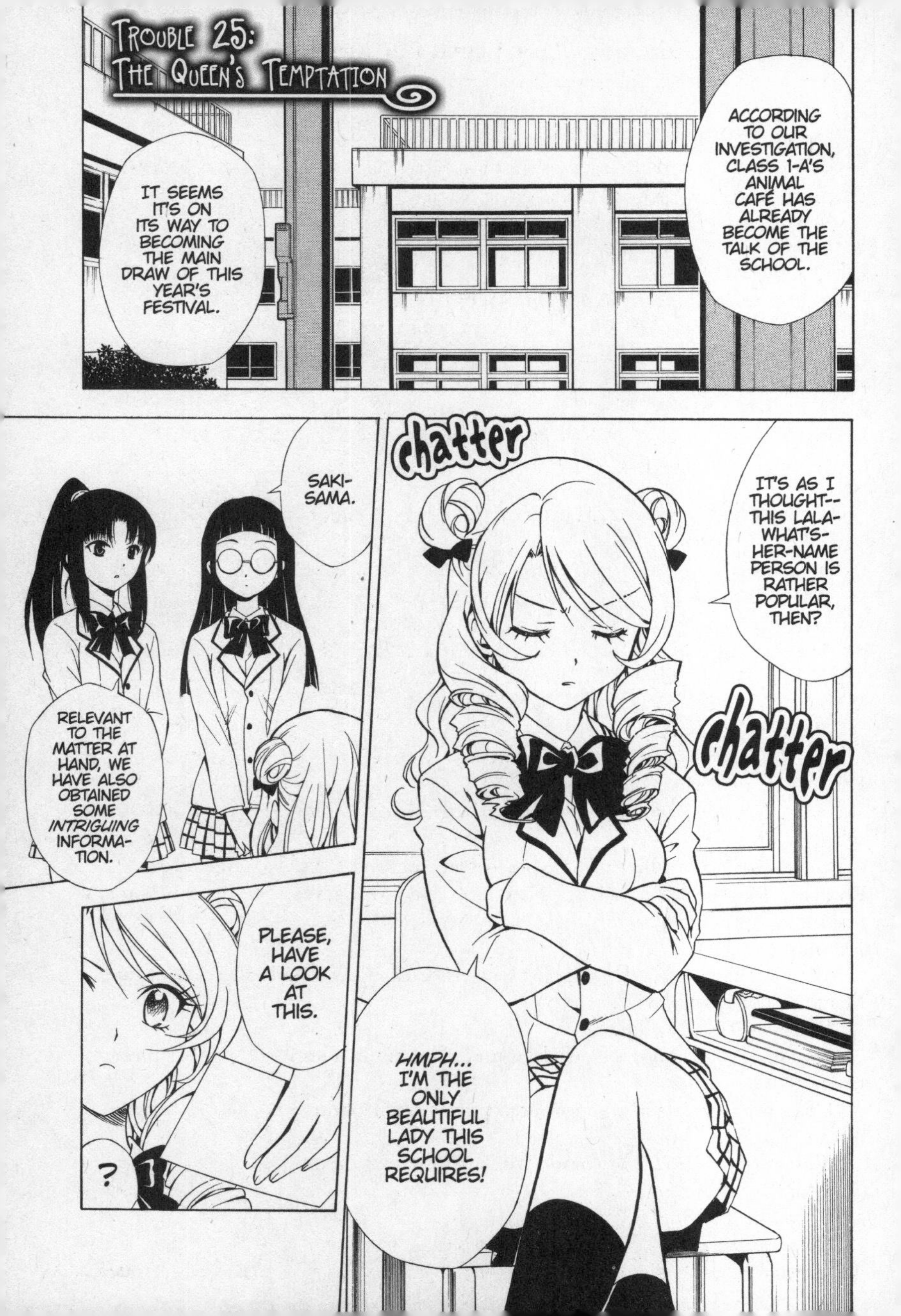

TROUBLE 25: THE QUEEN'S TEMPTATION
ACCORDING TO OUR INVESTIGATION, CLASS 1-A'S ANIMAL CAFÉ HAS ALREADY BECOME THE TALK OF THE SCHOOL.
IT SEEMS IT'S ON ITS WAY TO BECOMING THE MAIN DRAW OF THIS YEAR'S FESTIVAL.
chatter
IT'S AS I THOUGHT-- THIS LALA-WHAT'S-HER-NAME PERSON IS RATHER POPULAR, THEN?
chatter
HMPH... I'M THE ONLY BEAUTIFUL LADY THIS SCHOOL REQUIRES!
SAKI-SAMA.
RELEVANT TO THE MATTER AT HAND, WE HAVE ALSO OBTAINED SOME *INTRIGUING* INFORMATION.
PLEASE, HAVE A LOOK AT THIS.
?

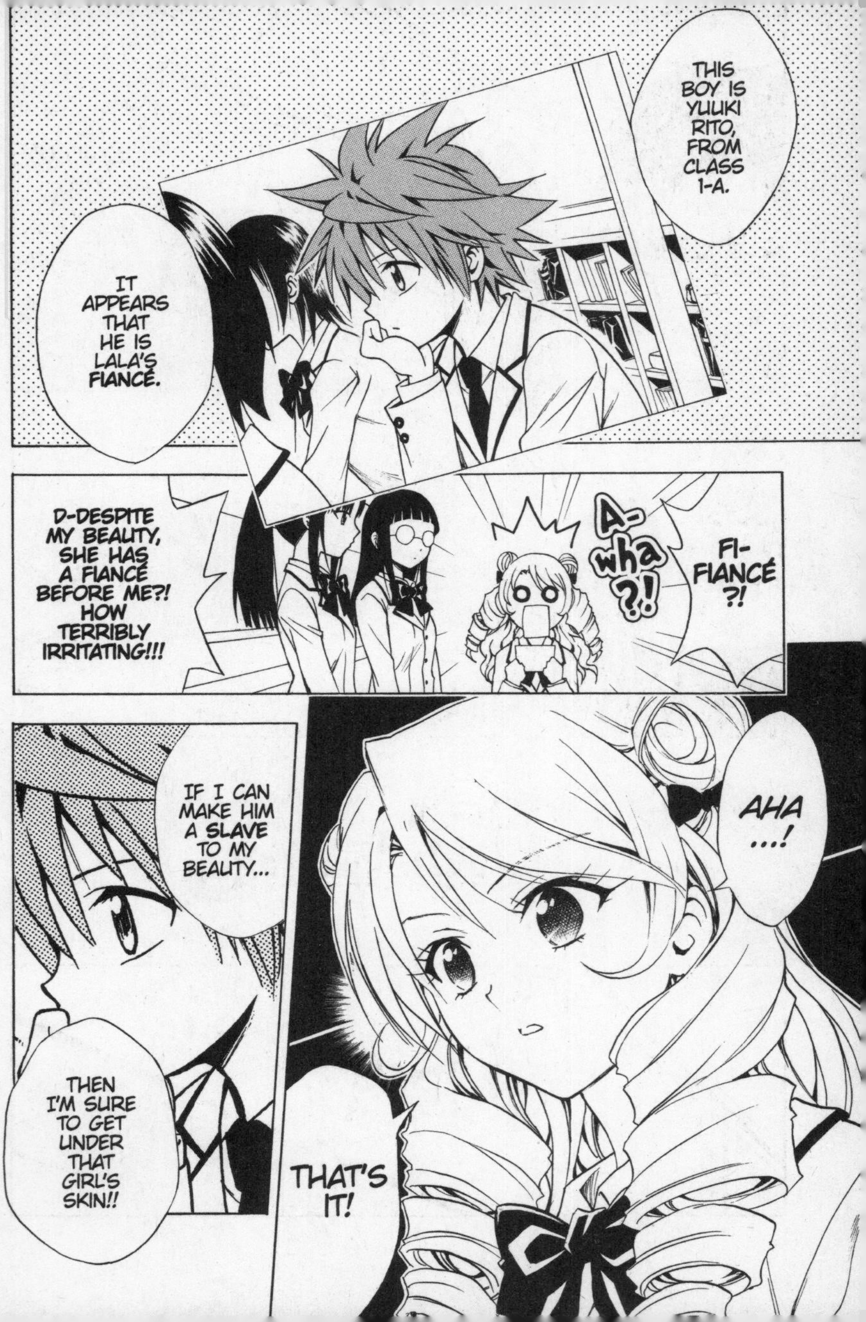
THIS BOY IS YUUKI RITO, FROM CLASS 1-A.
IT APPEARS THAT HE IS LALA'S FIANCÉ.
FI-FIANCÉ?!
A-wha?!
D-DESPITE MY BEAUTY, SHE HAS A FIANCÉ BEFORE ME?! HOW TERRIBLY IRRITATING!!!
AHA ...!
THAT'S IT!
IF I CAN MAKE HIM A SLAVE TO MY BEAUTY...
THEN I'M SURE TO GET UNDER THAT GIRL'S SKIN!!

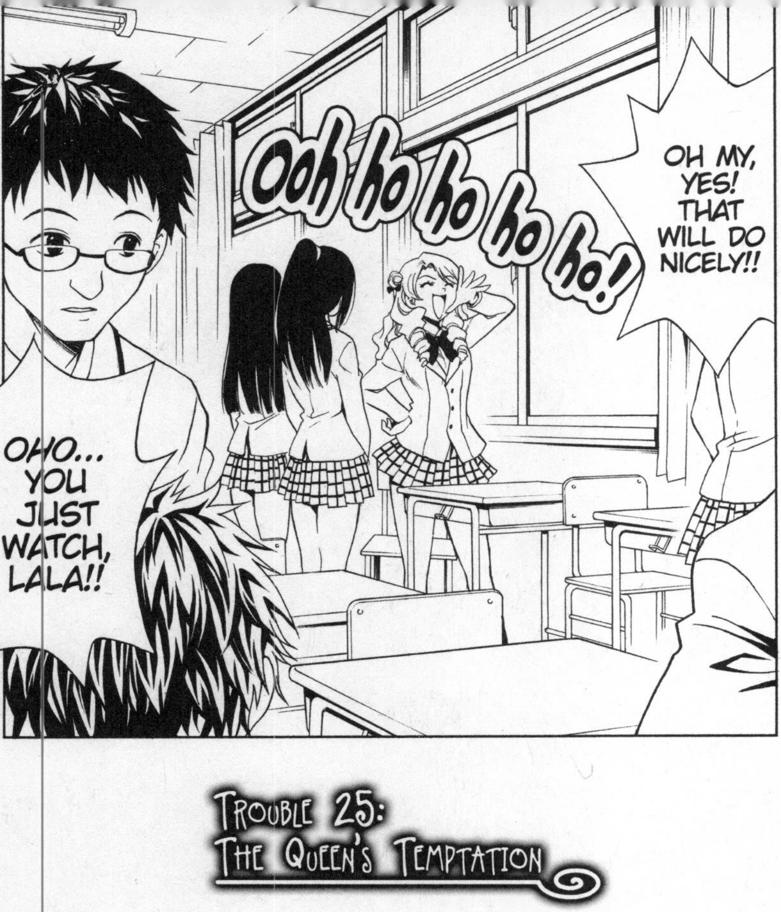
OH MY, YES! THAT WILL DO NICELY!!
Ooh ho ho ho ho ho!
OHO... YOU JUST WATCH, LALA!!

Trouble 25: The Queen's Temptation

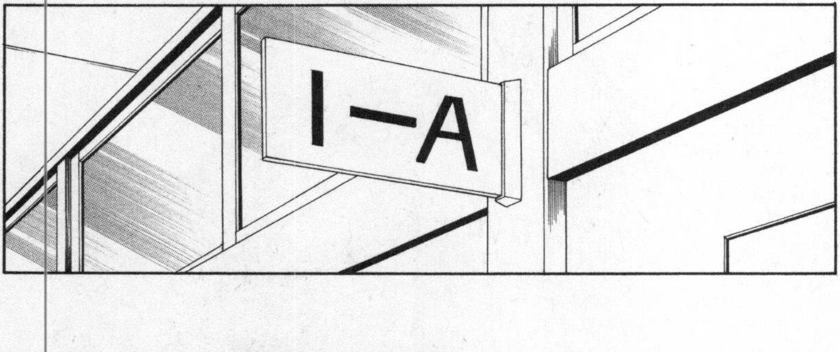
1-A

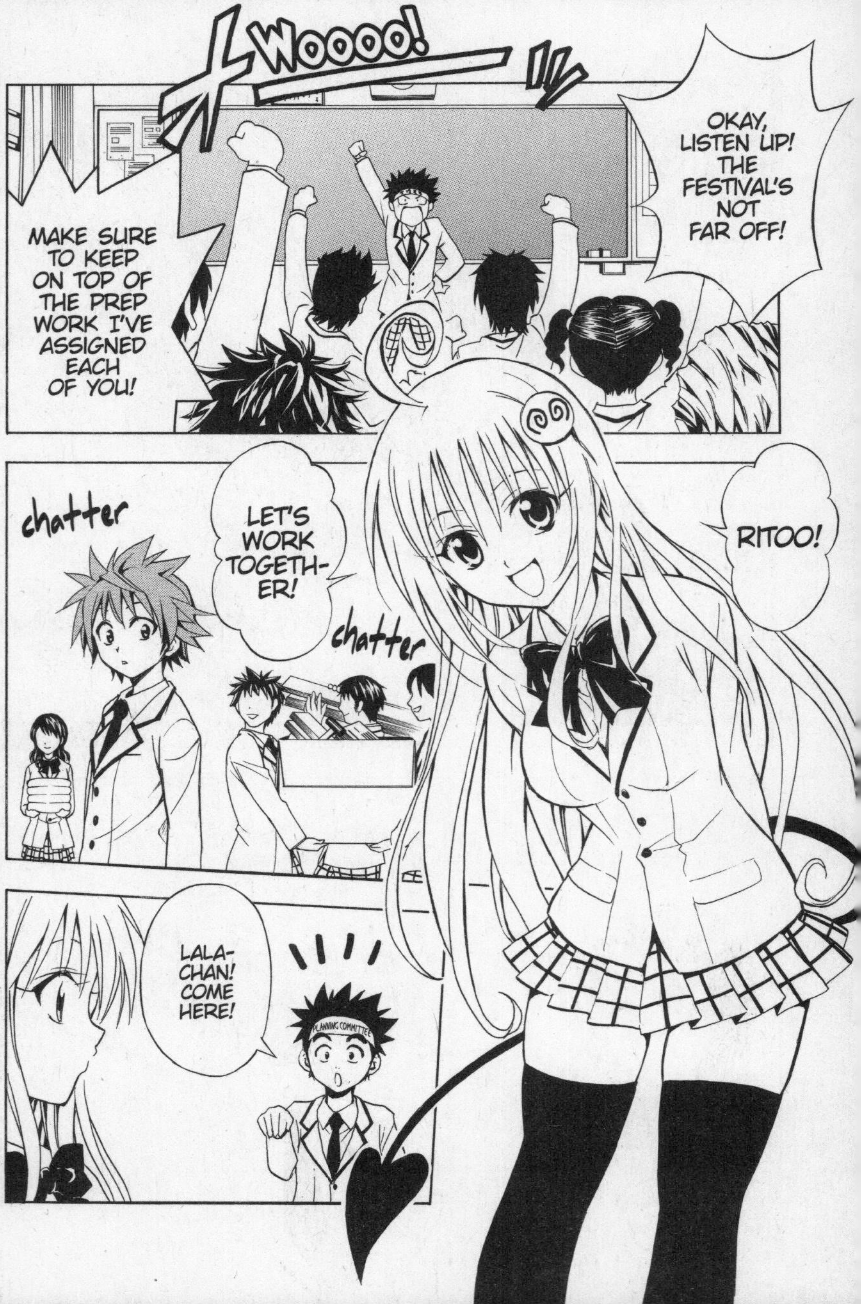
OKAY, LISTEN UP! THE FESTIVAL'S NOT FAR OFF!
WOOOO!
MAKE SURE TO KEEP ON TOP OF THE PREP WORK I'VE ASSIGNED EACH OF YOU!
RITOO!
LET'S WORK TOGETH-ER!
chatter
chatter
LALA-CHAN! COME HERE!
PLANNING COMMITTEE

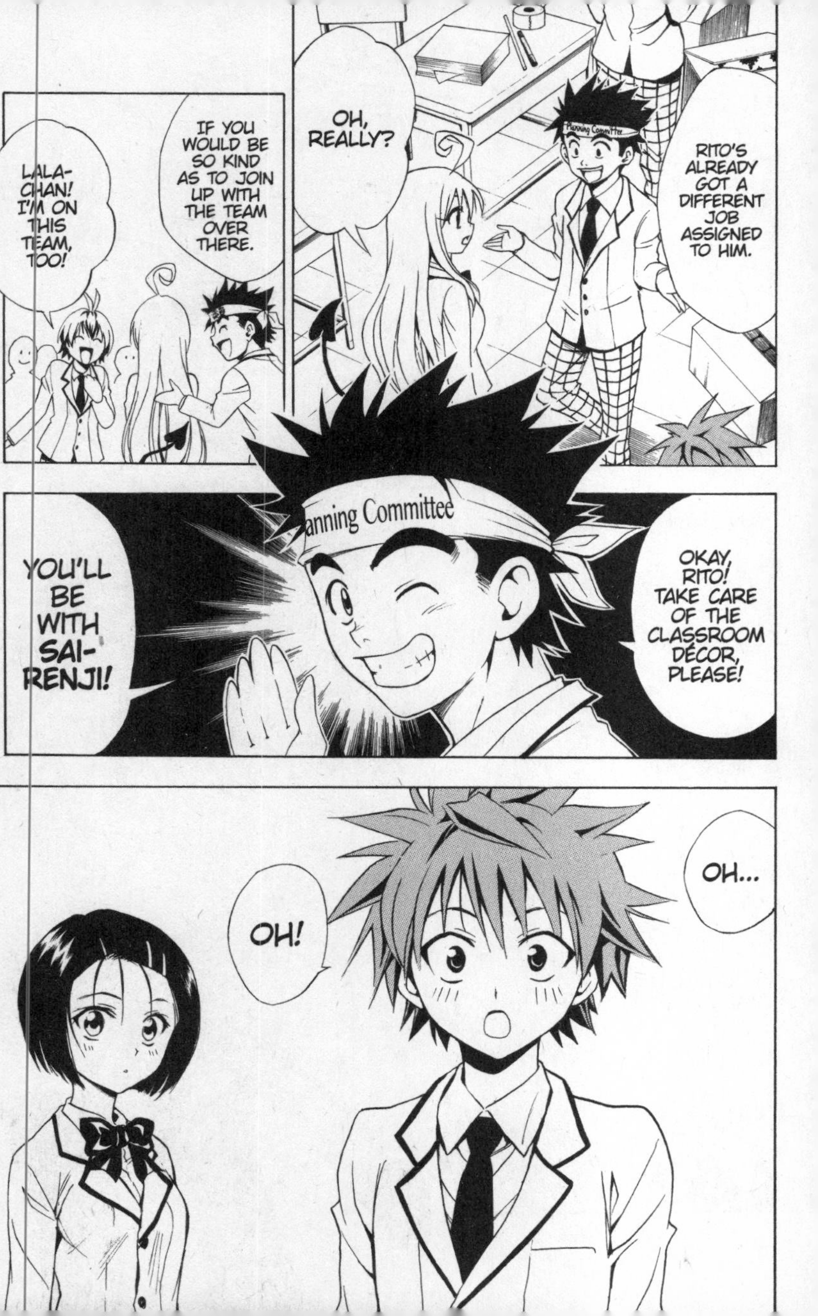
RITO'S ALREADY GOT A DIFFERENT JOB ASSIGNED TO HIM.
OH, REALLY?
IF YOU WOULD BE SO KIND AS TO JOIN UP WITH THE TEAM OVER THERE.
LALA-CHAN! I'M ON THIS TEAM, TOO!
OKAY, RITO! TAKE CARE OF THE CLASSROOM DÉCOR, PLEASE!
YOU'LL BE WITH SAI-RENJI!
OH...
OH!

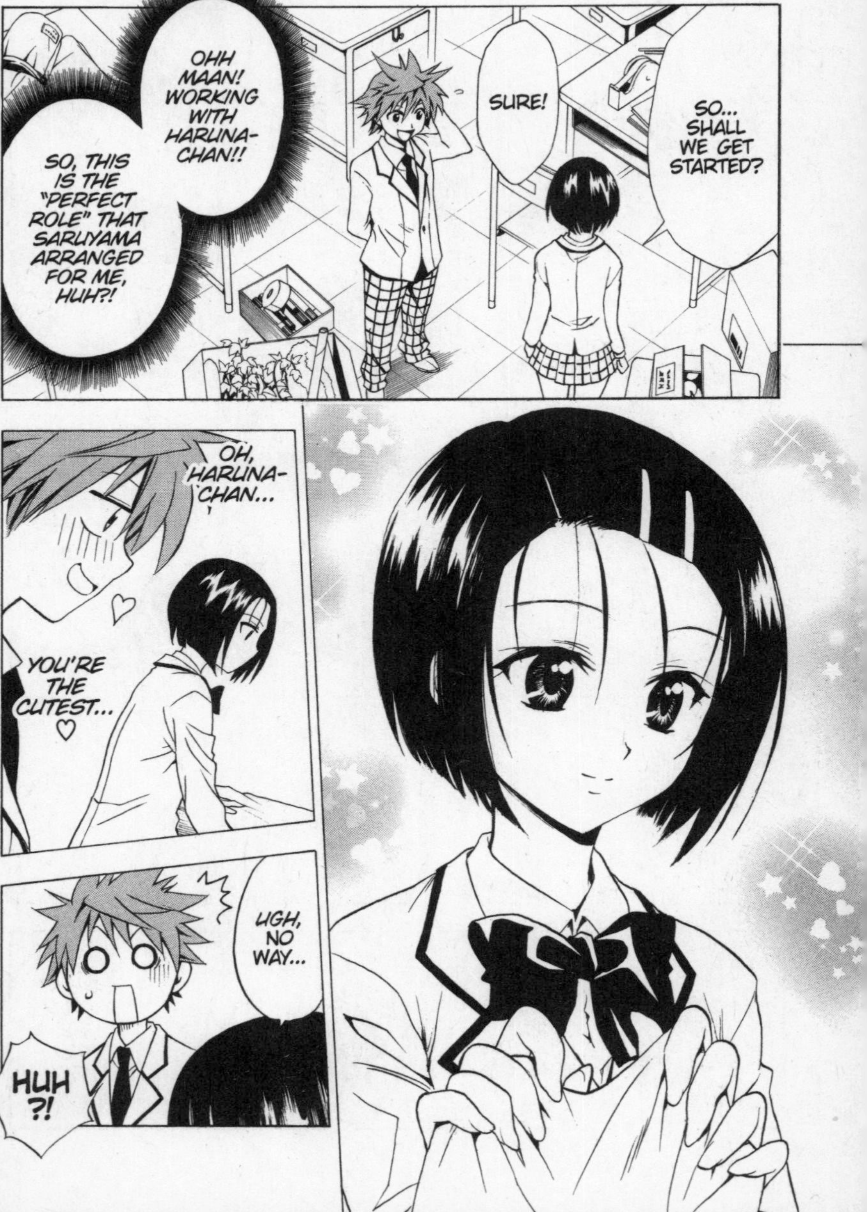
SO... SHALL WE GET STARTED?
SURE!
OHH MAAN! WORKING WITH HARUNA-CHAN!!
SO, THIS IS THE "PERFECT ROLE" THAT SARUYAMA ARRANGED FOR ME, HUH?!
OH, HARUNA-CHAN...
YOU'RE THE CUTEST... ♡
UGH, NO WAY...
HUH ?!

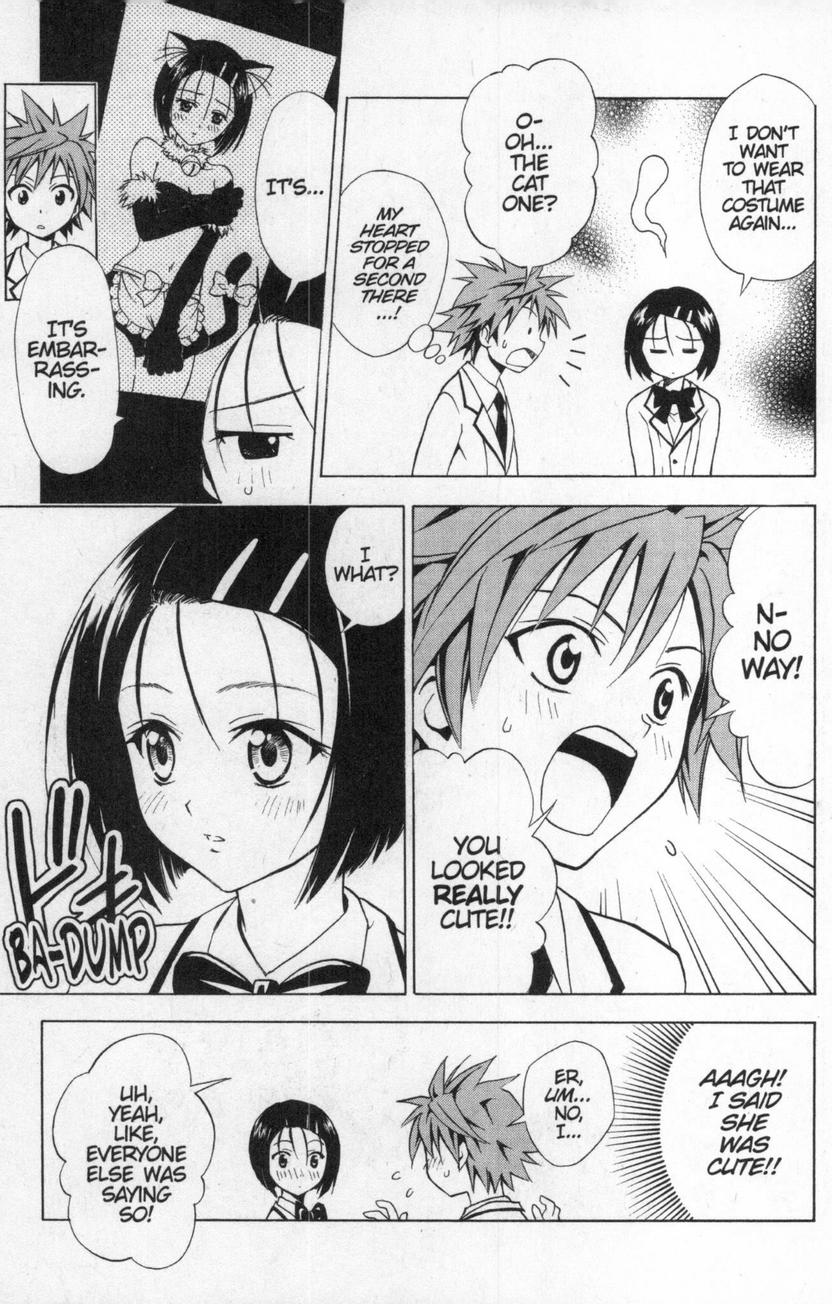

I DON'T WANT TO WEAR THAT COSTUME AGAIN...
O-OH... THE CAT ONE?
MY HEART STOPPED FOR A SECOND THERE ...!
IT'S...
IT'S EMBARRASSING.
N-NO WAY!
YOU LOOKED REALLY CUTE!!
I WHAT?
BA-DUMP
AAAGH! I SAID SHE WAS CUTE!!
ER, UM... NO, I...
UH, YEAH, LIKE, EVERYONE ELSE WAS SAYING SO!

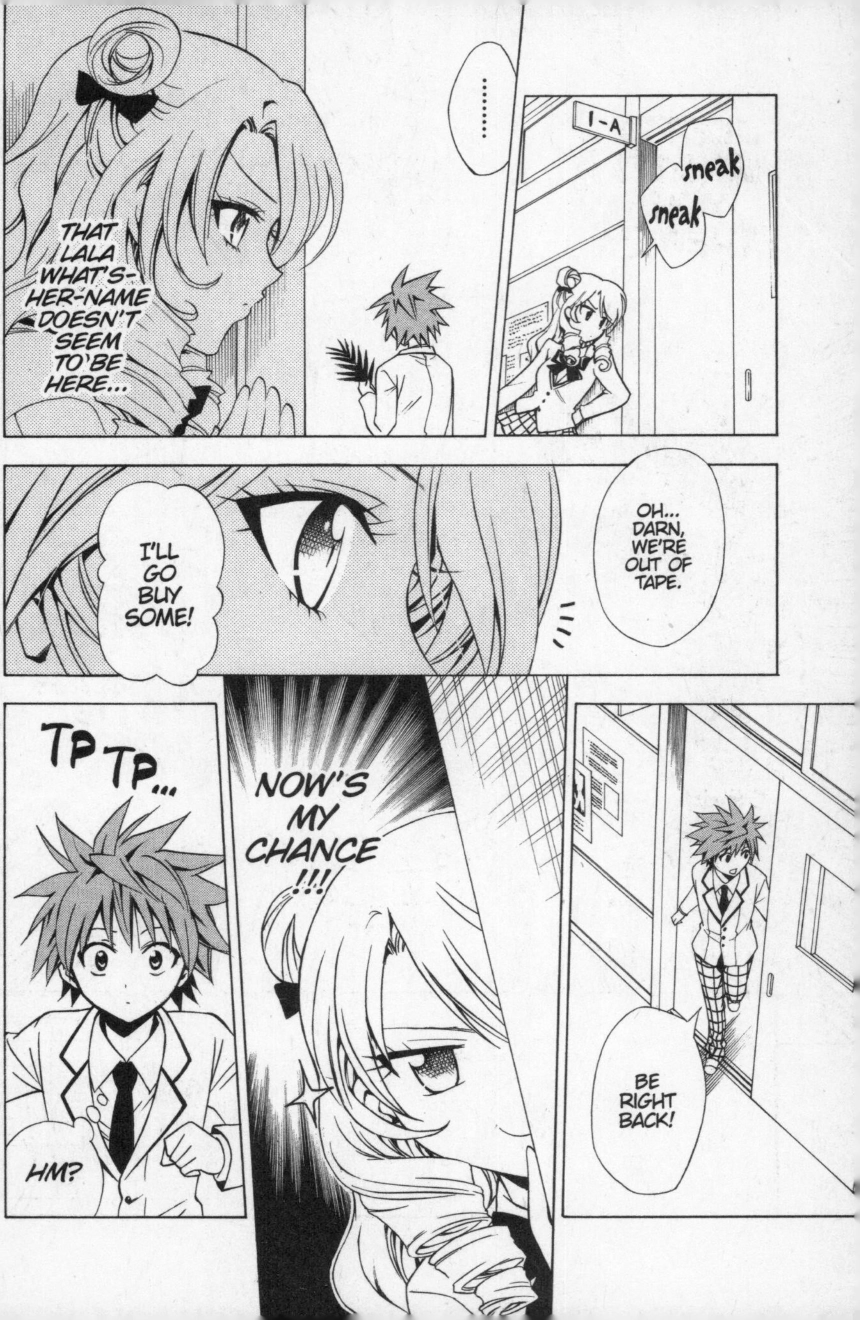
1-A
sneak
sneak
......
THAT LALA WHAT'S-HER-NAME DOESN'T SEEM TO BE HERE...
OH... DARN, WE'RE OUT OF TAPE.
I'LL GO BUY SOME!
BE RIGHT BACK!
NOW'S MY CHANCE !!!
TP TP...
HM?

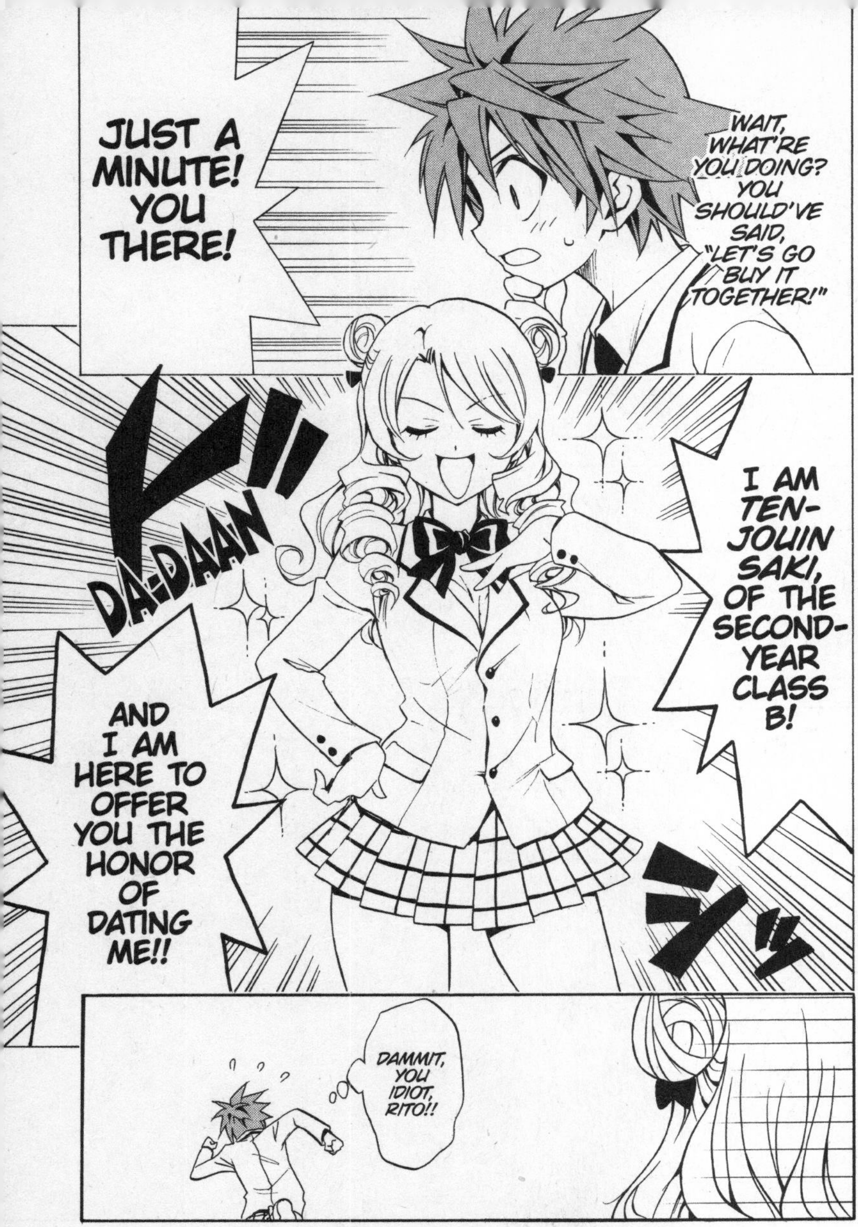
WAIT, WHAT'RE YOU DOING? YOU SHOULD'VE SAID, "LET'S GO BUY IT TOGETHER!"
JUST A MINUTE! YOU THERE!
I AM TEN-JOUIN SAKI, OF THE SECOND-YEAR CLASS B!
DA-DAAN
AND I AM HERE TO OFFER YOU THE HONOR OF DATING ME!!
DAMMIT, YOU IDIOT, RITO!!

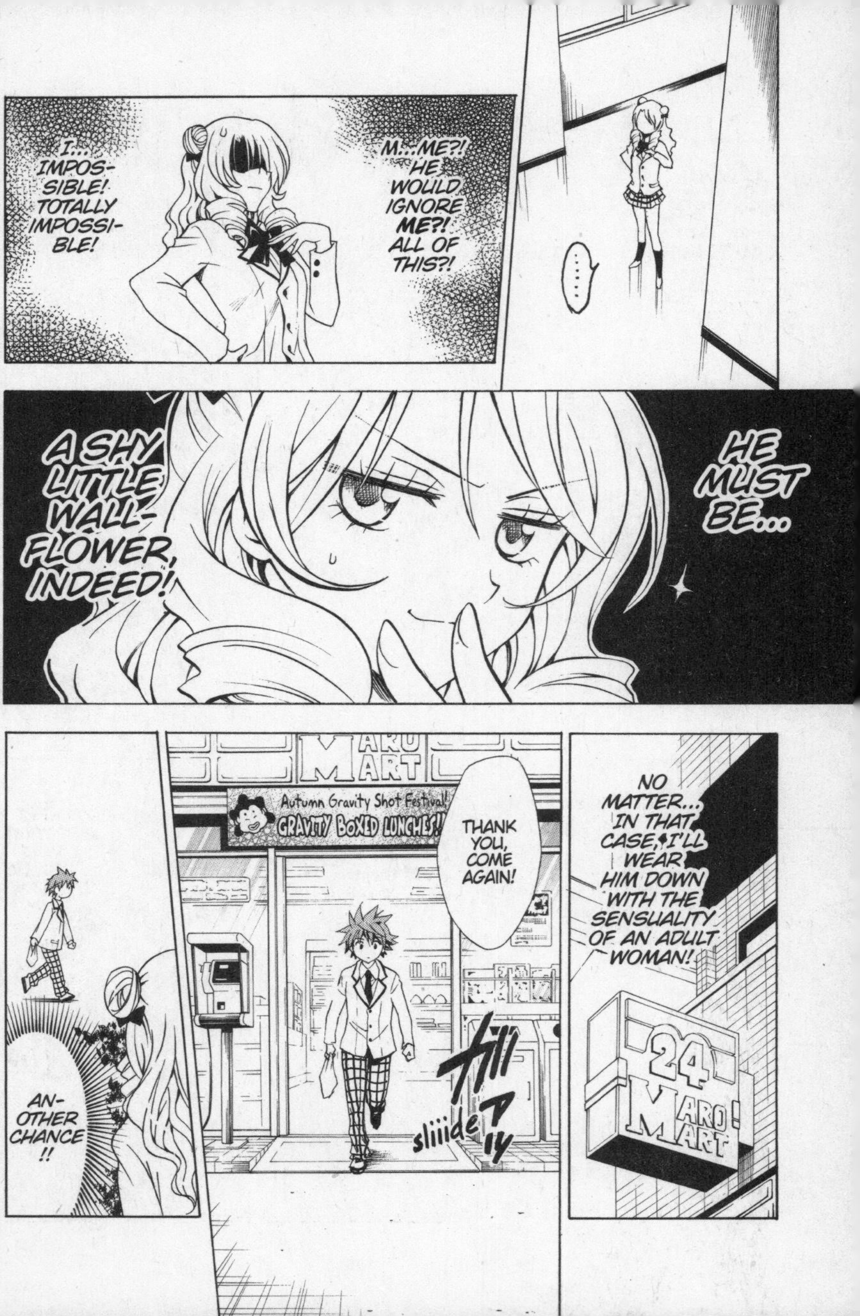
......
M...ME?! HE WOULD IGNORE ME?! ALL OF THIS?!
I... IMPOSSIBLE! TOTALLY IMPOSSIBLE!
HE MUST BE...
A SHY LITTLE WALLFLOWER, INDEED!
NO MATTER... IN THAT CASE, I'LL WEAR HIM DOWN WITH THE SENSUALITY OF AN ADULT WOMAN!
24
MARO MART
MARO MART
Autumn Gravity Shot Festival!
GRAVITY BOXED LUNCHES!!
THANK YOU, COME AGAIN!
sliiide
ANOTHER CHANCE!!

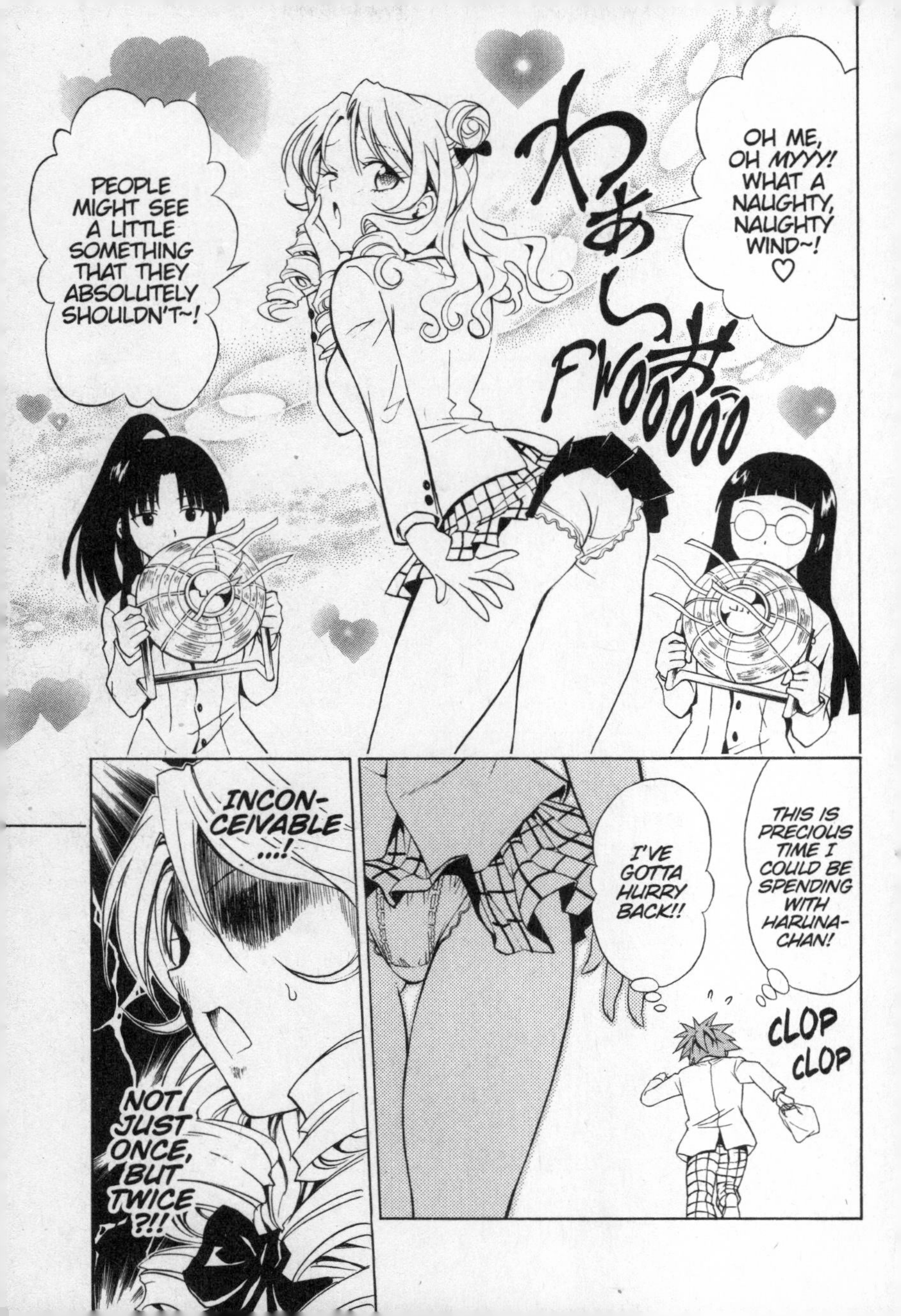
OH ME, OH MYYY! WHAT A NAUGHTY, NAUGHTY WIND~! ♡
わあらお
FWOOOOOOO
PEOPLE MIGHT SEE A LITTLE SOMETHING THAT THEY ABSOLULTELY SHOULDN'T~!
THIS IS PRECIOUS TIME I COULD BE SPENDING WITH HARUNA-CHAN!
I'VE GOTTA HURRY BACK!!
CLOP CLOP
INCON-CEIVABLE ...!
NOT JUST ONCE, BUT TWICE ?!!

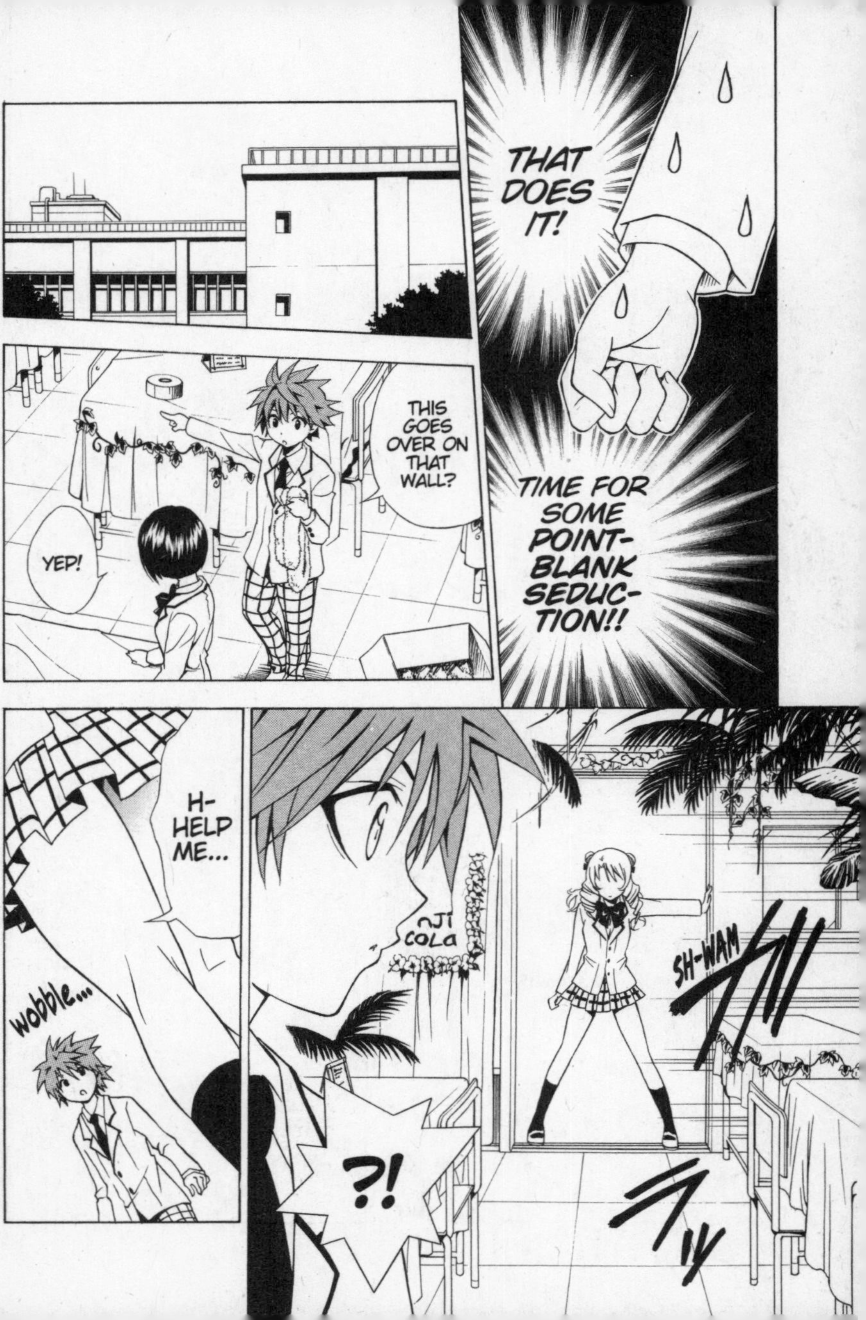
THAT DOES IT!
TIME FOR SOME POINT-BLANK SEDUCTION!!
THIS GOES OVER ON THAT WALL?
YEP!
SH-WAM
?!
COLA
H-HELP ME...
wobble...

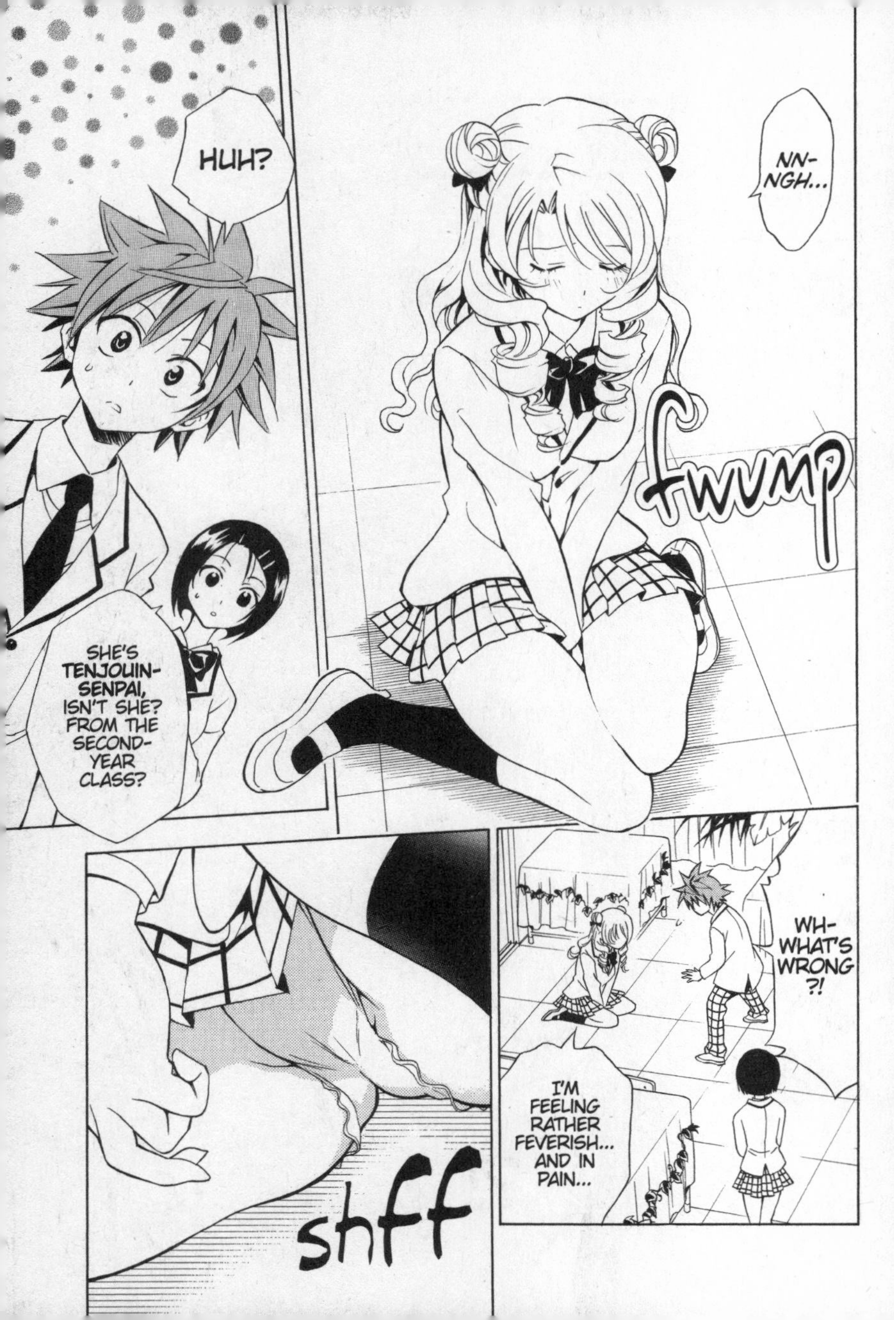
NN-NGH...
fwump
HUH?
SHE'S TENJOUIN-SENPAI, ISN'T SHE? FROM THE SECOND-YEAR CLASS?
WH-WHAT'S WRONG?!
I'M FEELING RATHER FEVERISH... AND IN PAIN...
shff

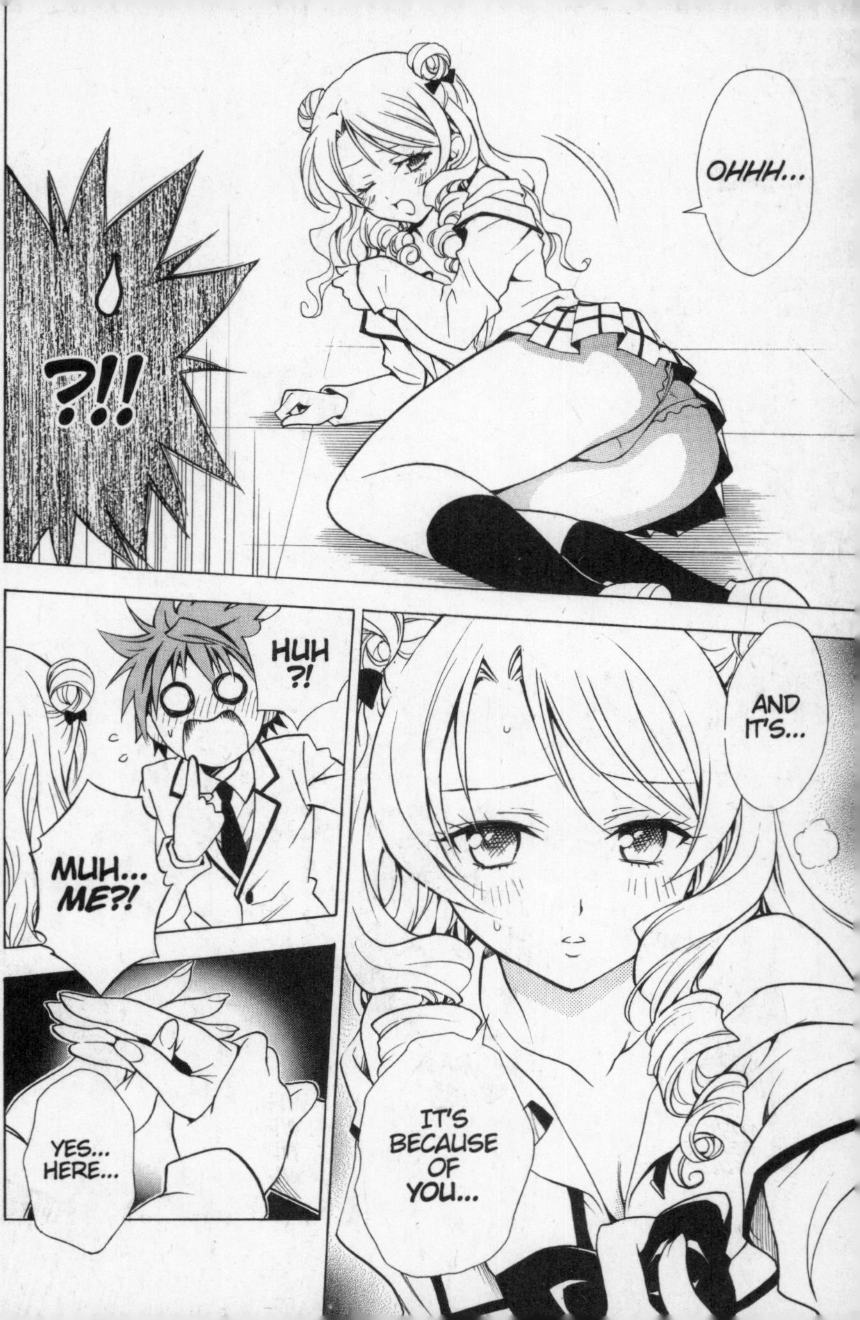
OHHH...
?!!
AND IT'S...
IT'S BECAUSE OF YOU...
HUH ?!
MUH... ME?!
YES... HERE...

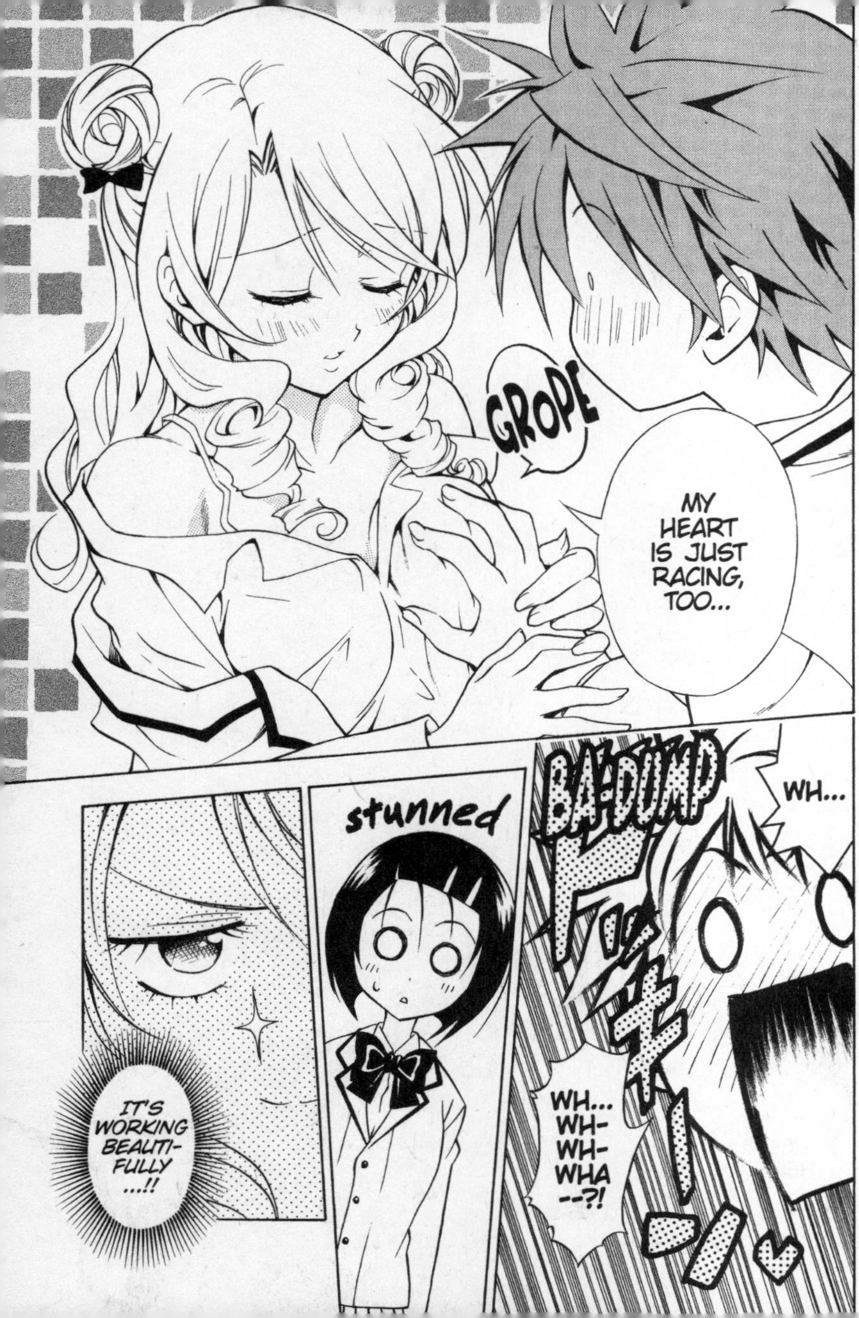
GROPE
MY HEART IS JUST RACING, TOO...
BA-DUMP
WH...
WH... WH-WH-WHA--?!
stunned
IT'S WORKING BEAUTI-FULLY ...!!

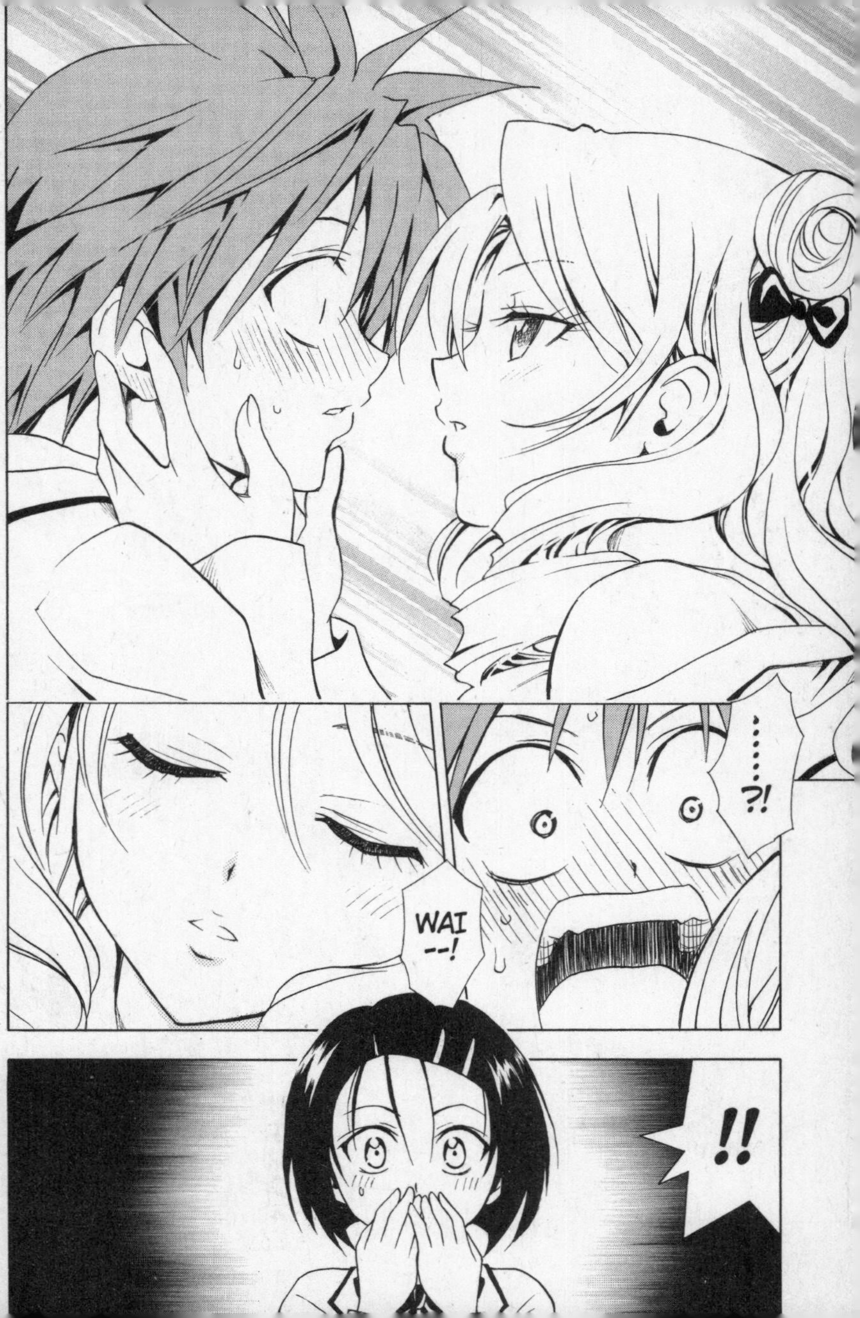
......?!
WAI--!
!!

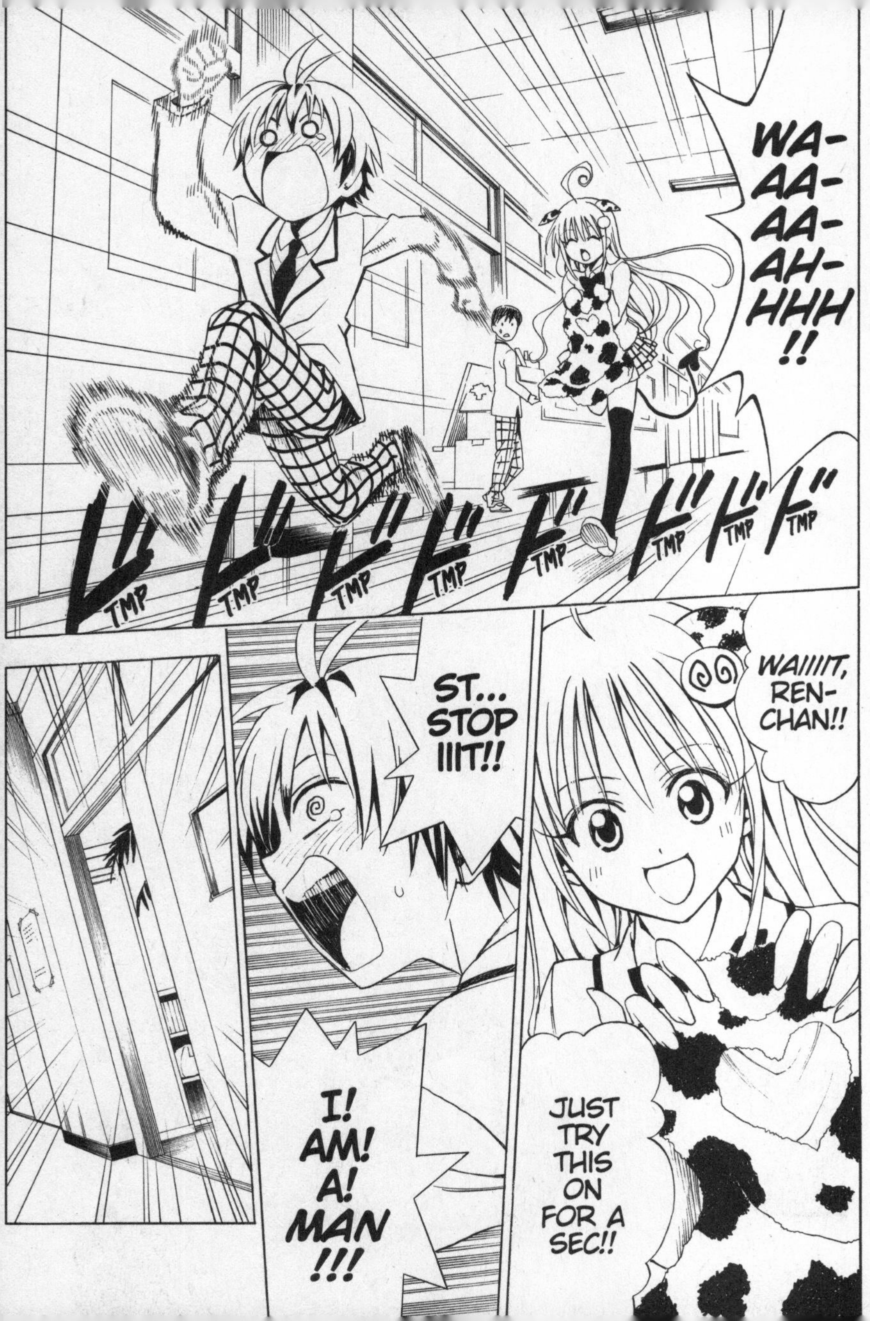
WA-AA-AA-AH-HHH!!
TMP TMP TMP TMP TMP TMP TMP TMP
WAIIIIT, REN-CHAN!!
JUST TRY THIS ON FOR A SEC!!
ST... STOP IIIIT!!
I! AM! A! MAN!!!

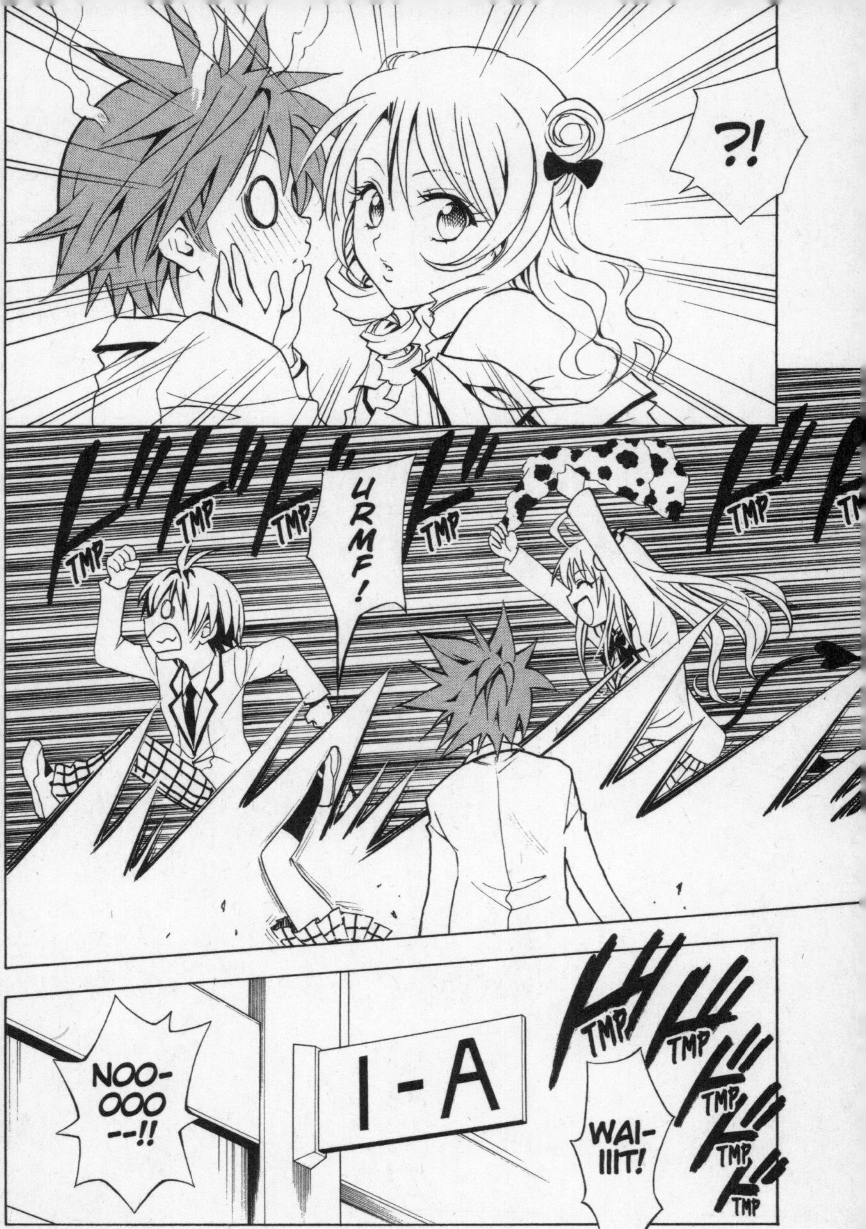
?!
TMP
TMP
URMF!
TMP
TMP
TMP
TMP
TMP
TMP
WAI-IIIT!
TMP
TMP
TMP
NOO-OOO--!!
I-A

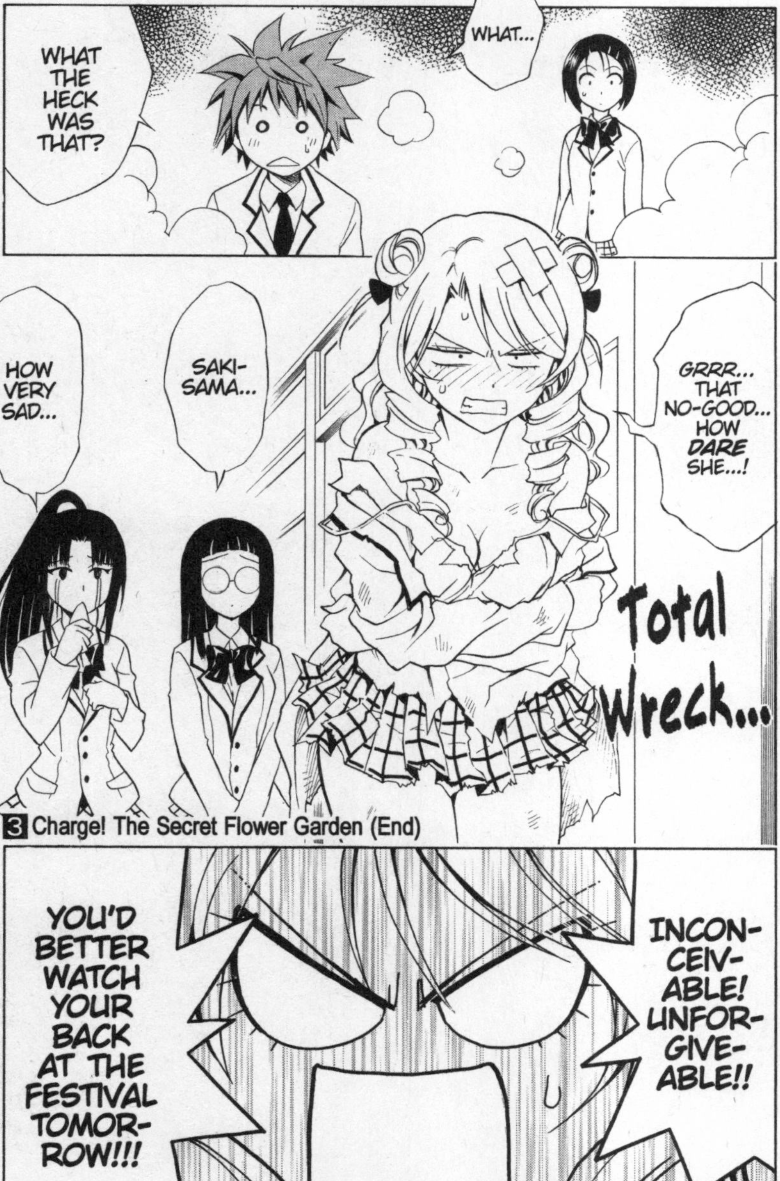
WHAT...
WHAT THE HECK WAS THAT?
GRRR... THAT NO-GOOD... HOW *DARE* SHE...!
Total Wreck...
SAKI-SAMA...
HOW VERY SAD...
INCON-CEIV-ABLE! UNFOR-GIVE-ABLE!!
YOU'D BETTER WATCH YOUR BACK AT THE FESTIVAL TOMOR-ROW!!!
3 Charge! The Secret Flower Garden (End)

To LOVE Ru

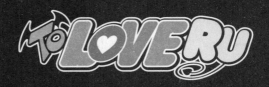

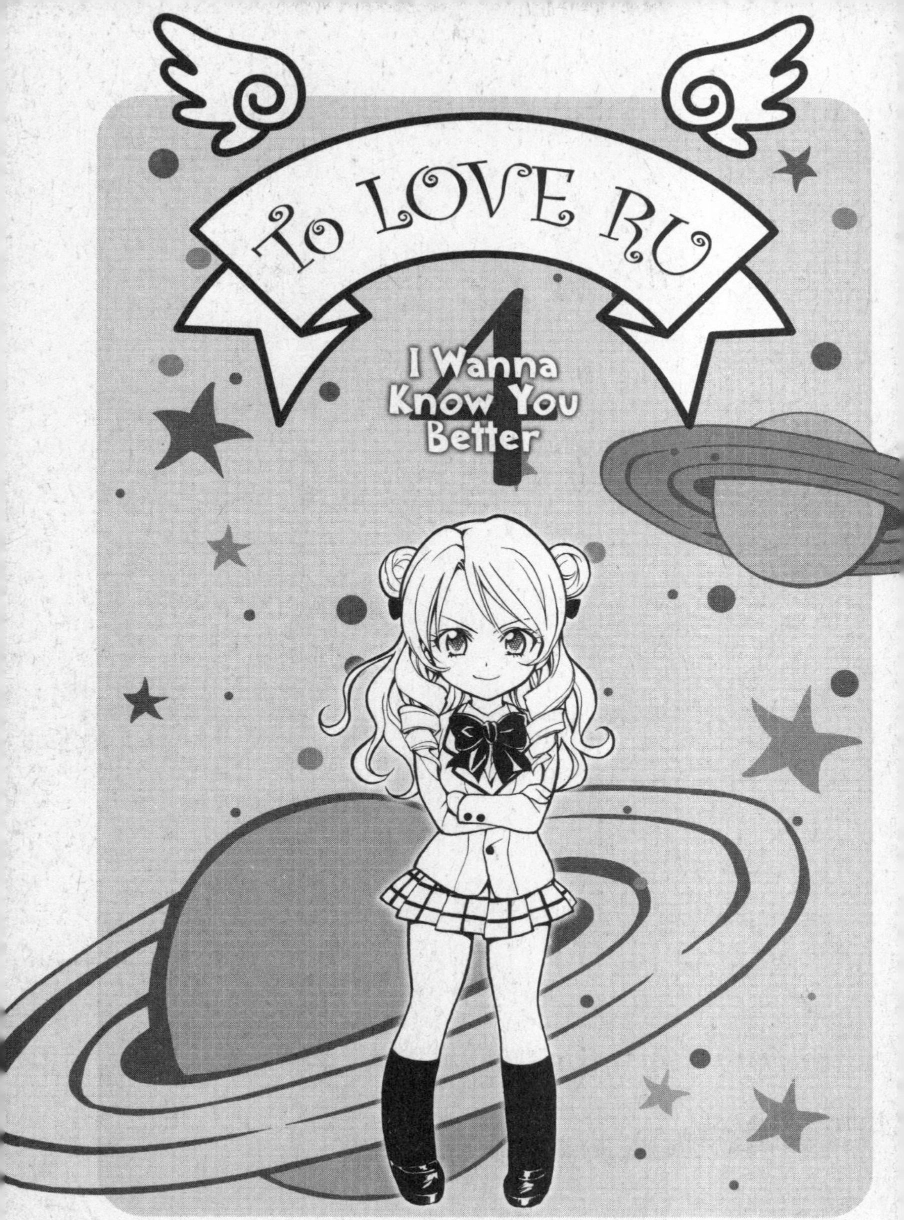
To LOVE RU
4
I Wanna Know You Better

Story: Saki Hasemi **Art: Kentaro Yabuki**

To LOVE Ru

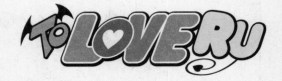

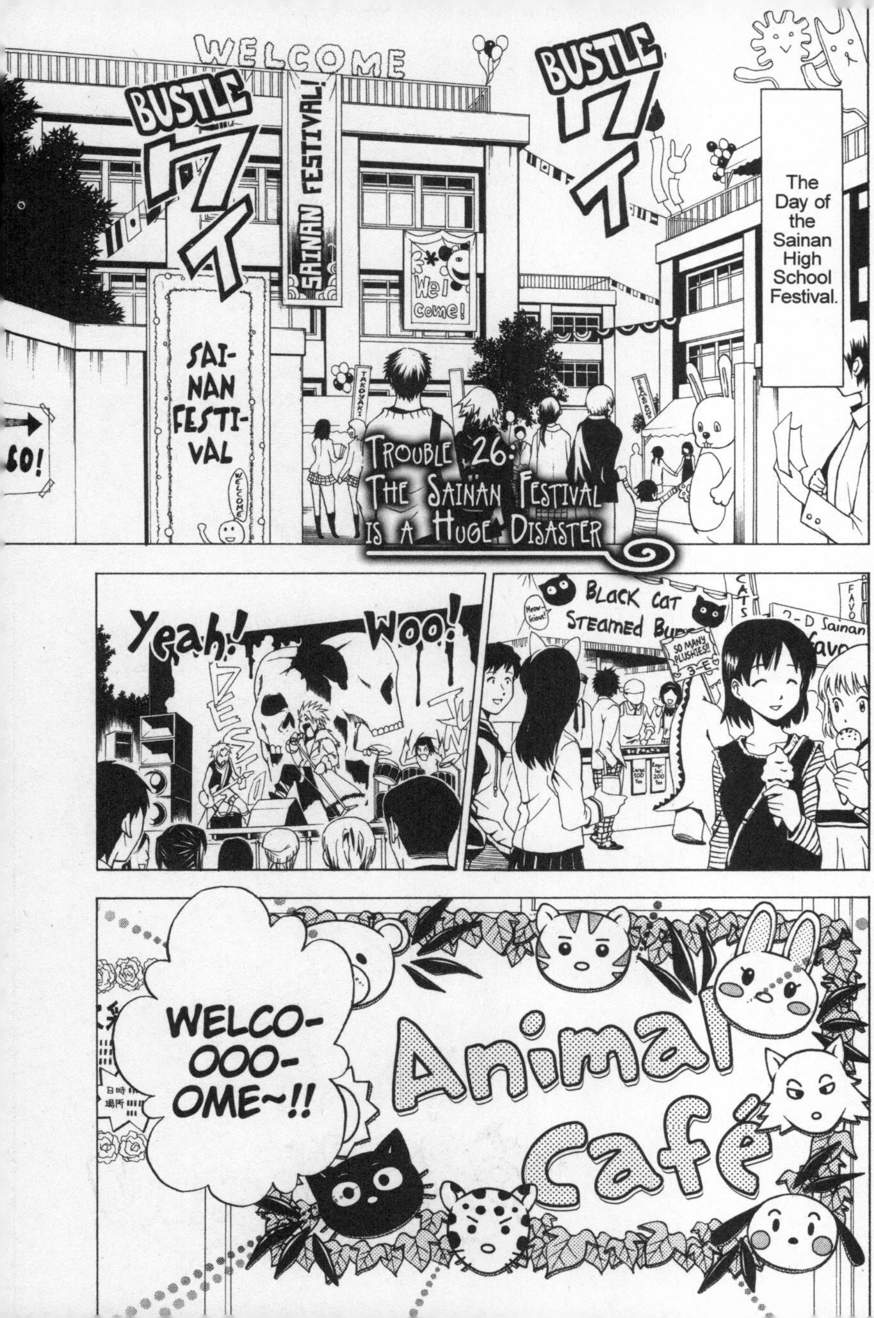

The Day of the Sainan High School Festival.
BUSTLE
BUSTLE
WELCOME
SAINAN FESTIVAL!
Wel come!
TAKOYAKI
SAI-NAN FESTI-VAL
WELCOME
GO!
TROUBLE 26: THE SAINAN FESTIVAL IS A HUGE DISASTER
CATS
2-D Sainan
BLACK CAT STEAMED BU
Meow-licious!
SO MANY PLUSHIES!! 3-E
Woo!
Yeah!
WELCO-OOO-OME~!!
Animal Café

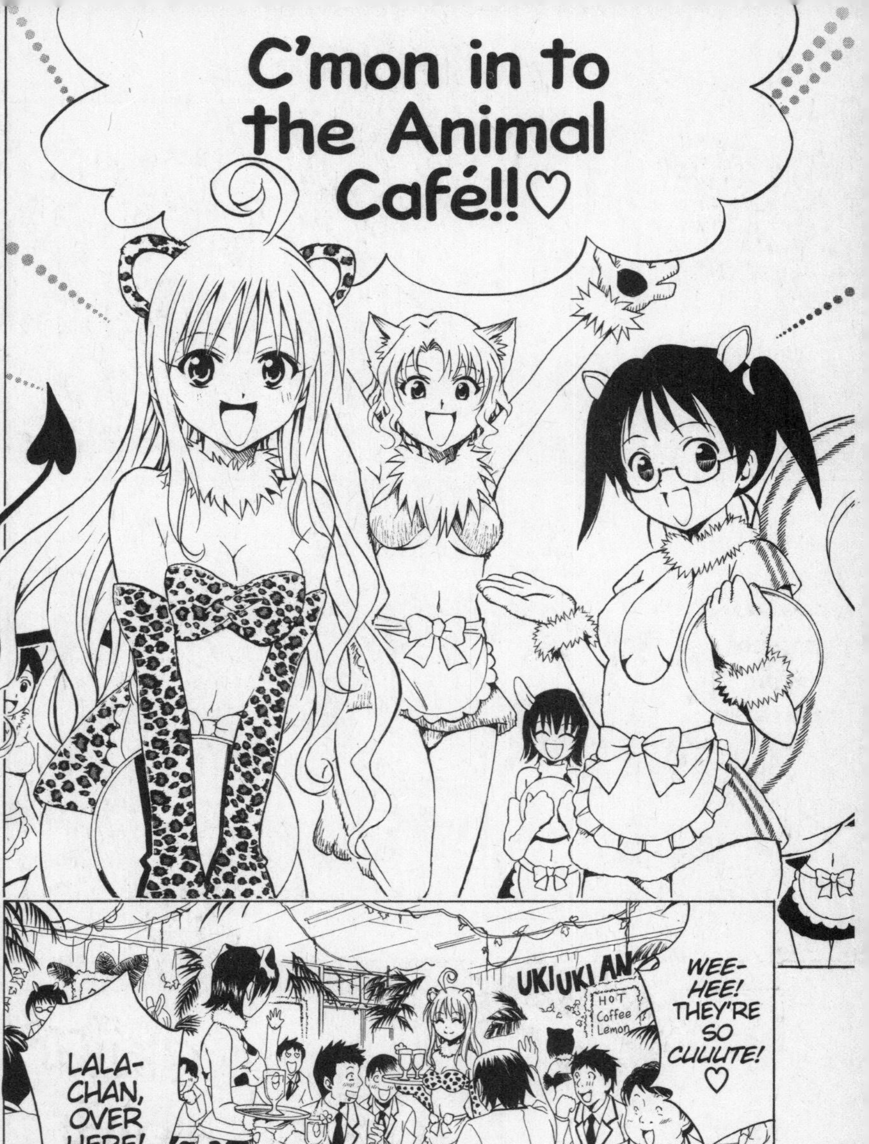
C'mon in to the Animal Café!!♡
WEE-HEE! THEY'RE SO CUUUTE! ♡
UKIUKI AN
HOT Coffee Lemon
LALA-CHAN, OVER HERE!

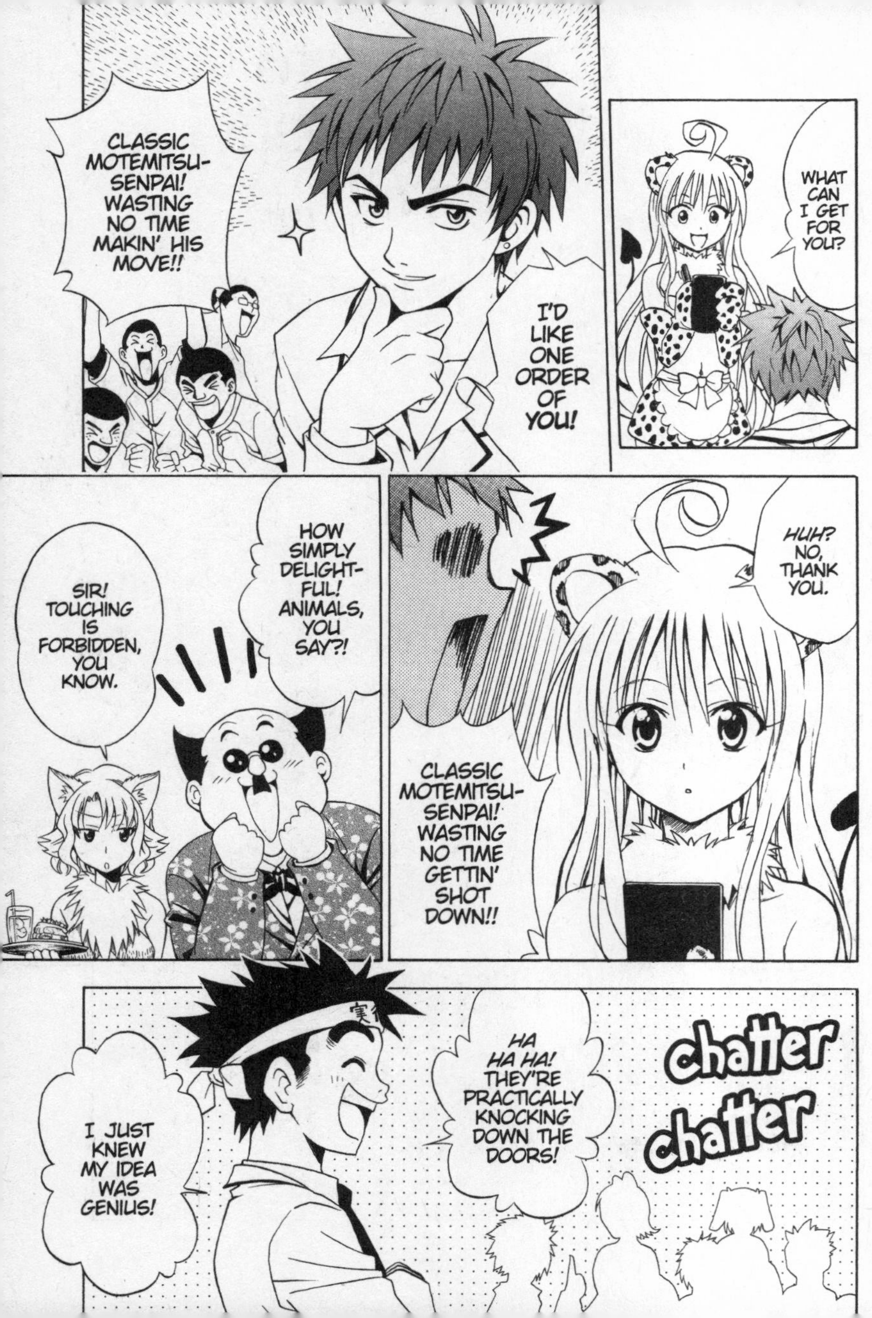
WHAT CAN I GET FOR YOU?
I'D LIKE ONE ORDER OF YOU!
CLASSIC MOTEMITSU-SENPAI! WASTING NO TIME MAKIN' HIS MOVE!!
HUH? NO, THANK YOU.
CLASSIC MOTEMITSU-SENPAI! WASTING NO TIME GETTIN' SHOT DOWN!!
HOW SIMPLY DELIGHT-FUL! ANIMALS, YOU SAY?!
SIR! TOUCHING IS FORBIDDEN, YOU KNOW.
chatter chatter
HA HA HA! THEY'RE PRACTICALLY KNOCKING DOWN THE DOORS!
I JUST KNEW MY IDEA WAS GENIUS!

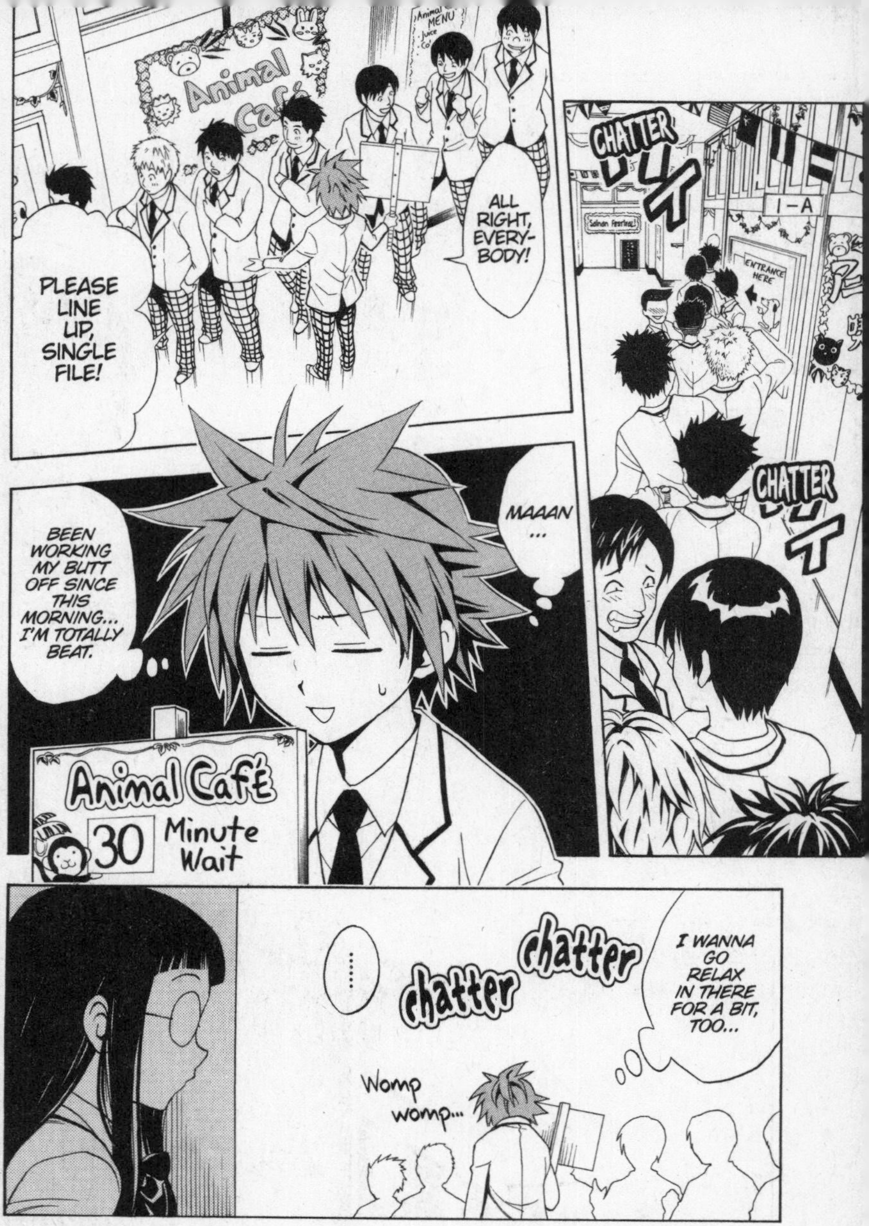
CHATTER
I-A
ENTRANCE HERE
CHATTER
Animal Café
ALL RIGHT, EVERYBODY!
PLEASE LINE UP, SINGLE FILE!
MAAAN...
BEEN WORKING MY BUTT OFF SINCE THIS MORNING... I'M TOTALLY BEAT.
Animal Café
30 Minute Wait
I WANNA GO RELAX IN THERE FOR A BIT, TOO...
chatter
chatter
Womp womp...
......

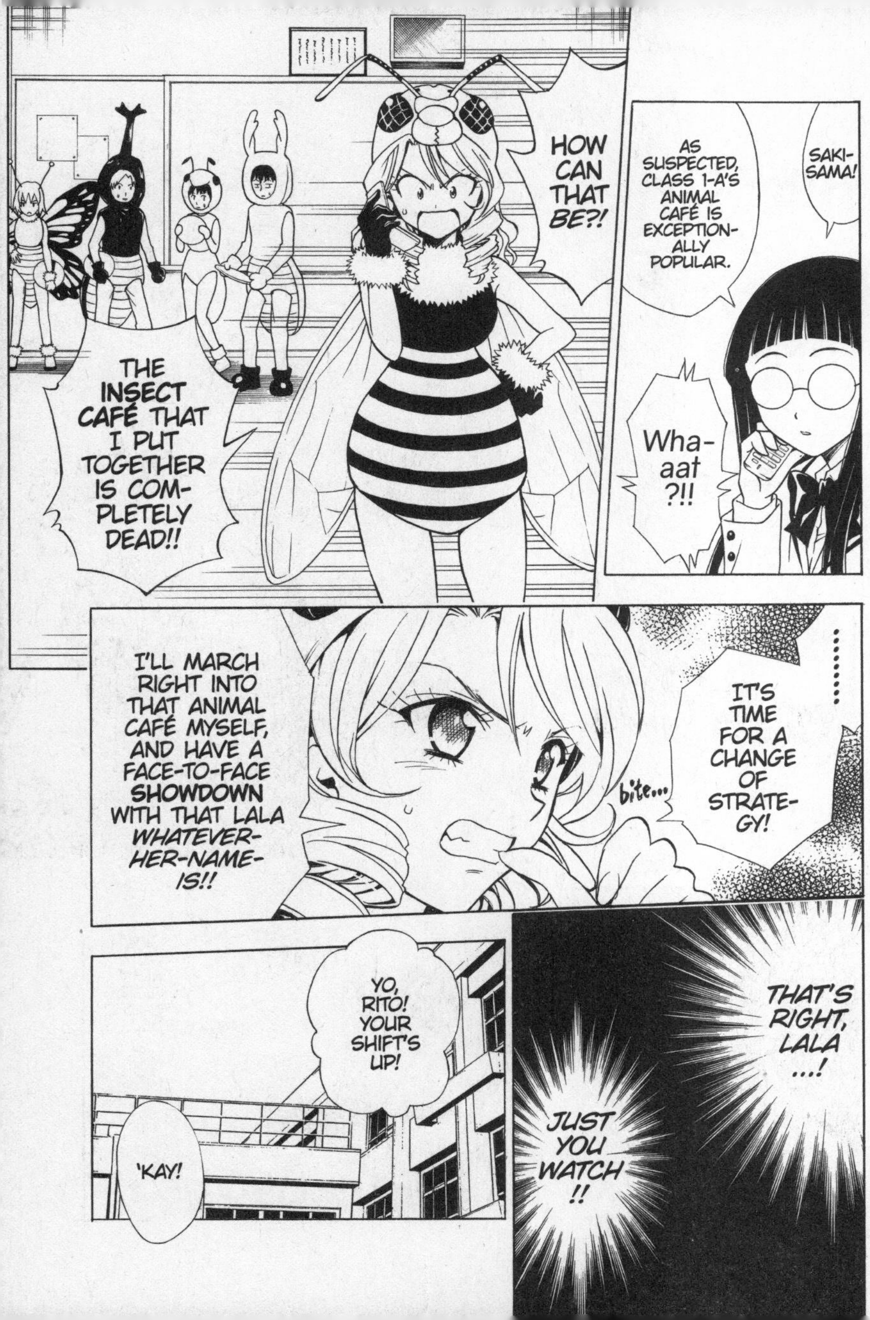
SAKI-SAMA!
AS SUSPECTED, CLASS 1-A'S ANIMAL CAFÉ IS EXCEPTION-ALLY POPULAR.
Wha-aat?!!
HOW CAN THAT BE?!
THE INSECT CAFÉ THAT I PUT TOGETHER IS COM-PLETELY DEAD!!
......
IT'S TIME FOR A CHANGE OF STRATE-GY!
bite...
I'LL MARCH RIGHT INTO THAT ANIMAL CAFÉ MYSELF, AND HAVE A FACE-TO-FACE SHOWDOWN WITH THAT LALA WHATEVER-HER-NAME-IS!!
THAT'S RIGHT, LALA ...!
JUST YOU WATCH !!
YO, RITO! YOUR SHIFT'S UP!
'KAY!

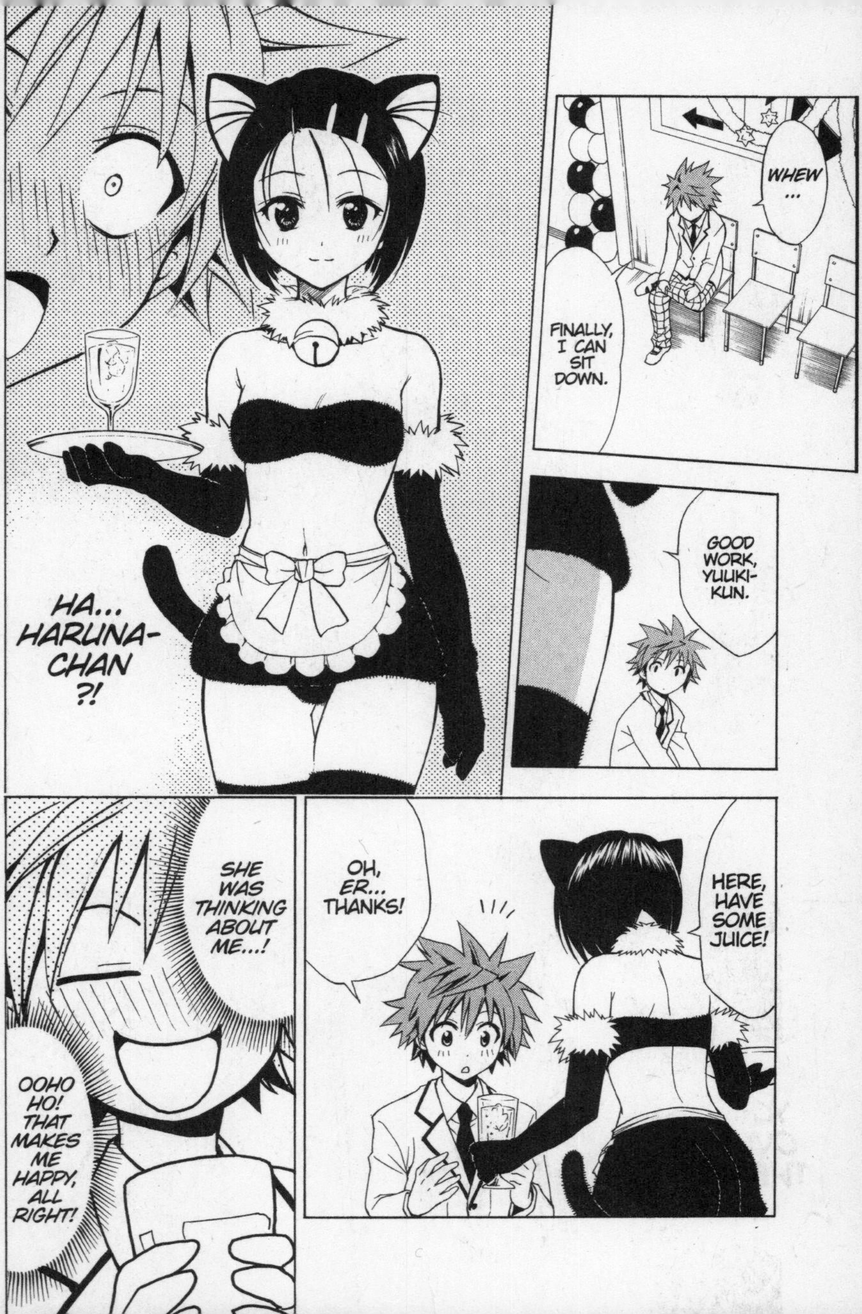
WHEW...
FINALLY, I CAN SIT DOWN.
GOOD WORK, YUUKI-KUN.
HA... HARUNA-CHAN?!
HERE, HAVE SOME JUICE!
OH, ER... THANKS!
SHE WAS THINKING ABOUT ME...!
OOHO HO! THAT MAKES ME HAPPY, ALL RIGHT!

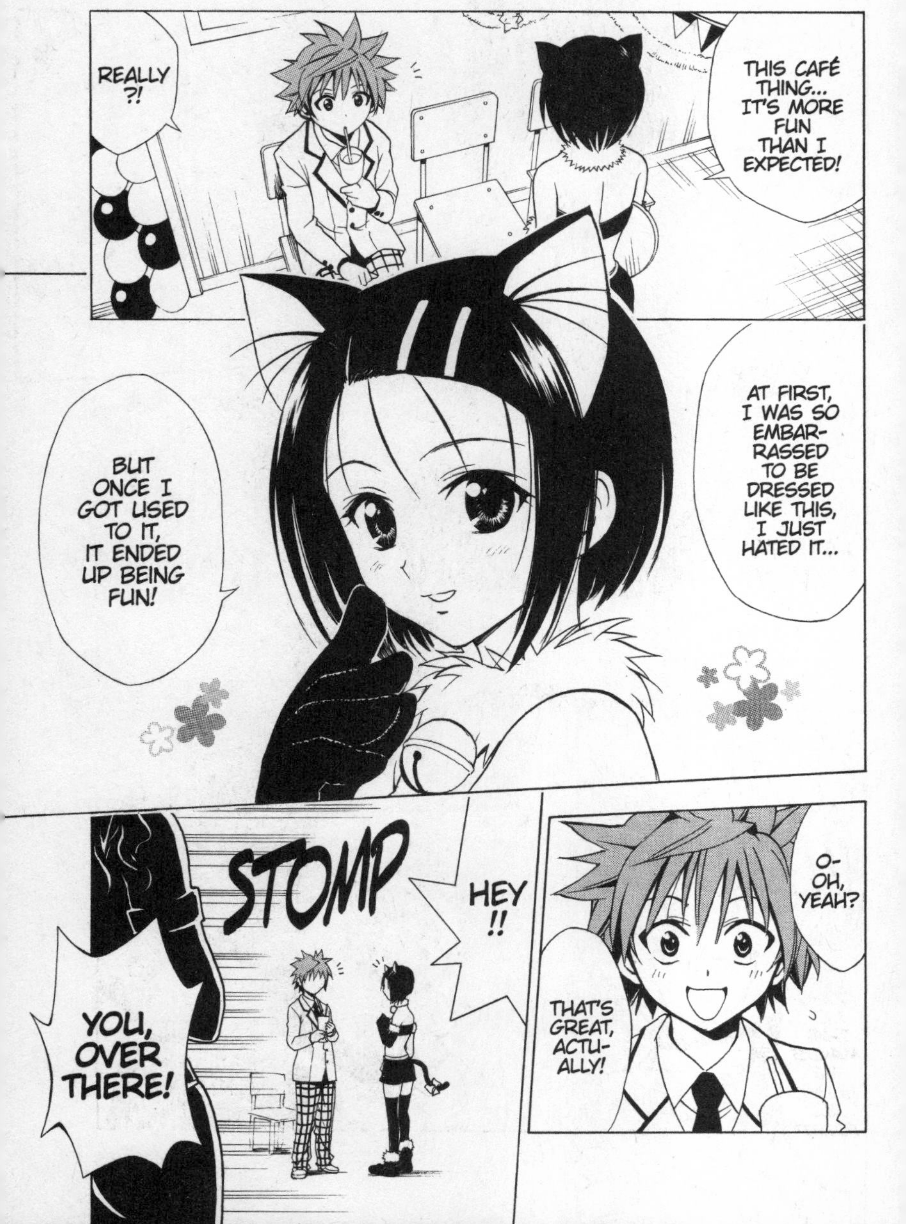

THIS CAFÉ THING... IT'S MORE FUN THAN I EXPECTED!
REALLY ?!
AT FIRST, I WAS SO EMBAR-RASSED TO BE DRESSED LIKE THIS, I JUST HATED IT...
BUT ONCE I GOT USED TO IT, IT ENDED UP BEING FUN!
O-OH, YEAH?
THAT'S GREAT, ACTU-ALLY!
STOMP
HEY !!
YOU, OVER THERE!

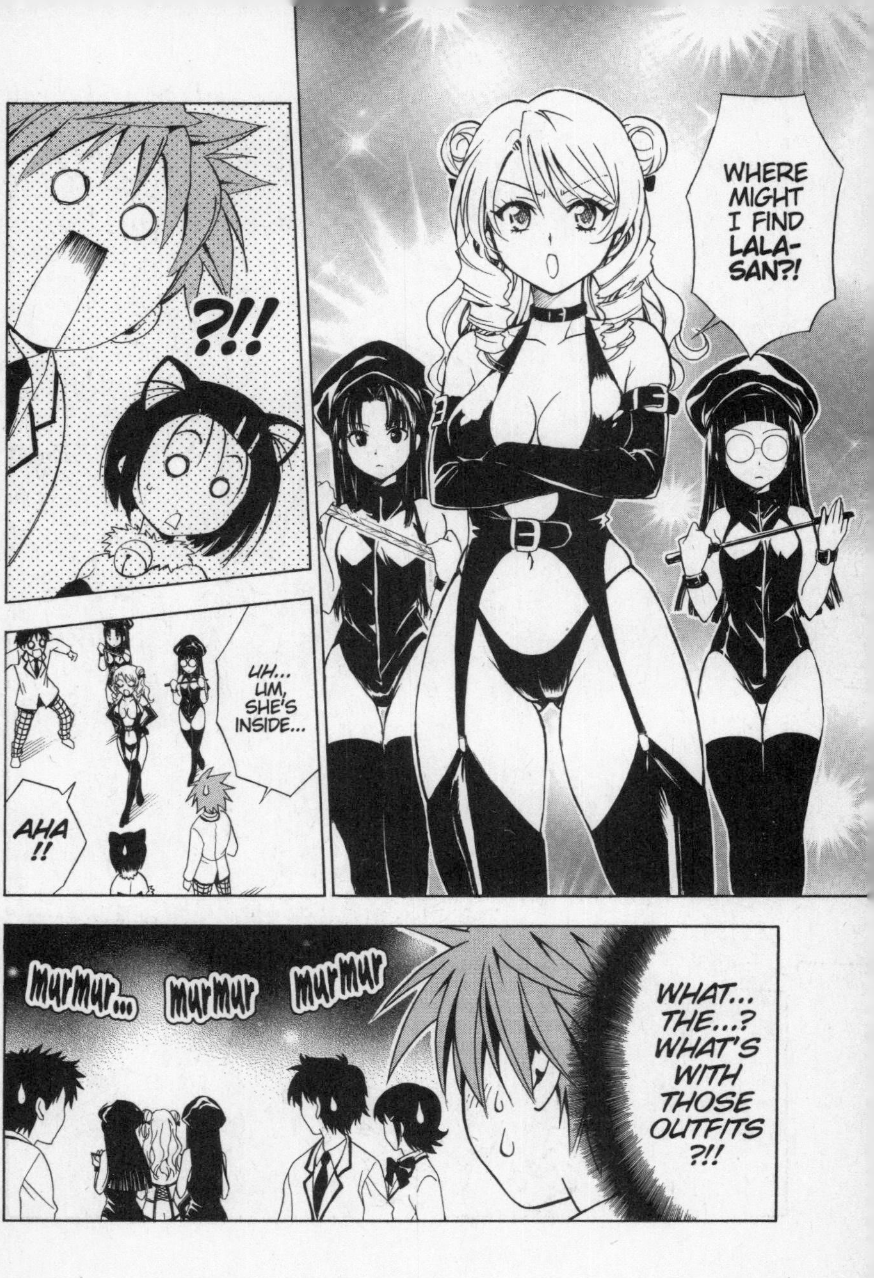
WHERE MIGHT I FIND LALA-SAN?!
?!!
UH... UM, SHE'S INSIDE...
AHA !!
WHAT... THE...? WHAT'S WITH THOSE OUTFITS ?!!
murmur... murmur murmur

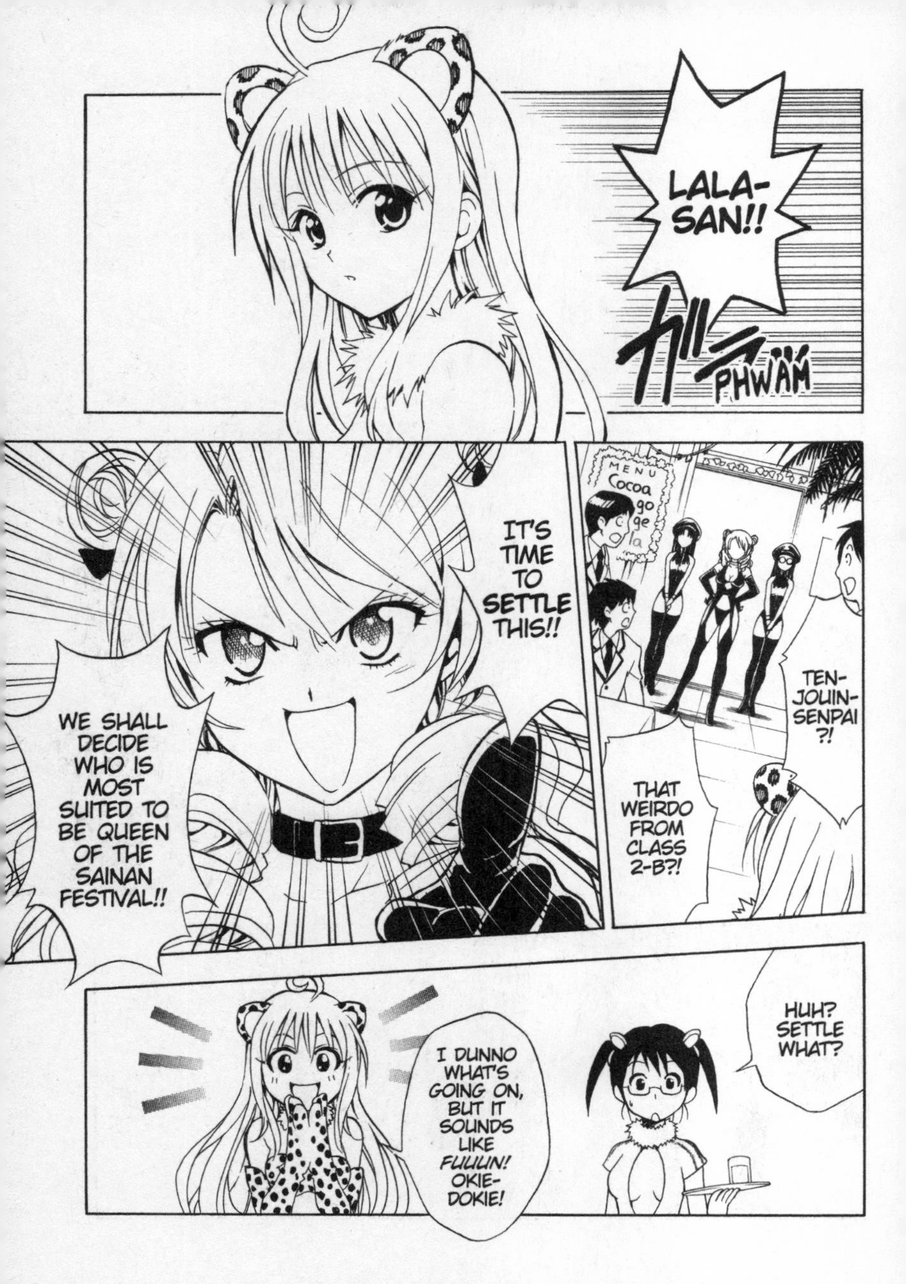
LALA-SAN!!
PHWAM
TEN-JOUIN-SENPAI?!
THAT WEIRDO FROM CLASS 2-B?!
MENU
Cocoa
IT'S TIME TO SETTLE THIS!!
WE SHALL DECIDE WHO IS MOST SUITED TO BE QUEEN OF THE SAINAN FESTIVAL!!
HUH? SETTLE WHAT?
I DUNNO WHAT'S GOING ON, BUT IT SOUNDS LIKE *FUUUN!* OKIE-DOKIE!

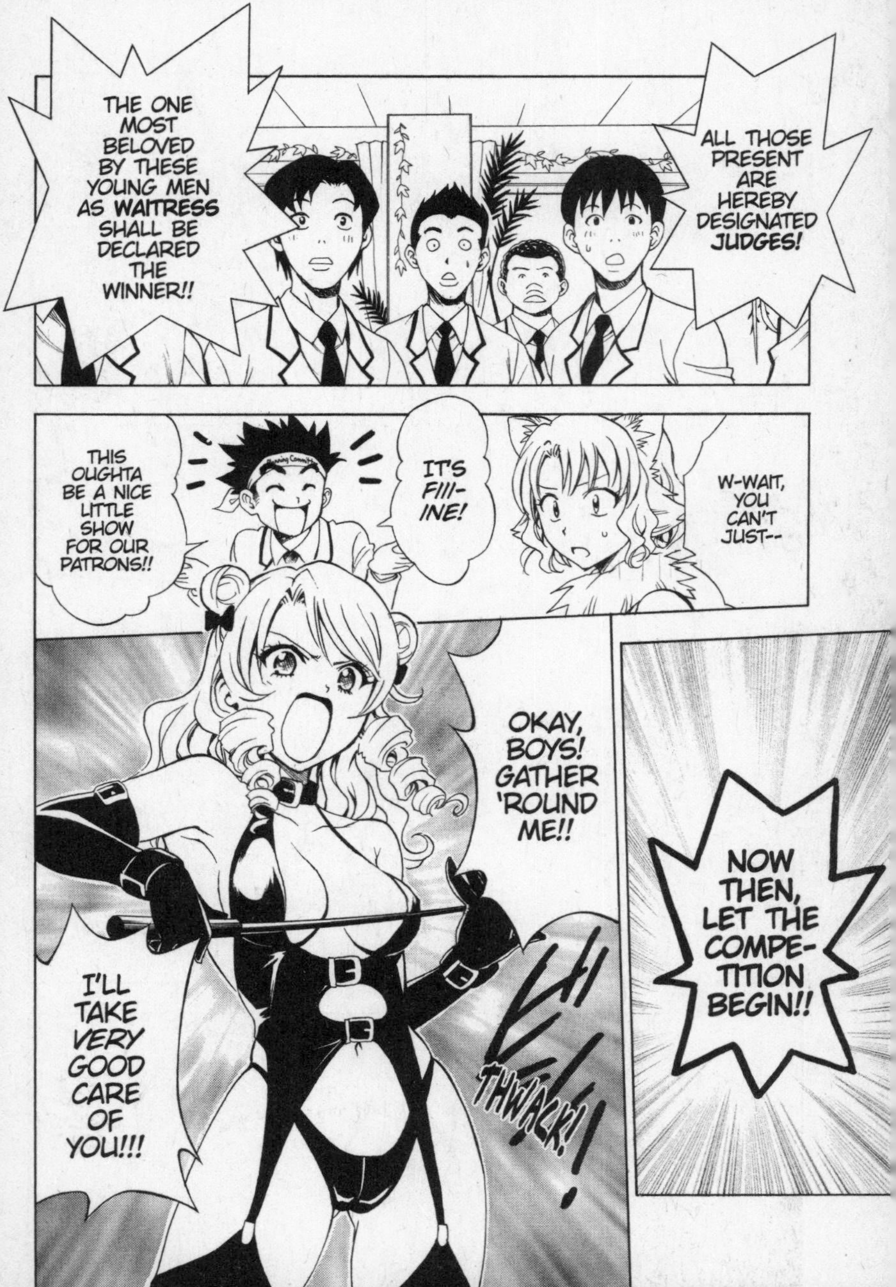
ALL THOSE PRESENT ARE HEREBY DESIGNATED JUDGES!
THE ONE MOST BELOVED BY THESE YOUNG MEN AS WAITRESS SHALL BE DECLARED THE WINNER!!
W-WAIT, YOU CAN'T JUST--
IT'S FIII-INE!
THIS OUGHTA BE A NICE LITTLE SHOW FOR OUR PATRONS!!
NOW THEN, LET THE COMPE-TITION BEGIN!!
OKAY, BOYS! GATHER 'ROUND ME!!
THWACK!
I'LL TAKE VERY GOOD CARE OF YOU!!!

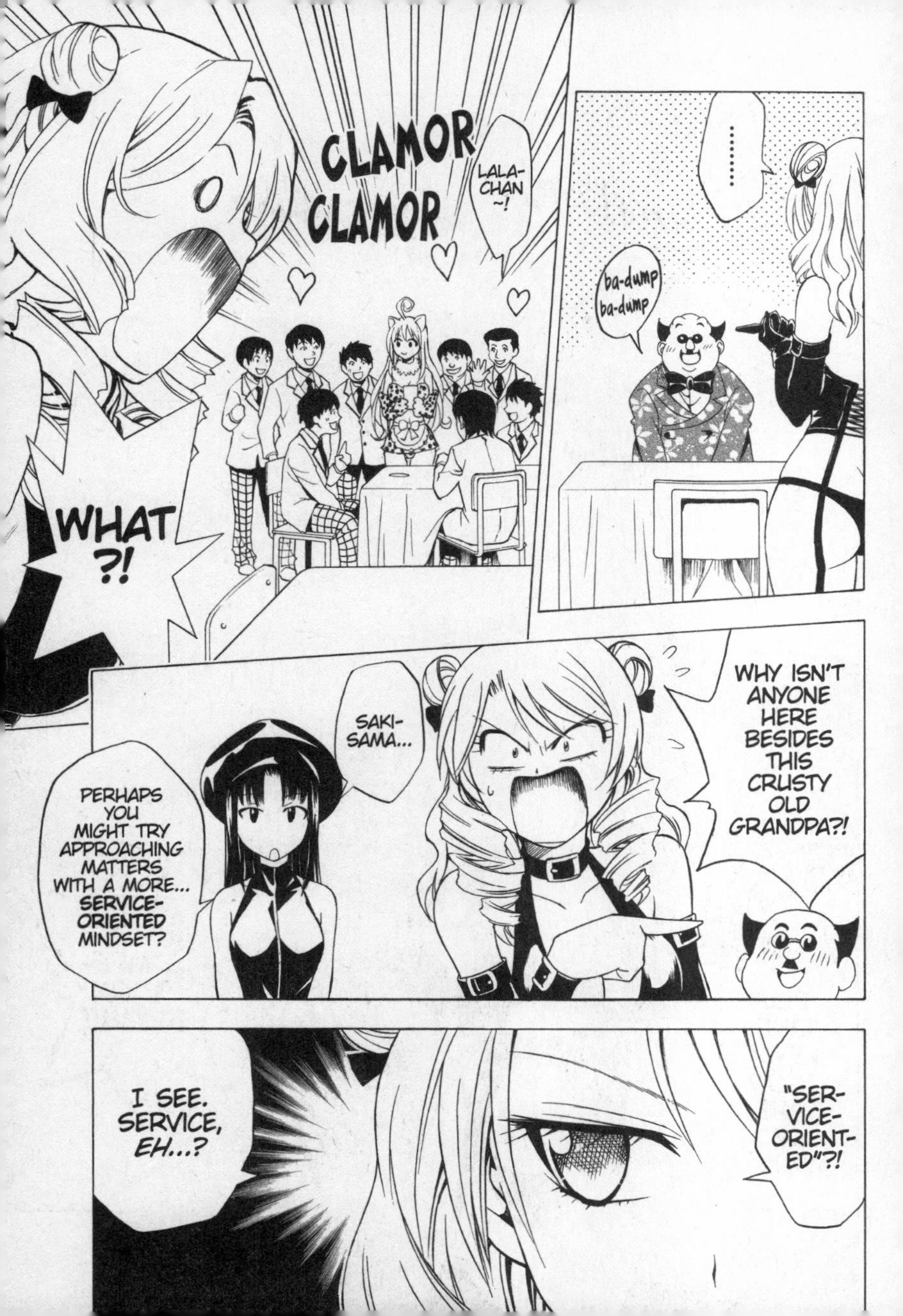
......
ba-dump ba-dump
CLAMOR CLAMOR
LALA-CHAN~!
WHAT?!
WHY ISN'T ANYONE HERE BESIDES THIS CRUSTY OLD GRANDPA?!
SAKI-SAMA...
PERHAPS YOU MIGHT TRY APPROACHING MATTERS WITH A MORE... SERVICE-ORIENTED MINDSET?
"SERVICE-ORIENTED"?!
I SEE. SERVICE, EH...?

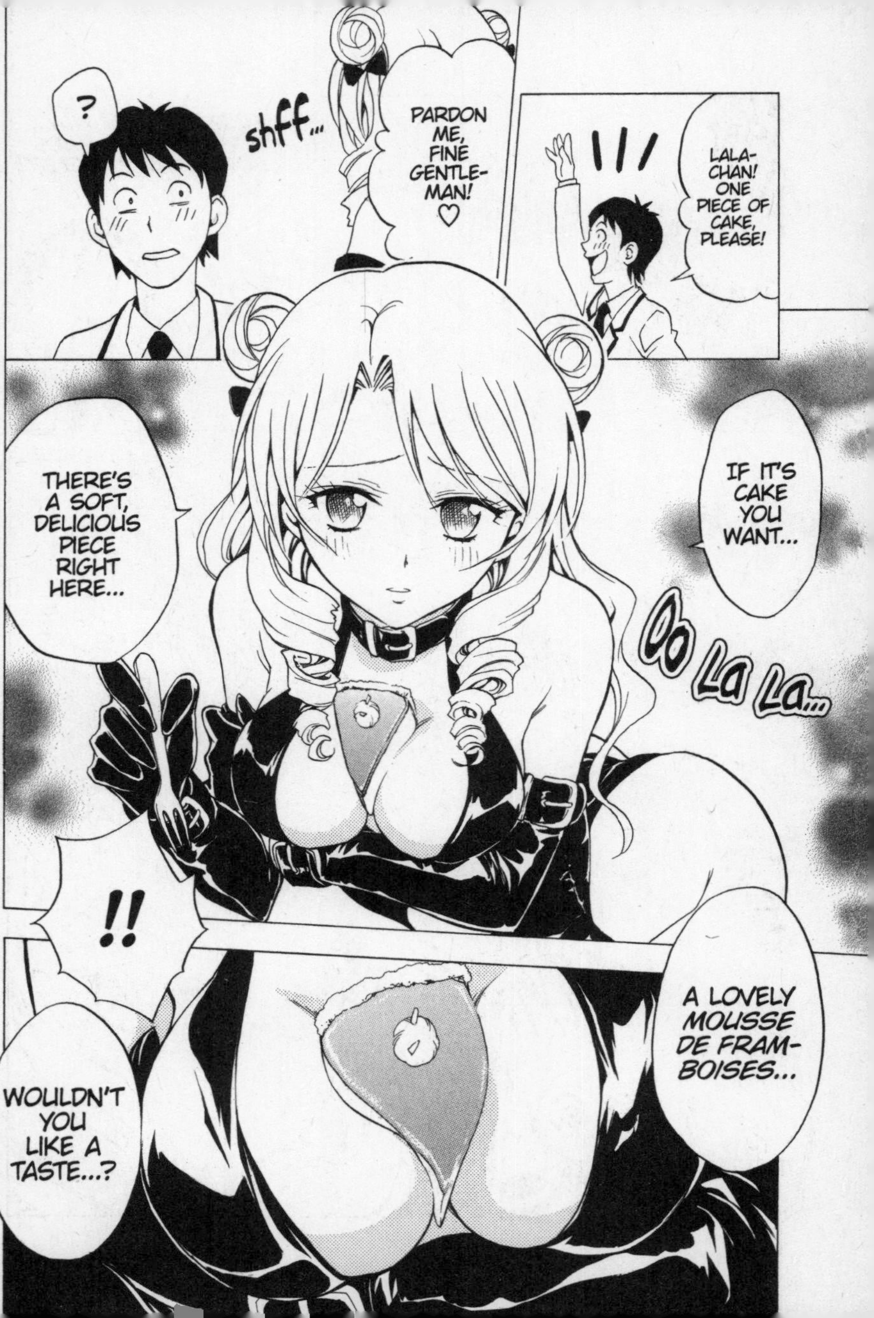
LALA-CHAN! ONE PIECE OF CAKE, PLEASE!
PARDON ME, FINE GENTLEMAN! ♡
shff...
?
IF IT'S CAKE YOU WANT...
Oo La La...
THERE'S A SOFT, DELICIOUS PIECE RIGHT HERE...
!!
A LOVELY MOUSSE DE FRAMBOISES...
WOULDN'T YOU LIKE A TASTE...?

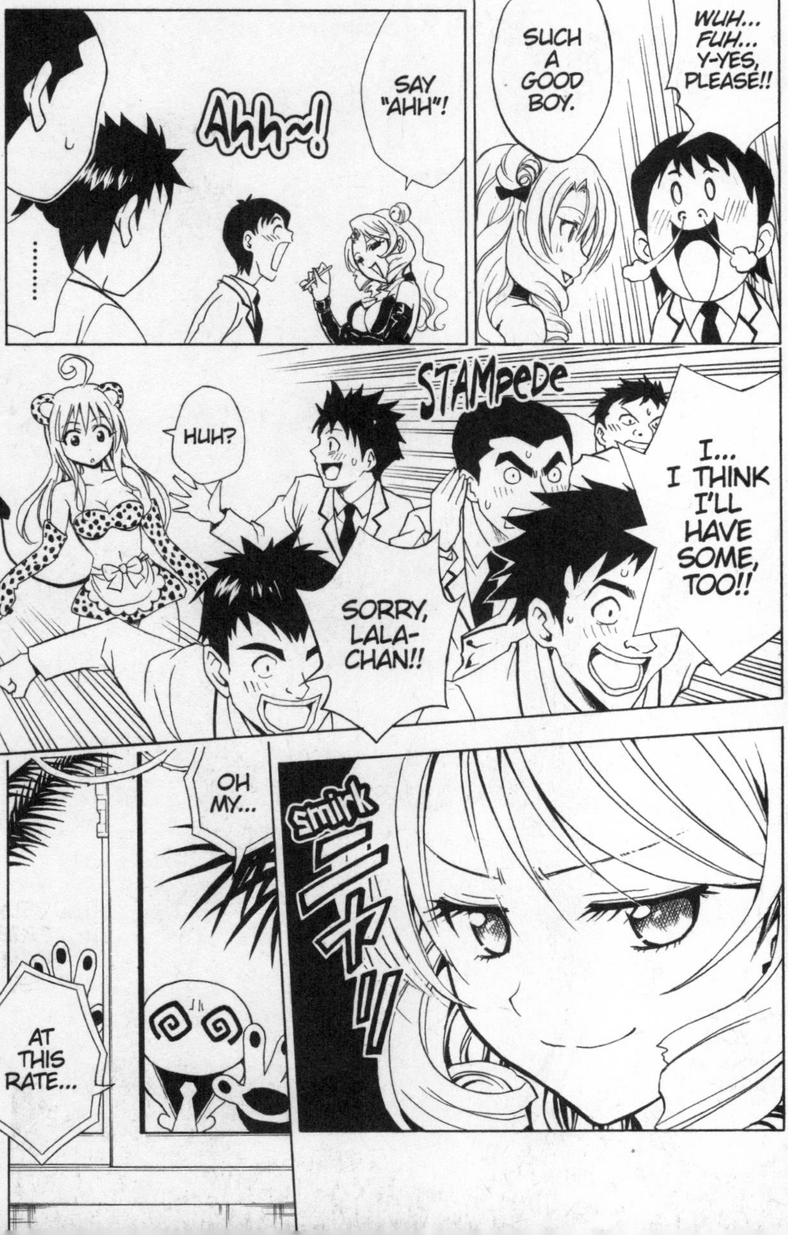
WUH... FUH... Y-YES, PLEASE!!
SUCH A GOOD BOY.
SAY "AHH"!
Ahh~!
......
STAMPEDE
I... I THINK I'LL HAVE SOME, TOO!!
SORRY, LALA-CHAN!!
HUH?
smirk
ニヤッ
OH MY...
AT THIS RATE...

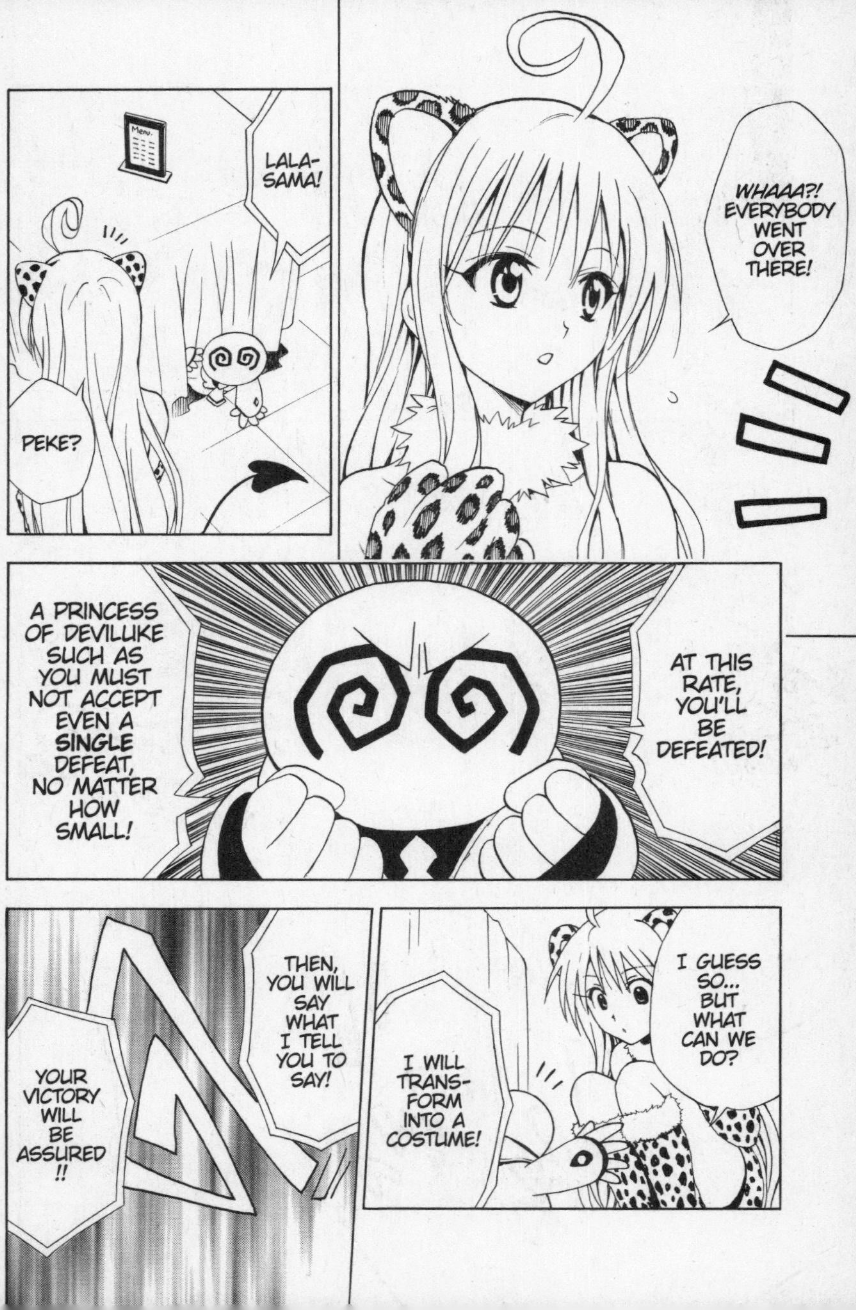
WHAAA?! EVERYBODY WENT OVER THERE!
LALA-SAMA!
PEKE?
AT THIS RATE, YOU'LL BE DEFEATED!
A PRINCESS OF DEVILUKE SUCH AS YOU MUST NOT ACCEPT EVEN A SINGLE DEFEAT, NO MATTER HOW SMALL!
I GUESS SO... BUT WHAT CAN WE DO?
I WILL TRANS-FORM INTO A COSTUME!
THEN, YOU WILL SAY WHAT I TELL YOU TO SAY!
YOUR VICTORY WILL BE ASSURED !!

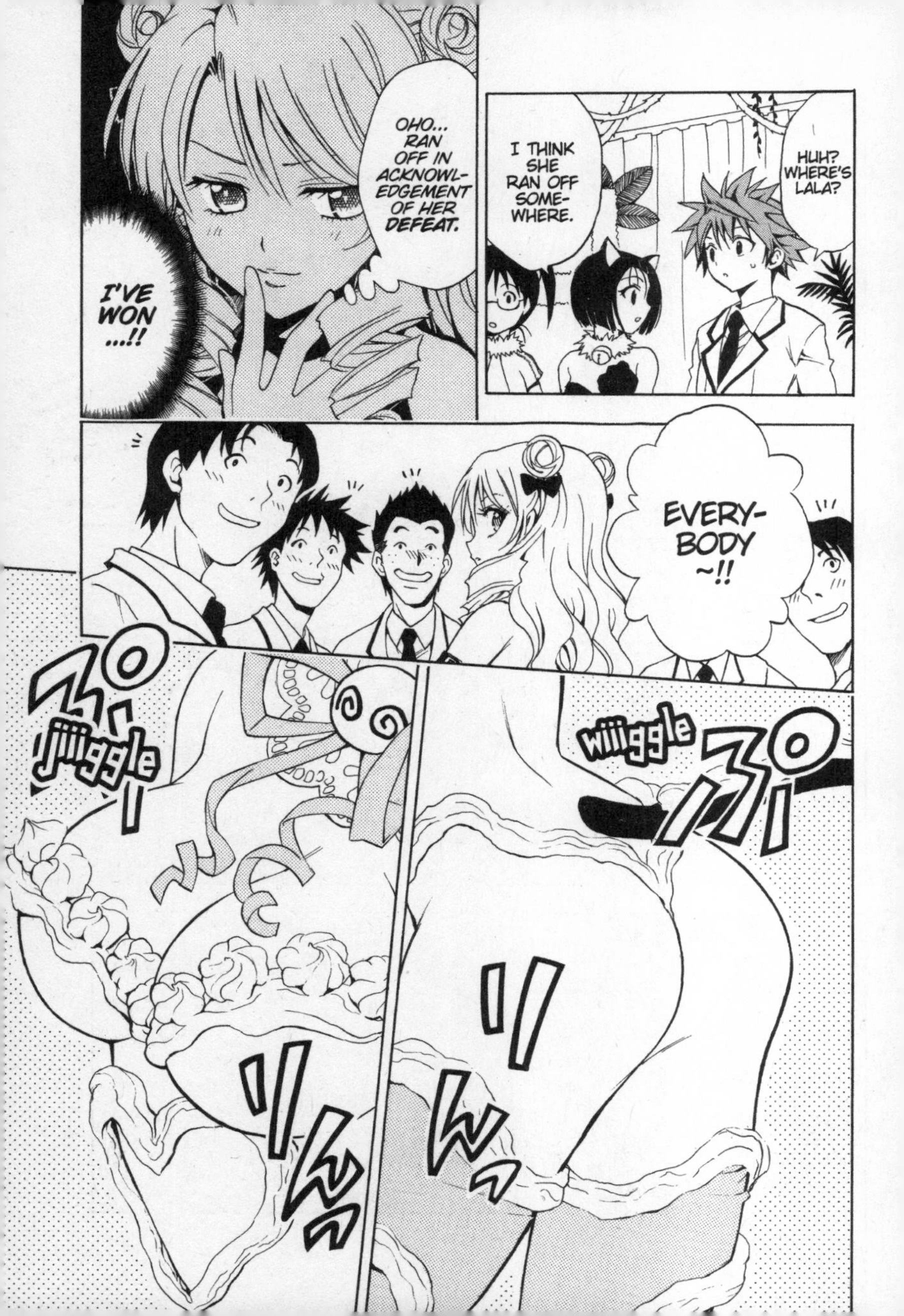
HUH? WHERE'S LALA?
I THINK SHE RAN OFF SOMEWHERE.
OHO... RAN OFF IN ACKNOWLEDGEMENT OF HER DEFEAT.
I'VE WON ...!!
EVERYBODY ~!!
wiiiggle
jiiiggle

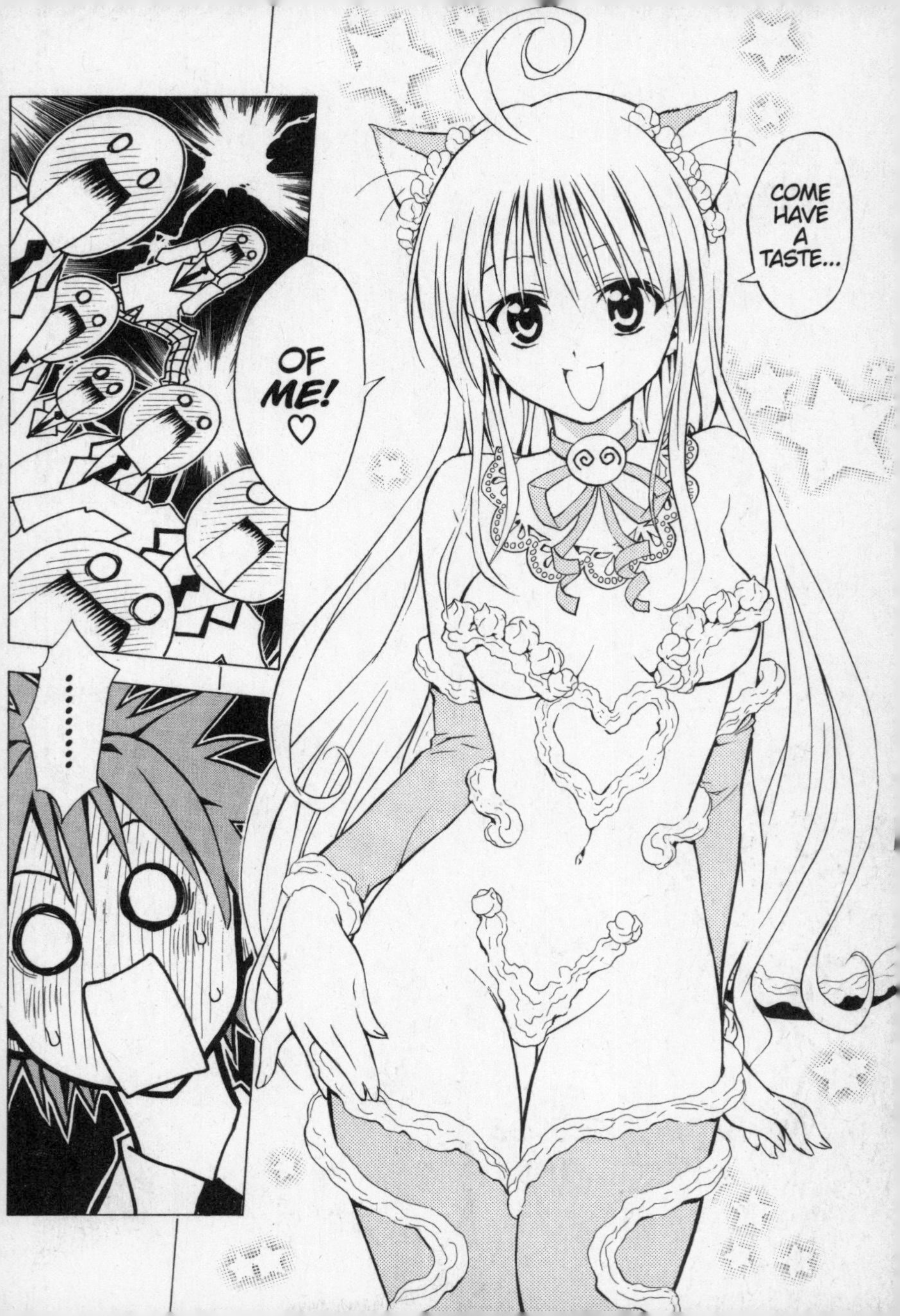
COME HAVE A TASTE...
OF ME! ♡
......

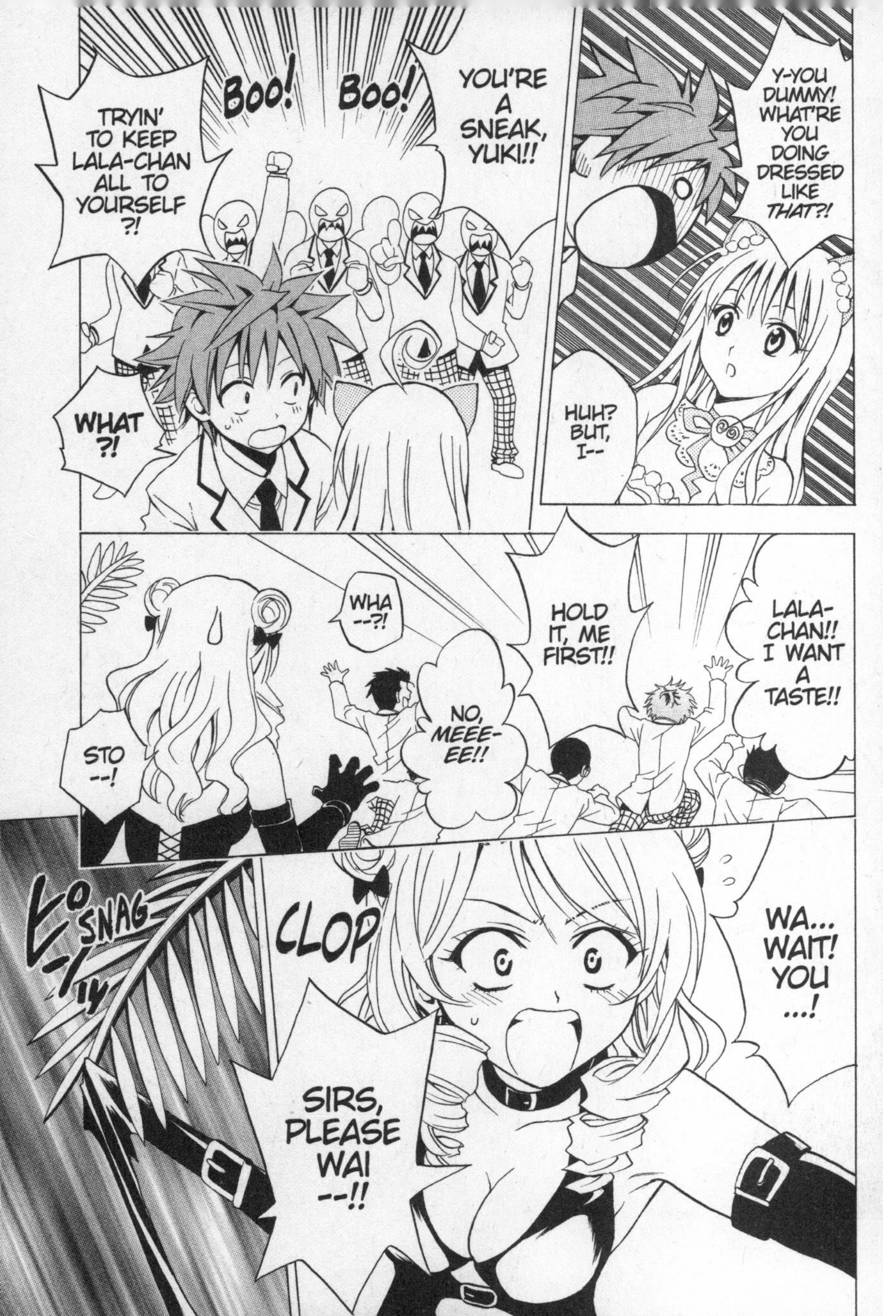
Y-YOU DUMMY! WHAT'RE YOU DOING DRESSED LIKE *THAT*?!
HUH? BUT, I--
YOU'RE A SNEAK, YUKI!!
BOO! BOO!
TRYIN' TO KEEP LALA-CHAN ALL TO YOURSELF ?!
WHAT ?!
LALA-CHAN!! I WANT A TASTE!!
HOLD IT, ME FIRST!!
WHA --?!
NO, MEEE-EE!!
STO --!
WA... WAIT! YOU ...!
CLOP
SNAG
SIRS, PLEASE WAI --!!

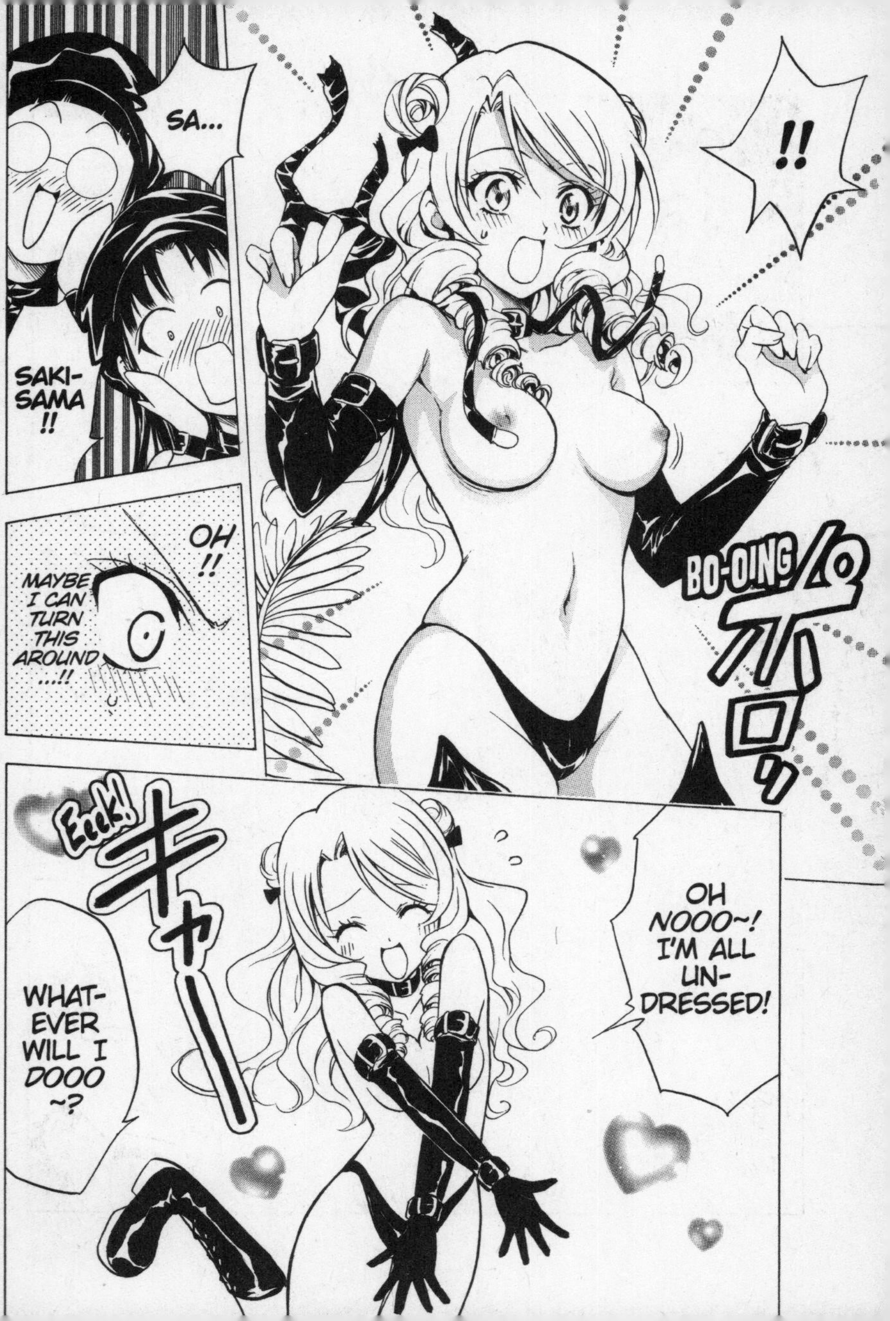
!!
BO-OING
ポロッ
SA...
SAKI-SAMA !!
OH !!
MAYBE I CAN TURN THIS AROUND ...!!
OH NOOO~! I'M ALL UN-DRESSED!
Eeek!
キャー
WHAT-EVER WILL I DOOO ~?

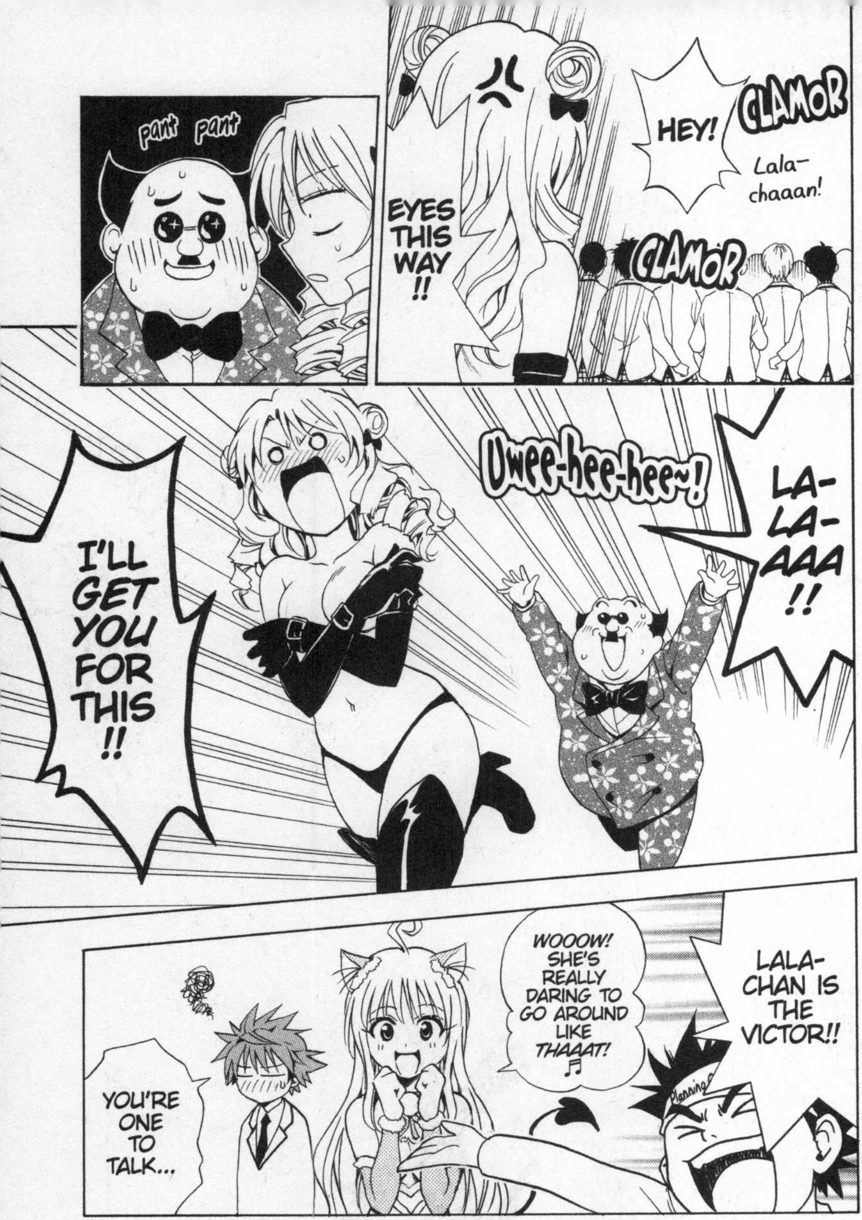
CLAMOR
HEY!
Lala-chaaan!
CLAMOR
EYES THIS WAY!!
pant pant
LA-LA-LAAA!!
Uwee-hee-hee~!
I'LL GET YOU FOR THIS!!
LALA-CHAN IS THE VICTOR!!
WOOOW! SHE'S REALLY DARING TO GO AROUND LIKE THAAAT! ♬
YOU'RE ONE TO TALK...

Character File 2

Tenjouin Saki

This time, we'll be discussing Tenjouin Saki. Even though the two of us have similar names, we didn't exactly intend for that to happen. It was just what we thought of based on Yabuki-san's drawing, so don't think about it too deeply *(ha ha)!*

☆Her Position as a Character

We had two reasons for creating Saki. The first was that we wanted to add a senpai-type character--someone who looks down on everyone from on high. So, we introduced her as someone older than Rito and company. The other reason was that her being a girl from the upper crust of society means she comes from a position of wealth. A character who doesn't hold back when it comes to speaking her mind, who also happens to be rich--that's a character who can be very convenient when it comes to advancing the story. Thanks to Saki and the power of her money, developing events for the story is super easy.

☆A Really Earnest Girl (So we think...)

When Saki first appears, she tries to get at Rito by using her sex appeal and basically behaves like a huge lady-pervert. However, she's really an earnest, straight-thinking girl at heart. Consider her behavior as the embodiment of a girl's earnest thinking, a girl who simply must be number one at whatever she chooses to do. Yeah, so, then... Maybe she's not really a pervert... I think. Following that same line of thinking, Yabuki-san added Saki's dialogue in Trouble 29 during the storyboarding stage.

☆Rin and Aya

A pair who admire Saki in such a way that they're always saying, "That's our Saki-sama!" Though, I really couldn't tell you exactly what that means! Eventually, I guess there will come a time when she supports them... Probably? On a somewhat related note, Aya and Rin are not twins.

☆How We Handle Her

Lately, it seems like every time we put Saki on the page, we're undressing her and making a victim out of her. In all honesty, she might be the number one victim in this entire manga. Nevertheless, as we move forward, we're going to depict her in a bright and positive way, so please offer her your warm encouragement!

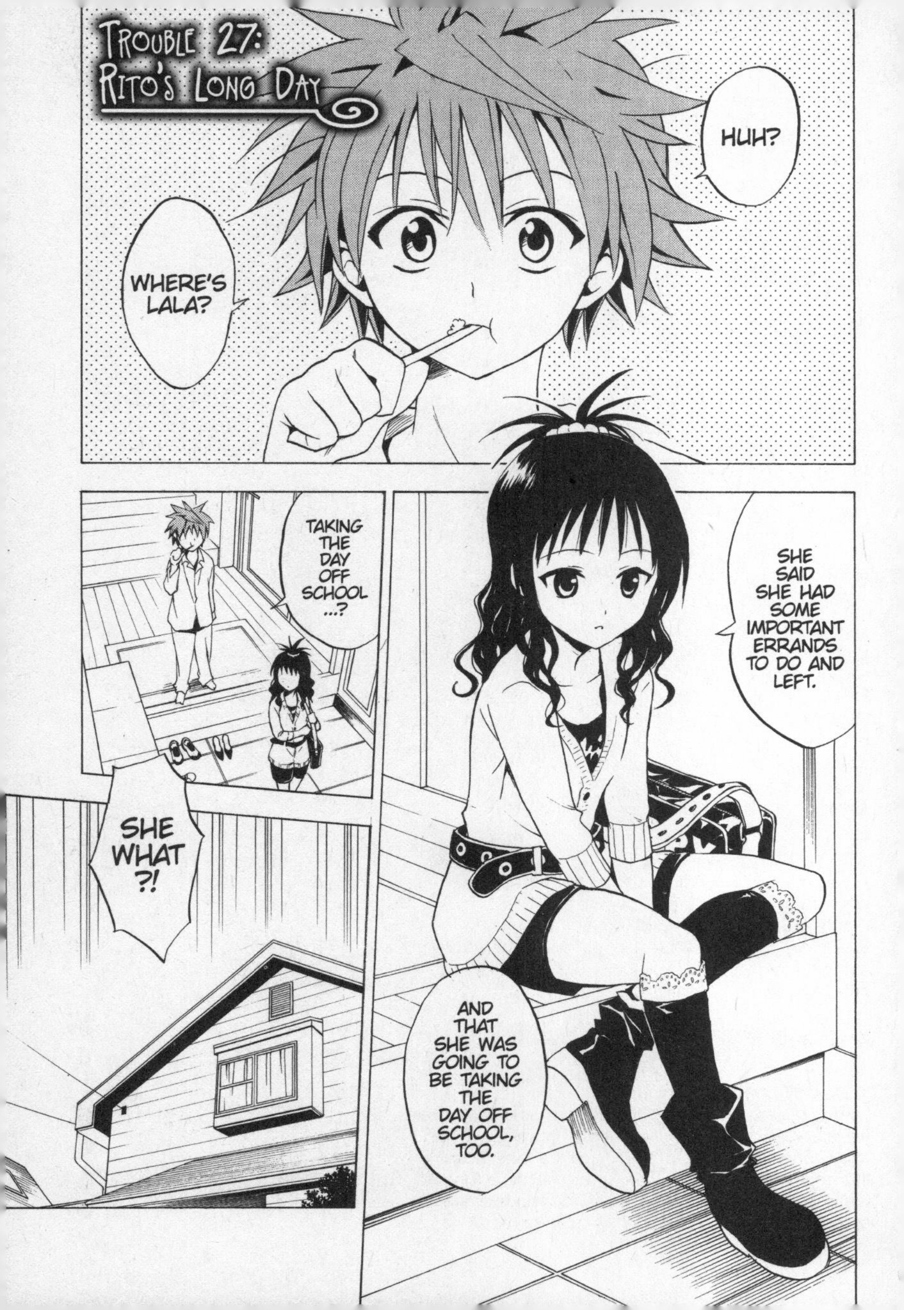
Trouble 27: Rito's Long Day
HUH?
WHERE'S LALA?
SHE SAID SHE HAD SOME IMPORTANT ERRANDS TO DO AND LEFT.
AND THAT SHE WAS GOING TO BE TAKING THE DAY OFF SCHOOL, TOO.
TAKING THE DAY OFF SCHOOL ...?
SHE WHAT ?!

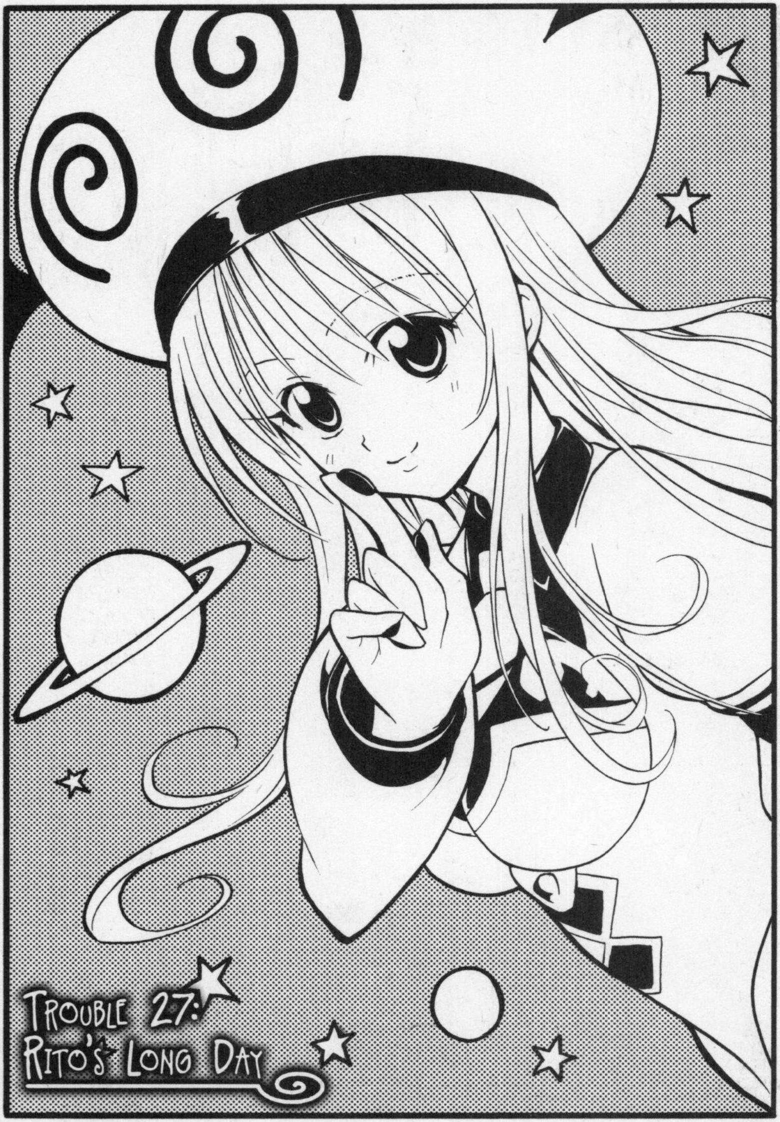
TROUBLE 27:
RITO'S LONG DAY

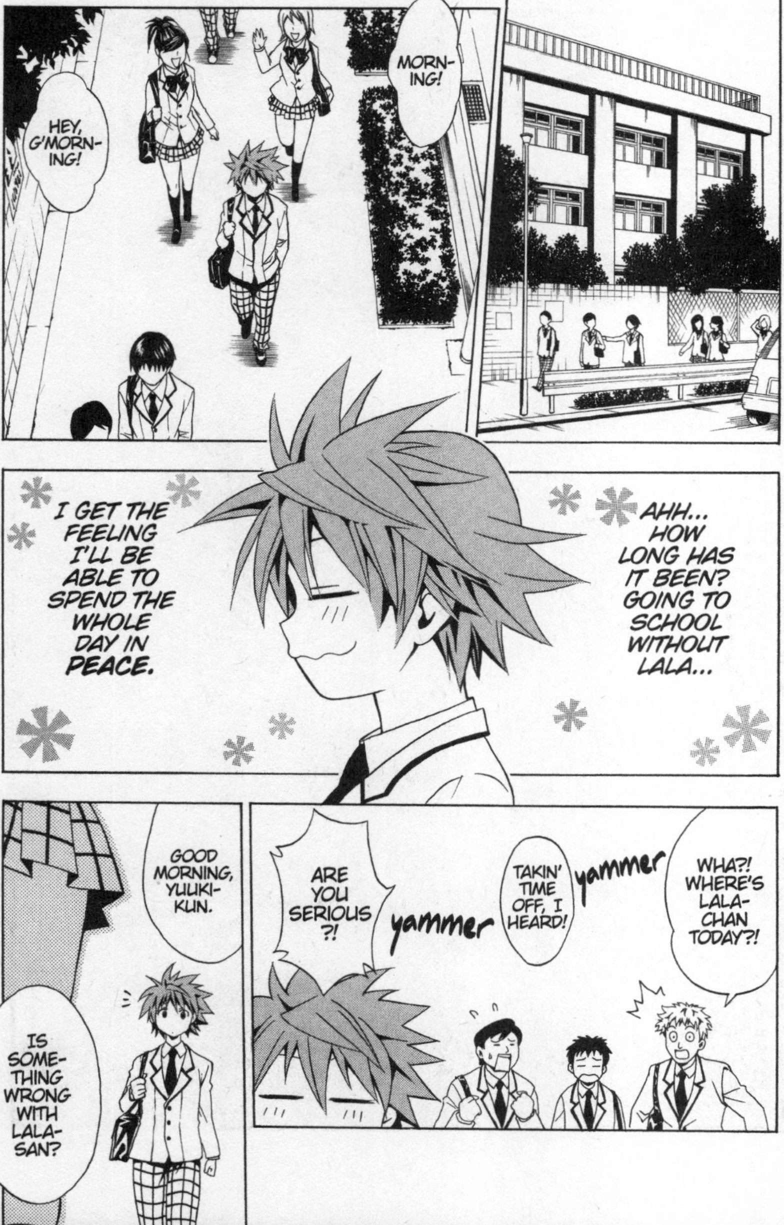
MORNING!
HEY, G'MORNING!
AHH... HOW LONG HAS IT BEEN? GOING TO SCHOOL WITHOUT LALA...
I GET THE FEELING I'LL BE ABLE TO SPEND THE WHOLE DAY IN PEACE.
WHA?! WHERE'S LALA-CHAN TODAY?!
yammer
TAKIN' TIME OFF, I HEARD!
yammer
ARE YOU SERIOUS?!
GOOD MORNING, YUUKI-KUN.
IS SOMETHING WRONG WITH LALA-SAN?

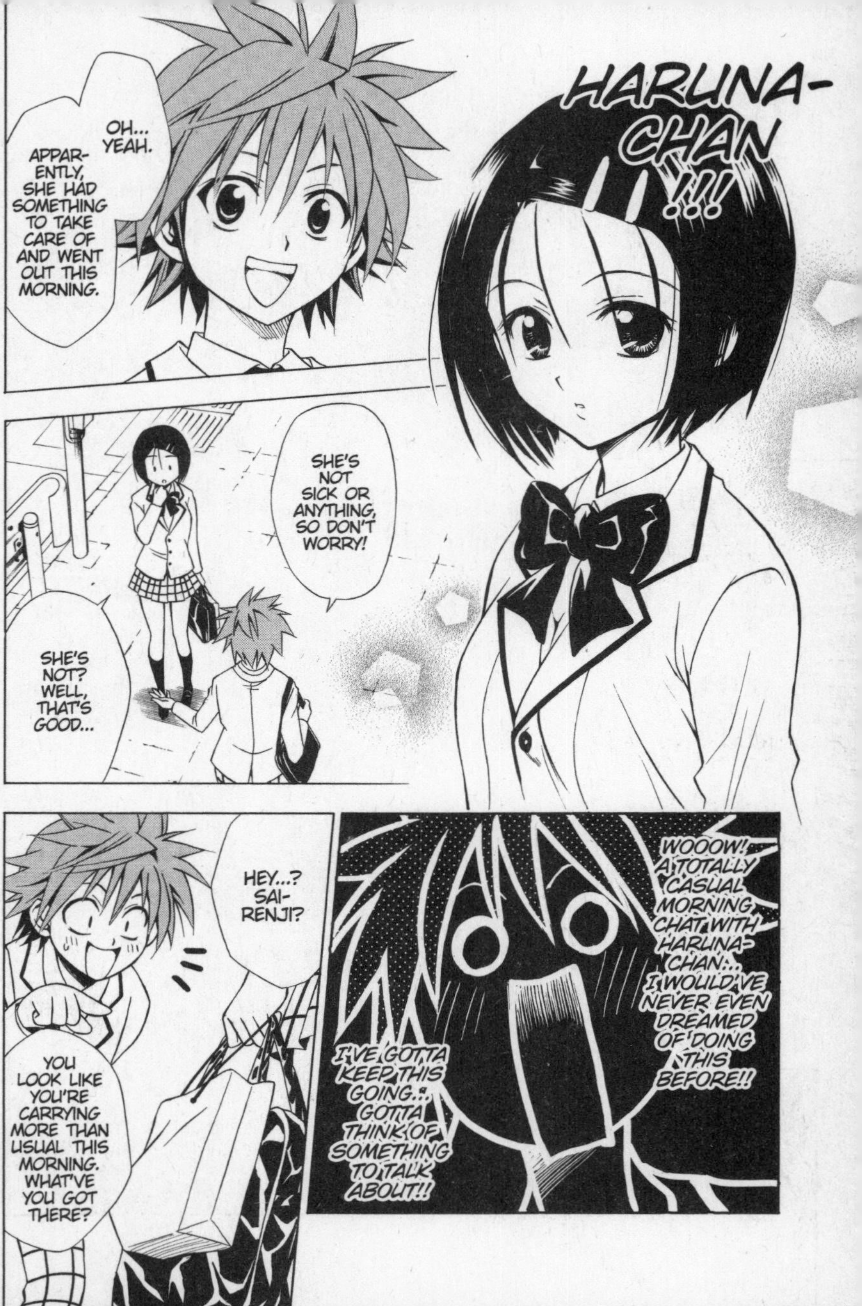
HARUNA-CHAN!!!
OH... YEAH.
APPARENTLY, SHE HAD SOMETHING TO TAKE CARE OF AND WENT OUT THIS MORNING.
SHE'S NOT SICK OR ANYTHING, SO DON'T WORRY!
SHE'S NOT? WELL, THAT'S GOOD...
WOOOW! A TOTALLY CASUAL MORNING CHAT WITH HARUNA-CHAN... I WOULD'VE NEVER EVEN DREAMED OF DOING THIS BEFORE!!
I'VE GOTTA KEEP THIS GOING... GOTTA THINK OF SOMETHING TO TALK ABOUT!!
HEY...? SAI-RENJI?
YOU LOOK LIKE YOU'RE CARRYING MORE THAN USUAL THIS MORNING. WHAT'VE YOU GOT THERE?

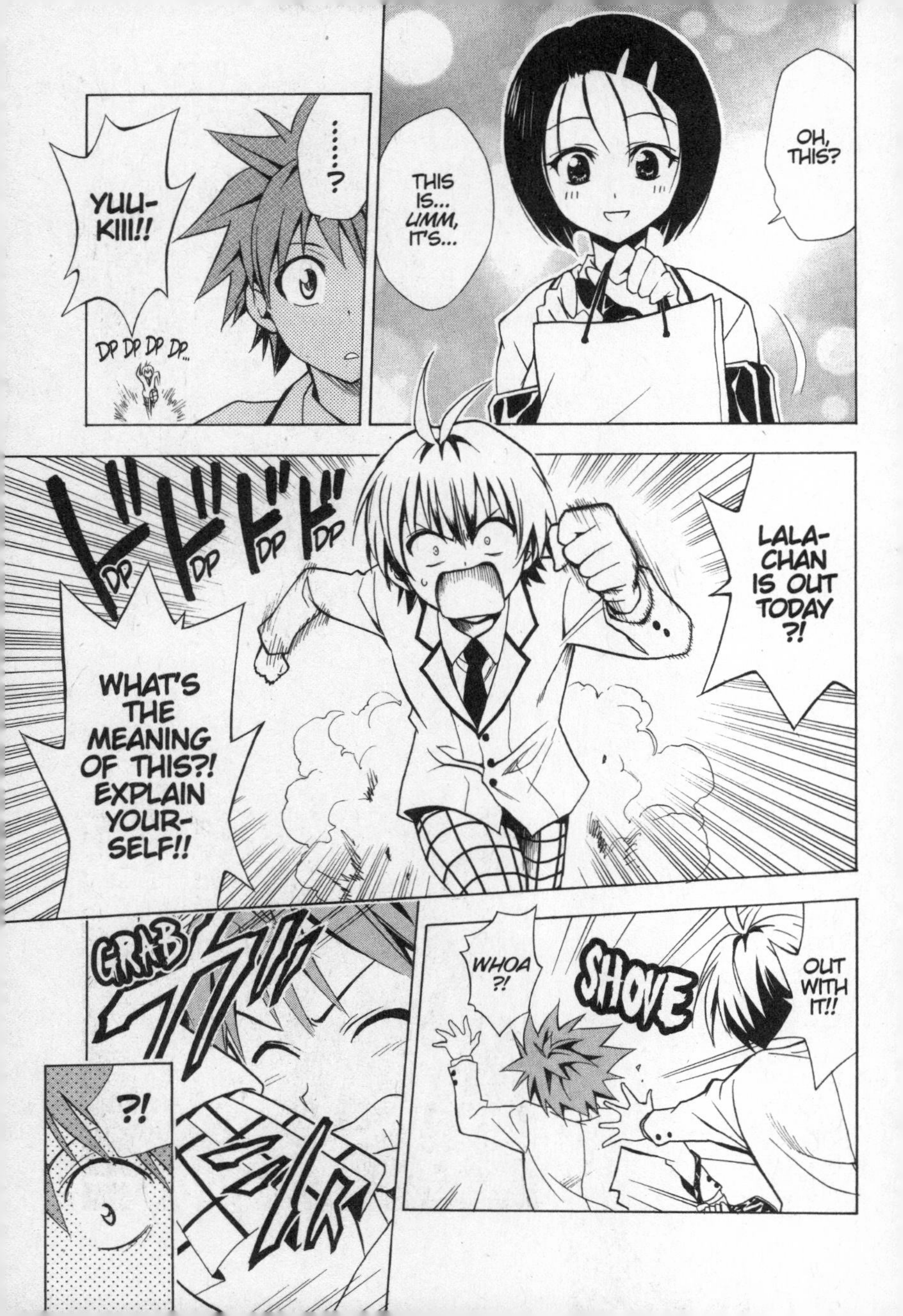

OH, THIS?
THIS IS... UMM, IT'S...
......?
YUU-KIIII!!
DP DP DP DP...
LALA-CHAN IS OUT TODAY?!
DP DP DP DP
WHAT'S THE MEANING OF THIS?! EXPLAIN YOUR-SELF!!
OUT WITH IT!!
SHOVE
WHOA?!
GRAB
?!

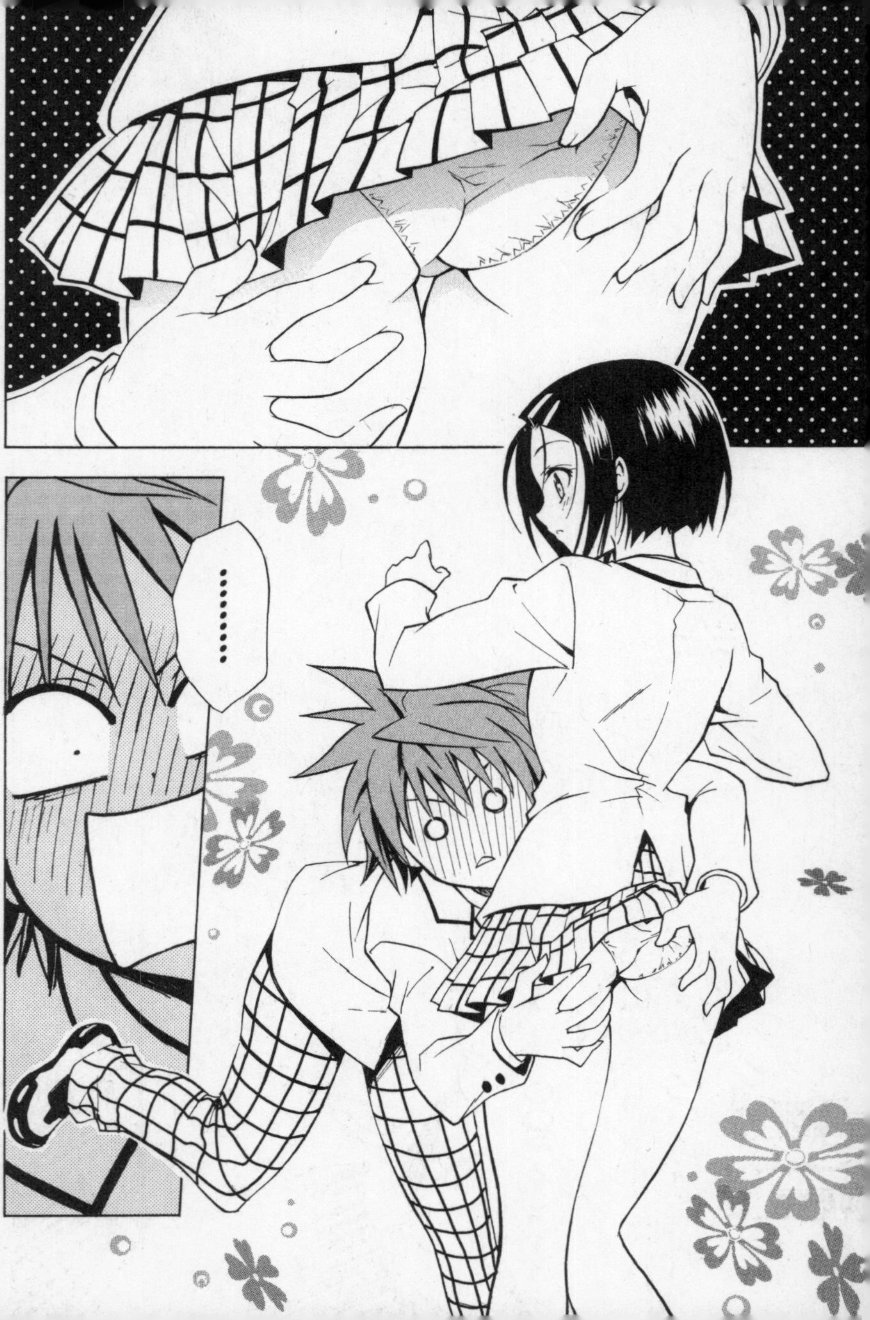
……

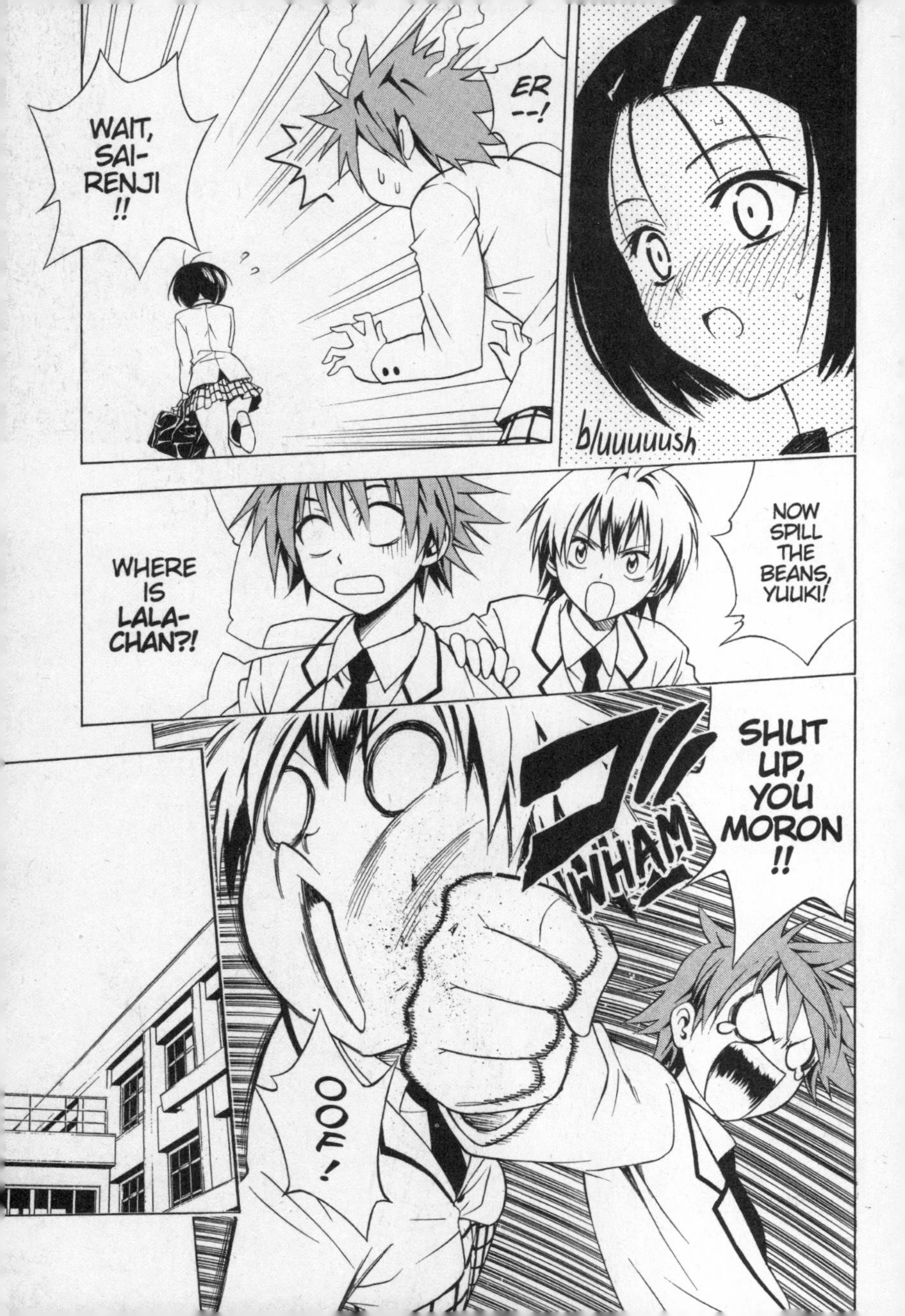
bluuuuush
ER --!
WAIT, SAI-RENJI !!
NOW SPILL THE BEANS, YUUKI!
WHERE IS LALA-CHAN?!
SHUT UP, YOU MORON !!
WHAM
OOF!

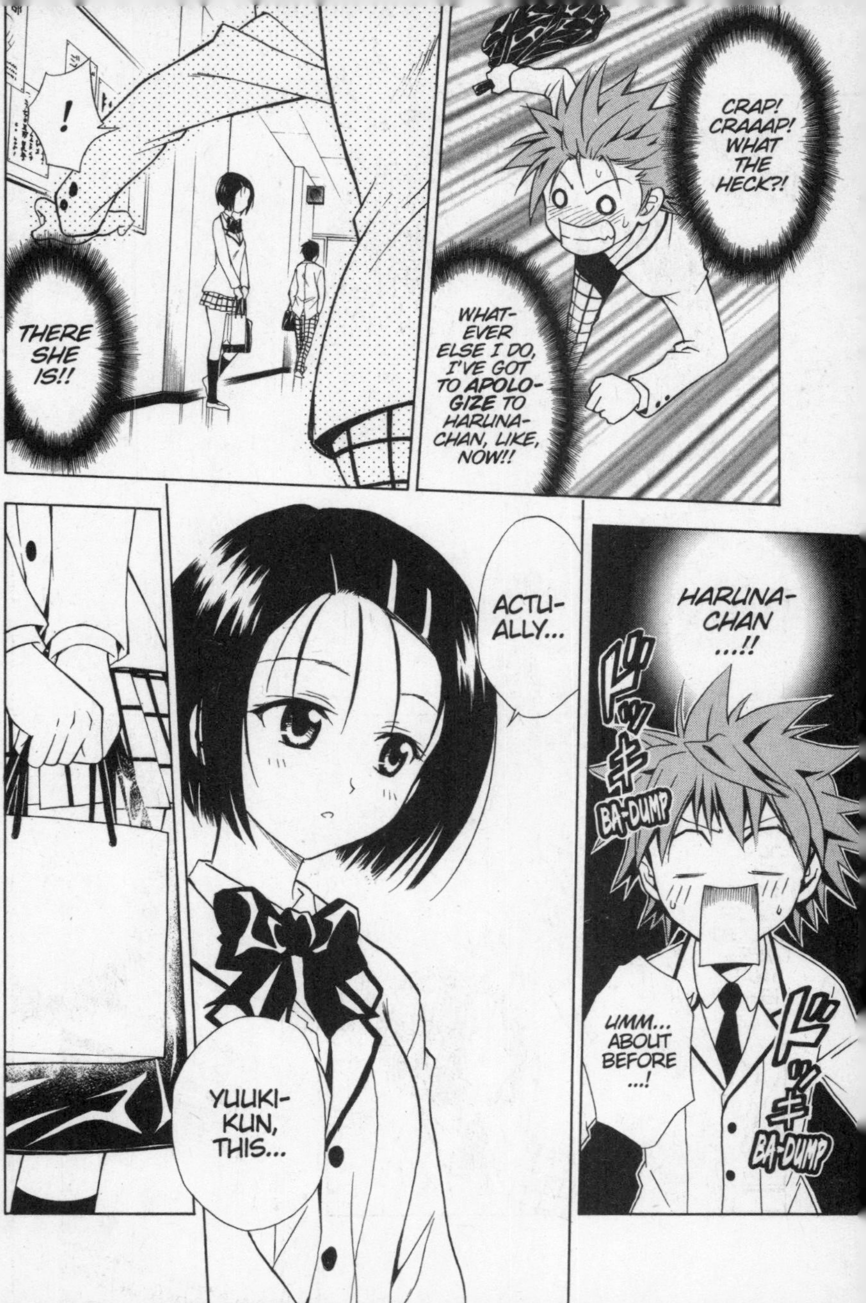
CRAP! CRAAAP! WHAT THE HECK?!
WHAT-EVER ELSE I DO, I'VE GOT TO **APOLOGIZE** TO HARUNA-CHAN, LIKE, NOW!!
!
THERE SHE IS!!
HARUNA-CHAN ...!!
BA-DUMP
UMM... ABOUT BEFORE ...!
BA-DUMP
ACTU-ALLY...
YUUKI-KUN, THIS...

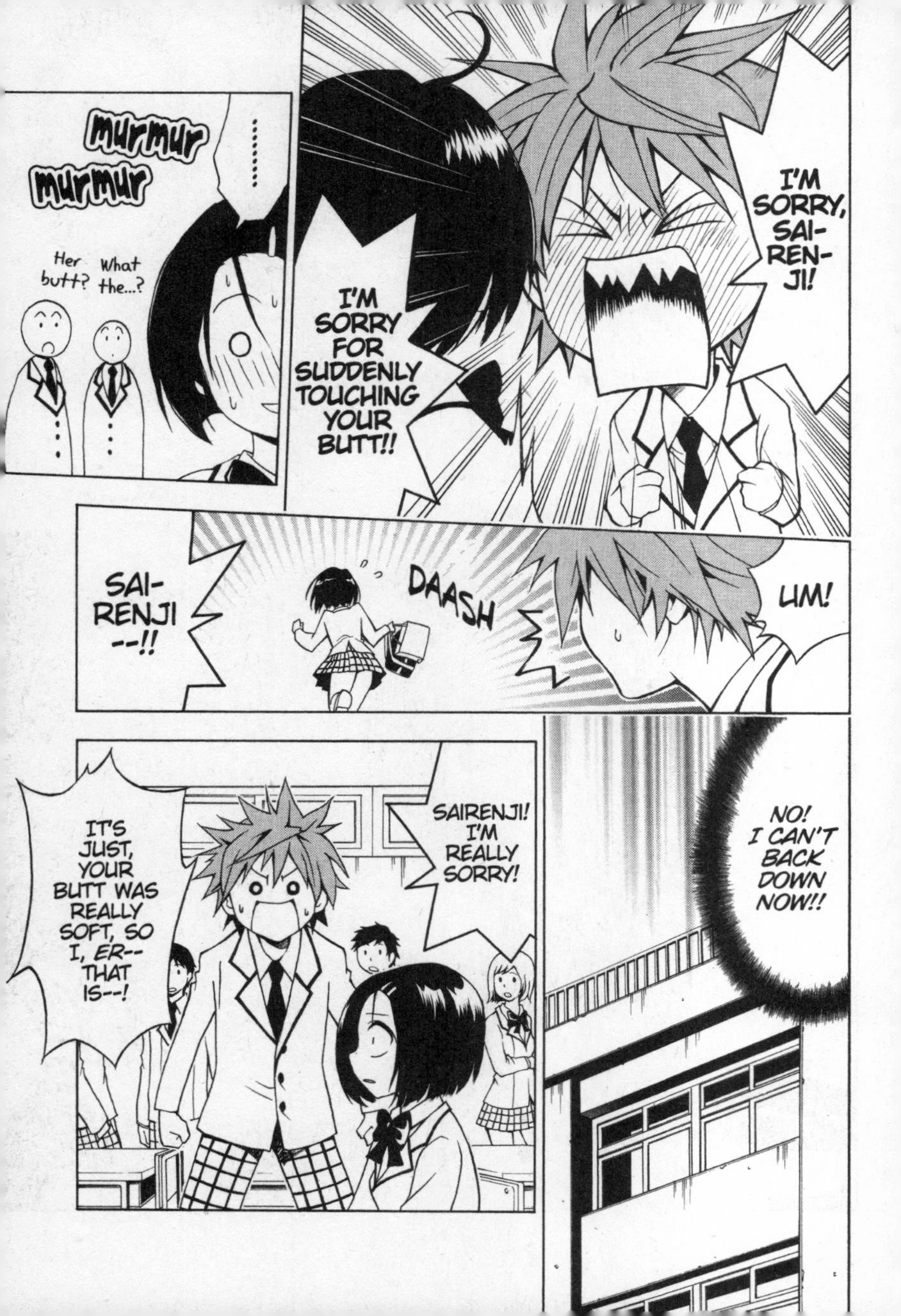
I'M SORRY, SAI-REN-JI!
I'M SORRY FOR SUDDENLY TOUCHING YOUR BUTT!!
......
murmur murmur
What the...?
Her butt?
UM!
DAASH
SAI-RENJI--!!
NO! I CAN'T BACK DOWN NOW!!
SAIRENJI! I'M REALLY SORRY!
IT'S JUST, YOUR BUTT WAS REALLY SOFT, SO I, *ER*-- THAT IS--!

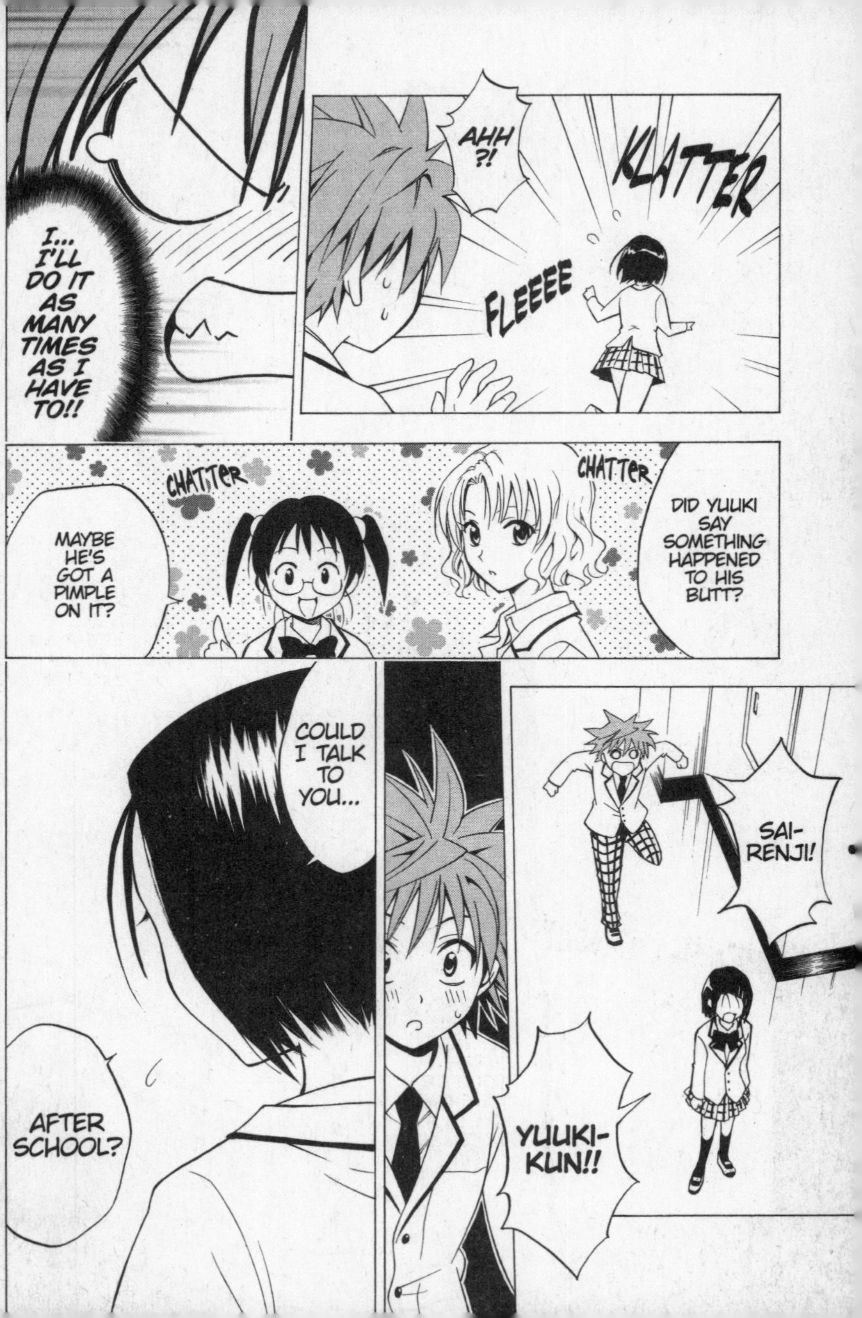
AHH ?!
KLATTER
FLEEEE
I... I'LL DO IT AS MANY TIMES AS I HAVE TO!!
CHATTER
DID YUUKI SAY SOMETHING HAPPENED TO HIS BUTT?
CHATTER
MAYBE HE'S GOT A PIMPLE ON IT?
SAI-RENJI!
YUUKI-KUN!!
COULD I TALK TO YOU...
AFTER SCHOOL?

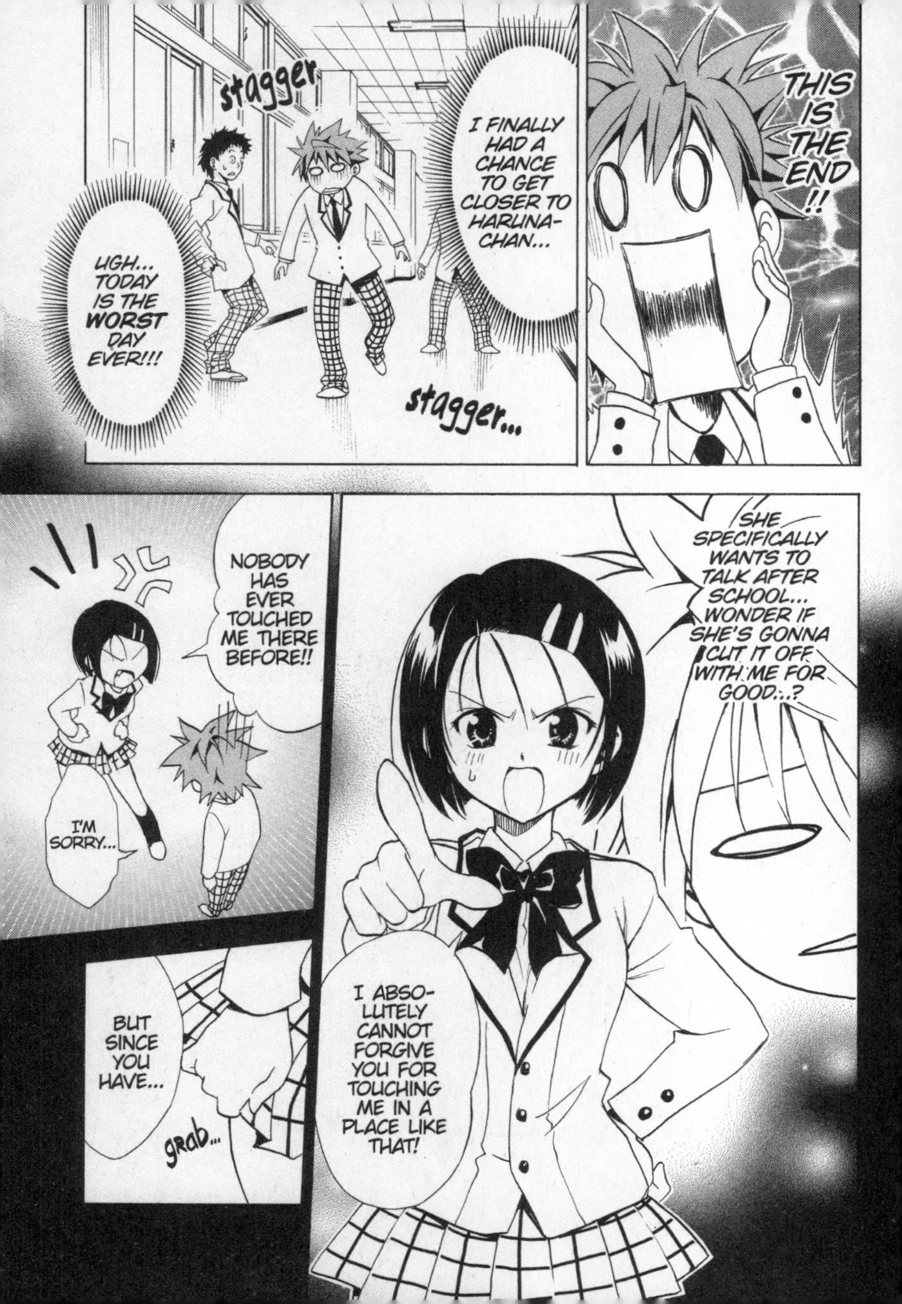
THIS IS THE END!!
I FINALLY HAD A CHANCE TO GET CLOSER TO HARUNA-CHAN...
stagger
UGH... TODAY IS THE WORST DAY EVER!!!
stagger...
SHE SPECIFICALLY WANTS TO TALK AFTER SCHOOL... WONDER IF SHE'S GONNA CUT IT OFF WITH ME FOR GOOD...?
I ABSO-LUTELY CANNOT FORGIVE YOU FOR TOUCHING ME IN A PLACE LIKE THAT!
NOBODY HAS EVER TOUCHED ME THERE BEFORE!!
I'M SORRY...
BUT SINCE YOU HAVE...
grab...

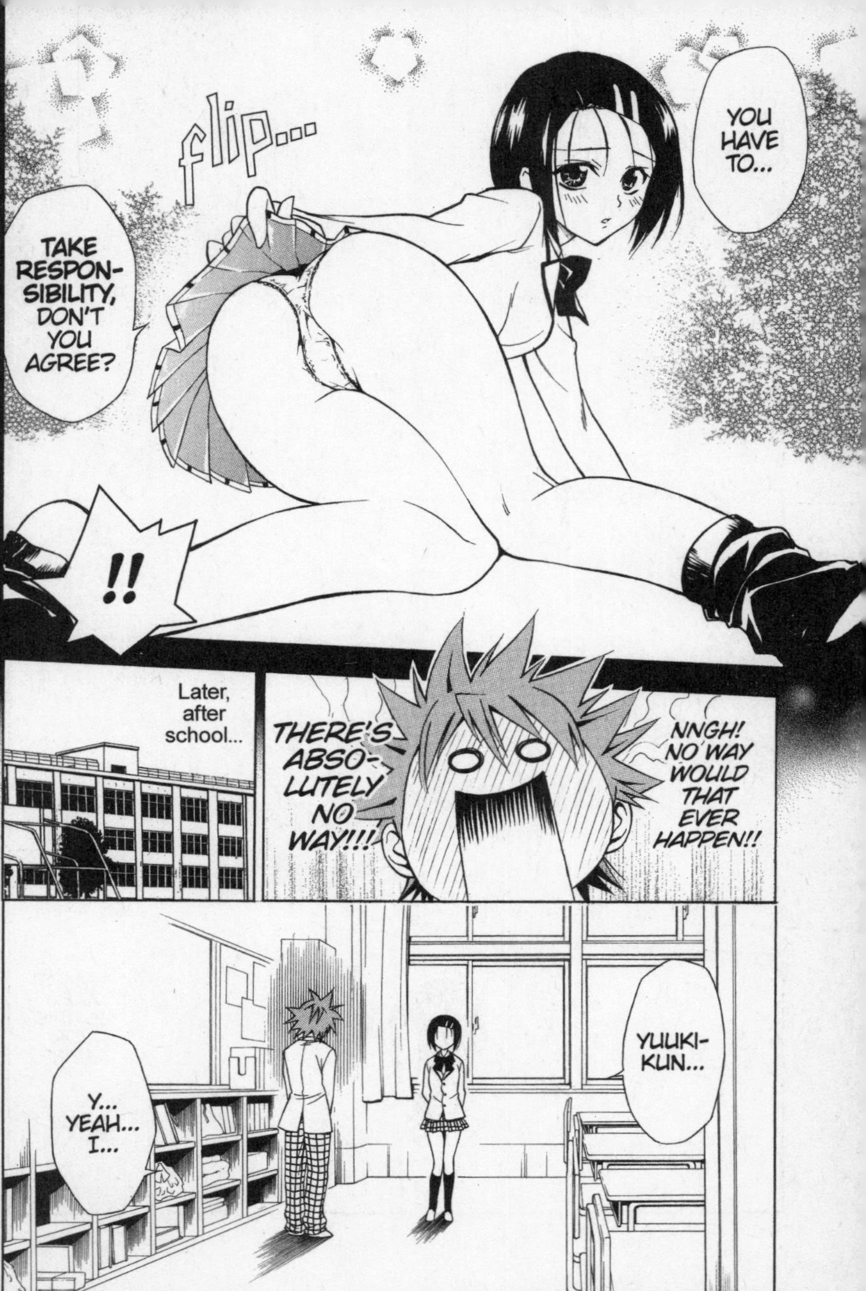
YOU HAVE TO...
flip...
TAKE RESPON-SIBILITY, DON'T YOU AGREE?
!!
NNGH! NO WAY WOULD THAT EVER HAPPEN!!
THERE'S ABSO-LUTELY NO WAY!!!
Later, after school...
YUUKI-KUN...
Y... YEAH... I...

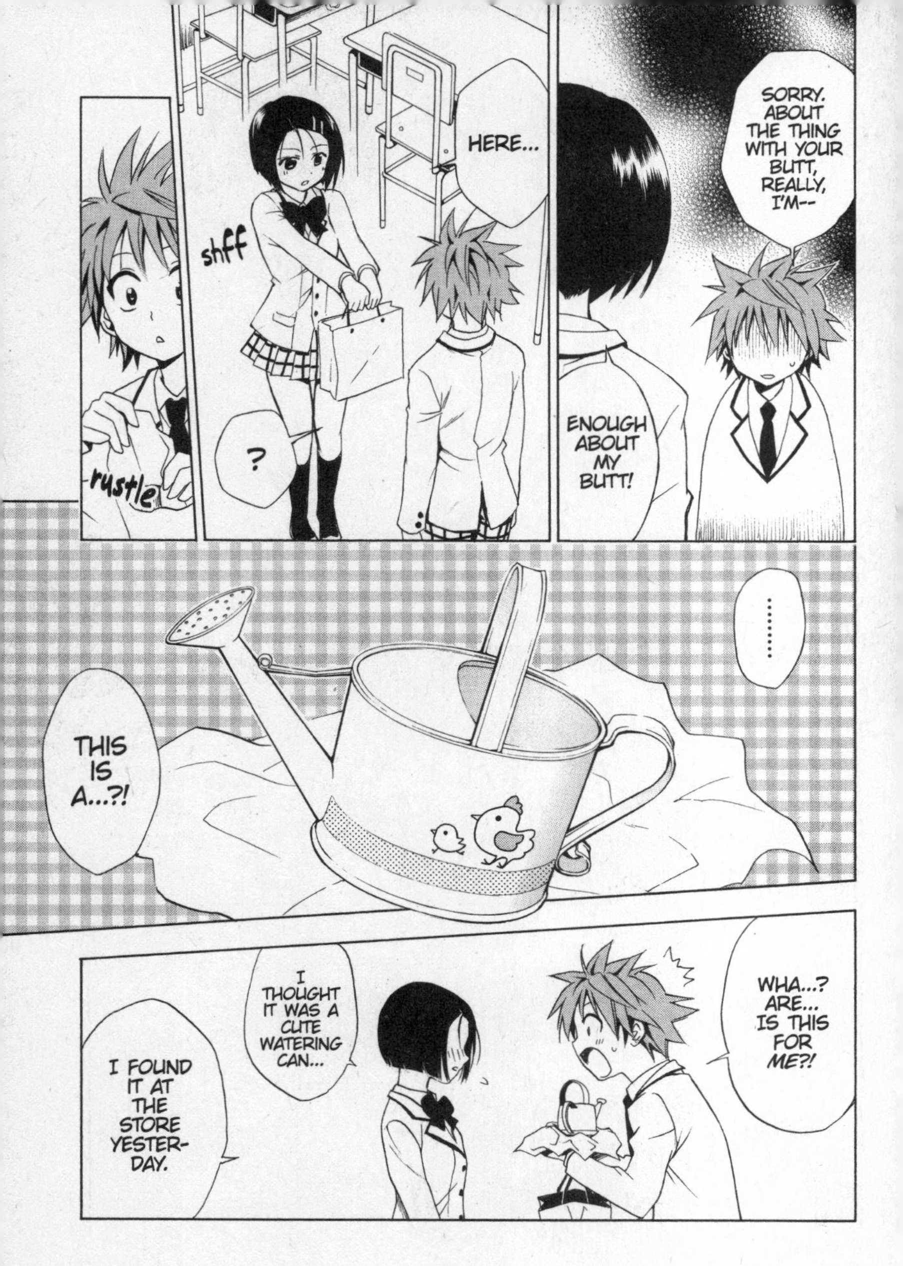
SORRY. ABOUT THE THING WITH YOUR BUTT, REALLY, I'M--
ENOUGH ABOUT MY BUTT!
HERE...
shff
?
rustle
......
THIS IS A...?!
WHA...? ARE... IS THIS FOR ME?!
I THOUGHT IT WAS A CUTE WATERING CAN...
I FOUND IT AT THE STORE YESTER-DAY.

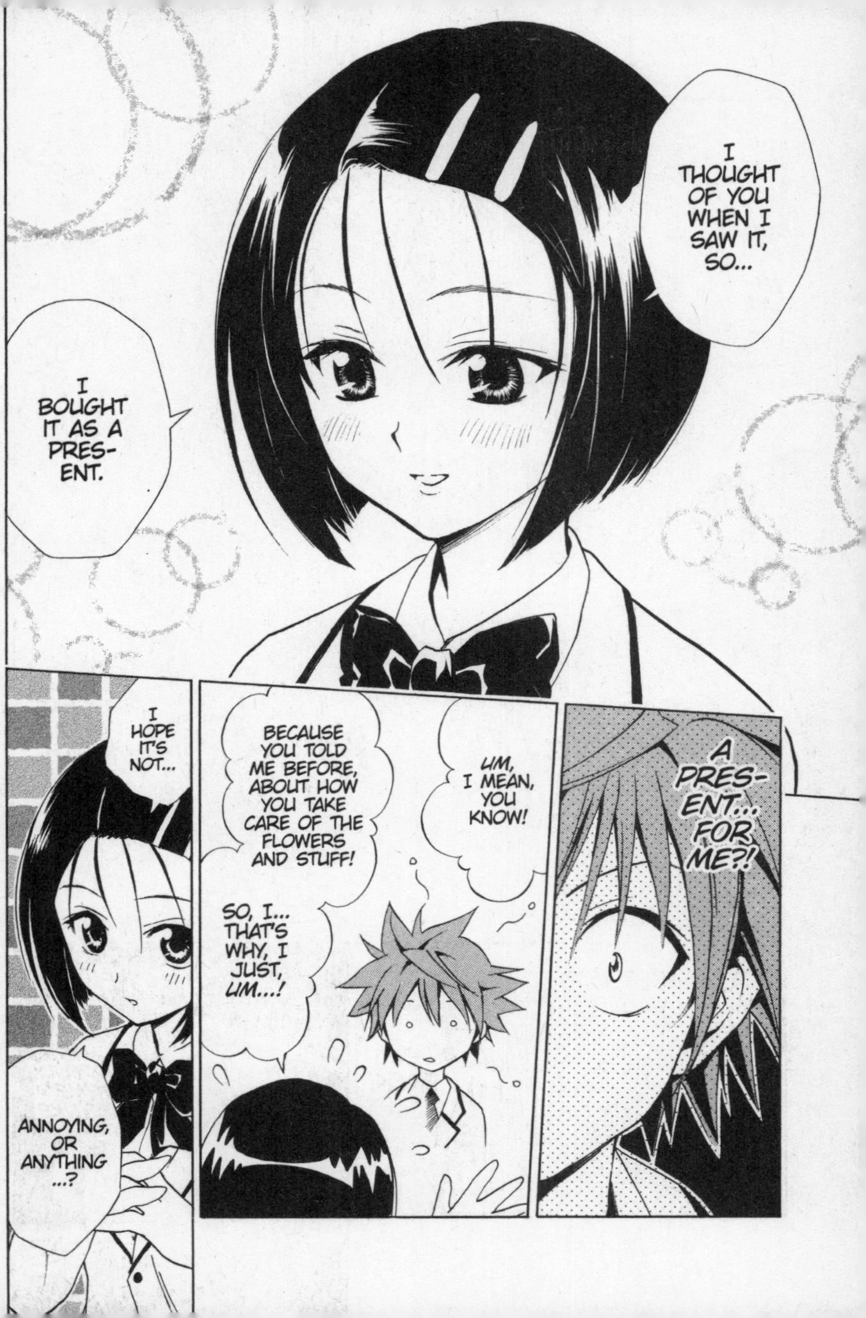
I THOUGHT OF YOU WHEN I SAW IT, SO...
I BOUGHT IT AS A PRESENT.
A PRESENT... FOR ME?!
UM, I MEAN, YOU KNOW!
BECAUSE YOU TOLD ME BEFORE, ABOUT HOW YOU TAKE CARE OF THE FLOWERS AND STUFF!
SO, I... THAT'S WHY, I JUST, UM...!
I HOPE IT'S NOT...
ANNOYING, OR ANYTHING ...?

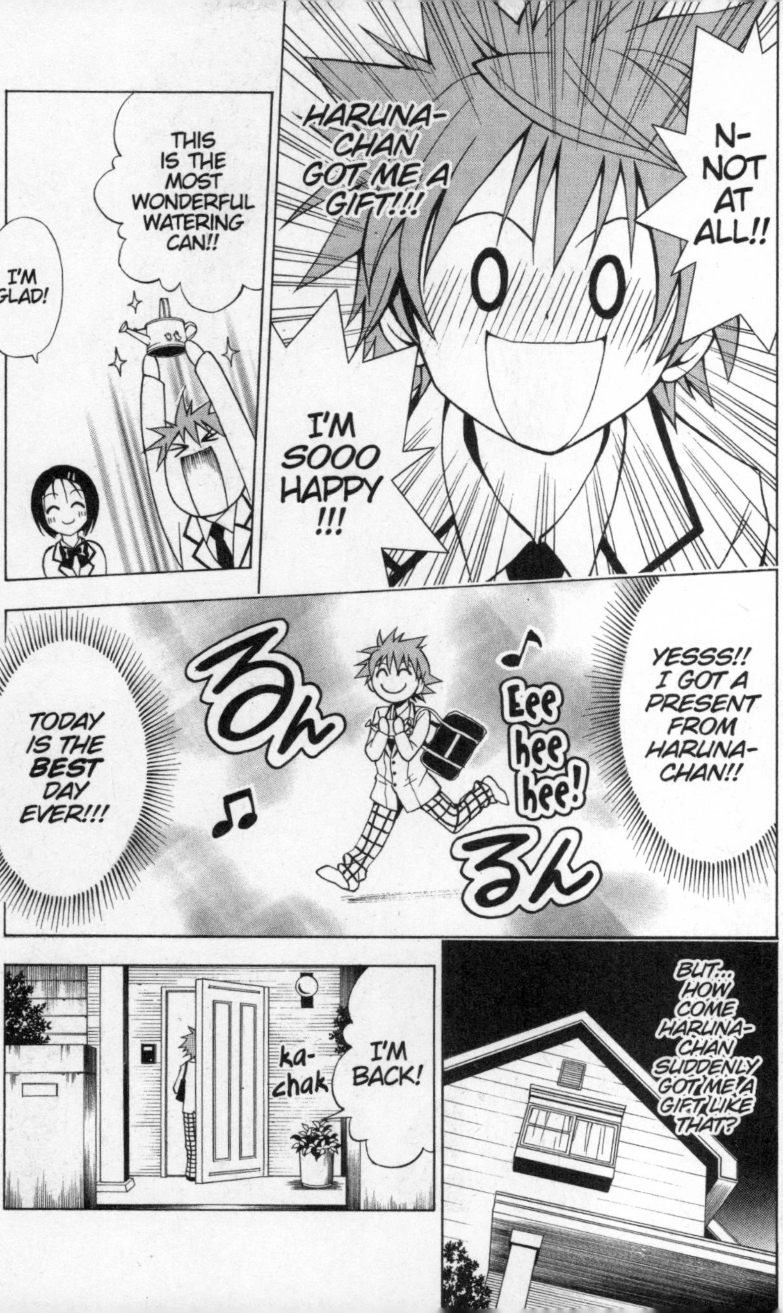
N-NOT AT ALL!!
HARUNA-CHAN GOT ME A GIFT!!!
I'M SOOO HAPPY!!!
THIS IS THE MOST WONDERFUL WATERING CAN!!
I'M GLAD!
YESSS!! I GOT A PRESENT FROM HARUNA-CHAN!!
Eee hee hee!
るん
るん
TODAY IS THE BEST DAY EVER!!!
BUT... HOW COME HARUNA-CHAN SUDDENLY GOT ME A GIFT LIKE THAT?
I'M BACK!
ka-chak

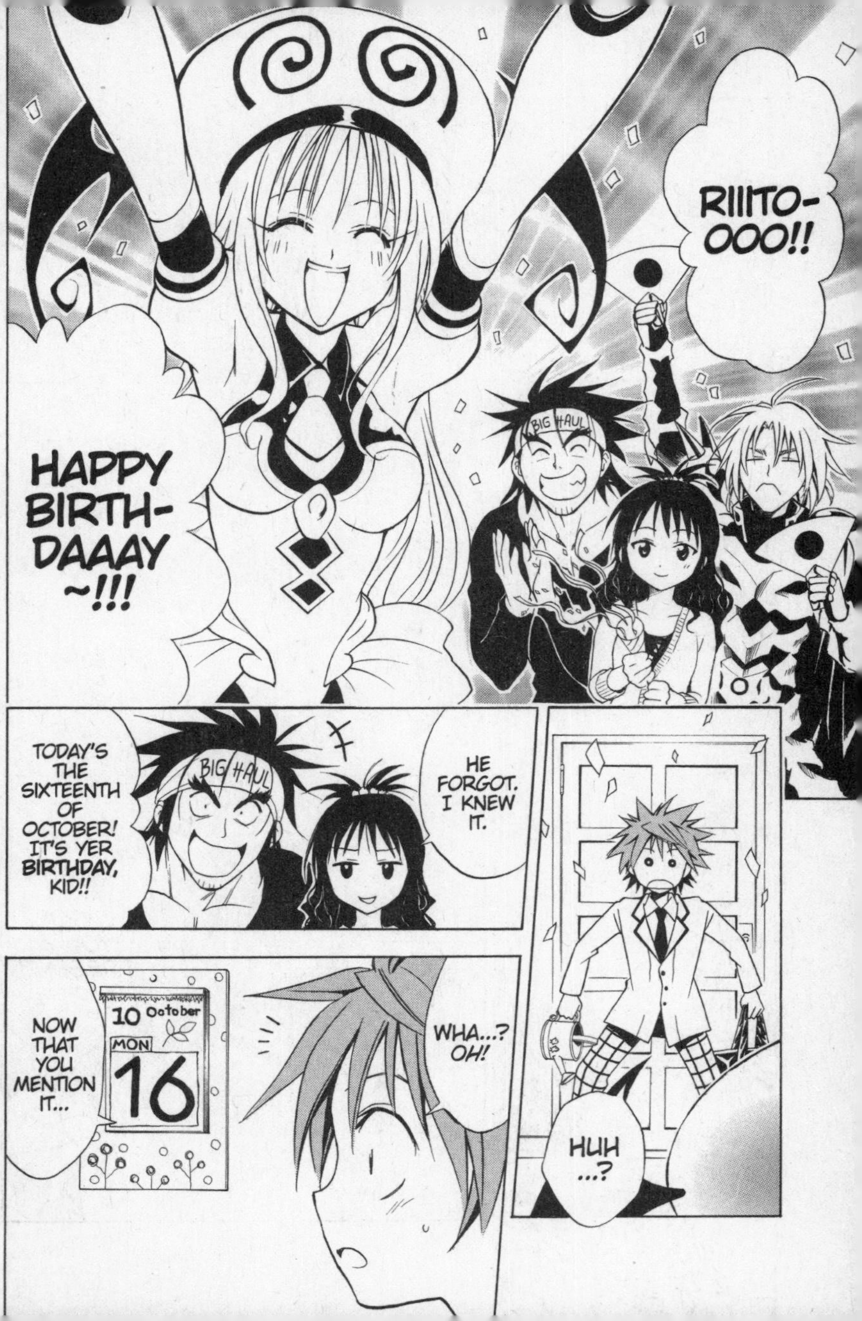
RIIITO-OOO!!
HAPPY BIRTH-DAAAY~!!!
BIG HAUL
HUH ...?
HE FORGOT. I KNEW IT.
TODAY'S THE SIXTEENTH OF OCTOBER! IT'S YER BIRTHDAY, KID!!
BIG HAUL
WHA...? OH!
10 October MON 16
NOW THAT YOU MENTION IT...

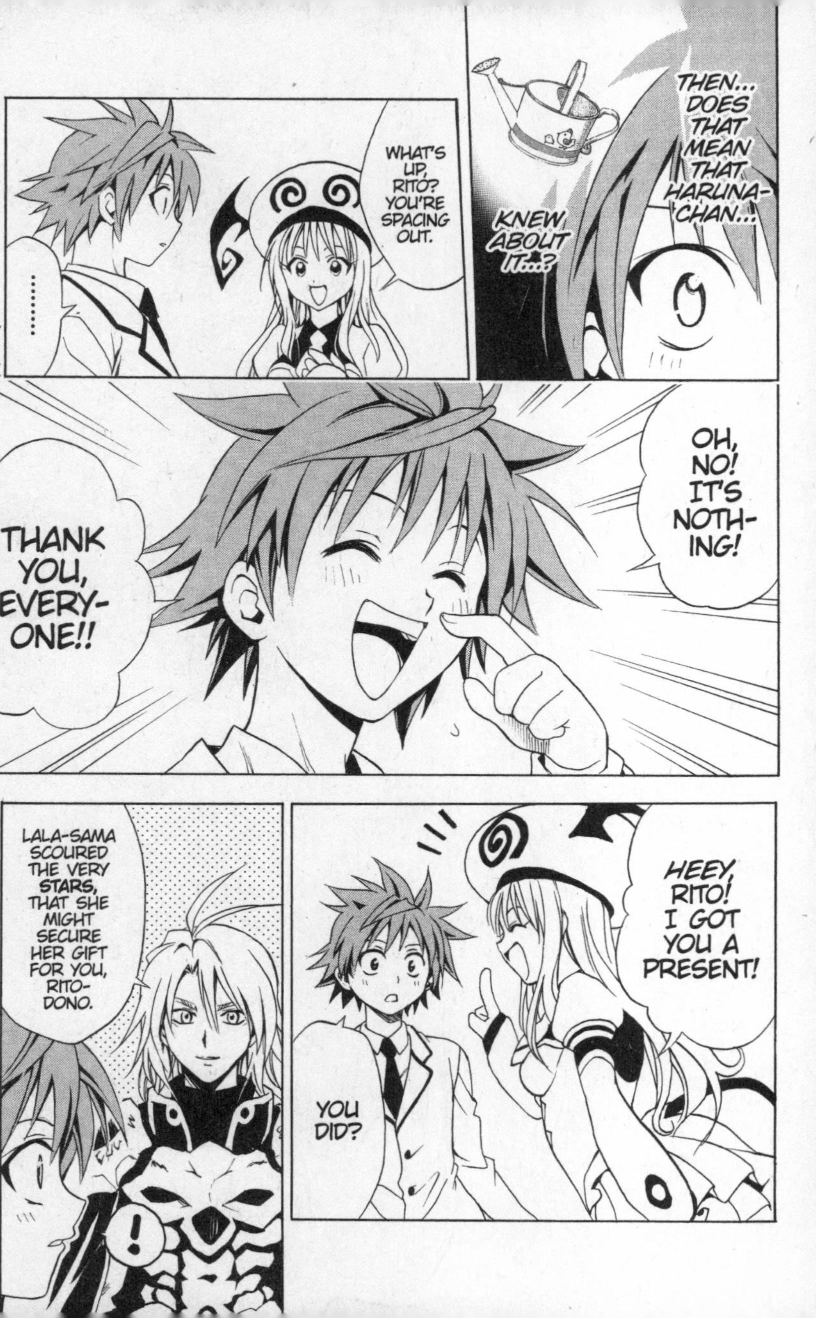
THEN... DOES THAT MEAN THAT HARUNA-CHAN...
KNEW ABOUT IT...?
WHAT'S UP, RITO? YOU'RE SPACING OUT.
......
OH, NO! IT'S NOTHING!
THANK YOU, EVERYONE!!
HEEY, RITO! I GOT YOU A PRESENT!
YOU DID?
LALA-SAMA SCOURED THE VERY STARS, THAT SHE MIGHT SECURE HER GIFT FOR YOU, RITO-DONO.
!

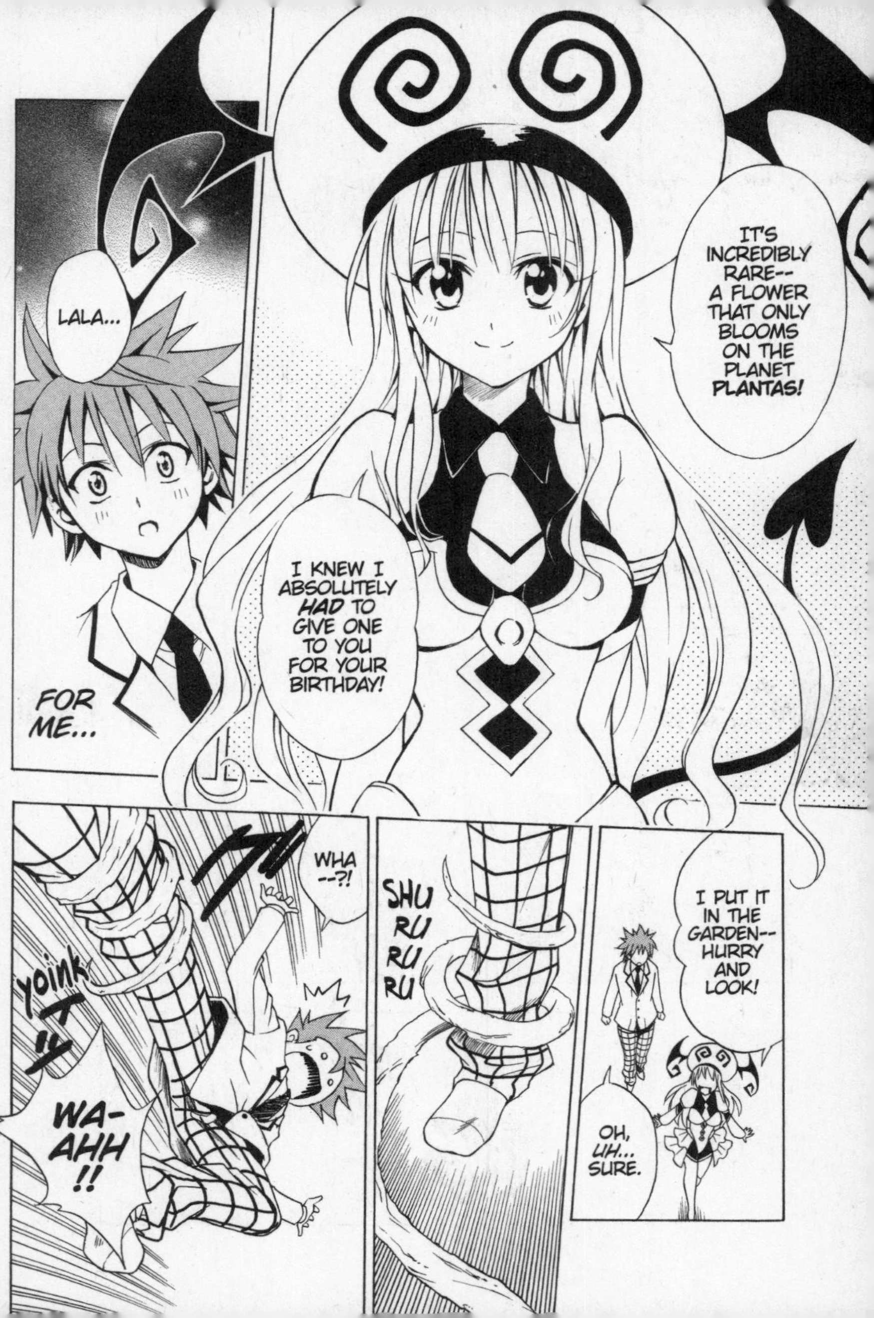
IT'S INCREDIBLY RARE-- A FLOWER THAT ONLY BLOOMS ON THE PLANET PLANTAS!
I KNEW I ABSOLUTELY HAD TO GIVE ONE TO YOU FOR YOUR BIRTHDAY!
LALA...
FOR ME...
I PUT IT IN THE GARDEN-- HURRY AND LOOK!
OH, UH... SURE.
SHU RU RU RU
WHA --?!
yoink
WA-AHH !!

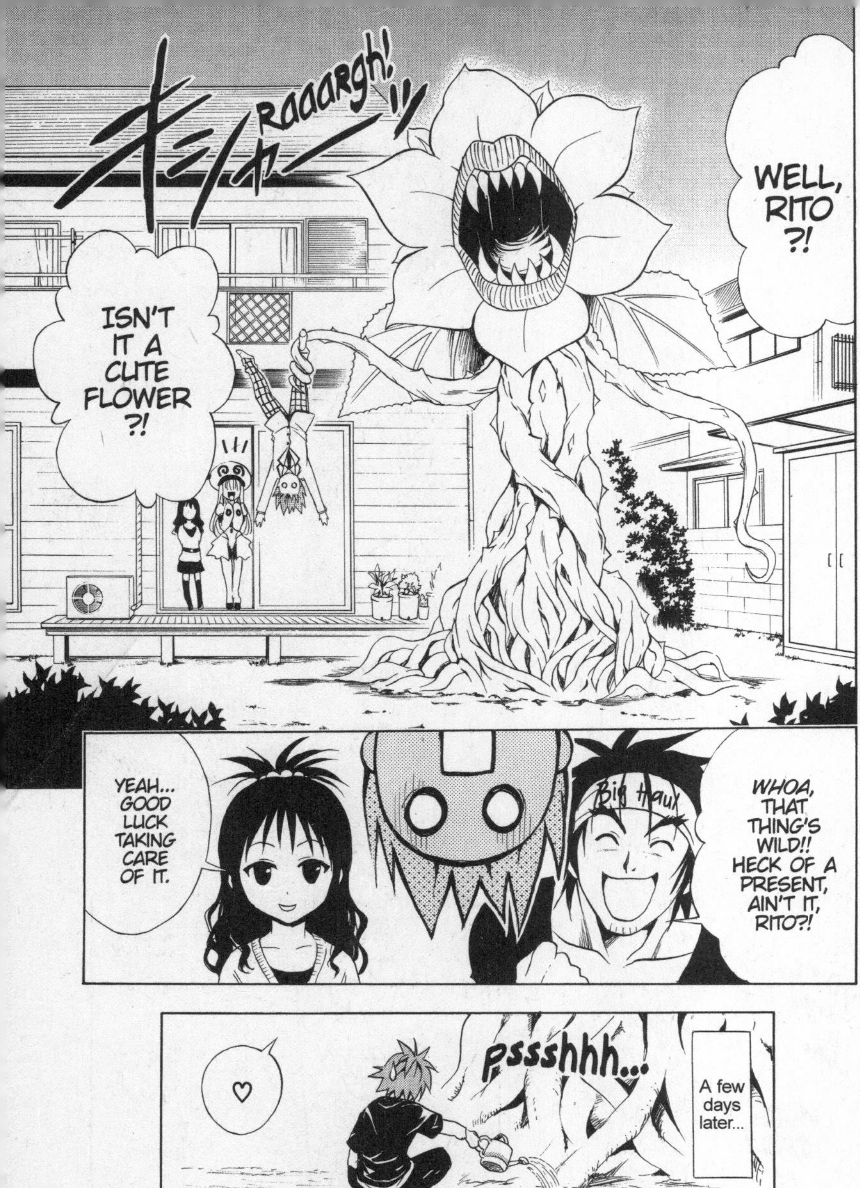
WELL, RITO?!
Raaaargh!
ISN'T IT A CUTE FLOWER?!
WHOA, THAT THING'S WILD!! HECK OF A PRESENT, AIN'T IT, RITO?!
YEAH... GOOD LUCK TAKING CARE OF IT.
A few days later...
Pssshhh...
♡

Character File

01
Yuuki Rito

We started our plan to write about the characters beginning in Volume 3. Since we skipped Volumes 1 and 2, we figured we'd do two this time and talk about Rito, as well!

● ● ● ● ● ● ● ● ● ● ● ● ● ● ● ● ● ●

☆As the Protagonist
When we were planning *To Love-Ru,* Yabuki-san had made up his mind about a few things. First, we had to have a love triangle (and the points had to be Rito, Lala, and Haruna). Second, Rito couldn't be a pervert. With all that being the case, Yabuki-san and I were pretty much in agreement as to the type of protagonist that we wanted. (For that matter, we were in agreement about the type of protagonist we really *didn't* like, too!

● ● ● ● ● ● ● ● ● ● ● ● ● ● ● ● ● ●

☆A Protagonist Boys Can Support
Yabuki-san and I really focused on developing Rito's character. We took care to portray him as someone whose actions weren't unpleasant or unlikeable. In fact, we were probably even more careful of this with the protagonist than we were with Lala and Haruna. Since *TLR* is serialized in a magazine for boys, lots of boys will be reading it. So, if male readers didn't support the protagonist, we'd be completely out of luck. We thought drawing cute girls would be meaningless if readers didn't support and like Rito. This might seem obvious, but the manga lives and dies by how well we handle it.

● ● ● ● ● ● ● ● ● ● ● ● ● ● ● ● ● ●

☆Growth as a Protagonist
In the beginning, Rito is completely unaccustomed to dealing with girls. However, by meeting the totally innocent and naïve Lala--as well as through his love for the girl of his dreams, Haruna-- he starts to grow, if only bit by bit. What form that growth takes, though, is connected with his decisions. I hope you'll enjoy seeing how that unfolds! Even we still aren't totally sure how it's all going to go--and we're his creators!

● ● ● ● ● ● ● ● ● ● ● ● ● ● ● ● ● ●

※ *Next time, we'll be covering the character on the cover of Volume 5 and Lala. We're taking a little break from Zastin's adventures.*

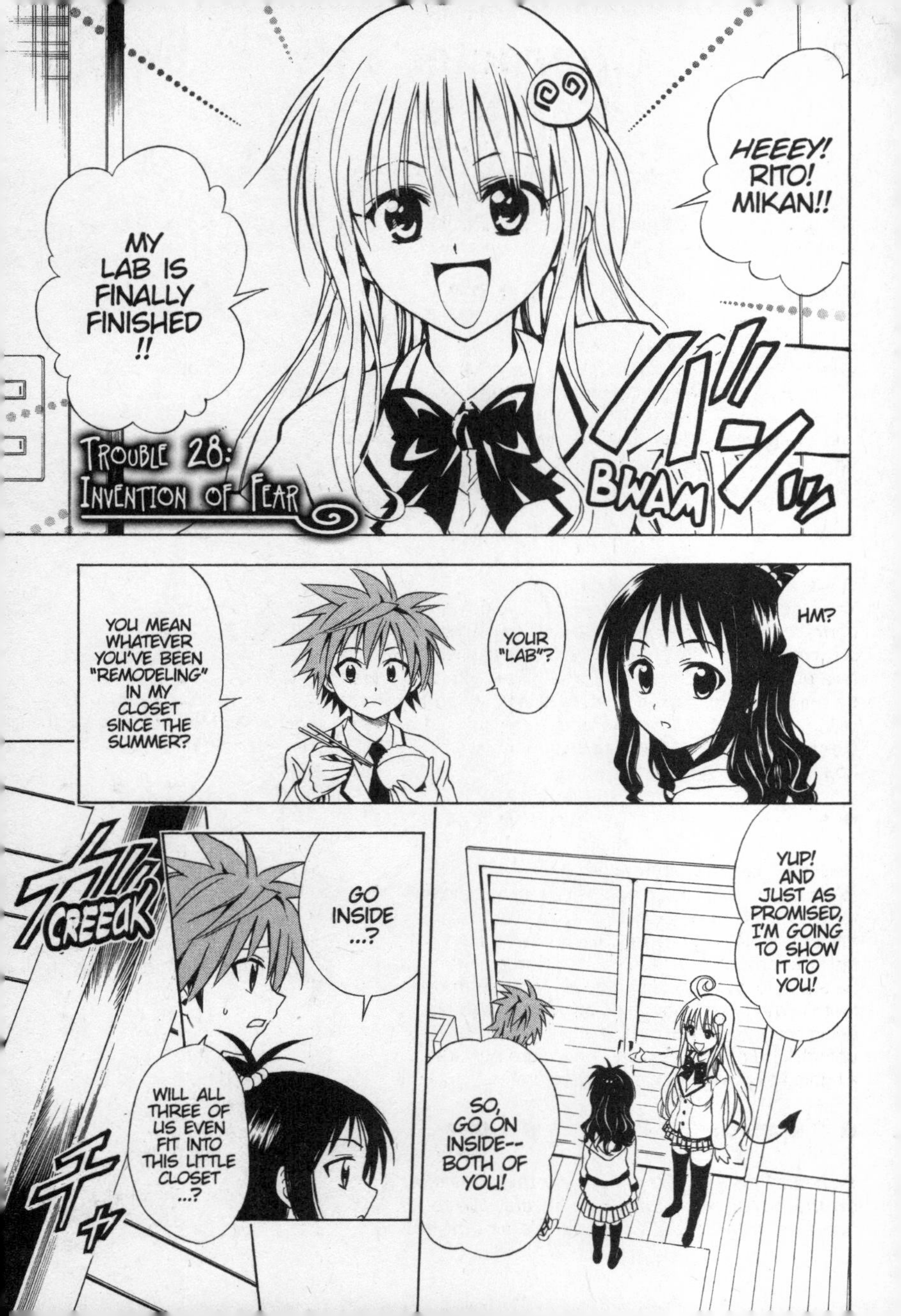
HEEEY! RITO! MIKAN!!
BWAM
MY LAB IS FINALLY FINISHED!!
Trouble 28: Invention of Fear
HM?
YOUR "LAB"?
YOU MEAN WHATEVER YOU'VE BEEN "REMODELING" IN MY CLOSET SINCE THE SUMMER?
YUP! AND JUST AS PROMISED, I'M GOING TO SHOW IT TO YOU!
SO, GO ON INSIDE--BOTH OF YOU!
GO INSIDE ...?
CREEEAK
WILL ALL THREE OF US EVEN FIT INTO THIS LITTLE CLOSET ...?

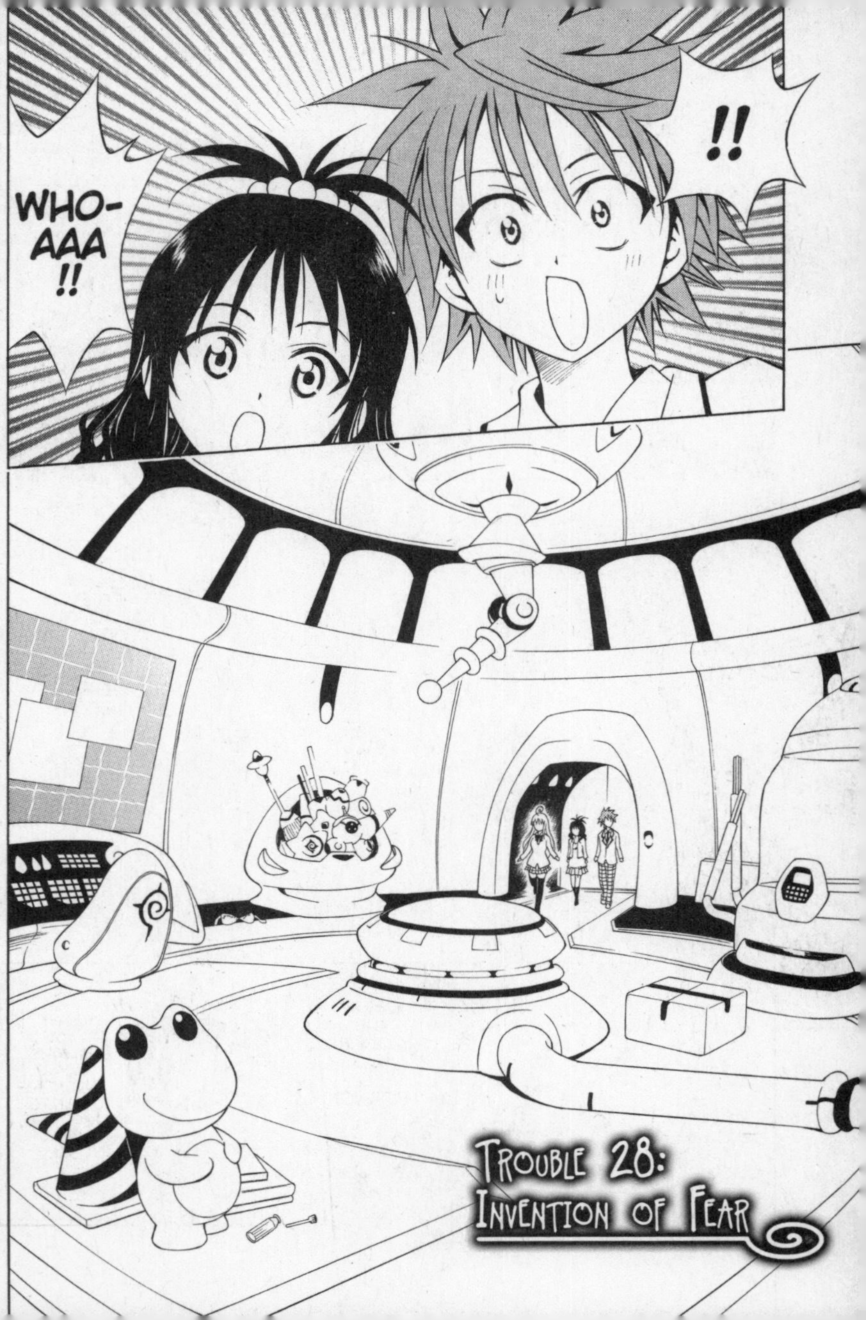
!!
WHO-AAA !!
Trouble 28:
Invention of Fear

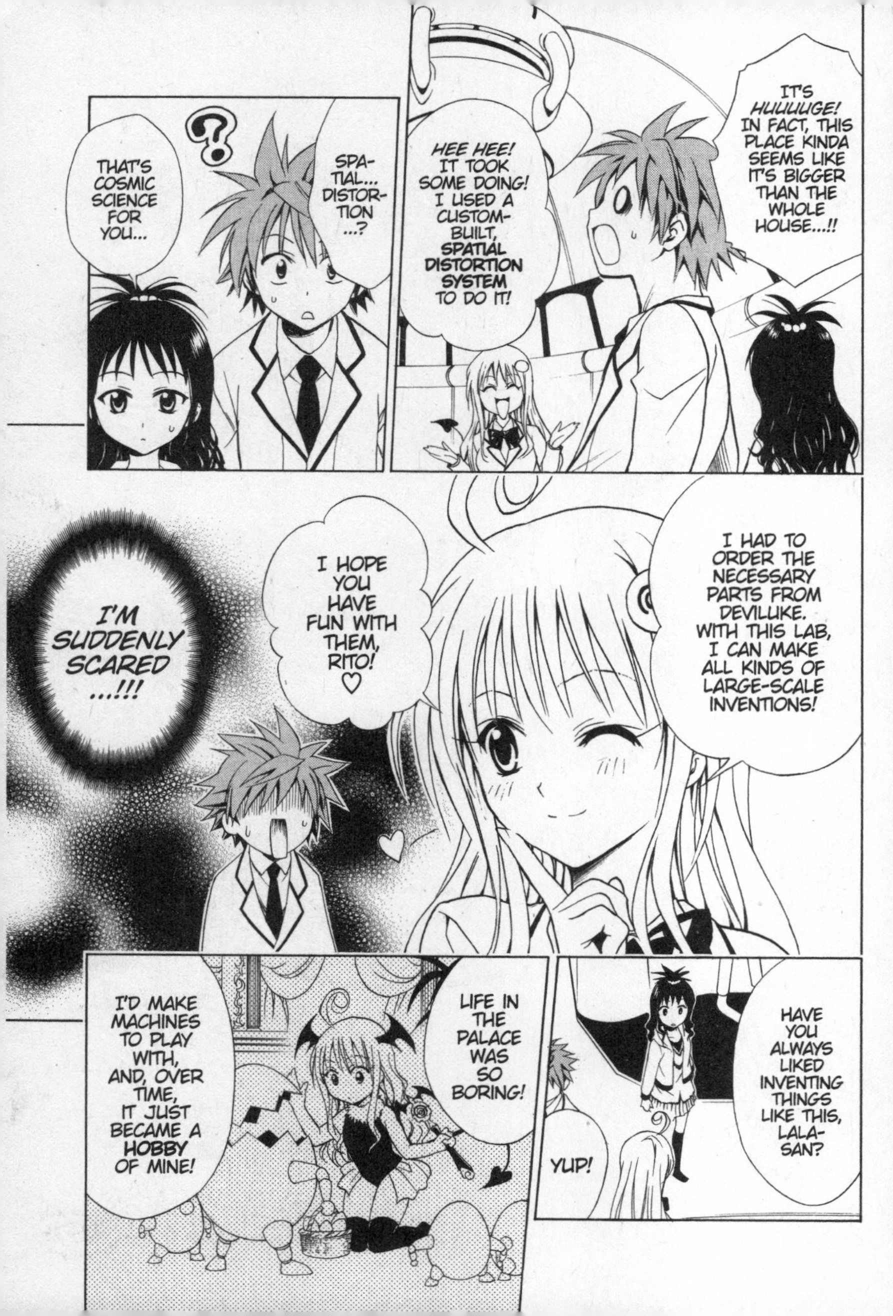
IT'S *HUUUUGE!* IN FACT, THIS PLACE KINDA SEEMS LIKE IT'S BIGGER THAN THE WHOLE HOUSE...!!
HEE HEE! IT TOOK SOME DOING! I USED A CUSTOM-BUILT, **SPATIAL DISTORTION SYSTEM** TO DO IT!
SPA-TIAL... DISTOR-TION ...?
?
THAT'S COSMIC SCIENCE FOR YOU...
I HAD TO ORDER THE NECESSARY PARTS FROM DEVILUKE. WITH THIS LAB, I CAN MAKE ALL KINDS OF LARGE-SCALE INVENTIONS!
I HOPE YOU HAVE FUN WITH THEM, RITO! ♡
I'M SUDDENLY SCARED ...!!!
HAVE YOU ALWAYS LIKED INVENTING THINGS LIKE THIS, LALA-SAN?
YUP!
LIFE IN THE PALACE WAS SO BORING!
I'D MAKE MACHINES TO PLAY WITH, AND, OVER TIME, IT JUST BECAME A **HOBBY** OF MINE!

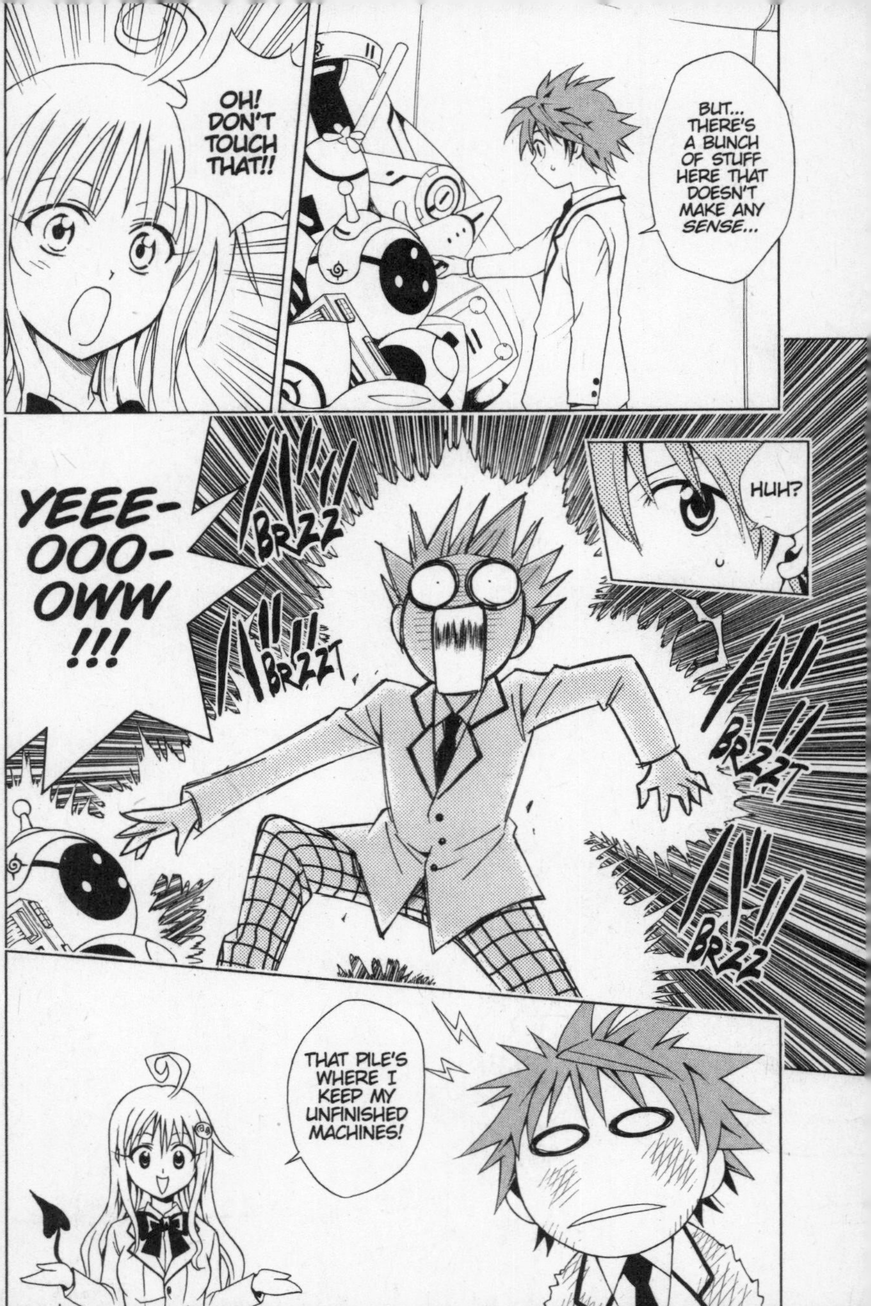
BUT... THERE'S A BUNCH OF STUFF HERE THAT DOESN'T MAKE ANY SENSE...
OH! DON'T TOUCH THAT!!
HUH?
BRZZ
YEEE-OOO-OWW!!!
BRZZT
BRZZT
BRZZ
THAT PILE'S WHERE I KEEP MY UNFINISHED MACHINES!

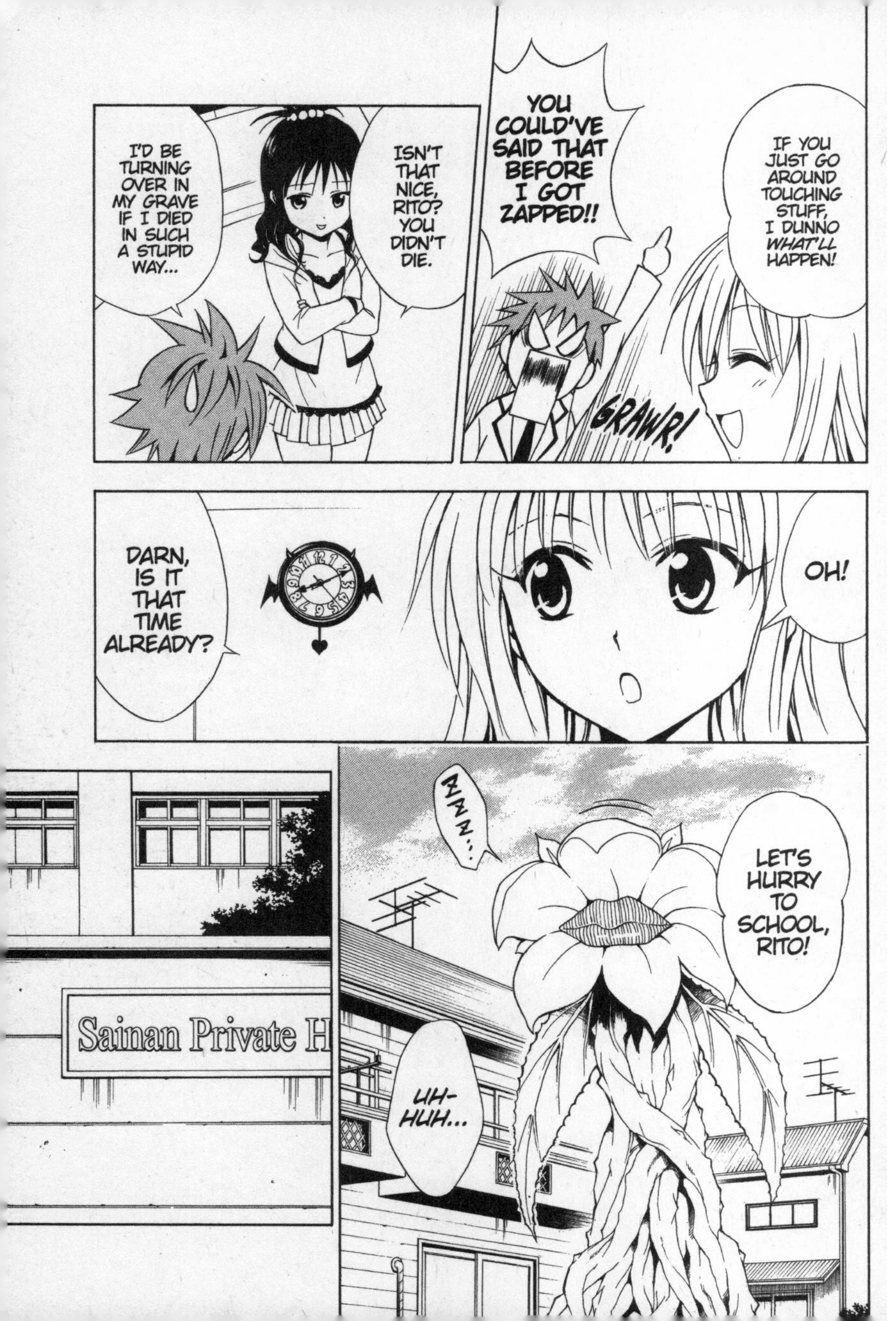
IF YOU JUST GO AROUND TOUCHING STUFF, I DUNNO *WHAT'LL* HAPPEN!
YOU COULD'VE SAID THAT BEFORE I GOT ZAPPED!!
GRAWR!
ISN'T THAT NICE, RITO? YOU DIDN'T DIE.
I'D BE TURNING OVER IN MY GRAVE IF I DIED IN SUCH A STUPID WAY...
OH!
DARN, IS IT THAT TIME ALREADY?
LET'S HURRY TO SCHOOL, RITO!
ZZZ...
UH-HUH...
Sainan Private H

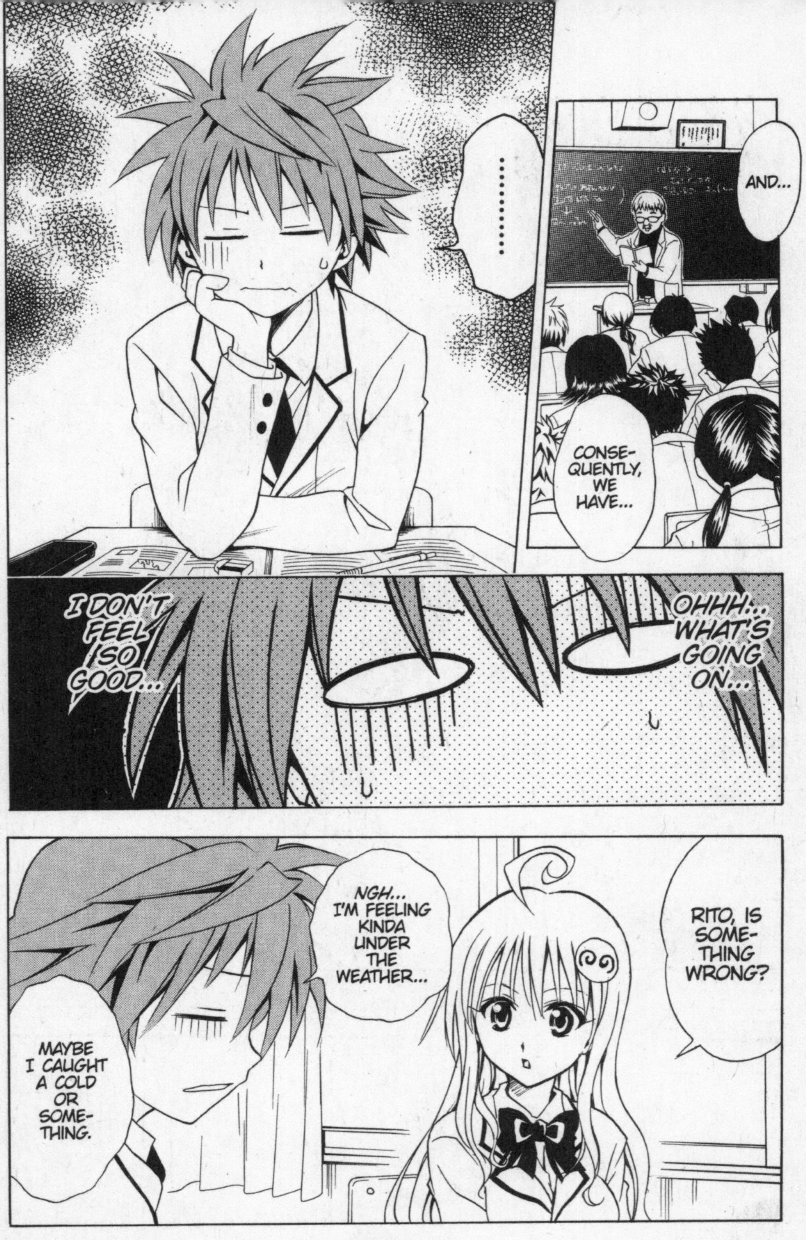
AND...
CONSE-QUENTLY, WE HAVE...
......
OHHH... WHAT'S GOING ON...
I DON'T FEEL SO GOOD...
RITO, IS SOME-THING WRONG?
NGH... I'M FEELING KINDA UNDER THE WEATHER...
MAYBE I CAUGHT A COLD OR SOME-THING.

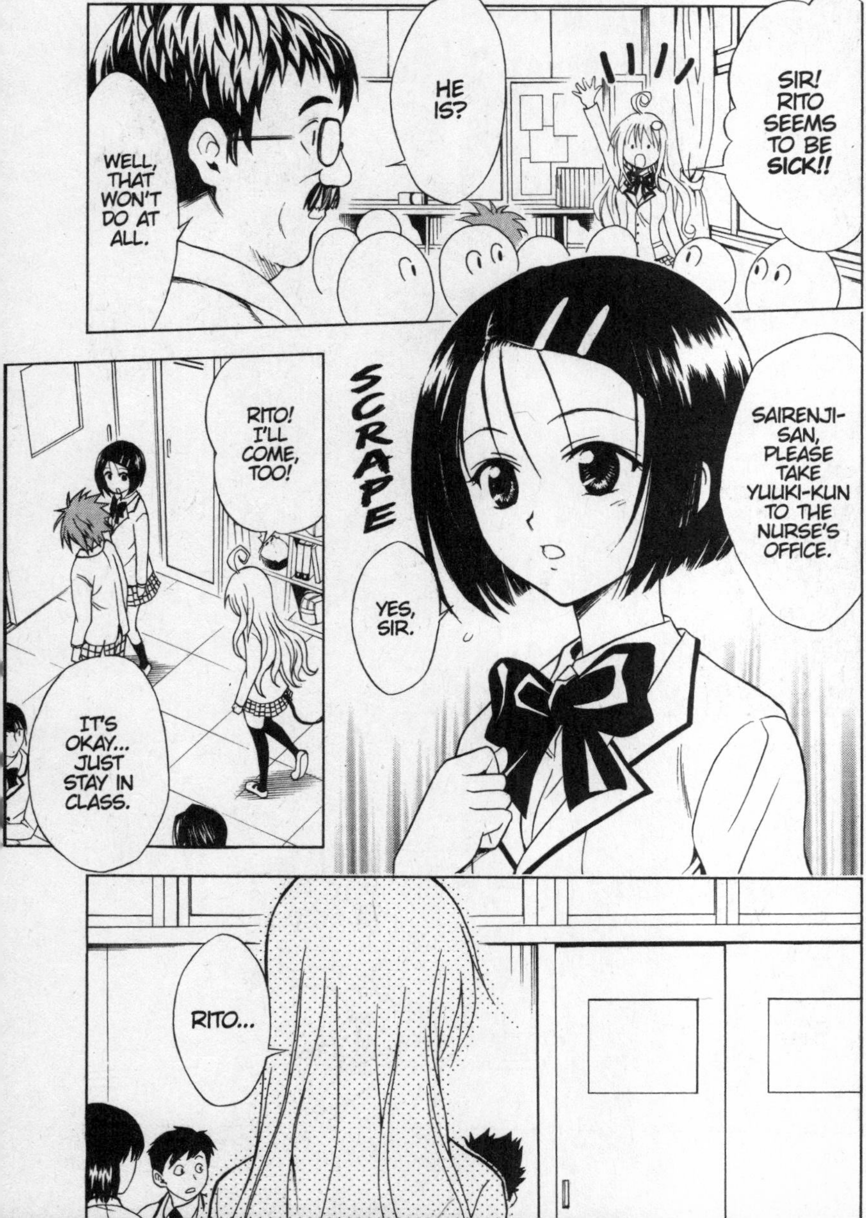
SIR! RITO SEEMS TO BE SICK!!
HE IS?
WELL, THAT WON'T DO AT ALL.
SAIRENJI-SAN, PLEASE TAKE YUUKI-KUN TO THE NURSE'S OFFICE.
SCRAPE
YES, SIR.
RITO! I'LL COME, TOO!
IT'S OKAY... JUST STAY IN CLASS.
RITO...

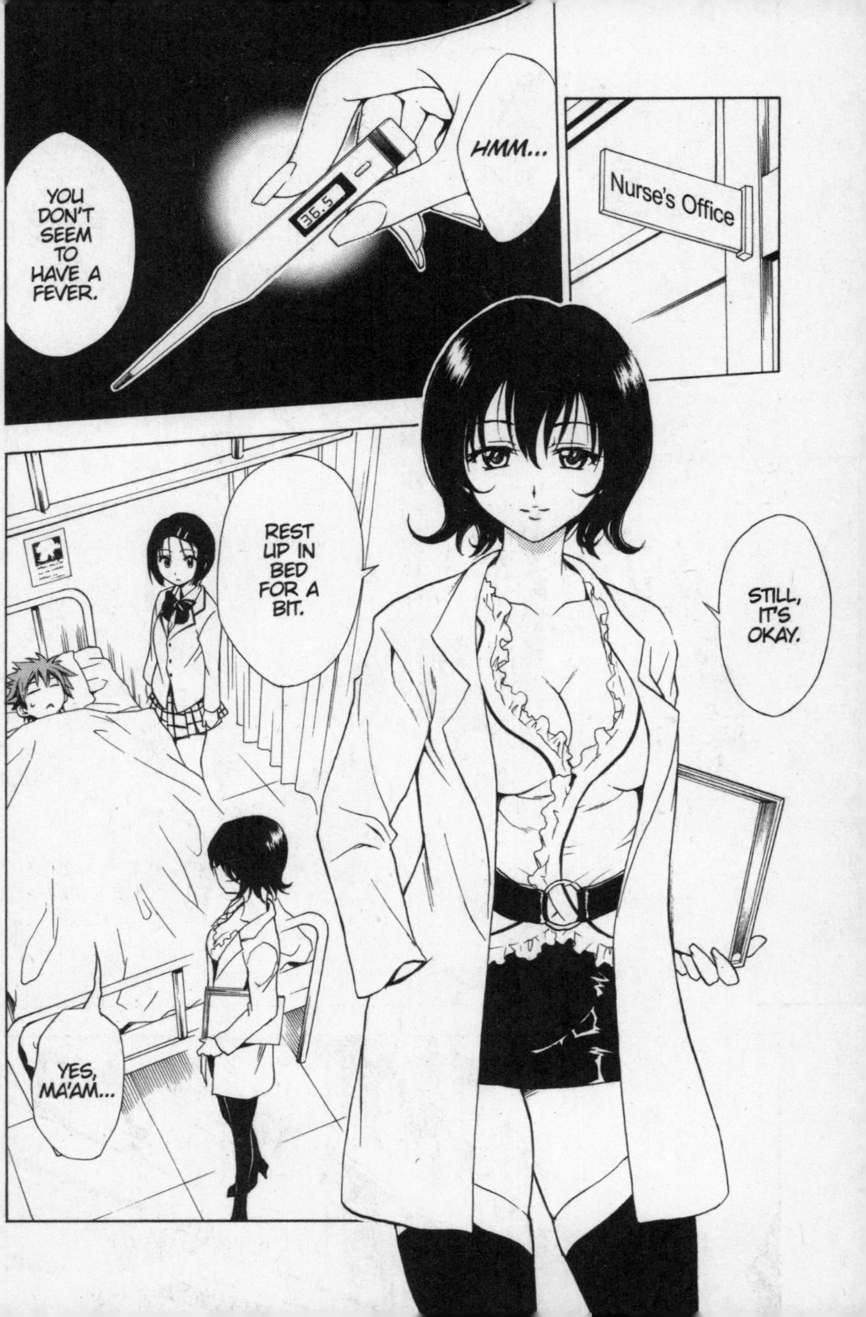
Nurse's Office
HMM...
36.5
YOU DON'T SEEM TO HAVE A FEVER.
STILL, IT'S OKAY.
REST UP IN BED FOR A BIT.
YES, MA'AM...

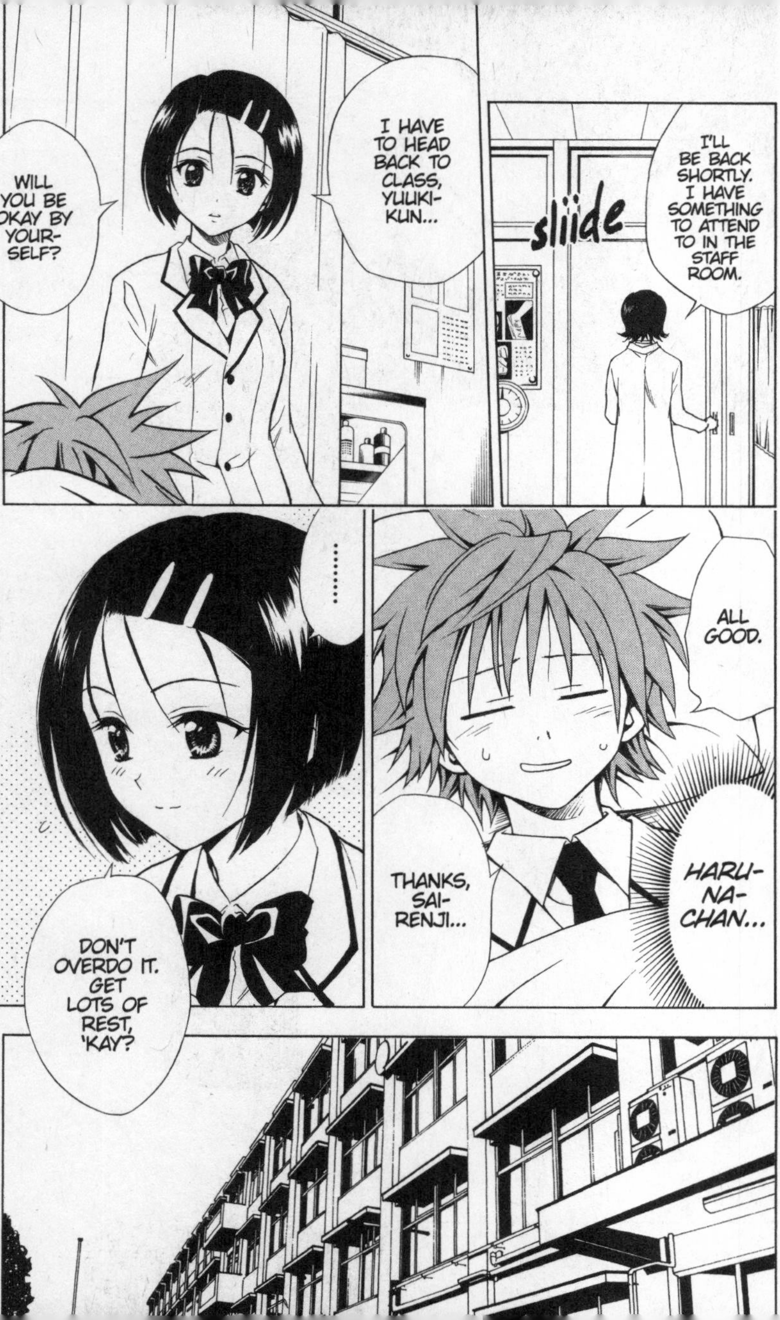
I'LL BE BACK SHORTLY. I HAVE SOMETHING TO ATTEND TO IN THE STAFF ROOM.
sliide
I HAVE TO HEAD BACK TO CLASS, YUUKI-KUN...
WILL YOU BE OKAY BY YOUR-SELF?
ALL GOOD.
HARU-NA-CHAN...
THANKS, SAI-RENJI...
......
DON'T OVERDO IT. GET LOTS OF REST, 'KAY?

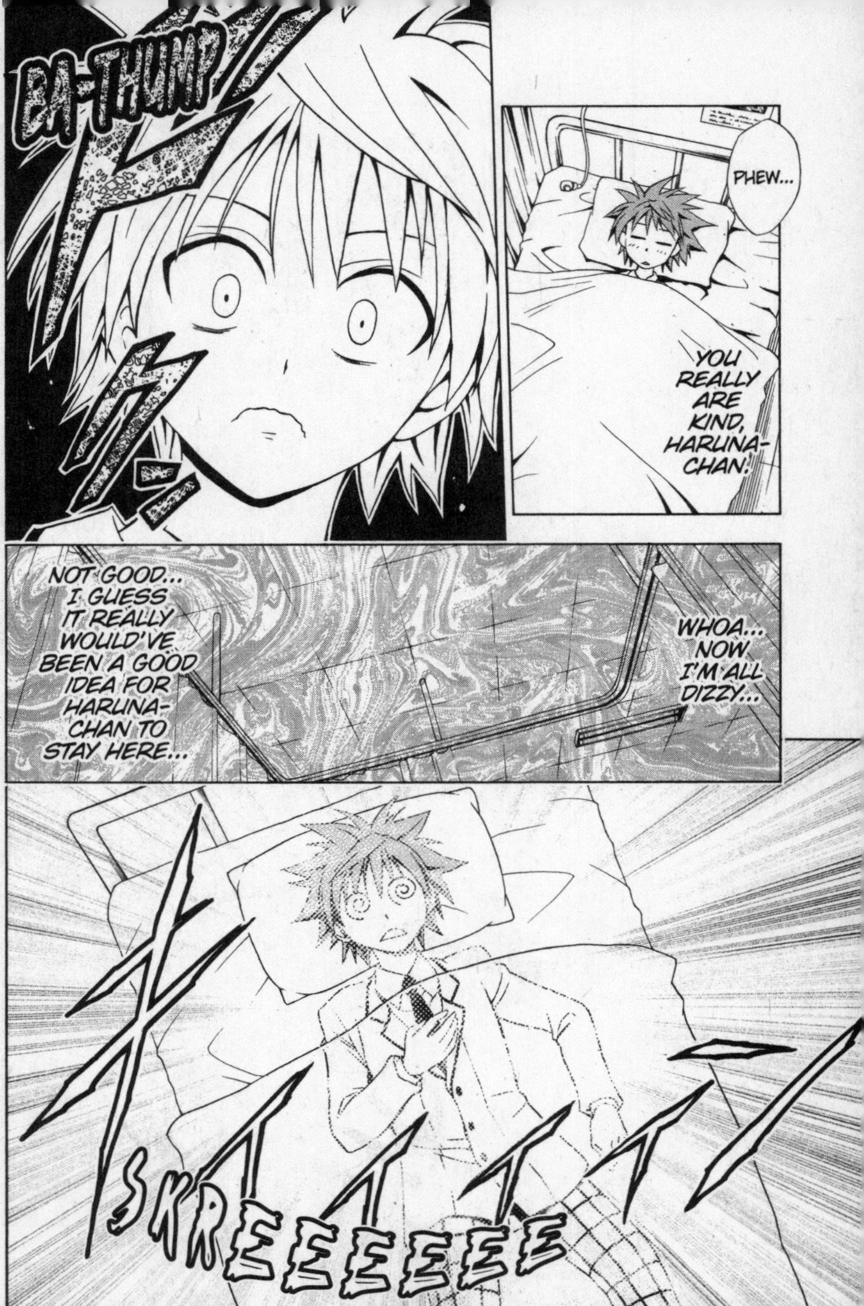
PHEW...
YOU REALLY ARE KIND, HARUNA-CHAN!
BA-THUMP
WHOA... NOW I'M ALL DIZZY...
NOT GOOD... I GUESS IT REALLY WOULD'VE BEEN A GOOD IDEA FOR HARUNA-CHAN TO STAY HERE...
SKREEEEEEE

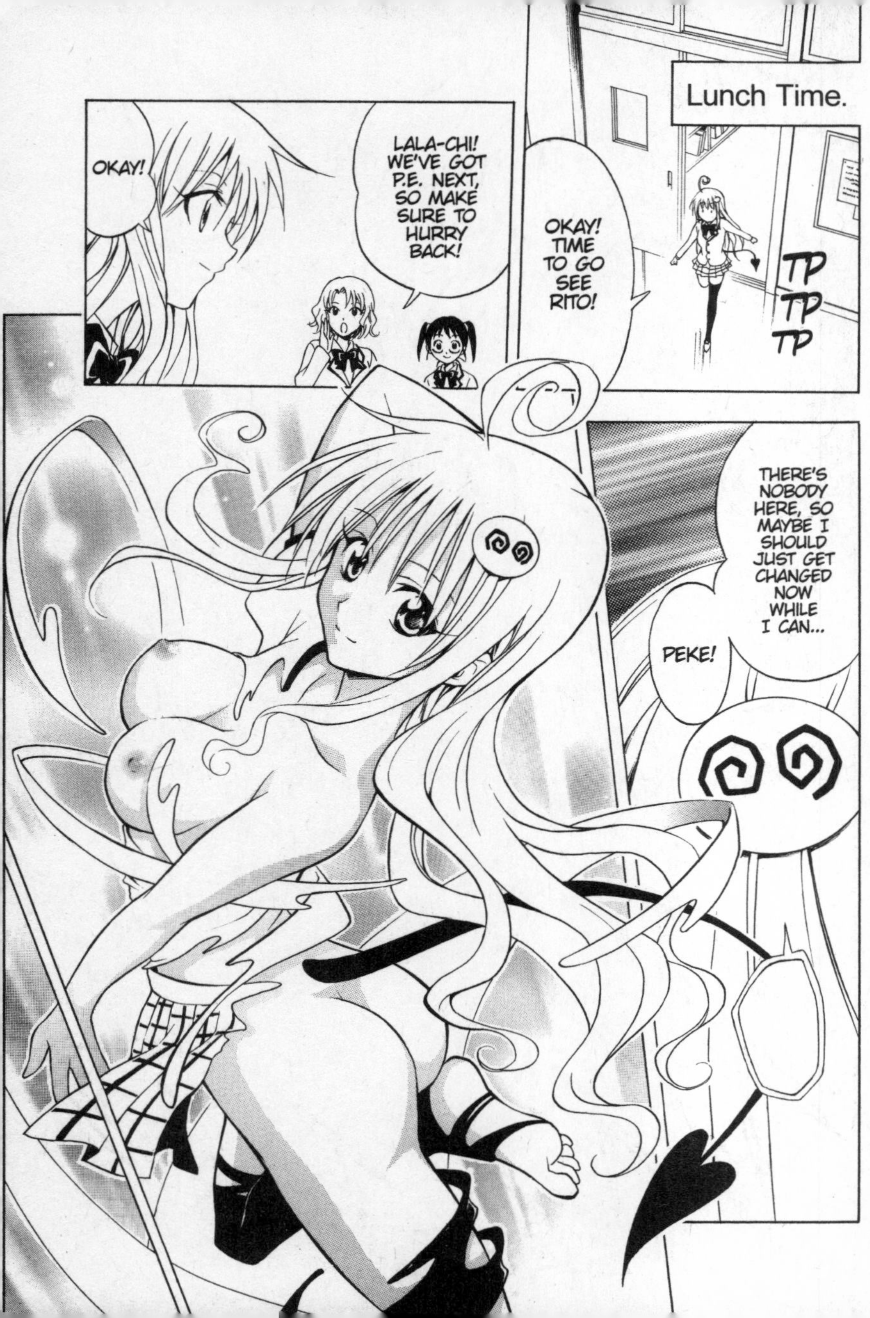
Lunch Time.
TP TP TP
OKAY! TIME TO GO SEE RITO!
LALA-CHI! WE'VE GOT P.E. NEXT, SO MAKE SURE TO HURRY BACK!
OKAY!
THERE'S NOBODY HERE, SO MAYBE I SHOULD JUST GET CHANGED NOW WHILE I CAN...
PEKE!

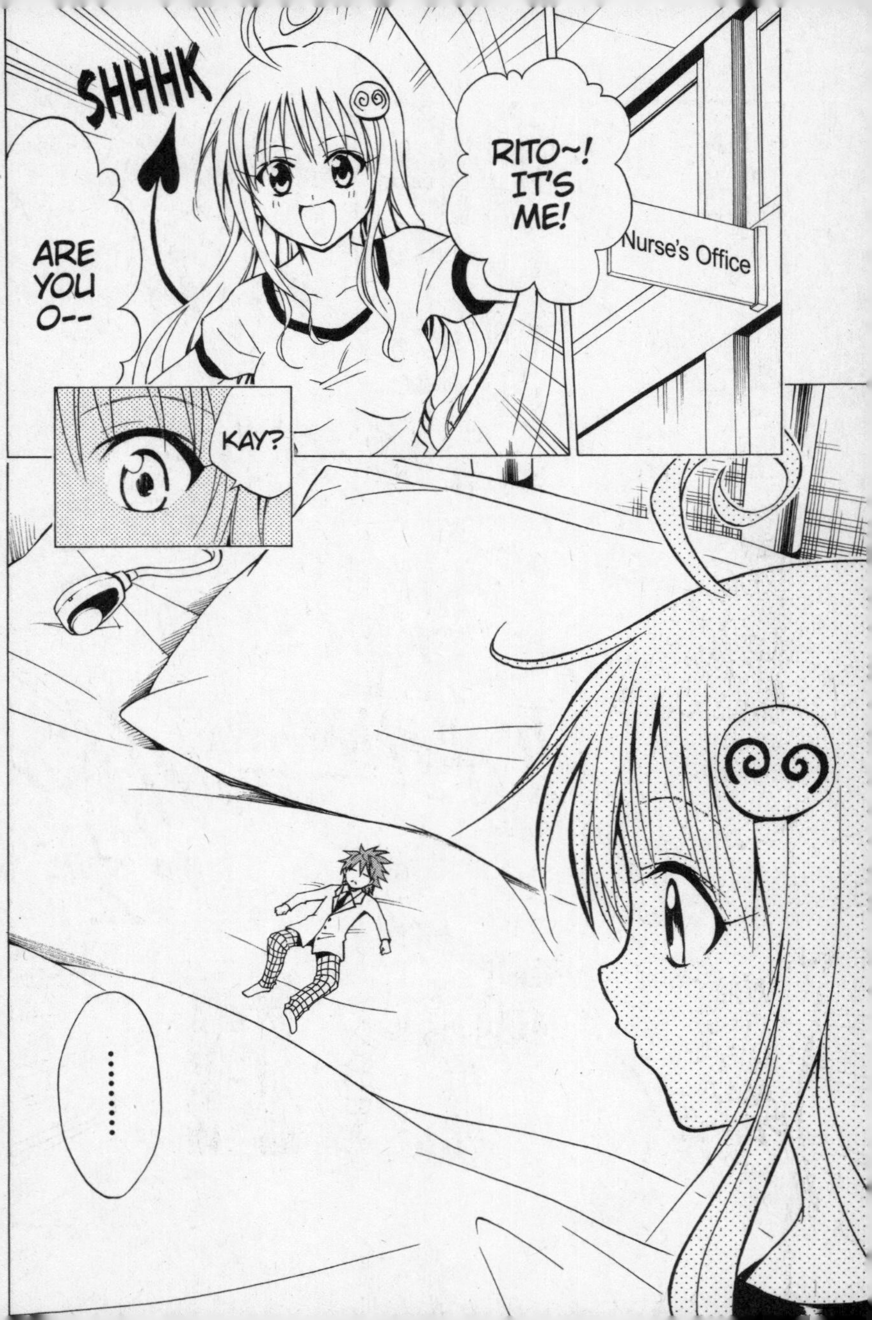
SHHHK
RITO~! IT'S ME!
Nurse's Office
ARE YOU O--
KAY?
....

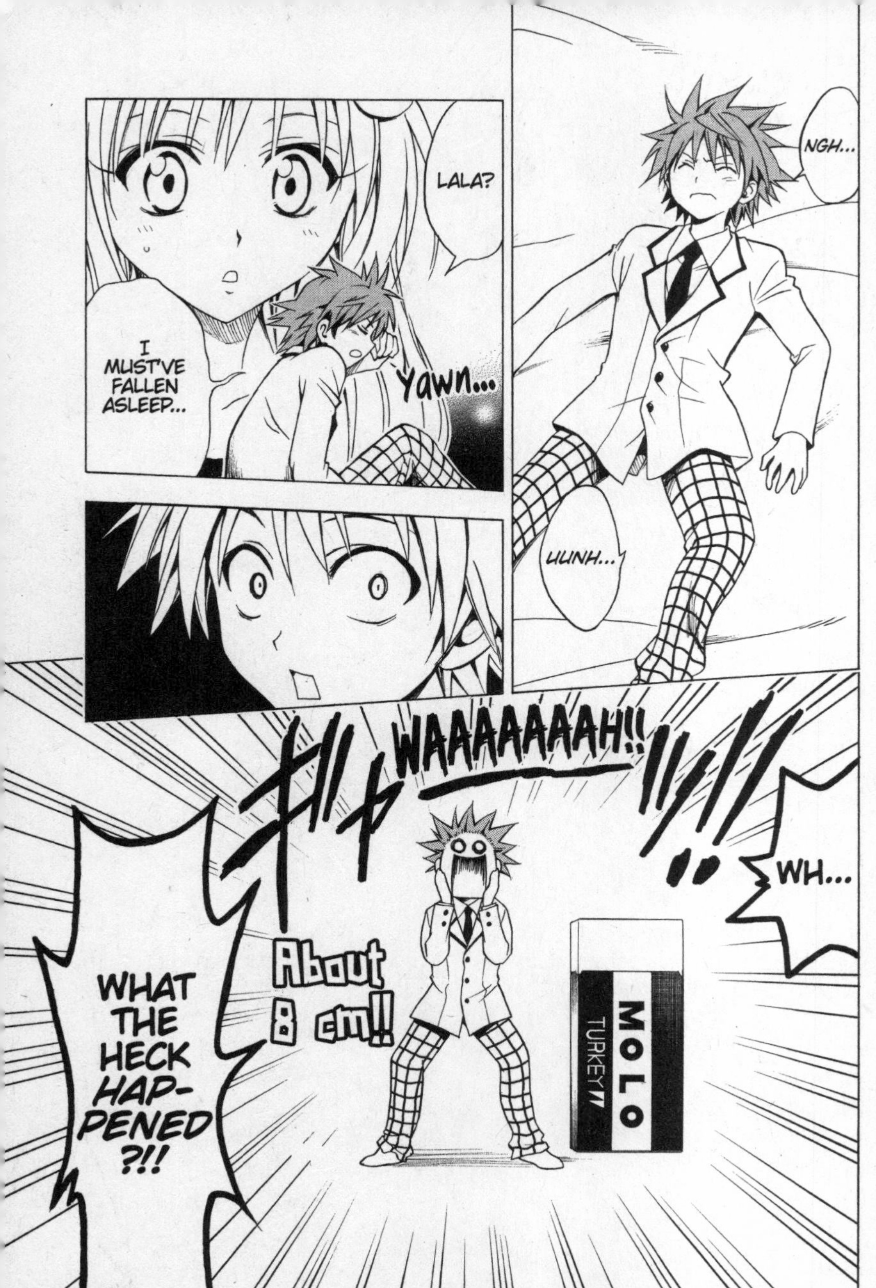
NGH...
UUNH...
LALA?
I MUST'VE FALLEN ASLEEP...
Yawn...
WAAAAAAAH!!
WH...
MOLO
TURKEY
About 8 cm!!
WHAT THE HECK HAP-PENED?!!

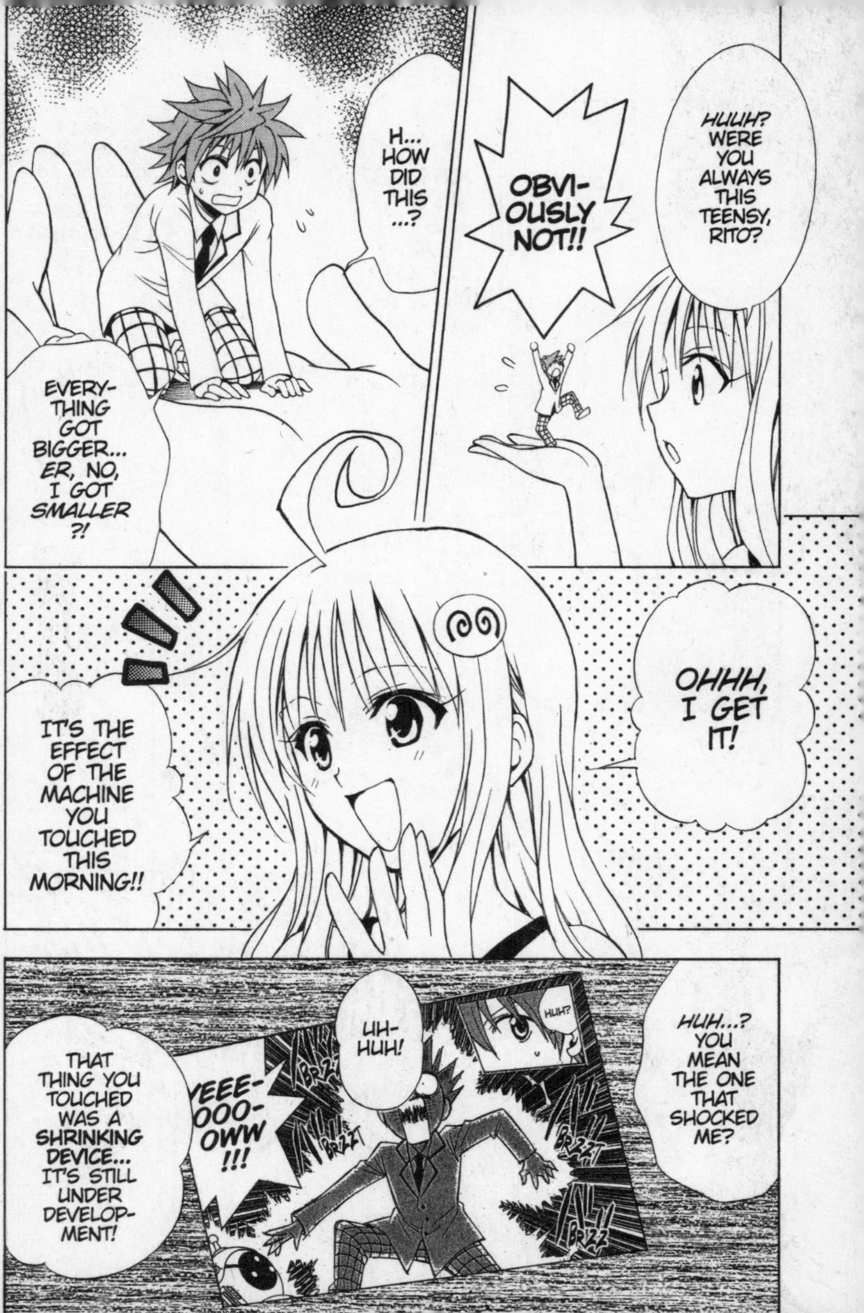
HUUH? WERE YOU ALWAYS THIS TEENSY, RITO?
OBVI-OUSLY NOT!!
H... HOW DID THIS ...?
EVERY-THING GOT BIGGER... ER, NO, I GOT SMALLER ?!
OHHH, I GET IT!
IT'S THE EFFECT OF THE MACHINE YOU TOUCHED THIS MORNING!!
HUH...? YOU MEAN THE ONE THAT SHOCKED ME?
HUH?
UH-HUH!
YEEE-OOO-OWW !!!
THAT THING YOU TOUCHED WAS A SHRINKING DEVICE... IT'S STILL UNDER DEVELOP-MENT!

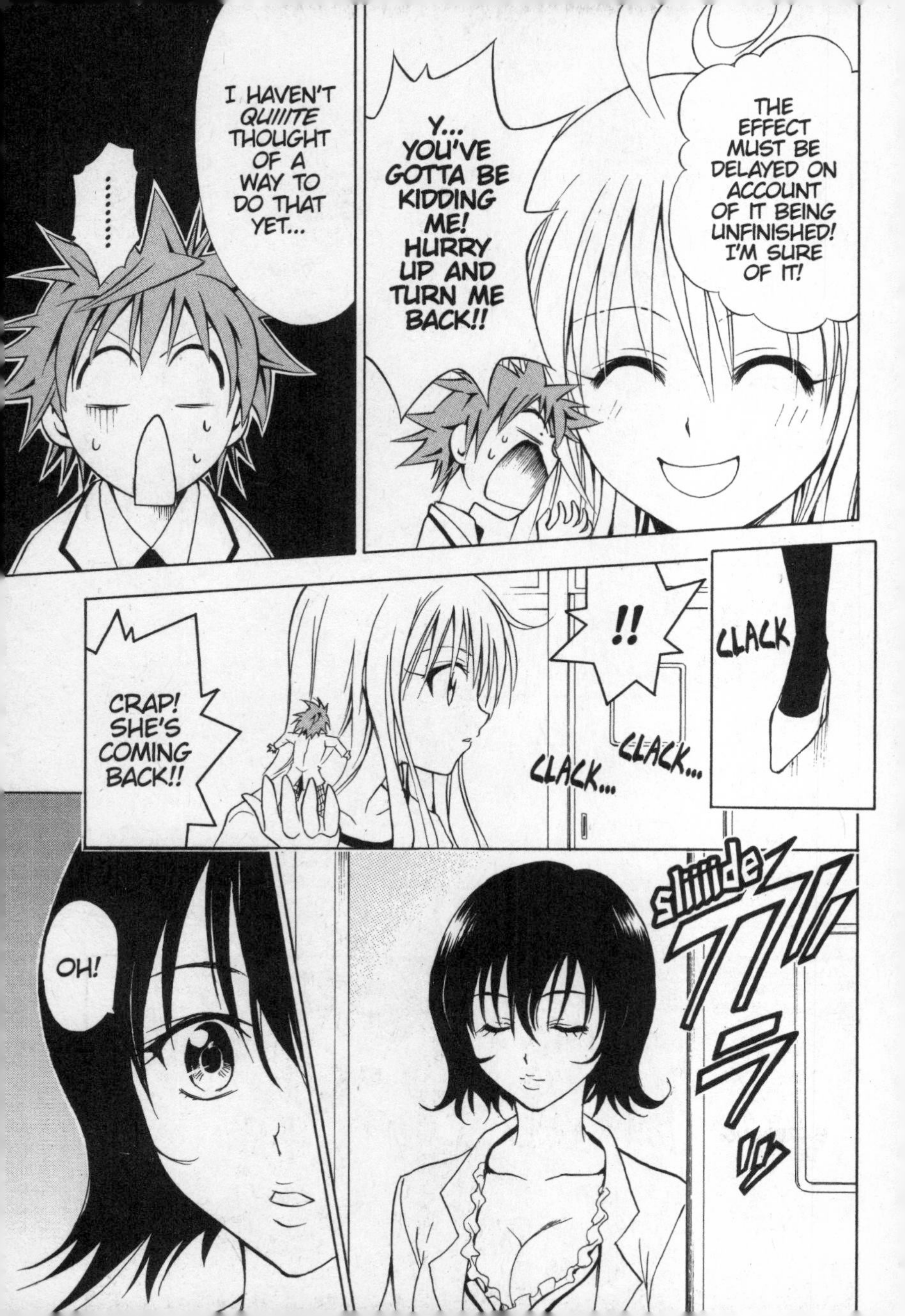
THE EFFECT MUST BE DELAYED ON ACCOUNT OF IT BEING UNFINISHED! I'M SURE OF IT!
Y... YOU'VE GOTTA BE KIDDING ME! HURRY UP AND TURN ME BACK!!
I HAVEN'T QUIIIITE THOUGHT OF A WAY TO DO THAT YET...
......
CLACK
!!
CLACK...
CLACK...
CRAP! SHE'S COMING BACK!!
sliiiide
OH!

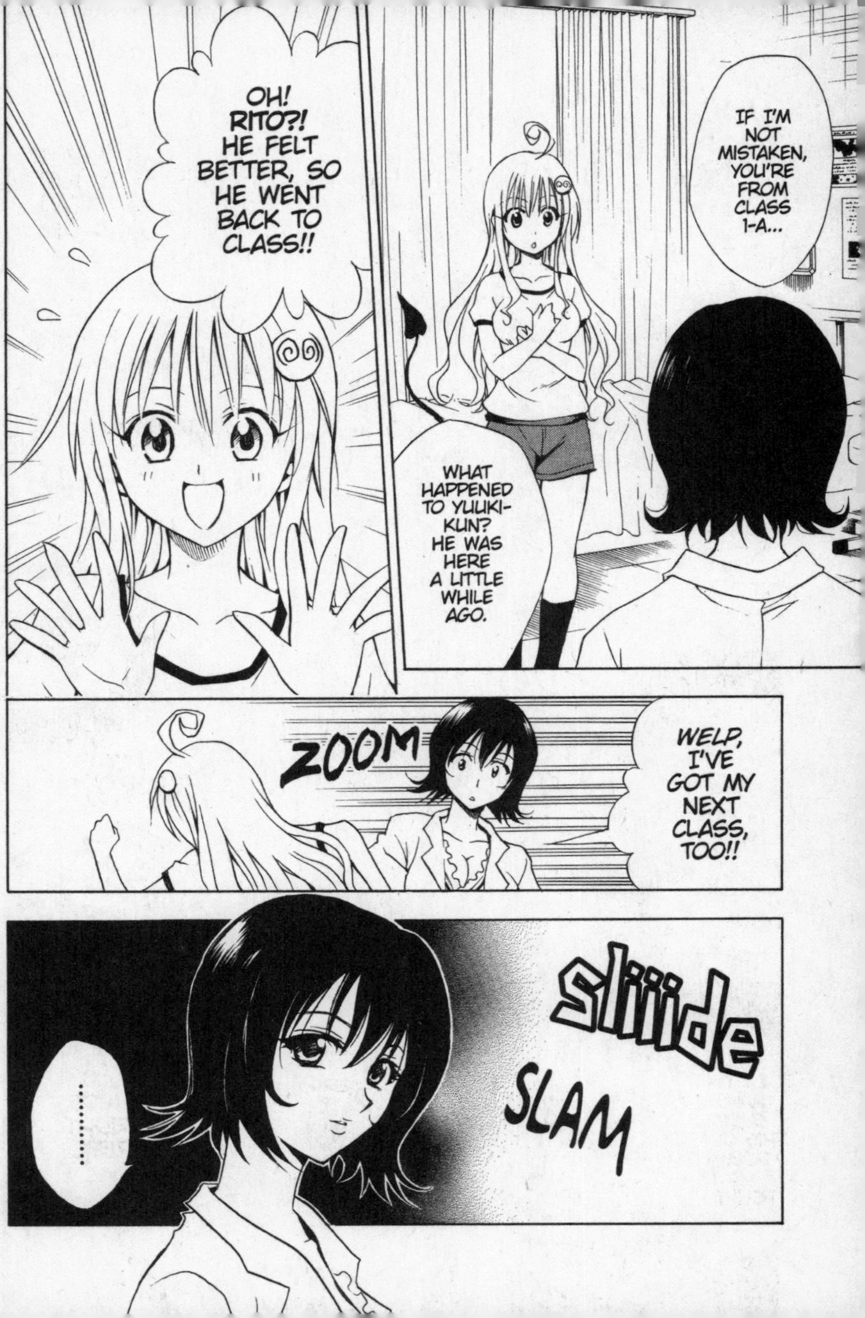

IF I'M NOT MISTAKEN, YOU'RE FROM CLASS 1-A...
WHAT HAPPENED TO YUUKI-KUN? HE WAS HERE A LITTLE WHILE AGO.
OH! RITO?! HE FELT BETTER, SO HE WENT BACK TO CLASS!!
WELP, I'VE GOT MY NEXT CLASS, TOO!!
ZOOM
sliiide
SLAM
......

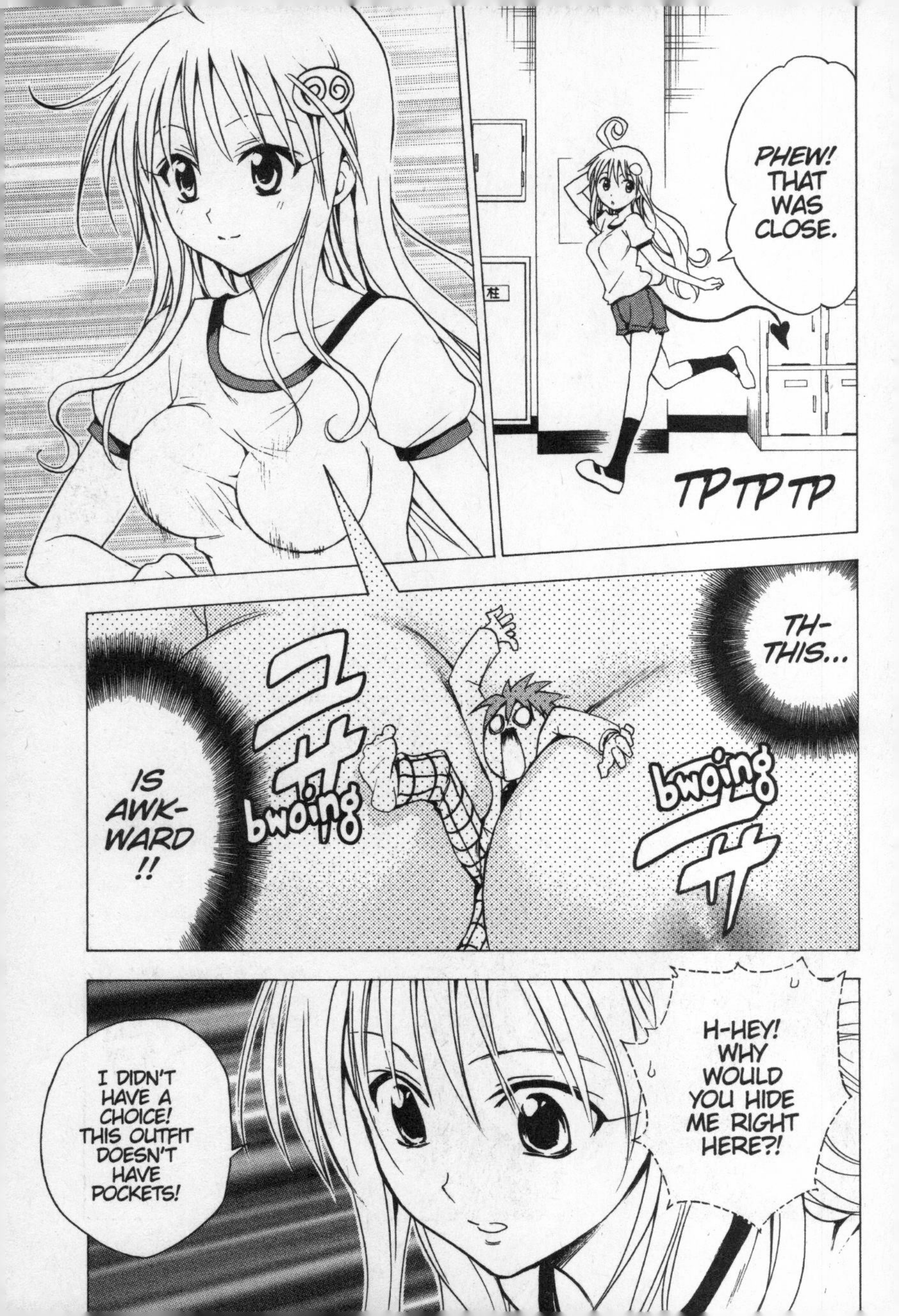
PHEW! THAT WAS CLOSE.
TP TP TP
TH-THIS...
bwoing
ユサ
ユサ
bwoing
IS AWK-WARD!!
H-HEY! WHY WOULD YOU HIDE ME RIGHT HERE?!
I DIDN'T HAVE A CHOICE! THIS OUTFIT DOESN'T HAVE POCKETS!

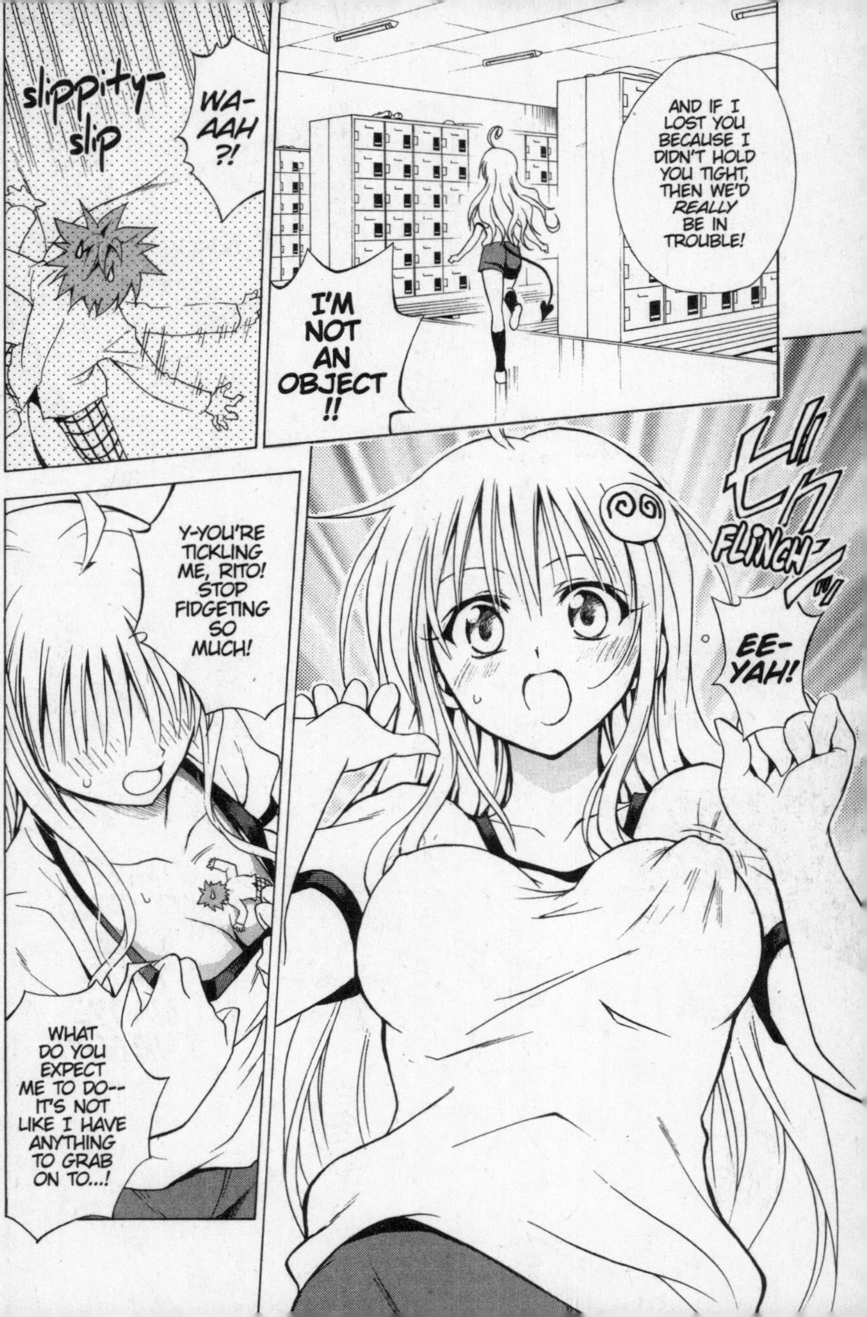
AND IF I LOST YOU BECAUSE I DIDN'T HOLD YOU TIGHT, THEN WE'D *REALLY* BE IN TROUBLE!
I'M NOT AN OBJECT!!
WA-AAH?!
slippity-slip
FLINCH
EE-YAH!
Y-YOU'RE TICKLING ME, RITO! STOP FIDGETING SO MUCH!
WHAT DO YOU EXPECT ME TO DO--IT'S NOT LIKE I HAVE ANYTHING TO GRAB ON TO...!

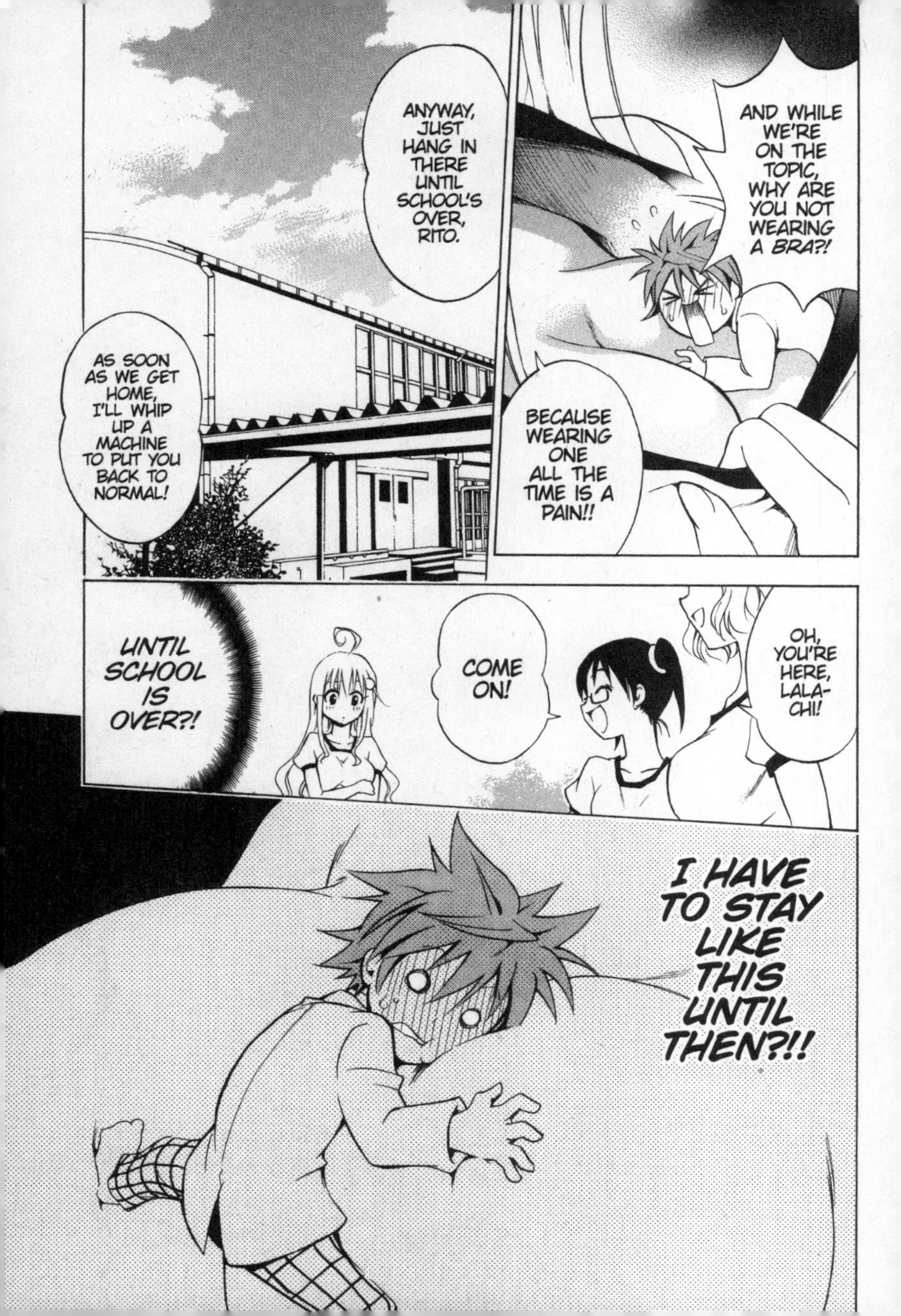
AND WHILE WE'RE ON THE TOPIC, WHY ARE YOU NOT WEARING A *BRA*?!
BECAUSE WEARING ONE ALL THE TIME IS A PAIN!!
ANYWAY, JUST HANG IN THERE UNTIL SCHOOL'S OVER, RITO.
AS SOON AS WE GET HOME, I'LL WHIP UP A MACHINE TO PUT YOU BACK TO NORMAL!
OH, YOU'RE HERE, LALA-CHI!
COME ON!
UNTIL SCHOOL IS OVER?!
I HAVE TO STAY LIKE THIS UNTIL THEN?!!

To LOVE Ru

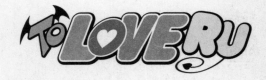

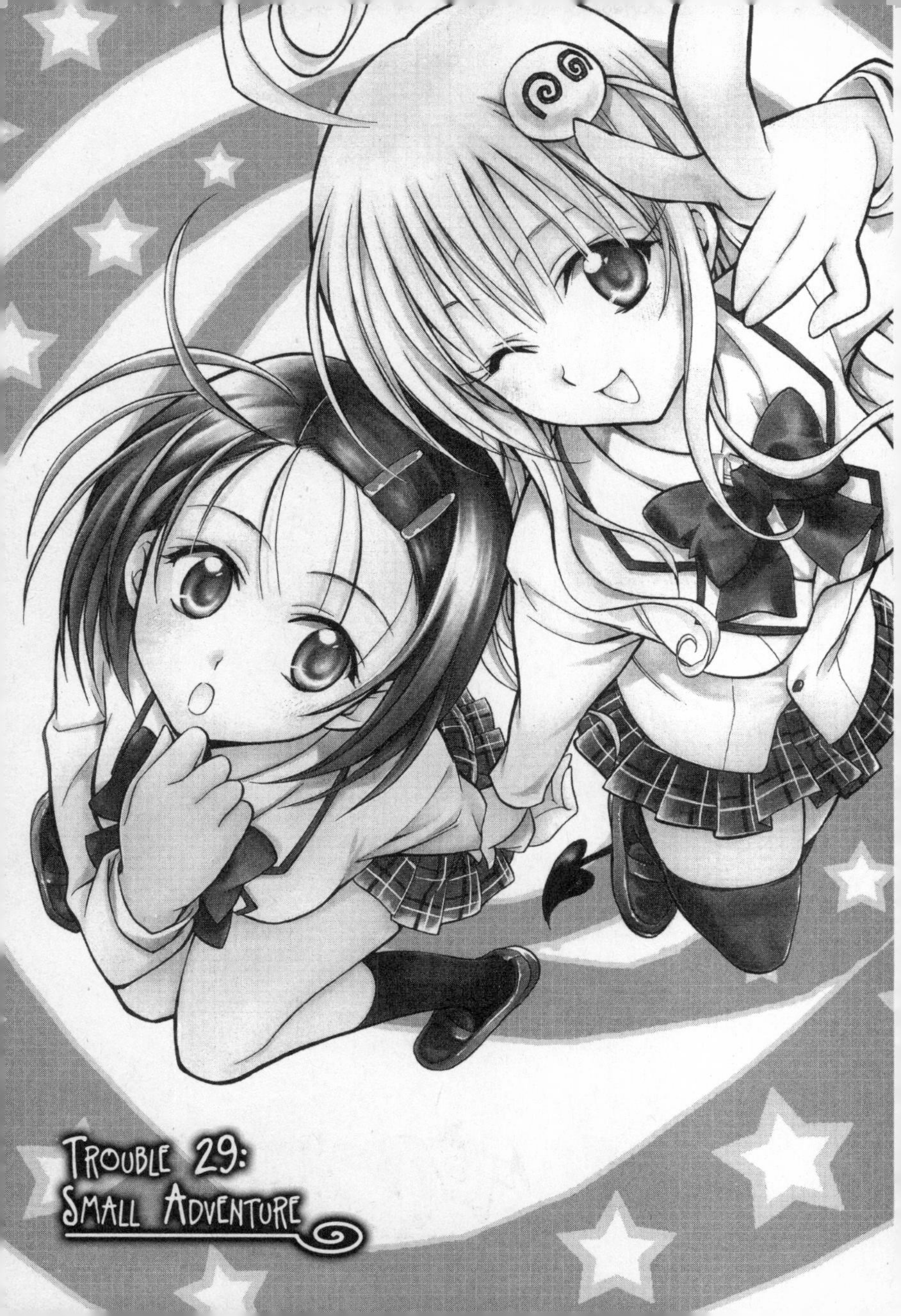
Trouble 29:
Small Adventure

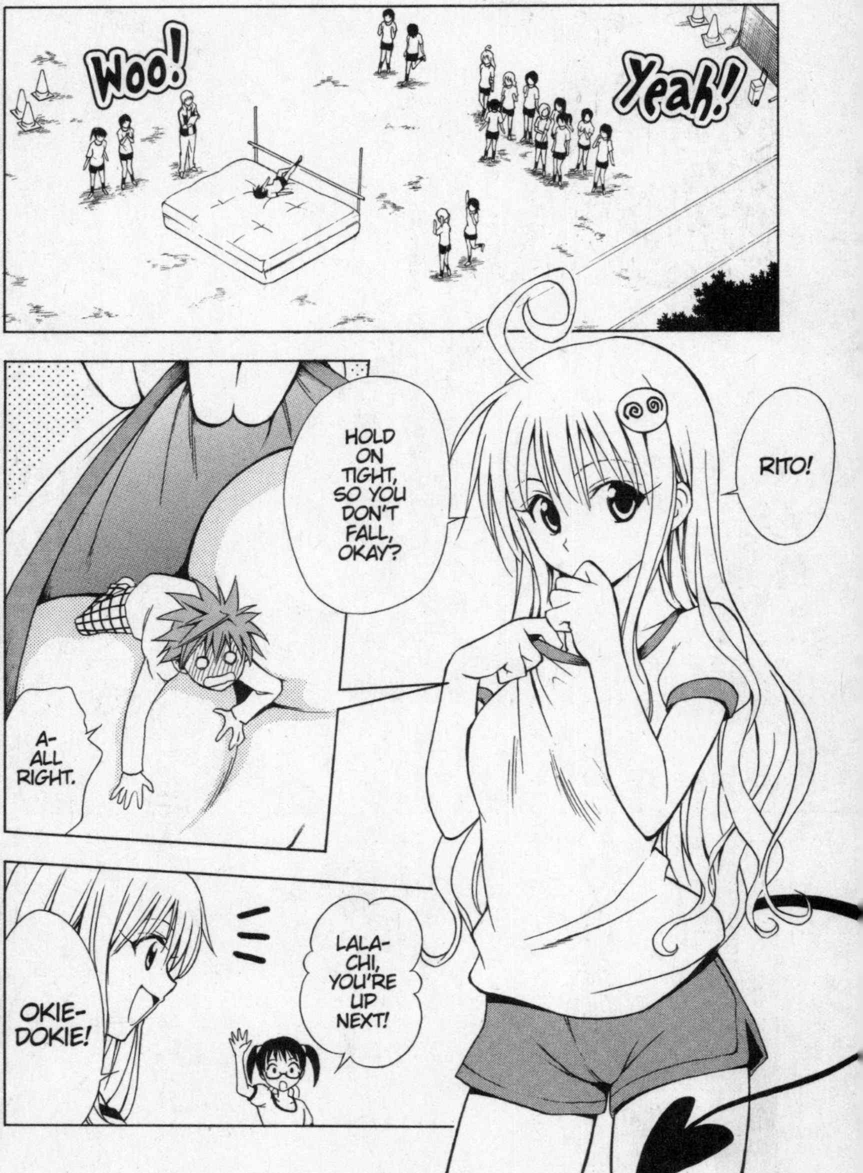
Yeah!
Woo!
RITO!
HOLD ON TIGHT, SO YOU DON'T FALL, OKAY?
A-ALL RIGHT.
LALA-CHI, YOU'RE UP NEXT!
OKIE-DOKIE!

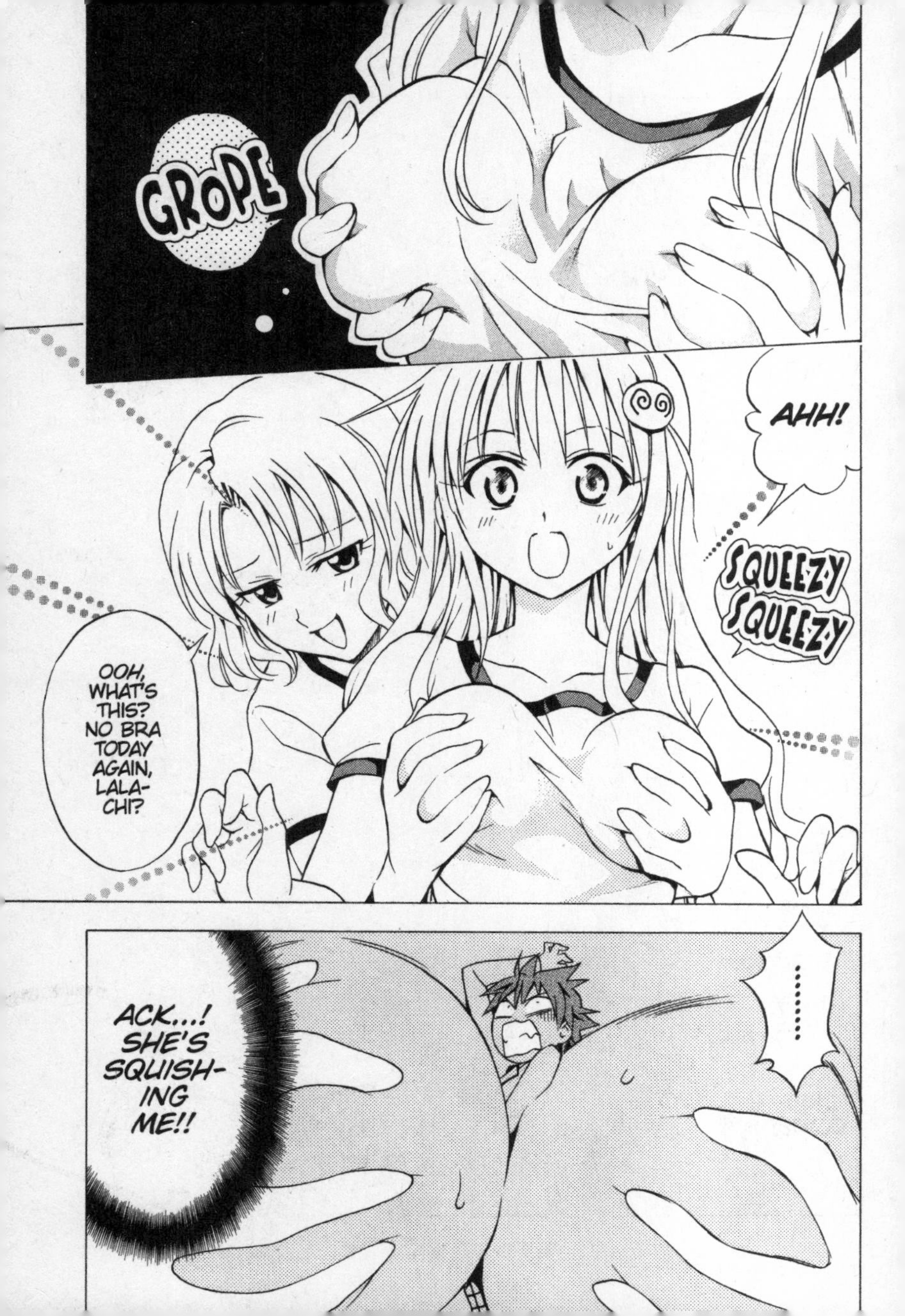
GROPE
AHH!
SQUEEZY SQUEEZY
OOH, WHAT'S THIS? NO BRA TODAY AGAIN, LALA-CHI?
......!
ACK...! SHE'S SQUISH-ING ME!!

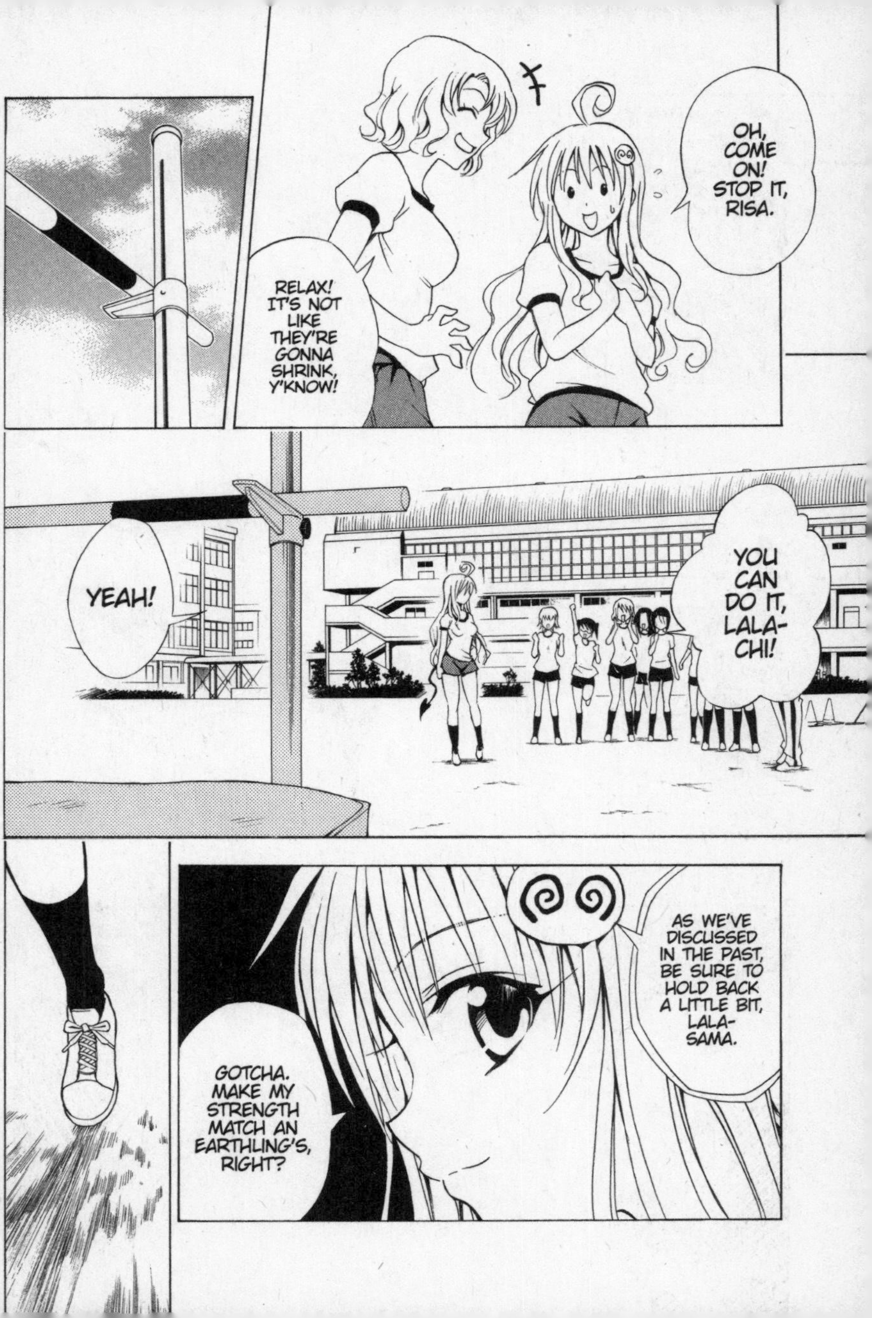
OH, COME ON! STOP IT, RISA.
RELAX! IT'S NOT LIKE THEY'RE GONNA SHRINK, Y'KNOW!
YOU CAN DO IT, LALA-CHI!
YEAH!
AS WE'VE DISCUSSED IN THE PAST, BE SURE TO HOLD BACK A LITTLE BIT, LALA-SAMA.
GOTCHA. MAKE MY STRENGTH MATCH AN EARTHLING'S, RIGHT?

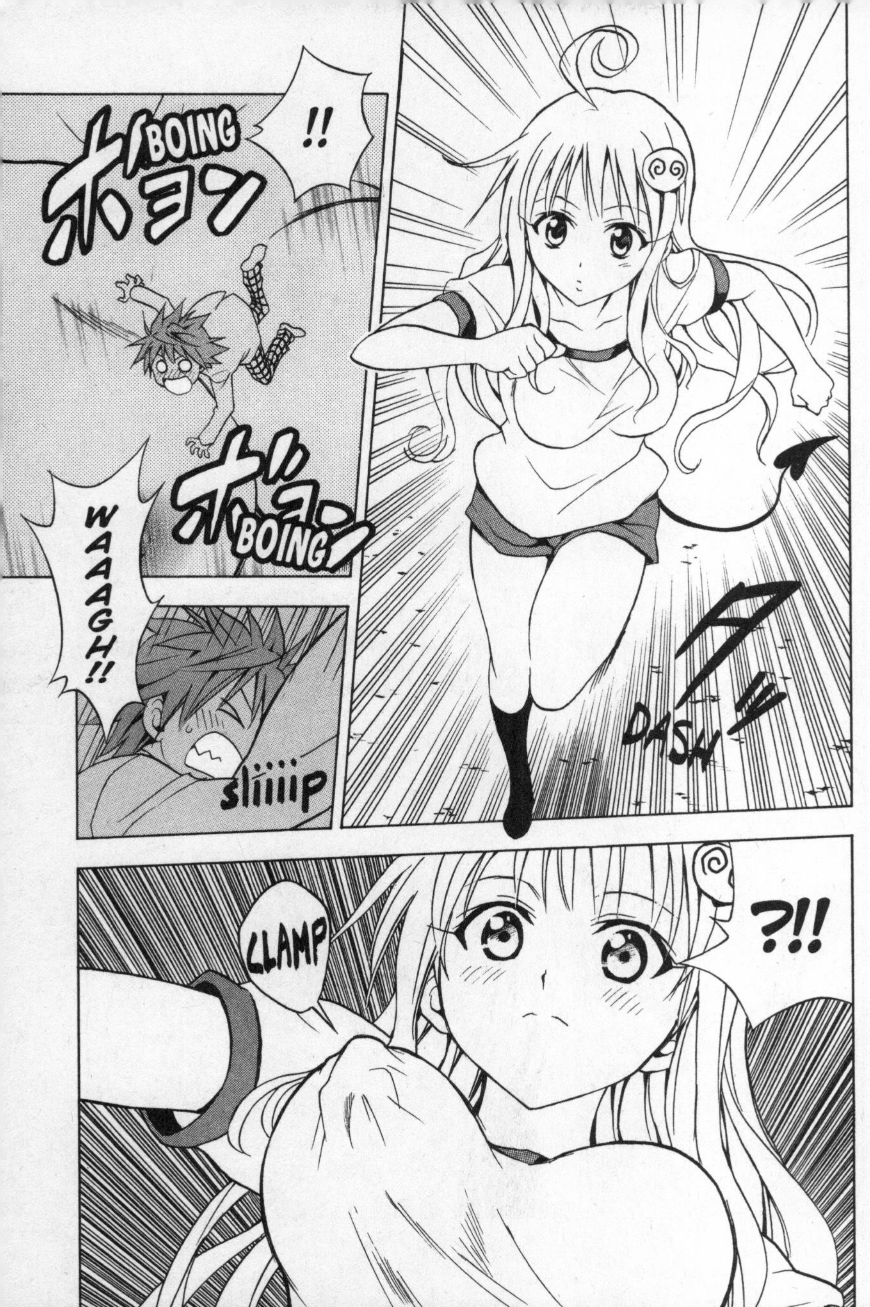
DASH
!!
ホヨン
BOING
BOING
WAAAAGH!!
sliiiip
?!!
CLAMP

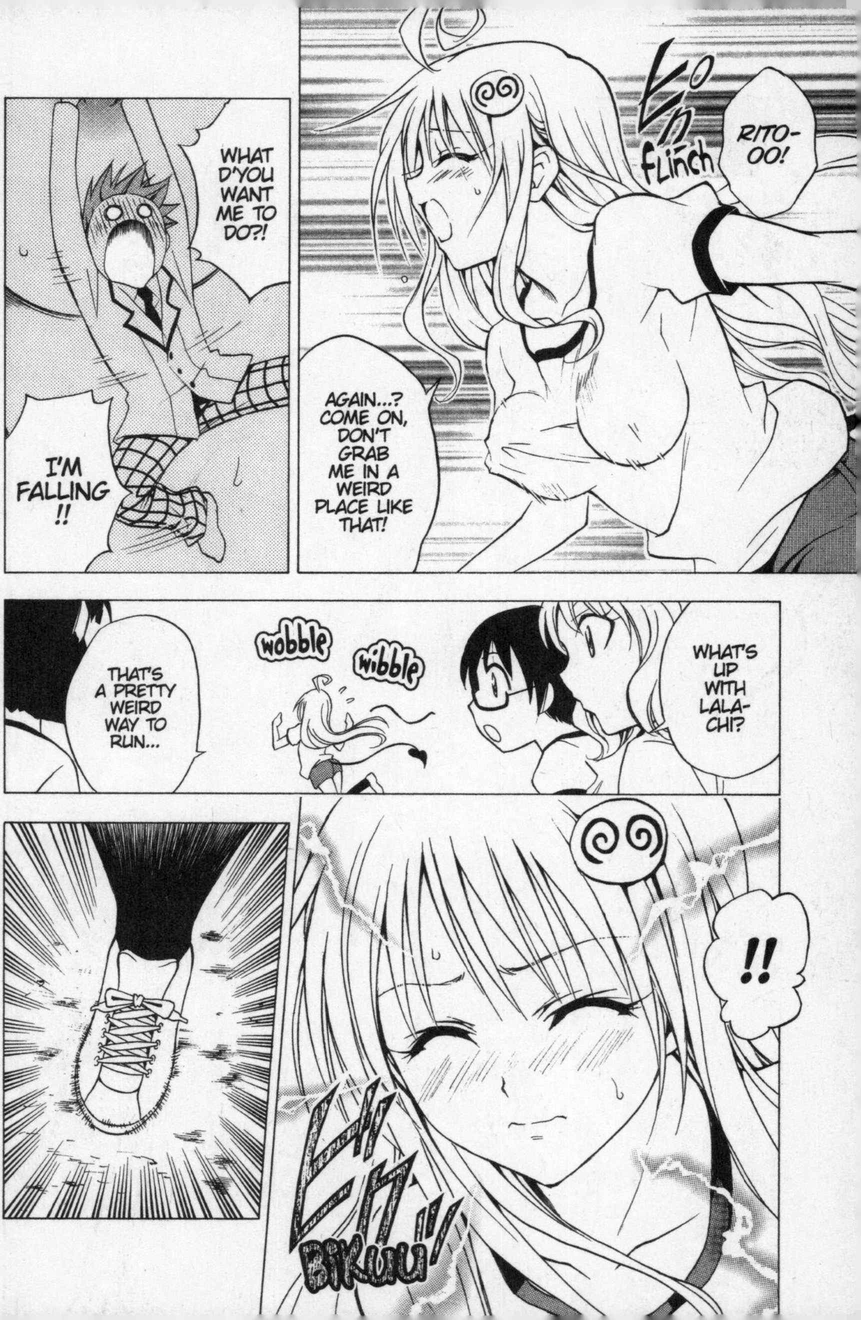
RITO-OO!
Flinch
AGAIN...? COME ON, DON'T GRAB ME IN A WEIRD PLACE LIKE THAT!
WHAT D'YOU WANT ME TO DO?!
I'M FALLING!!
WHAT'S UP WITH LALA-CHI?
wibble
wobble
THAT'S A PRETTY WEIRD WAY TO RUN...
!!
BIKUU!

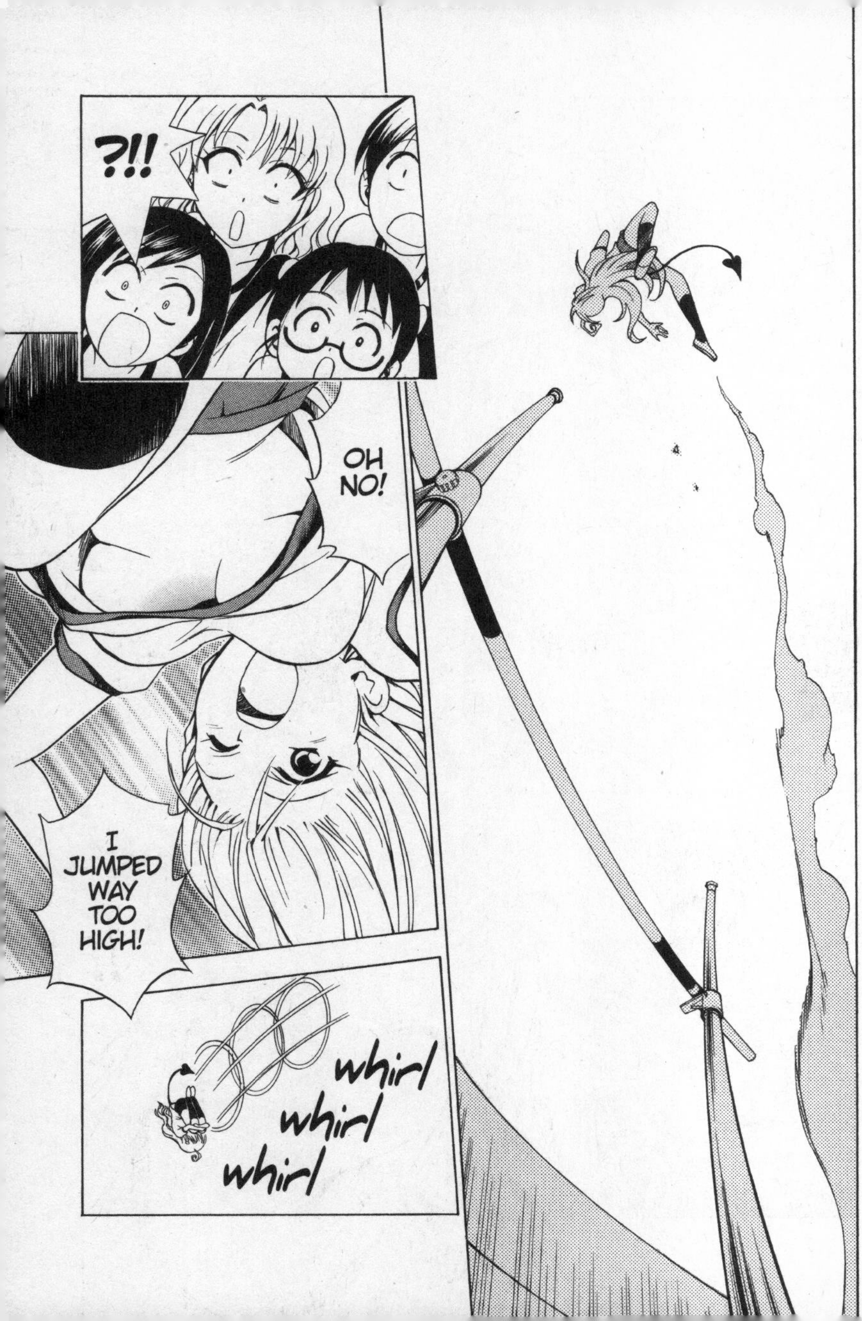
?!!
OH NO!
I JUMPED WAY TOO HIGH!
whirl
whirl
whirl

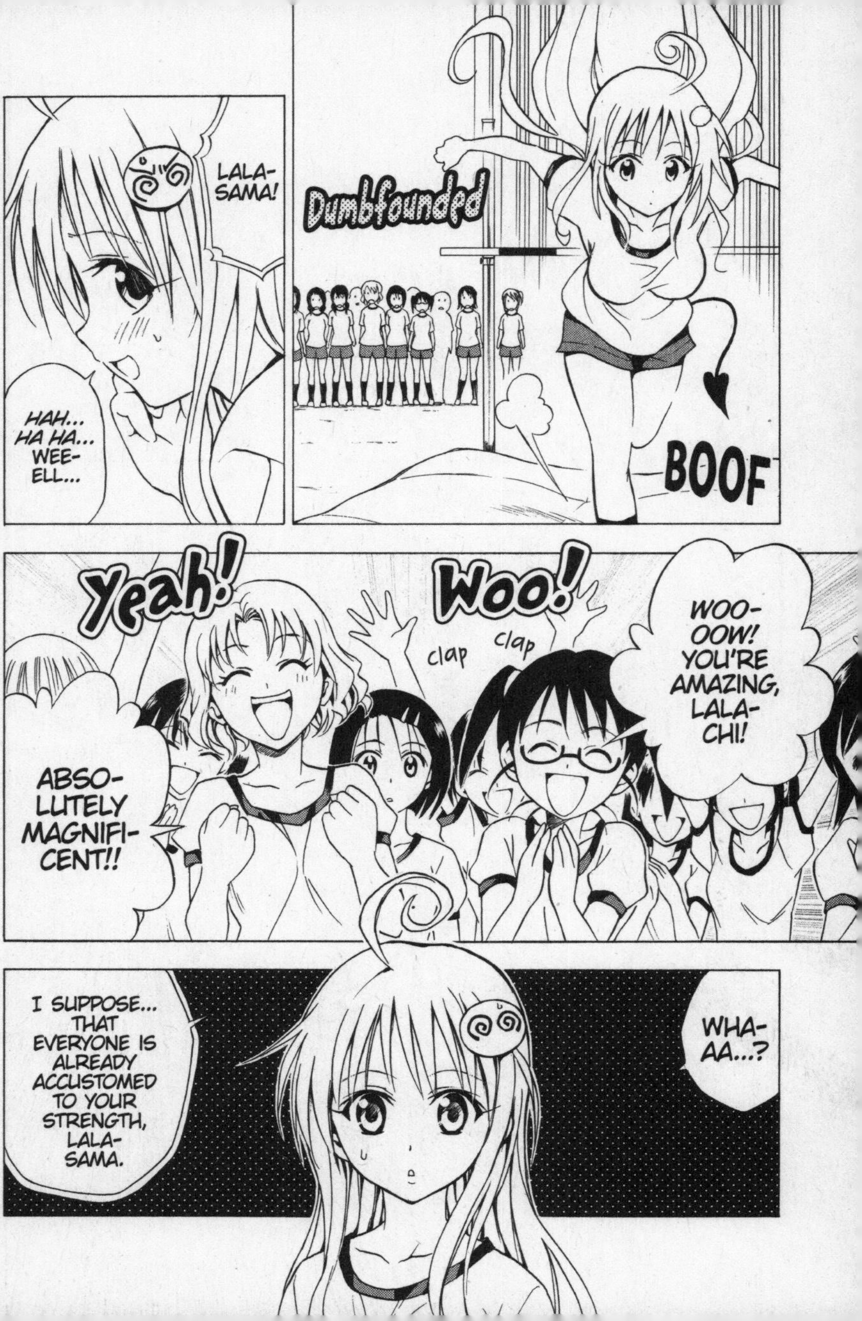
Dumbfounded
BOOF
LALA-SAMA!
HAH... HA HA... WEE-ELL...
WOO-OOW! YOU'RE AMAZING, LALA-CHI!
Woo!
clap
clap
Yeah!
ABSO-LUTELY MAGNIFI-CENT!!
WHA-AA...?
I SUPPOSE... THAT EVERYONE IS ALREADY ACCUSTOMED TO YOUR STRENGTH, LALA-SAMA.

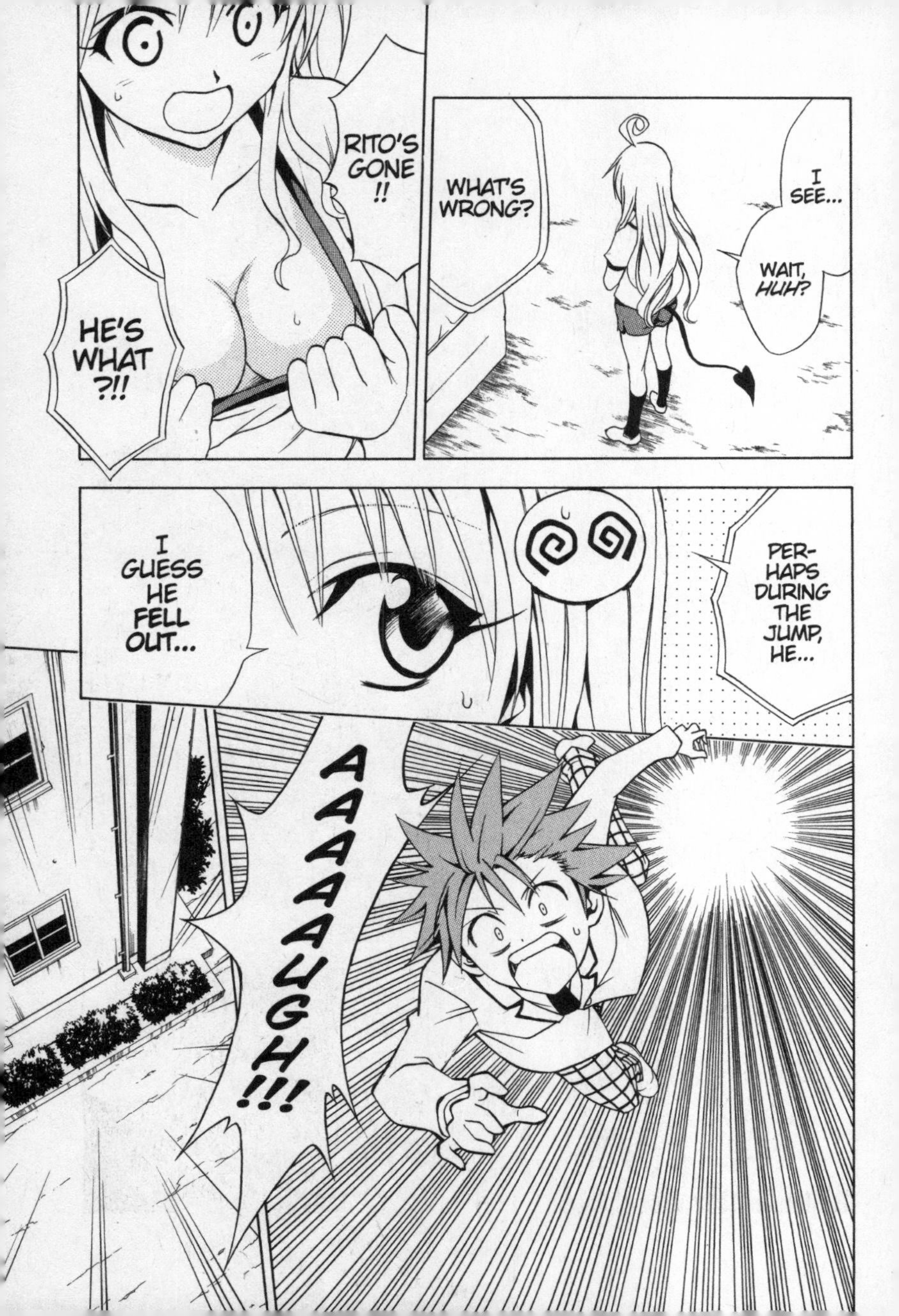
I SEE...
WAIT, HUH?
WHAT'S WRONG?
RITO'S GONE !!
HE'S WHAT ?!!
PER-HAPS DURING THE JUMP, HE...
I GUESS HE FELL OUT...
AAAAAAUGH!!!

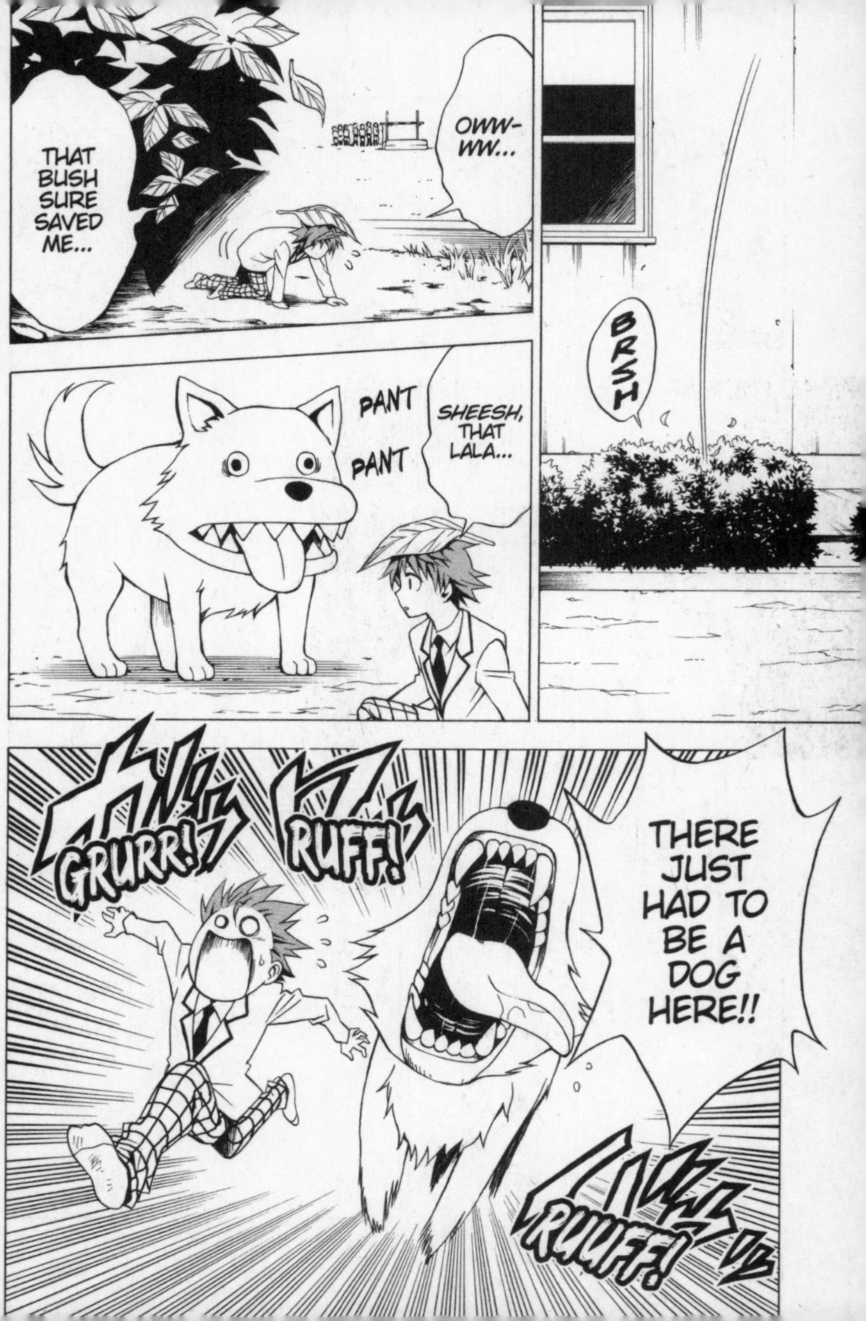
BRSH
OWW-WW...
THAT BUSH SURE SAVED ME...
SHEESH, THAT LALA...
PANT
PANT
THERE JUST HAD TO BE A DOG HERE!!
RUFF!
GRURR!
RUUFF!

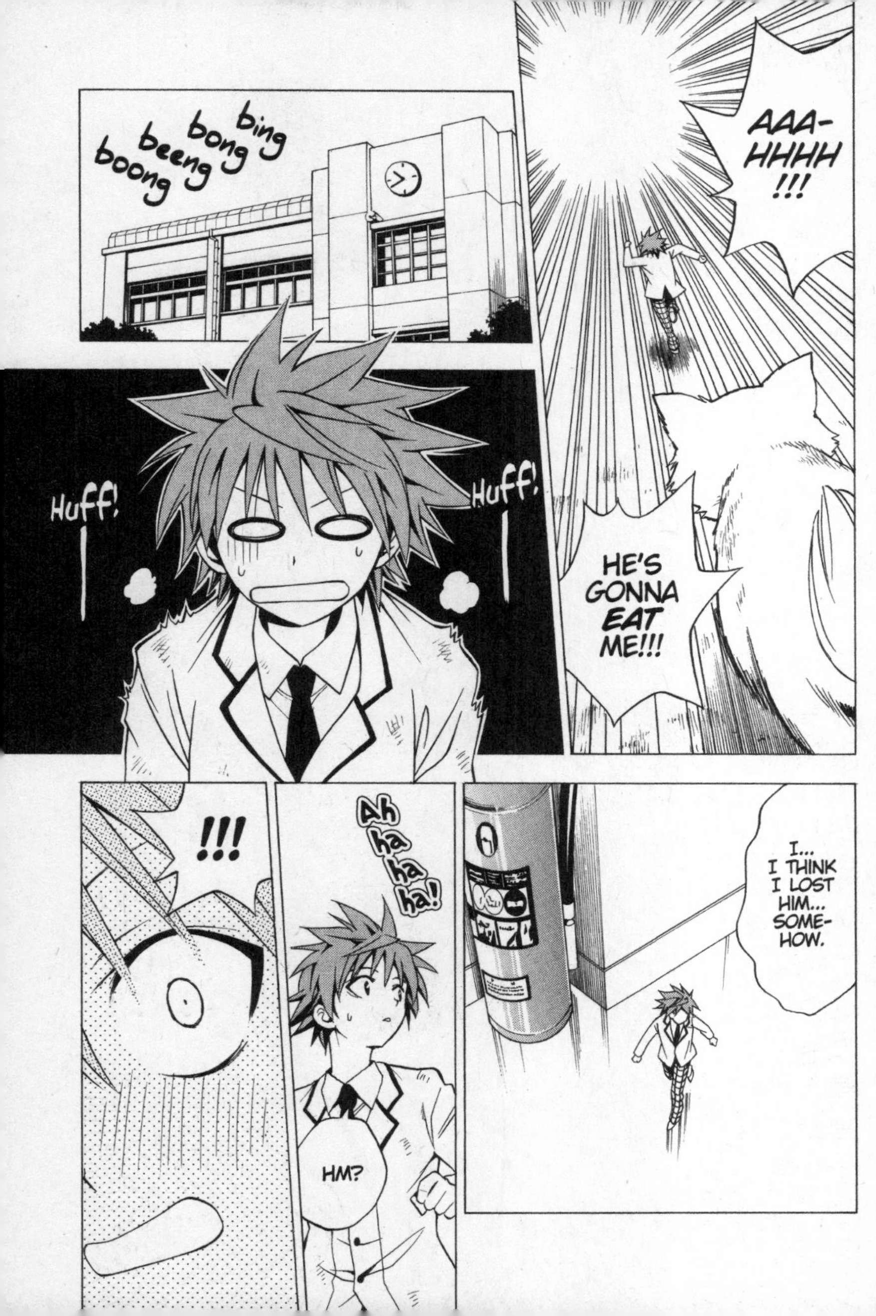
AAA-HHHH!!!
HE'S GONNA EAT ME!!!
bing bong beeng boong
Huff!
Huff!
I... I THINK I LOST HIM... SOMEHOW.
Ah ha ha ha!
HM?
!!!

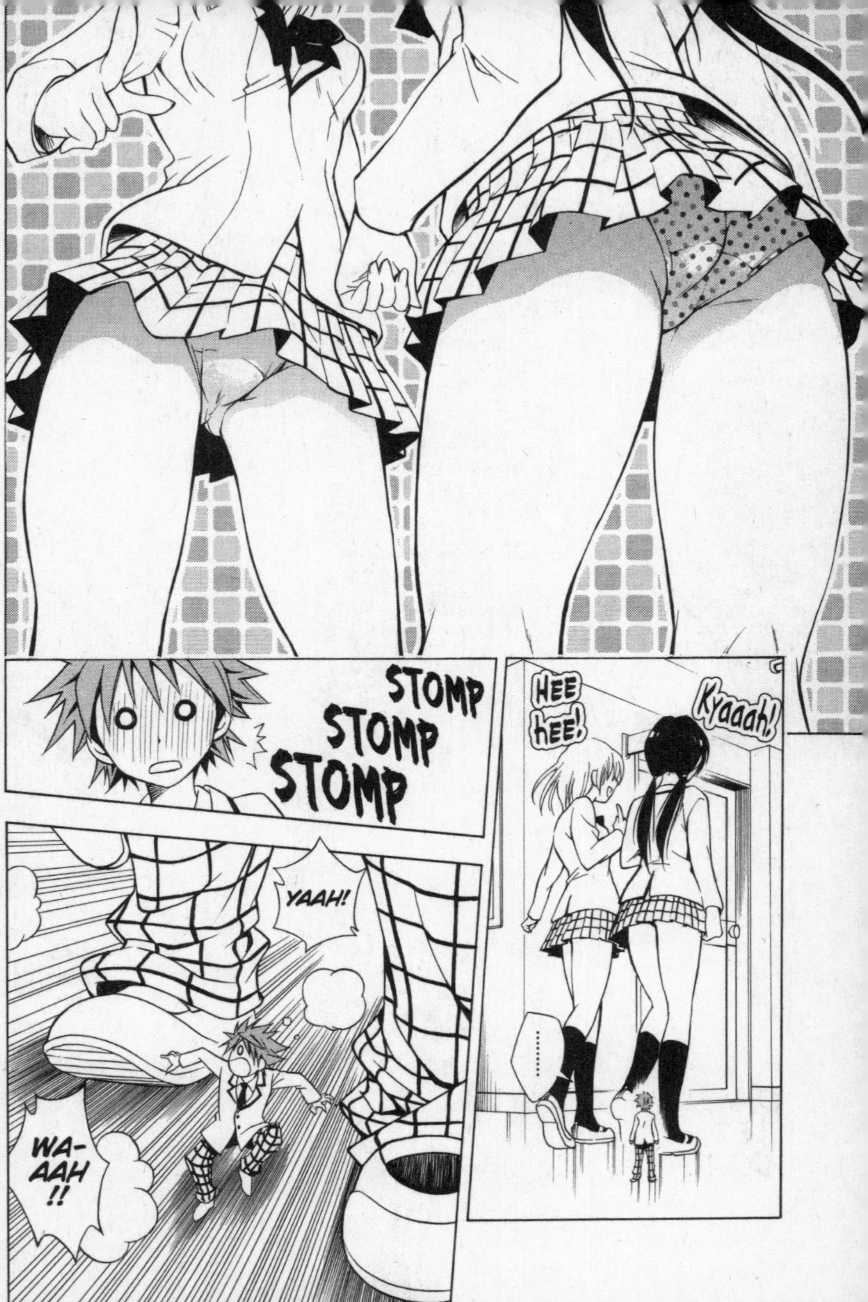
Kyaaah!
HEE hee!
......
STOMP
STOMP
STOMP
YAAH!
WA-AAH!!

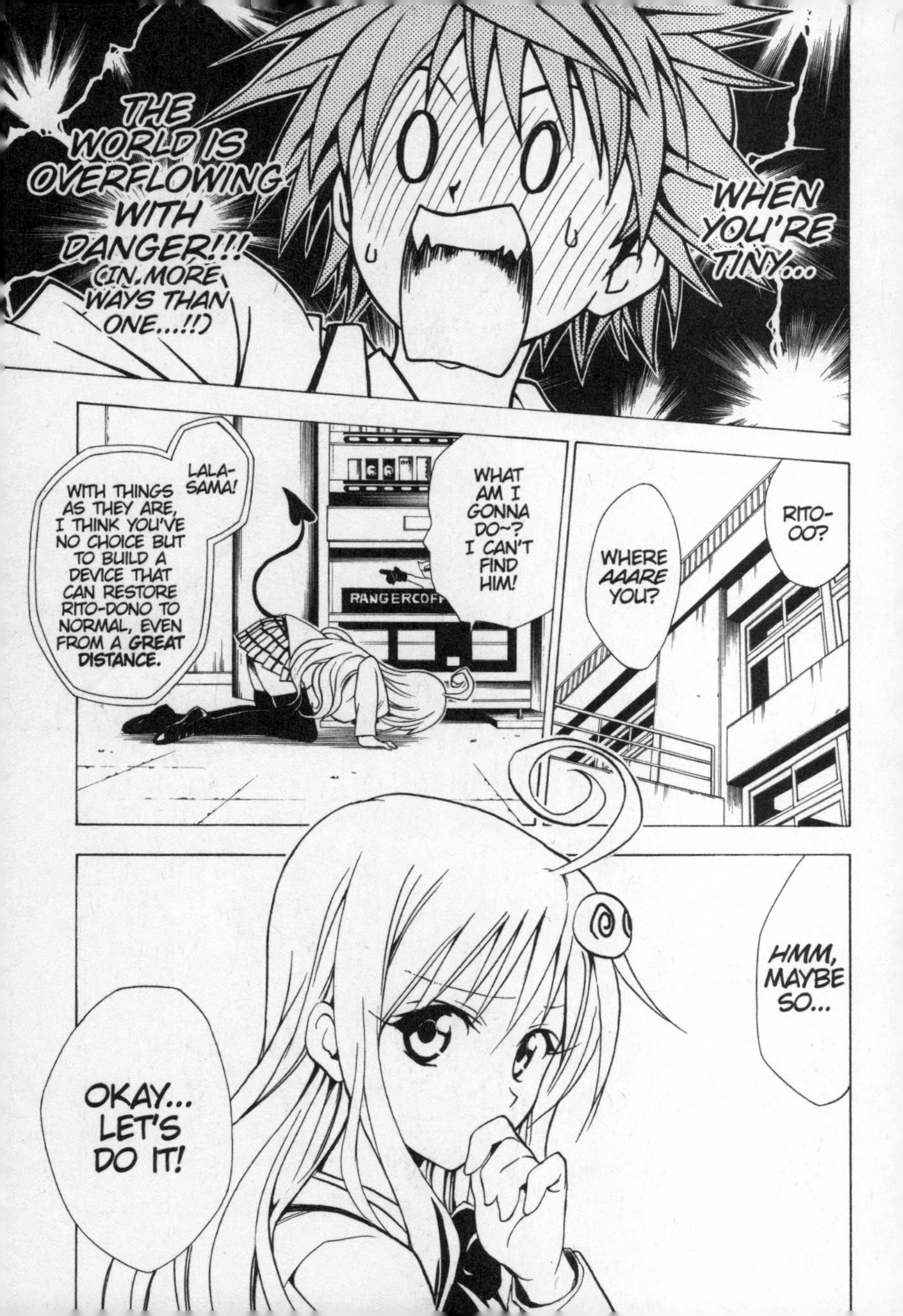
WHEN YOU'RE TINY...
THE WORLD IS OVERFLOWING WITH DANGER!!!
(IN MORE WAYS THAN ONE...!!)
RITO-OO?
WHERE AAARE YOU?
WHAT AM I GONNA DO~? I CAN'T FIND HIM!
RANGERCOFF
LALA-SAMA!
WITH THINGS AS THEY ARE, I THINK YOU'VE NO CHOICE BUT TO BUILD A DEVICE THAT CAN RESTORE RITO-DONO TO NORMAL, EVEN FROM A GREAT DISTANCE.
HMM, MAYBE SO...
OKAY... LET'S DO IT!

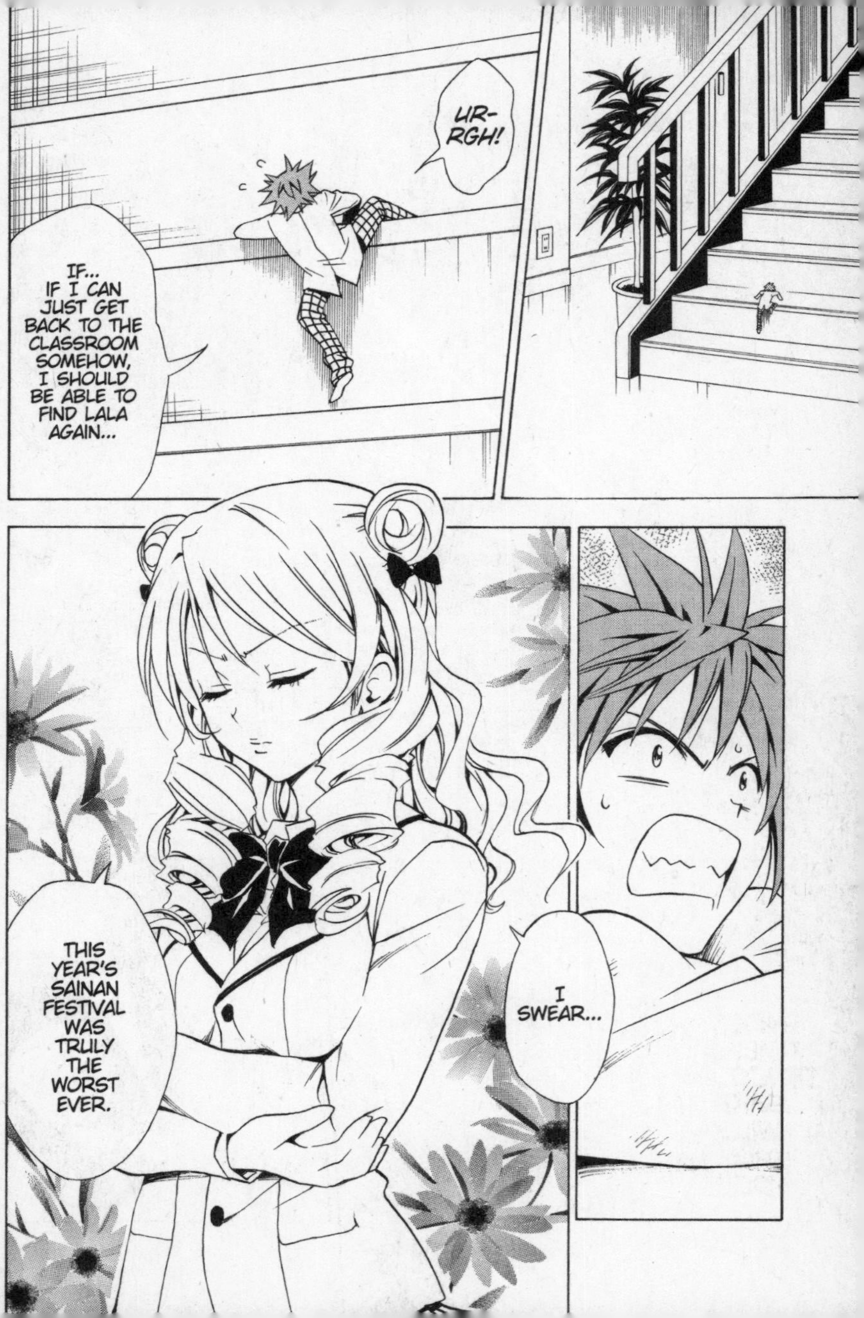
UR-RGH!
IF... IF I CAN JUST GET BACK TO THE CLASSROOM SOMEHOW, I SHOULD BE ABLE TO FIND LALA AGAIN...
I SWEAR...
THIS YEAR'S SAINAN FESTIVAL WAS TRULY THE WORST EVER.

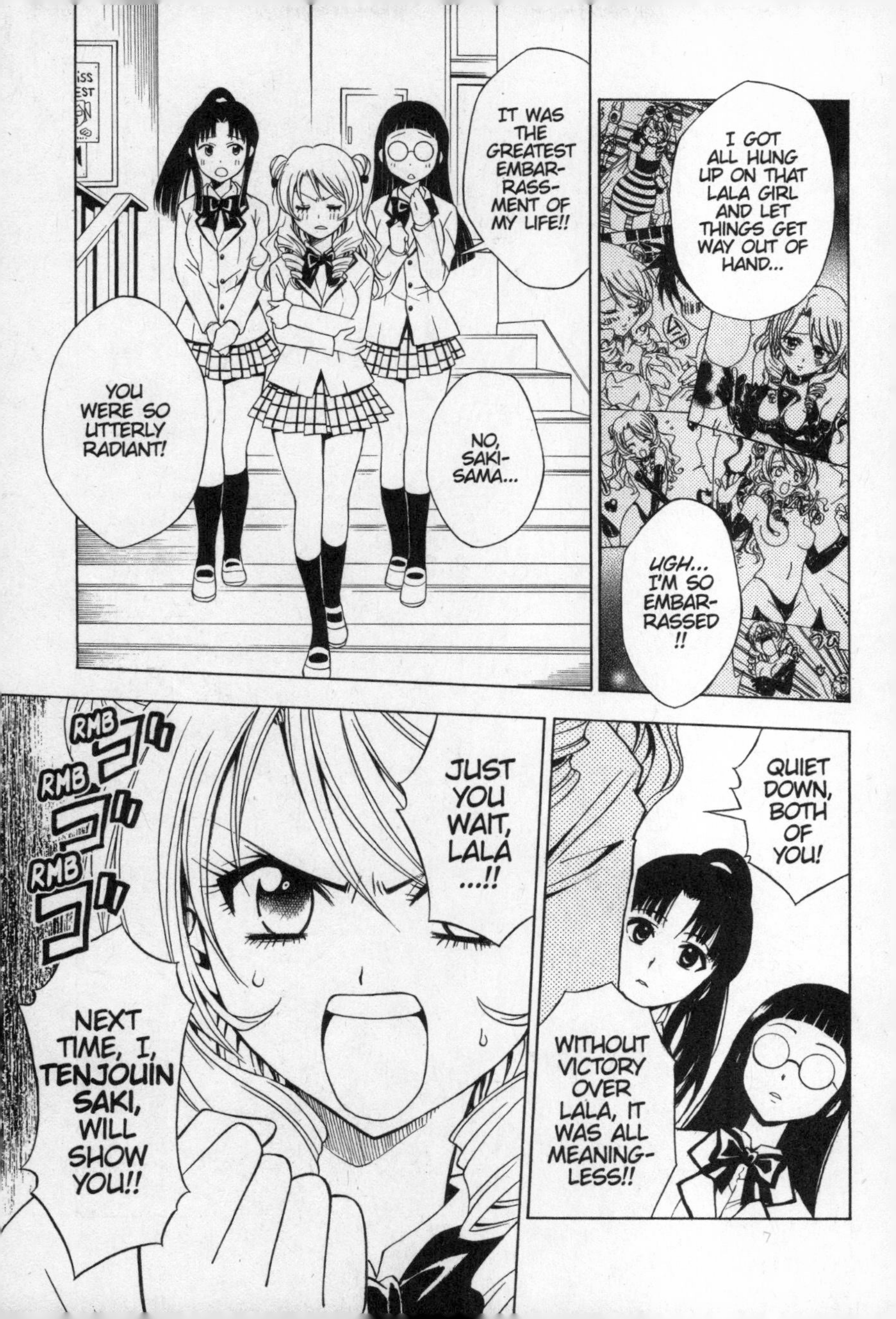
I GOT ALL HUNG UP ON THAT LALA GIRL AND LET THINGS GET WAY OUT OF HAND...
UGH... I'M SO EMBARRASSED!!
IT WAS THE GREATEST EMBARRASSMENT OF MY LIFE!!
NO, SAKI-SAMA...
YOU WERE SO UTTERLY RADIANT!
QUIET DOWN, BOTH OF YOU!
WITHOUT VICTORY OVER LALA, IT WAS ALL MEANINGLESS!!
JUST YOU WAIT, LALA...!!
RMB
RMB
RMB
NEXT TIME, I, TENJOUIN SAKI, WILL SHOW YOU!!

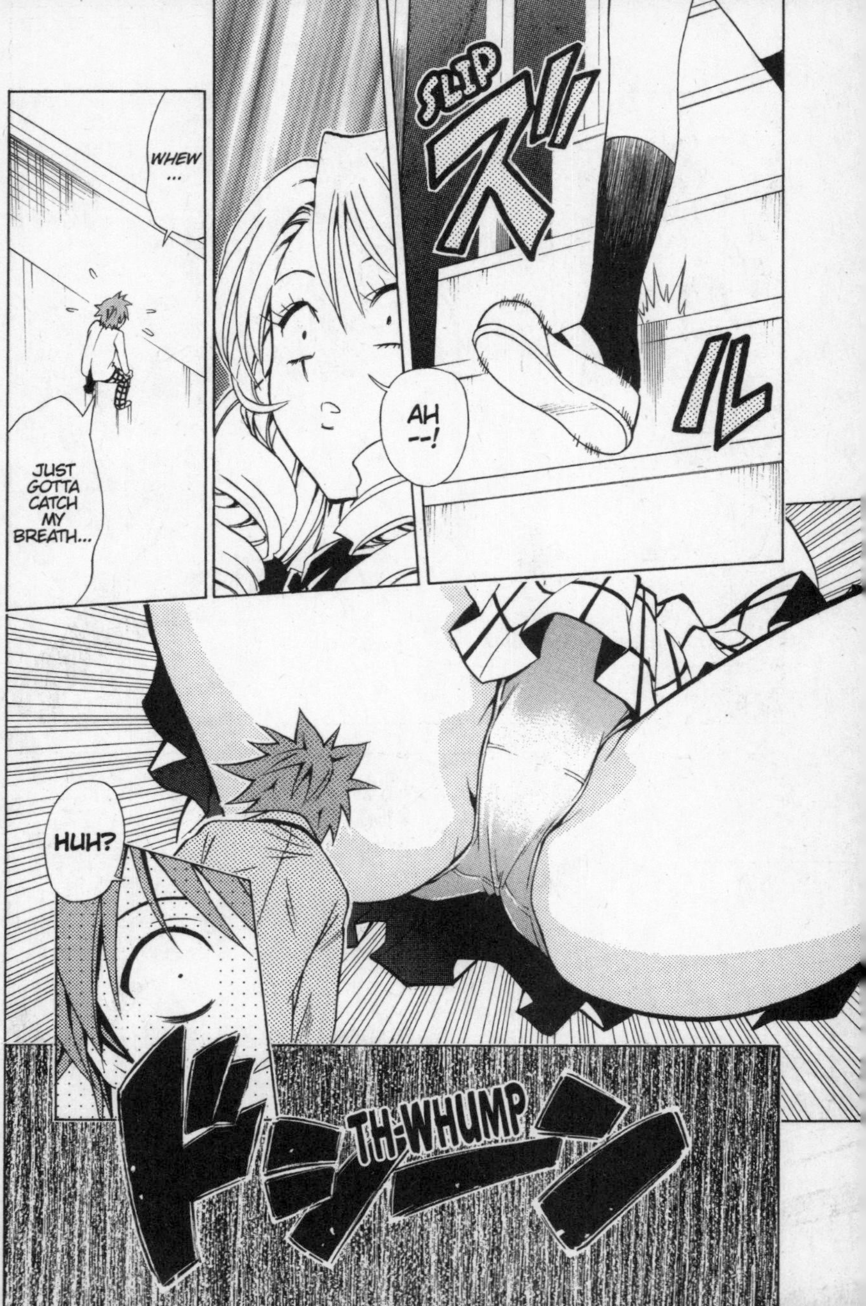
SLIP
AH --!
WHEW ...
JUST GOTTA CATCH MY BREATH...
HUH?
TH-WHUMP

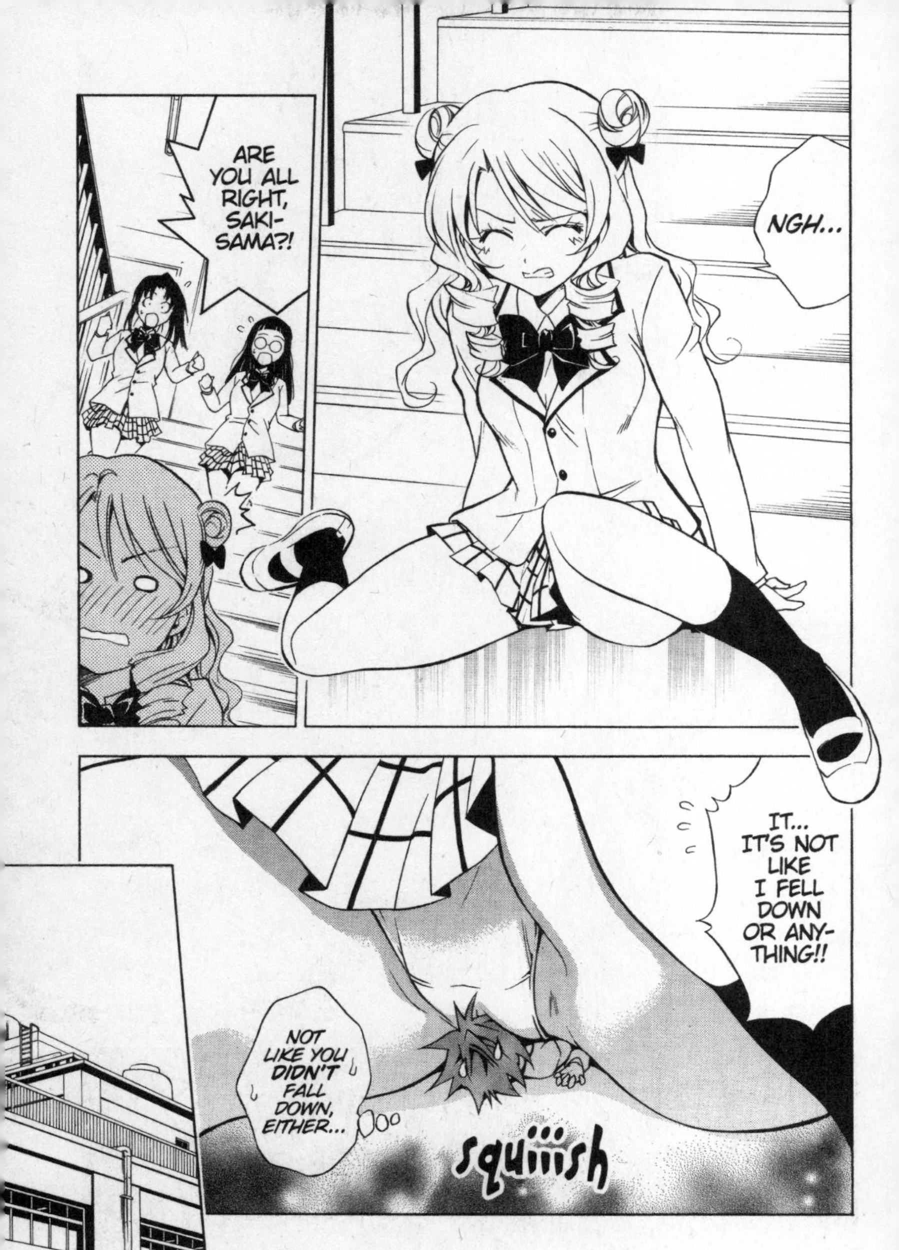
NGH...
ARE YOU ALL RIGHT, SAKI-SAMA?!
IT... IT'S NOT LIKE I FELL DOWN OR ANY-THING!!
NOT LIKE YOU DIDN'T FALL DOWN, EITHER...
squiiish

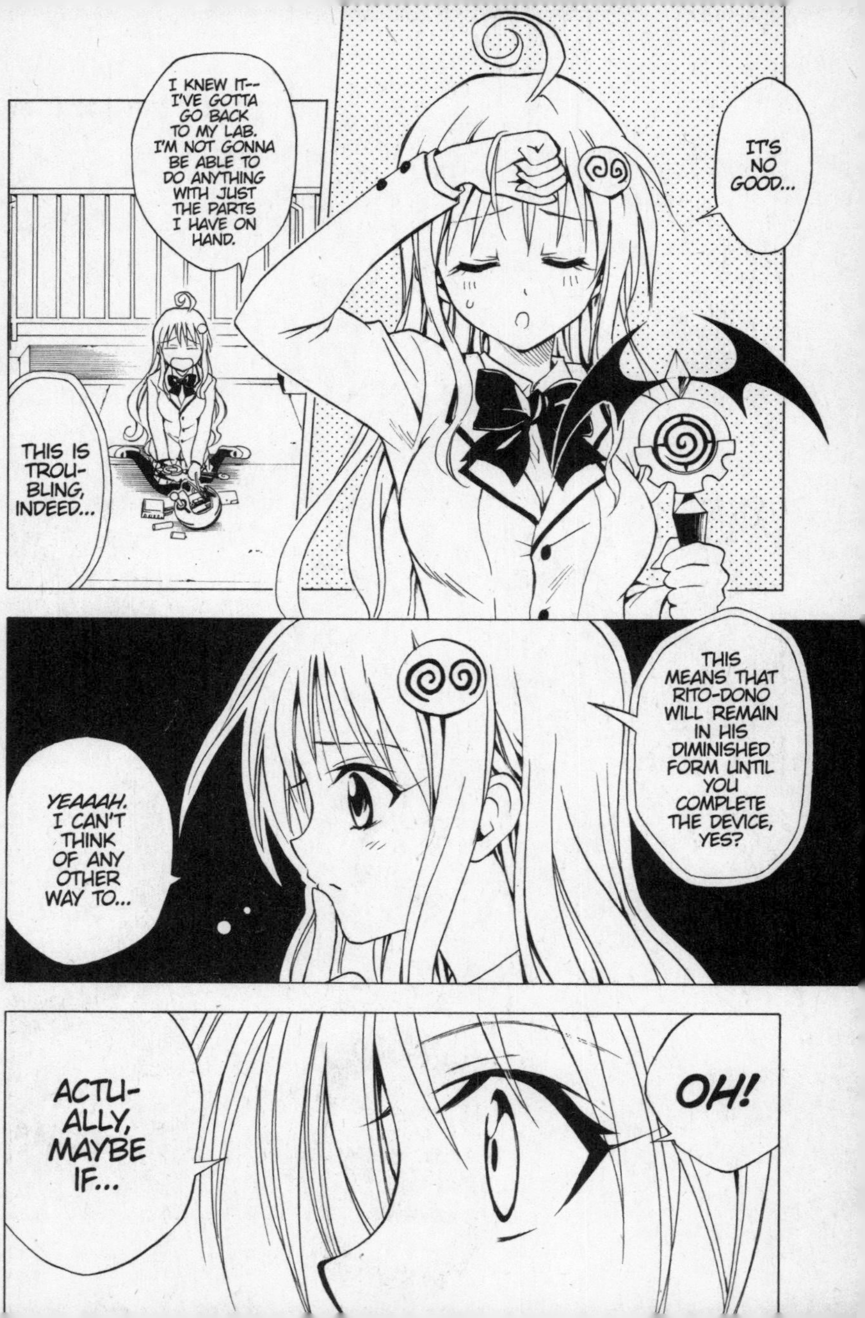
IT'S NO GOOD...
I KNEW IT-- I'VE GOTTA GO BACK TO MY LAB. I'M NOT GONNA BE ABLE TO DO ANYTHING WITH JUST THE PARTS I HAVE ON HAND.
THIS IS TROU-BLING, INDEED...
THIS MEANS THAT RITO-DONO WILL REMAIN IN HIS DIMINISHED FORM UNTIL YOU COMPLETE THE DEVICE, YES?
YEAAAH. I CAN'T THINK OF ANY OTHER WAY TO...
OH!
ACTU-ALLY, MAYBE IF...

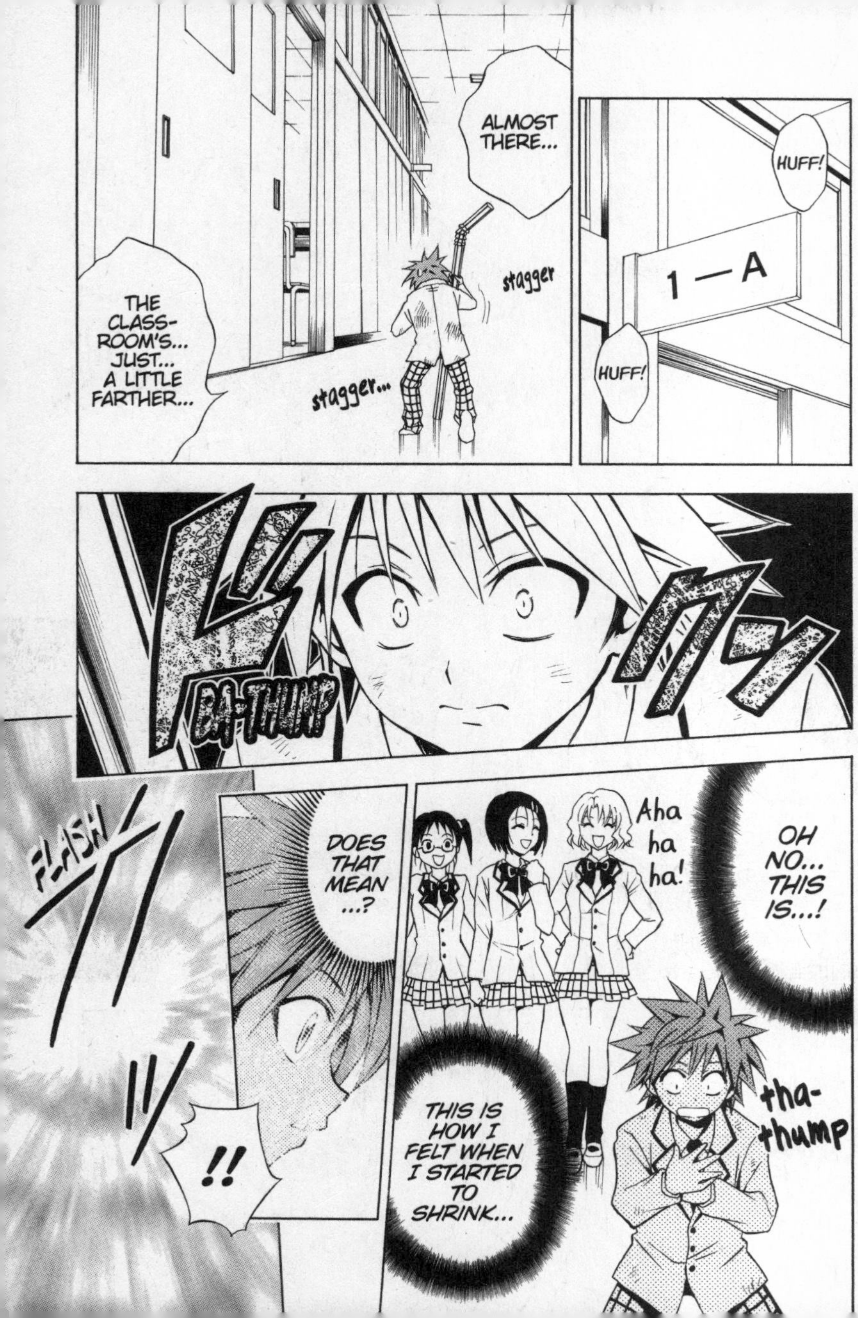

HUFF!
1 — A
HUFF!
ALMOST THERE...
stagger
THE CLASS-ROOM'S... JUST... A LITTLE FARTHER...
stagger...
BA-THUMP
OH NO... THIS IS...!
Aha ha ha!
tha-thump
THIS IS HOW I FELT WHEN I STARTED TO SHRINK...
DOES THAT MEAN ...?
FLASH
!!

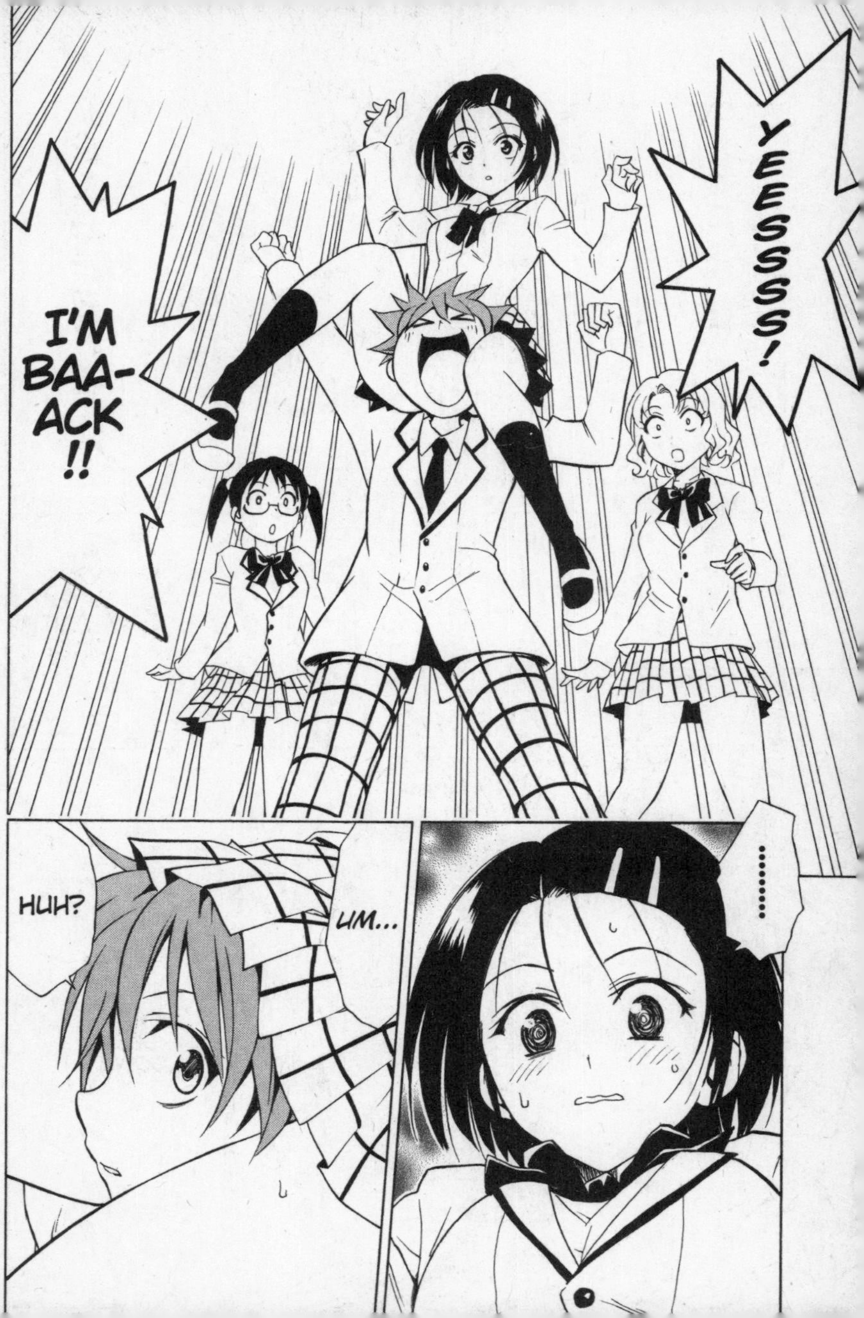
YEESSSSS!
I'M BAAA-ACK!!
......
UM...
HUH?

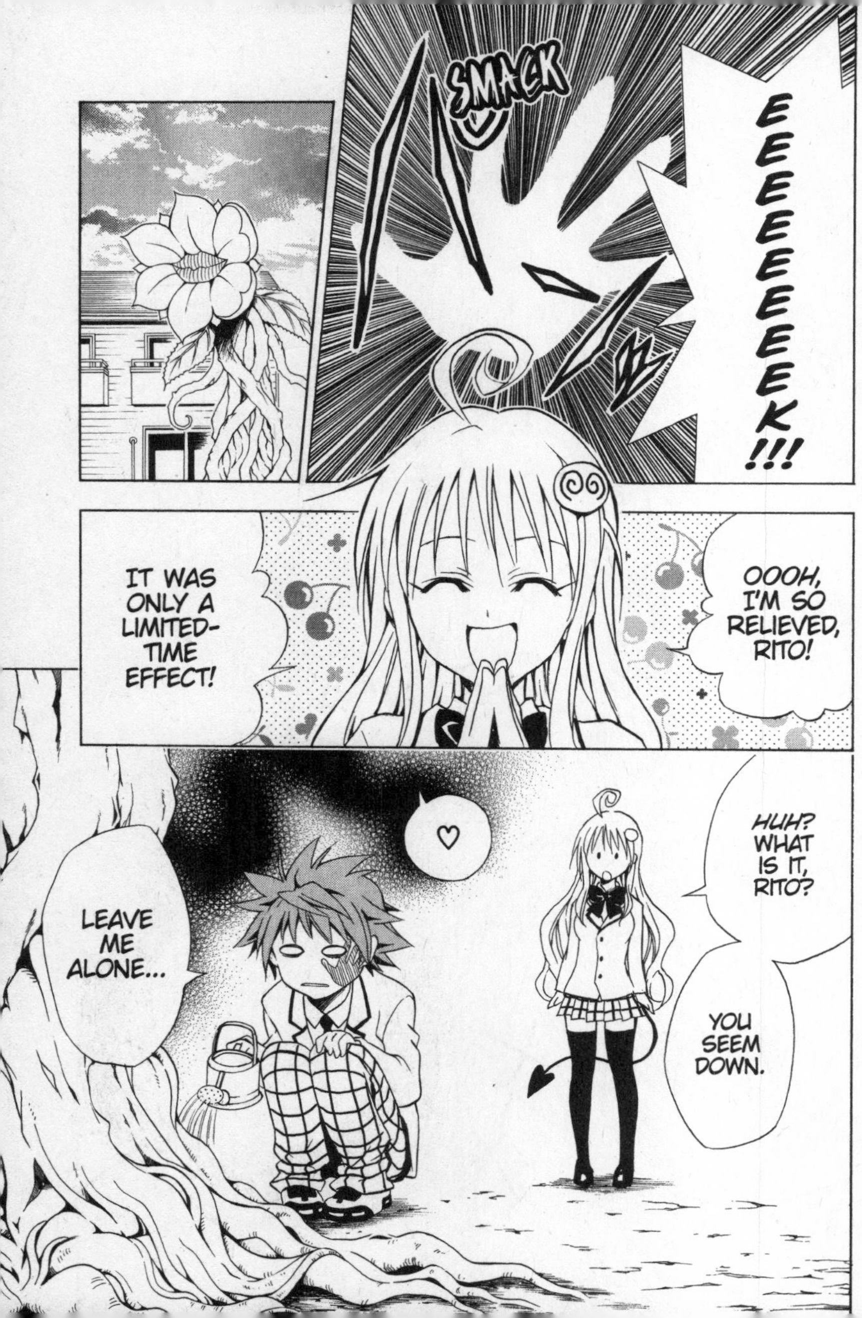
SMACK
EEEEEEEEEK!!!
OOOH, I'M SO RELIEVED, RITO!
IT WAS ONLY A LIMITED-TIME EFFECT!
HUH? WHAT IS IT, RITO?
YOU SEEM DOWN.
LEAVE ME ALONE...

To LOVE Ru

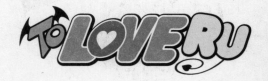

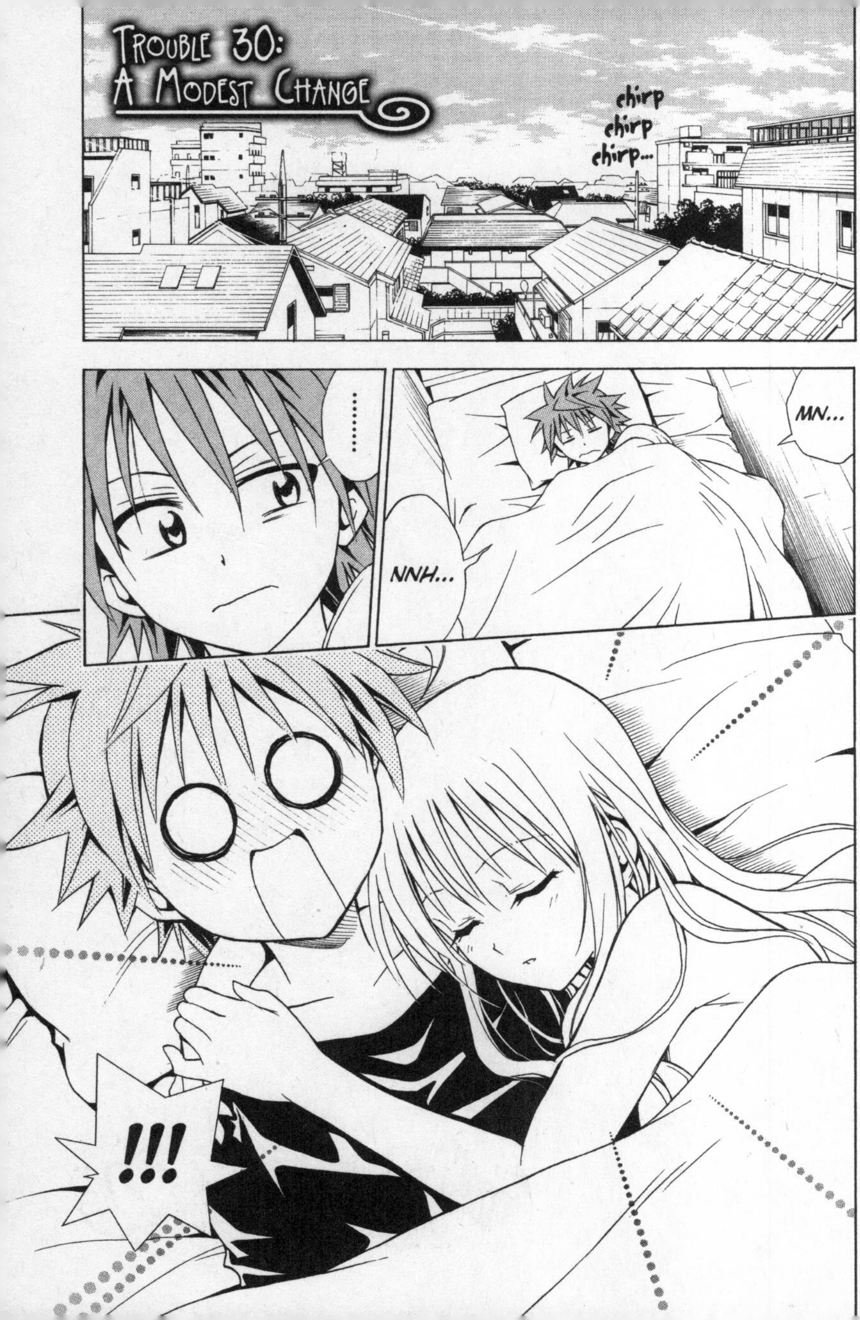
TROUBLE 30:
A MODEST CHANGE
chirp
chirp
chirp...
MN...
NNH...
......
!!!

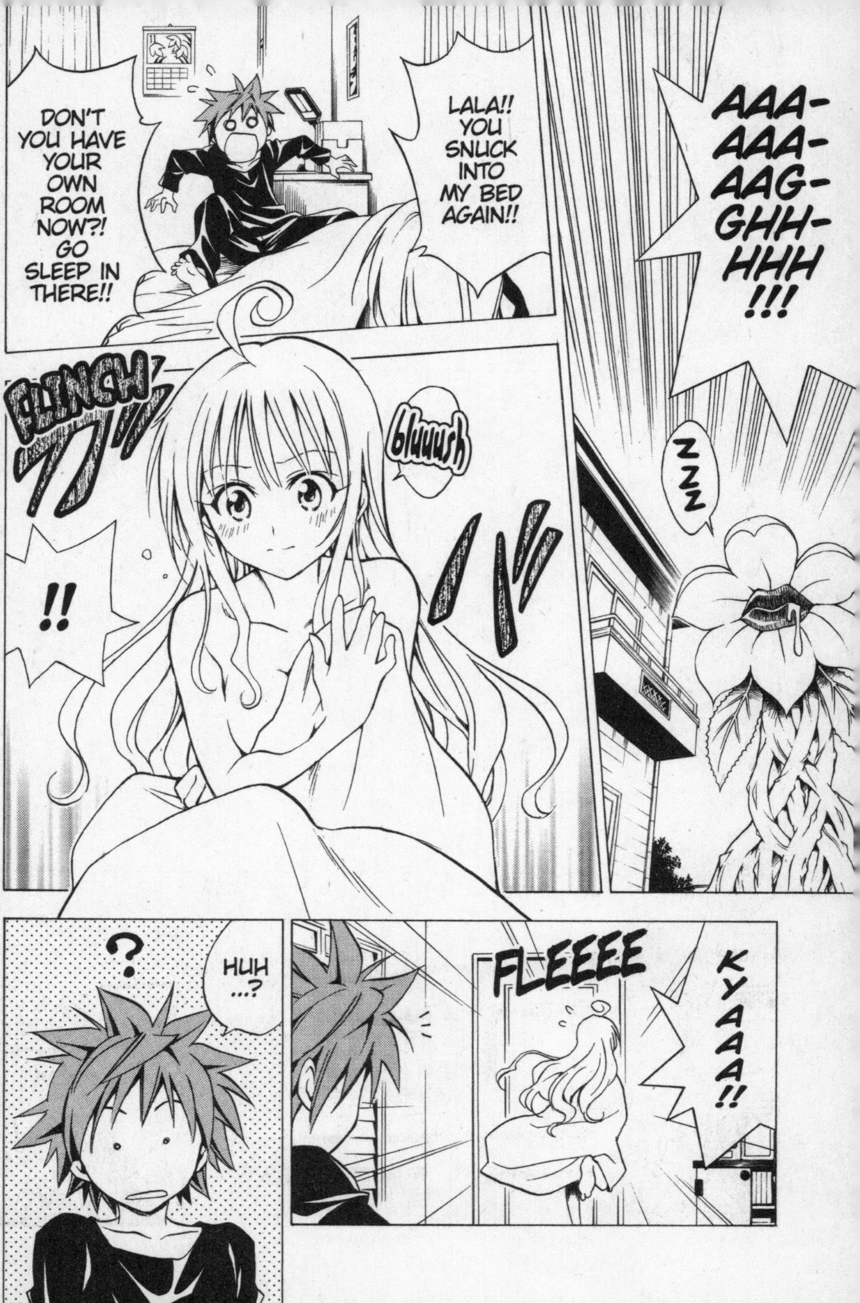
AAA-AAA-AAG-GHH-HHH!!!
ZZZ
LALA!! YOU SNUCK INTO MY BED AGAIN!!
DON'T YOU HAVE YOUR OWN ROOM NOW?! GO SLEEP IN THERE!!
bluuush
FLINCH
!!
KYAAAA!!
FLEEEE
HUH ...?
?

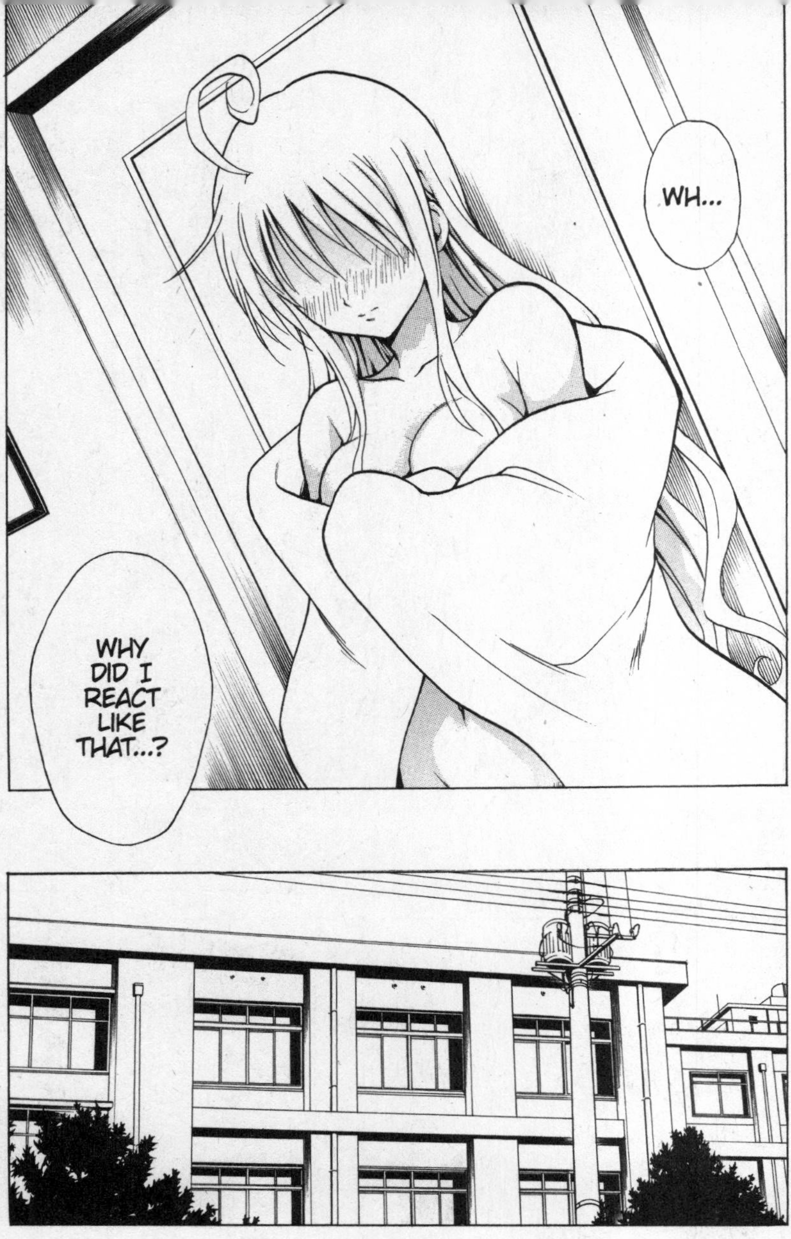
WH...
WHY DID I REACT LIKE THAT...?

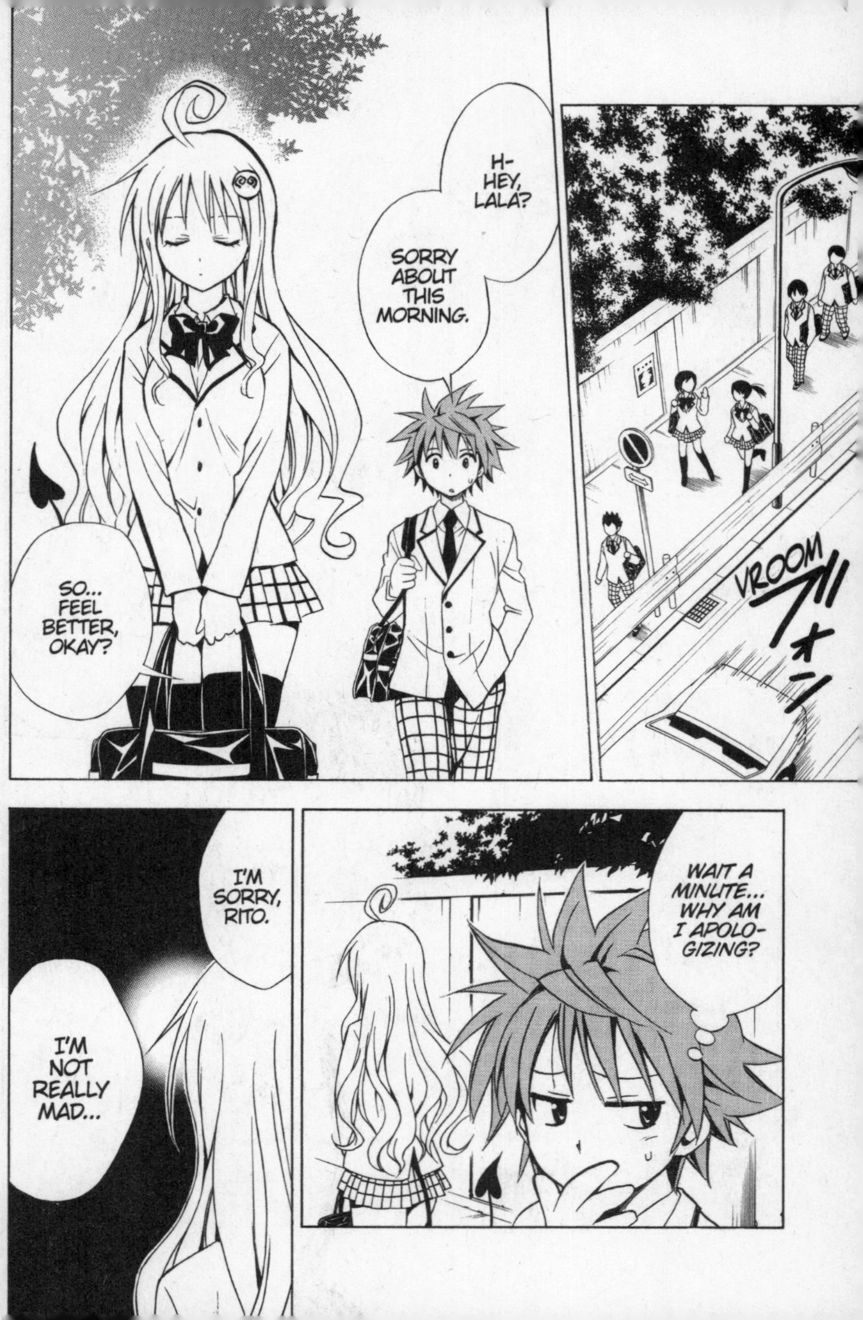
VROOM
H-HEY, LALA?
SORRY ABOUT THIS MORNING.
SO... FEEL BETTER, OKAY?
WAIT A MINUTE... WHY AM I APOLOGIZING?
I'M SORRY, RITO.
I'M NOT REALLY MAD...

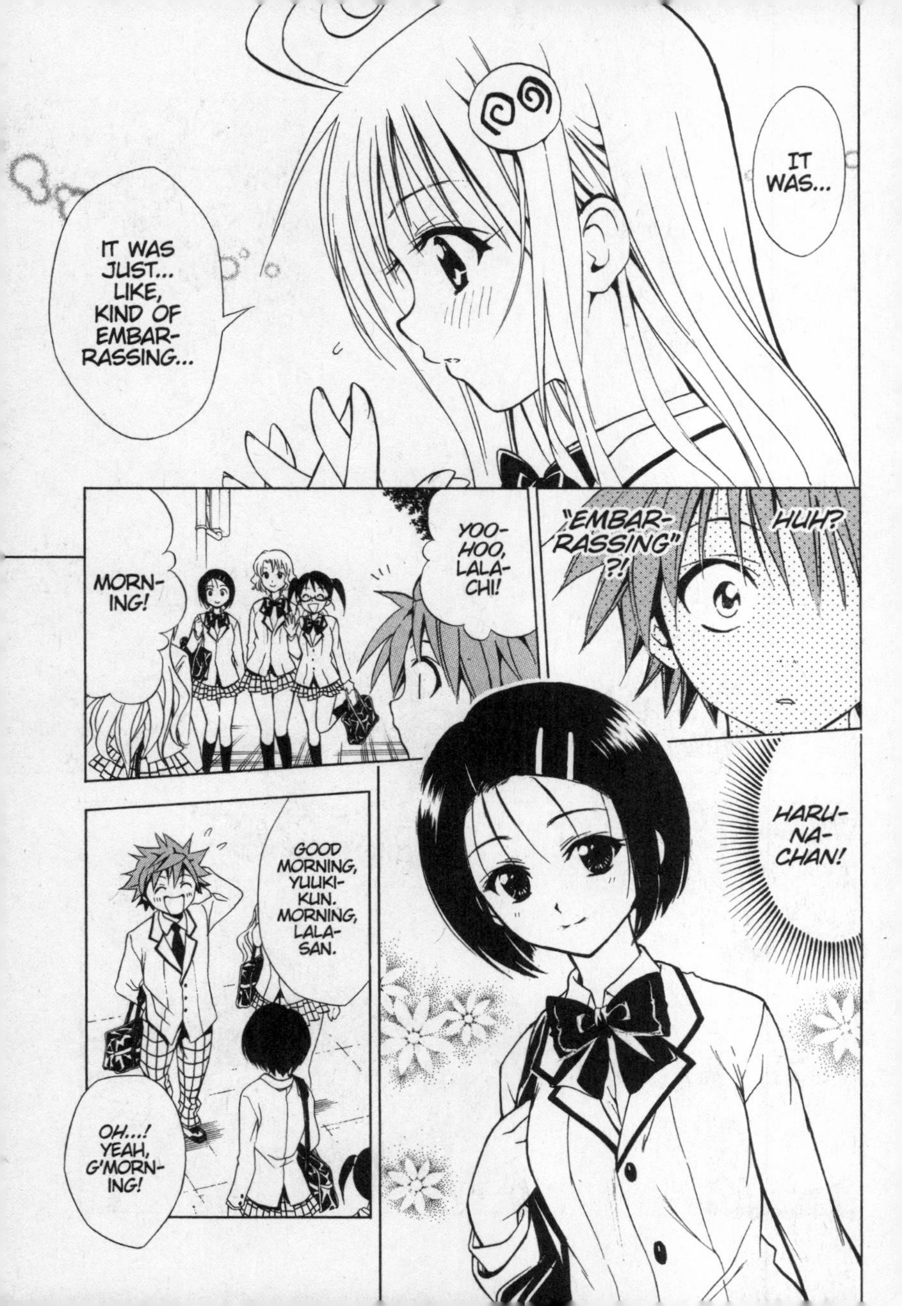
IT WAS...
IT WAS JUST... LIKE, KIND OF EMBAR-RASSING...
HUH?
"EMBAR-RASSING"?!
YOO-HOO, LALA-CHI!
MORN-ING!
HARU-NA-CHAN!
GOOD MORNING, YUUKI-KUN. MORNING, LALA-SAN.
OH...! YEAH, G'MORN-ING!

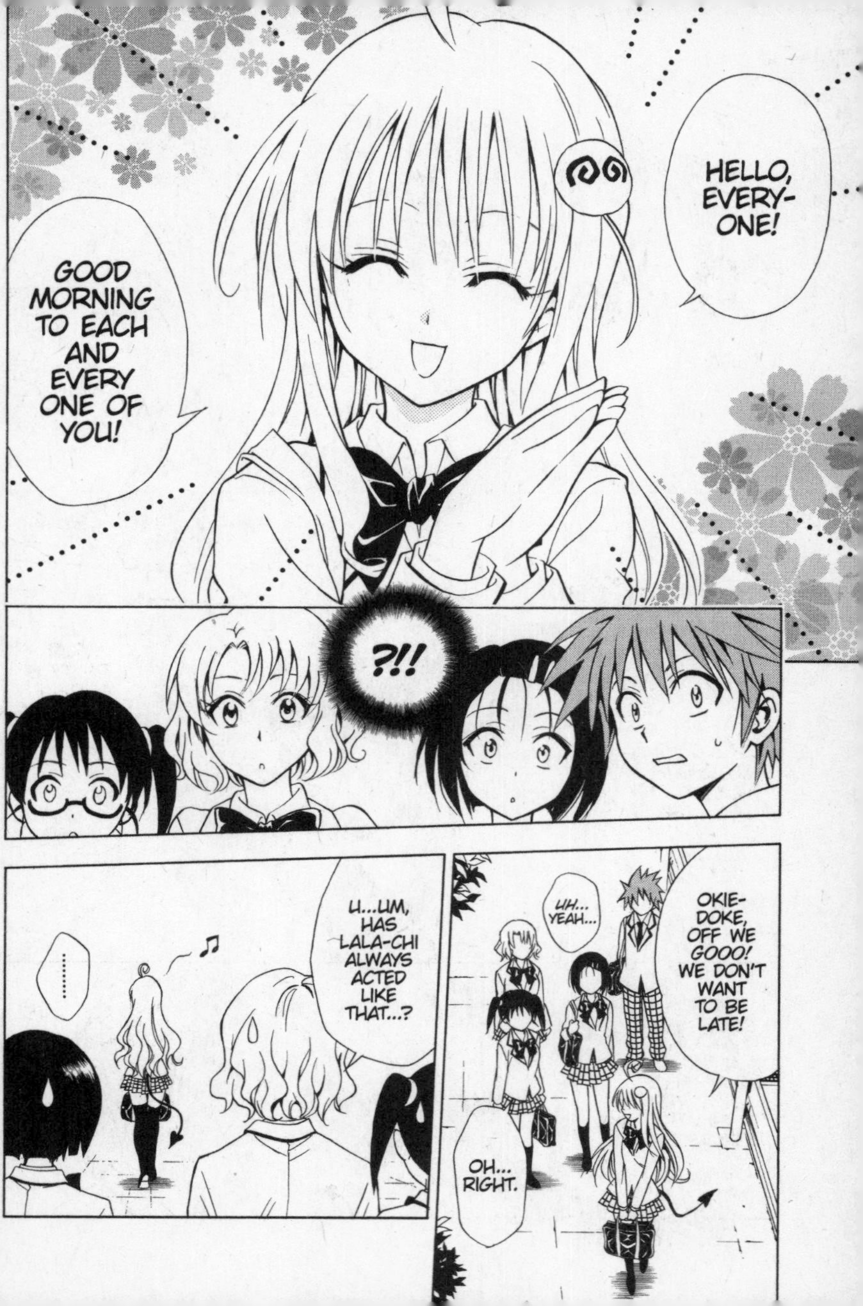
HELLO, EVERY-ONE!
GOOD MORNING TO EACH AND EVERY ONE OF YOU!
?!!
OKIE-DOKE, OFF WE GOOO! WE DON'T WANT TO BE LATE!
UH... YEAH...
OH... RIGHT.
U...UM, HAS LALA-CHI ALWAYS ACTED LIKE THAT...?
♪
......

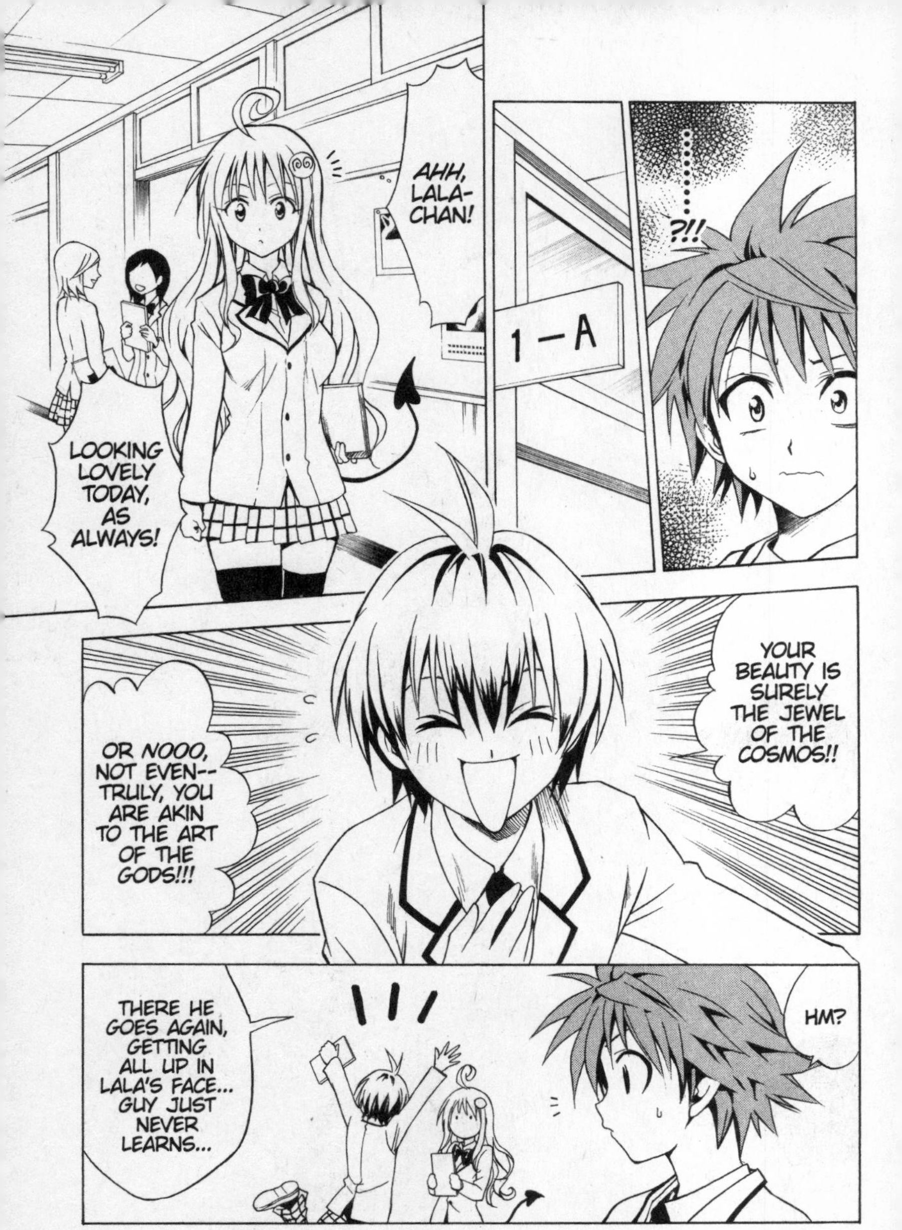
?!!
1-A
AHH, LALA-CHAN!
LOOKING LOVELY TODAY, AS ALWAYS!
YOUR BEAUTY IS SURELY THE JEWEL OF THE COSMOS!!
OR NOOO, NOT EVEN-- TRULY, YOU ARE AKIN TO THE ART OF THE GODS!!!
HM?
THERE HE GOES AGAIN, GETTING ALL UP IN LALA'S FACE... GUY JUST NEVER LEARNS...

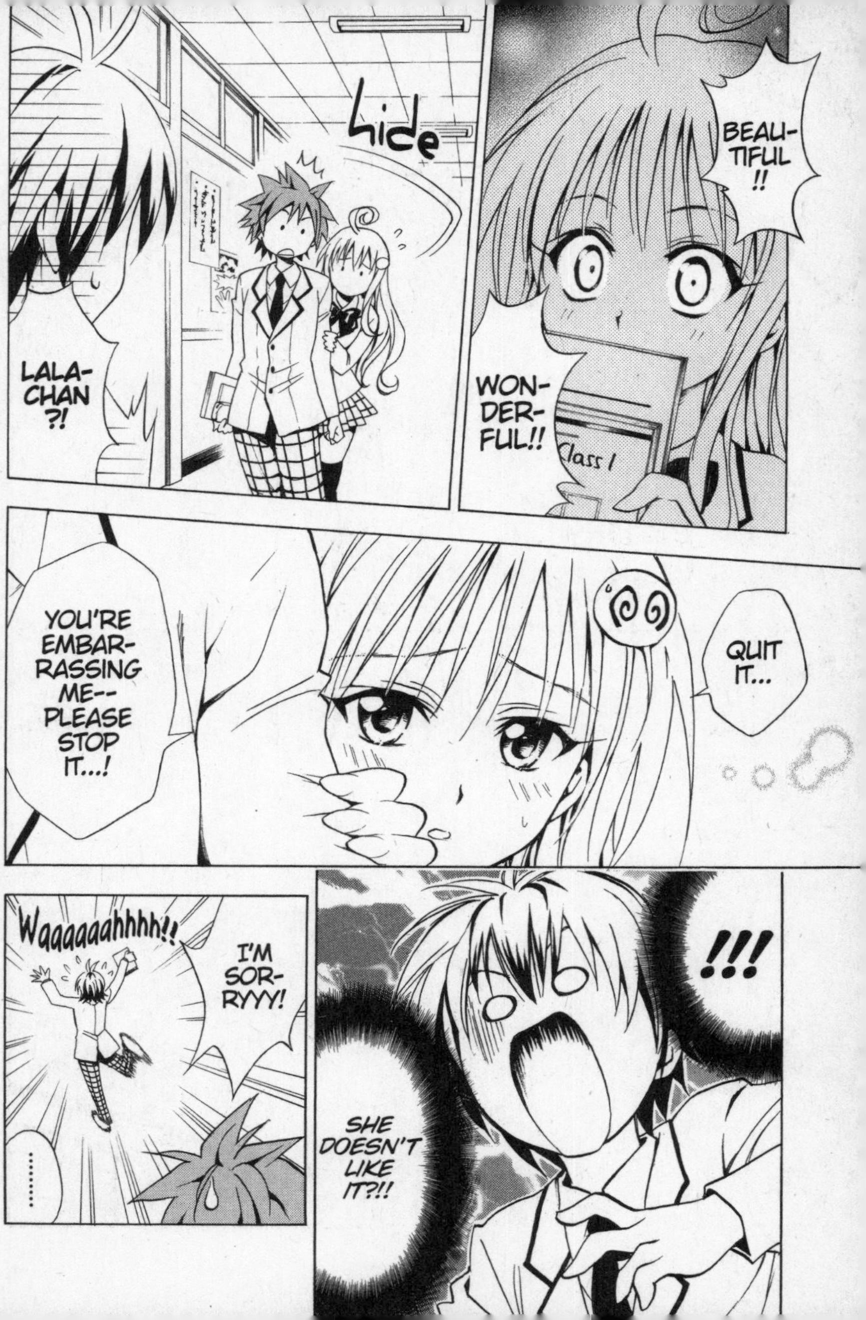
BEAUTIFUL!!
WONDERFUL!!
Class 1
Hide
LALA-CHAN?!
QUIT IT...
YOU'RE EMBARRASSING ME--PLEASE STOP IT...!
!!!
SHE DOESN'T LIKE IT?!!
Waaaaaahhhh!!
I'M SORRYYY!
......

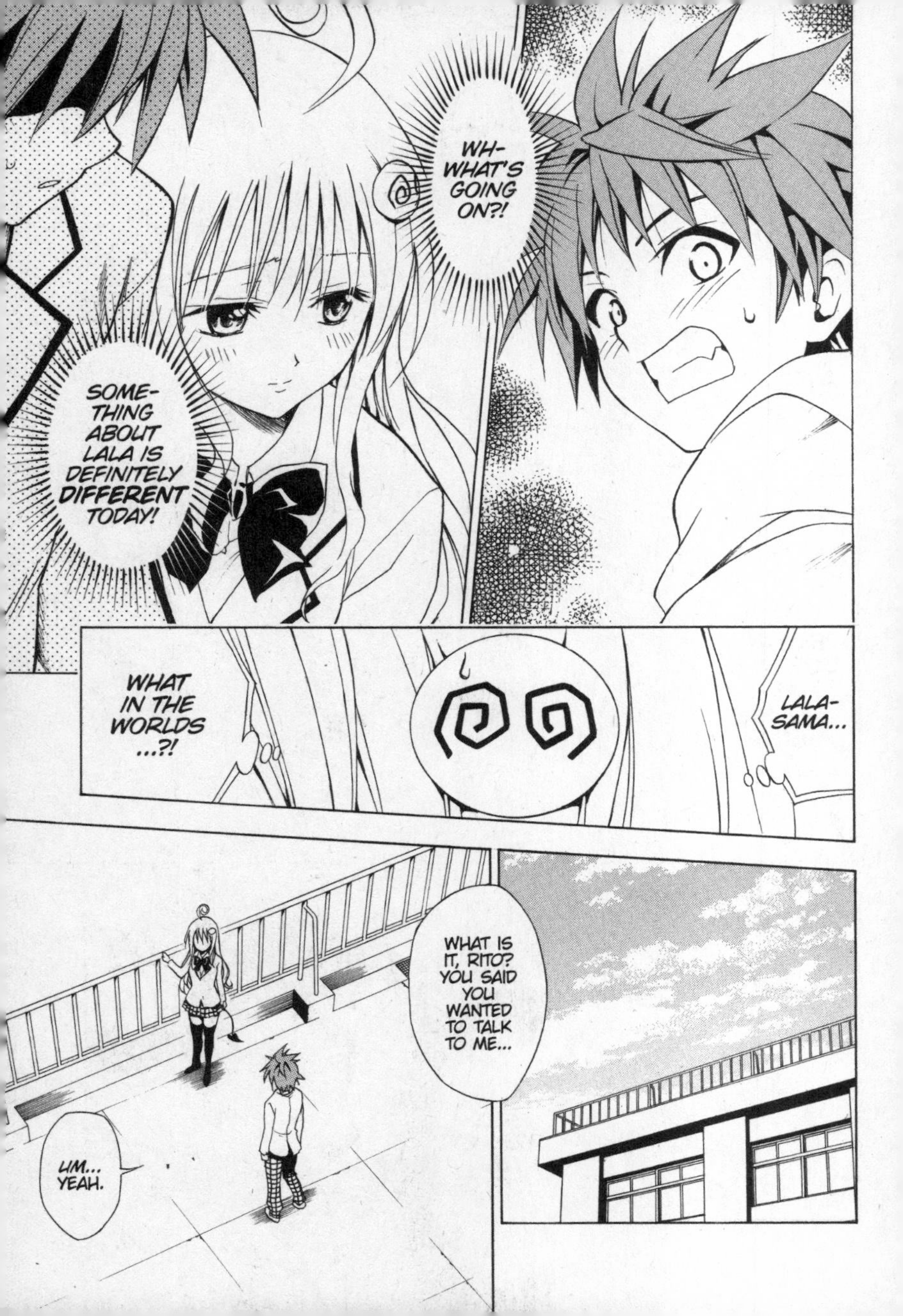
WH- WHAT'S GOING ON?!
SOME-THING ABOUT LALA IS DEFINITELY DIFFERENT TODAY!
LALA-SAMA...
WHAT IN THE WORLDS ...?!
WHAT IS IT, RITO? YOU SAID YOU WANTED TO TALK TO ME...
UM... YEAH.

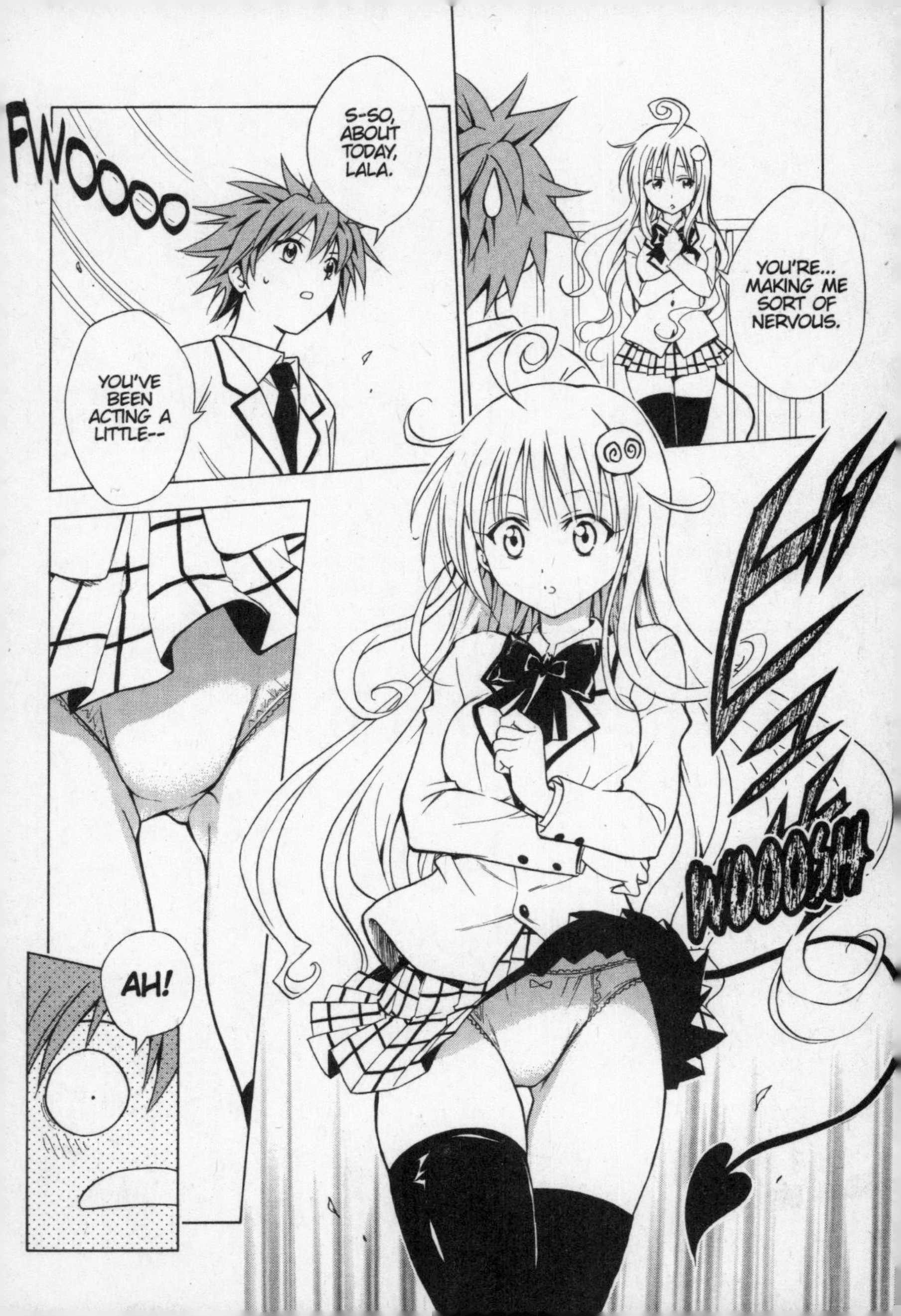
YOU'RE... MAKING ME SORT OF NERVOUS.
S-SO, ABOUT TODAY, LALA.
FWOOOOO
YOU'VE BEEN ACTING A LITTLE--
WOOOSH
AH!

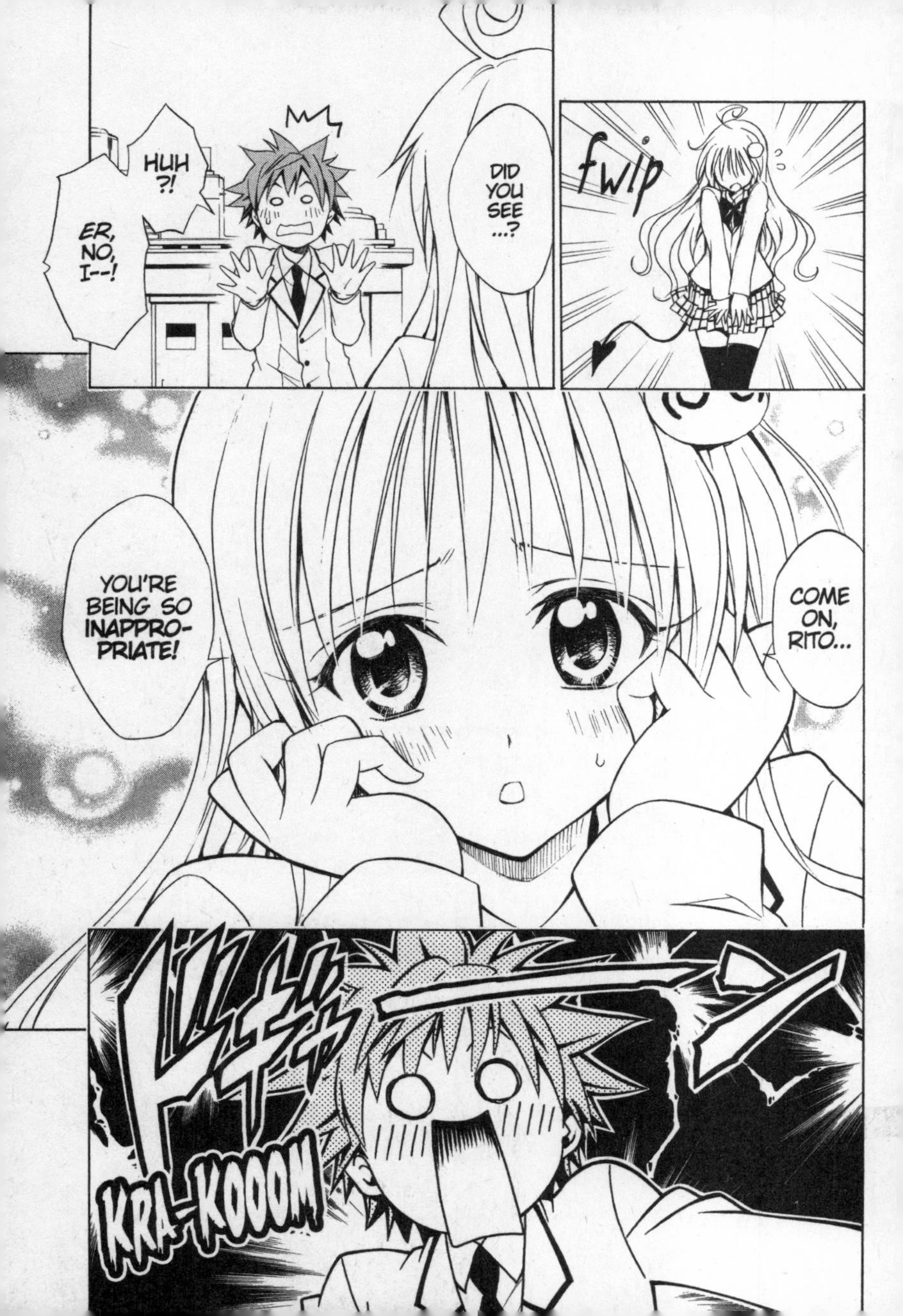
fwip
DID YOU SEE ...?
HUH ?!
ER, NO, I--!
COME ON, RITO...
YOU'RE BEING SO INAPPRO-PRIATE!
KRA-KOOM

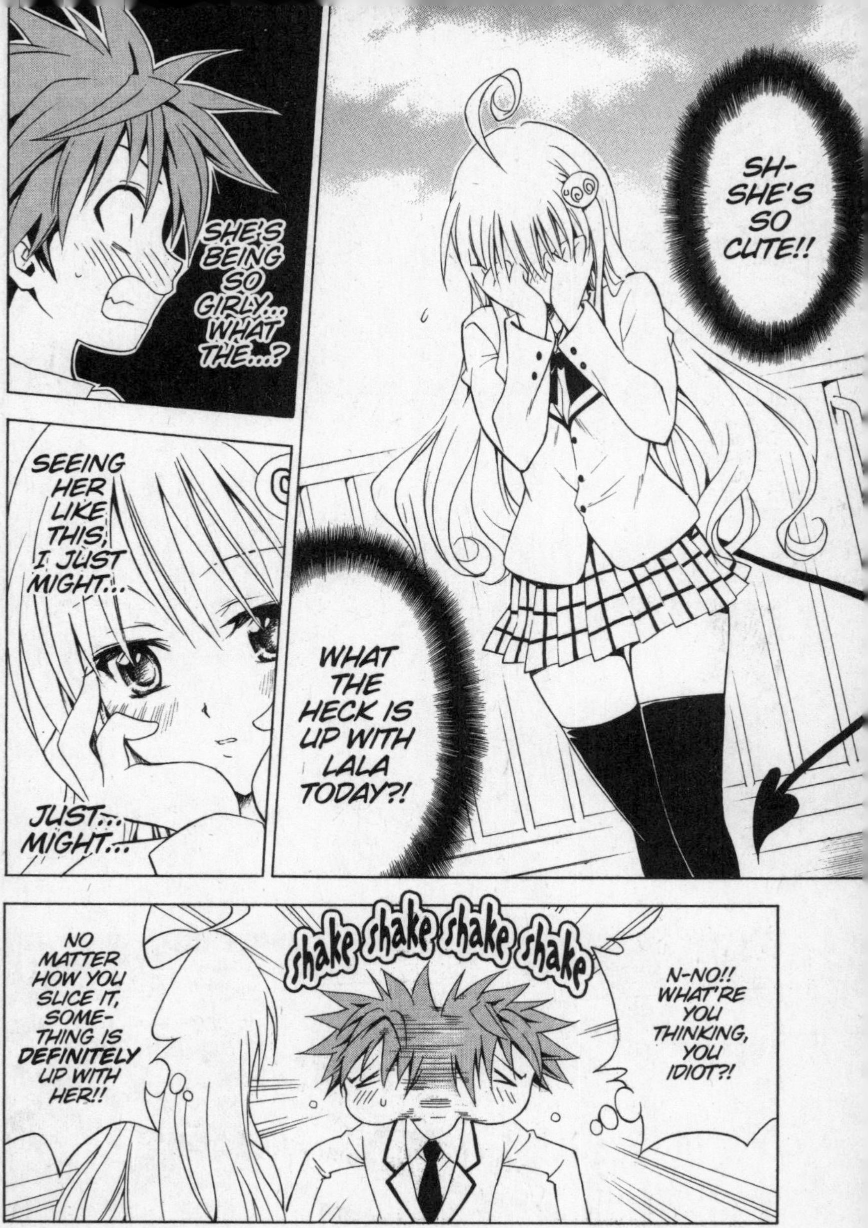
SH-SHE'S SO CUTE!!
WHAT THE HECK IS UP WITH LALA TODAY?!
SHE'S BEING SO GIRLY... WHAT THE...?
SEEING HER LIKE THIS, I JUST MIGHT...
JUST... MIGHT...
N-NO!! WHAT'RE YOU THINKING, YOU IDIOT?!
shake shake shake shake
NO MATTER HOW YOU SLICE IT, SOME-THING IS DEFINITELY UP WITH HER!!

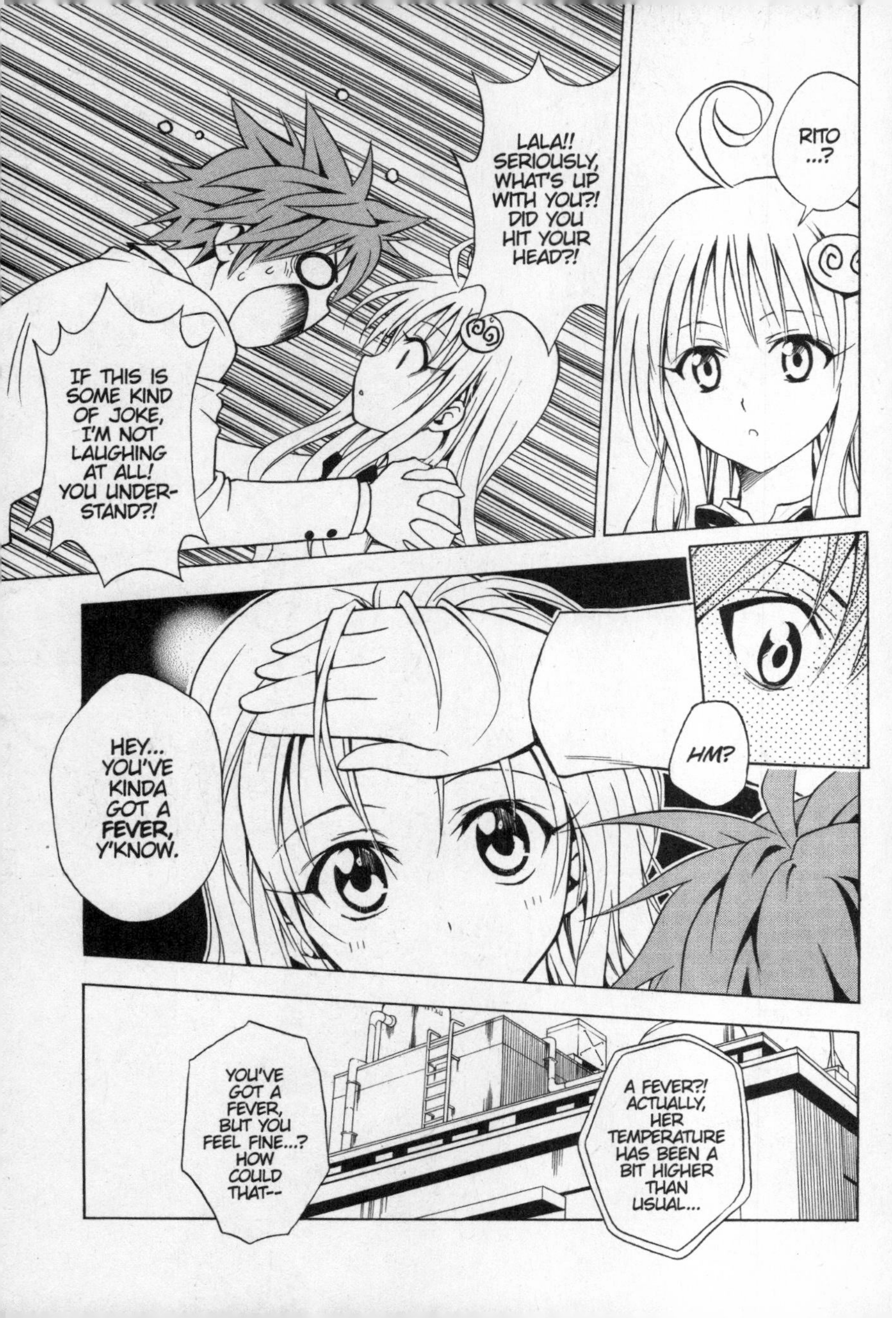
RITO ...?
LALA!! SERIOUSLY, WHAT'S UP WITH YOU?! DID YOU HIT YOUR HEAD?!
IF THIS IS SOME KIND OF JOKE, I'M NOT LAUGHING AT ALL! YOU UNDER-STAND?!
HM?
HEY... YOU'VE KINDA GOT A FEVER, Y'KNOW.
A FEVER?! ACTUALLY, HER TEMPERATURE HAS BEEN A BIT HIGHER THAN USUAL...
YOU'VE GOT A FEVER, BUT YOU FEEL FINE...? HOW COULD THAT--

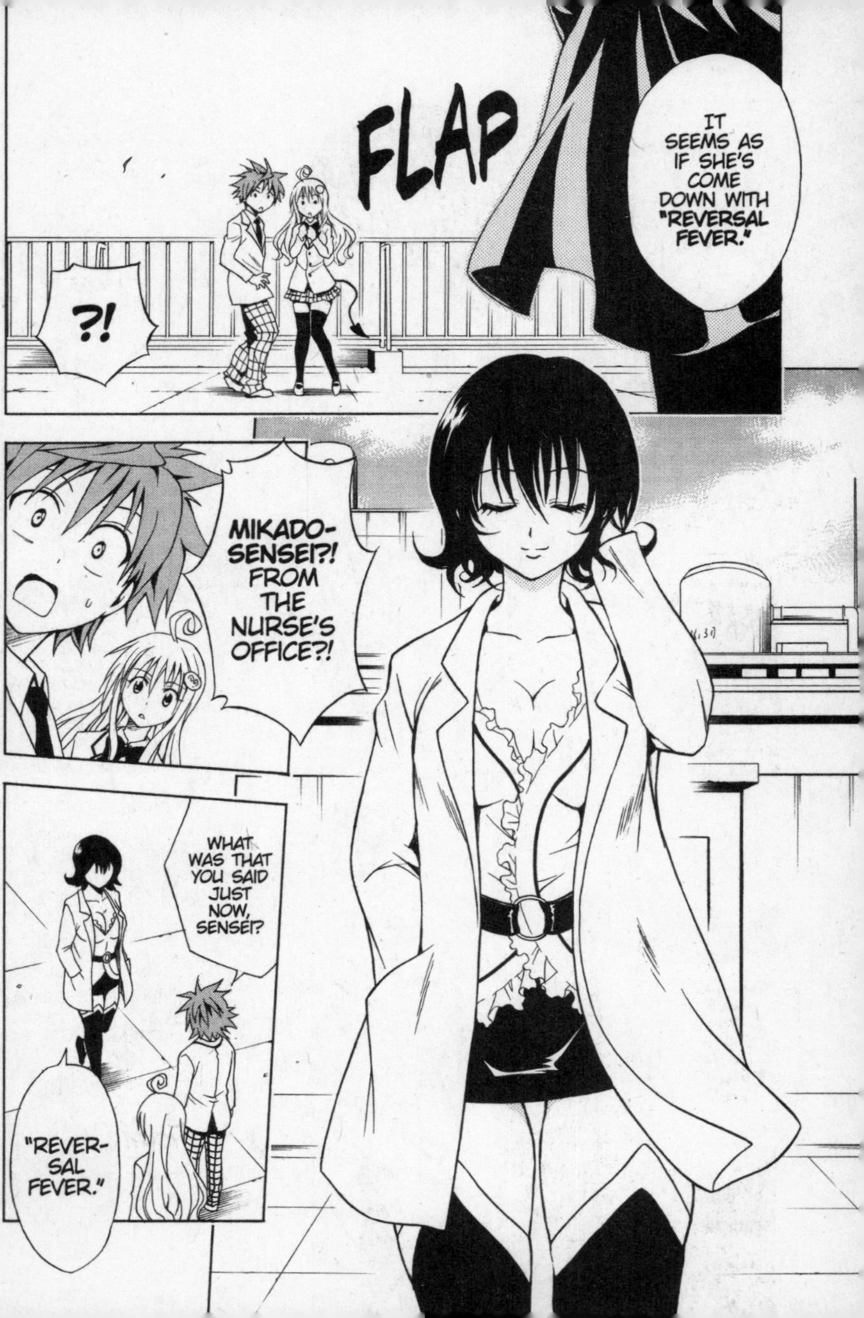
IT SEEMS AS IF SHE'S COME DOWN WITH "REVERSAL FEVER."
FLAP
?!
MIKADO-SENSEI?! FROM THE NURSE'S OFFICE?!
WHAT WAS THAT YOU SAID JUST NOW, SENSEI?
"REVER-SAL FEVER."

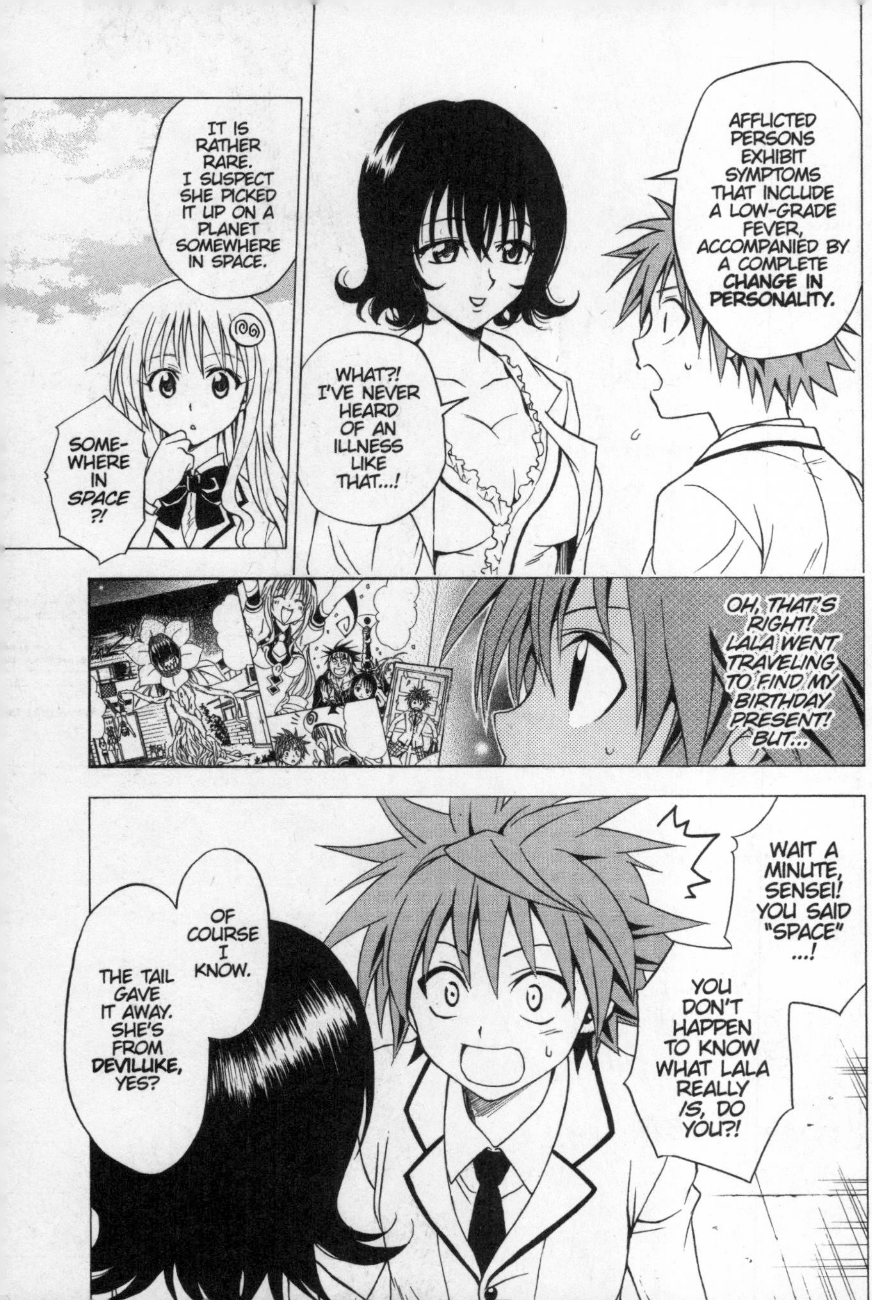

AFFLICTED PERSONS EXHIBIT SYMPTOMS THAT INCLUDE A LOW-GRADE FEVER, ACCOMPANIED BY A COMPLETE CHANGE IN PERSONALITY.
WHAT?! I'VE NEVER HEARD OF AN ILLNESS LIKE THAT...!
IT IS RATHER RARE. I SUSPECT SHE PICKED IT UP ON A PLANET SOMEWHERE IN SPACE.
SOME-WHERE IN SPACE ?!
OH, THAT'S RIGHT! LALA WENT TRAVELING TO FIND MY BIRTHDAY PRESENT! BUT...
WAIT A MINUTE, SENSEI! YOU SAID "SPACE" ...!
YOU DON'T HAPPEN TO KNOW WHAT LALA REALLY IS, DO YOU?!
OF COURSE I KNOW.
THE TAIL GAVE IT AWAY. SHE'S FROM DEVILUKE, YES?

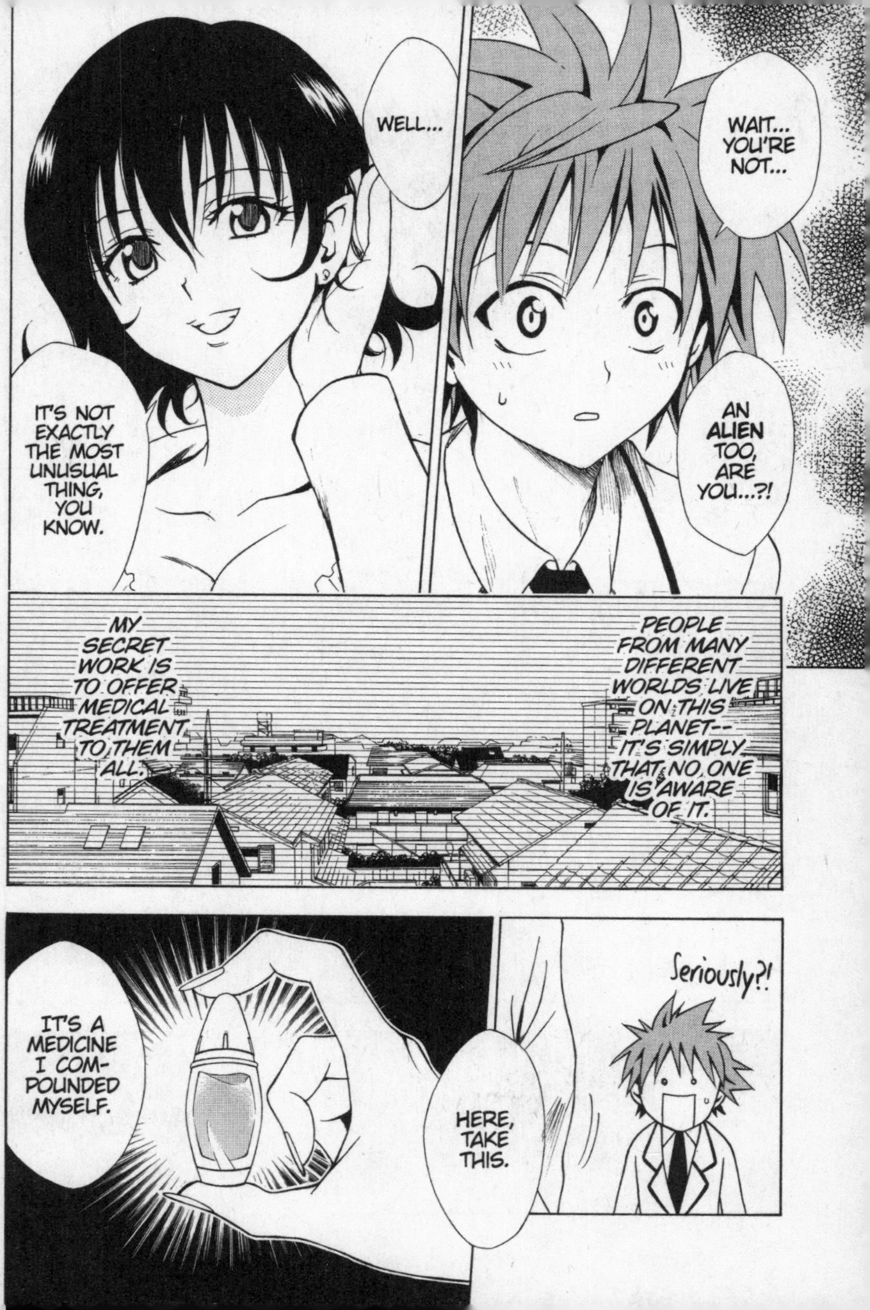
WAIT... YOU'RE NOT...
AN ALIEN TOO, ARE YOU...?!
WELL...
IT'S NOT EXACTLY THE MOST UNUSUAL THING, YOU KNOW.
PEOPLE FROM MANY DIFFERENT WORLDS LIVE ON THIS PLANET-- IT'S SIMPLY THAT NO ONE IS AWARE OF IT.
MY SECRET WORK IS TO OFFER MEDICAL TREATMENT TO THEM ALL.
Seriously?!
HERE, TAKE THIS.
IT'S A MEDICINE I COMPOUNDED MYSELF.

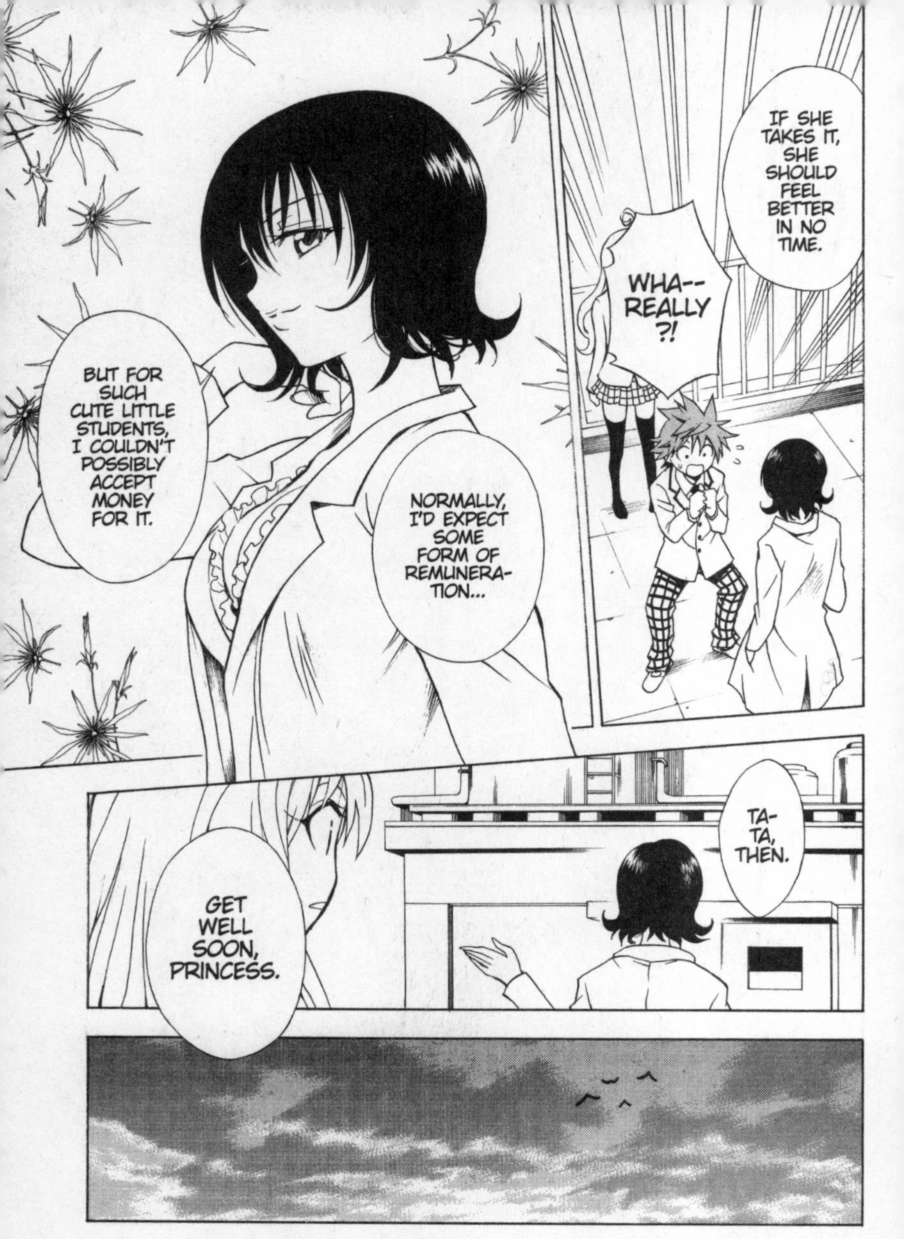
IF SHE TAKES IT, SHE SHOULD FEEL BETTER IN NO TIME.
WHA-- REALLY ?!
NORMALLY, I'D EXPECT SOME FORM OF REMUNERA-TION...
BUT FOR SUCH CUTE LITTLE STUDENTS, I COULDN'T POSSIBLY ACCEPT MONEY FOR IT.
TA-TA, THEN.
GET WELL SOON, PRINCESS.

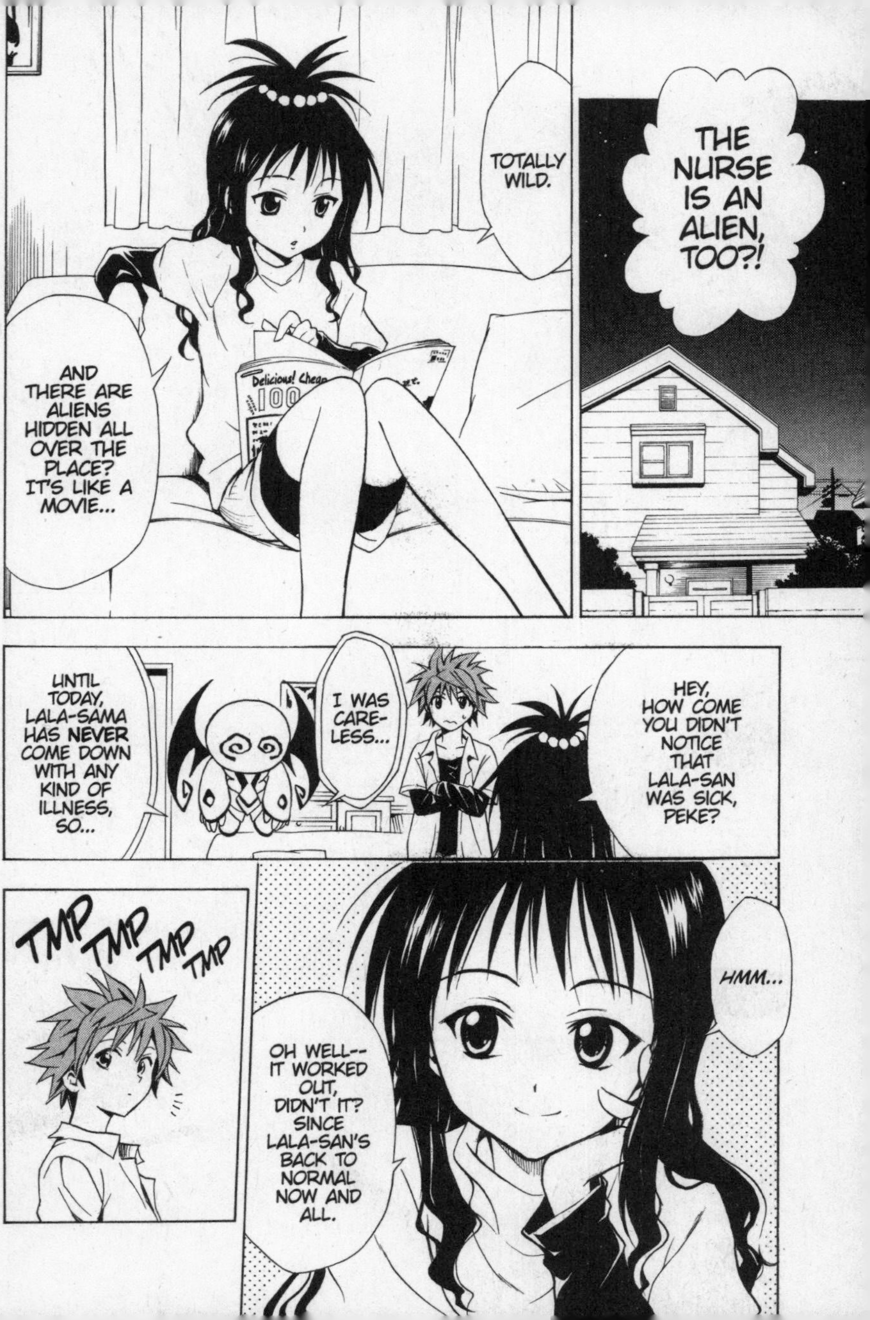
THE NURSE IS AN ALIEN, TOO?!
TOTALLY WILD.
Delicious!
AND THERE ARE ALIENS HIDDEN ALL OVER THE PLACE? IT'S LIKE A MOVIE...
HEY, HOW COME YOU DIDN'T NOTICE THAT LALA-SAN WAS SICK, PEKE?
I WAS CARELESS...
UNTIL TODAY, LALA-SAMA HAS NEVER COME DOWN WITH ANY KIND OF ILLNESS, SO...
HMM...
OH WELL-- IT WORKED OUT, DIDN'T IT? SINCE LALA-SAN'S BACK TO NORMAL NOW AND ALL.
TMP TMP TMP TMP

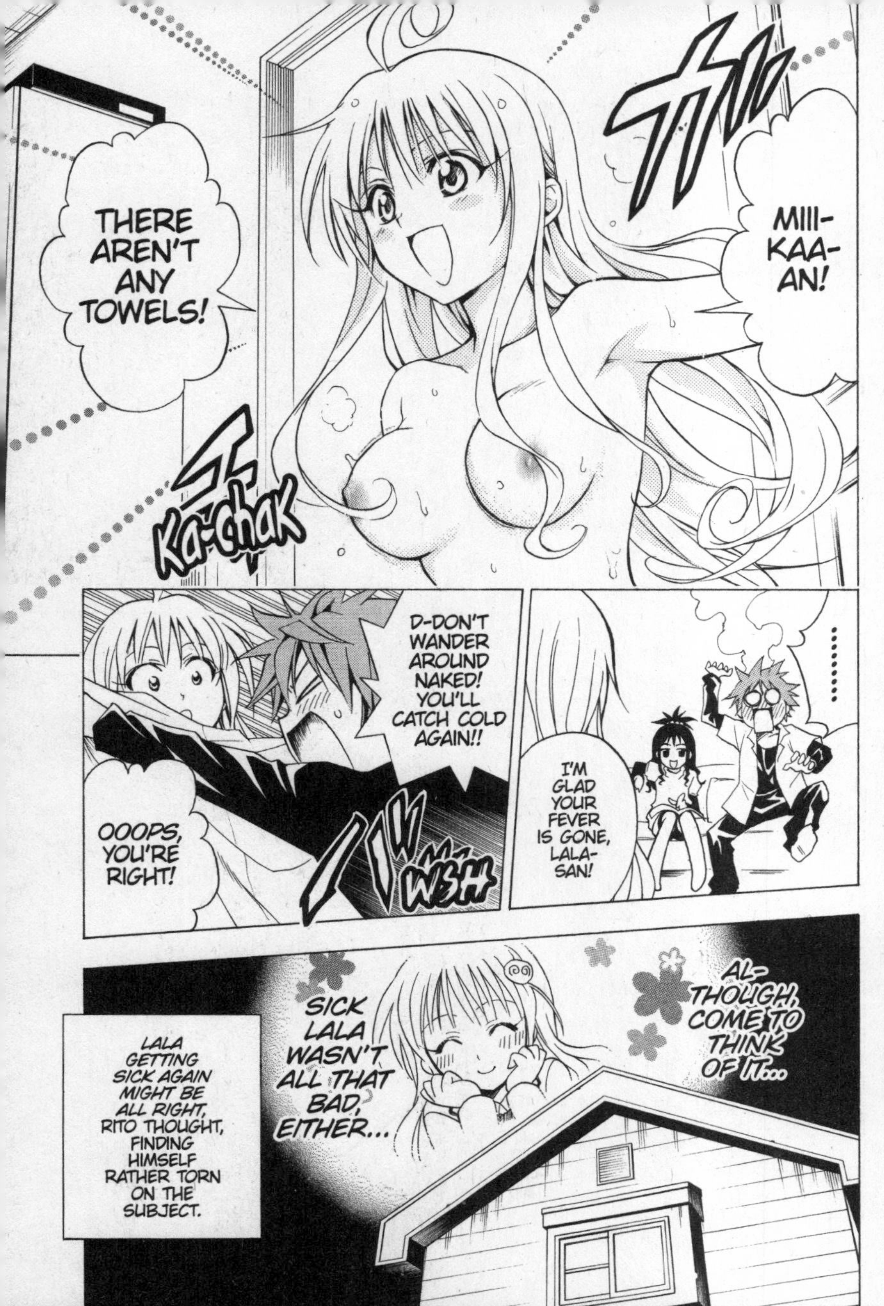
MIII-
KAA-
AN!
THERE AREN'T ANY TOWELS!
KA-CHAK
......
I'M GLAD YOUR FEVER IS GONE, LALA-SAN!
D-DON'T WANDER AROUND NAKED! YOU'LL CATCH COLD AGAIN!!
OOOPS, YOU'RE RIGHT!
WSH
AL-THOUGH, COME TO THINK OF IT...
SICK LALA WASN'T ALL THAT BAD, EITHER...
LALA GETTING SICK AGAIN MIGHT BE ALL RIGHT, RITO THOUGHT, FINDING HIMSELF RATHER TORN ON THE SUBJECT.

To LOVE Ru

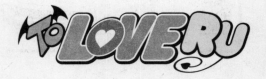

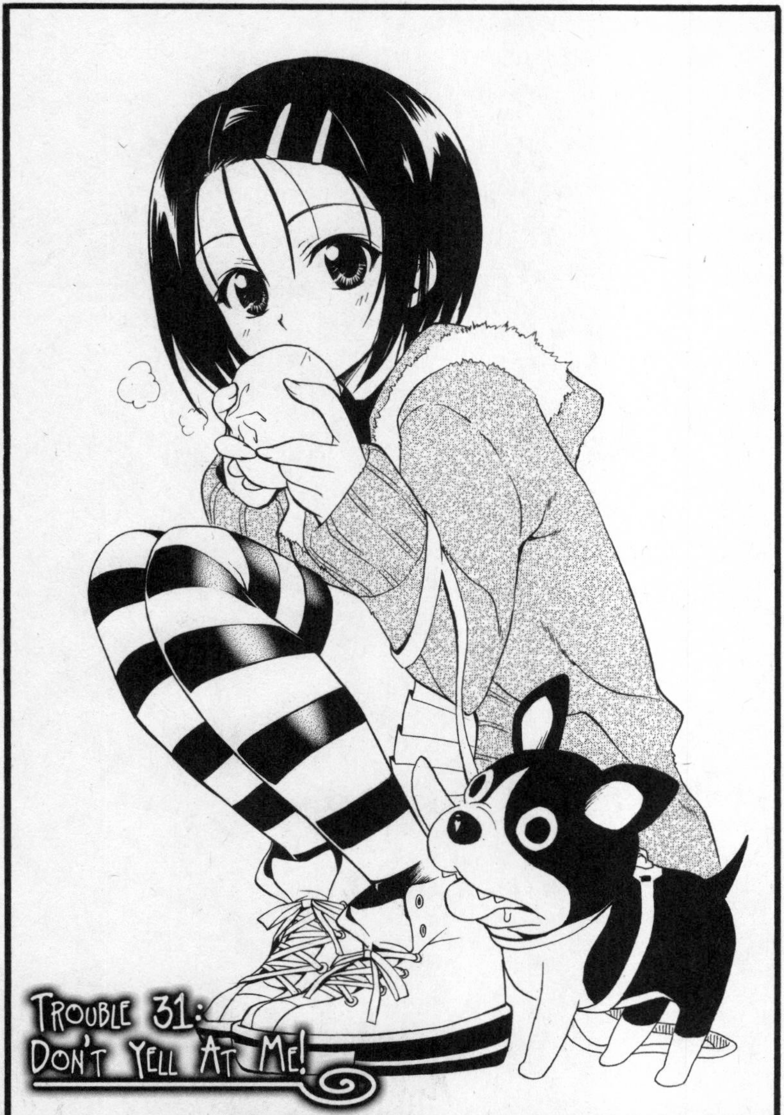
Trouble 31:
Don't Yell At Me!

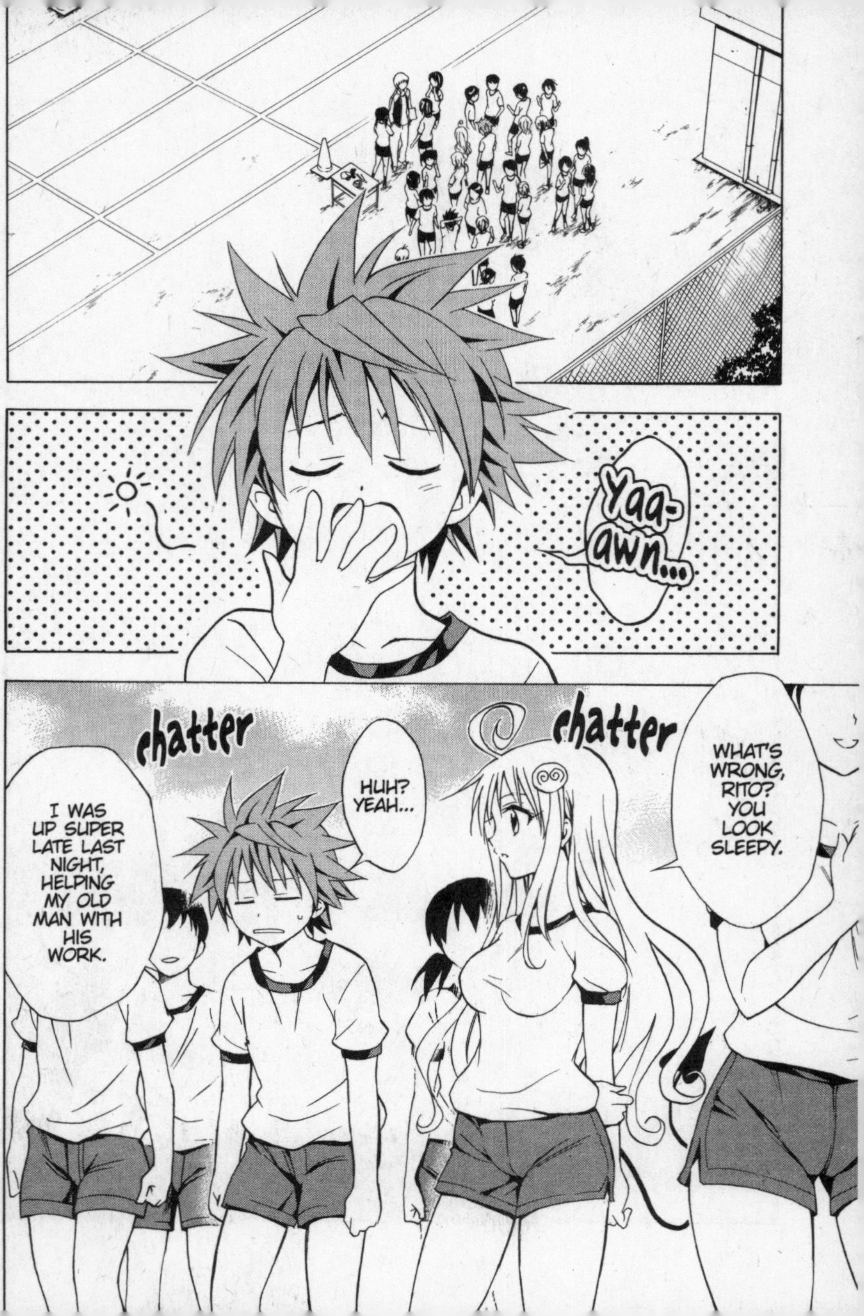
Yaa-awn...
chatter
WHAT'S WRONG, RITO? YOU LOOK SLEEPY.
HUH? YEAH...
chatter
I WAS UP SUPER LATE LAST NIGHT, HELPING MY OLD MAN WITH HIS WORK.

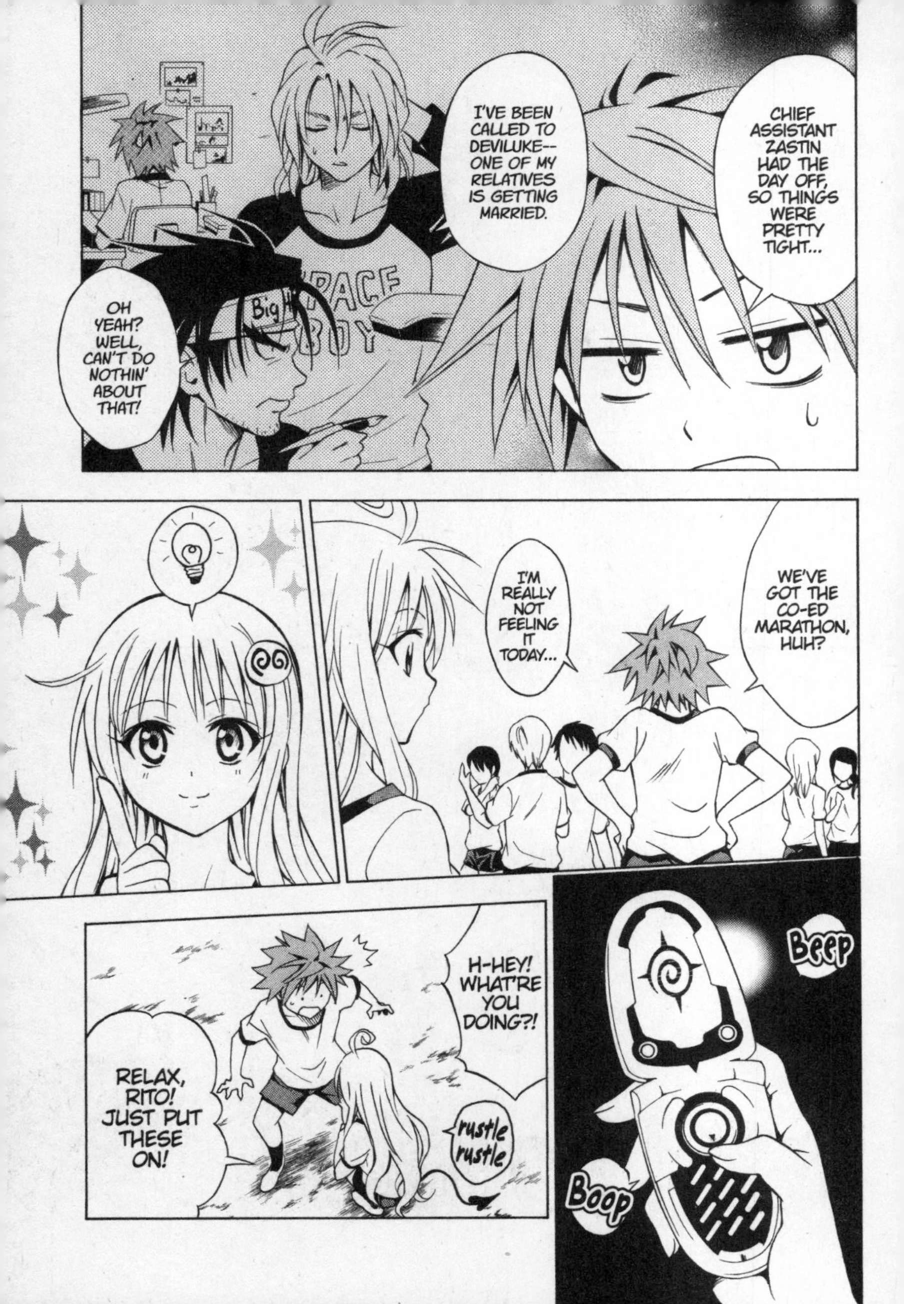
CHIEF ASSISTANT ZASTIN HAD THE DAY OFF, SO THINGS WERE PRETTY TIGHT...
I'VE BEEN CALLED TO DEVILUKE-- ONE OF MY RELATIVES IS GETTING MARRIED.
OH YEAH? WELL, CAN'T DO NOTHIN' ABOUT THAT!
WE'VE GOT THE CO-ED MARATHON, HUH?
I'M REALLY NOT FEELING IT TODAY...
Beep
Boop
H-HEY! WHAT'RE YOU DOING?!
RELAX, RITO! JUST PUT THESE ON!
rustle rustle

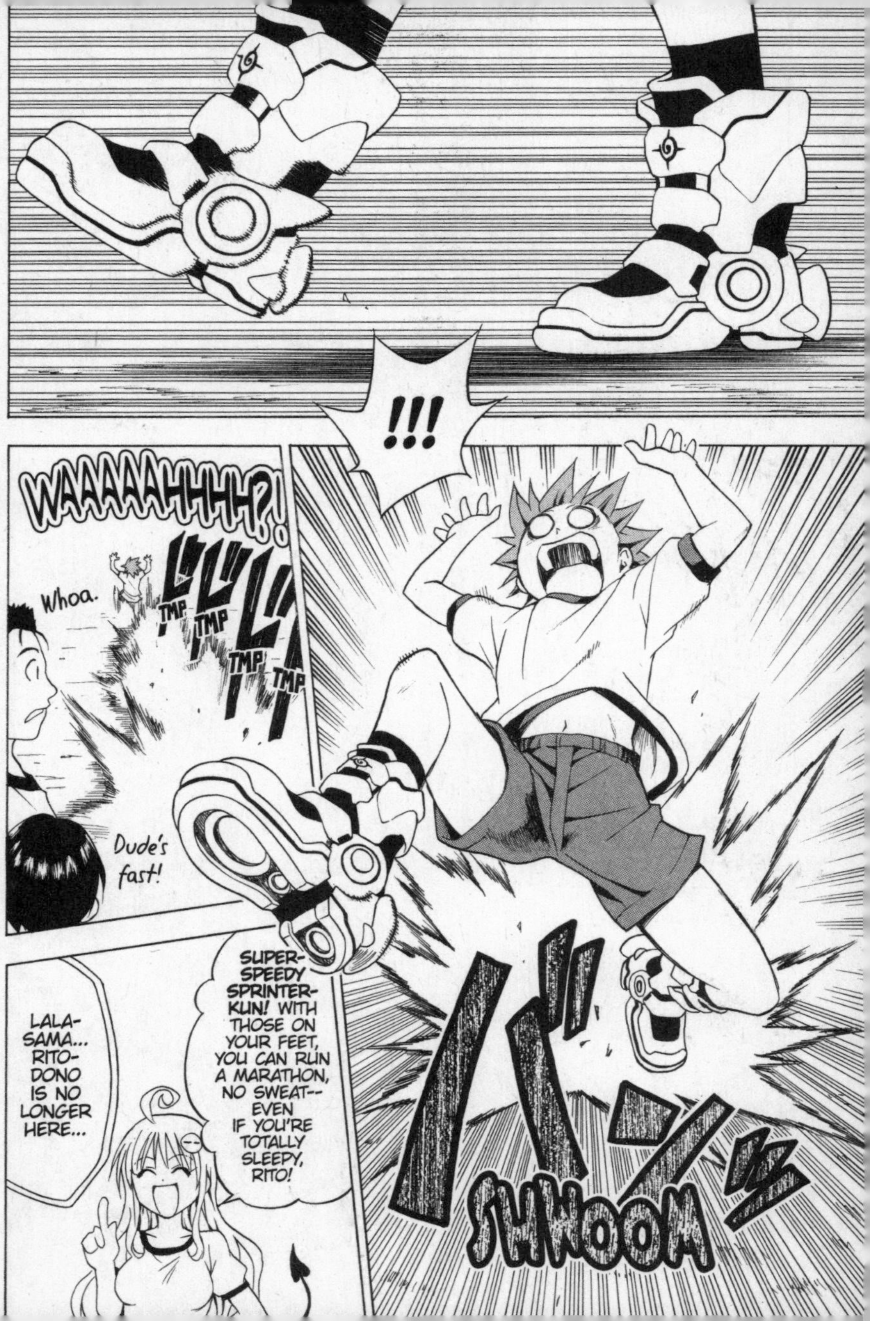
!!!
SHWOOM
WAAAAAHHHH?!
TMP TMP TMP TMP
Whoa.
Dude's fast!
SUPER-SPEEDY SPRINTER-KUN! WITH THOSE ON YOUR FEET, YOU CAN RUN A MARATHON, NO SWEAT--EVEN IF YOU'RE TOTALLY SLEEPY, RITO!
LALA-SAMA... RITO-DONO IS NO LONGER HERE...

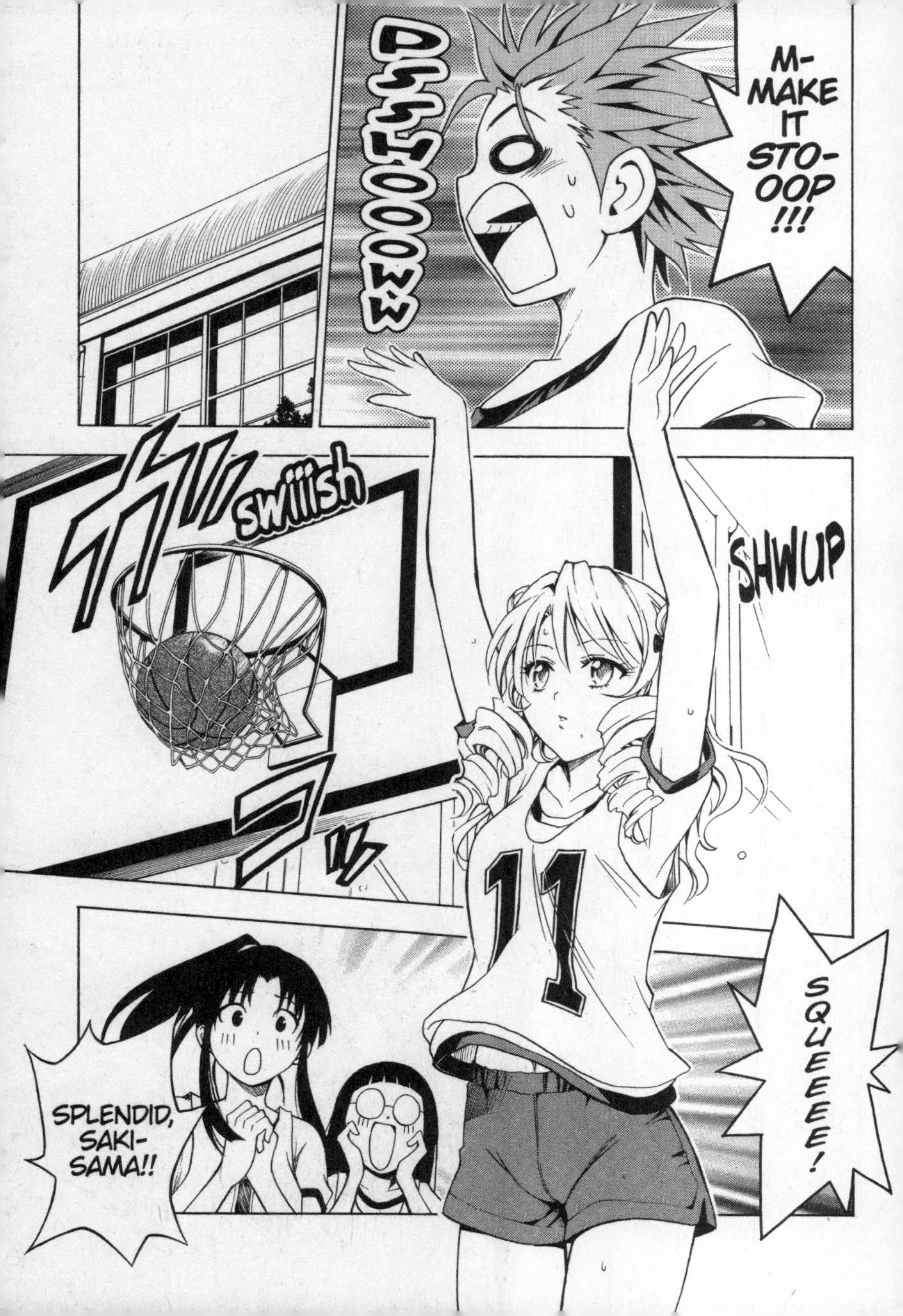
M-MAKE IT STO-OOP!!!
DSSHOOOOWW
SHWUP
swiiish
SQUEEEEE!
SPLENDID, SAKI-SAMA!!

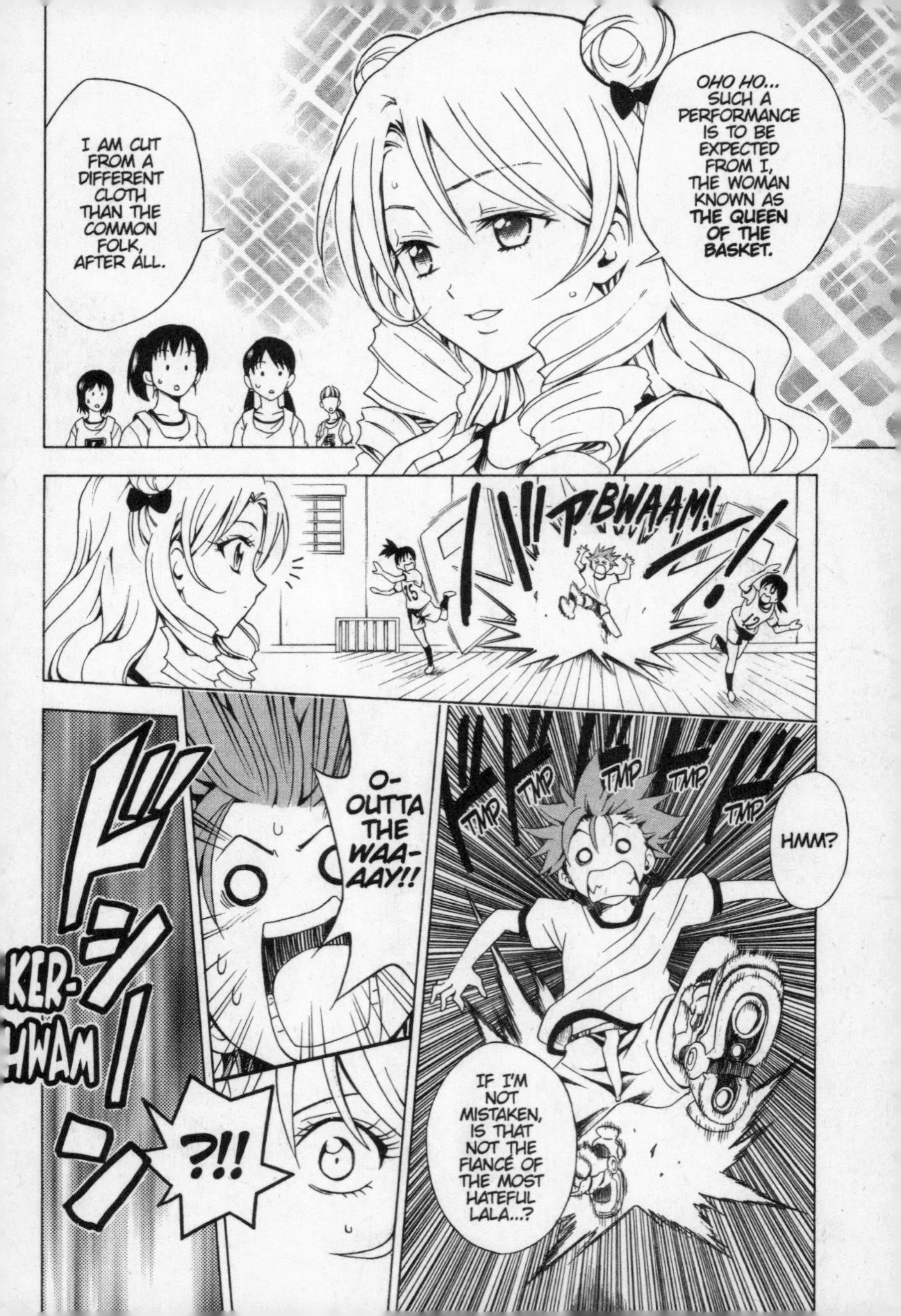
OHO HO... SUCH A PERFORMANCE IS TO BE EXPECTED FROM I, THE WOMAN KNOWN AS THE QUEEN OF THE BASKET.
I AM CUT FROM A DIFFERENT CLOTH THAN THE COMMON FOLK, AFTER ALL.
PBWAAM!
HMM?
TMP TMP TMP TMP TMP TMP
IF I'M NOT MISTAKEN, IS THAT NOT THE FIANCÉ OF THE MOST HATEFUL LALA...?
O-OUTTA THE WAAAAY!!
KER-
HWAM
?!!

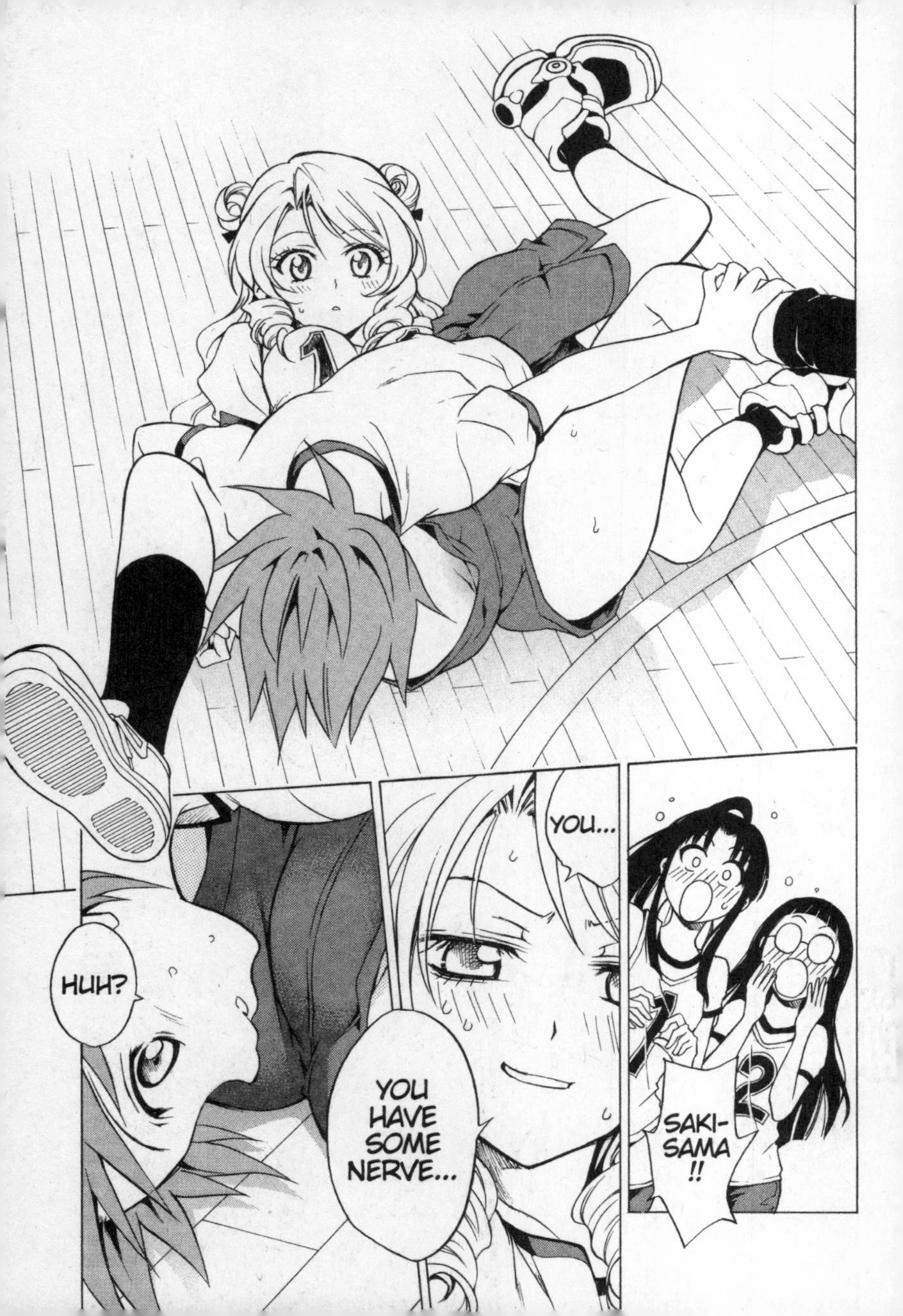
SAKI-SAMA !!
YOU...
YOU HAVE SOME NERVE...
HUH?

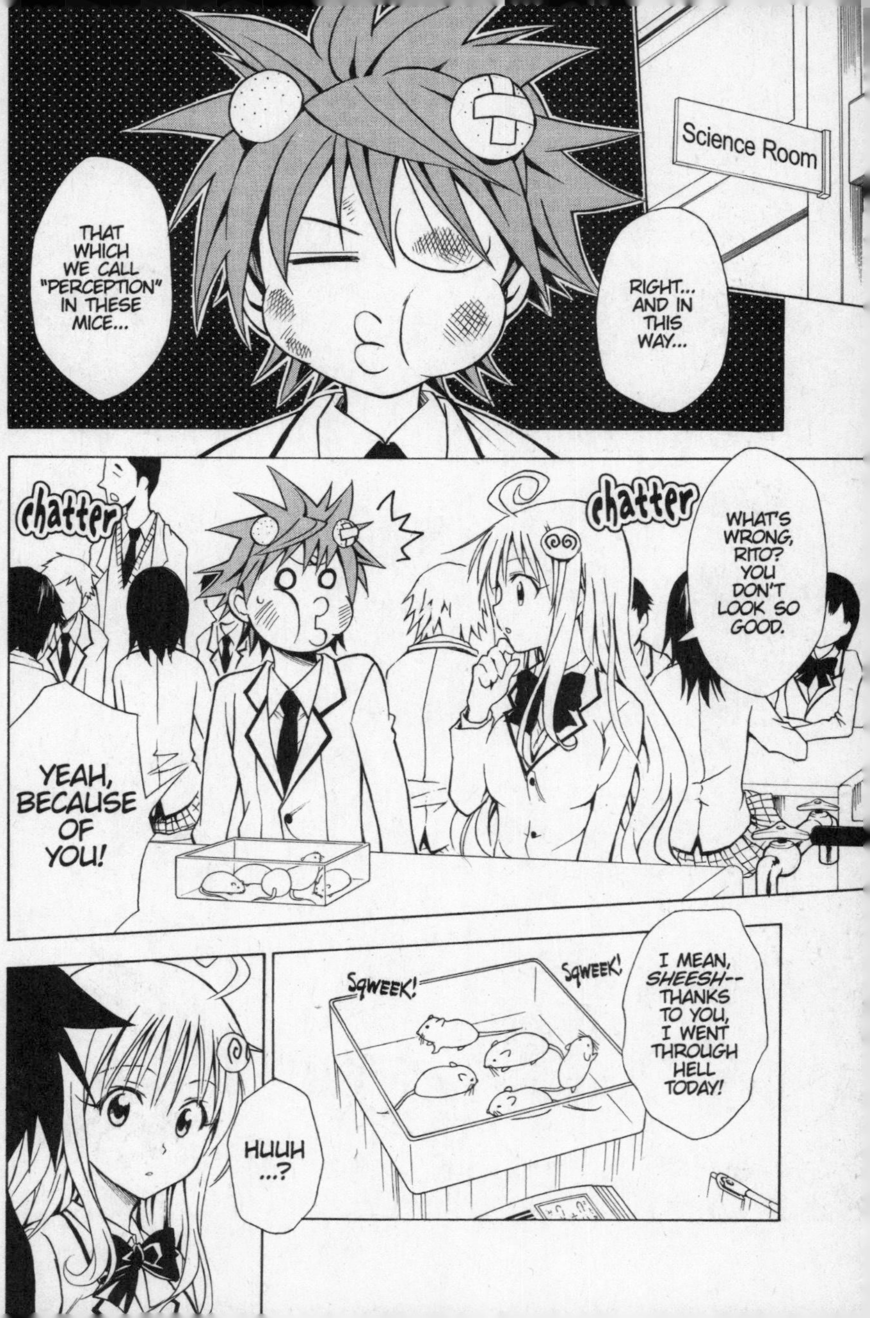
Science Room
THAT WHICH WE CALL "PERCEPTION" IN THESE MICE...
RIGHT... AND IN THIS WAY...
chatter
WHAT'S WRONG, RITO? YOU DON'T LOOK SO GOOD.
chatter
YEAH, BECAUSE OF YOU!
I MEAN, SHEESH-- THANKS TO YOU, I WENT THROUGH HELL TODAY!
Sqweek!
Sqweek!
HUUH ...?

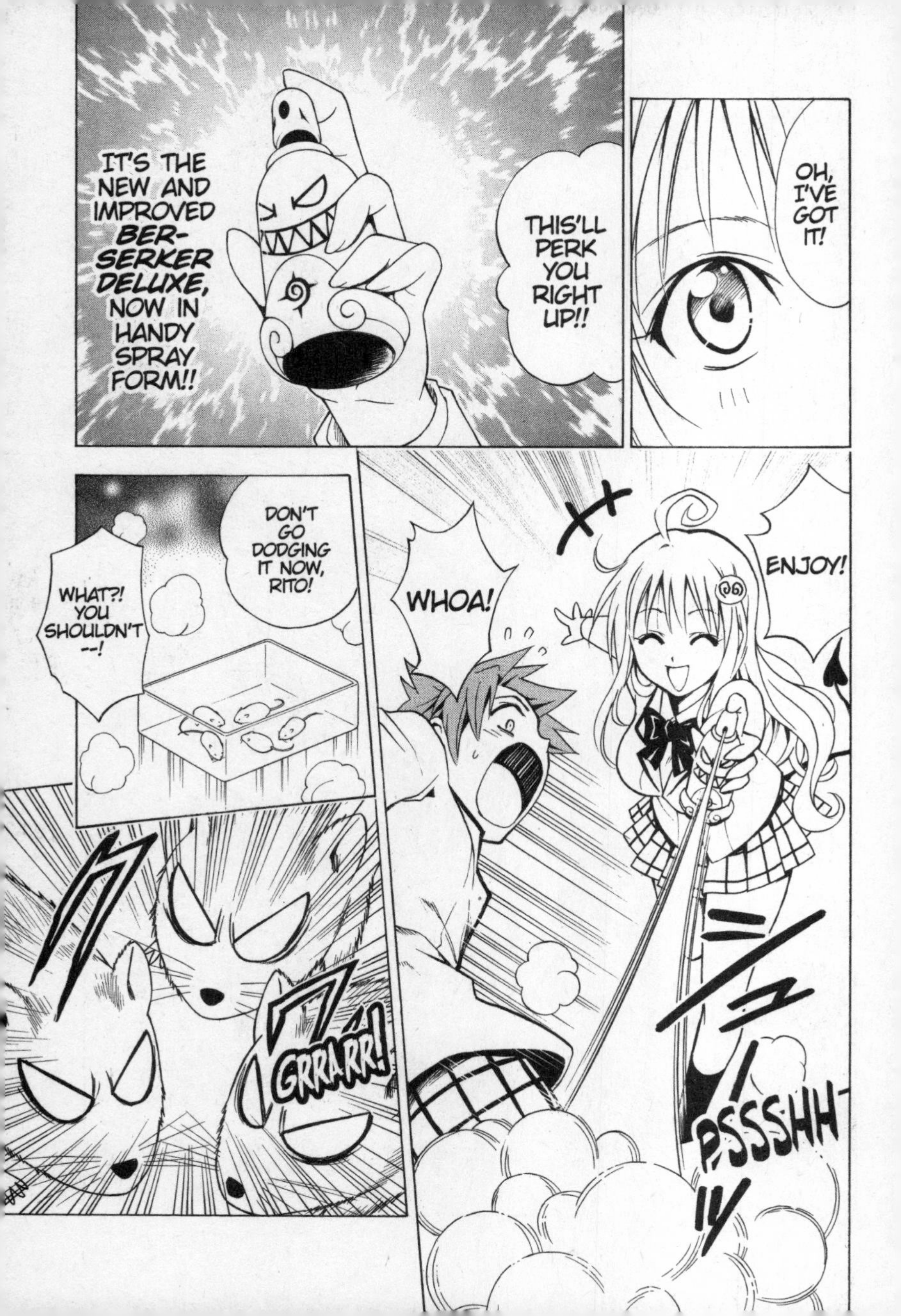
OH, I'VE GOT IT!
THIS'LL PERK YOU RIGHT UP!!
IT'S THE NEW AND IMPROVED BER-SERKER DELUXE, NOW IN HANDY SPRAY FORM!!
ENJOY!
WHOA!
DON'T GO DODGING IT NOW, RITO!
PSSSHH
WHAT?! YOU SHOULDN'T --!
GRRARR!

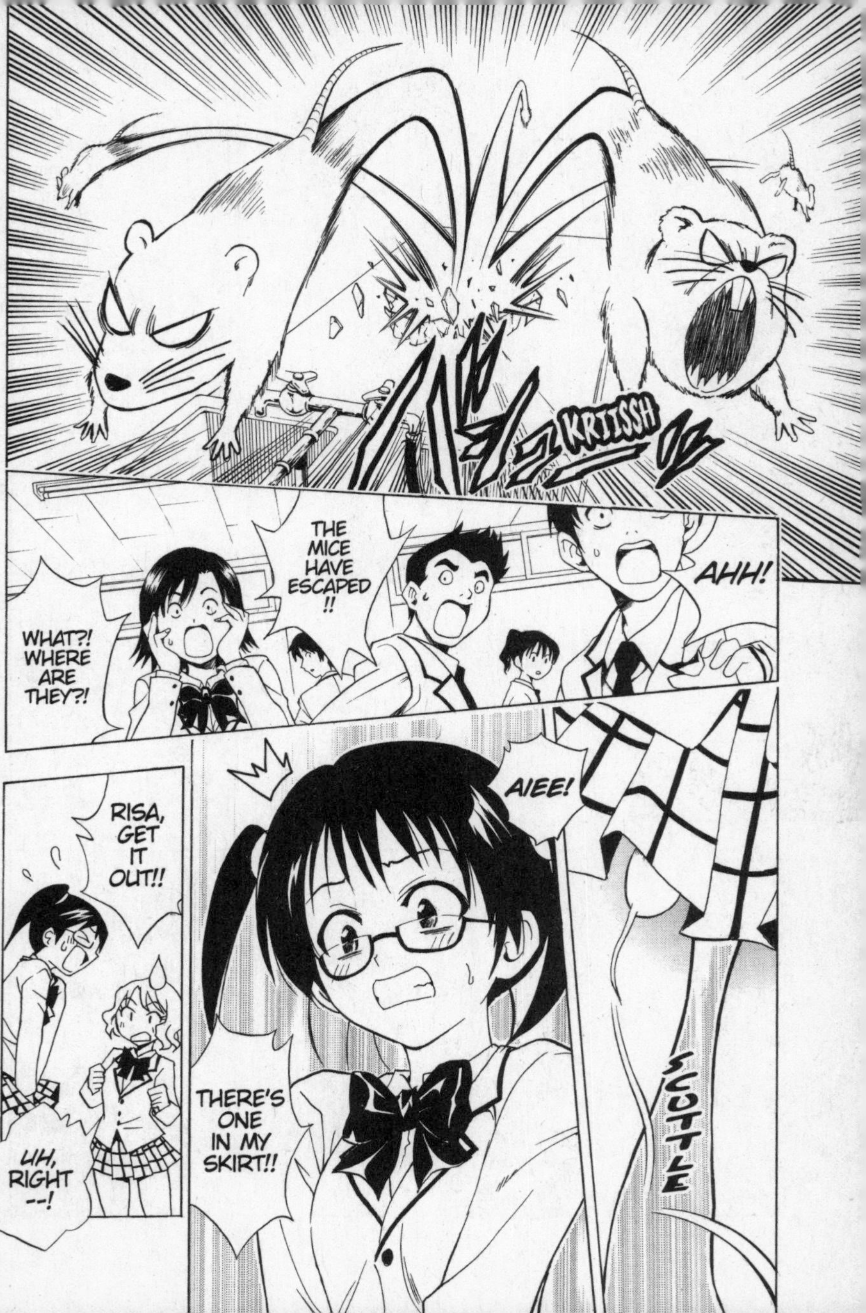
KRIISSH
AHH!
THE MICE HAVE ESCAPED!!
WHAT?! WHERE ARE THEY?!
AIEE!
THERE'S ONE IN MY SKIRT!!
SCUTTLE
RISA, GET IT OUT!!
UH, RIGHT--!

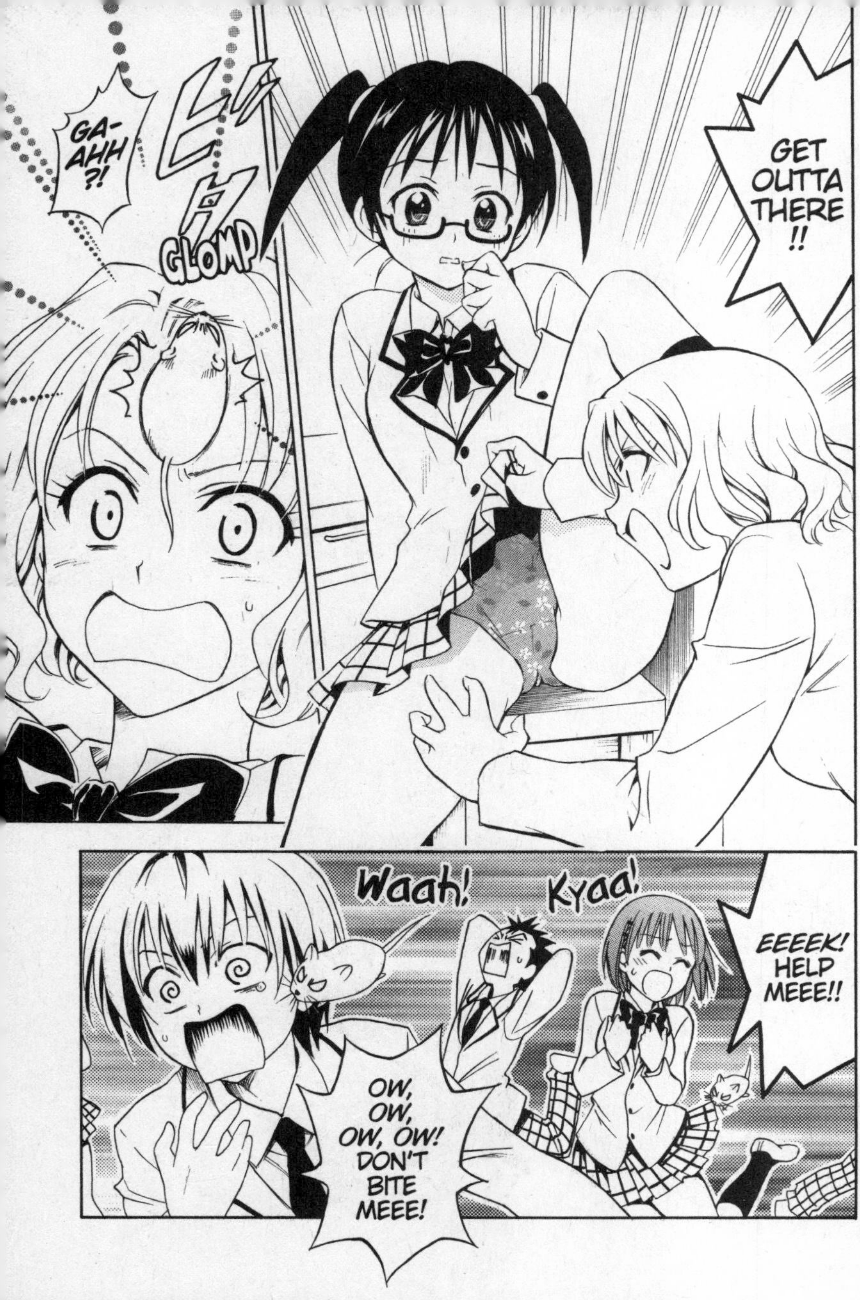
GET OUTTA THERE!!
GLOMP
GA-AHH?!
EEEEK! HELP MEEE!!
Kyaa!
Waah!
OW, OW, OW, OW! DON'T BITE MEEE!

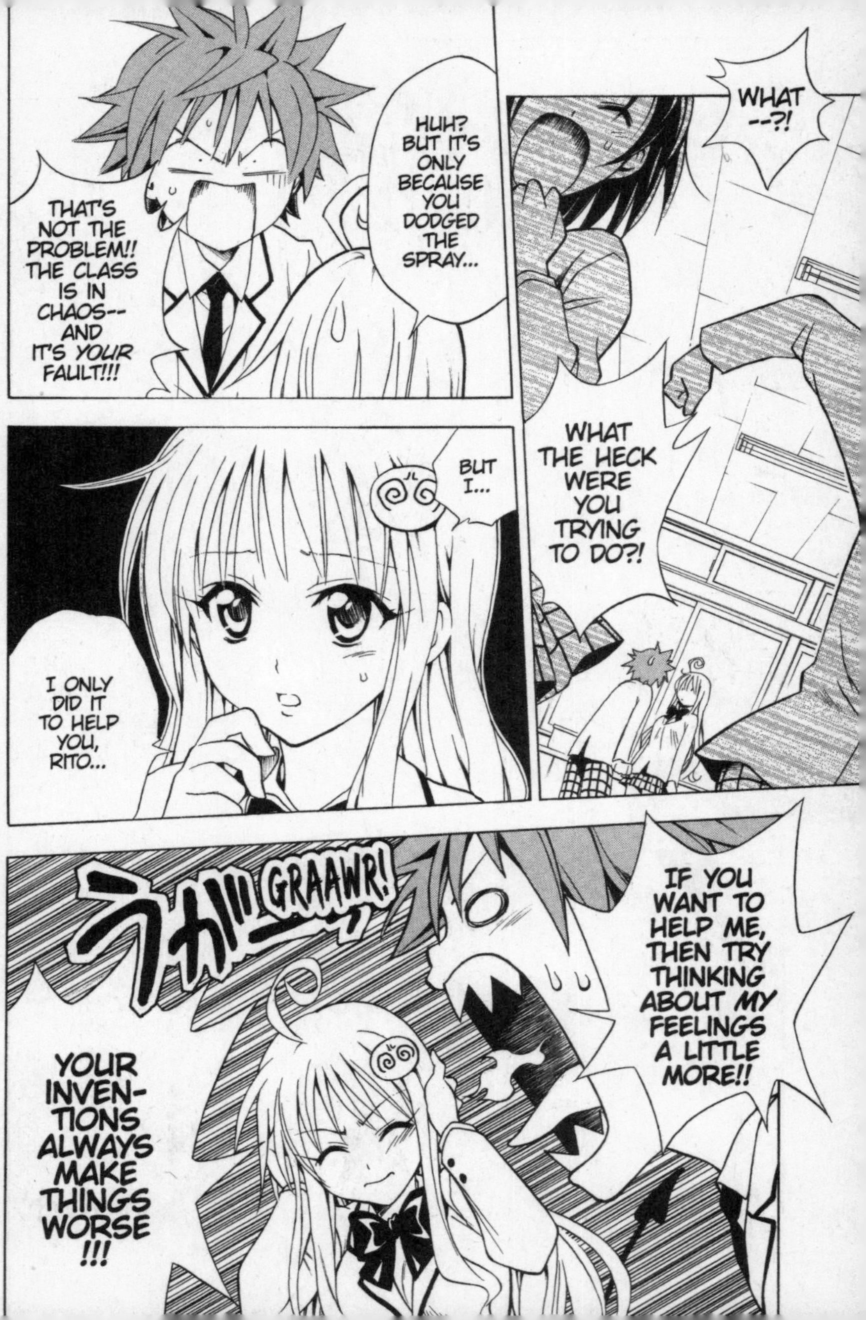
WHAT --?!
WHAT THE HECK WERE YOU TRYING TO DO?!
HUH? BUT IT'S ONLY BECAUSE YOU DODGED THE SPRAY...
THAT'S NOT THE PROBLEM!! THE CLASS IS IN CHAOS-- AND IT'S *YOUR* FAULT!!!
BUT I...
I ONLY DID IT TO HELP YOU, RITO...
IF YOU WANT TO HELP ME, THEN TRY THINKING ABOUT *MY* FEELINGS A LITTLE MORE!!
うがーっ GRAAWR!
YOUR INVENTIONS ALWAYS MAKE THINGS WORSE!!!

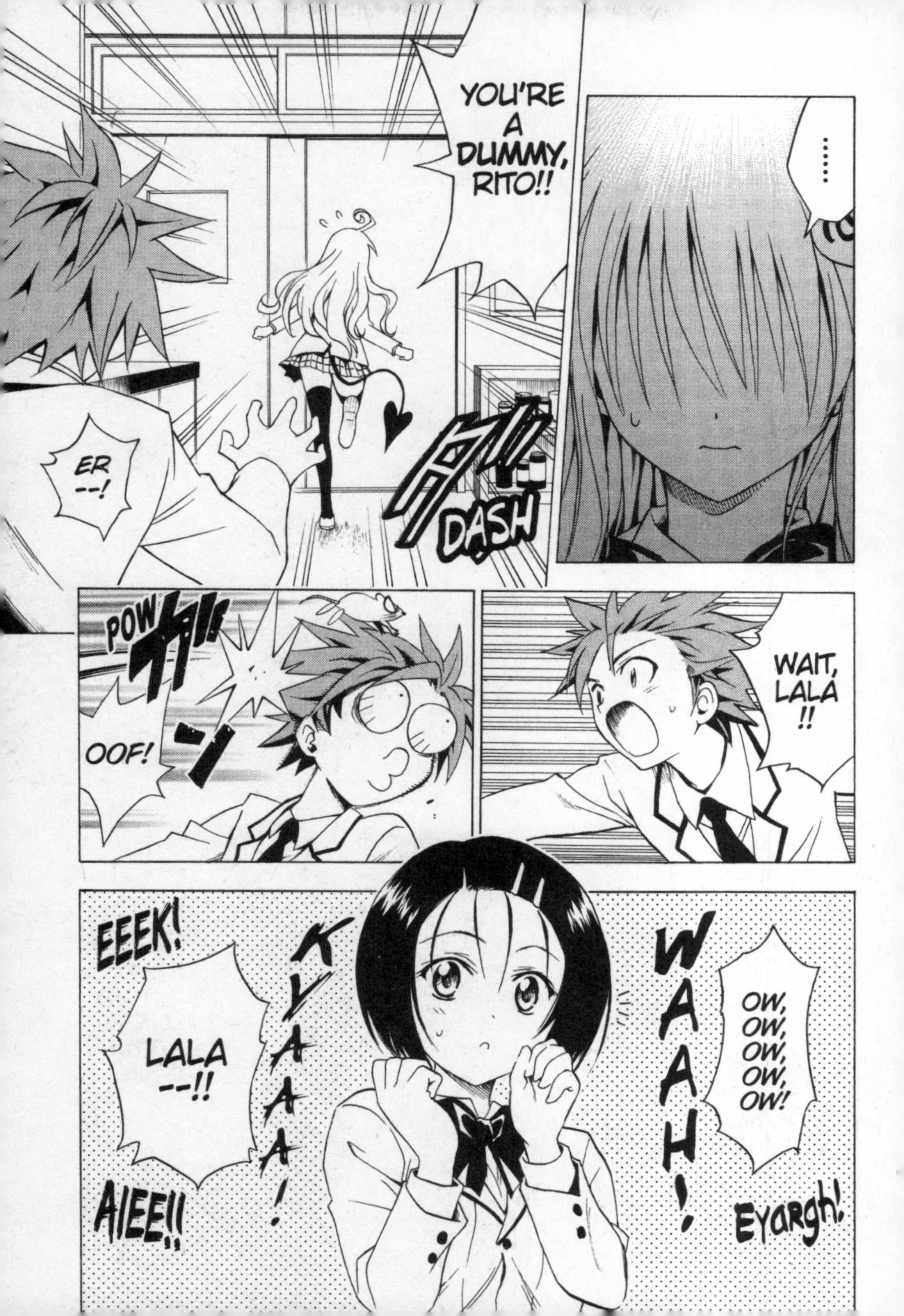
......
YOU'RE A DUMMY, RITO!!
DASH
ER--!
WAIT, LALA!!
POW
OOF!
OW, OW, OW, OW, OW!
WAAH!
Eyargh!
KYAAAA!
LALA--!!
EEEK!
AIEE!!

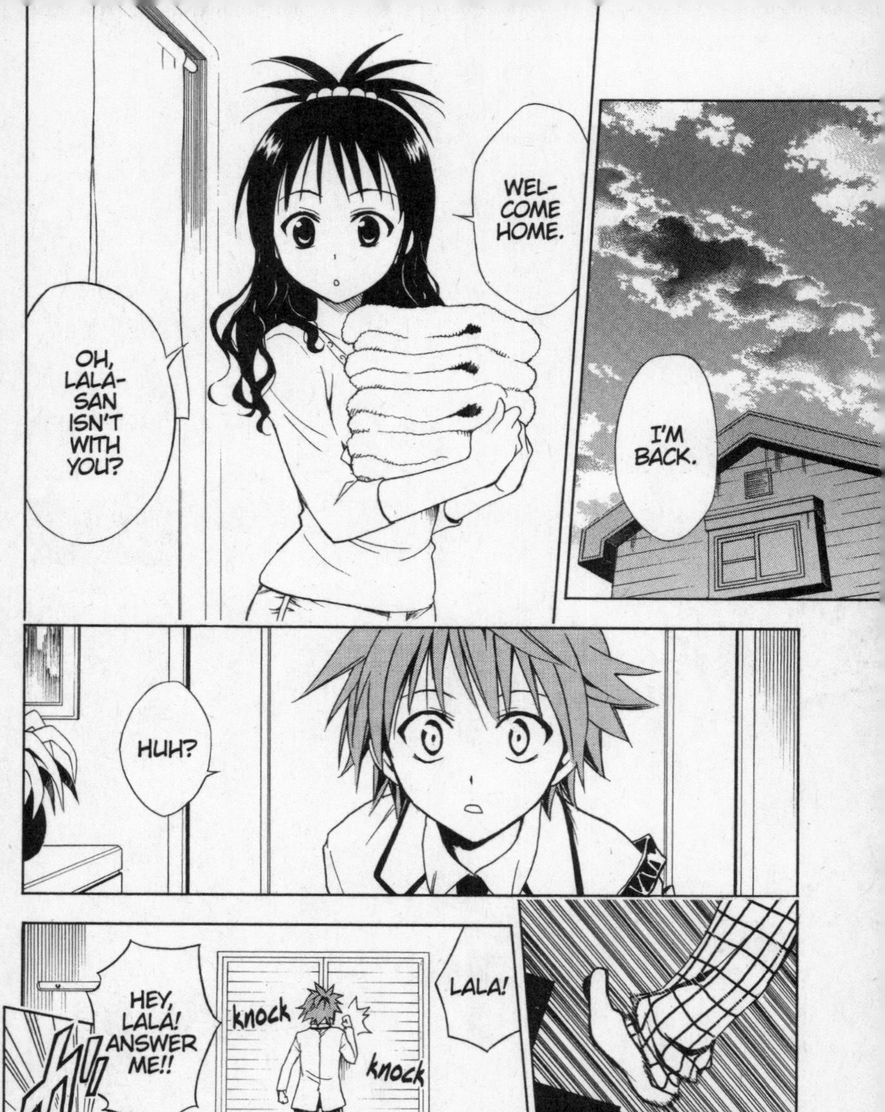
I'M BACK.
WEL-COME HOME.
OH, LALA-SAN ISN'T WITH YOU?
HUH?
LALA!
HEY, LALA! ANSWER ME!!
knock
knock
KA-CHAK

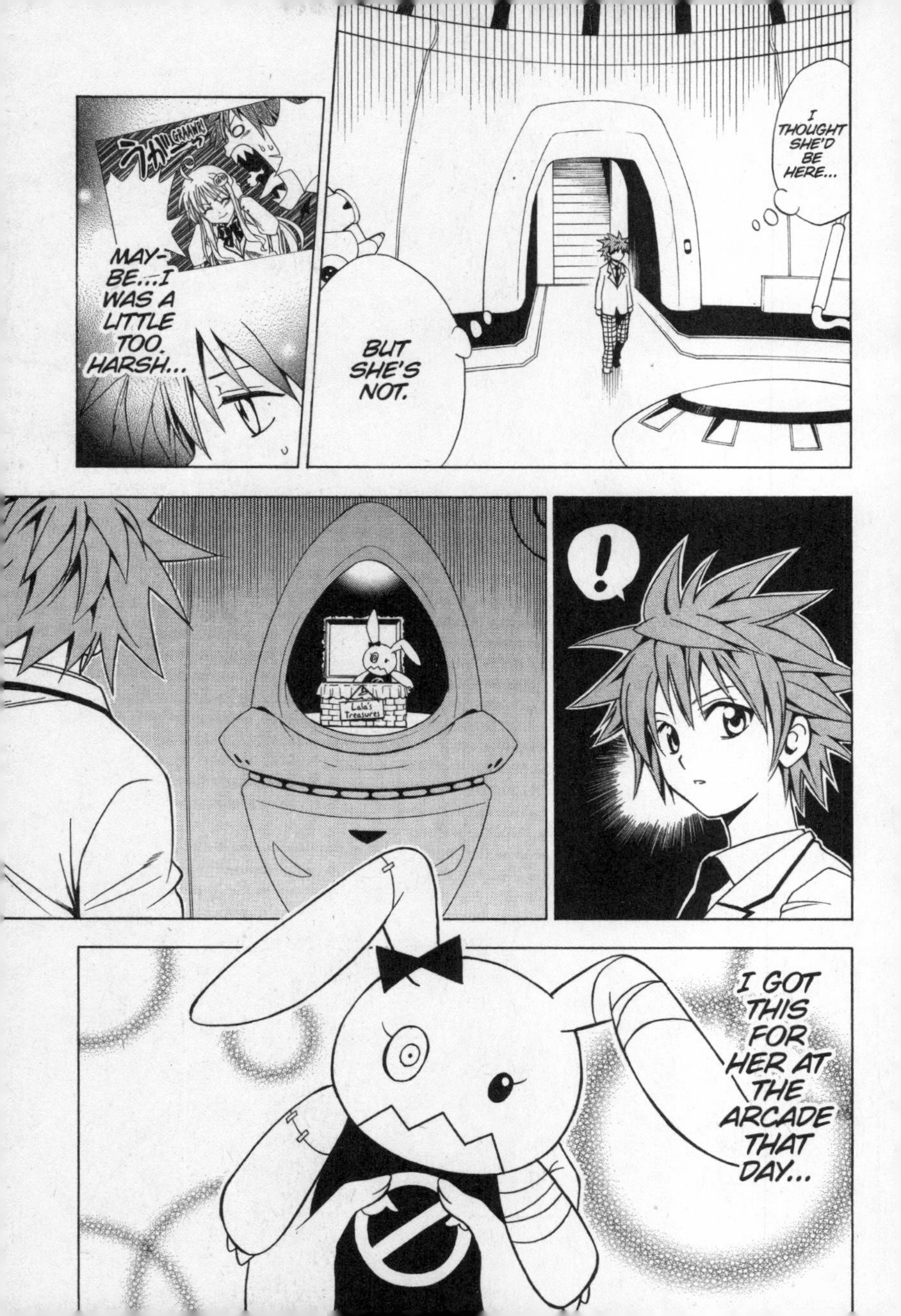
I THOUGHT SHE'D BE HERE...
BUT SHE'S NOT.
GRAAWR!
MAY-BE...I WAS A LITTLE TOO. HARSH...
!
Lala's Treasures
I GOT THIS FOR HER AT THE ARCADE THAT DAY...

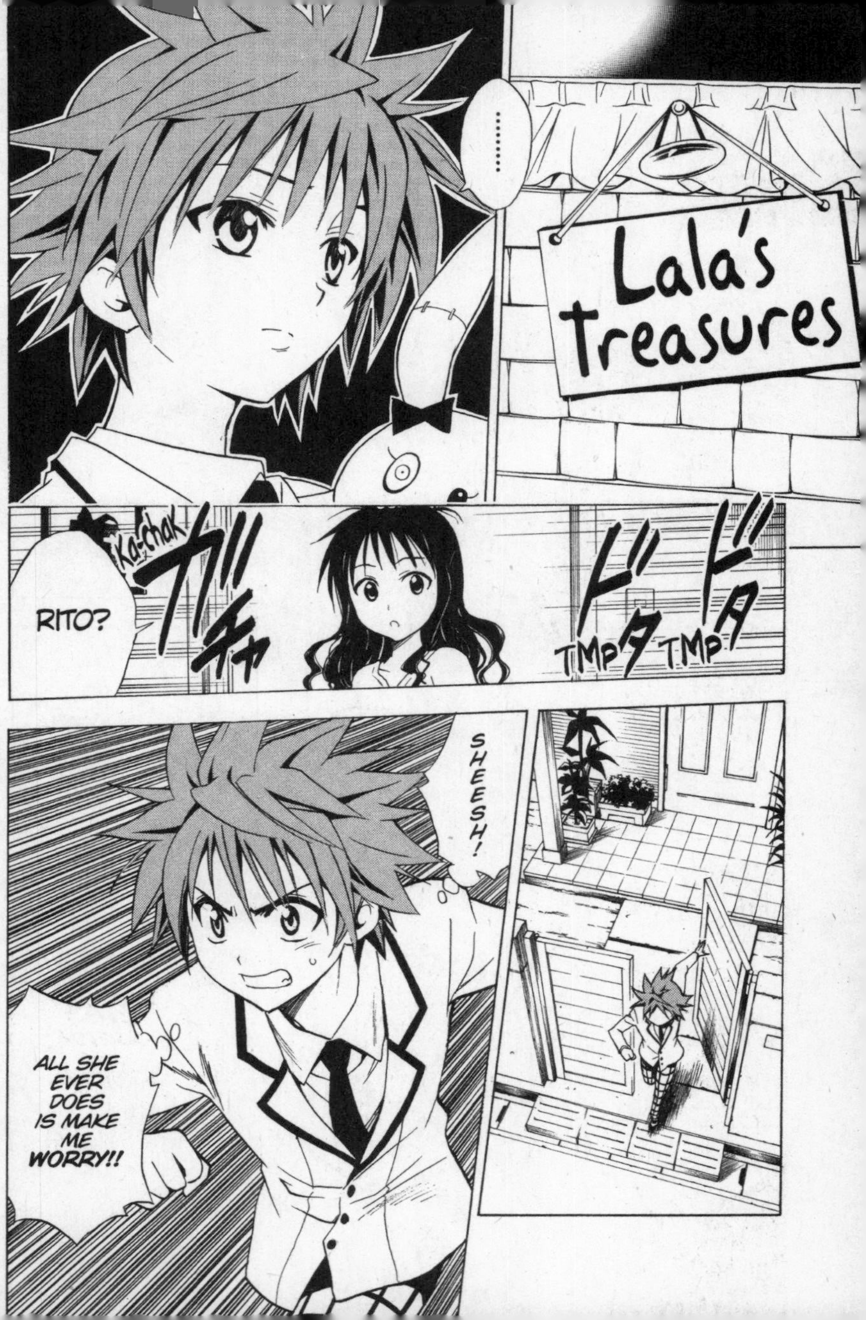
Lala's Treasures
......
ドタ ドタ
TMP TMP
ガチャ
Ka-chak
RITO?
SHEESH!
ALL SHE EVER DOES IS MAKE ME WORRY!!

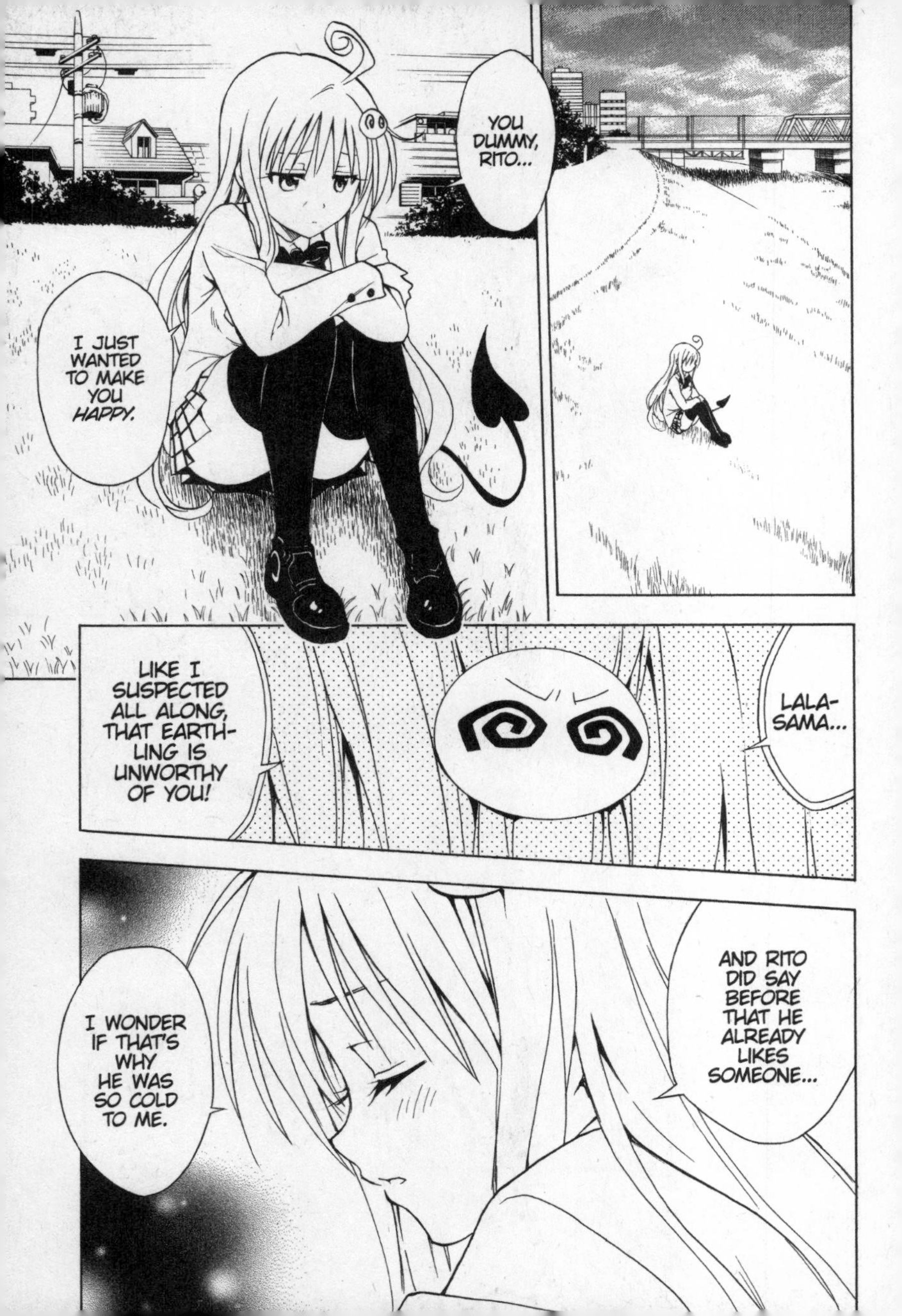
YOU DUMMY, RITO...
I JUST WANTED TO MAKE YOU *HAPPY.*
LALA-SAMA...
LIKE I SUSPECTED ALL ALONG, THAT EARTHLING IS UNWORTHY OF YOU!
AND RITO DID SAY BEFORE THAT HE ALREADY LIKES SOMEONE...
I WONDER IF THAT'S WHY HE WAS SO COLD TO ME.

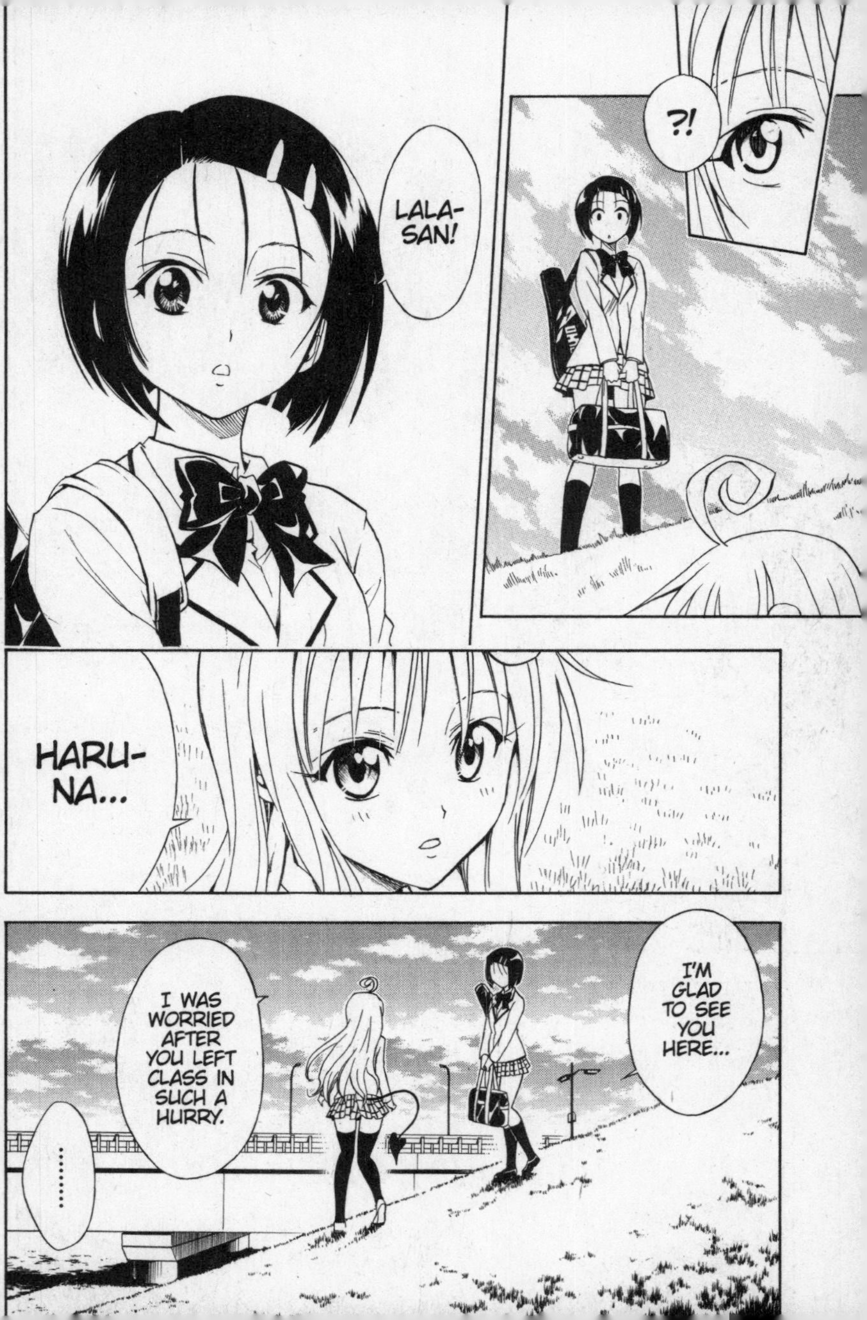
?!
LALA-SAN!
HARU-NA...
I'M GLAD TO SEE YOU HERE...
I WAS WORRIED AFTER YOU LEFT CLASS IN SUCH A HURRY.
....

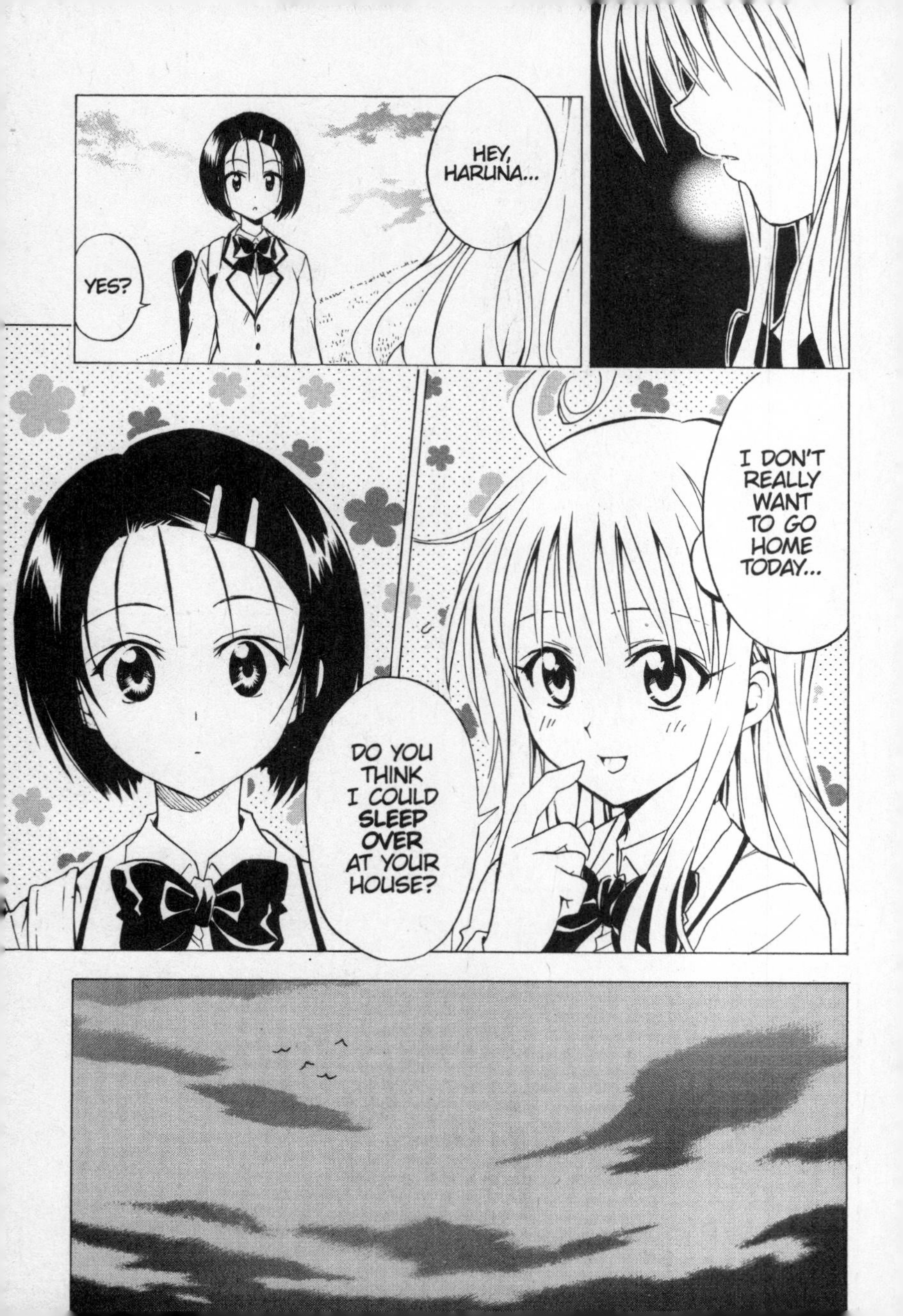
HEY, HARUNA...
YES?
I DON'T REALLY WANT TO GO HOME TODAY...
DO YOU THINK I COULD SLEEP OVER AT YOUR HOUSE?

To LOVE Ru

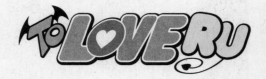

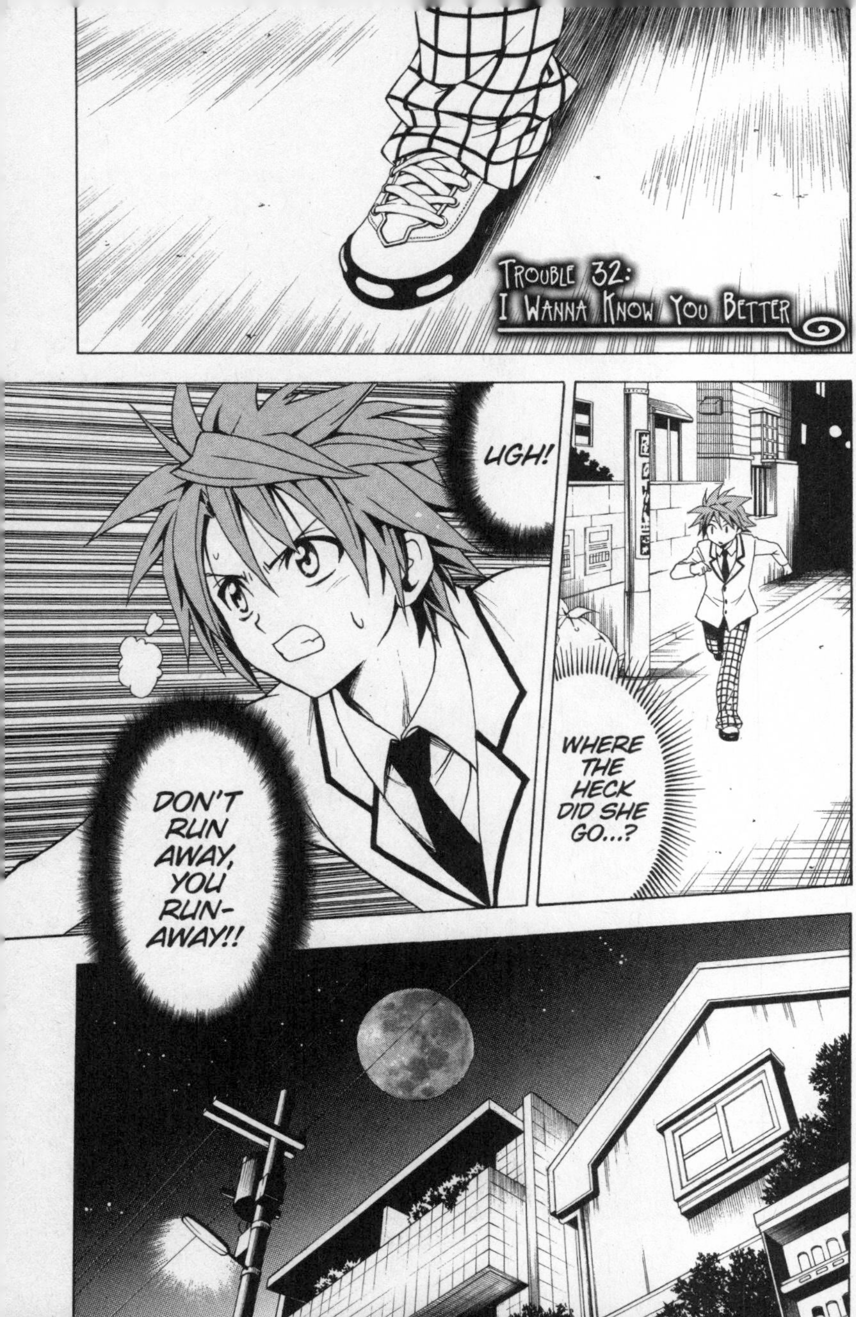
TROUBLE 32:
I WANNA KNOW YOU BETTER
WHERE THE HECK DID SHE GO...?
UGH!
DON'T RUN AWAY, YOU RUN-AWAY!!

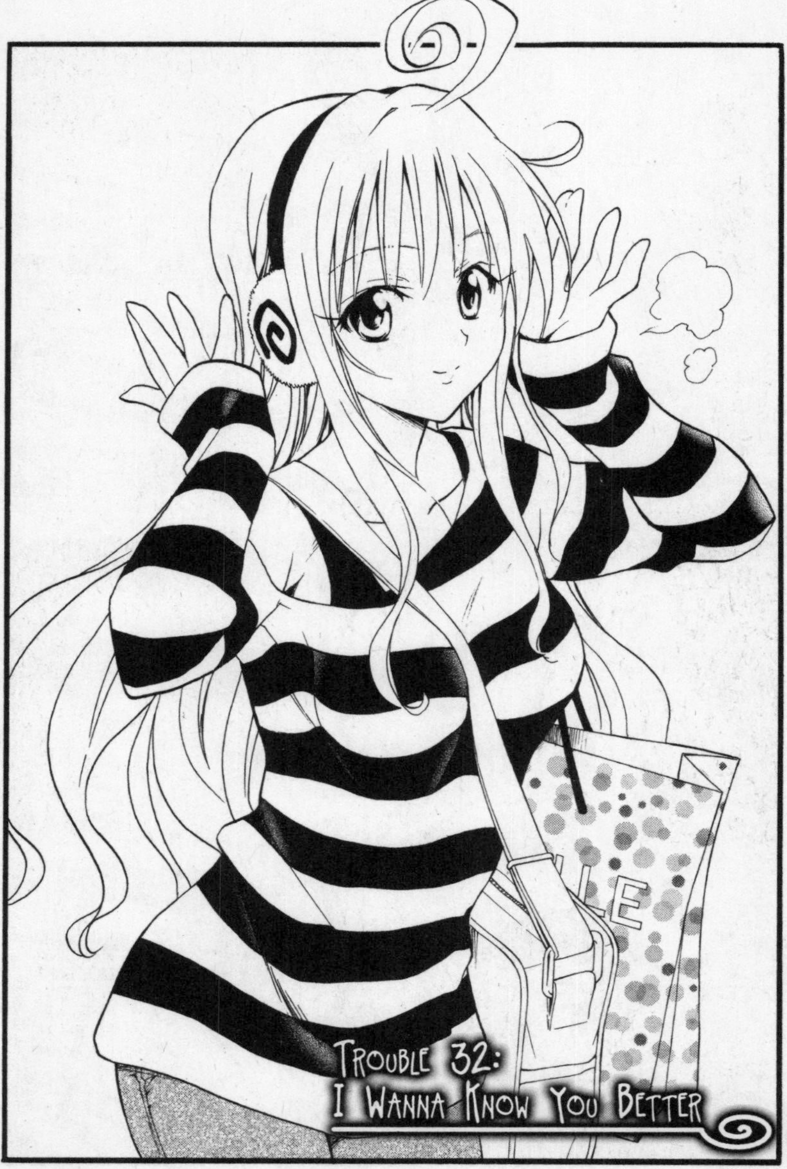
Trouble 32:
I Wanna Know You Better

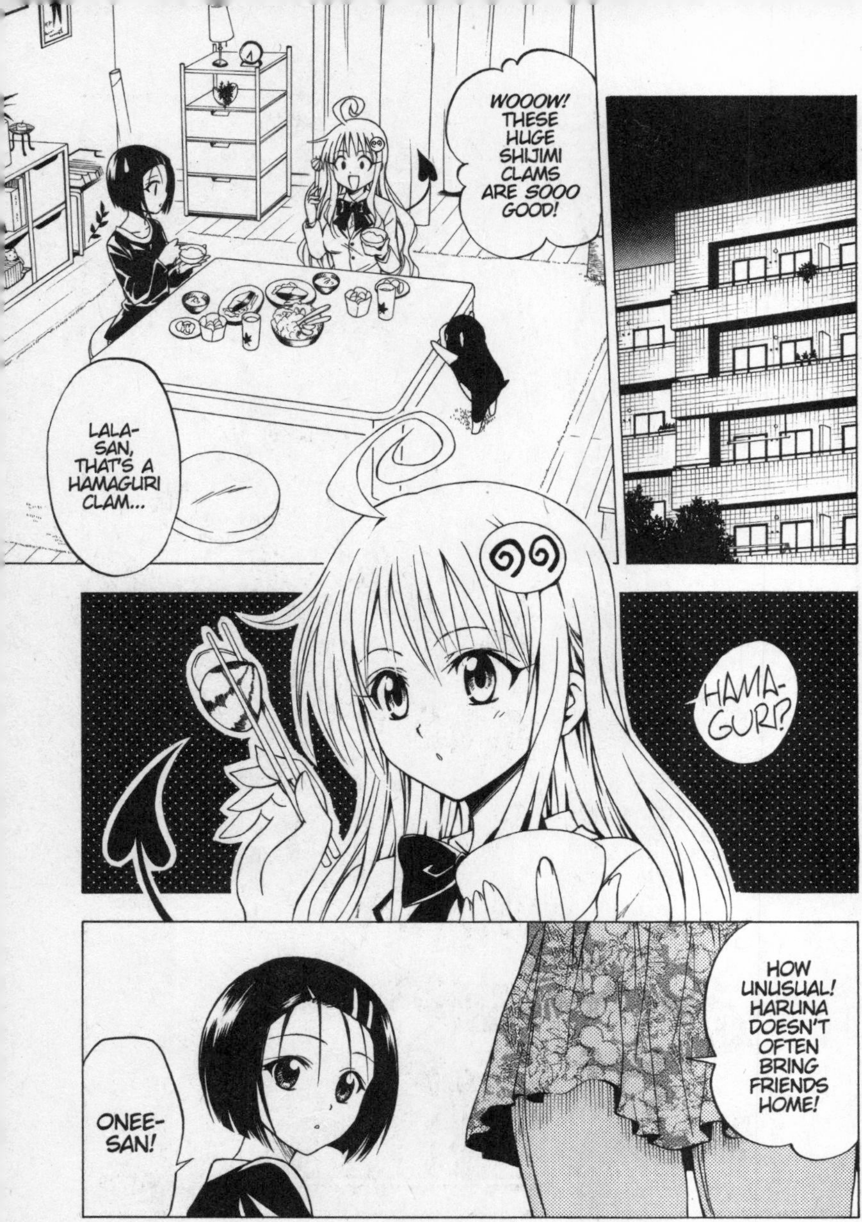
WOOOW! THESE HUGE SHIJIMI CLAMS ARE SOOO GOOD!
LALA-SAN, THAT'S A HAMAGURI CLAM...
HAMA-GURI?
HOW UNUSUAL! HARUNA DOESN'T OFTEN BRING FRIENDS HOME!
ONEE-SAN!

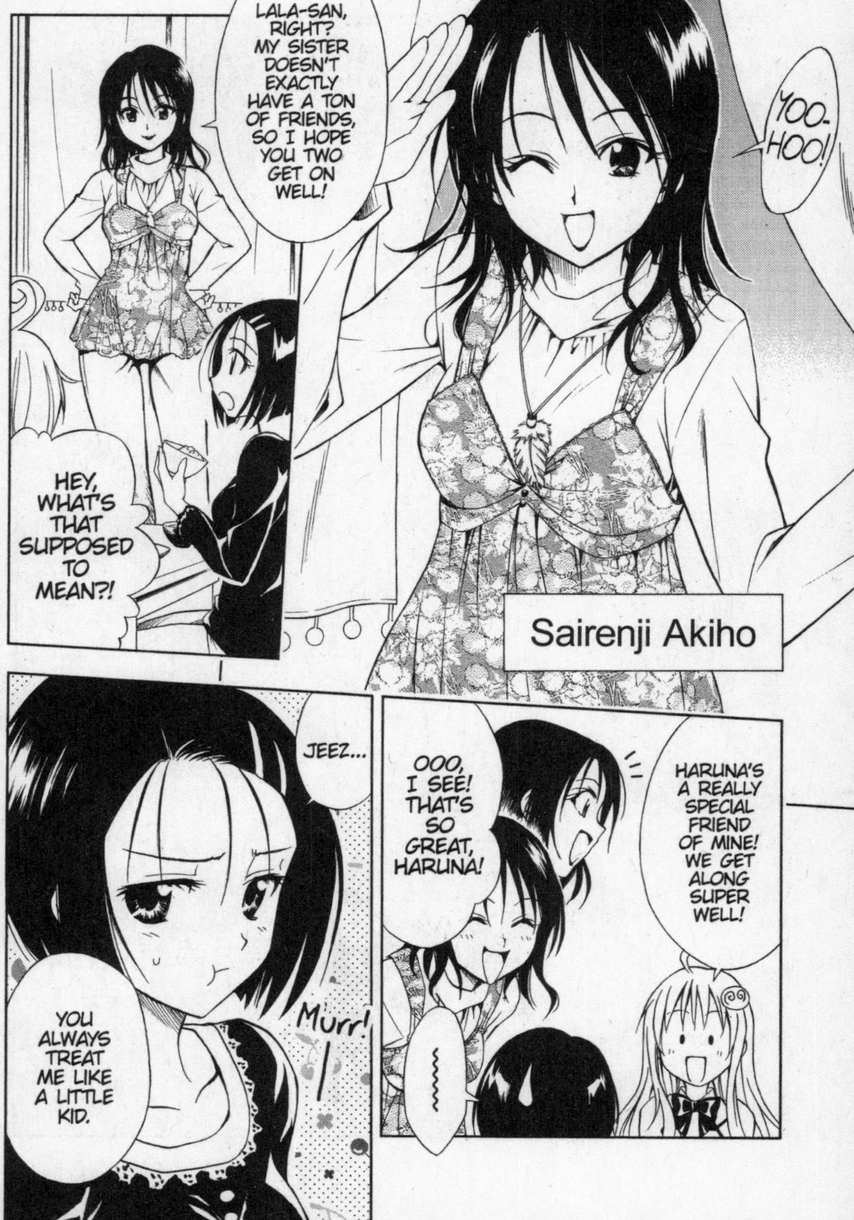
YOO-HOO!
Sairenji Akiho
LALA-SAN, RIGHT? MY SISTER DOESN'T EXACTLY HAVE A TON OF FRIENDS, SO I HOPE YOU TWO GET ON WELL!
HEY, WHAT'S THAT SUPPOSED TO MEAN?!
HARUNA'S A REALLY SPECIAL FRIEND OF MINE! WE GET ALONG SUPER WELL!
OOO, I SEE! THAT'S SO GREAT, HARUNA!
......
JEEZ...
Murr!
YOU ALWAYS TREAT ME LIKE A LITTLE KID.

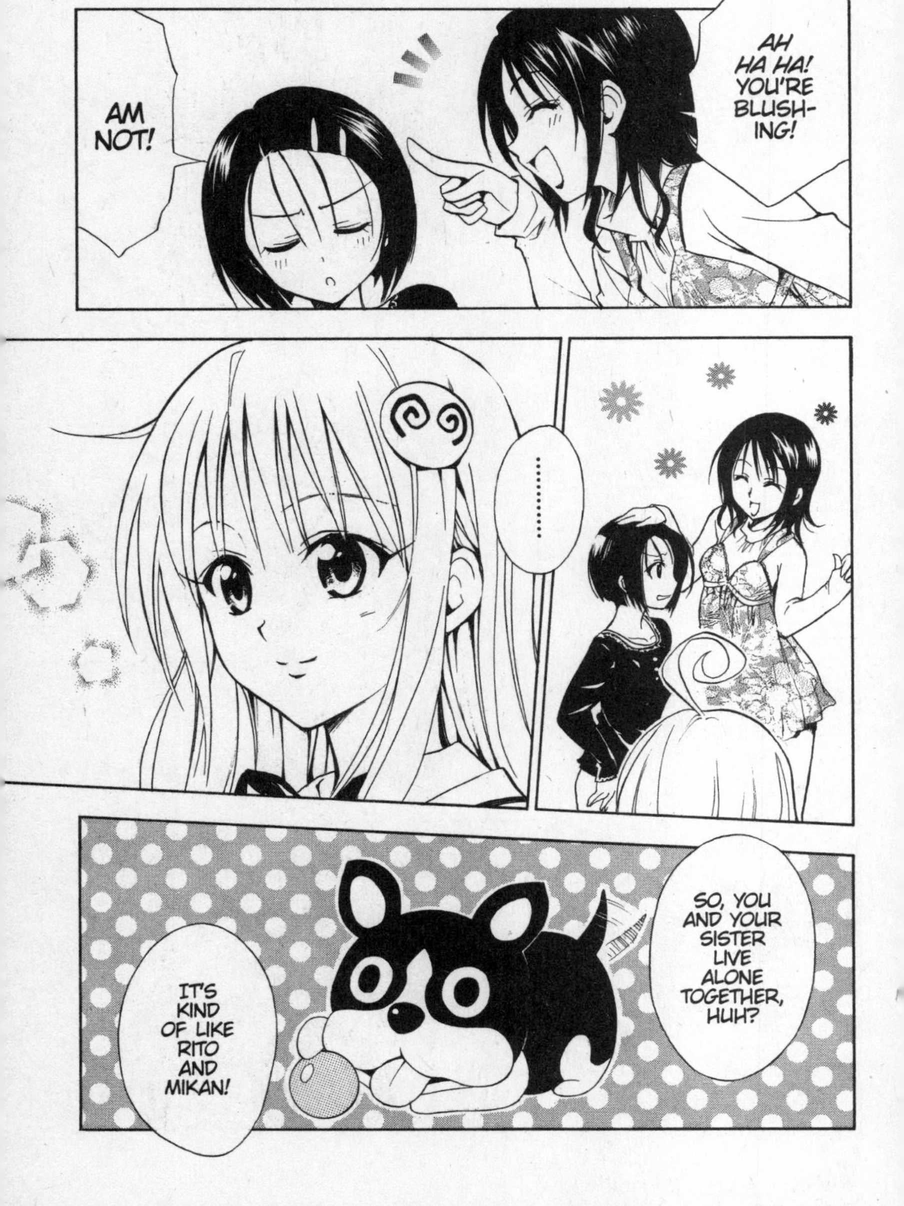
AH HA HA! YOU'RE BLUSH-ING!
AM NOT!
......
SO, YOU AND YOUR SISTER LIVE ALONE TOGETHER, HUH?
IT'S KIND OF LIKE RITO AND MIKAN!

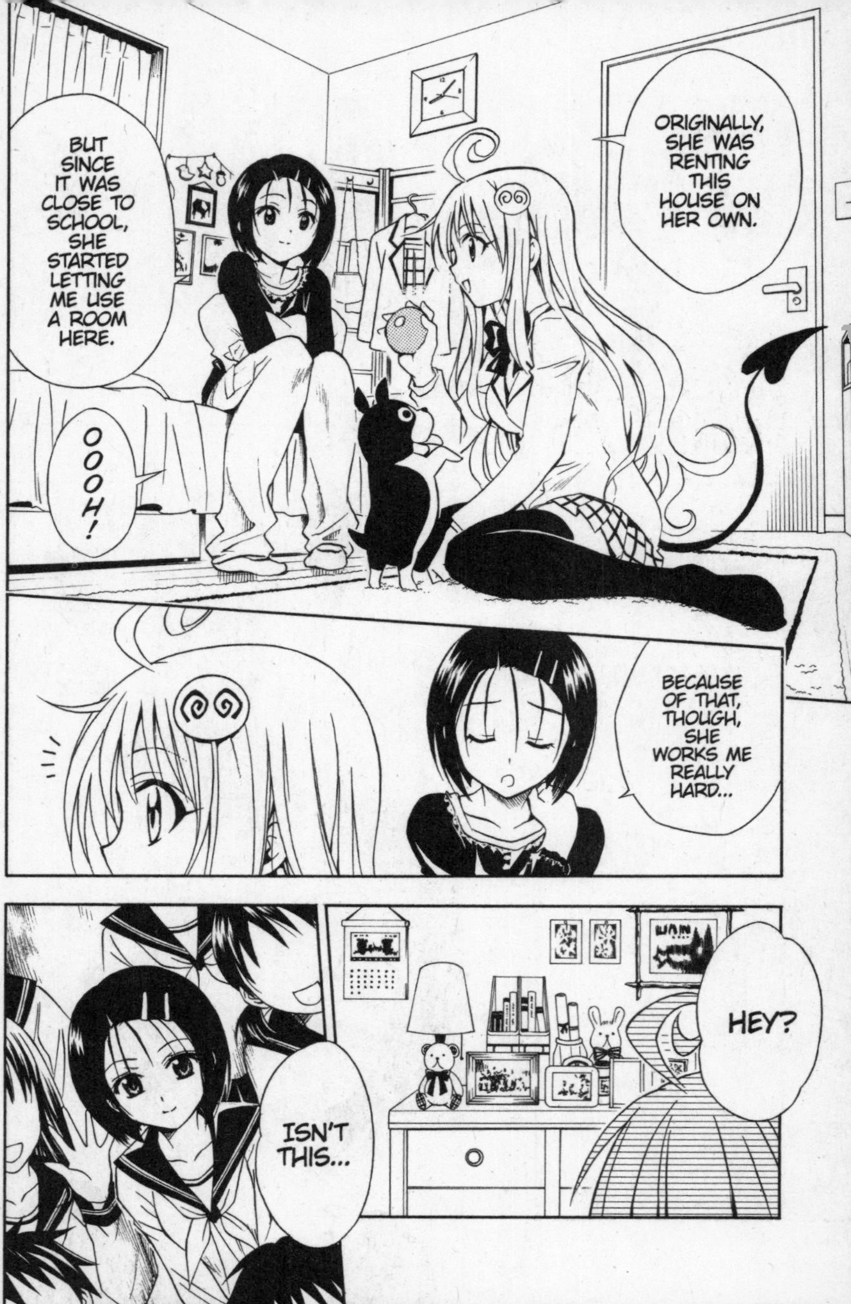
ORIGINALLY, SHE WAS RENTING THIS HOUSE ON HER OWN.
BUT SINCE IT WAS CLOSE TO SCHOOL, SHE STARTED LETTING ME USE A ROOM HERE.
OOOOH!
BECAUSE OF THAT, THOUGH, SHE WORKS ME REALLY HARD...
HEY?
ISN'T THIS...

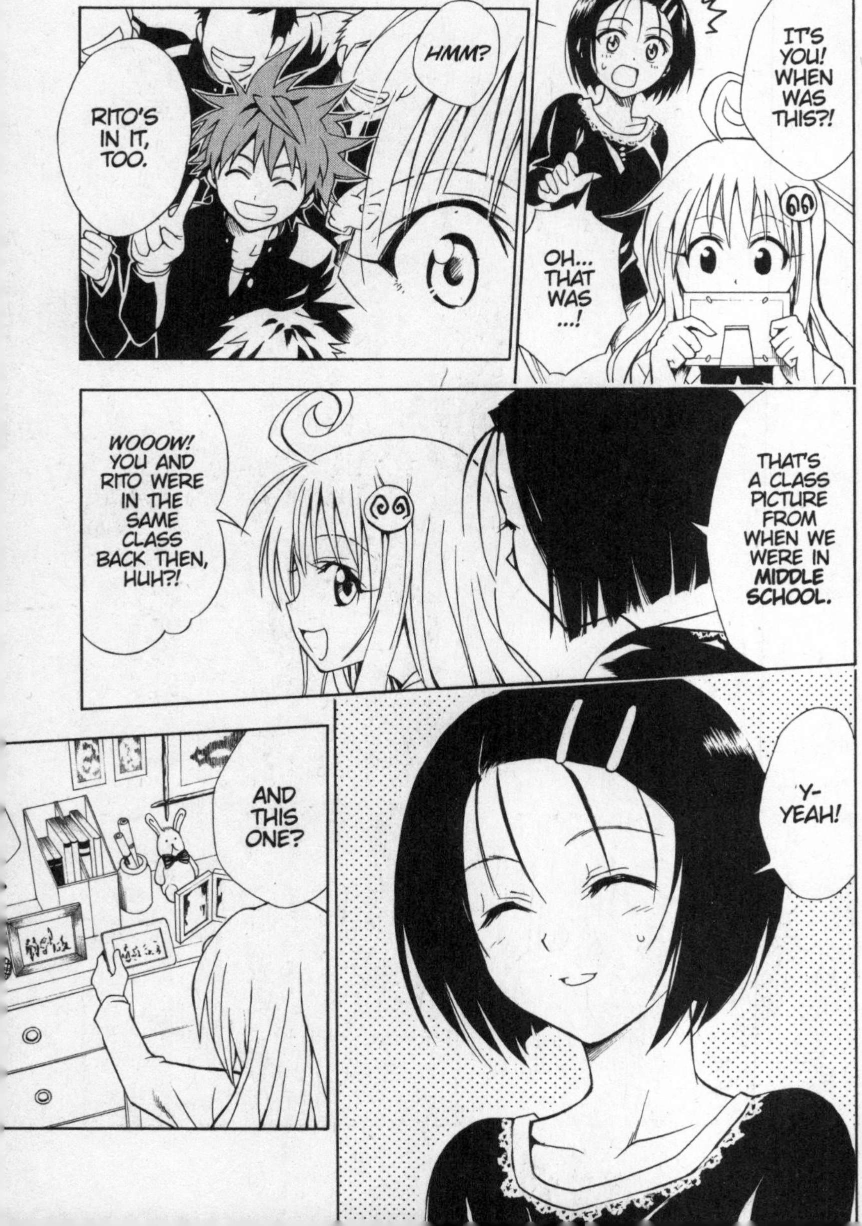
IT'S YOU! WHEN WAS THIS?!
OH... THAT WAS ...!
HMM?
RITO'S IN IT, TOO.
THAT'S A CLASS PICTURE FROM WHEN WE WERE IN MIDDLE SCHOOL.
WOOOW! YOU AND RITO WERE IN THE SAME CLASS BACK THEN, HUH?!
Y-YEAH!
AND THIS ONE?

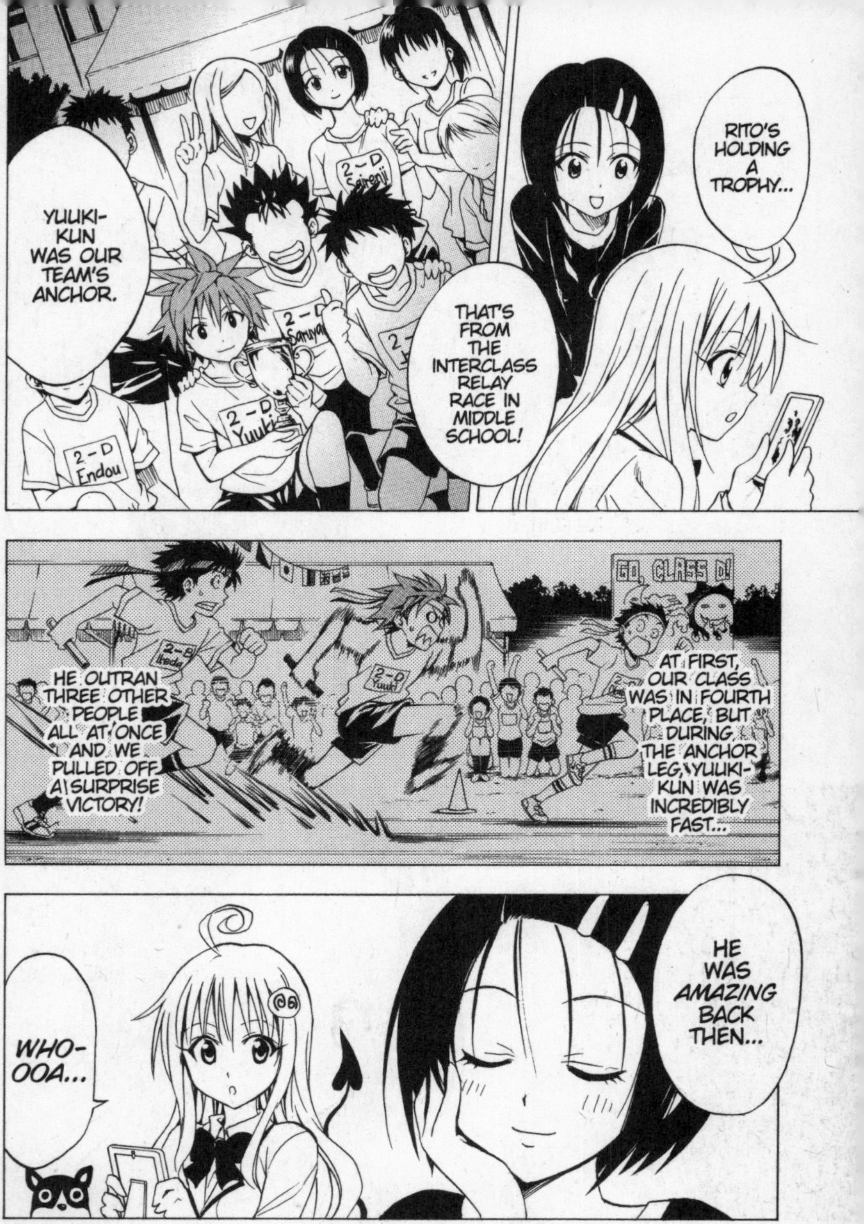
RITO'S HOLDING A TROPHY...
THAT'S FROM THE INTERCLASS RELAY RACE IN MIDDLE SCHOOL!
2-D Sairenji
YUUKI-KUN WAS OUR TEAM'S ANCHOR.
2-D Yuuki
2-D Endou
GO, CLASS D!
AT FIRST, OUR CLASS WAS IN FOURTH PLACE, BUT DURING THE ANCHOR LEG, YUUKI-KUN WAS INCREDIBLY FAST...
2-D Yuuki
HE OUTRAN THREE OTHER PEOPLE ALL AT ONCE AND WE PULLED OFF A SURPRISE VICTORY!
HE WAS AMAZING BACK THEN...
WHO-OOA...

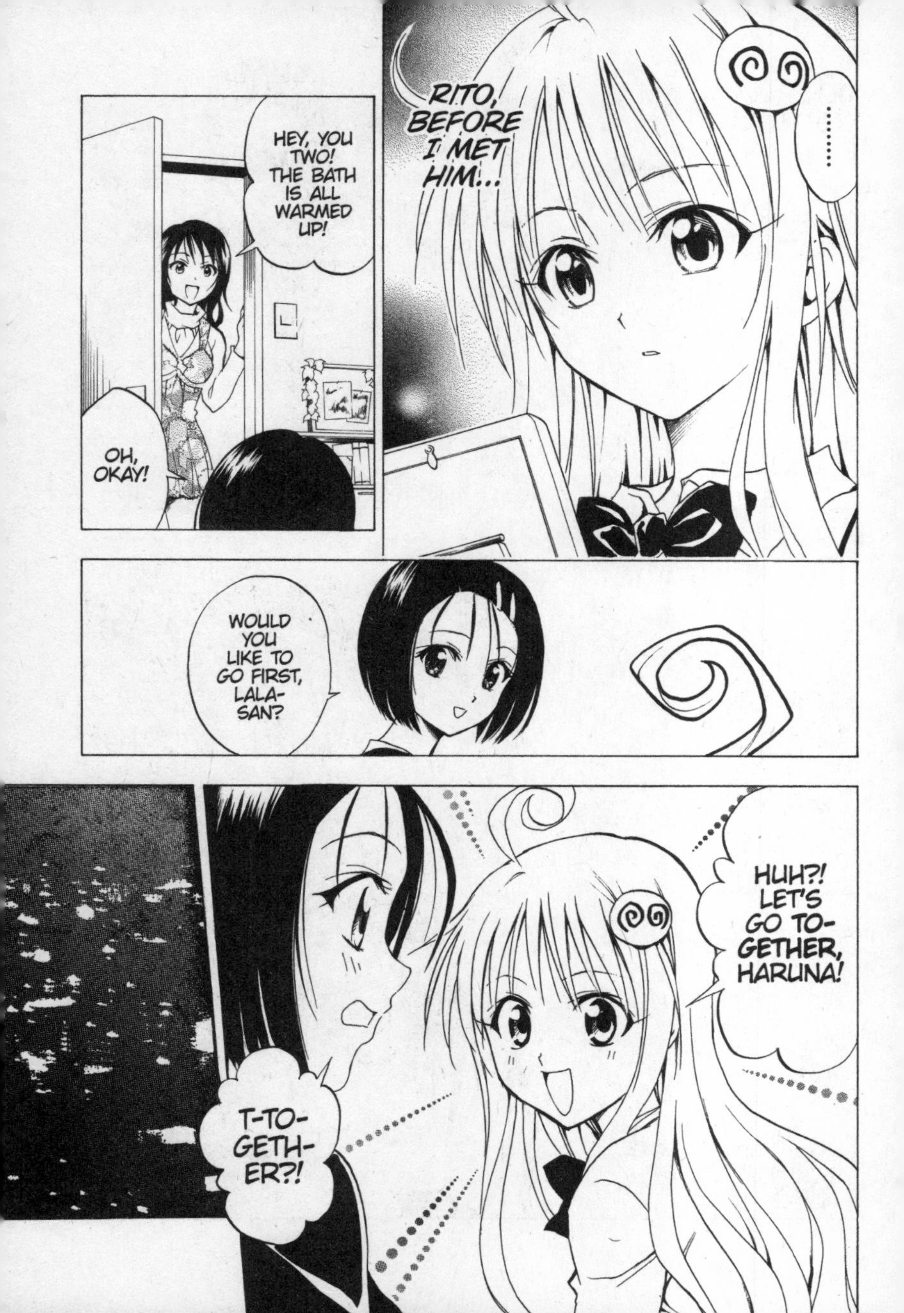
......
RITO, BEFORE I MET HIM...
HEY, YOU TWO! THE BATH IS ALL WARMED UP!
OH, OKAY!
WOULD YOU LIKE TO GO FIRST, LALA-SAN?
HUH?! LET'S GO TOGETHER, HARUNA!
T-TOGETHER?!

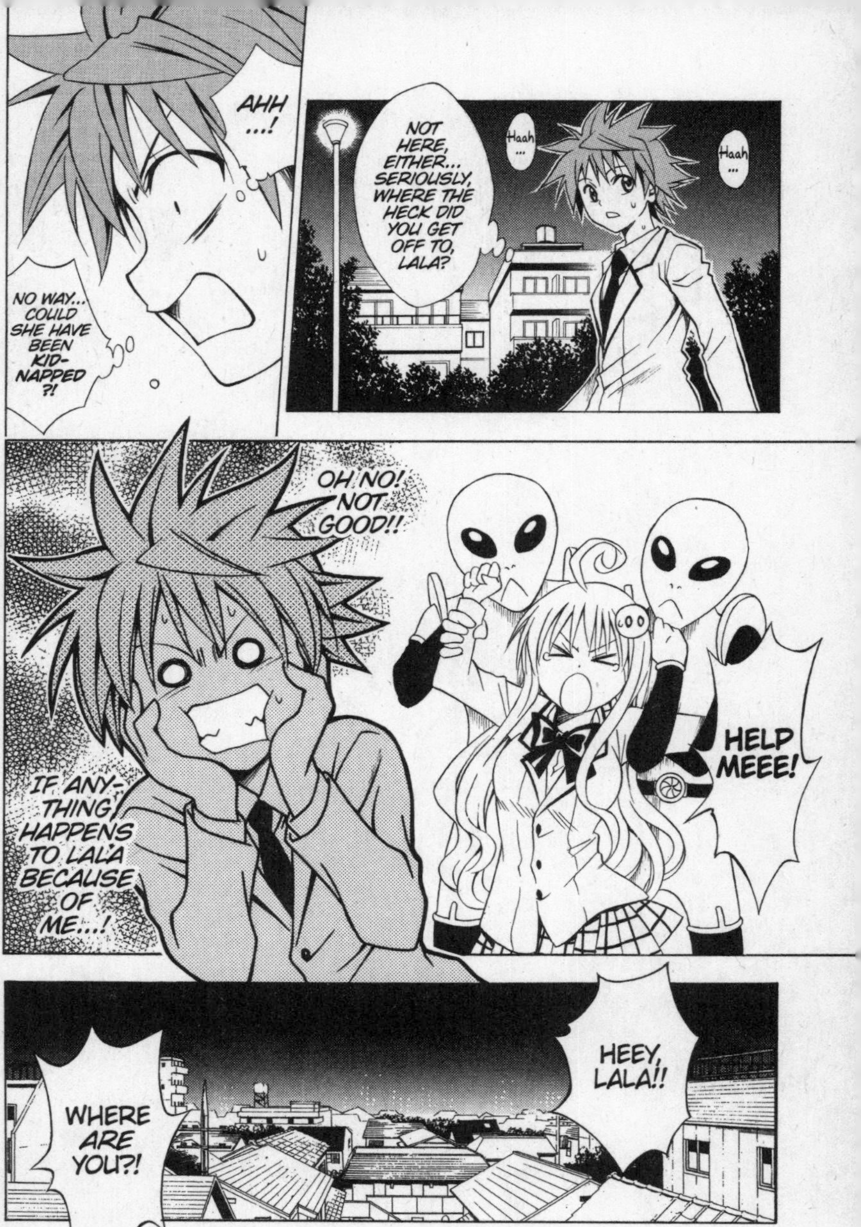
Haah ...
Haah ...
NOT HERE, EITHER... SERIOUSLY, WHERE THE HECK DID YOU GET OFF TO, LALA?
AHH ...!
NO WAY... COULD SHE HAVE BEEN KID-NAPPED ?!
OH NO! NOT GOOD!!
HELP MEEE!
IF ANY-THING HAPPENS TO LALA BECAUSE OF ME...!
HEEY, LALA!!
WHERE ARE YOU?!

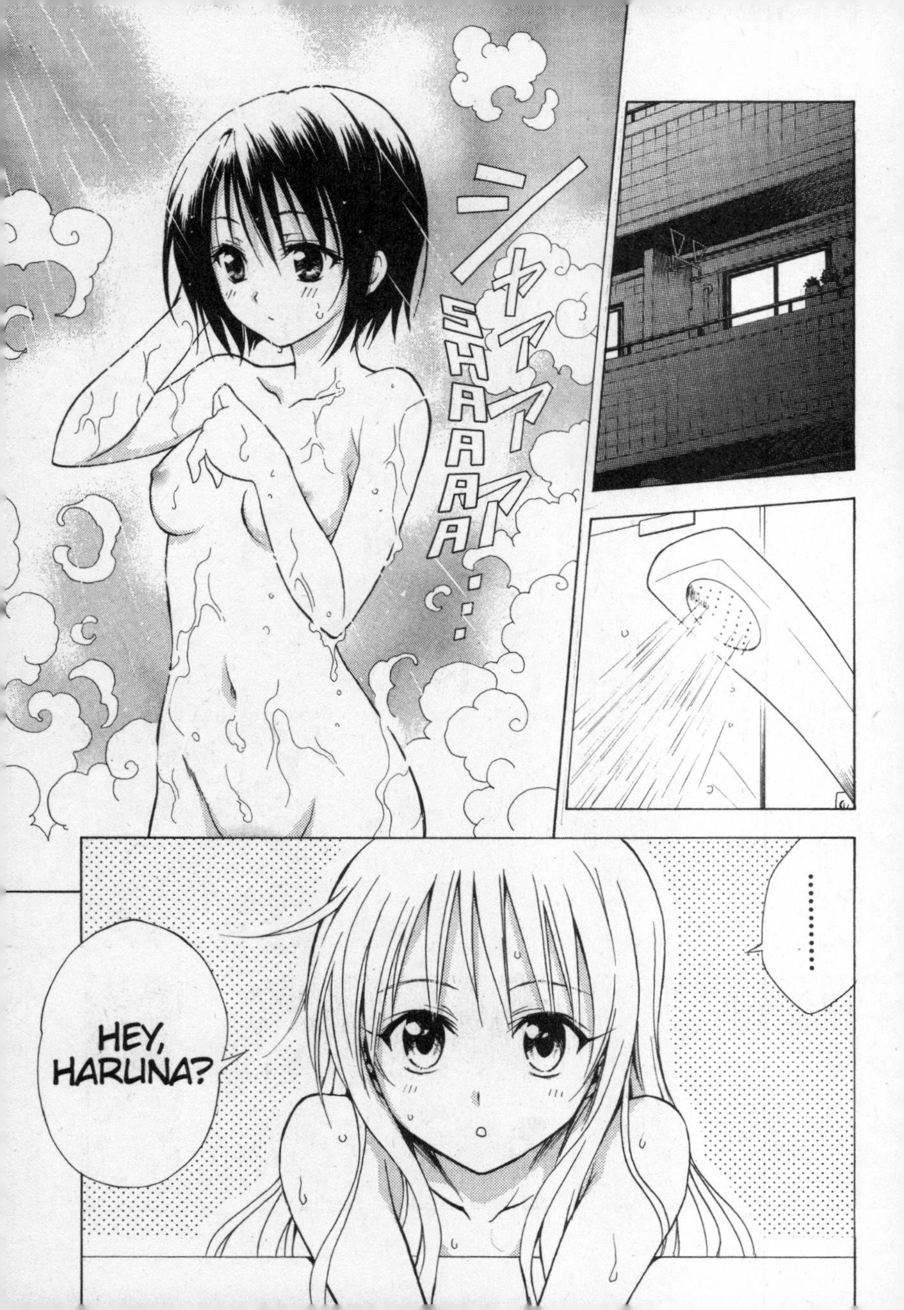
シャアアア
SHAAAAA...
......
HEY, HARUNA?

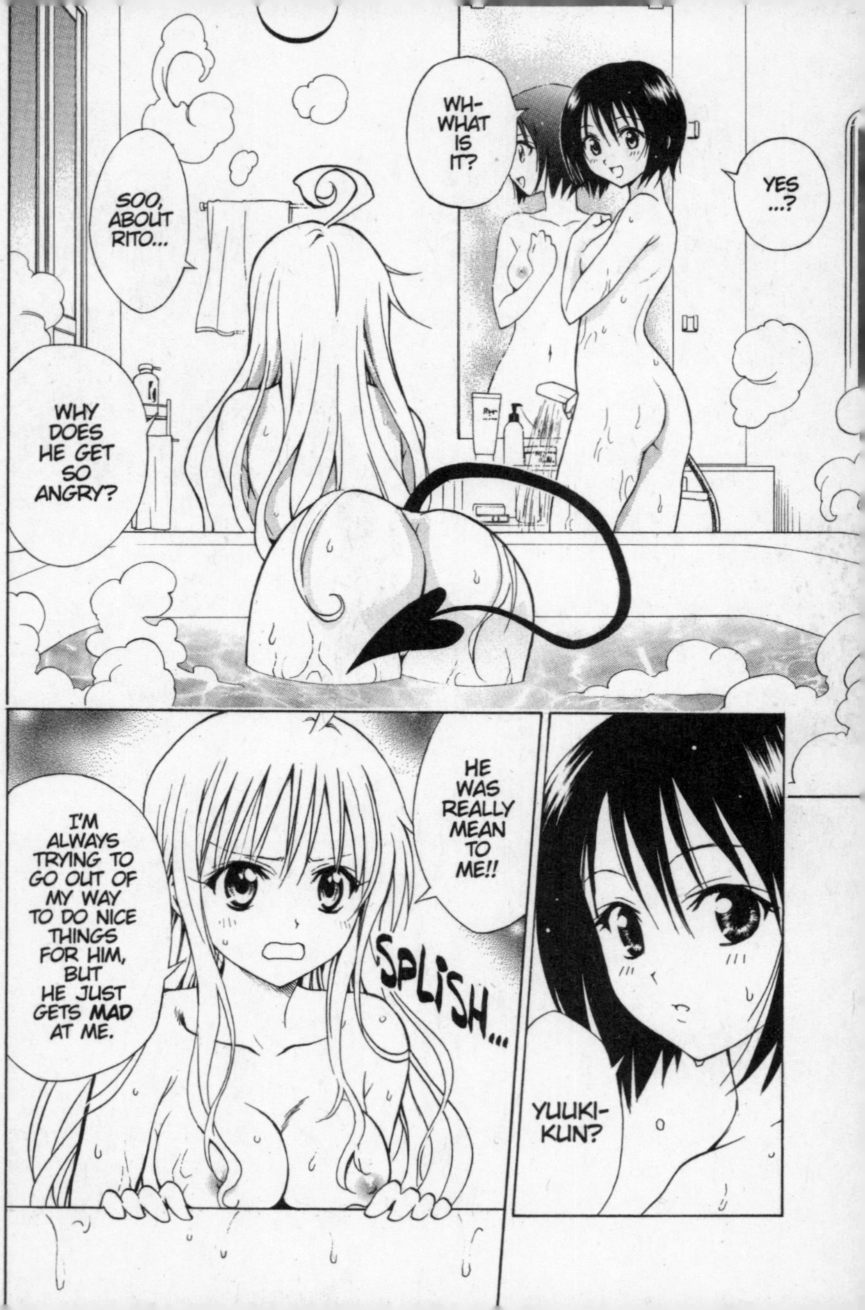

YES ...?
WH- WHAT IS IT?
SOO, ABOUT RITO...
WHY DOES HE GET SO ANGRY?
YUUKI-KUN?
HE WAS REALLY MEAN TO ME!!
I'M ALWAYS TRYING TO GO OUT OF MY WAY TO DO NICE THINGS FOR HIM, BUT HE JUST GETS MAD AT ME.
SPLISH...

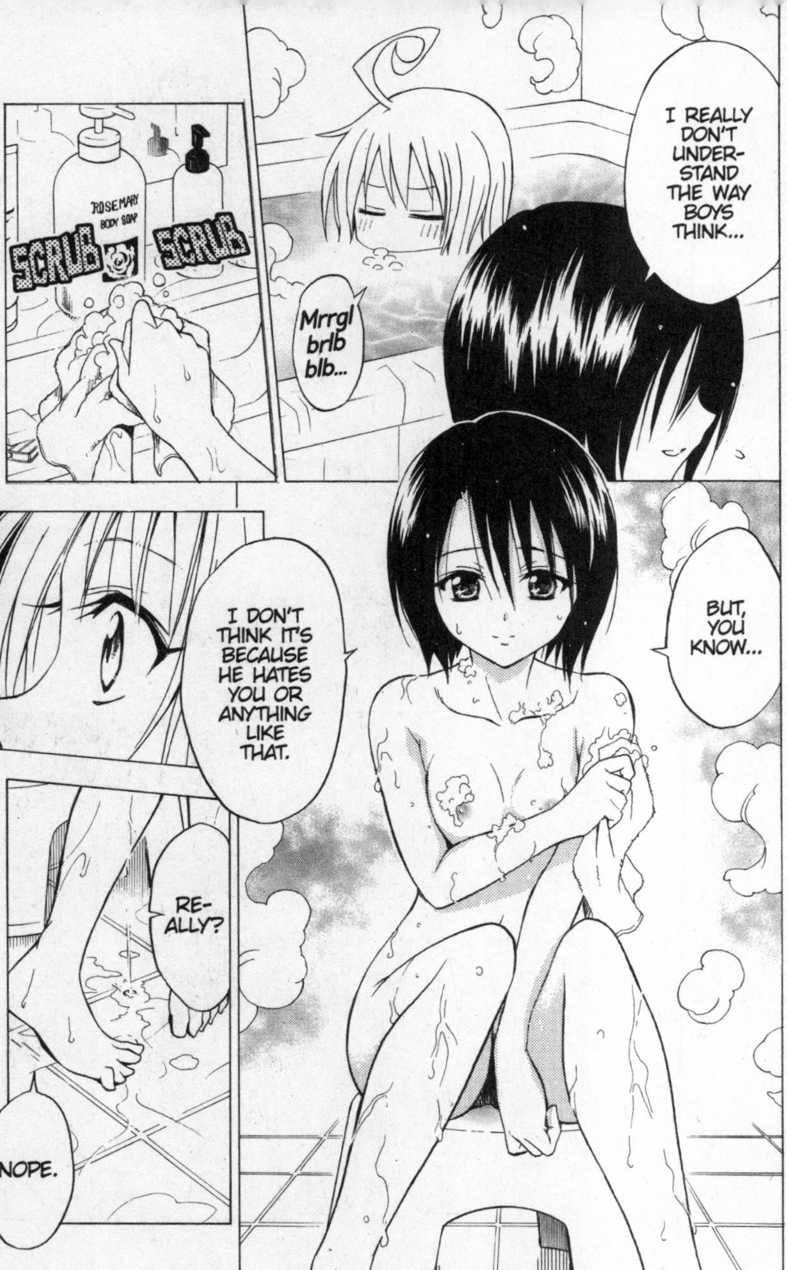
I REALLY DON'T UNDER-STAND THE WAY BOYS THINK...
Mrrgl brlb blb...
ROSEMARY BODY SOAP
SCRUB SCRUB
BUT, YOU KNOW...
I DON'T THINK IT'S BECAUSE HE HATES YOU OR ANYTHING LIKE THAT.
RE-ALLY?
NOPE.

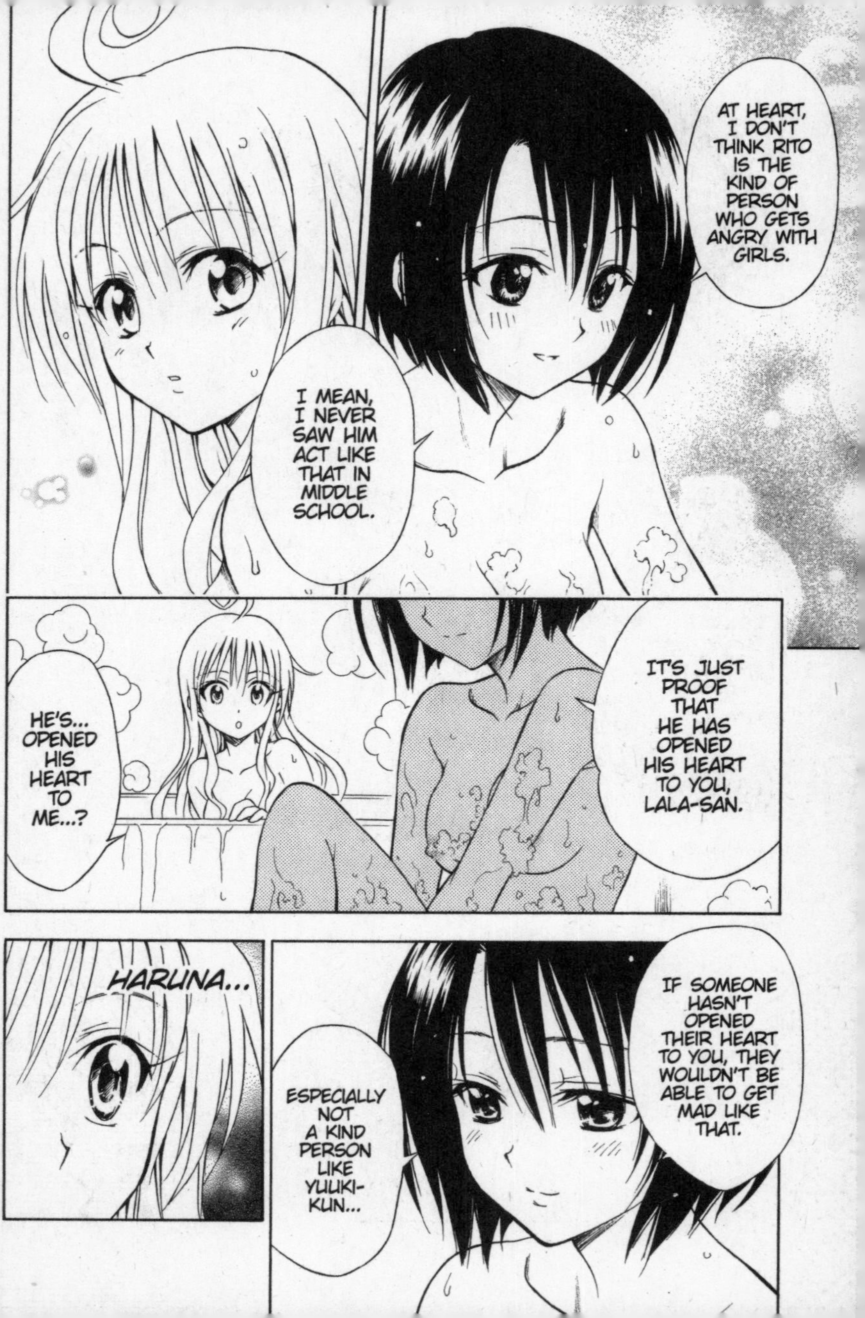
AT HEART, I DON'T THINK RITO IS THE KIND OF PERSON WHO GETS ANGRY WITH GIRLS.
I MEAN, I NEVER SAW HIM ACT LIKE THAT IN MIDDLE SCHOOL.
IT'S JUST PROOF THAT HE HAS OPENED HIS HEART TO YOU, LALA-SAN.
HE'S... OPENED HIS HEART TO ME...?
IF SOMEONE HASN'T OPENED THEIR HEART TO YOU, THEY WOULDN'T BE ABLE TO GET MAD LIKE THAT.
ESPECIALLY NOT A KIND PERSON LIKE YUUKI-KUN...
HARUNA...

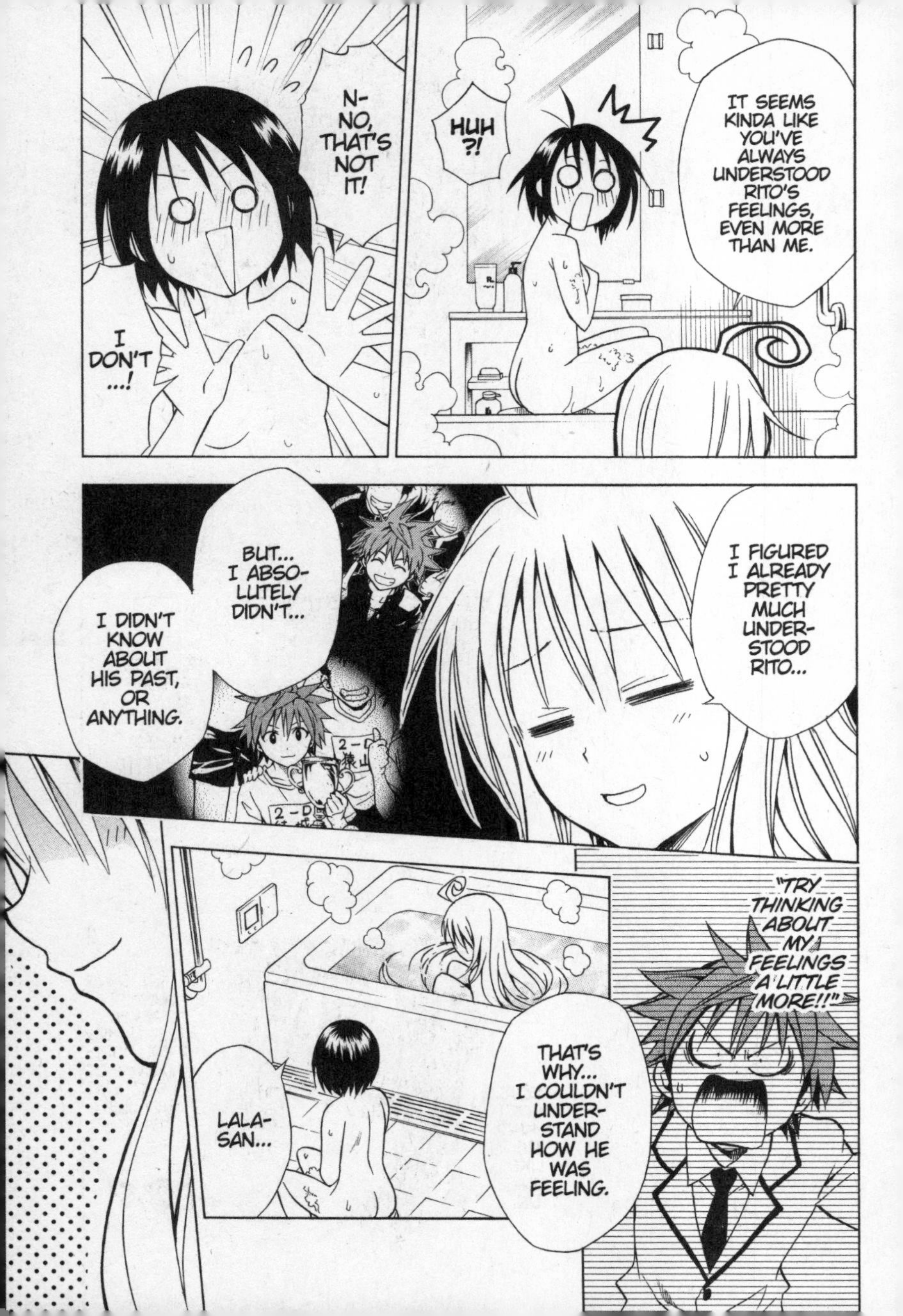
IT SEEMS KINDA LIKE YOU'VE ALWAYS UNDERSTOOD RITO'S FEELINGS, EVEN MORE THAN ME.
HUH ?!
N-NO, THAT'S NOT IT!
I DON'T ...!
I FIGURED I ALREADY PRETTY MUCH UNDER-STOOD RITO...
BUT... I ABSO-LUTELY DIDN'T...
I DIDN'T KNOW ABOUT HIS PAST, OR ANYTHING.
"TRY THINKING ABOUT MY FEELINGS A LITTLE MORE!!"
THAT'S WHY... I COULDN'T UNDER-STAND HOW HE WAS FEELING.
LALA-SAN...

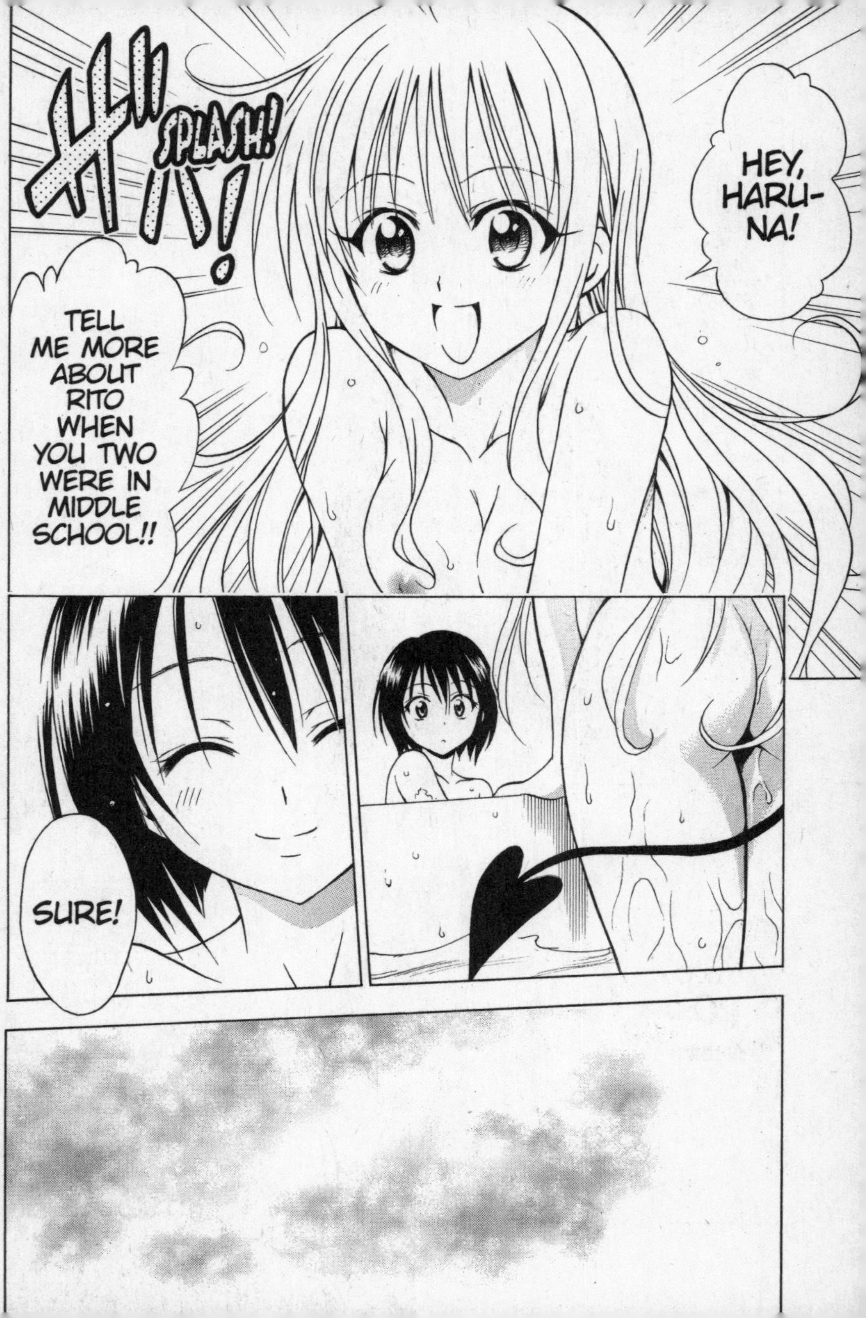
HEY, HARU-NA!
SPLASH!
TELL ME MORE ABOUT RITO WHEN YOU TWO WERE IN MIDDLE SCHOOL!!
SURE!

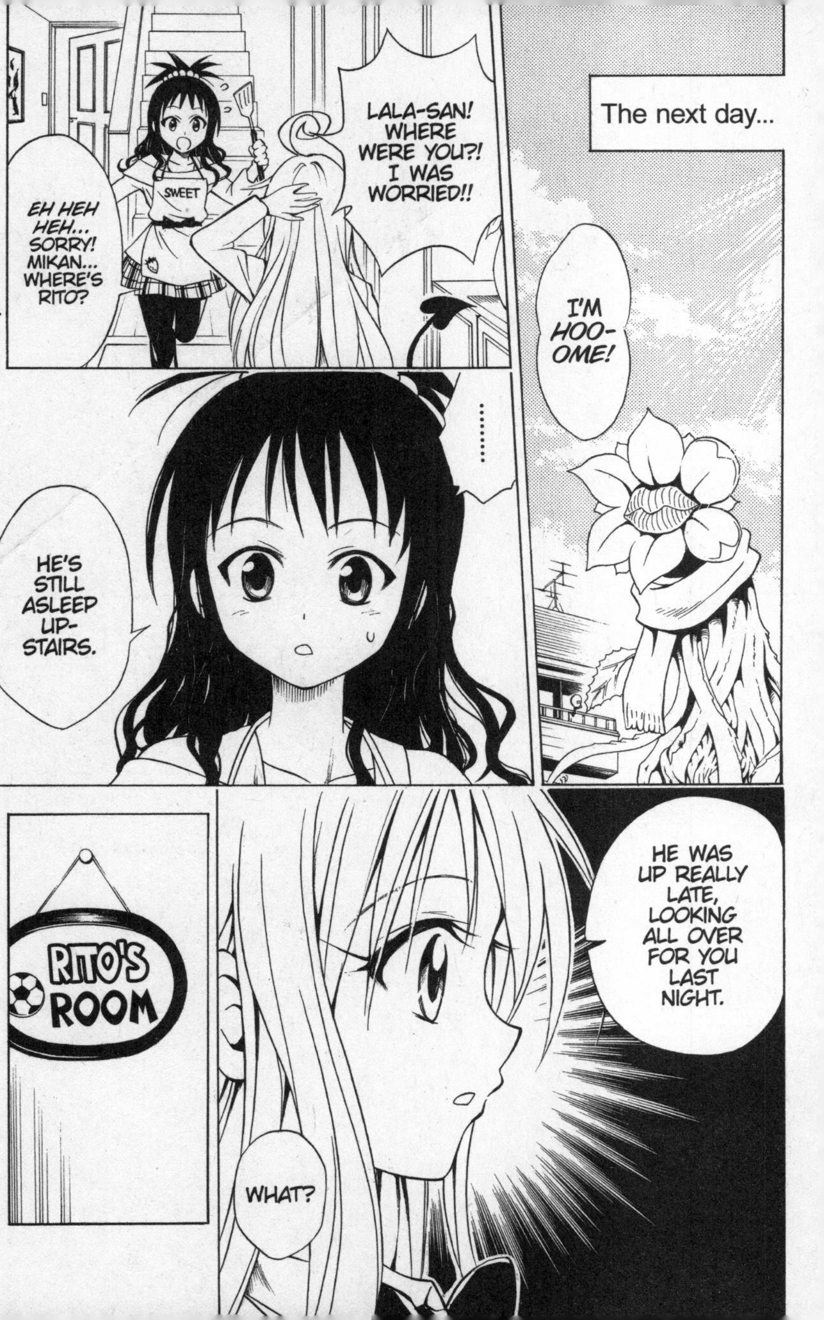
The next day...
I'M HOO-OME!
LALA-SAN! WHERE WERE YOU?! I WAS WORRIED!!
EH HEH HEH... SORRY! MIKAN... WHERE'S RITO?
......
HE'S STILL ASLEEP UP-STAIRS.
HE WAS UP REALLY LATE, LOOKING ALL OVER FOR YOU LAST NIGHT.
WHAT?
RITO'S ROOM

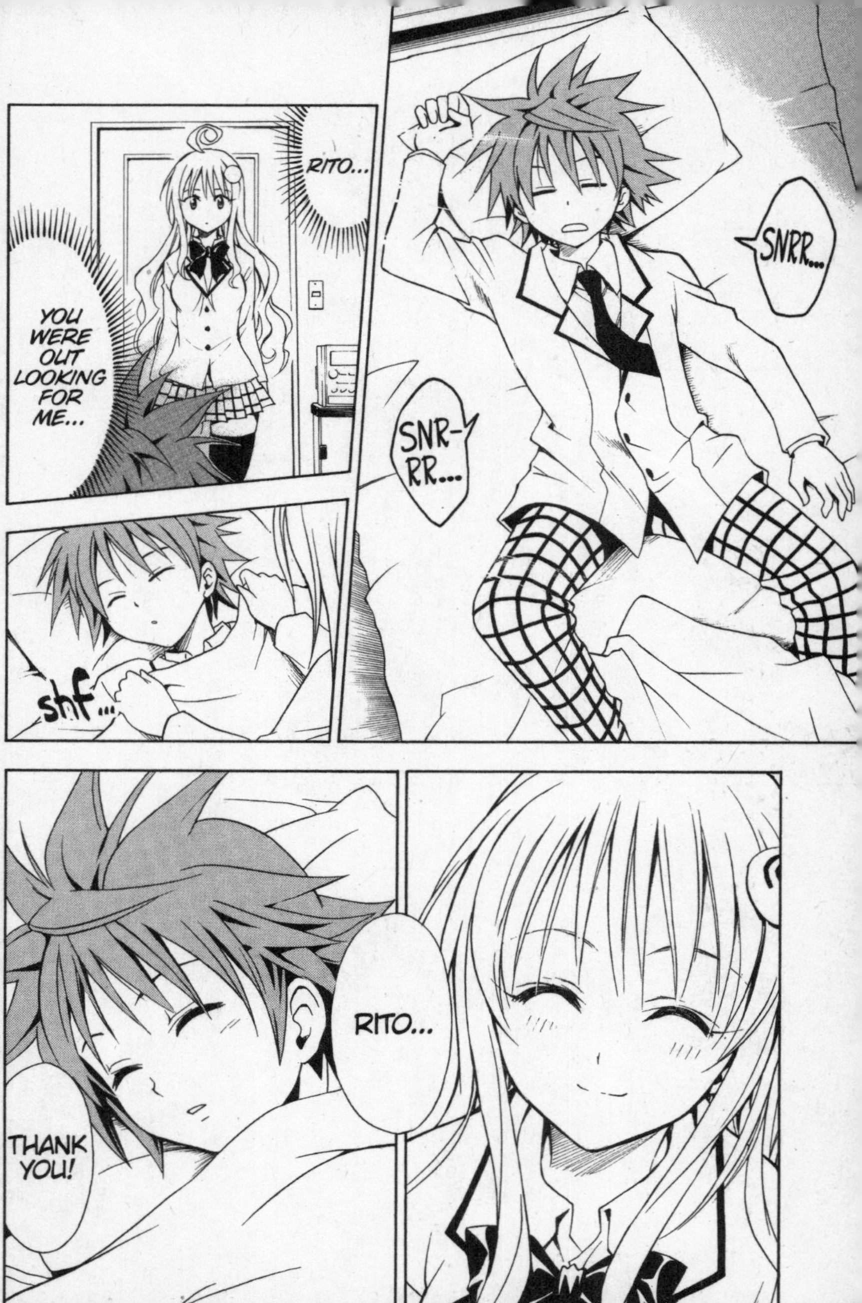

SNRR...
SNR-RR...
RITO...
YOU WERE OUT LOOKING FOR ME...
shf...
RITO...
THANK YOU!

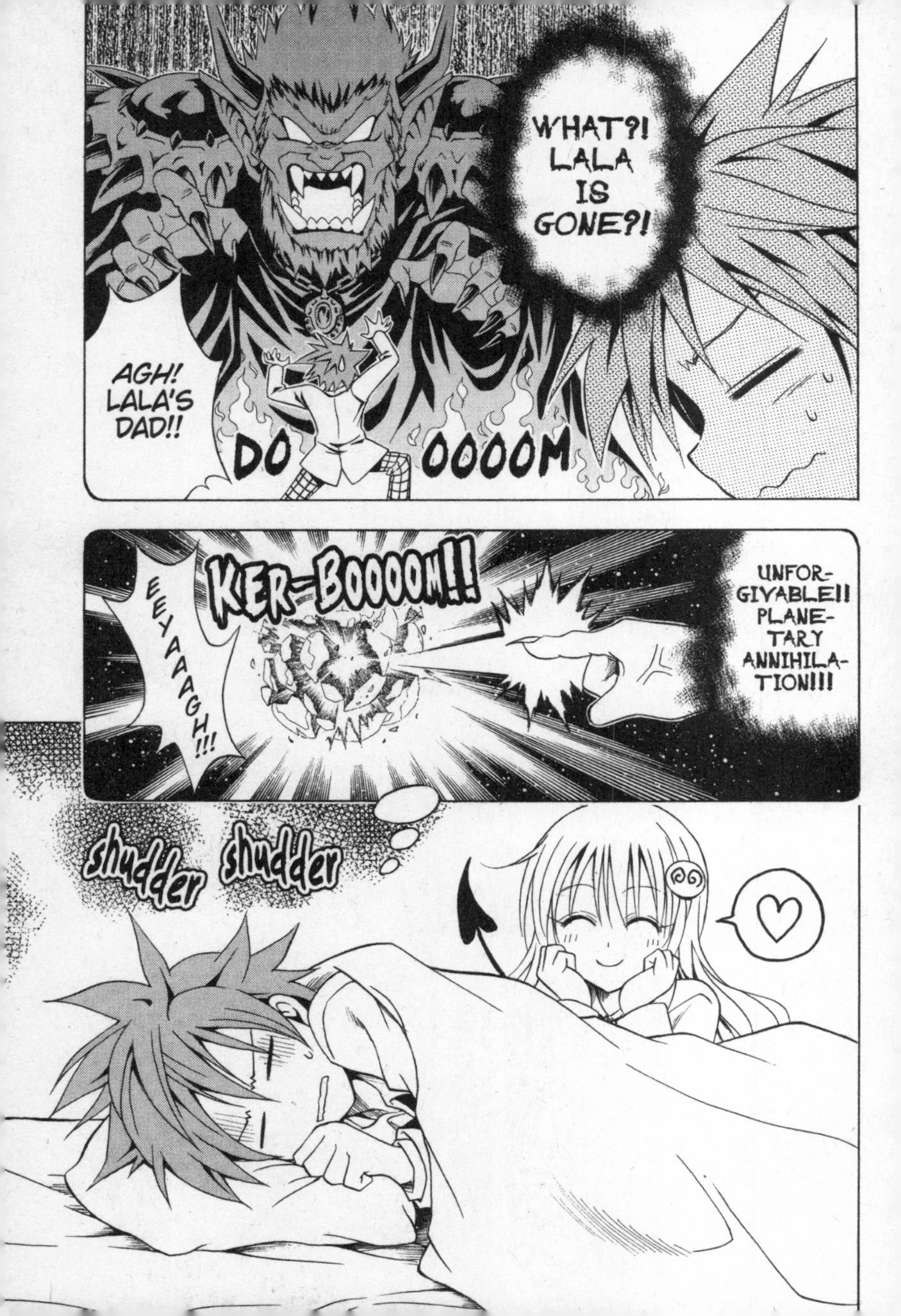
WHAT?! LALA IS GONE?!
AGH! LALA'S DAD!!
DOOOOOM
UNFORGIVABLE!! PLANETARY ANNIHILATION!!!
KER-BOOOOM!!!
EEYAAAAGH!!!
♡
shudder shudder

To LOVE Ru

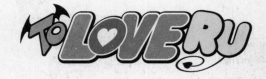

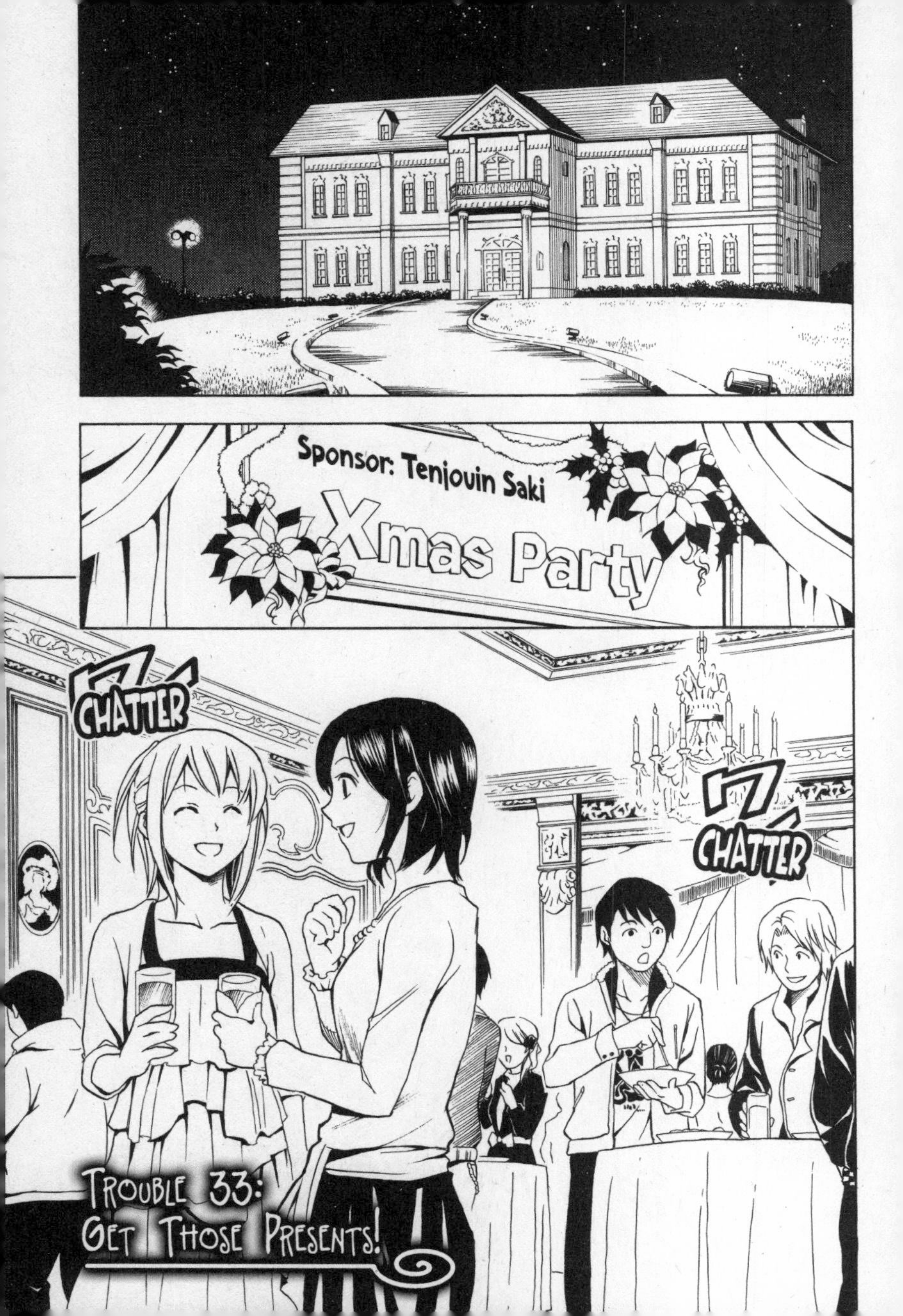
Sponsor: Tenjouin Saki
Xmas Party
CHATTER
CHATTER
Trouble 33:
Get Those Presents!

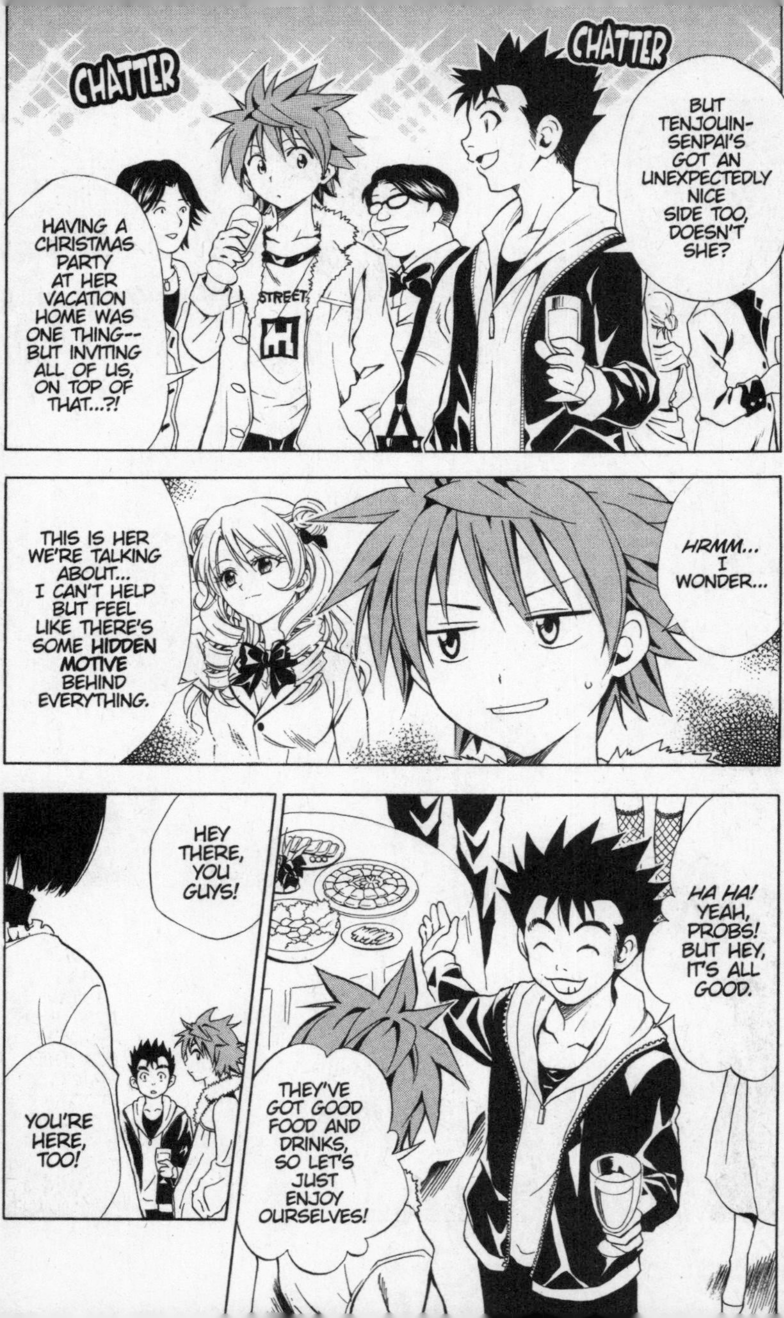
CHATTER
BUT TENJOUIN-SENPAI'S GOT AN UNEXPECTEDLY NICE SIDE TOO, DOESN'T SHE?
CHATTER
HAVING A CHRISTMAS PARTY AT HER VACATION HOME WAS ONE THING-- BUT INVITING ALL OF US, ON TOP OF THAT...?!
STREET
HRMM... I WONDER...
THIS IS HER WE'RE TALKING ABOUT... I CAN'T HELP BUT FEEL LIKE THERE'S SOME HIDDEN MOTIVE BEHIND EVERYTHING.
HA HA! YEAH, PROBS! BUT HEY, IT'S ALL GOOD.
THEY'VE GOT GOOD FOOD AND DRINKS, SO LET'S JUST ENJOY OURSELVES!
HEY THERE, YOU GUYS!
YOU'RE HERE, TOO!

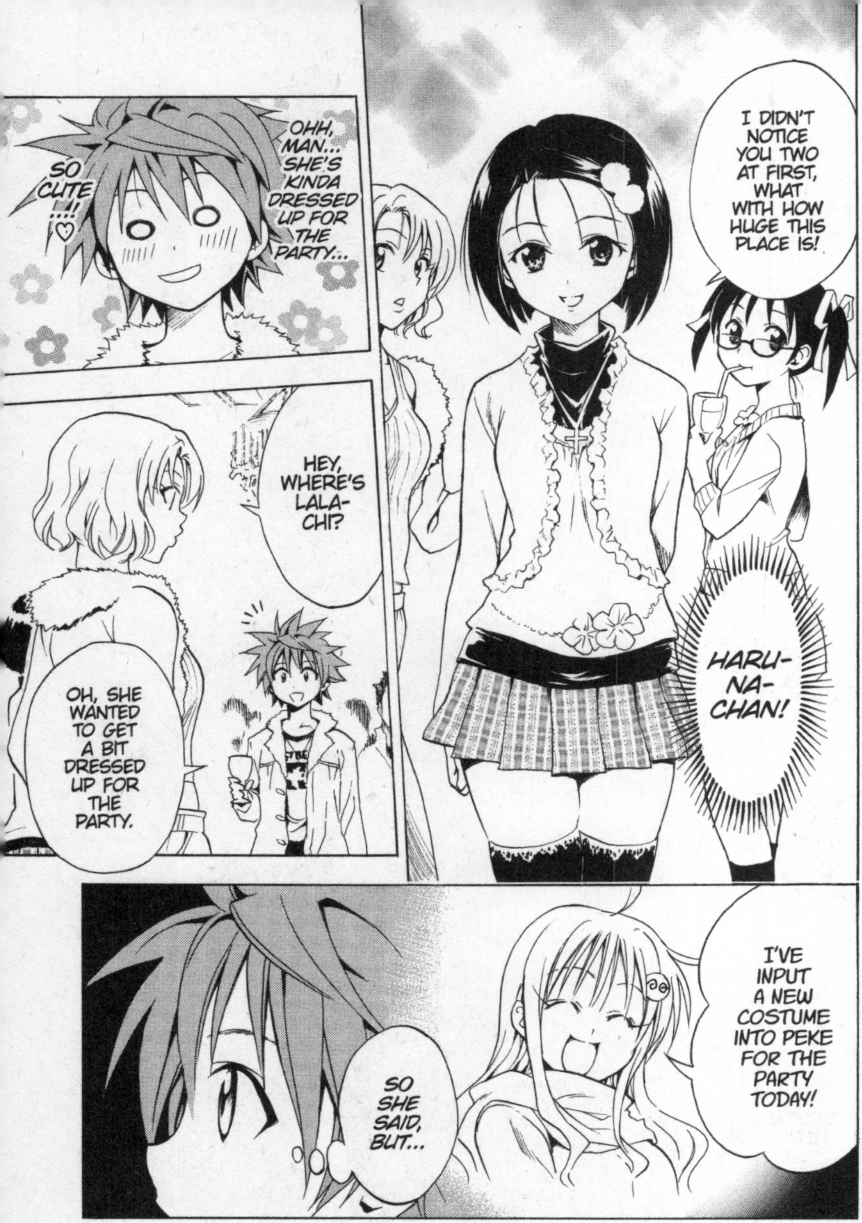
I DIDN'T NOTICE YOU TWO AT FIRST, WHAT WITH HOW HUGE THIS PLACE IS!
HARU-NA-CHAN!
OHH, MAN... SHE'S KINDA DRESSED UP FOR THE PARTY...
SO CUTE!!! ♡
HEY, WHERE'S LALA-CHI?
OH, SHE WANTED TO GET A BIT DRESSED UP FOR THE PARTY.
I'VE INPUT A NEW COSTUME INTO PEKE FOR THE PARTY TODAY!
SO SHE SAID, BUT...

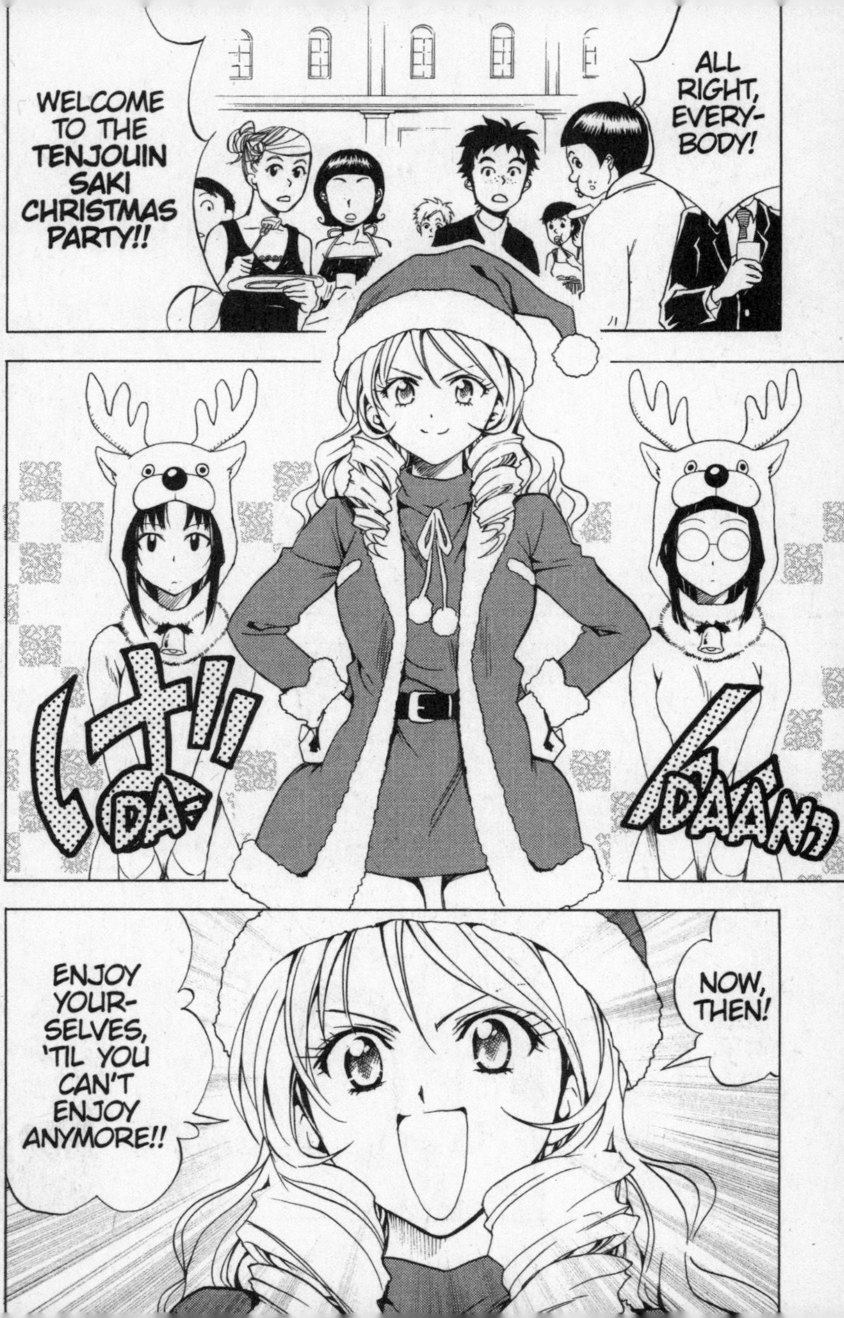
ALL RIGHT, EVERY-BODY!
WELCOME TO THE TENJOUIN SAKI CHRISTMAS PARTY!!
DA-
DAAAN
NOW, THEN!
ENJOY YOUR-SELVES, 'TIL YOU CAN'T ENJOY ANYMORE!!

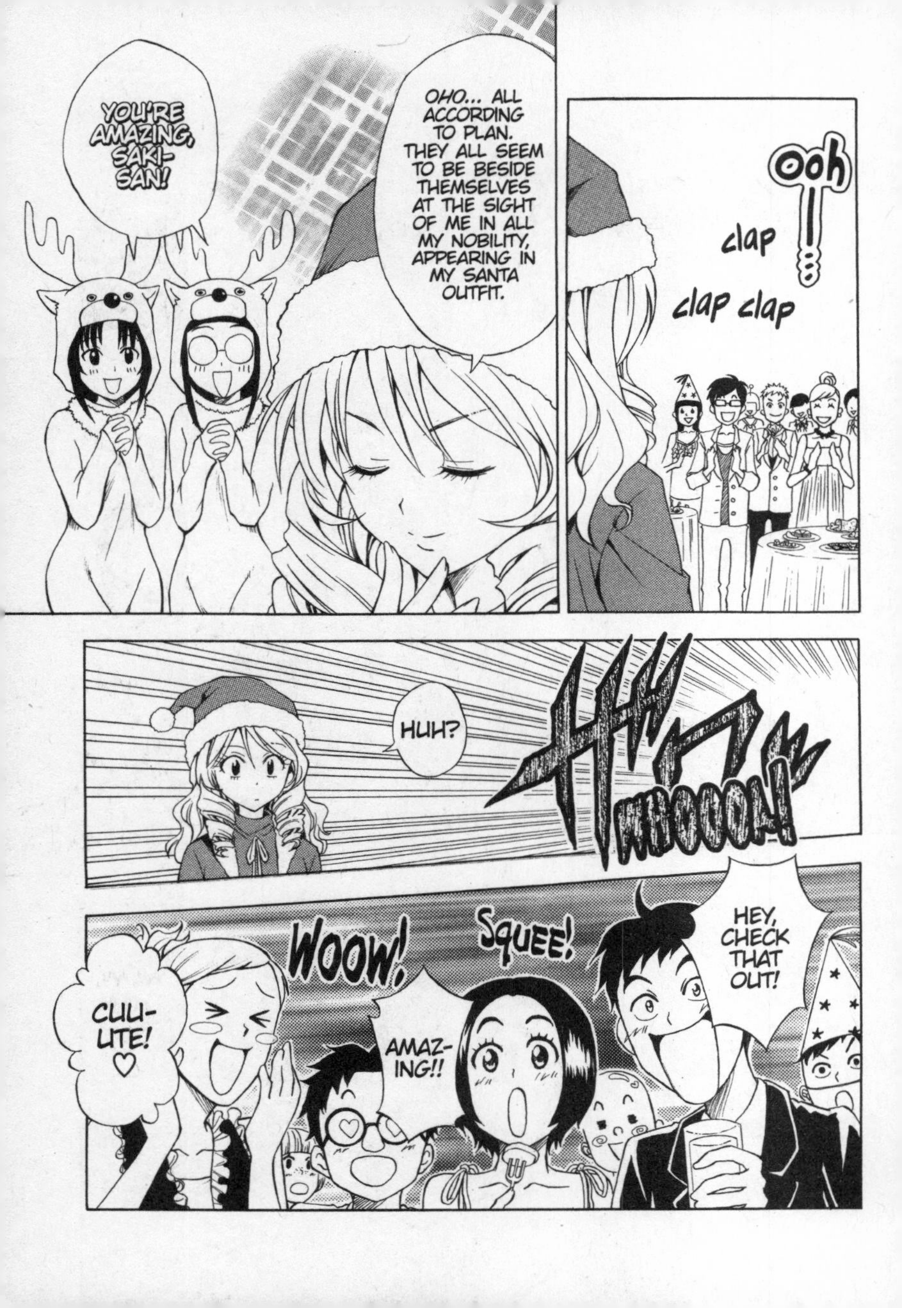
Ooh!...
clap
clap clap
OHO... ALL ACCORDING TO PLAN. THEY ALL SEEM TO BE BESIDE THEMSELVES AT THE SIGHT OF ME IN ALL MY NOBILITY, APPEARING IN MY SANTA OUTFIT.
YOU'RE AMAZING, SAKI-SAN!
WHOOOM!
HUH?
HEY, CHECK THAT OUT!
SQUEE!
AMAZ-ING!!
WOOW!
CUUU-UTE! ♡

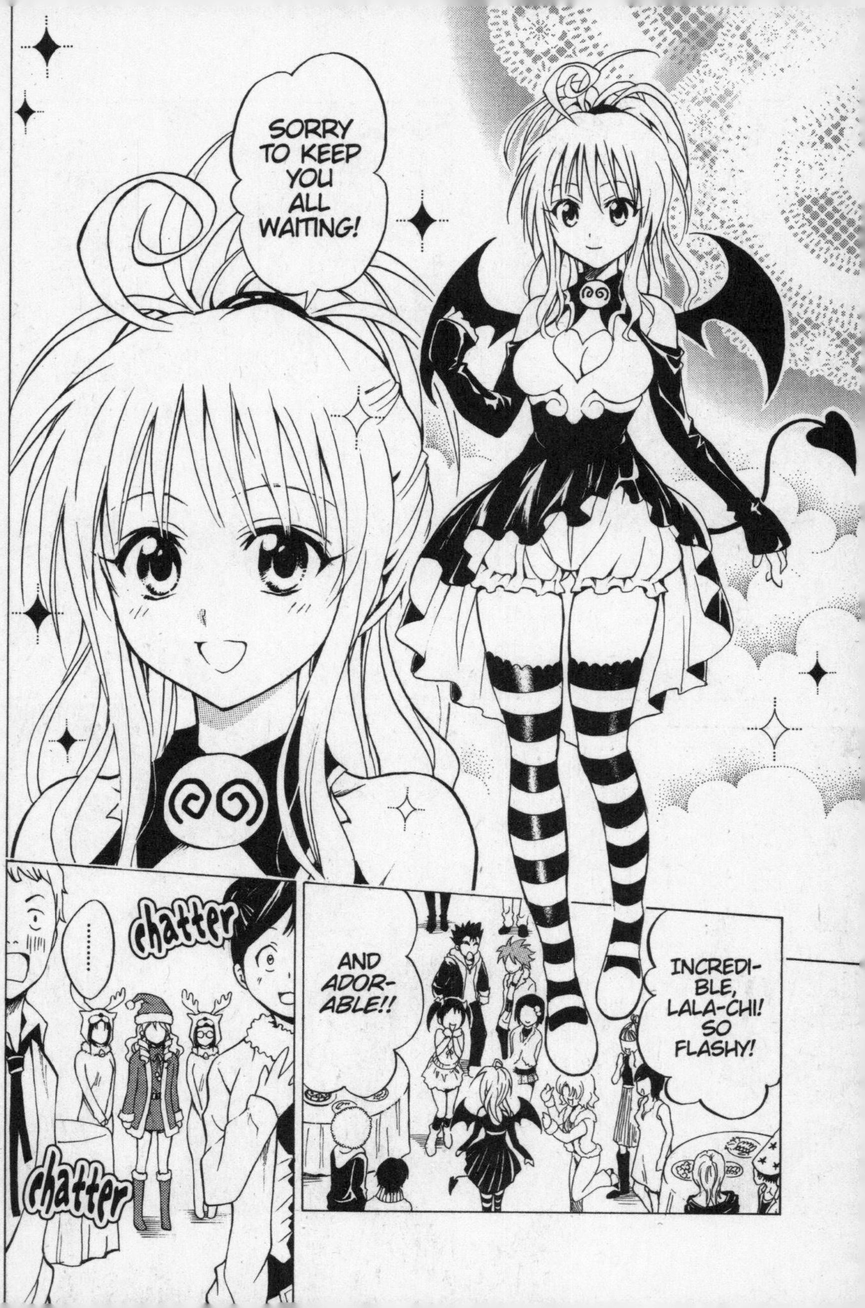
SORRY TO KEEP YOU ALL WAITING!
INCREDI-BLE, LALA-CHI! SO FLASHY!
AND ADOR-ABLE!!
chatter
......
chatter

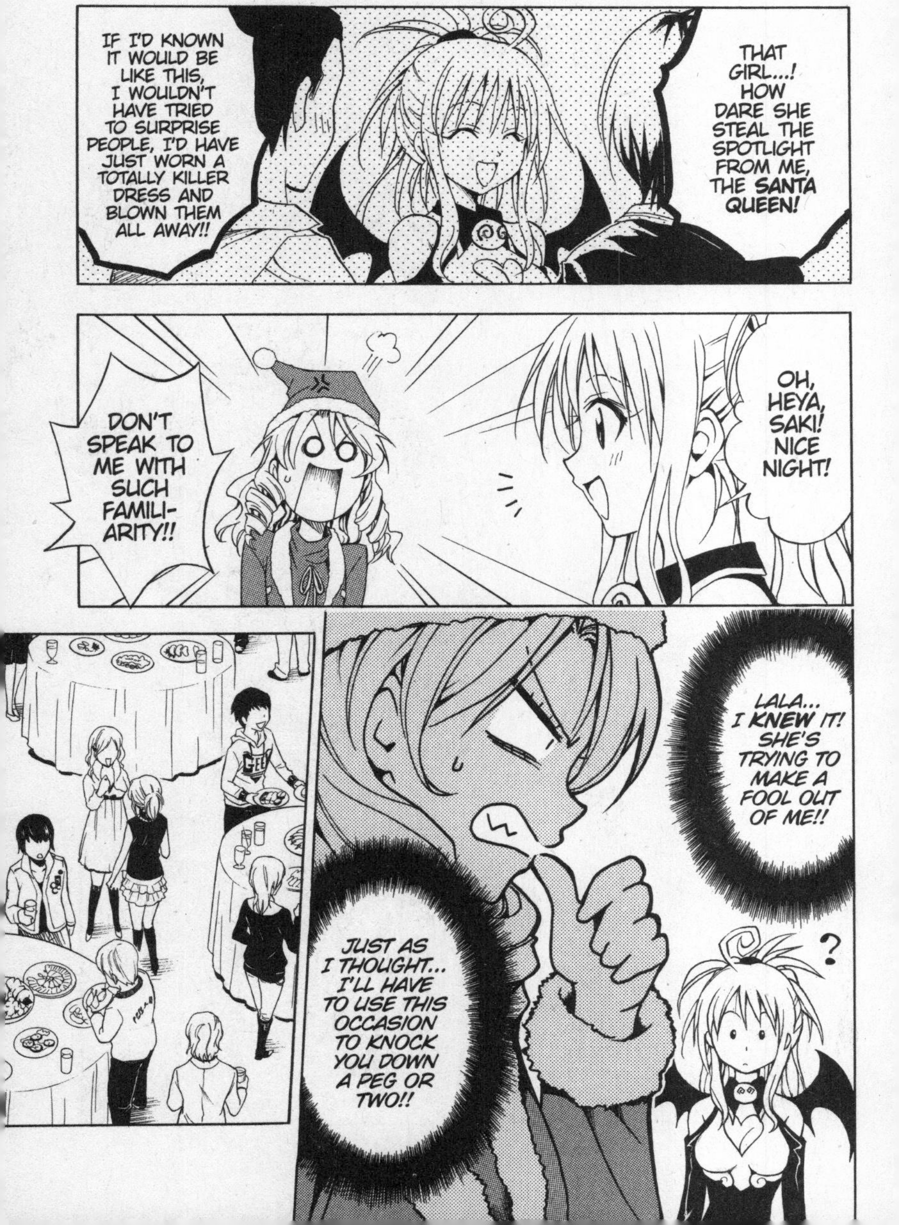
THAT GIRL...! HOW DARE SHE STEAL THE SPOTLIGHT FROM ME, THE SANTA QUEEN!
IF I'D KNOWN IT WOULD BE LIKE THIS, I WOULDN'T HAVE TRIED TO SURPRISE PEOPLE, I'D HAVE JUST WORN A TOTALLY KILLER DRESS AND BLOWN THEM ALL AWAY!!
OH, HEYA, SAKI! NICE NIGHT!
DON'T SPEAK TO ME WITH SUCH FAMILI-ARITY!!
LALA... I KNEW IT! SHE'S TRYING TO MAKE A FOOL OUT OF ME!!
?
JUST AS I THOUGHT... I'LL HAVE TO USE THIS OCCASION TO KNOCK YOU DOWN A PEG OR TWO!!

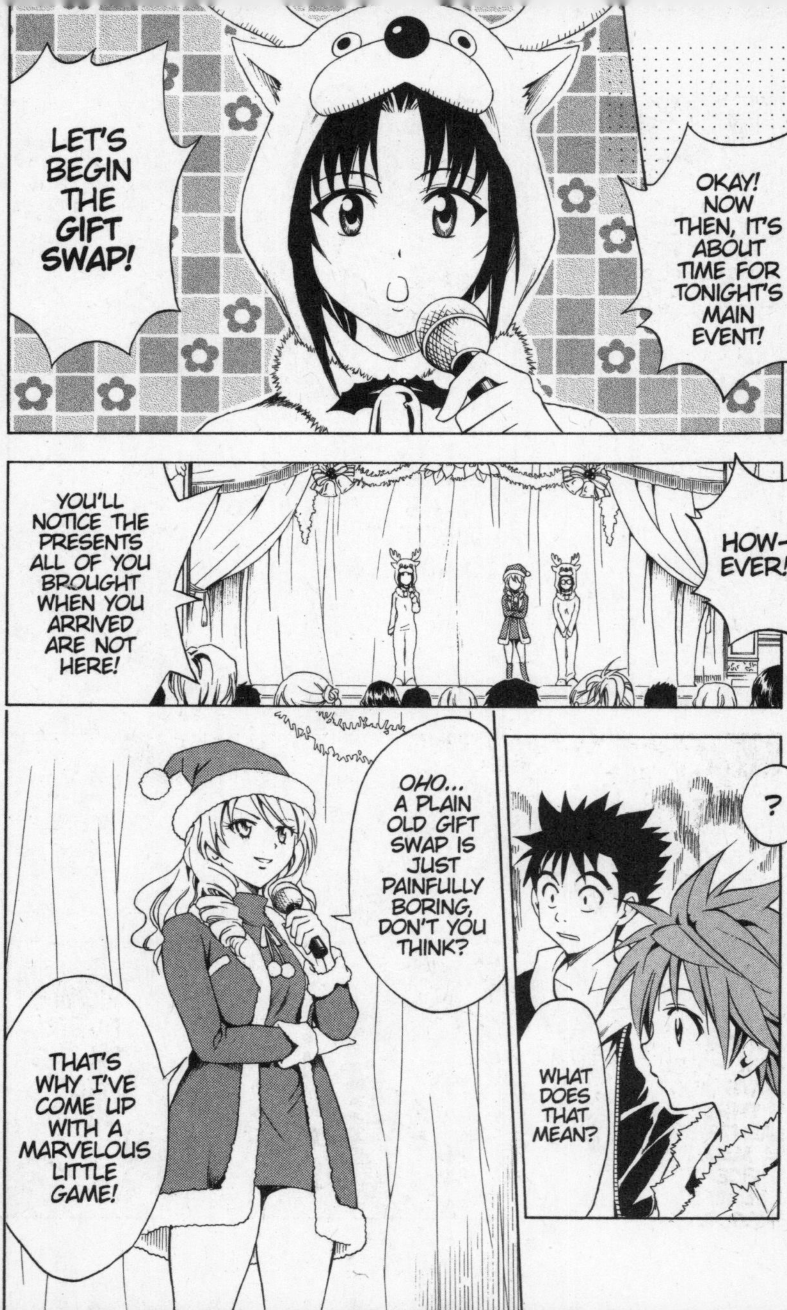
OKAY! NOW THEN, IT'S ABOUT TIME FOR TONIGHT'S MAIN EVENT!
LET'S BEGIN THE GIFT SWAP!
HOW-EVER!
YOU'LL NOTICE THE PRESENTS ALL OF YOU BROUGHT WHEN YOU ARRIVED ARE NOT HERE!
?
WHAT DOES THAT MEAN?
OHO... A PLAIN OLD GIFT SWAP IS JUST PAINFULLY BORING, DON'T YOU THINK?
THAT'S WHY I'VE COME UP WITH A MARVELOUS LITTLE GAME!

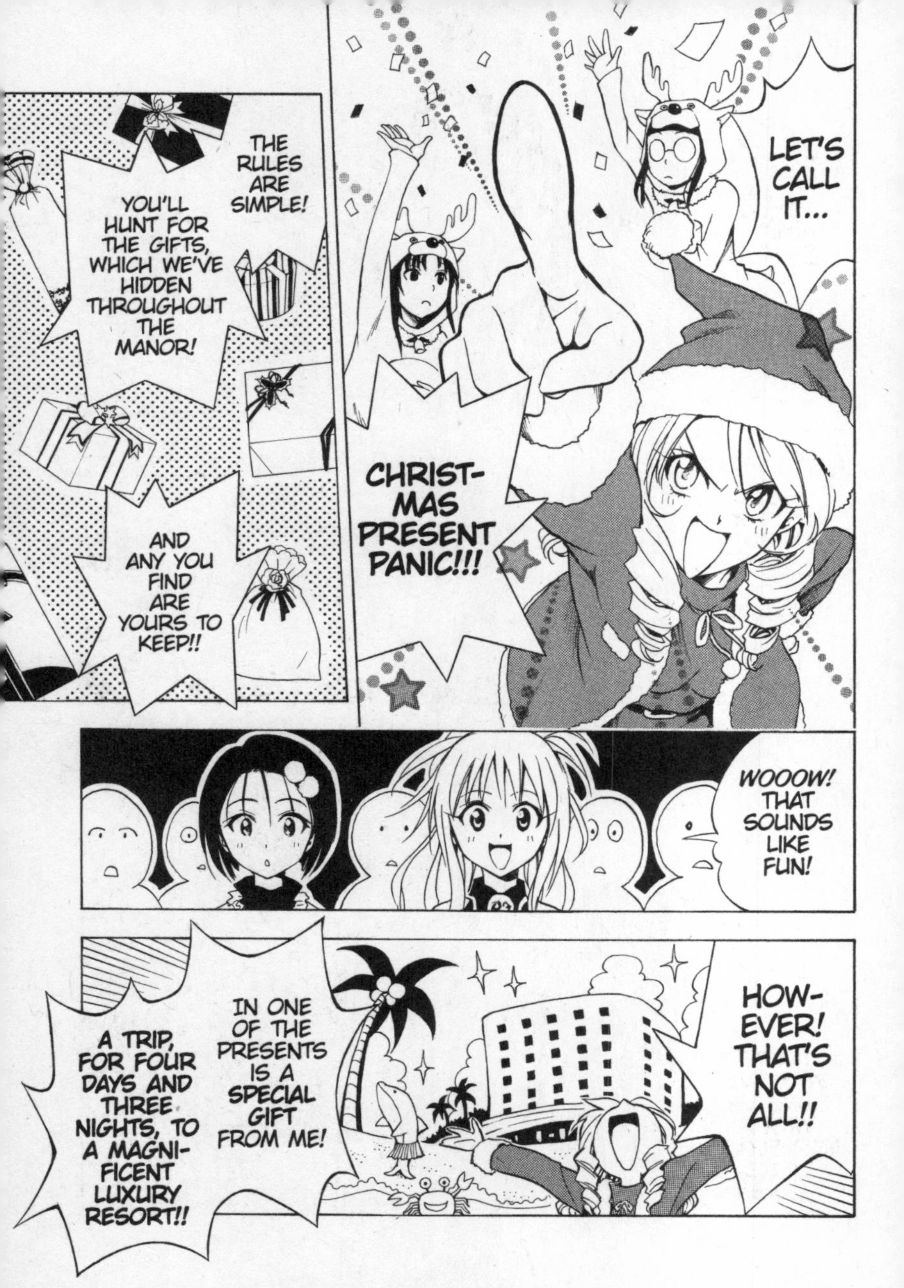
LET'S CALL IT...
CHRISTMAS PRESENT PANIC!!!
THE RULES ARE SIMPLE!
YOU'LL HUNT FOR THE GIFTS, WHICH WE'VE HIDDEN THROUGHOUT THE MANOR!
AND ANY YOU FIND ARE YOURS TO KEEP!!
WOOOW! THAT SOUNDS LIKE FUN!
HOWEVER! THAT'S NOT ALL!!
IN ONE OF THE PRESENTS IS A SPECIAL GIFT FROM ME!
A TRIP, FOR FOUR DAYS AND THREE NIGHTS, TO A MAGNIFICENT LUXURY RESORT!!

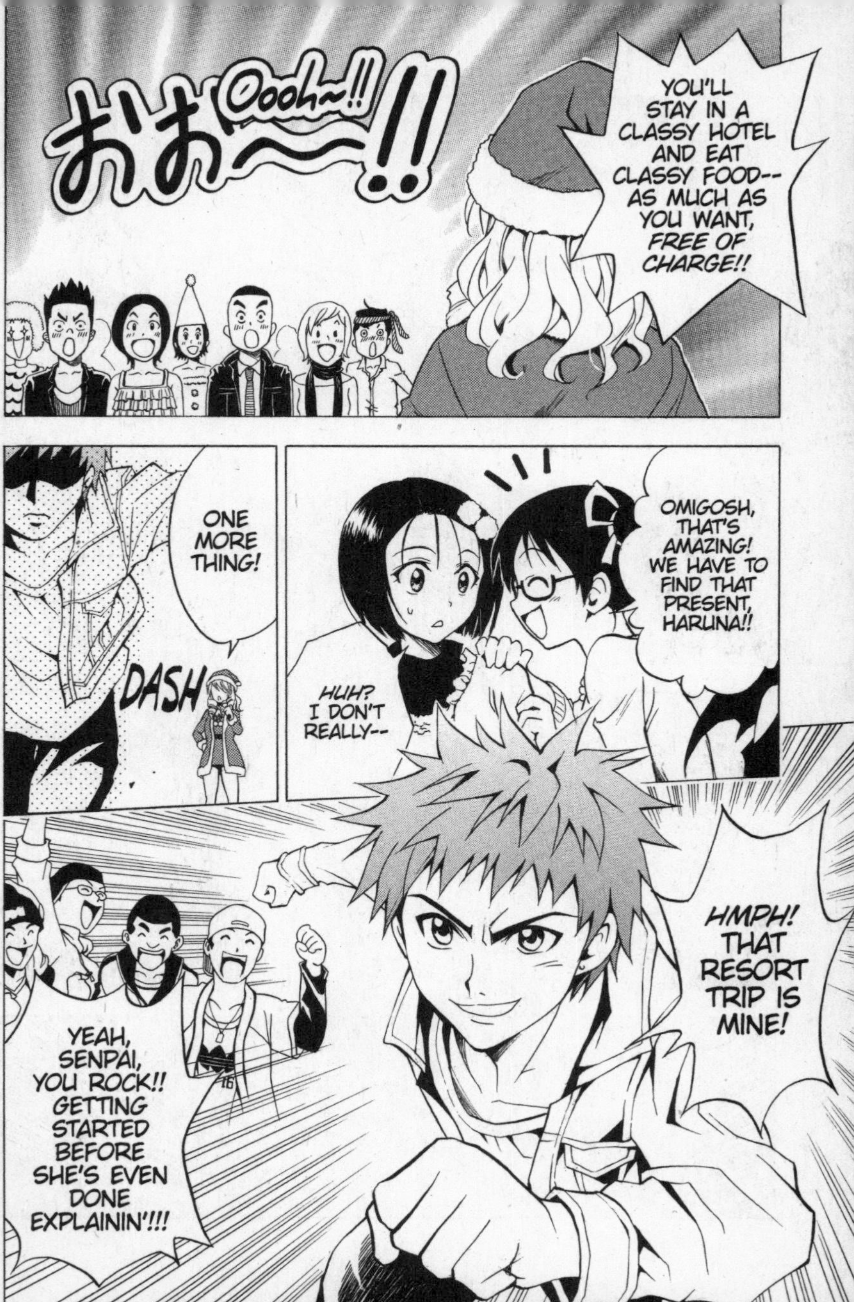
YOU'LL STAY IN A CLASSY HOTEL AND EAT CLASSY FOOD-- AS MUCH AS YOU WANT, FREE OF CHARGE!!
おお〜〜!!
Oooh~!!
OMIGOSH, THAT'S AMAZING! WE HAVE TO FIND THAT PRESENT, HARUNA!!
HUH? I DON'T REALLY--
ONE MORE THING!
DASH
HMPH! THAT RESORT TRIP IS MINE!
YEAH, SENPAI, YOU ROCK!! GETTING STARTED BEFORE SHE'S EVEN DONE EXPLAININ'!!!

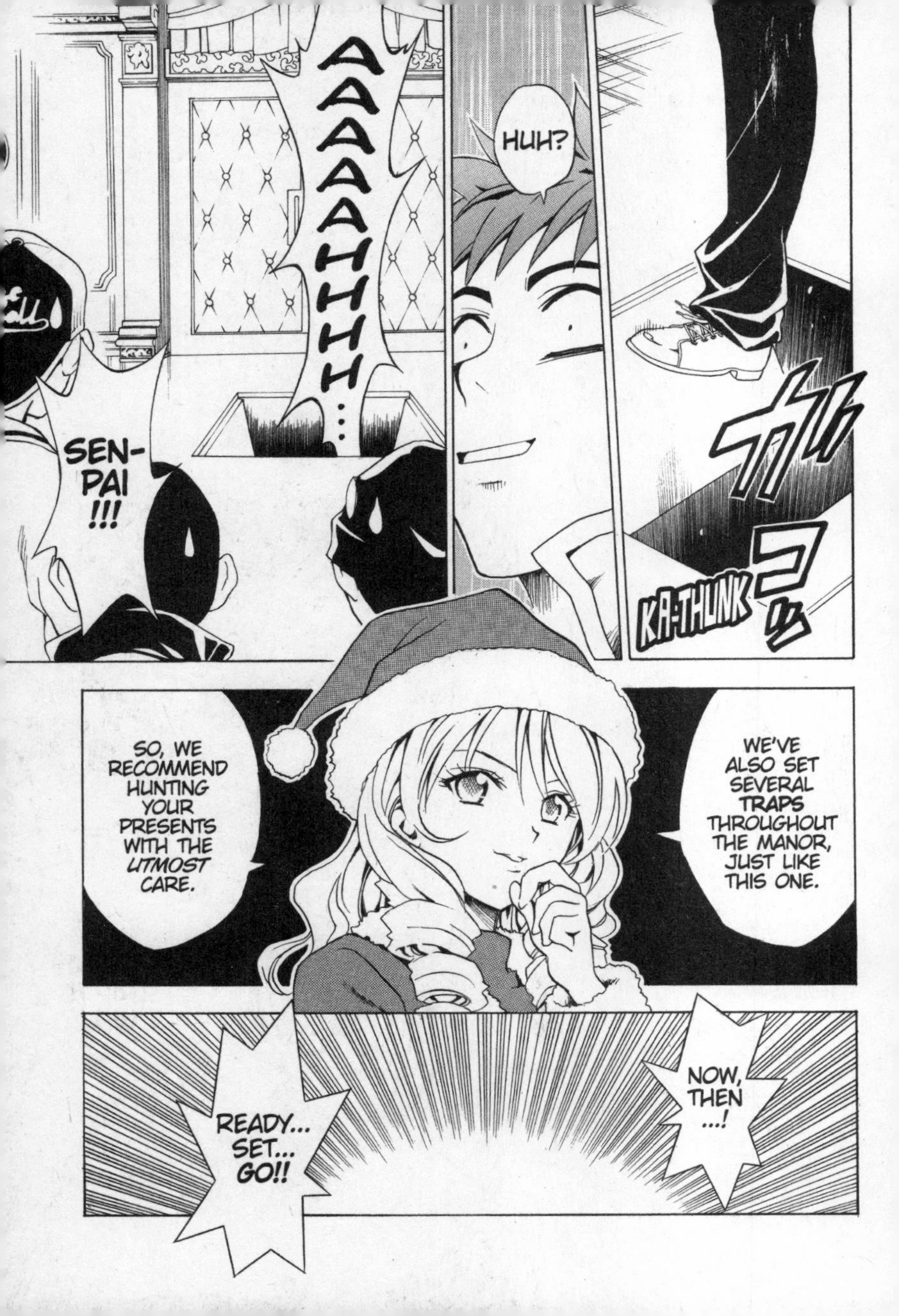
KA-THUNK
HUH?
AAAAAHHHH...
SEN-PAI!!!
WE'VE ALSO SET SEVERAL TRAPS THROUGHOUT THE MANOR, JUST LIKE THIS ONE.
SO, WE RECOMMEND HUNTING YOUR PRESENTS WITH THE *UTMOST* CARE.
NOW, THEN ...!
READY... SET... GO!!

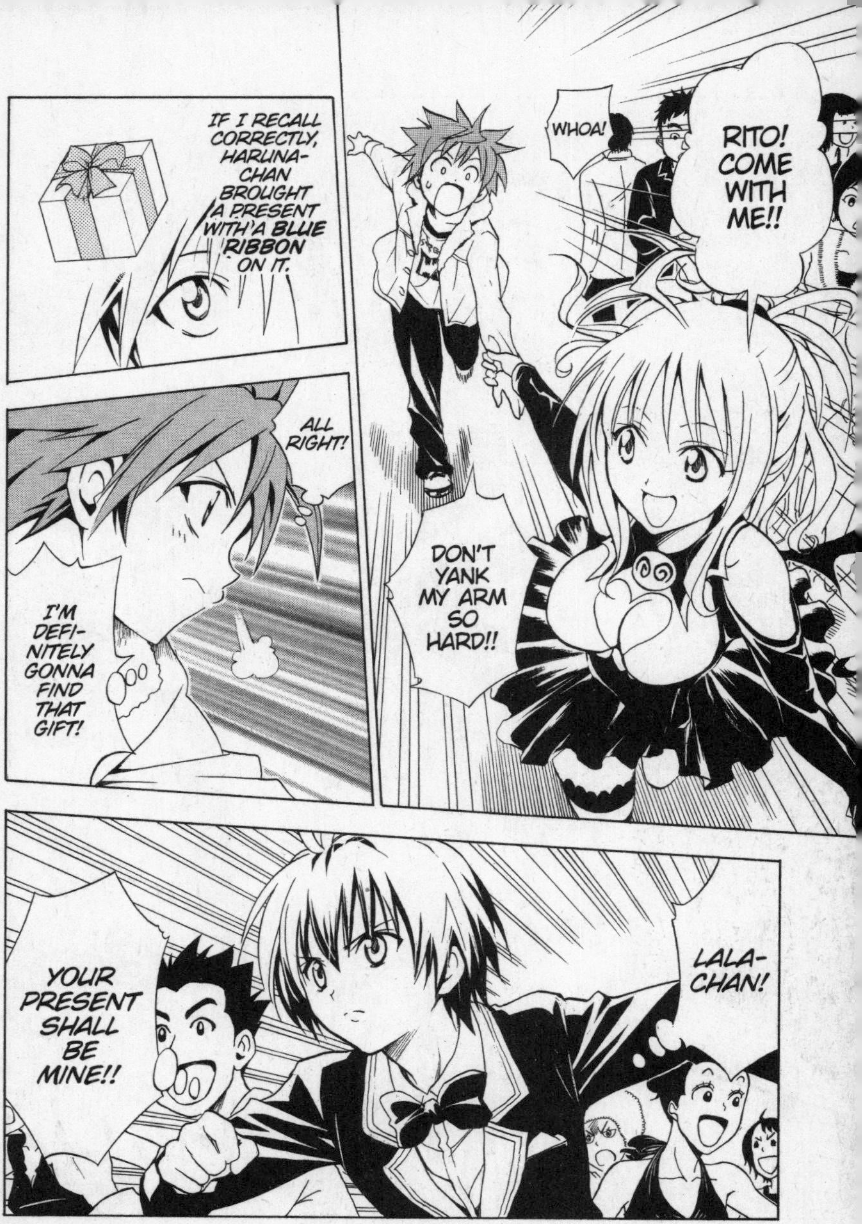
RITO! COME WITH ME!!
WHOA!
DON'T YANK MY ARM SO HARD!!
IF I RECALL CORRECTLY, HARUNA-CHAN BROUGHT A PRESENT WITH A BLUE RIBBON ON IT.
ALL RIGHT!
I'M DEFINITELY GONNA FIND THAT GIFT!
LALA-CHAN!
YOUR PRESENT SHALL BE MINE!!

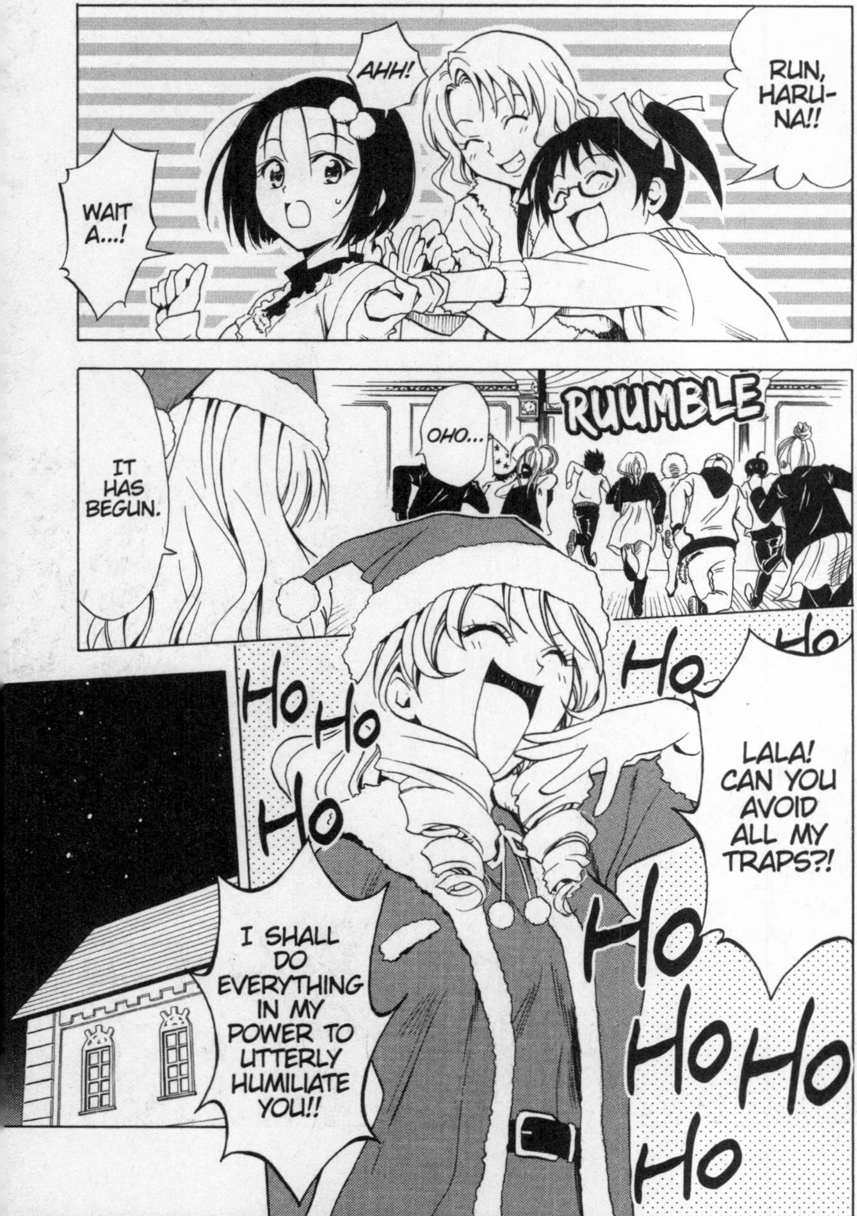
RUN, HARU-NA!!
AHH!
WAIT A...!
RUUMBLE
OHO...
IT HAS BEGUN.
Ho
Ho
LALA! CAN YOU AVOID ALL MY TRAPS?!
Ho Ho Ho Ho
I SHALL DO EVERYTHING IN MY POWER TO UTTERLY HUMILIATE YOU!!
Ho Ho
Ho

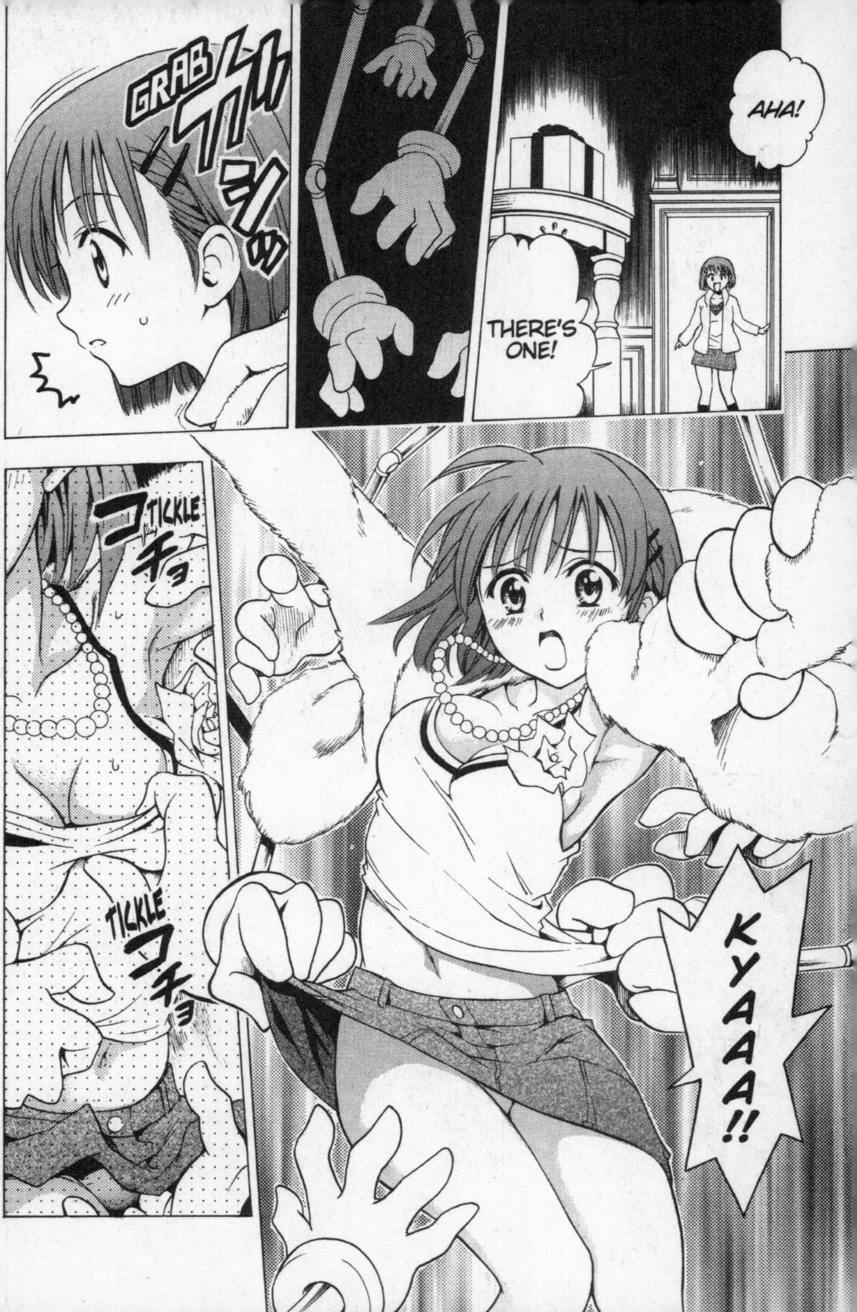
AHA!
THERE'S ONE!
GRAB
KYAAAA!!
TICKLE
TICKLE

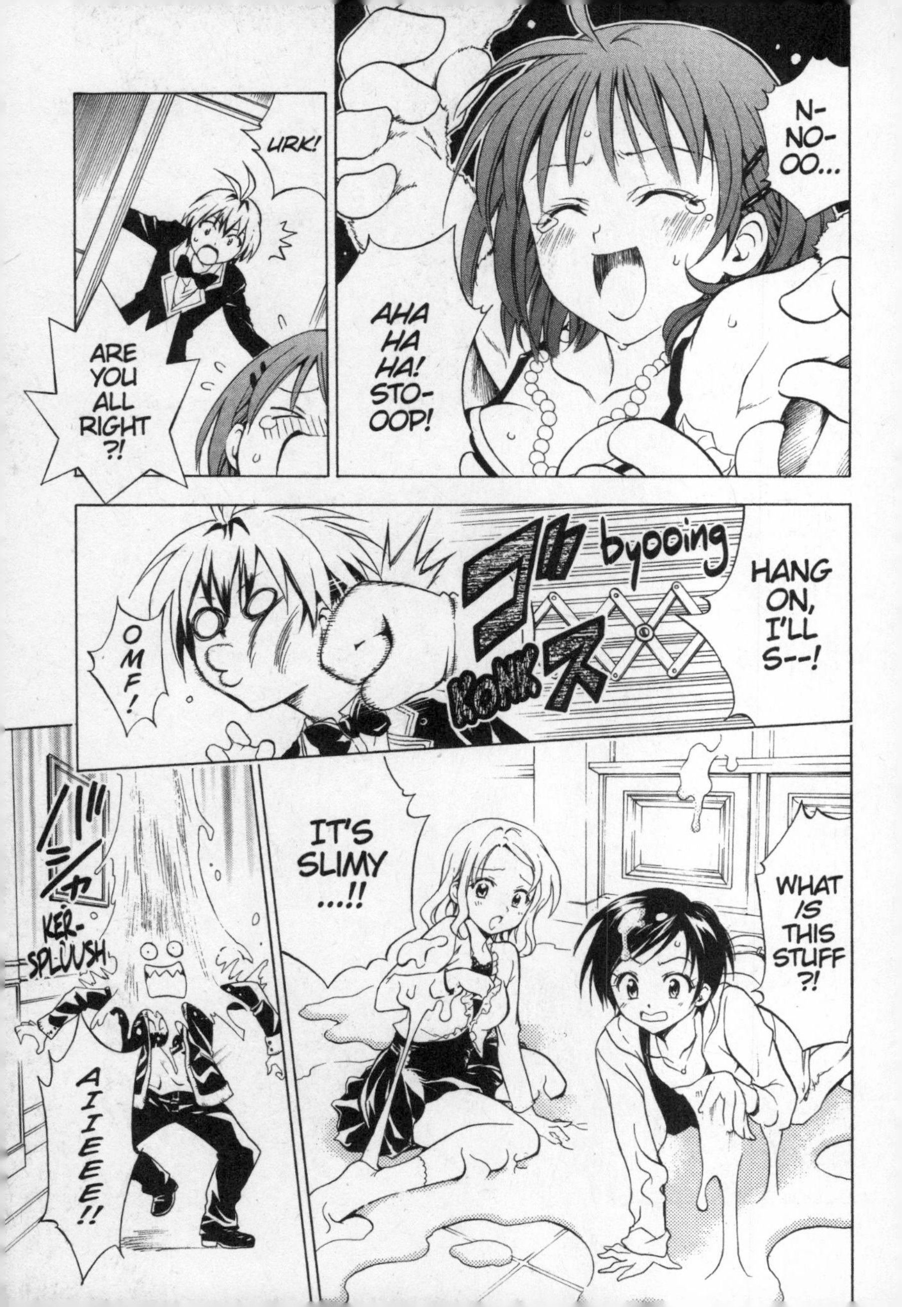
N-NO-OO...
AHA HA HA! STO-OOP!
URK!
ARE YOU ALL RIGHT?!
HANG ON, I'LL S--!
byooing
KONK
OMF!
WHAT IS THIS STUFF?!
IT'S SLIMY...!!
KER-SPLUUSH
AIIEEEE!!

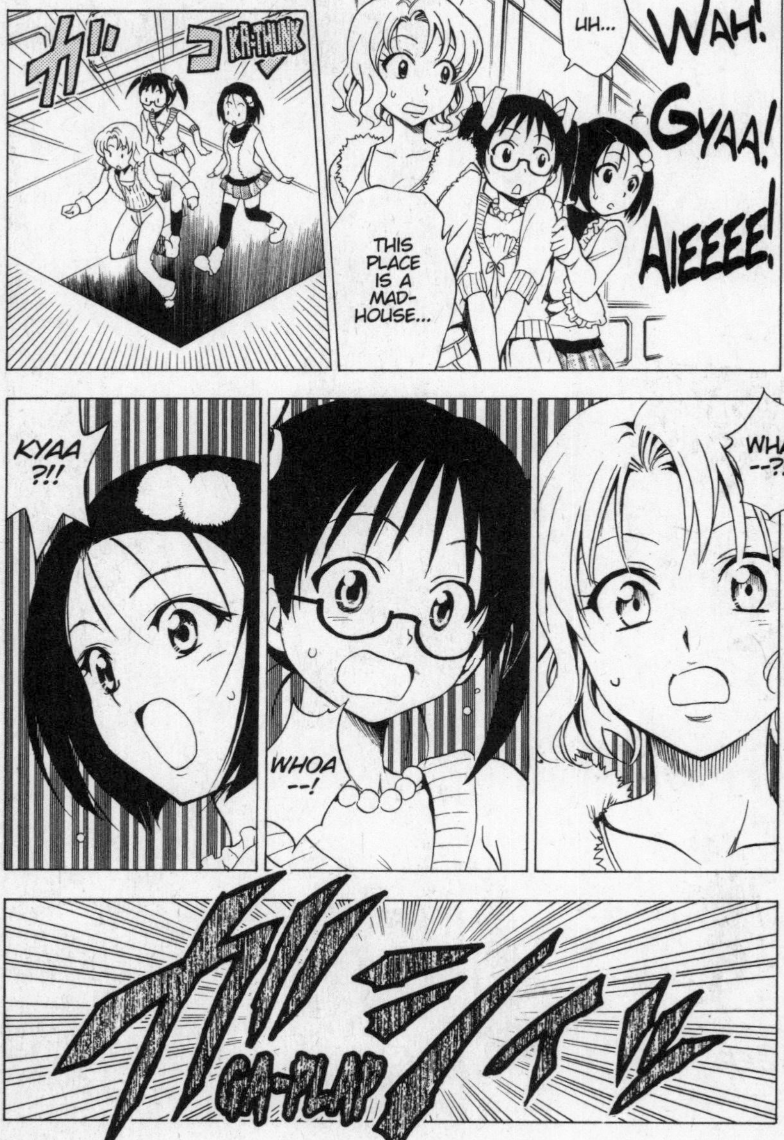
WAH!
GYAA!
AIEEEE!
UH...
THIS PLACE IS A MAD-HOUSE...
KA-THUNK
WHA--?!
WHOA--!
KYAA?!!
CA-FLIP

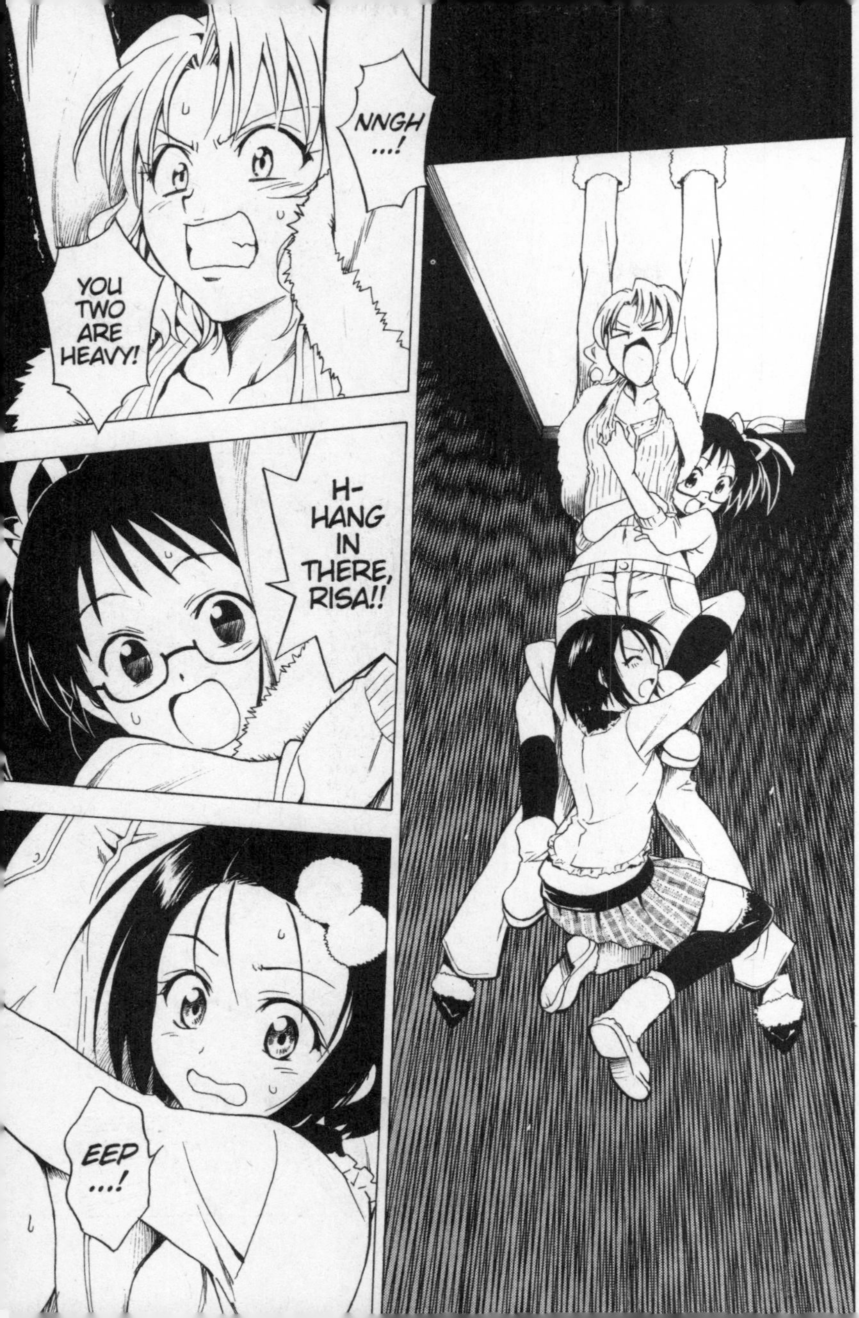
NNGH ...!
YOU TWO ARE HEAVY!
H- HANG IN THERE, RISA!!
EEP ...!

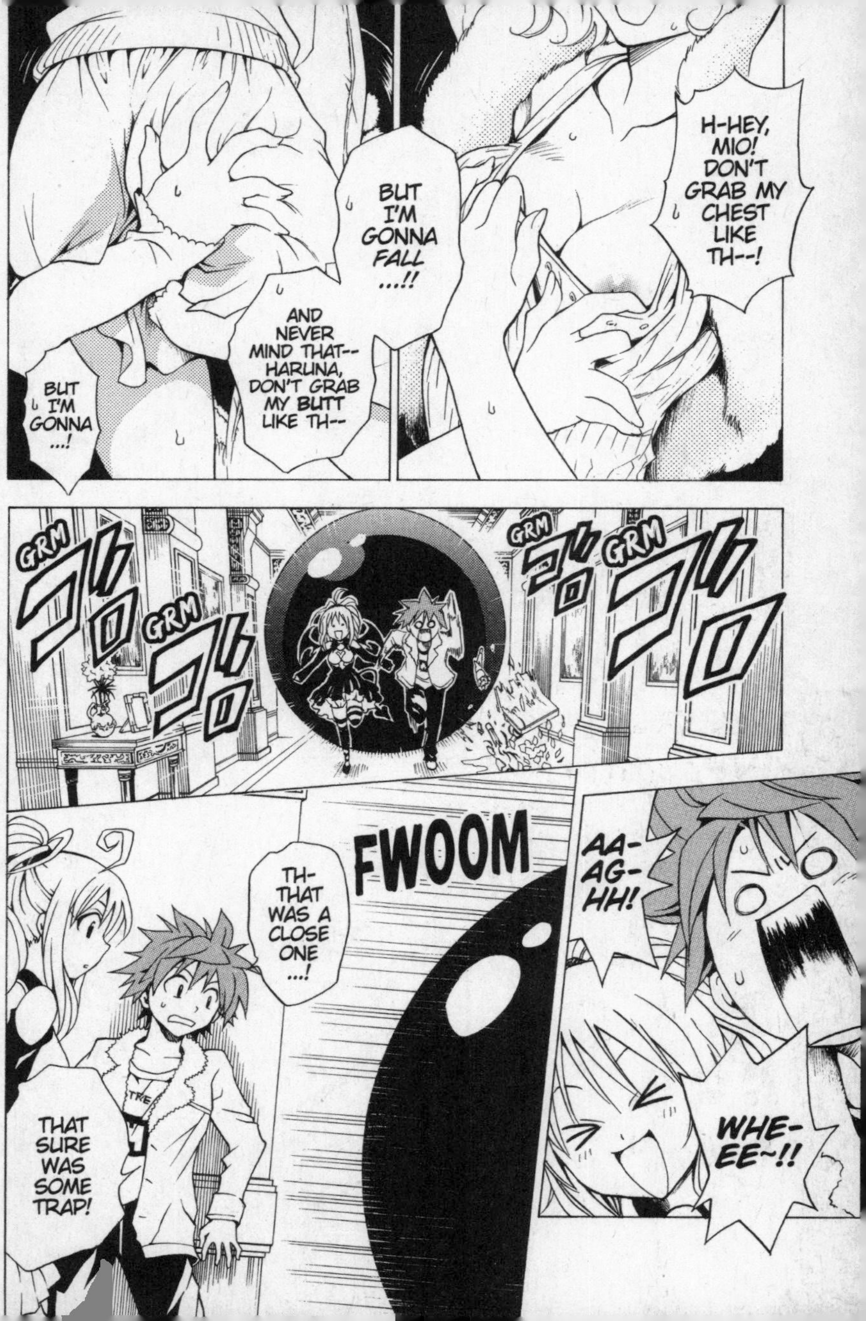
H-HEY, MIO! DON'T GRAB MY CHEST LIKE TH--!
BUT I'M GONNA FALL ...!!
AND NEVER MIND THAT-- HARUNA, DON'T GRAB MY BUTT LIKE TH--
BUT I'M GONNA ...!
GRM
GRM
GRM
GRM
AA-AG-HH!
WHEE-EE~!!
FWOOM
TH-THAT WAS A CLOSE ONE ...!
THAT SURE WAS SOME TRAP!

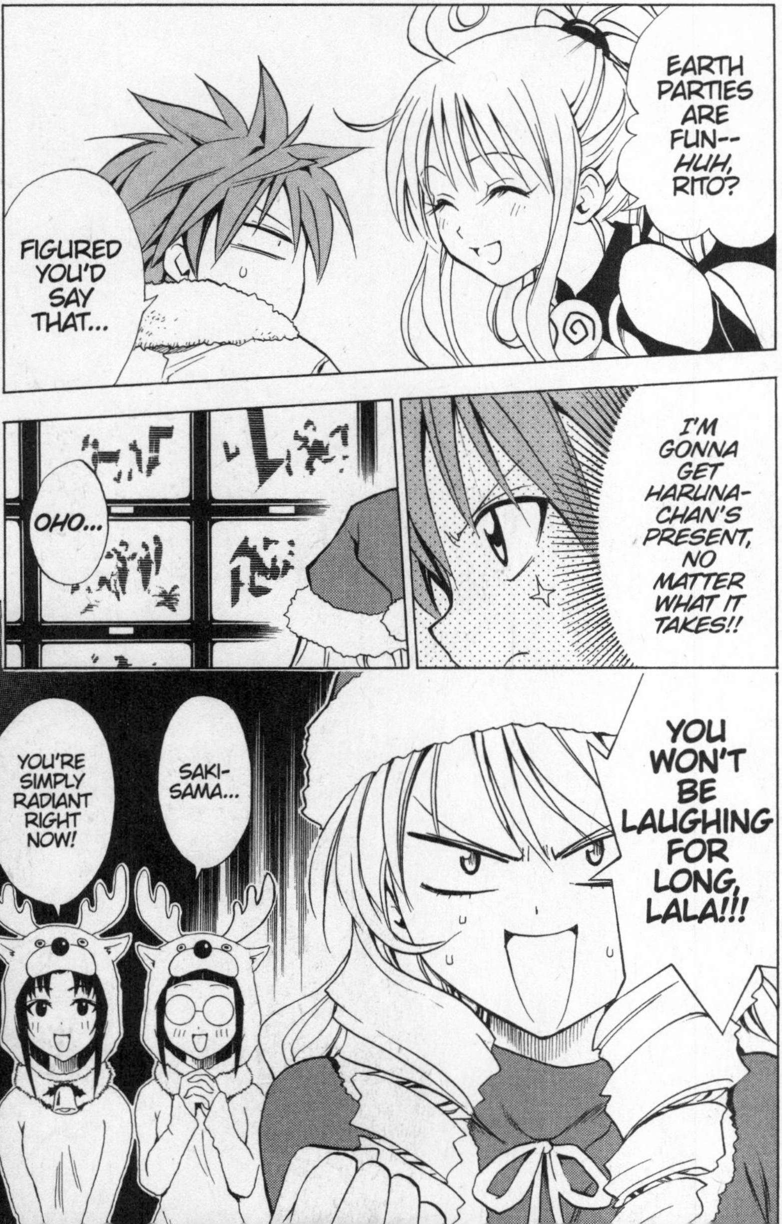
EARTH PARTIES ARE FUN-- HUH, RITO?
FIGURED YOU'D SAY THAT...
I'M GONNA GET HARUNA-CHAN'S PRESENT, NO MATTER WHAT IT TAKES!!
OHO...
YOU WON'T BE LAUGHING FOR LONG, LALA!!!
SAKI-SAMA...
YOU'RE SIMPLY RADIANT RIGHT NOW!

To LOVE Ru

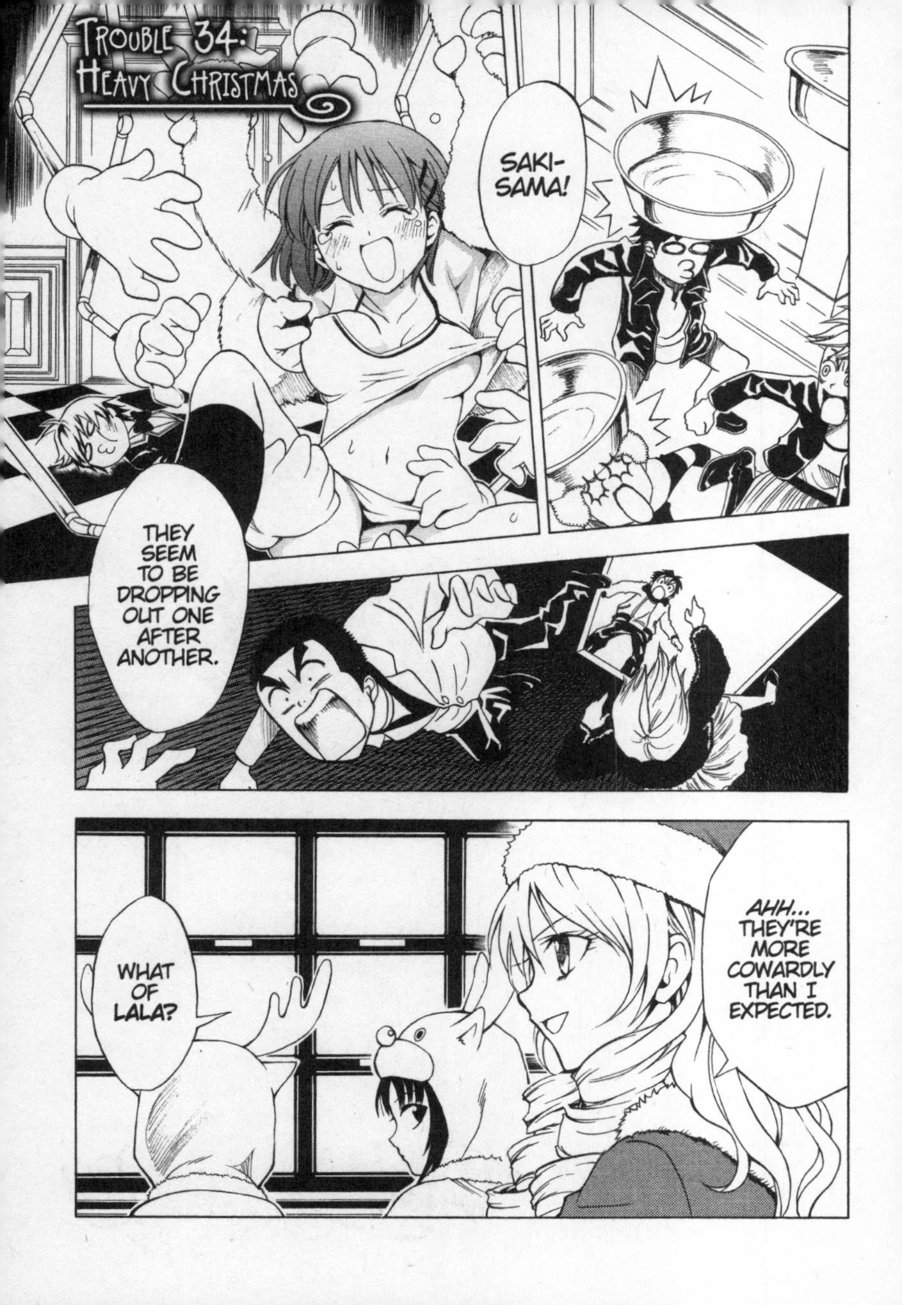
SAKI-SAMA!
Trouble 34: Heavy Christmas
THEY SEEM TO BE DROPPING OUT ONE AFTER ANOTHER.
AHH... THEY'RE MORE COWARDLY THAN I EXPECTED.
WHAT OF LALA?

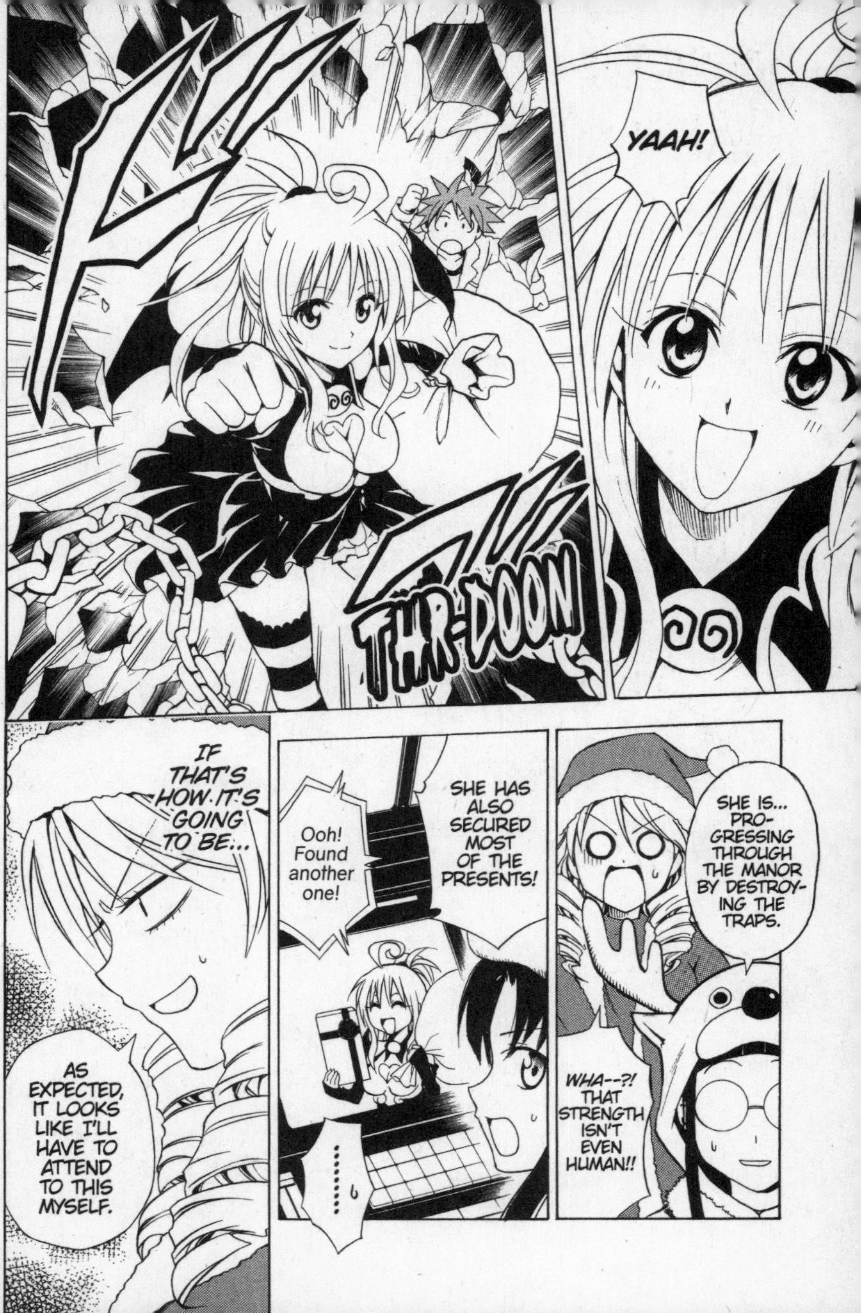
YAAH!
THR-DOON
SHE IS... PRO-GRESSING THROUGH THE MANOR BY DESTROY-ING THE TRAPS.
WHA--?! THAT STRENGTH ISN'T EVEN HUMAN!!
SHE HAS ALSO SECURED MOST OF THE PRESENTS!
Ooh! Found another one!
......
IF THAT'S HOW IT'S GOING TO BE...
AS EXPECTED, IT LOOKS LIKE I'LL HAVE TO ATTEND TO THIS MYSELF.

Trouble 34: Heavy Christmas

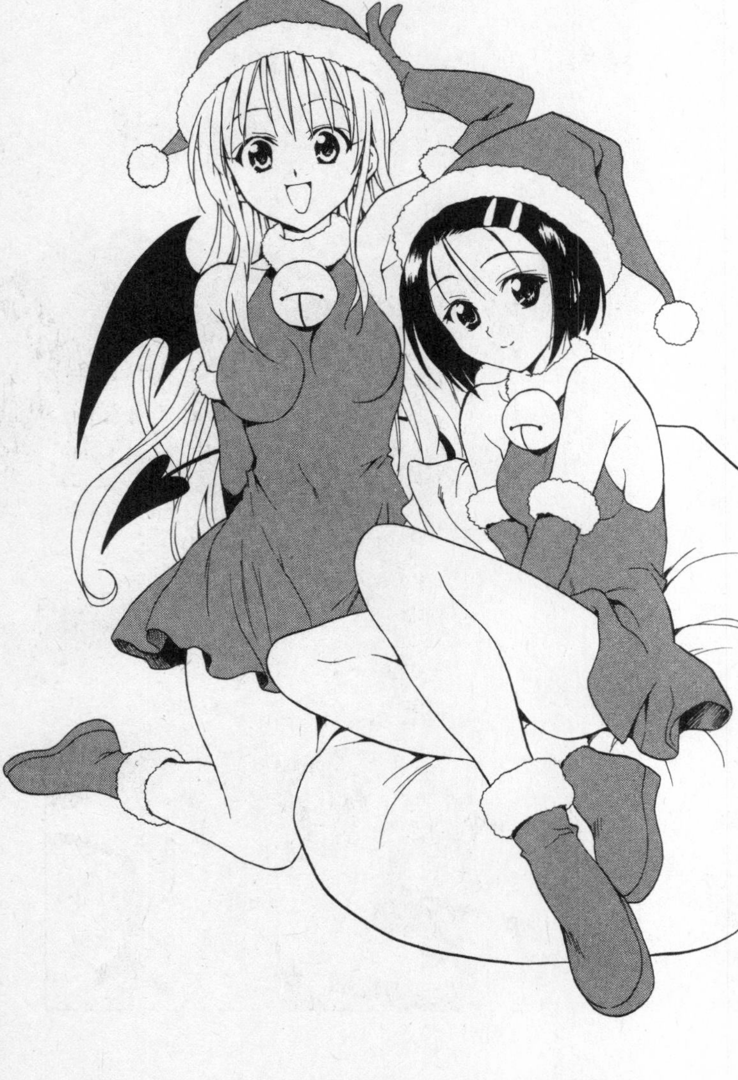

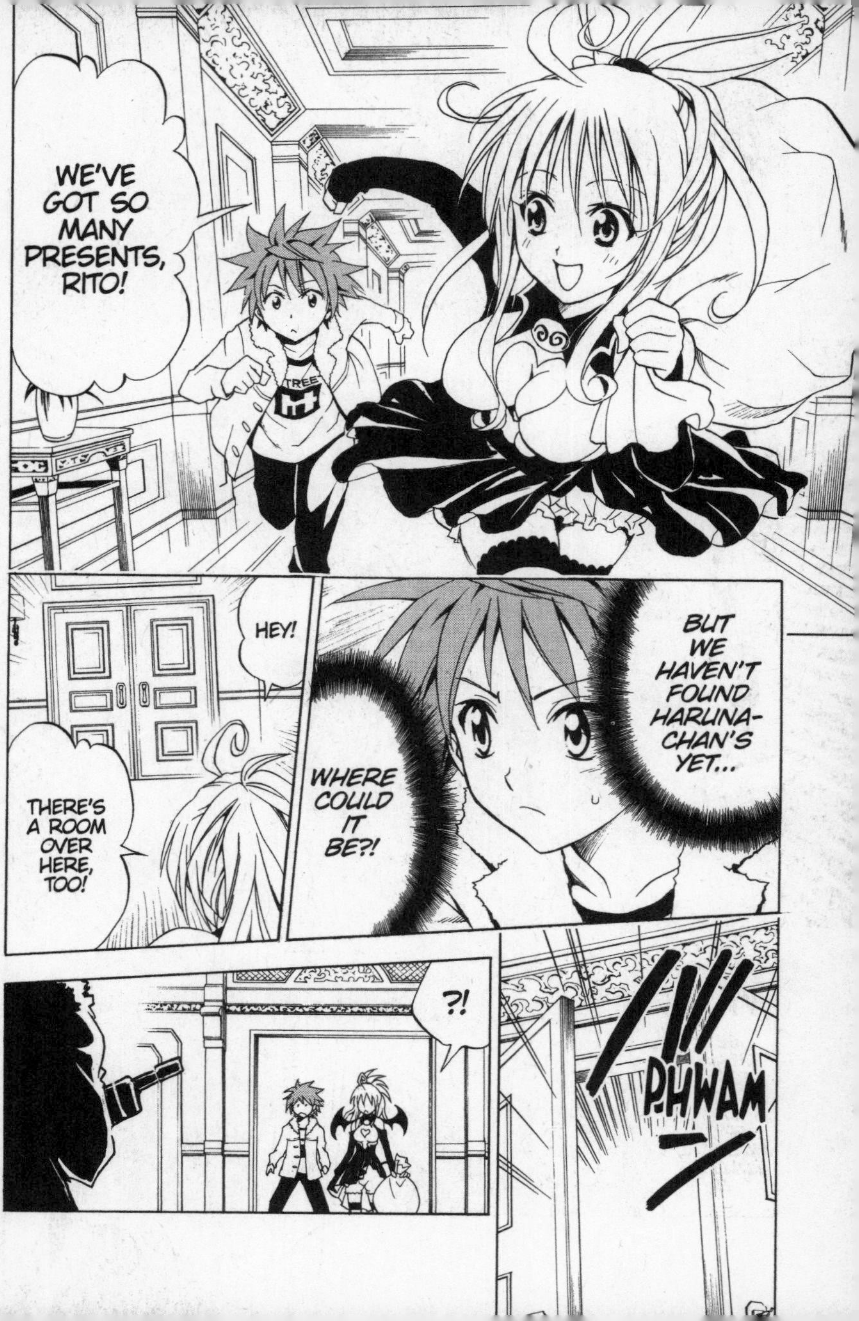
WE'VE GOT SO MANY PRESENTS, RITO!
BUT WE HAVEN'T FOUND HARUNA-CHAN'S YET...
WHERE COULD IT BE?!
HEY!
THERE'S A ROOM OVER HERE, TOO!
PHWAM
?!

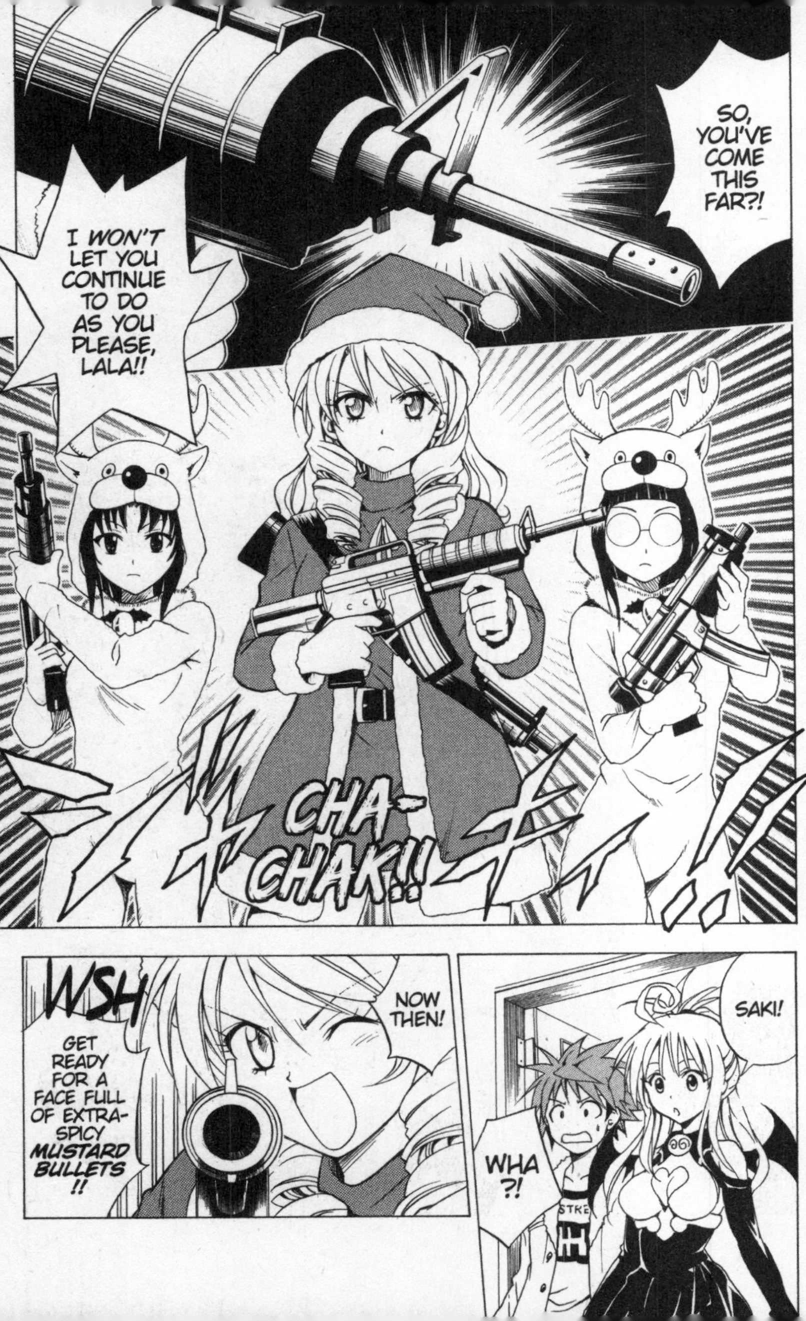
SO, YOU'VE COME THIS FAR?!
I *WON'T* LET YOU CONTINUE TO DO AS YOU PLEASE, LALA!!
CHA-CHAK!!
SAKI!
WHA ?!
NOW THEN!
WSH
GET READY FOR A FACE FULL OF EXTRA-SPICY *MUSTARD BULLETS* !!

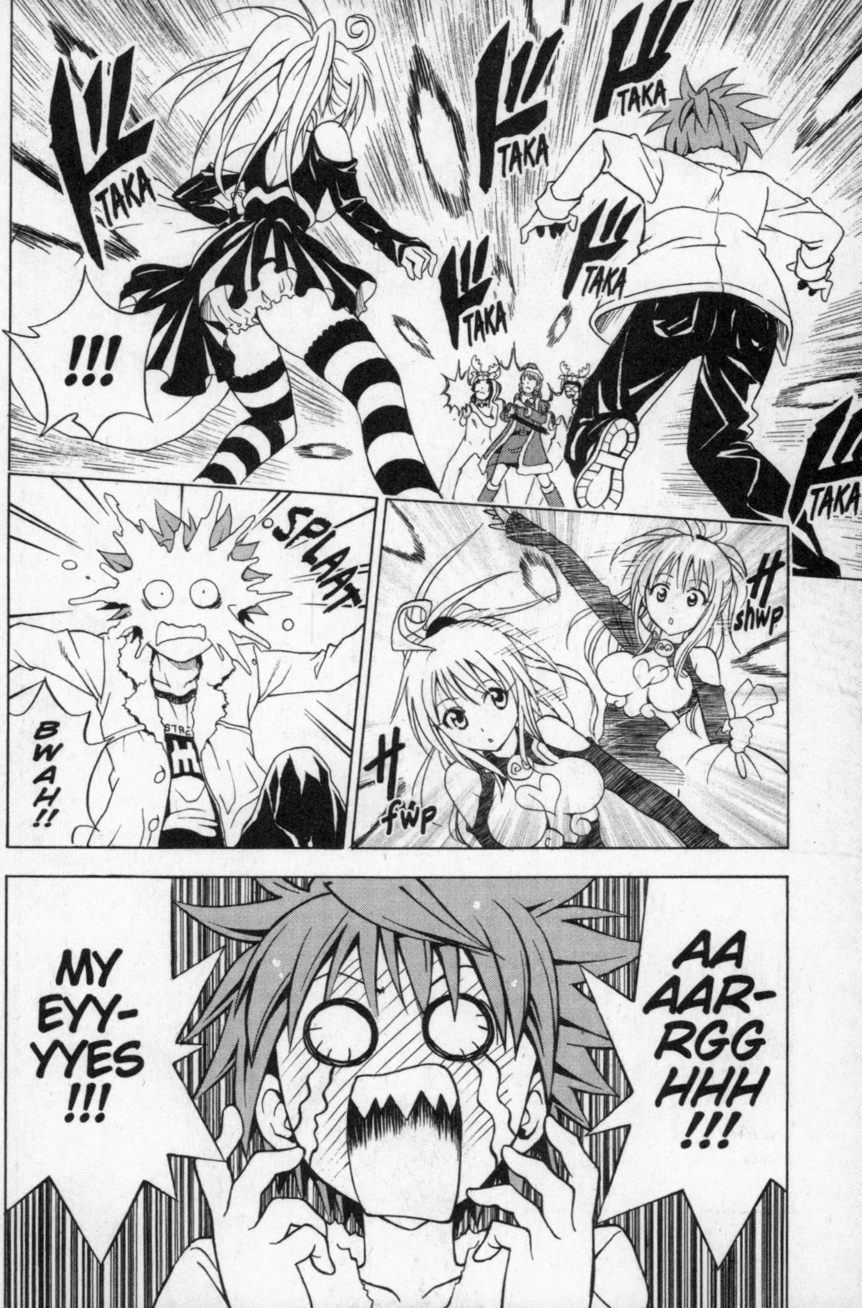
TAKA
TAKA
TAKA
TAKA
TAKA
TAKA
TAKA
!!!
shwp
fwp
SPLAAT
BWAH!!
AAAARRGGHHH!!!
MY EYYYYES!!!

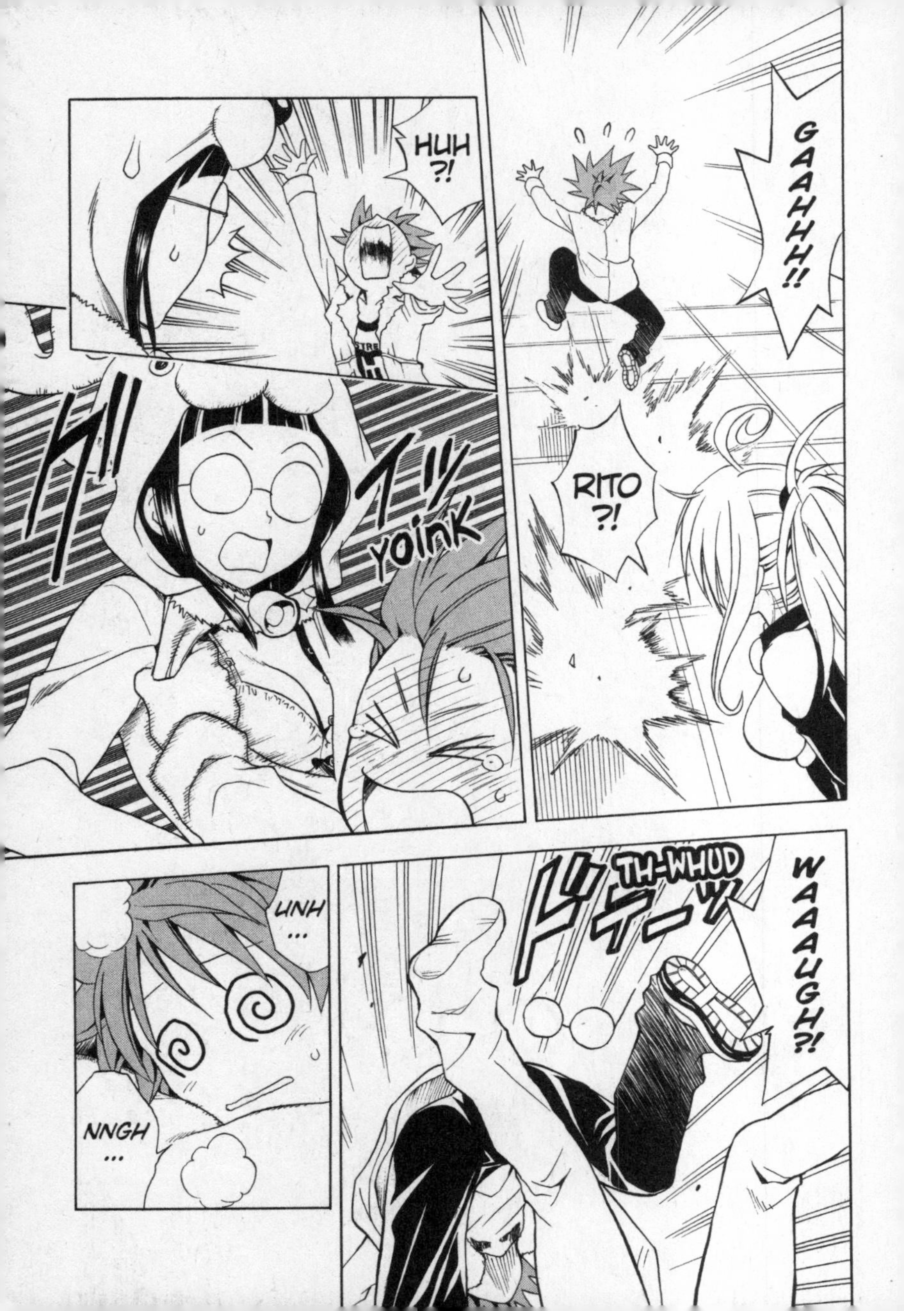
GAAHHH!!
RITO?!
HUH?!
YOINK
WAAAAUGH?!
TH-WHUD
UNH...
NNGH...

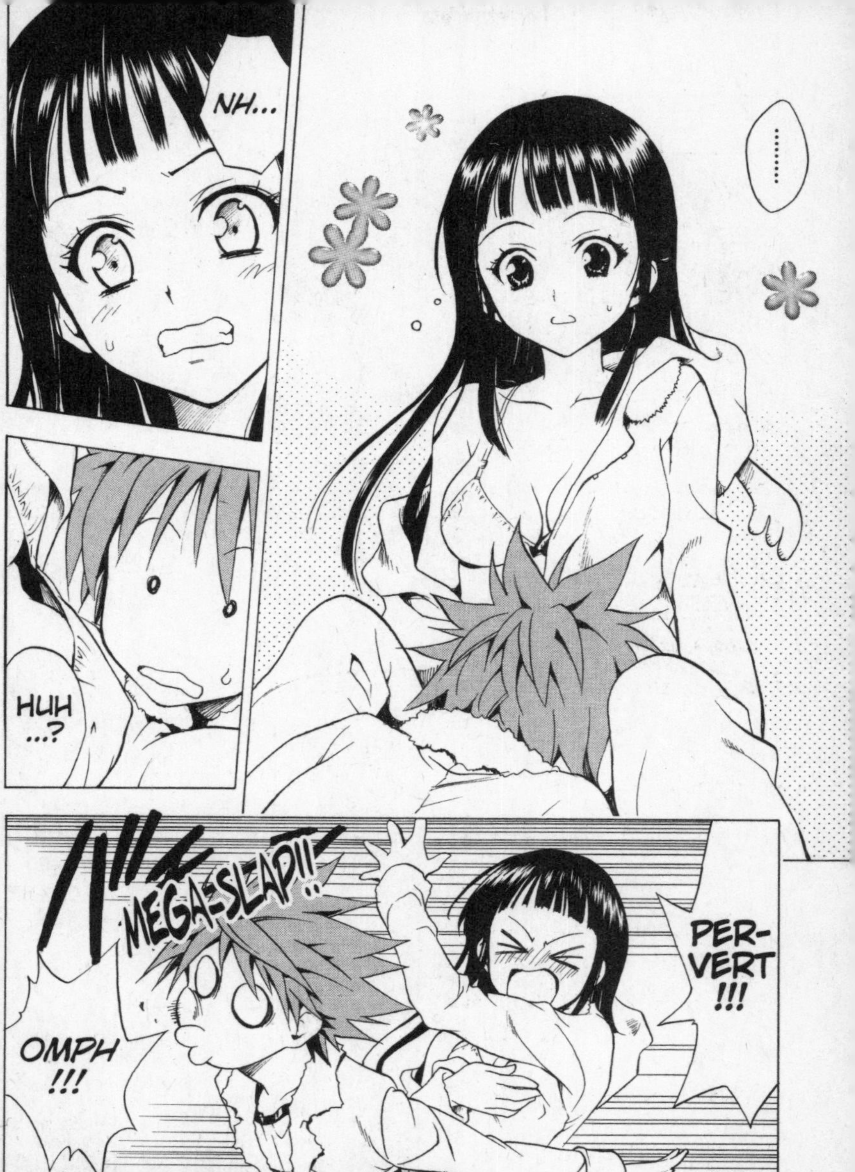
......
NH...
HUH ...?
PER-VERT !!!
MEGA-SLAP!!
OMPH !!!

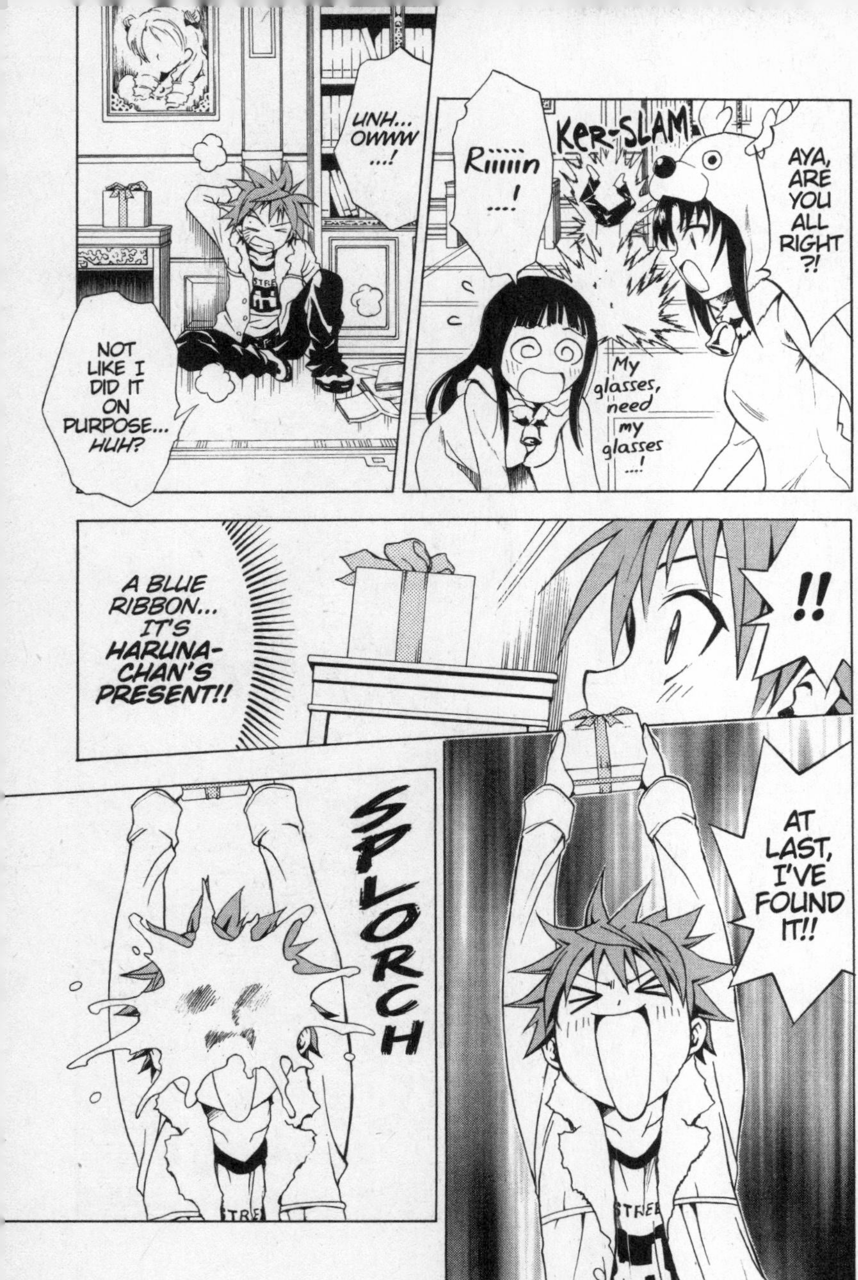
AYA, ARE YOU ALL RIGHT?!
KER-SLAM
Riiiiin ....!
...My glasses, need my glasses ...!
UNH... OWWW ...!
NOT LIKE I DID IT ON PURPOSE... HUH?
!!
A BLUE RIBBON... IT'S HARUNA-CHAN'S PRESENT!!
AT LAST, I'VE FOUND IT!!
SPLORCH

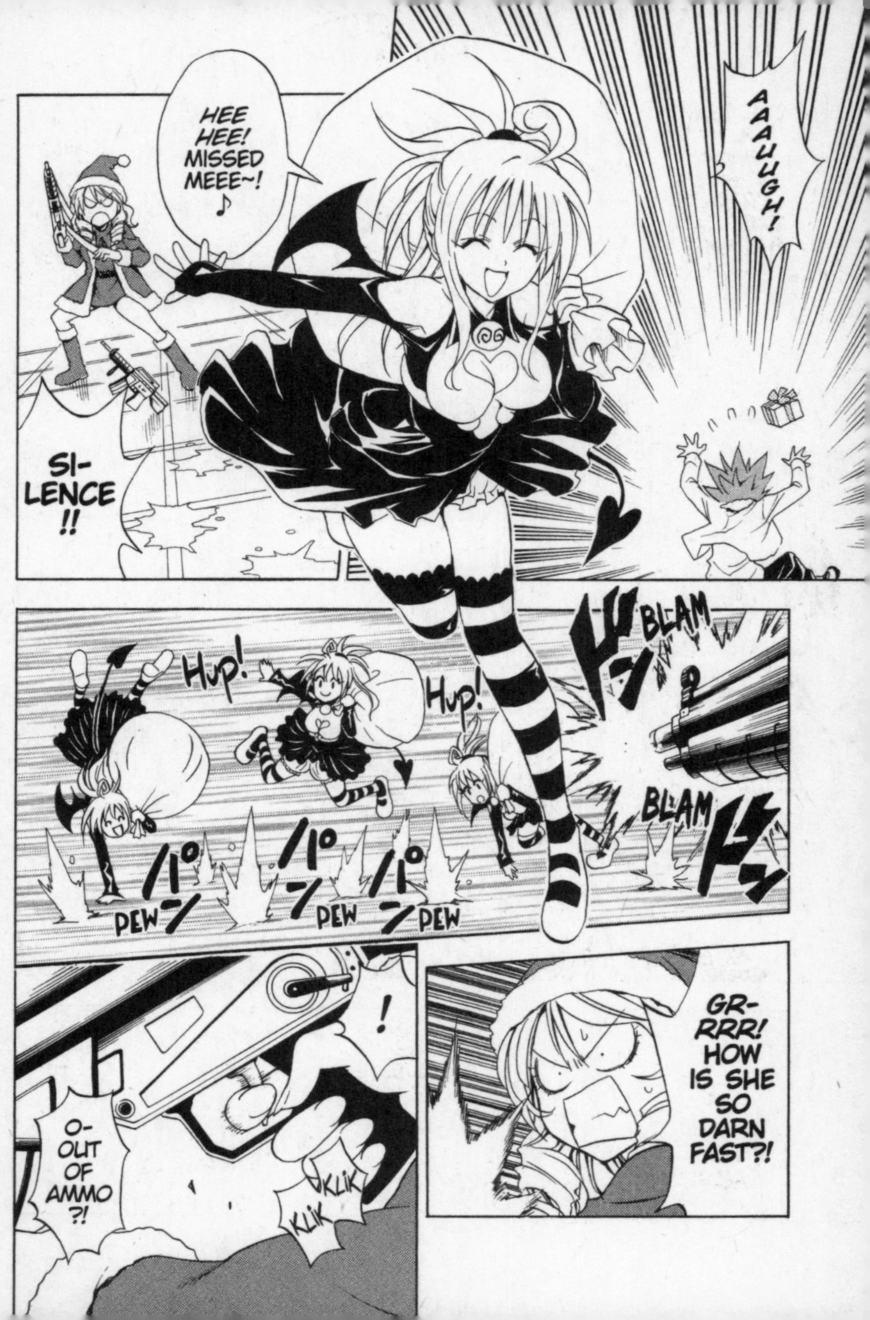
AAAUGH!
HEE HEE! MISSED MEEE~! ♪
SI-LENCE!!
BLAM
Hup!
Hup!
BLAM
PEW
PEW
PEW
GR-RRR! HOW IS SHE SO DARN FAST?!
!
O-OUT OF AMMO?!
KLIK
KLIK

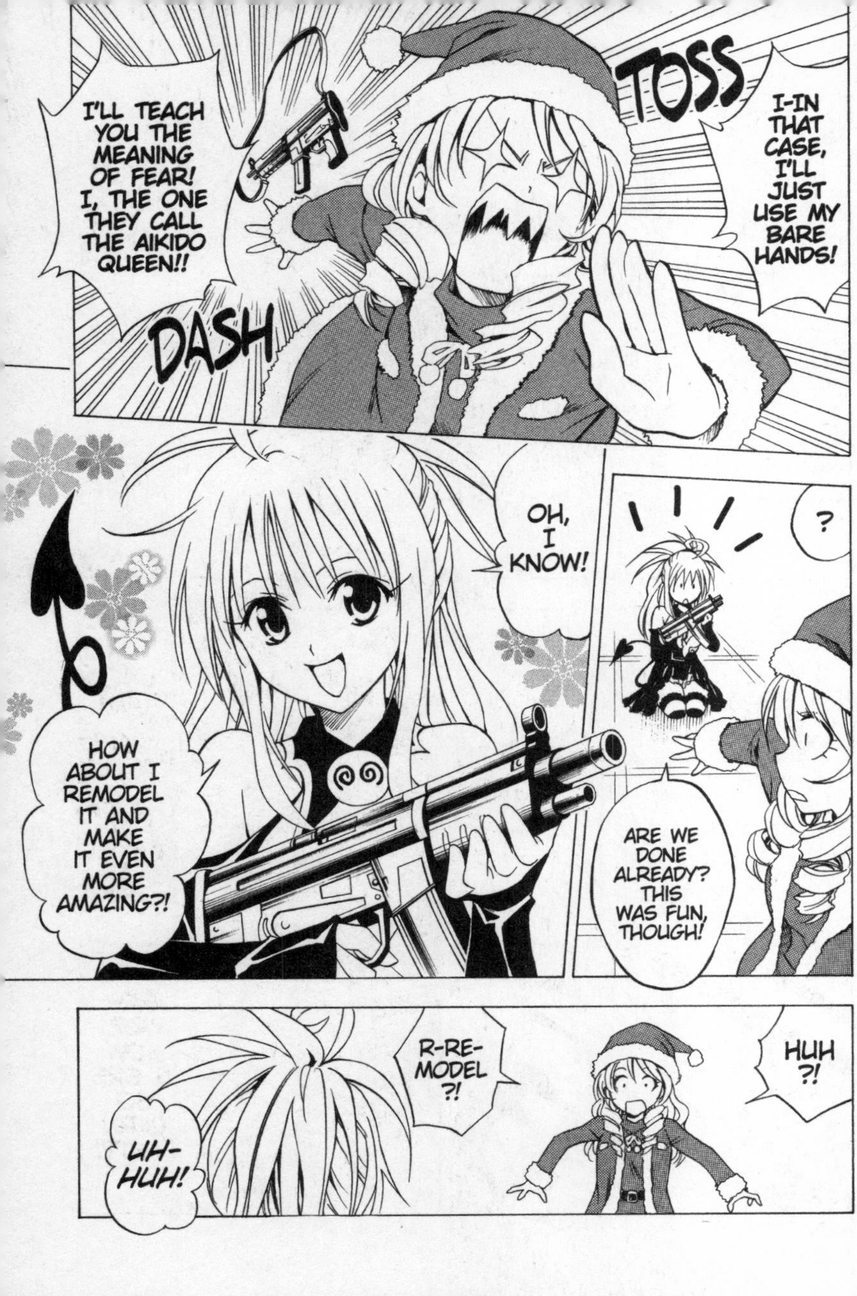
TOSS
I-IN THAT CASE, I'LL JUST USE MY BARE HANDS!
I'LL TEACH YOU THE MEANING OF FEAR! I, THE ONE THEY CALL THE AIKIDO QUEEN!!
DASH
?
ARE WE DONE ALREADY? THIS WAS FUN, THOUGH!
OH, I KNOW!
HOW ABOUT I REMODEL IT AND MAKE IT EVEN MORE AMAZING?!
HUH ?!
R-RE-MODEL ?!
UH-HUH!

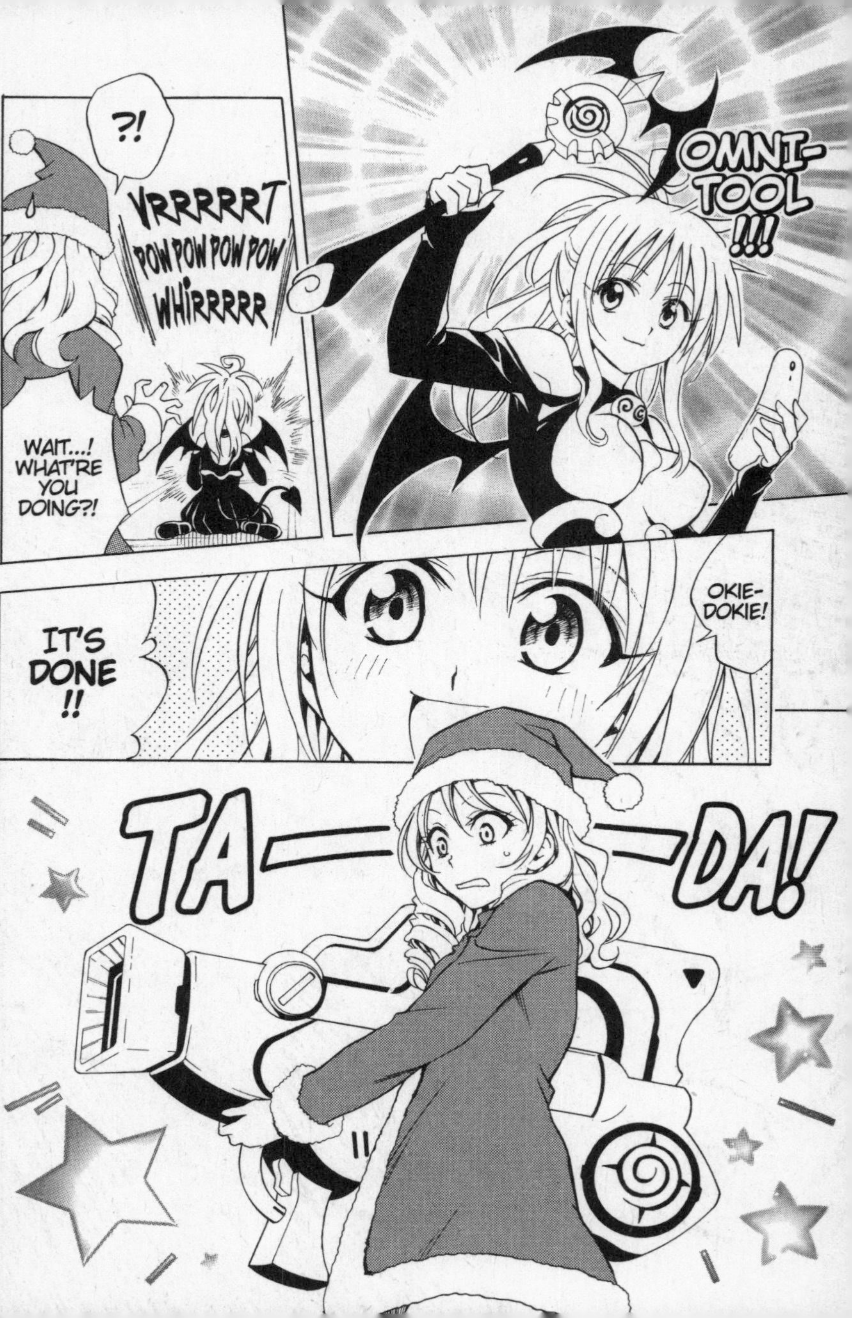
OMNI-TOOL!!!
?!
VRRRRRT
POW POW POW POW
WHIRRRRR
WAIT...! WHAT'RE YOU DOING?!
OKIE-DOKIE!
IT'S DONE!!
TA———DA!

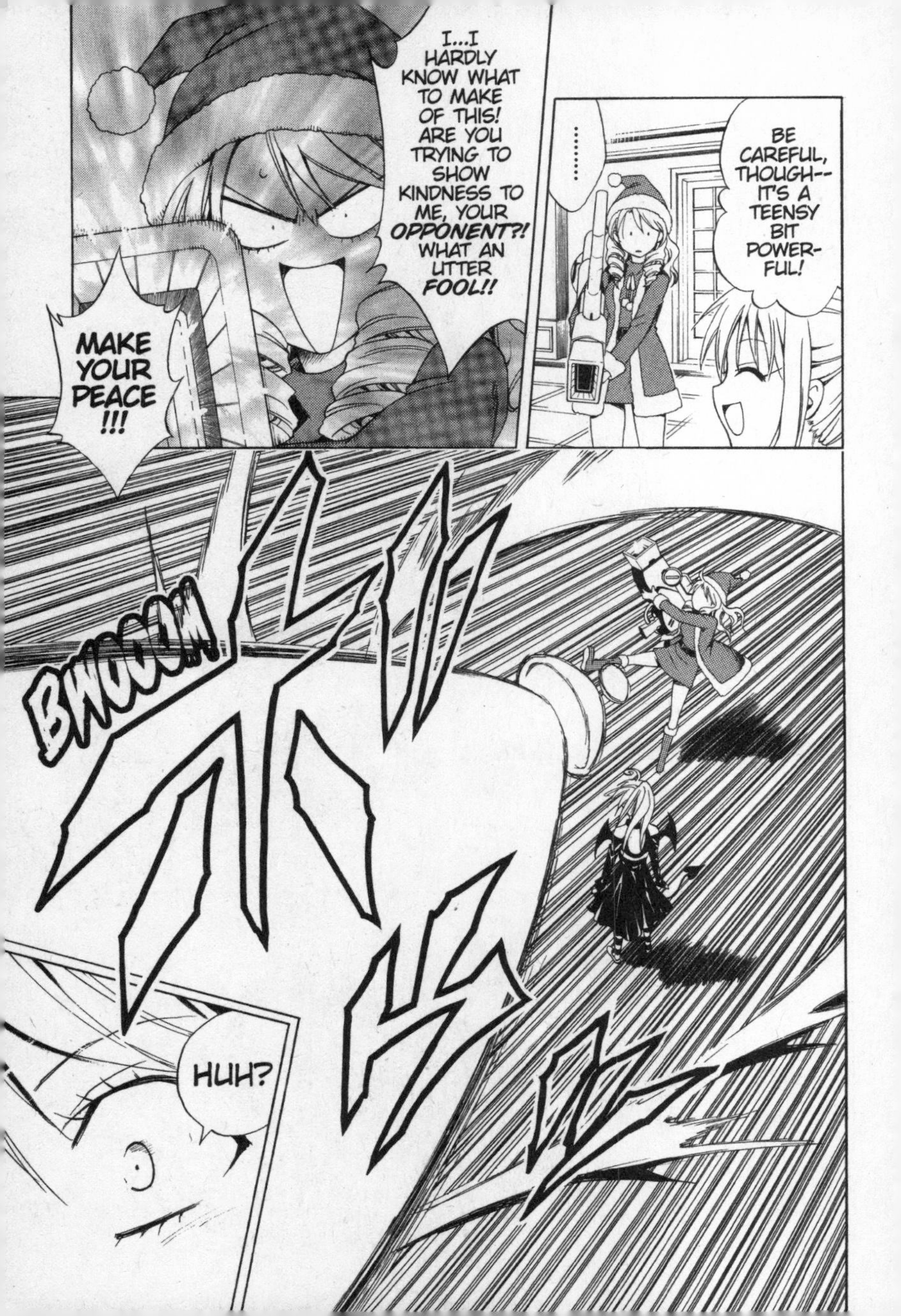
BE CAREFUL, THOUGH-- IT'S A TEENSY BIT POWER-FUL!
……
I...I HARDLY KNOW WHAT TO MAKE OF THIS! ARE YOU TRYING TO SHOW KINDNESS TO ME, YOUR *OPPONENT*?! WHAT AN UTTER *FOOL!!*
MAKE YOUR PEACE !!!
BWOOOM
HUH?

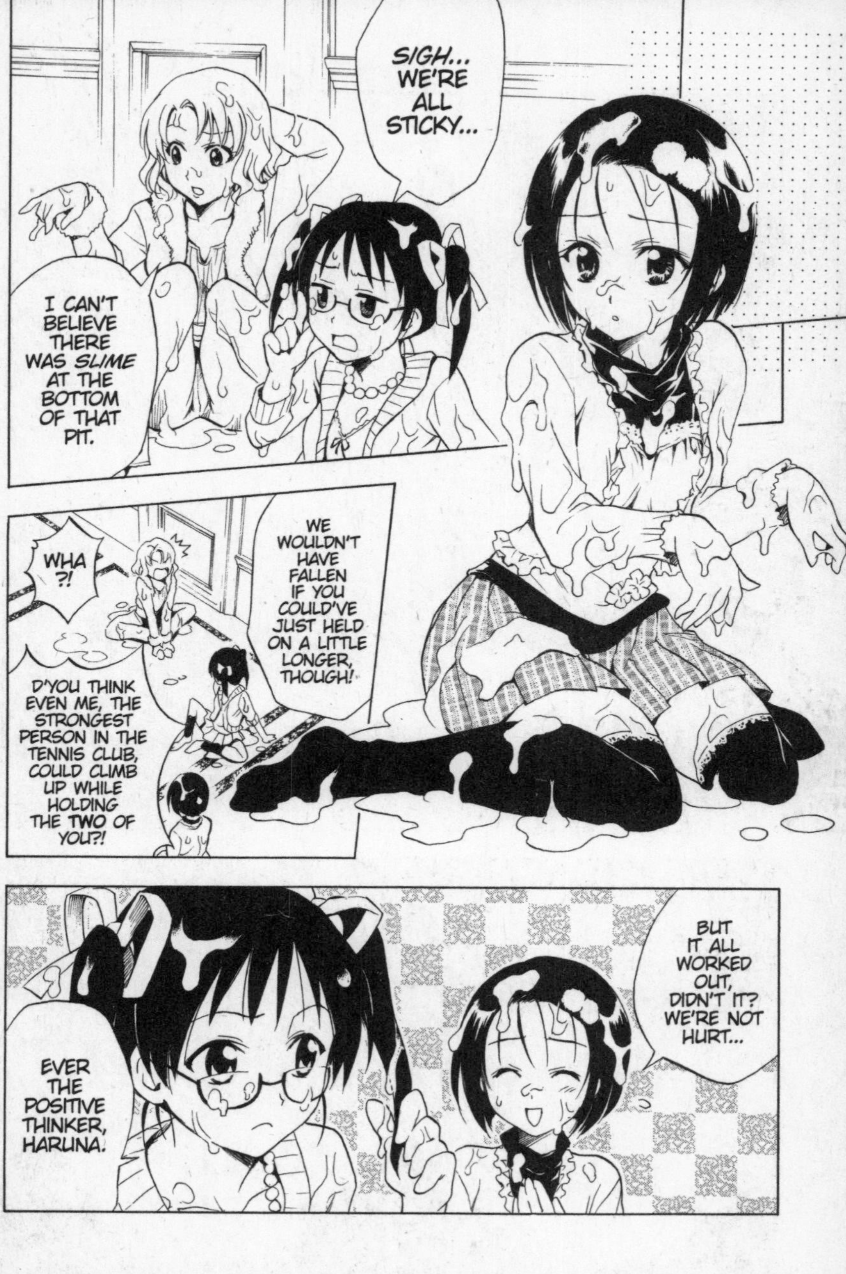
SIGH... WE'RE ALL STICKY...
I CAN'T BELIEVE THERE WAS *SLIME* AT THE BOTTOM OF THAT PIT.
WE WOULDN'T HAVE FALLEN IF YOU COULD'VE JUST HELD ON A LITTLE LONGER, THOUGH!
WHA ?!
D'YOU THINK EVEN ME, THE STRONGEST PERSON IN THE TENNIS CLUB, COULD CLIMB UP WHILE HOLDING THE TWO OF YOU?!
BUT IT ALL WORKED OUT, DIDN'T IT? WE'RE NOT HURT...
EVER THE POSITIVE THINKER, HARUNA.

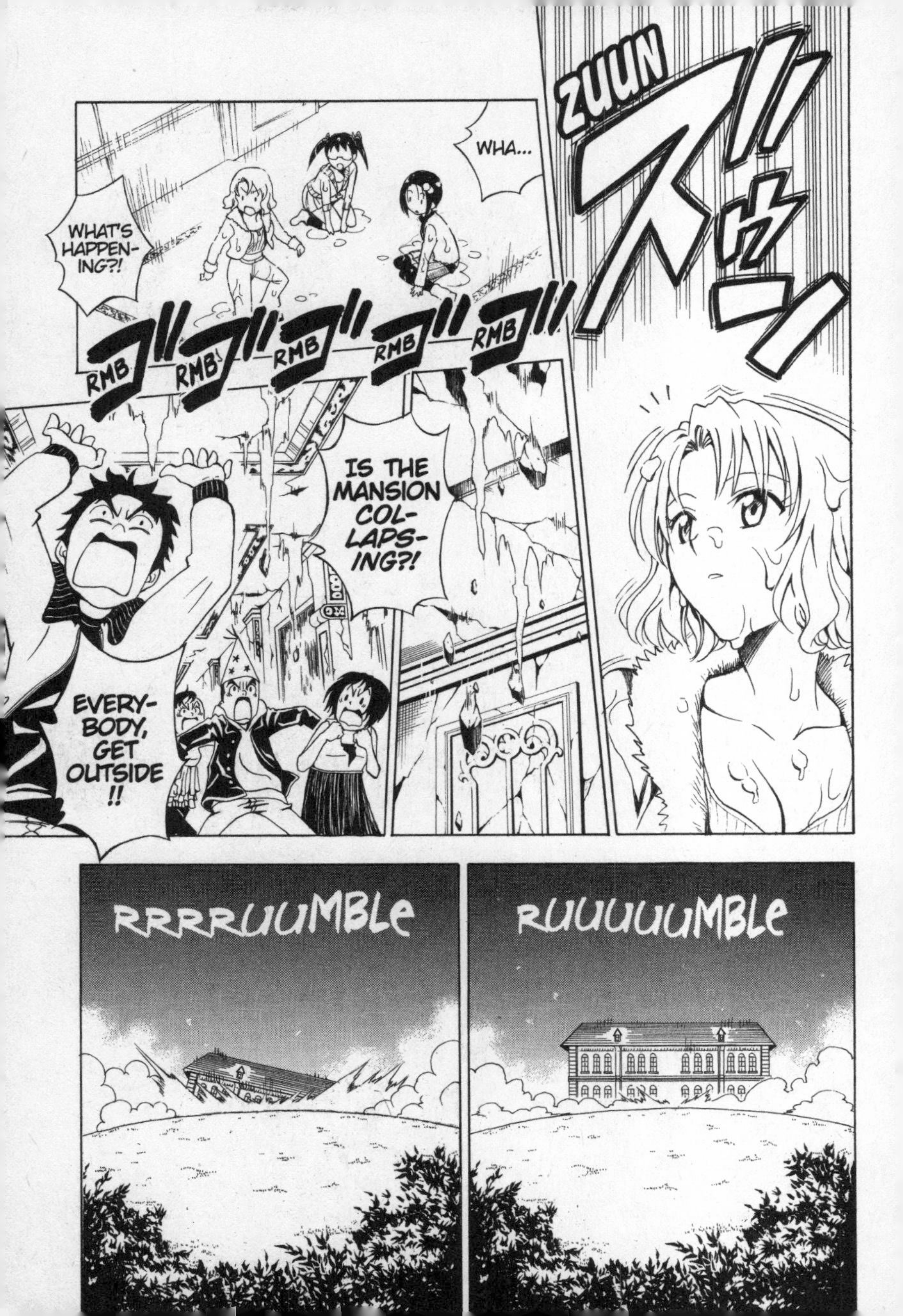
ZUUN
WHA...
WHAT'S HAPPENING?!
RMB RMB RMB RMB RMB
IS THE MANSION COL-LAPS-ING?!
EVERY-BODY, GET OUTSIDE !!
RUUUUUMBLE
RRRRUUMBLE

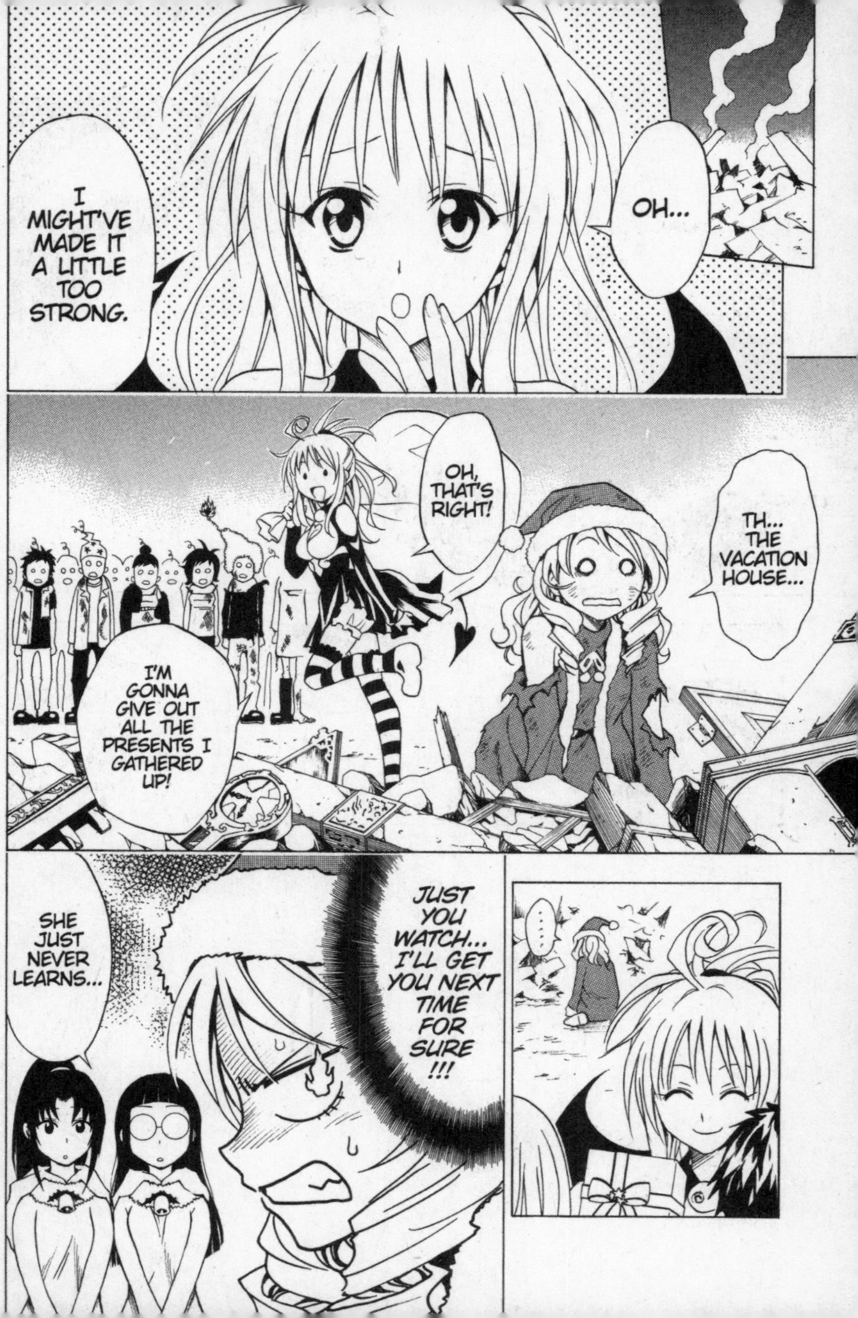
OH...
I MIGHT'VE MADE IT A LITTLE TOO STRONG.
TH... THE VACATION HOUSE...
OH, THAT'S RIGHT!
I'M GONNA GIVE OUT ALL THE PRESENTS I GATHERED UP!
......
JUST YOU WATCH... I'LL GET YOU NEXT TIME FOR SURE!!!
SHE JUST NEVER LEARNS...

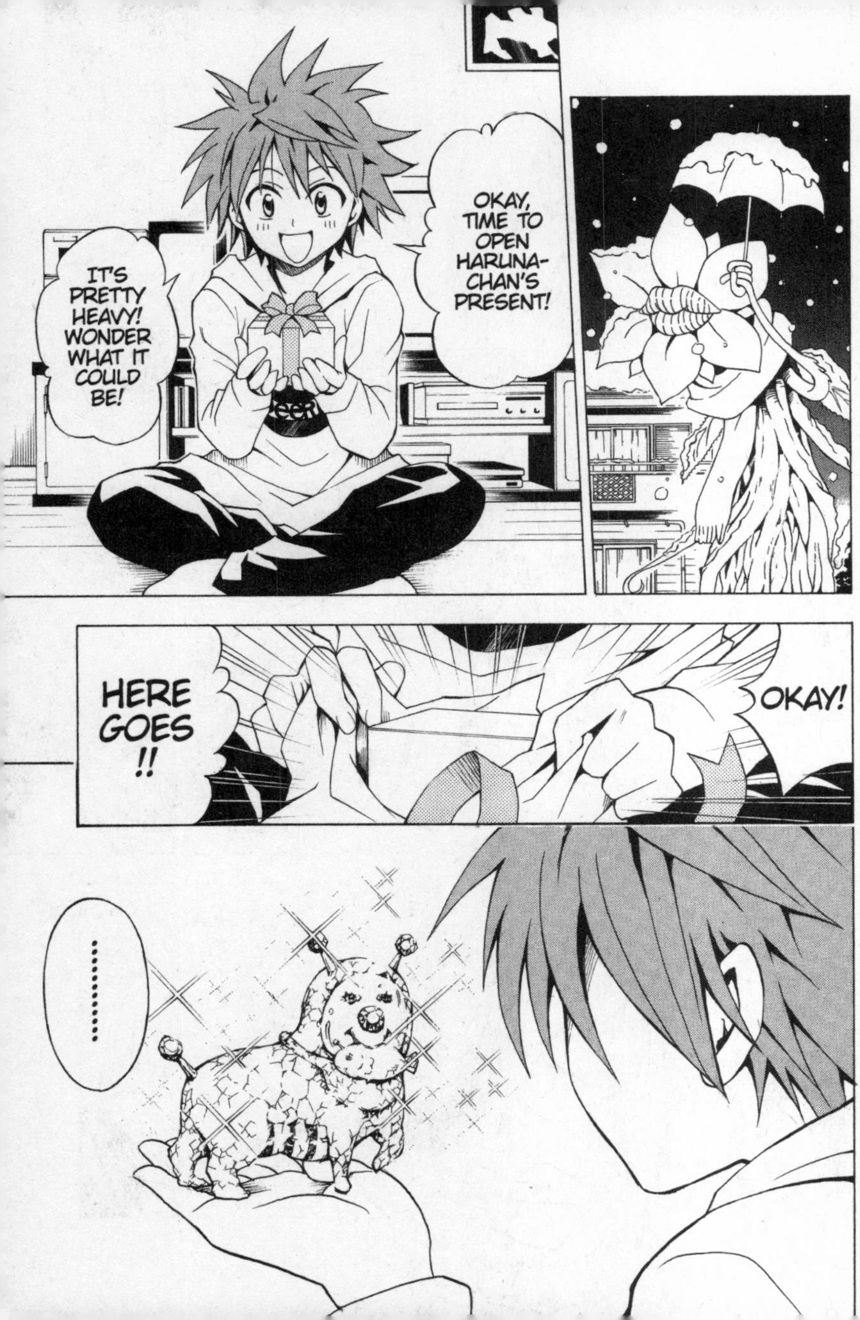
OKAY, TIME TO OPEN HARUNA-CHAN'S PRESENT!
IT'S PRETTY HEAVY! WONDER WHAT IT COULD BE!
OKAY!
HERE GOES!!
....

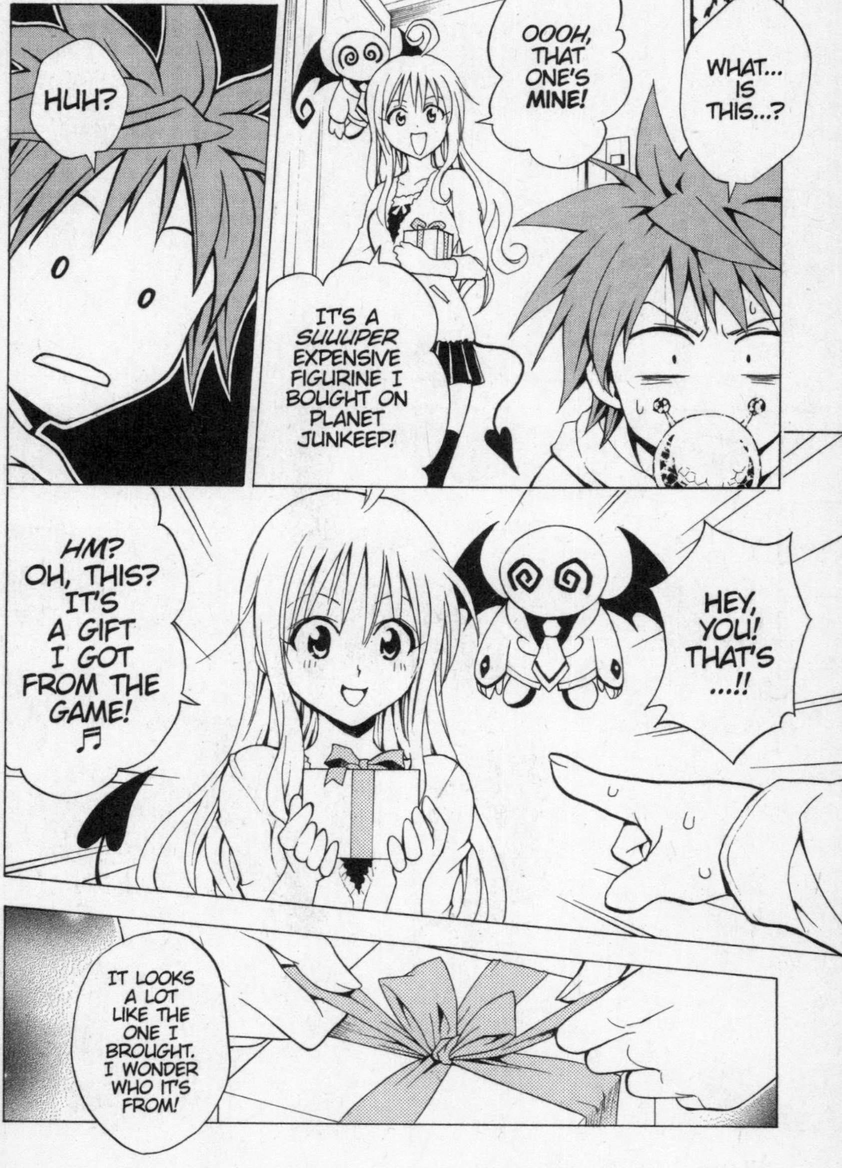
WHAT... IS THIS...?
OOOH, THAT ONE'S MINE!
IT'S A *SUUUPER* EXPENSIVE FIGURINE I BOUGHT ON PLANET JUNKEEP!
HUH?
HEY, YOU! THAT'S ...!!
HM? OH, THIS? IT'S A GIFT I GOT FROM THE GAME! ♬
IT LOOKS A LOT LIKE THE ONE I BROUGHT. I WONDER WHO IT'S FROM!

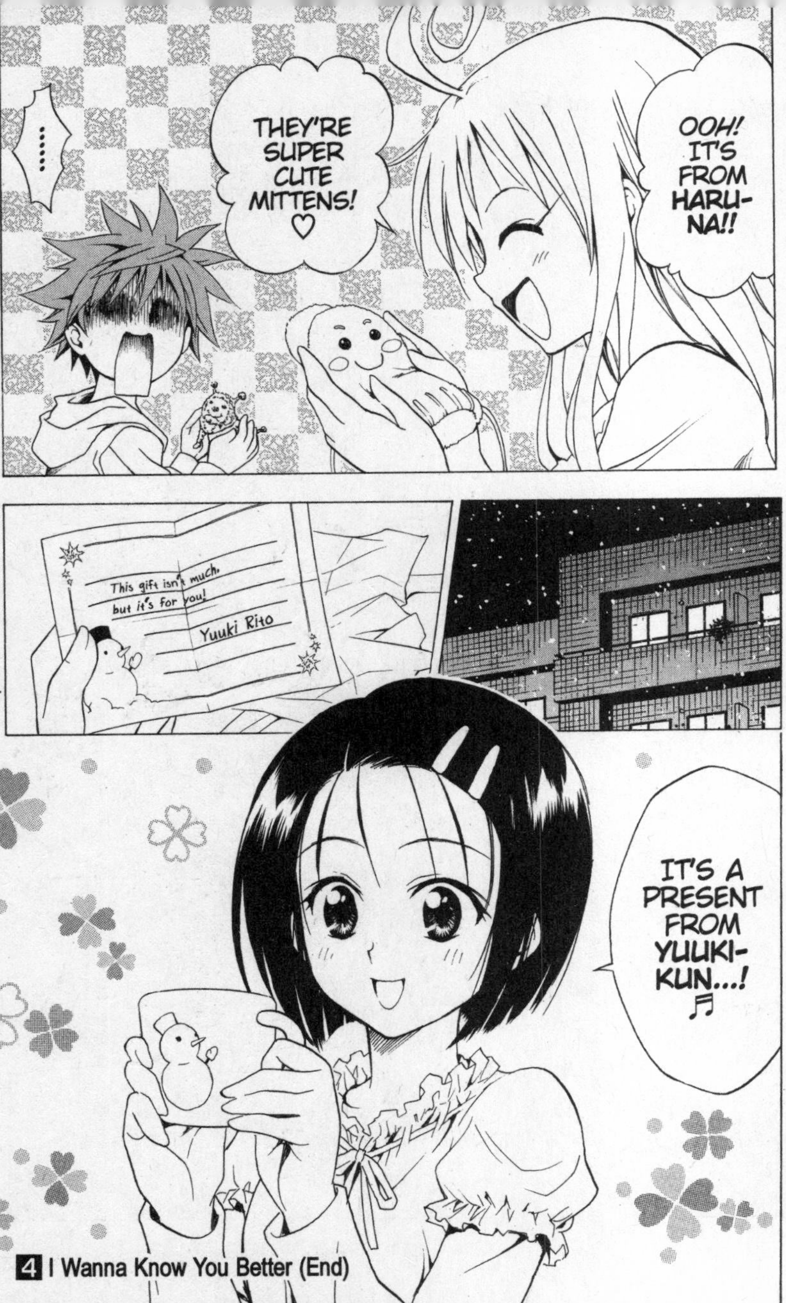
OOH! IT'S FROM HARU-NA!!
THEY'RE SUPER CUTE MITTENS! ♡
......
This gift isn't much, but it's for you!
Yuuki Rito
IT'S A PRESENT FROM YUUKI-KUN...! ♬

4 I Wanna Know You Better (End)

To LOVE Ru

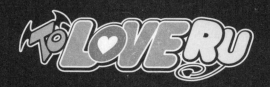

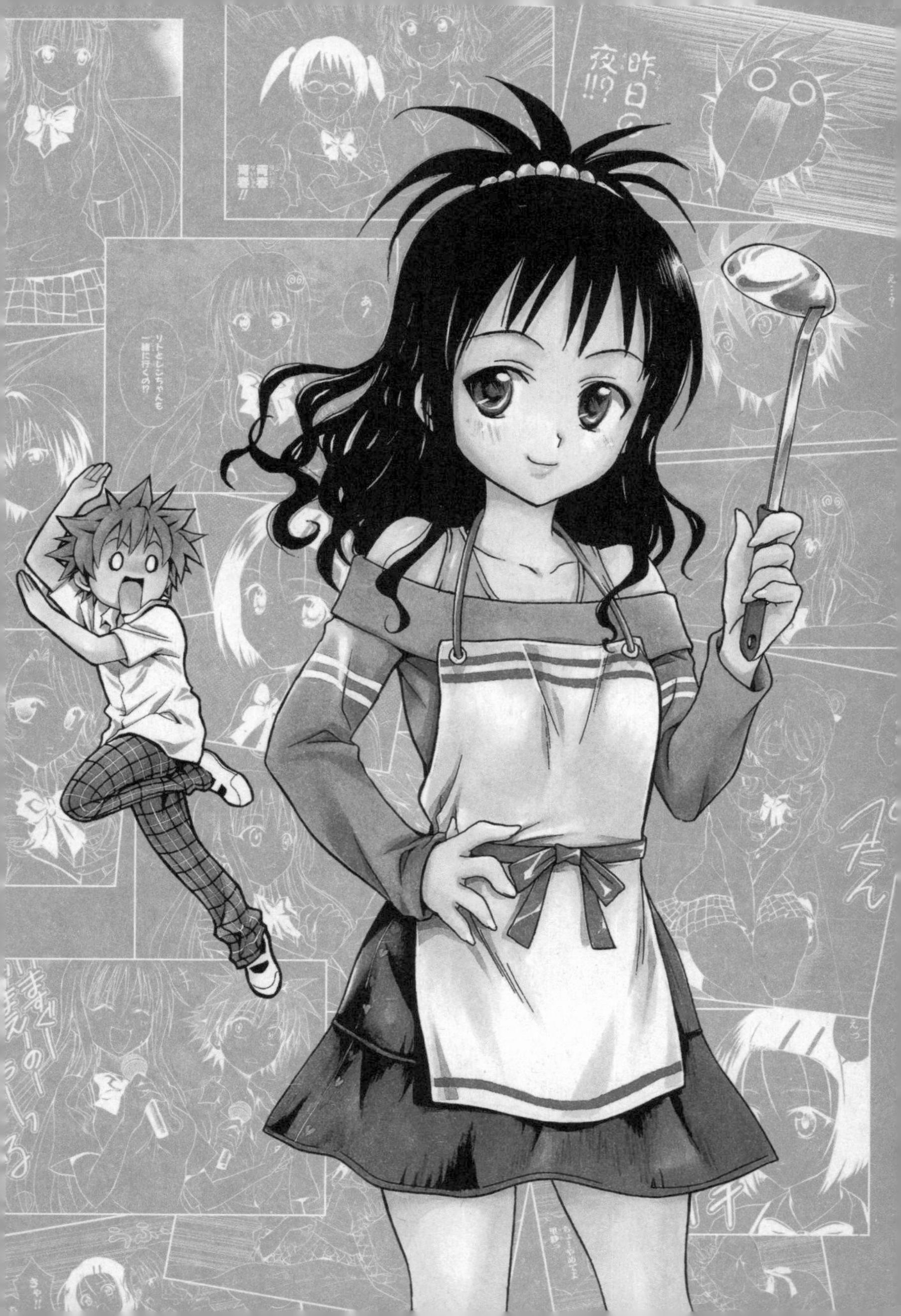

昨日の夜!!?

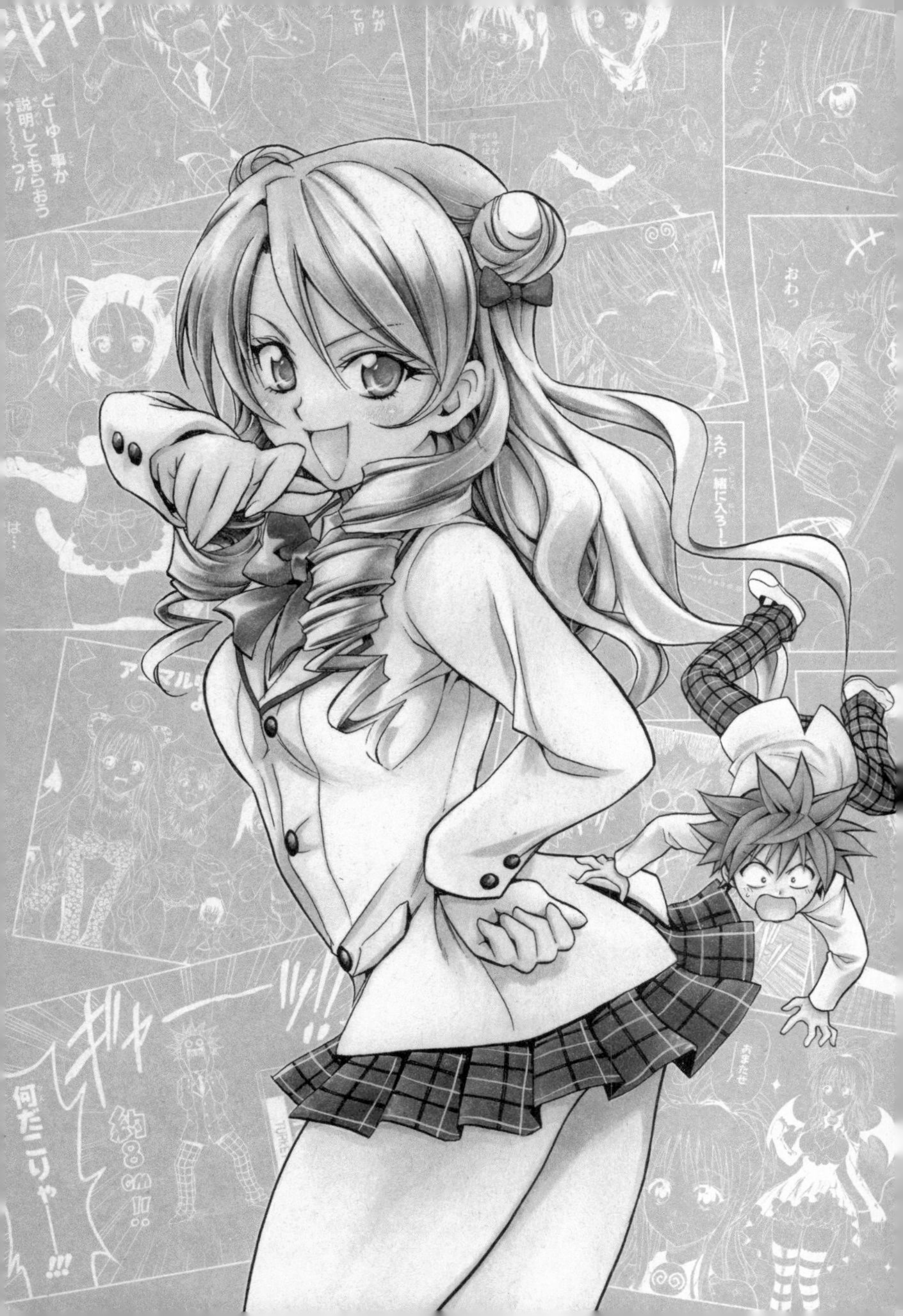

おわっ
え?一緒に入ろーよ
どーゆー事か説明してもらおうっ!!
約8cm!!
ギャー!!
何だこりゃー!!!

To LOVE Ru

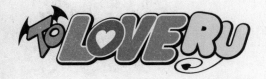

SEVEN SEAS' GHOST SHIP PRESENTS

TO LOVE RU

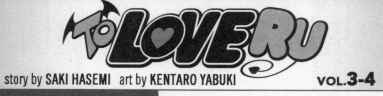

story by SAKI HASEMI art by KENTARO YABUKI

VOL.3-4

TRANSLATION
Alex Gaspard

ADAPTATION
J.P. Sullivan

LETTERING AND LAYOUT
Paweł Szczęszek

LOGO DESIGN
Larry Kotef

COVER DESIGN
Nicky Lim

PROOFREADER
Janet Houck
Tom Speelman

ASSISTANT EDITOR
Jenn Grunigen

PRODUCTION ASSISTANT
CK Russell

PRODUCTION MANAGER
Lissa Pattillo

EDITOR-IN-CHIEF
Adam Arnold

PUBLISHER
Jason DeAngelis

TO LOVE RU VOL. 3-4

First published in Japan in 2006 by SHUEISHA Inc., Tokyo.
English translation rights arranged by SHUEISHA Inc.
through TOHAN CORPORATION, Tokyo.

ISBN: 978-1-947804-06-7

Printed in Canada

First Printing: January 2018

10 9 8 7 6 5 4 3 2 1

FOLLOW US ONLINE: *www.ghostshipmanga.com*

READING DIRECTIONS

This book reads from ***right to left***, Japanese style. If this is your first time reading manga, you start reading from the top right panel on each page and take it from there. If you get lost, just follow the numbered diagram here. It may seem backwards at first, but you'll get the hang of it! Have fun!!

1
2
3
4
5
6
7
8
9

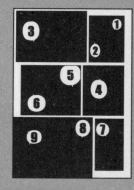